Rowdy

✳ Rowdy *racing in the Mediterranean at Le Voile d' Antibes, Panerai Trophy. Antibes, France, June 6, 2009. (© Ph. Carlhant)*

✳ Rowdy *racing in the Mediterranean at Le Voile d'Antibes, Panerai Trophy. Antibes, France, June 6, 2009. (© Ph. Carlhant)*

Rowdy

by
Christopher Madsen

Santa Barbara, California
2015

ISBN: 978-0-9960260-0-0

Library of Congress Control Number: 2014905162

Cover and Text Designer: Terri Wright (www.terriwright.com)
Copy Editor: Barbara Willette

Cover photo, *Rowdy,* May 1931.
© Mystic Seaport, Rosenfeld Collection, Mystic, CT, # 45657F

Title page photo, *Rowdy,* May 1921.
© Mystic Seaport, Rosenfeld Collection, Mystic, CT, # 29588F

Dedicated to my twin daughters
Sophia and Claire,
and their big sister, Chloe

Foreword

When I found *Rowdy* in 1998, her 83-year-old hull was so badly deteriorated that her bilge pumps ran nearly continuously to keep up with the profusion of leaks through the rotten planks. As I began to rebuild the boat, I also began to research her history and, as of this writing, am in my sixteenth year of an unfolding story.

My search led me from the West Coast to the East Coast as I investigated maritime museums, historical societies, historic yacht clubs, archived newspaper articles by the thousands, old court cases still in boxes in musty library vaults, and scores of vintage books, both general to the war and sailing and specific to *Rowdy* and her owner Holland Sackett Duell. I also conducted numerous personal interviews including those with Holland's 93-year-old daughter Harriet-Anne and with Halsey Herreshoff, whose grandfather designed and built *Rowdy*.

It was immediately obvious to me that this was a story not only about *Rowdy*, but more substantively about her first owner, Holland Sackett Duell. Hardly a day went by when I didn't uncover some new fact about his life or his yacht. The snail's pace at which all the little pieces came together was most enjoyably accompanied by the sense of reading a book in slow motion. It was the most marvelous and intricate story—an adventure of love and war, of power and politics, of fortunes and mansions, and the link that drew me into the story: an adventure of the sea.

In fact, it was not until some years after I had completed the restoration and seen *Rowdy* off to Monaco, where she once again became a world class-champion, that I realized the biggest event in my life was not the boat, but the window that she had provided into her past. *Rowdy* had opened a portal in time, through which, I had the good fortune of becoming intimately acquainted with a group of most remarkable people, just as the last flickering light of their story was about to fade out. I have endeavored to base every element of this book on actual, true-life facts and events and to portray the story of these people's lives as accurately as possible. Throughout the book are extensive footnotes citing my sources, which fully support the material presented in this story.

In the spirit of a good book that one wants never to end, I encourage anyone who can contribute any further information to contact me, in hopes of a second, even richer edition.

— *Chris Madsen*
 rowdystory@yahoo.com

Many Thanks to All

Having spent over sixteen years reaching out to anyone and everyone who might have any information about this story, it would take a separate book to thank all the wonderful people who have come forward.

I owe at least a million thanks to the entire Duell family, the relatives of *Rowdy's* original owner, Holland Sackett Duell. Despite their busy lives, they all rallied to my requests for information with enthusiasm, teamwork, and the type of support I would expect only from my immediate family. They dug up sailing trophies, had copies made of artwork, located vintage photographs, traveled across the country to personally visit me and *Rowdy*, and much, much more. They are a remarkable group of people whom I feel very fortunate to have met.

What a blessing and privilege it was to have met and enjoyed a correspondence with Harriet-Anne (Duell) Pierson, known as "Hanny," Holland's only child still living at the time I began my research. Her passing truly marked the end of an era, but what she shared with me during the course of a lovely friendship, through phone calls and letters and one meeting aboard *Rowdy*, contributed substantially toward breathing life back into this story as it teetered on a precipice, in peril of disappearing from memory and becoming lost to this world for all time.

Cherry Taylor, as a young girl, knew *Rowdy's* owner as "Uncle Holland," who was best friends with her parents. Cherry and I also enjoyed a rich friendship, active in phone calls and correspondence by mail. She not only shared with me stories of flying and sailing and skiing with Holland, but also sent me photographs, each of which felt to me like the discovery of a lost treasure.

Sharon (Winn) Stewart was 19 years old when, in 1963, she set sail aboard *Rowdy* with her parents and brother from Florida, en route to San Diego via the Panama Canal. Who would believe that a box of over twenty letters that her mother wrote along the way could still be intact? And how amazing that Sharon would be gracious and trusting enough to mail me the entire box of fifty-year-old letters that documented the trip! She also sent me newspaper articles and photographs, and she addressed my every question through e-mails, letters, and phone calls. THANK YOU, Sharon!!!

Many people knew of *Rowdy* after she left the Duell family and went to the Great Lakes. I only wish there was space to list and thank everyone who called me to contribute information. Please know that I will never forget you and your generosity.

On the technical side:

Thanks to Kurt Hasselbalch at the Massachusetts Institute of Technology for providing the dozens of technically drawn ship's plans that helped to restore *Rowdy* to her original plan.

Thanks to Mystic Seaport for locating and providing vintage photographs of *Rowdy* from the Rosenfeld Collection. The copyrighted photos may be purchased from them at Mystic Seaport, 75 Greenmanville Avenue, Mystic, CT 06355 or by contacting them at (860)572-5383 or www.rosenfeldcollection.org.

Thanks to Mariners' Museum for providing vintage photographs of *Rowdy* from the Levick Collection. The copyrighted photos may be purchased from them at Mariners' Museum, 100 Museum Drive, Newport News, VA 23601 or by contacting them at (757)596-2222 or www.marinersmuseum.org.

Thanks to the New York Times for allowing the reprint of so many wonderful, vintage articles headlining *Rowdy's* racing successes.

Thanks to the Herreshoff Marine Museum for providing historical information about *Rowdy*.

Thanks to Halsey Herreshoff for welcoming me to his town on a research trip and showing me his New York 40, *Rugosa II*.

Thanks to Cannell Boatyard in Camden, Maine, and the New York Yacht Club consortium for allowing me to see the New York 40 *Marilee* during her renovation.

Thank you to the Yale Alumni Association for providing me with biographical information on Holland Duell. Specifically, I thank Christine Baird for forwarding my letter to the address on file for Holland's daughter, which allowed me the chance to get to know Hanny.

Thanks to the New York Public Library for pulling so many items out of special collections and archival storage vaults.

Thanks to James Robinson Taylor for the marvelous photos he provided of *Rowdy* racing in the Mediterranean. His work may be viewed at http://www.jrtphoto.com.

Thanks to Philippe Carlhant for the two dynamic *Rowdy* photos that precede the title page. His work may be viewed at http://www.carlhant.net.

Thanks to Greg Singley for the commissioned oil paintings "Pirate Gun" and "Christmas Dinner at the Hotel Ritz, Paris." His work may be viewed at http://gregsingley.com.

Additional thanks to the New York Yacht Club, Larchmont Yacht Club, Eastern Yacht Club, American Yacht Club, Smithsonian Institution, Newport Historical Society, Historical Society of Pennsylvania, Westchester County Historical Society, Wisconsin Historical Society, New York Historical Society, Larchmont Historical Society, WACO Historical Society, Waukesha County Museum, Mystic Seaport, Mariners' Museum, Chrysler Museum of Art, National Park Service, Theodore Roosevelt Birthplace, National Park Service, Thomas Edison National Historic Park, Massachusetts Institute of Technology, Herreshoff Marine Museum, Yale University, Hamilton College, Wright State University, Library of Congress, National Archives and Administration, New York Library, New York Public Library for the Performing Arts, Longwood Public Library, Detroit Free Press, Cumberland Times-News, Santa Barbara News Press, Tonawanda News, U-T San Diego newspaper, Daily Breeze, New York Times, New York Post, Bonnier Corp.

And for getting dirty in the boatyard, thanks to shipwrights Alan Richter, Curt and Jason Beltz, and John Dye; Larry Driver on metals; Tony Athens and Bill Kennish on propulsion; Les Weatheral on electronics; and surveyors Skip Riley and Ross Hubbard.

Special thanks to my amazing copy editor, Barbara Willette, and my wonderful book designer, Terri Wright (http://www.terriwright.com), for turning my rough project into the polished, professional book that I had envisioned.

My most sincere thanks,

Christopher Madsen
January 2015

Table of Contents

Chapter

The Beginning

*H*ow curious it is that sometimes the most innocuous-seeming event can have such a profound effect on one's life. What at the time seems like the most inconsequential decision or action can carry the unintended consequence of redirecting the entirety of one's life path to the polar opposite of what it would have been otherwise. Yet at the time, the moment sneaks by under the radar, obscured in the noise of daily activities. The words that you are reading right now would not exist, the events that have defined my life for the past fifteen years would never have taken place, and my twin daughters would never have been so much as a twinkle in my eye had it not been for one such event. A casual thought in the middle of a busy day prompted me to make a phone call that I never dreamed would have any bearing on the course of my life. I was wrong.

I am not an author by profession and never would have envisioned myself writing a piece of nonfiction, although I have always enjoyed reading books based on true stories. For me, they deliver substance and depth immeasurably beyond those of pure fiction. But in 1998, a seemingly harmless event set off a chain reaction that would result in my becoming involved in such a true-life adventure — an adventure of a world at war, power and politics at the highest levels, the birth of Hollywood, fortunes and mansions, love and romance, scandalous affairs, and the link that drew me into the story: an adventure of the sea.

I'm not sure exactly when I first fell in love with the ocean. It is such a huge part of my life and enjoyment that it's hard to believe there are people who have lived their entire lives without ever seeing an ocean. As early as I can remember, there were lazy summer days spent searching for funny-looking sea creatures in tide pools. The warmth of the sun, the lapping of the waves, and the occasional drone of an overhead plane all filled my senses as my mother, father, older sister, and I enjoyed long, playful days accented with the occasional thrill of a captured starfish or baby octopus.

Although my mother was always a full participant in the fun, it was my dad, without question, who was the initiator. Mother actually couldn't swim because she had lost an eardrum to scarlet fever as a child. But my father had always been around the water, and his enjoyment of it was contagious. He had been born in Shanghai, China, while his parents were on a business trip from what was at the time their home in the Philippines. No, I'm not Chinese or Filipino. My grandfather was a U.S. citizen of Danish ancestry who was the president of a large import–export company. Consequently, my father had a unique childhood, growing up outside of Manila and, for fun, playing in jungles and swimming and fishing in tropical waters. From that upbring-

✳ *My dad, anthropologist*
William Madsen

ing undoubtedly sprang his love for tropical adventures and oceans, which he carried throughout his life. That energy flowed out of him in later years and into my sister and me through such bedtime stories as *The Swiss Family Robinson*, *The Adventures of Doctor Doolittle*, and *Robinson Crusoe* as well as through our many family vacations to warm, tropical destinations.

Mom and Dad shared a fascination with travel and seeing the world. They were both anthropologists, and drafting in the flight path of their travel adventures was magical for a young kid. Before I was 18, I had explored Mayan ruins in the jungles of the Yucatan, ridden camels to the pyramids of Egypt, walked the Coliseum in Rome, safaried in Africa, and posed by a snake charmer in India so Father could get a picture of me next to the man's cobra. This is but a small sample of our adventures. But above all, I thrived on vacations that featured the beach and the ocean. My father and I snorkeled the Great Barrier Reef, swam with turtles in Hawaii, and deep-sea fished in Mexico. We had so much fun in the water, on the water, and on warm, sunny beaches beside the water that the ocean became part of my required environment. It was a seed that, once planted, blossomed within me and inspired many daydreams of faraway tropical paradises and small sailing ships. I bought my first boat when I was 18 and have had one ever since.

If ever there was a place for turning recreational boaters into seasoned sailors, it would be my home of the past 45 years, Santa Barbara, California. I find it hard to imagine a more ideal place on this planet to live. Nestled between the Santa Ynez Mountains and expansive white sand beaches, a small pocket of relatively flat land holds an intimate little city of stucco buildings, red tile roofs, and colorful gardens.

A forty-five-minute drive takes one over the mountain range to beautiful Lake Cachuma, where a glorious day can be had renting an outboard or houseboat and watching deer while navigating the many small coves tucked into rolling oak-covered hills. The little snack stand on the hill above the boat rental docks operates at a slow country pace, producing anything from bacon and eggs to night crawlers, fish-hooks, and salmon eggs to ham-and-cheese sandwiches with chips and sodas, these last always making their way on board when Father and I went out on trout fishing trips. We would wait on the wooden picnic benches for the deli to finish making our lunches while the wonderful breakfast smells from the grill steamed and warmed the crisp early morning air. The glassy stillness of the shimmering lake in the soft amber light, before there was the slightest rustle of a breeze, was magnificent, beckoning us to become a part of the experience. For me, the delay before we could finally be on our boat in the midst of that beauty, melting into the splendid scenery while perhaps entertaining lazy daydreams of Tom Sawyer or Huckleberry Finn, always seemed an agonizingly long one.

All of this beauty is set within the confines of the Santa Ynez Valley, a sprawling expanse of gently rolling hills with a very light scattering of gnarled old oak trees. Top-quality wines come from the many vineyards, which compete for space with miniature horse ranches, ostrich ranches, alpaca ranches, upscale estates, and Cold Springs Tavern, the historic log cabin stagecoach stop turned gourmet restaurant.

The Santa Barbara locals tend to be an exceptionally healthy and active group. Nature trails abound, and there are forever outdoor athletic events such as bike rides, cancer walks, triathlons, and dog parades—if you can call that an athletic event. On the more leisurely side, there are innumerable sidewalk cafes, tastefully decorated gift shops, theaters for movies and stage performances, art galleries, a world-class art museum, and many fun special events.

My mother spent the second half of her life fighting to maintain building codes that would preserve our low-key Spanish architecture and uniform building plan. Although Santa Barbara is only an hour and a half north of Hollywood and Los Angeles, it doesn't sport a single billboard. Also noticeably absent are high-rises, neon lights, and any distasteful commercial advertising. It is peaceful, quiet, and serene. Outside of the downtown area, you would be hard pressed to find a spot anywhere in the world with a higher concentration of beautiful, spacious, wooded estates or such an abundance of red tile roofs.

Yet for all the attractions Santa Barbara offers, what has always occupied my energies more than anything else is the ocean. When I was a young boy of 8, my father took me sailing on a friend's small wooden sailboat in the San Francisco Bay, and from that moment on, there was no turning back—I was a sailor.

My first boat, which I purchased for $500, was a wood cabin cruiser about 18 feet long with a Johnson outboard. I had been on many boats with my father and figured that credential gave me license to be a captain. The reality was that I didn't know the first thing about boating or seamanship. Luckily, in my case, learning by immersion turned out to be forgiving of my many shortcomings.

The first time my friend John and I backed the boat and trailer into the water at the marina launching ramp, we wanted to mimic the veterans who slammed on the brakes at the last minute of descent so that the boat would slide off the trailer into the water, saving them the trouble of pushing it

✴ *Chris Madsen sailing in San Francisco Bay with Dad on his friend's boat*

off. Either their boats were lighter than mine or their trucks were heavier than my van because when I braked hard on that algae-covered, sloping concrete, the boat, trailer, and van all went into a slow, steady skid that didn't end until my rear tires and tailpipe were under water. John and I proudly ignored the few jeers because the boat floated off the trailer without any pushing, just as planned—well, almost.

Flush with success, we left the marina and, for my first experience as captain, went to sea. Being 18, we headed straight for More Mesa, a clothing-optional beach, where we dropped anchor and basked in the glory. It was a short-lived glory, however, because in less than five minutes, we noticed that our anchor was dragging and we were almost in the surf zone. There wouldn't be much of a story if the engine had started, but of course it didn't. It turned over but wouldn't fire up. As the breaking waves got closer, I scrambled to pull off the engine cover and, one by one, remove the spark plugs, sand the dirty tips, and reinstall them, the last one to John's nervous "Hurry up, man!" The engine fired, and we reanchored, enjoyed the rest of the day, and went home, not realizing that there had been anything the least bit unpolished about our performance.

Coastal cruising and fishing were fun, but what I really wanted was to make it out to the islands. From east to west, Anacapa, Santa Cruz, Santa Rosa, and San

Miguel, the last which is forty miles from shore, form Channel Islands National Park. The islands are completely undeveloped with the exception of a few ranger stations. The nearest to Santa Barbara, Santa Cruz Island, is twenty miles offshore, twenty miles long, and about ten miles wide.

I sold the cabin cruiser and bought a 21-foot Santana sailboat. The heavy lead keel had to be cranked up and the mast folded down for the boat to fit on the trailer. Youth, I think, is oblivious to work done in the pursuit of fun because, looking back, that was a lot of work! By this time, I had taken some classes in sailing and seamanship.

The Santa Barbara Channel, running between the mainland and the islands, is rated as one of the most dangerous waterways in the world because of the cross-currents that are formed as currents wrap around the islands and because of dangerous reefs, fog, and occasional strong offshore Santa Ana winds. But with my newly acquired nautical schooling and no lack of confidence, I decided to sail single-handed out to Santa Cruz Island. How bad could it get? I figured that if it got too rough, I could just turn around and head home. Luckily, it didn't. It was the perfect trip. The winds gradually picked up along the way, giving me the chance to test my skills at reducing sail. The little boat sliced through the water and bounced over the waves. There was a little bit of play in the 550-pound lead keel at its point of attachment, and occasionally a large wave would cause the keel to make an unnervingly loud side-to-side clunking noise, but I convinced myself that was okay and probably perfectly normal. I'm actually still not sure about that.

Four and a half hours after putting to sea, I made anchor in Potato Bay on Santa Cruz Island. It's a cute little anchorage, just big enough for one boat, and with steep, protecting cliffs on all sides, it affords excellent shelter, though it provides no access to the island for hiking. But I enjoyed the calm anchorage, had a nice dinner, and woke early the next morning in order to get back across the channel before the weather got rough. My small outboard absolutely refused to start that morning, and I had no radio on the boat, so my only option was to hoist sail and hurriedly pull anchor as I sailed out. The maneuver would have been much easier with two people, but everything went fine, as did the trip home. By early afternoon, I had completed my first of what would become hundreds of trips to the islands.

Over the ensuing years, I had many boats. They seemed to get bigger, and I oscillated between powerboats and sailboats.

In 1987, at the age of 32, my wife Peggy, whom I had been with for ten years, died after an extended illness. I was affected not just emotionally but also physically, to the point that I was sure there was something wrong with me, and I pressed doctors to identify some underlying cause such as cancer or a heart condition. I scoffed at their diagnosis that stress could be the root of my symptoms of fatigue, palpitations, and body aches and cramps. For the past fourteen years, I had owned and operated a swimming pool business in Santa Barbara. With Peggy's passing and uncertain of my own future health, I decided it was time to sell the business, buy a bigger boat, and sail to Tahiti.

I bought a beautiful cutter-rigged Valiant 40 and went back to school to take classes in celestial navigation, meteorology, advanced first aid, and French (since Tahiti is in French Polynesia). *Rejoyce* was a phenomenal boat, fast and graceful but built heavy and strong. This was a boat that you could take anywhere in the world. This was the boat you would want to be on if you had to face a hurricane or other large storm. I sailed that boat every chance I got. I knew every nut and bolt, every rope and wire, every piece of electrical and plumbing, every possible sail configuration.

More often than not, I would take her out to the islands by myself and camp out for as long as I could, moving from anchorage to anchorage until I had to be back for work. I enjoyed the time alone on the ocean. It was healing. Until you have been on a boat by yourself in the middle of the ocean, it is doubtful that anyone could adequately explain the feeling.

My favorite spot aboard *Rejoyce* was all the way forward on the extreme tip of the bow. With the autopilot set, I would sit there holding the forestay, my legs dangling off to either side. The silence, complete but for the wind on the sails and the lapping of the waves against the bow as it gracefully sliced through the water, was hypnotic. To sit atop a vessel of that size and tonnage sliding through the water so quietly and gracefully and in such harmony with the elements, charging along with nothing more than the sea breeze to provide power, was awe-inspiring. From my perch on the bow, I often looked straight down at dolphins, which would roll over just enough to look back up at me as they glided from port to starboard and back again. In the glassy calm of one trip, I observed two gray whales, the barnacles visible on their backs, swimming slowly toward each other from opposite directions. At the last minute, they rolled onto their sides so that they could slowly rub bellies as they passed, in what I guessed was some kind of courtship dance.

In that setting, all alone in the middle of such a vastness of ocean, which by all rights should feel like a cold, uninviting void, surprisingly there comes an almost spiritual feeling of awe and wonder at the magnificence of the planet on which we live. It is a place where a sailor feels an almost personal connection with the whole of the earth. A friend of mine who is a diver said that when he's out there, "it feels like being with God." I fully understand the feeling he expressed.

My favorite of all of the spots on all of the islands is the Pelican Bay anchorage on Santa Cruz Island. It is right in the middle of the island on the side facing Santa Barbara, so from the marina it is a straight shot out. A good-sized anchorage that will accommodate about fifty boats, it indents sharply into the island with sheer, towering cliffs on all sides, making it a calm spot in the roughest of weather. Some places just plain have personality. Pelican Bay, alive and wild and beautiful, overflows with it. In ancient times, Pelican Bay was the site of a large Chumash Indian village, and in the 1920s, a local family accommodated paying guests at a fishing camp that they built there. One can still see stonework and traces of foundations from several wood cabins that had perched atop the bluffs. The twenty miles of sea between Pelican Bay and Santa Barbara make it feel isolated and a world unto itself—a vibrant world.

The island is of a volcanic nature from some ancient fissure. The solid conglomerate of porous red and black rock is visible only on the exposed edges of 100-foot cliffs, which have been cut out by the erosion of the sea, and in the steep-walled canyons, which harbor little streams cascading sharply down to the water's edge. The remainder of the island is blanketed with a dark, fertile soil that supports an abundant diversity of plant life. In places, the island is barren and arid. In contrast, the deep ravine, whose creek empties just to the side of the anchorage, hosts a luxuriant wood of large, very old eucalyptus trees. In their cool shade grow many varieties of flowering vines, and large sword ferns adorn the small rock pools along the creek, which seems always to be occupied by plump, happy pollywogs. Many spots on the hillsides are covered with dense thickets of bent and twisted manzanita bushes, with shiny red bark that feels smooth and oily to the hand.

On the hillside immediately above the anchorage and running all the way to the top of the island is a thick wooded grove of Santa Cruz Island pines. They grow nowhere else in the world. They are relatively tall but are not straight like sequoias. Instead, they grow bent and gnarled and weathered, as you would expect of a tree on a windswept island. They hold an abundance of cones and have spread an undisturbed carpet of needles on the ground. To be on an island twenty miles offshore, high on a hillside, perched atop a large boulder in the midst of a magnificent pine forest and, at the same time, to be enjoying a bird's-eye view of the ocean below stretching out to the distant mainland is magical.

Santa Cruz Island rises abruptly from sea level to an altitude of 2,450 feet. A hike to the top can be made by carefully selecting routes along the ridgetops and avoiding the creeks with their impassable box canyons. I have summited the island in many places and each time had sore muscles for days afterwards.

Regardless of the activity, every trip I have made to the islands has been a mini-adventure with many surprises. On one occasion, while relaxing on a bluff and taking in the beauty of the setting, my friend and I spotted a pod of pilot whales moving in our direction, close to shore. We hurried down to the dinghy and raced out into their path just in time to watch in excited amazement as their 20-foot white forms passed in crystal clear water directly beneath us and surfaced on both sides of us. I later read an account in a sailing magazine of a solo sailor in a 27-foot fiberglass sloop whose boat may have bumped a pilot whale or perhaps made a mother feel threatened. Whatever the cause, the result was a continual ramming of the boat by the pod until the hull split and the boat sank. Even with that knowledge, I wouldn't trade my experience for a million dollars—but I also wouldn't pay a dollar to repeat it.

Santa Cruz Island used to be home to large numbers of wild pigs and boars. After one particularly rough crossing to the island, a friend and I arrived at Pelican Bay and dropped anchor just before dark. Feeling the effects of the rough seas, we rowed to the little rock shelf that is used as a landing, dragged the dinghy above the high water mark, and hiked up the narrow, foot-wide path that switchbacks up the volcanic rock cliffs to the bluff above. Feeling refreshed after a couple hours of lying on our backs stargazing, we began the hike back down the path, not realizing that a large male boar had previously descended and was grazing on seaweed on the shelf below. I think we and the boar became aware of each other's presence at the same time when we were about halfway down. My friend and I were first startled by a deep, agitated snorting sound, immediately followed by a clackety chorus of rapidly stampeding hoofs. In his haste to exit the scene, the boar charged past us as we screamed, the narrowness of the path forcing him to smash against our legs and, at the same time, affording us a firsthand view of what boar tusks and the straight standing black bristles on a boar's back look like up close. I wouldn't pay a dollar to repeat that experience either.

If Santa Cruz Island is beautiful, the water is incomparable. It is usually crystal clear in varying shades of emerald and sapphire. Beneath the surface, the cliffs con-

✳ Rejoyce *at anchor in Pelican Bay, Santa Cruz Island, 1988*

tinue their vertical descent for 10 or 15 feet to a bottom of sand strewn with rocks and boulders. The sun playing through forests of seaweed adds to the vibrant colors and accents the many fish that swim about, including California's spectacular state fish, the garibaldi, which is about 10 inches long and solid gold in color. Lobsters abound in these waters, as do playful sea lions, crabs, abalone, and a multitude of species of fish. The island is a worldwide diving destination, and I have enjoyed many hours of underwater exploration there.

On one dive, I found a 40-pound anchor that must have been cut free by a boat in trouble—and recently, because it was still in perfect condition. Despite the difficulty of swimming that large an anchor back to the boat, I did so because I knew that I could easily sell it for a decent price. After I got it home, it sat in my garage for a year, but I finally placed an ad in the paper, and someone immediately called saying that he wanted to buy it. He didn't have a car and wanted me to drive it to his house. We agreed on a price of $40, and I agreed to drive it over to him. When I pulled up in front of the old Victorian house, I stared in disbelief. Ten-foot flames were spreading across the front of it, and there wasn't another soul in sight. I called 911, grabbed a hose, and began to douse the flames. When I banged on the door to let the guy know his house was on fire, he had no idea. After the fire department arrived and knocked a hole in the house to extinguish the flames inside the wall, he gave me $50 for the anchor. I had only twenties on me, so I put the $50 in my top pocket, and we walked together to the corner market to get his $10 change. When we got there, I found that the $50 had fallen out of my pocket on the way. We backtracked but never found it. So the upshot of the story was this:

> I labored to swim that anchor to my boat.
> I stored it in my garage for a year.
> I paid to advertise it in the paper.
> I drove it to the buyer's house.
> I saved the buyer's house from burning down.
> And in the end, the whole thing cost *me* $10. I'm
>   glad I don't do salvage for a living!

Well, plans are plans, and I never did sail to Tahiti. At the time, the real estate market was just starting its ascent, and I didn't want to get left behind, so I sold the boat, bought a house, and flew to Tahiti instead, pondering on the flight over whether I had "sold out." The in-flight movie, cocktail, and roasted almonds all helped to convince me that spending part of a day in the air versus weeks at sea was a wise move.

My time with *Rejoyce* was a wonderful chapter in my life, and I really honed my skills as a sailor. After Peggy's death, the boat almost immediately helped me to have fun and enjoy life again. Coincidently, in those months, all my physical symptoms, which I assumed reflected some underlying terminal condition, miraculously faded away. This convinced me that stress can indeed have an effect on the body.

Real estate went in the right direction, and I eventually traded up to a house that perfectly fit my personality. The house itself was 1960s style and begging to be updated, but it was located atop a mesa with unobstructed, panoramic views of the beach, marina, and all four islands, not to mention sunrises and sunsets. The entire side of the house facing the ocean was floor-to-ceiling glass with the most beautiful ocean and island views.

I have always enjoyed construction, so I went to work gutting the house, adding a bedroom and bathroom, and generally updating everything. Most of the time, I had a large dumpster parked in front of the house for construction debris. One day, my neighbor approached me as I was throwing some trash in.

"Chris I've got a favor to ask of you," he said.

"What can I do for you?" I replied.

"I have an old rowboat under my house that I've been planning on rebuilding. The problem is, it's been ten years now, and I just don't think I'll ever get around to it."

"Don't look at me," I said. "I'm going into project therapy if I ever finish this one."

"Actually, I was just going to ask if I could pay you to throw it in your dumpster."

"Sure. Throw it in the dumpster, but I'm not taking your money. You've put up with all my noise. It's the least I can do. I'll even help you carry it up here."

We carried the rowboat out from under his house, but as we approached the dumpster, a thought crossed my mind, and I suggested that we just leave the boat on my front lawn. I had remembered an acquaintance who had a nonprofit corporation. He helped rehabilitate people with drug and alcohol problems by involving them in boating and teaching them how to restore boats. People would donate used boats to him in exchange for a tax write-off. I didn't know much about him, but it seemed like a good cause and possibly a good home for the rowboat, so I picked up the phone. I PICKED UP THE PHONE. **I PICKED UP THE PHONE!!!**

At that moment, the heavens should have shouted down, "You're not just picking up the phone. You are kicking over a giant domino that is going to knock over another domino and then another and another, sending your life off in an altogether unplanned, unforeseen direction."

Alas, the heavens lay silent and so, as alluded to in my opening words and without the slightest inkling that the action I was about to take would irrevocably alter my life's course, I dialed the number.

Hello, Rowdy

THE VOICE ON THE OTHER END of the phone said, "Hello?"

"Jack," I said, "this is Chris Madsen, Josie's friend. Do you remember me?"

"Chris, how are things?"

"Well I don't get to work on boats every day like some lucky people. Otherwise, life is good."

"You would not believe!" he exclaimed. "You should see the boat I'm sitting on right now."

"It's only nine o'clock in the morning, and you're already on a boat?"

"A 59-foot Herreshoff sloop named *Rowdy*."

"Captain Nat or his son?" I asked.

In the late 1800s, Nathanael Herreshoff had started the Herreshoff Manufacturing Company, which, thanks to his genius, became the most famous boat builder of all time. The company was later taken over and run with a good, yet less stellar reputation by his son, L. Francis Herreshoff.

Jack said, "Captain Nat built her in 1916 for the New York Yacht Club."

In a flash, I forgot why I had even called. Classic Herreshoffs with any kind of pedigree are coveted collectors' items for people who are wealthy enough to afford them. It was like hearing someone on the phone telling you that he was had just found a piece of paper that was covered in equations and signed by a guy named Einstein or happened to be looking at a cute little painting signed by someone named Picasso.

"Really! What kind of shape is she in?" I asked.

"Well, that's a sad, sad story. Actually, her *shape* is beautiful, her lines are spectacular, but her condition is just about terminal — a lot of rotten wood. I'm pumping water out of the bilge right now. We're in Channel Islands Harbor. You ought to come down and have a look. You don't get the chance to see many boats like this these days."

Channel Islands Harbor is in Oxnard, about a 45-minute drive south of Santa Barbara. I quickly calculated whether I had time in my day to make the trip.

"Today's tight," I said. "How are you looking next week?"

"If we still have her," he replied. "It's too big of a project for us to hang onto. We're just going to polish her up and try to find a buyer."

"What do you think she'll sell for?"

"The monthly slip fees are killing me. I just need to stop expenses, so I'll probably sell her for about $5,000."

A 59-foot Herreshoff, which I know would normally go in the $1,000,000-plus range, for $5,000? I felt like I had just won the lottery!

"Tell you what," I said. "If I come down around noon today, can you take a few minutes off to have lunch together?"

Jack said lunch would be fine. Having altogether forgotten the original reason for my call, I hung up without ever mentioning the rowboat.

Oxnard, if I were to be kind, I would say is a work in progress. Many of the buildings are old, designed in the 1960s and even then of only modest origins. Some have cinderblock walls decorated by taggers, as Oxnard has a large gang presence. Most of the schools have perimeter chain link fences with locking gates and security guards. The sprawling, flat landscape includes a patchwork of giant rectangular plots of soil dedicated to agriculture. Oxnard is the strawberry capital of California, and the breeze often communicates, in no kind way, when a mammoth load of fertilizer has been dumped and spread over one of those large fields.

But much effort has gone into giving the city a facelift, and there are scattered developments, many gated, with beautiful two-story townhouses and attractive landscaping. The one area where the city has excelled is at the Channel Islands Marina. The engineered development is sprawling, and its channels travel inland for an extended distance. Within the overall development and waterways, which branch off like individual streets beckoning to curious explorers, there are several boatyards, individual marinas, waterfront restaurants, yacht clubs, shops, and exclusive waterfront communities complete with individual slips for the homeowner's boats. I have enjoyed renting a little electric boat and spending a full day exploring up and down all the different channels and avenues, looking at the variety of boats, shops, and restaurants.

They say you only have seconds to make a first impression. To be honest, when I arrived at the marina and saw *Rowdy*, my first impression of her was so decidedly mixed that I would equate it to seeing a beautiful purebred dog that had been beaten, abused, neglected, and left to die in a pitiful state. *Rowdy* seemed to look up at me with big, sad puppy eyes, behind which the grace and beauty and massive strength of her lines took my breath away. At 22 tons, she seemed to me to be not a boat but a small SHIP! Her form was all that remained to convey her pedigree, for everything else had been desecrated. The wood decks had been covered with fiberglass and painted. The bowsprit was missing. The boom had been cut to half its original length. Every bit of original hardware and every original hatch had been removed and replaced with insultingly cheap and absolutely inappropriate items. The rigging was wrong. There were no sails. The hull was a mess of peeling paint, punctuated with bleeding rust spots and large areas of visible dry rot.

If I have a personality flaw, it is that I tend to be the eternal optimist. I appreciate the good in things to such a point that it is very easy for me to overlook the bad. So at that moment, while I know I glanced over all the flaws, my gaze was held by the clean design of her flush deck, with no built-up cabin, and her long, graceful sweeping shear. I could picture how easily and quickly her bow, with its immensely long overhang, must have sliced through the water in her heyday. Looking at her sleek yet sad appearance, I saw nothing but potential and the obvious signature of her master designer, Captain Nat Herreshoff.

Nathanael Greene Herreshoff, an accomplished sailor, started the Herreshoff Manufacturing Company in Bristol, Rhode Island, in 1878, along with his brother

John. A genius by any measure, Nat Herreshoff was undisputedly the greatest yacht designer of all time. He brought speed and grace to yachting, building a worldwide reputation that earned him the nickname "The Wizard of Bristol." His designs absolutely dominated the sport of sailing, decade after decade. He was untouchable. Between 1893 and 1934, every winning America's Cup yacht was built by Herreshoff. They included many legendary names:

Vigilant – 1893 (designed and built by Herreshoff)
Defender – 1895 (designed and built by Herreshoff)
Columbia – 1899, 1901 (designed and built by Herreshoff)
Reliance – 1903 (designed and built by Herreshoff)
Resolute – 1920 (designed and built by Herreshoff)
Enterprise – 1930 (designed by Starling Burgess, built by Herreshoff)
Rainbow – 1934 (designed by Starling Burgess, built by Herreshoff)

Herreshoff was an innovator, and his inventions and patents forever changed the world of yachting. To name just a few:

He invented the modern-day sail track and slide systems.
He invented the folding propeller.
He received the first U.S. patent on catamaran sailboats.
He introduced screw fastenings for planking to the United States.
He developed light, hollow steel spars combined with scientific rigging.
He invented the cross-cut sail with cloths
    running at right angles to the leech.
He invented the streamline-shaped bulk and fin keels.
He developed the long overhangs on sailing yachts that allow
    for more sail, greater speed, and better stability.

He designed universally accepted racing tables.
He developed nearly all methods of light wood hull construction.
He developed below-deck winches (*Reliance*, 1903).
He developed the method of splicing rope to wire.

His innovations were far from being limited to recreational sailing boats. In the power arena:

He built the first torpedo boats for the U.S. Navy.
He developed the first light steam engine and fast torpedo boats.
He designed more types of steam engines than anyone else.
He designed the web frame and longitudinal construction for metal
    hulls, afterward patented and known as the Isherwood System.
He developed the flat stern form of steam yachts, making them
    capable of being driven at high speed/length ratios.

Herreshoff was prolific, and because of his many accomplishments, he was one of the few people ever to have been made an honorary member of the New York Yacht Club, his name being listed immediately before those of His Majesty King George V of England and the Prince of Wales. I had seen many pictures of Herreshoff's yachting designs in books and museums, but they were only pictures. As I stood looking at the genuine article, everything inside me was crying out to find a way to own that boat.

I'm sure I was already sold, but I tried to look only casually curious as I called to Jack, "Permission to come aboard?"

"You made it, great. Come take a look."

"Well I must say this is a lot of boat. What do you know about it?"

"It's a New York 40. Even though she is 59 feet on deck, she's called a New York 40 because she's 40 feet at the waterline, and she was built for the New York Yacht Club. In 1916, Herreshoff built twelve of them for the club, to be raced against each other as a class. Beyond that, I don't know anything about her history. I got her from a lady who wanted to restore her but ended up running out of funds, so she donated *Rowdy* to us for a tax write-off."

We looked the boat over, and the only thing the outside had going for it was that it was in better condition than the inside, which was dark and damp and had a musty smell. Fresh water dripping down the inside of the hull indicated how high the bilgewater must have been before being recently pumped out.

Over lunch, I found that Jack was not interested in the rowboat that had been responsible for initiating this saga. But I was interested in *Rowdy* and gave Jack his full asking price of $5,000 in exchange for a receipt, written on the back of a business card. Then began the learning curve. Oh, how much simpler life would be if you could be born knowing it all — but how much less interesting.

The Boatyard

$\mathcal{W}$ITH LOTS OF CARPENTRY EXPERIENCE and lots of boating experience, I was prepared to jump in, all guns blazing, do a first-class restoration, and be sailing *Rowdy* in six months. I scheduled the boatyard to haul her into their yard for what I said would be an extended period of work. I had to wait several weeks for an available space, so I kept busy with maintenance and began to play around with research.

Because Nat Herreshoff was such an important figure in maritime history, the Massachusetts Institute of Technology has built an extensive archive containing many of his drawings, patents, and ship plans, including those for the New York 40—not just one plan, but hundreds! I discovered that there were hull plans, sail plans, deck plans, a plan for the skylight hatch, and even a plan that detailed Herreshoff's patented hinge for that skylight. The MIT archive was a gold mine for the project. There is no room for artistic expression on a proper vintage yacht restoration. Every detail has to be as close to original as humanly possible. So I ordered full-sized copies of all of the plans. I wanted to see every detail of every part of that boat from the original layout. Thus began what would become a torrential outpouring of money—beyond anything I would have imagined (and I have a good imagination).

I hounded and pestered anyone I could get on the phone to find additional details about the boat and ended up hitting another gold mine. Collections of photographs from two of the top boating photographers of *Rowdy*'s era were archived on the East Coast, and copies of individual pictures were available for purchase. Both the Rosenfeld Collection and the Edwin Levick Collection are indexed, and after requesting searches, I was told that each collection had numerous photographs of *Rowdy* by herself and with other New York 40s. It was more money out the window, but I didn't blink an eye. How exciting was the prospect of seeing actual photos of her from the 1920s and earlier! How absolutely thrilling to see what she would have looked like at her very best, pressing hard to win a race! Perhaps I would be able to see the people on deck. I thought it would be fascinating to find anything out about the original owner.

I contacted the Herreshoff Marine Museum and spoke with Halsey Herreshoff, Captain Nat's grandson. I learned that as well as the twelve New York 40s built in 1916, two more were built in 1926. Halsey had restored one of them, *Rugosa II*, which he sailed regularly. He had previously been the town administrator of Bristol, Rhode Island, and had a busy schedule, but he was extremely gracious and invited me to come visit him and see his boat any time. He told me that *Marilee*, also built in 1926, was currently being restored in Camden, Maine, but very few of the original twelve New York 40s were still around. Halsey was able to send me a copy of the original order card for *Rowdy*, which was still on file in the museum. She was ordered in 1915 for $10,000 with an extra $280 to have the wheel option instead of a tiller, and the buyer's name was Holland Sackett Duell.

I hadn't anticipated any sort of reaction on discovering the original owner's name. Perhaps if it had been Bob Smith, the impact would have been less dramatic. But there was something about seeing that name in front of me—Holland Sackett Duell—on a piece of paper, tangible. It wasn't just a name. It represented a person, a personality, who at one time must have had an immensely close and active connection with *Rowdy*. Even in her current run-down, beat-up condition, when I stepped aboard her, *Rowdy* filled me with a feeling of being captain, the captain of a substantial, strong, graceful little ship, and with yearning to lean her over in a wind and plow her bow through long, rolling ocean swells. For a man who was a member of the New York Yacht Club, racing her as a new boat against a class of sister ships, the thrill must have been immense.

At that moment, I knew that the scope of my project had doubled. It was no longer just about researching the boat, trying to find boat plans and old sailing photos. In a flash, it became obvious to me that I had been looking at only half of the story. I now had a burning curiosity about *Rowdy's* owner and a realization that this project was not just about bringing *Rowdy* back to life but also about resurrecting the story of Holland Sackett Duell.

Getting the boat sailing was my immediate priority, but at every opportunity, I continued to press hard to research the boat, and I began to find references to her in many books and magazine articles. She seemed to have had a fairly famous racing history. I spent an exorbitant amount of time on the Internet trying to discover anything about Duell or *Rowdy*, and while I was constantly finding helpful little clues for *Rowdy*, I was coming up pretty much empty for Duell.

The day came when *Rowdy* was scheduled to be hauled out onto the dry land of the boatyard. A travel lift cannot be used for a boat as large as *Rowdy*; instead, a boatyard will use a marine railway, which is a sloped concrete ramp with railroad tracks that extends into the water. A large cradle with supporting sides and railroad wheels is lowered underwater, a boat is driven through the water to a point above the cradle, and then cradle and boat are pulled out with a hydraulic cable system. That morning, I tied up to the courtesy dock, somewhat wound up with anxious butterflies but not expecting what came next. The yard foreman looked at *Rowdy*, shook his head, and invited me into the office.

"Chris, I know we scheduled this a long time ago, but I didn't realize the condition of the boat, and I don't want it in my yard."

Stunned silence. Disbelief. Am I going to be stuck with a boat and no place to rebuild it?

"Why?" I asked.

"I think she's too far gone. If she doesn't break up and fall apart under her own weight when we pull her out of the water, I think you would run out of money long before you could ever finish rebuilding her, in which case we would need to call in a bulldozer, break her up, and haul away the remains at a cost to us of about $5,000. It's happened to me too many times."

You son of a —!, I thought. *You are in no position to judge my abilities or my character. If anything, you should have looked at the boat before promising me a spot in your yard.*

"Larry, I know I will see the job through," I said. "But listen. If it comes to that, I have the funds to dispose of the boat. You won't get stuck with the bill."

"I just don't want to take the chance. I can't tell you how many people come into this yard, excited as a school kid about the deal they got on a wooden boat. People have no idea how much work, time, and money are involved in fixing a boat like that. One by one, they lose a ton of money, learn their lesson, and never do it again. But I've got to watch it over and over again and pick up the pieces when they walk away, and I don't want to do that again."

"I understand your point. It's your yard, and you make the rules. How about if I give you an extra $5,000 as a deposit? That way, if I walk, you're covered."

To my monumental relief, he saw my logic, took my money, and put the boat on blocks in the yard after she refused to fall apart on the haul-out as he had half-expected. A mad flurry of activity ensued. Because her decks towered 13 feet above the ground, two levels of scaffolding were erected completely around her. To protect her from the elements, I built an enormous bubble out of PVC pipe and tarps that covered the entire boat from the ground up, leaving standing room on deck.

One thing I have learned in business is that you don't have to be an expert to excel at something as long as you surround yourself with experts. So I called in the best wooden boat surveyor I could find to size the project up and, I hoped, follow it through. Don spent hours going over and through the boat. First, he tapped on the hull with a special wooden mallet and put chalk X's on the planks that returned a dull thud, indicating that they were rotten and needed to be replaced. When, to my dismay, the entire hull seemed to be a solid wall of X's, he systematically moved through the inside inspecting deck beams, frames ("ribs" to the layman), engine, electrical, plumbing, and a host of other items, all of which he noted on the inspection forms.

I had expected Don to congratulate me on my purchase and to compliment me on what a rare treasure I now owned. Instead, he pretty much echoed the opinion of the yard foreman: "Chris, I've seen this too many times. People get into these wooden boat projects, and they end up being drained of every penny they have. I've seen marriages end in divorce, houses lost, and lives ruined. My suggestion to you is write a check for $5,000, have the boat broken up and hauled away, and cut your losses and walk."

With that input, I did the only thing that made any sense at the time: I fired him and looked for another surveyor. Maritime Surveyors was my next choice. The company was highly respected and had lots of wooden boat experience. Skip Riley approached the project with much more enthusiasm and optimism, while at the same time stressing the enormity of the undertaking and making sure I understood it. He was enamored of the boat and saw huge value in preserving such a gem of maritime history.

Of all the things Skip did throughout that project, what he did next was perhaps the most valuable. He told me, "You are going to need a full-time shipwright on this project, someone who has lived and breathed wooden boats. Unless this boat is rebuilt properly, it's going to go down as a colossal waste of your time and money and the loss of an important boat. I've got someone in mind for you. He has worked in Maine. He

✻ Rowdy *rotten hull.*

has taught in Washington, and right now he is working at a local boatyard doing work that holds no interest for him whatsoever. I think he would enjoy being involved in a project of this caliber. His name's Alan. I'll see if I can get him to give you a call. He's good. He's really good."

Alan joined the project and started off with gusto. He was the guy all right. Alan knew everything about vintage wooden boats. He knew the people who orbited in that sphere, and he had resources for planking wood, for hardware, and even for foundries for some of the bronze hardware that we had to have custom cast.

The first step was to tear off all the bad wood. It was disheartening, as the dumpster filled with broken pieces of rotten wood, to watch *Rowdy*'s form assume that of a decrepit skeleton.

But piles of new planking wood were ordered from Washington, teak decking was ordered from Florida, and I acquired appropriate antique hardware as I could find it. I hired two marine cabinetmakers to help with the interior, a marine metal shop for the many custom metal projects, and an engine company to custom design a new propulsion system. I put in twelve to fourteen hours a day on that boat, seven days a week, month after month, and soon the months turned into years. Almost every piece of framing on the boat was either replaced or doubled up. Ninety percent of the planks and the entire deck were replaced. A new rudder and bowsprit were installed, as were completely new electrical, plumbing, navigational, and propulsion systems.

For the first year, I commuted back and forth every day from Santa Barbara. My girlfriend at the time always had trouble reaching me because it was difficult for me to hear my cell phone over all the power tools. She was the jealous sort and became suspicious that I was having an affair, which of course I would never do. But to make it easier for her to reach me, I got a vibrating pager. Unfortunately, that system failed to elicit swift enough replies from me, and the relationship ended.

It was a challenging time for me that also saw me picking up speeding tickets in the haste of my morning commute to the boat. When I got the fourth one, I thought I had reached the limit and my license would be suspended. I actually wept after the officer gave me the ticket and drove away. It would have been a crippling blow to have lost my transportation. Luckily, no mention was ever made of suspending my license, but it was scary enough to whip me into submission, and to this day I don't speed. To top things off, money was flying out of my account in all directions at an alarming and somewhat depressing rate. That was the low point of the project for me. It was becoming a struggle logistically, financially, and emotionally.

I decided to rent out my house in Santa Barbara and live on the boat. This ended up being a very good move. It saved money. It saved travel time. The interior of *Rowdy* was spacious and had become quite livable, and I woke up every morning to the smell of salt air and the singing of sea gulls. My daily routine began with a social chat session at the coffee and doughnut shop next door and included a 5:00 p.m. beer break with all the other guys in the yard when they called it quits for the day. One day I made friends with a pigeon that roosted by the boat. Before long, she was comfortable enough to land on my finger when I fed her, and she

✳ *Pile of rotten wood.*

soon earned the name "Tricksy" by performing little tricks to earn my handouts. She remained my friend throughout the project.

Eventually, there seemed to be light at the end of the tunnel. Every bit of the restoration had been done with painstaking attention to detail, and the results were spectacular. I had put together photo albums of vintage photos of *Rowdy* that I had collected, and she was now starting to resemble that earlier self. Taking advantage of Halsey Herreshoff's invitation, I had traveled to Rhode Island to study his boat. (I still owe him lunch if he ever makes it to Santa Barbara.) I also visited *Marilee* in the boatyard in Camden, Maine. I had acquired so much information on *Rowdy* and the New York 40 class that I felt there could be very little else, if anything, that I could be doing in my quest to bring her back to life.

The other half of the story, that of the original owner, remained my missing link. One evening, I decided to look over the Rosenfeld photos with a magnifying glass. There was one photo that had been taken on a calm day, obviously from another boat, given the closeness of the shot and the somewhat elevated perspective of the camera. There seemed to be about five people in and around the cockpit. As I moved the magnifying glass in, expecting no more than a blurred view, I was greeted by an amazingly high level of resolution, none of which was lost as I moved in closer and closer. And there, gazing forward from the helm, was Holland Sackett Duell. I will never forget the moment I was first able to lay eyes on the original owner of *Rowdy*.

✳ *Fourth of July, 1920 sail aboard* Rowdy.

He was a handsome man with a strong chin, focused eyes, neatly trimmed hair, and a well-formed physique, sporting a formal suit and a captain's cap.

Seeing the image caused me to redouble my efforts to track down any kind of history about the man. One day during an Internet search, I got a hit for a Holland Duell, which I initially thought to dismiss because he was a New York state senator. Such a person, I thought, would probably not have the time or interest for sailing. But I was following up all leads, and the reference said that he had attended Yale. I contacted the Association of Yale Alumni, and their records showed a Holland Duell who had five children, four of whom were deceased. They didn't know whether the fifth was dead or alive, but they did have an address, and if I wanted to write a letter of inquiry and mail it to the association, they would forward the letter. So I wrote a letter saying something to the effect of "I am rebuilding a boat and trying to determine the original owner. His name was Holland Duell. I know that your father was named Holland Duell. Did your father ever own a sailboat named *Rowdy*?"

By that time, I had framed an enlargement of that photo and displayed it belowdecks in the main salon. It posed far more questions than it answered. Before I acquired it, I'd had only the name Holland Sackett Duell, which after so much time was starting to feel somewhat mythical. Now I found myself looking at the photo every time I walked past it, face to face not only with an image that proved his real-life existence, but also with the faces of four other people who must have been in some way involved in his life. I was tormented by the question "What was their relationship and why, after all this time, could I still not find a doorway into this past?" Little did I know what was waiting for me just around the corner.

Hanny

I HAD NO IDEA, as my ringing phone called me away from the boat, that I was about to have one of the most memorable conversations of my life.

"Hello," I said.

A frail woman's voice on the other end replied, "I hear you're fixing up my father's boat."

It was eight simple little words. It took a minuscule two seconds out of the entirety of my allotted time in this world. Yet the thunderous percussion of those words reverberates over and over in my mind—fondly, indeed very fondly, because for me, that was the moment when this story truly began. "I hear you're fixing up my father's boat" marked the opening of a door through which I came to share so many details of the triumphs, struggles, intimacies, joys, and sorrows of an intertwined group of people whose lives had already come and passed.

Yet just as the triggers for life-changing events are rarely recognized for their true weighting at the moment of occurrence, I was immediately caught off balance, unable to fully process those words as I inquisitively replied, "Who is this?"

"You sent me a letter," she said.

"Through Yale." My intonation was half questioning, half making a statement of fact.

Playfully, she asked, "Have you got it?"

"If your father was Holland Duell, I believe your name must be Harriet Anne Duell."

"My father was Holland Duell, and if I may call you Chris, I would like for you to call me Hanny."

My disorientation was gone. All of the detective work that I had done for the past few years was now crystal clear at the front of my mind. This was the only real lead I'd had to finding out who the original owner of the boat might have been. I knew that the name of the original owner and the name of this woman's father were the same, but was it the same Holland Duell or were they two different people? I felt that I was about to explode with an out-of-control swelling of nervous excitement, anxiety, and suspense. I absolutely could not contain myself within the proper formalities of polite conversation. I asked, or maybe blurted, "Did your father own a boat named *Rowdy?*"

I was probably in a fetal position bracing for the response when she replied, "Yes. He loved that boat."

I believe I actually laughed aloud. I'm not really sure why. I just felt such immeasurable happiness in the moment that that's how it came out. She may have thought it inappropriate, but she made no indication of offense. Throughout the call, she impressed me as having a very gracious and sophisticated yet playful demeanor. At last my doorway to *Rowdy*'s past had opened, and I was stepping through it. As far as I knew, this was the only person on the planet who had firsthand knowledge of *Rowdy* in her early years, and here she was, welcoming me in conversation. It was truly remarkable! I had a million questions, and I asked her the one burning at the top of my mind: "Did you ever sail aboard *Rowdy*?"

"Yes, as a child, often. They were wonderful times."

That conversation was the beginning of what became a beautiful, close, and ongoing friendship. We wrote back and forth and spoke on the phone often, and what we shared helped to satisfy needs that for both of us required attention. In a way, I almost got to know her father, and in a way, sometimes painful, sometimes heartfelt, she was able to revisit his memory and reconnect with her father and *Rowdy*.

That first conversation was no more than fifteen minutes long and ended with Hanny saying, "Well, Chris, I need to get some rest. At 92 years old, one gets tired very easily. I am Father's only living child, but if you would please send me your address, I will put you in touch with my son and many of Father's other grandchildren, who may also be able to help you."

From there, the story blossomed. I corresponded with Duells from all over the country. Many actually flew out to California to see *Rowdy* in the boatyard, and all enthusiastically volunteered whatever information they could offer.

A pleasant surprise came one day, about two years after Hanny's first phone call, when her son Robert called to say that his mother wanted to come out and see *Rowdy* and meet me in person. Of course I said that I would be thrilled. As the date drew nearer, we tried to figure out how Hanny could see the top of the boat. We toyed with the idea of pulling back the tarps and constructing some kind of platform on which the yard forklift could raise her. The yard foreman was less than receptive to that idea. We decided to figure it out when Hanny arrived at the boat.

It was a beautiful sunny day when Hanny and her son Robert showed up. There was a freshness of ocean smells in the salt air and barely a breath of the prevailing sea breeze. It was nice to meet at last in person, and Hanny's appearance was well matched to her personality. There was no mistaking that she was in her nineties, but there was a strength and grace about her that age could not suppress. She had a strong square jaw, a straight mouth, high cheekbones, and a youthful twinkle in her eyes.

Following warm introductions, we almost immediately migrated toward *Rowdy* Without discussion, Hanny went straight for the 10-foot rolling metal stepladder and grabbed the handrail as if that had been the plan all along.

You have to picture the wheels of the stepladder resting on an uneven, highly eroded blacktop surface, causing it to teeter back and forth with increasing motion as one's feet neared the top. From there, care had to be taken when stepping off the stepladder and onto the upper scaffolding, which was made of springy 2" × 10"s, laid three wide and a full 9 feet off the ground. Yet that upper layer of scaffolding was only as high as *Rowdy*'s waterline. There, precariously resting on the scaffolding, a half-broken ancient 6-foot wooden stepladder slanted up and rested against *Rowdy*'s top deck rail.

For years I had scrambled up and down this pathway all day long, but I would never consider it even remotely safe enough for a 93-year-old woman to attempt.

But Hanny expressed that she wanted to go to the top of the rolling metal stepladder. You don't say no in that situation, and we nervously went to her assistance. As she summited the ladder and stepped onto the scaffolding, she turned and put the flat palm of her outstretched hand against *Rowdy*'s hull, as if tenderly touching the cheek of a long-lost loved one. The moment lingered briefly with nothing said as her mouth curved into an effortless smile, and then, in a single movement, her hand went from the hull to the rickety wooden stepladder. I couldn't help being amused at her commanding determination. After an admiring laugh slipped out, I asked, "Are you going up?"

"If I may have your permission."

"Let me go up first so I can take your hand."

It was one slow, careful step at a time followed by a roll off the ladder and up onto the deck. Wow! She had not been aboard *Rowdy* for 83 years! By this time, most of the deck and interior were finished, so what she was seeing closely paralleled her memories. It was wonderful to see in her eyes the excitement of the moment. Forgetting the limits of her age, she scrambled down the 5-foot companionway ladder into *Rowdy*'s main salon.

The interior was incredibly rich and luxurious. This had been a gentleman's yacht, and I followed every detail of the plans to portray that. The floors were teak. The raised panel bulkheads and doors were made of varnished old-growth mahogany. In contrast with plantation-grown mahogany, the old, slow-growing wood is darker with beautiful deep, rich shades of red and burgundy. Trying to find worthy wood seemed a never-ending treasure hunt. Hardware such as toilets and sink pumps were all rebuilt brass antiques. Light in the main salon cascaded down through a large overhead butterfly hatch, illuminating a folding table of the finest mahogany, which was detailed by ornate woodwork and brass hardware. The accompanying bench seats were a burgundy-colored tuck and roll. On the wall hung a reproduction of an oil painting of *Rowdy* done by Lars Thorsen in 1926 and a reproduction of a watercolor of her painted by Fred Cozzens in 1916. Aft of the salon were a head, galley, navigation station, port bunk, and engine compartment.

Forward of the salon was the captain's stateroom, complete with a beveled glass library and liquor cabinet. Forward of that was another head and then the forward bow cabin.

Hanny immediately went to the folding table in the main salon and, sitting down, rubbed her hand back and forth on it. More than anything else below decks,

✳ *Main salon aboard* Rowdy

✳ *Captain's stateroom aboard* Rowdy

that one item triggered something that took her back to her days as a child playing on the boat. It's funny how a smell, a certain sound, or a funny insignificant little object can trigger that kind of memory recall and immediately transport you back in time.

"Chris, you have done a fantastic job," she said. "It's marvelous. I am absolutely floored."

"How do you like the copies of the paintings?" I asked. She had helped to locate originals among relatives. They in turn had had reproductions made for me, the oil being reproduced with oil on canvas and the watercolor being done on linen.

She leaned forward, staring at them, and replied, "I would never guess they're not originals."

"Thank you for your help. I love having them onboard."

It was at that moment that the framed enlargement of *Rowdy* on her 1920 Fourth of July sail caught Hanny's eye, prompting an involuntary shudder. As she reached for the photograph, I noticed a slight tremble in her hand that had not been there before. I supposed, ever so incorrectly, that she was startled at unexpectedly seeing an image of her father.

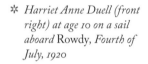

✻ Harriet Anne Duell (front right) at age 10 on a sail aboard Rowdy, *Fourth of July, 1920*

"Is that your father at the helm?" I asked.

The long pause before her reply caused me to wonder whether she had not heard me or perhaps found my question to be in some way inappropriate and was not going to acknowledge it. I was relieved that her tone was very pleasant when she replied, "Yes, that's my father, and the little girl on the right is me."

Before I had a chance to ask about the other people in the photo, Hanny set it down on the counter and stepped away, saying, "Your mother must be very proud."

Oddly, she had not stood the picture back up but had laid it flat, face down. At the time I didn't even think to question the gesture. I simply answered her question. "She thinks I'm crazy for taking this on, but I think she admires my determination and commitment to see it through."

"I would like to meet her someday. When do you think you might have *Rowdy* sailing?"

"I'm hoping she will be in the water within a year, and then it will probably be another three or four months before we're sailing."

"What do you plan to do when she is all finished?"

"I probably won't keep her long. I have financed a good portion of the project, and it's going to go beyond what I feel I can justify for a luxury item at this time in my life."

"So you will sell her. When do you think you will do that?"

"First I need to finish every last detail, enter her in some races, and enjoy some payback trips to the Channel Islands. What I would like to do along the way is put together a book detailing her history. Most of her value lies in the fact that she is a Herreshoff design. I have enough to write a history of Herreshoff and of the New York 40 Class, but I think it would be very valuable to this project if I could document *Rowdy*'s racing history, especially if she ever won any important races. Do you know anything of her racing history?"

"Father loved to race."

"Do you know any details or if he ever won any major races?"

"Would it be all right if we went up and talked on deck?"

"Absolutely. Let me help you."

She stood up slowly, partially bent over for a moment, then straightened and made her way up the companionway.

She sat down on a shelf on the starboard side of the companionway hatch and continued: "Chris, you have done a marvelous job on this project, and I can see that you have dedicated a huge portion of your life to it. I understand in order to add value, you want to document the racing history, and you will then feel that you have brought this project to fruition, and you can offer someone the complete package."

✳ *Looking aft from main salon aboard* Rowdy

✳ *Port quarter berth aboard* Rowdy

✳ *Harriet Anne (Duell) Pierson—"Hanny"—at age 93, aboard* Rowdy *in 2002 for the first time in 83 years. I didn't notice until months later, when comparing photos, that she chose to sit in the same spot she had as a child of 10, back in 1920.*

✳ *Holland Duell's open cockpit Waco plane (Photo courtesy of Holland Duell's granddaughter Susan Duell and her son Mitch Higgins)*

✳ *Holland S. Duell on horseback . (Photo courtesy of Holland Duell's granddaughter Susan Duell and her son Mitch Higgins)*

I nodded.

"Now listen very carefully to me," she said. "I mean this in the kindest and most helpful way, but you have only scratched the surface. There is so much more to this story than you can imagine. My father was a remarkable man. Both his father and his grandfather were rather famous attorneys who at times each held important government positions and each served terms as the United States Commissioner of Patents. Father had a distinguished career in business and politics. When World War 1 came, he fought and led men bravely, and was highly decorated for extraordinary heroism. Everyone in the sailing community knew and respected him. In his later years, he transitioned from sailing to flying and had many forced landings in his open cockpit Waco due to mechanical failures, but he had a cool head and always managed to pull it off. He was a man of adventure and steel nerves.

"There was never a moment when Father was not excited about life and living it to the fullest. He loved to play tennis and dance and ride horses, and he learned to ski in his sixties. He was a caring person who enjoyed doing things for other people, and with his lovely sense of humor, he was always wonderful company. When I look back at all he did, I find it absolutely amazing how much living he packed into a single lifetime.

"My father owned this boat for 24 years, longer than any of the other New York 40s were owned. Much of his life revolved around it and was intertwined with it. If this boat could talk, we would both probably learn volumes more about my father. Every boat has a personality. My father was the heart and soul of *Rowdy*. You cannot possibly understand the way this boat raced and competed based simply on a list of races she may have won or placed in. To have your 'complete package,' to gain a feel for how this boat was raced and sailed, you will need insight into how my father lived life."

My excitement had been rising as she spoke. She understood! It wasn't just the dry facts I wanted, but a sense of the living man.

"This has been an incredible experience. I thank you, and I hope to continue our conversation soon, but right now I need to get some rest. I am going to leave you with something. I hope it will address some of the questions I'm sure I have just raised."

With that, she handed me a book-sized package neatly wrapped in old brown wrapping paper and taped closed. I thanked Hanny and Robert both and walked them back to the car. As anxious as I had been for them to arrive, I was now equally anxious for them to be gone so I could examine the contents of the mysterious package.

The Journal

I made myself comfortable in the main salon, laid the package on the table, and opened it, having no idea what to expect. It was immediately obvious that this was a journal of some sort, written by Hanny's father. What was not so obvious to me was that the words that lay before me, like a time machine, were about to whisk me back into the past, allowing me to connect with—no, to become fully immersed, on a most personal level, in—the incredibly colorful life of *Rowdy's* original owner. At the time I would have never fathomed the depth of familiarity and connection I would eventually develop toward this man. Nor could I have guessed how getting to know his life so intimately would affect my feelings toward *Rowdy* and the entire project. But as I read, along with the first words began my first steps into the epochal adventure of the life of Holland Sackett Duell. ❦

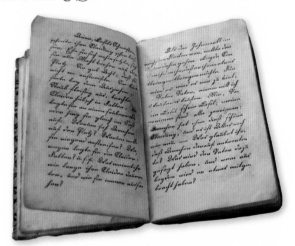

❦ I should explain that what I was about to read—what Holland Duell wrote and published in 1920—was not an actual diary but a book titled *The History of the 306th Field Artillery*. In helping to tell his story on the following pages, I have supplemented his writings with many additional facts, which I have acquired from numerous regimental histories and other sources as specified in the footnotes. I took exacting care to include only details and events that Holland Duell would have experienced personally during the war. My research yielded so many colorful, intimate and personal experiences that I decided to present them on the following pages in the form of a diary, as if told in the words of Holland Duell.

With the benefit of hindsight and the resources of innumerable books written immediately after the war, I believe that this is the most detailed accounting ever written on the history of the 306th Field Artillery, 77th Division.

Part 1
Training Camps

(MAY 11, 1917 - APRIL 22, 1918)

The event which I have, for some time, deemed inevitable has finally taken place, and with it, every soul on this planet should be concerned that, as a consequence, their life stands to be permanently and irrevocably altered. The winds of war have finally blown across the Atlantic and are bearing down upon the American people. Just weeks ago, on April 6, 1917, every paper in the nation had ushered in news that the United States had declared war with Germany. I have no doubt our participation will be an earth-shaking event that will challenge, if not threaten, the very backbone and foundation of our country, yet it is the right thing to do, and I plan to volunteer my energies to help in the cause.

For the last three years President Woodrow Wilson has resisted any measure of U.S. involvement in the European war and has officially declared the U.S. neutral. So despite the growing moral pressure to join in and do our part for the free world, we have sat on the side lines with a woefully ill prepared military, as if in hopes that if we could just hold our breath long enough somehow the whole thing would roll up and blow away without the U.S having to become involved.

But, with the declaration of war, the United States will now send the largest army it has ever assembled overseas to support the Allies. Like a schoolboy who wait-ed until the last minute to start his homework, the United States, having made the decision to go to war, is now beginning a mad scramble to build a war machine, a process that by all rights should have been going on for years.

Here we have made the decision to send a million-man army to Europe, and not only do we not have a million-man army, we do not have officers to train a million-man army. We do not have camps to house and train that many troops. We do not have weapons, uniforms, medical supplies, or any semblance of the litany of necessities we will need to achieve our ambitions. But now that we have made our decision and we are firm in our conviction to go to war, we are jumping around like a nation of jackrabbits brainstorming and blundering through billions of logistical challenges, the solving of which will lead to the attainment of our aspired fighting force.

Plattsburg Officer Training Camp
(MAY 11, 1917 – AUGUST 15, 1917)

Across the country, construction of huge training camps for the troops is already beginning. Thousands of new officers will have to enter and graduate from officer training camps before the troop training camps are finished in order for there to be enough officers available to train the troops. It has been determined that 10,000 additional officers will be needed to accomplish this.[1] Fourteen military bases will be converted into officer training camps. Each camp will be limited to a maximum of 2,500 prospective officers.[2] The enlisted men are inducted into the army by conscription, meaning that they are drafted.[3] Men aspiring to be officers have to apply and, if accepted, will attend one of the fourteen officers' training camps.[4]

✳ *Platsberg Officer's Training Camp (old postcard)*

Immediately after the April 6, 1917, declaration of war by the United States, I applied for Plattsburg Officer's Training Camp.[5] Plattsburg is rich in a history that embodies the spirit of America. The sound defeat of the British in the 1814 Battle of Plattsburg brought an end to the War of 1812. Ulysses S. Grant was stationed at Plattsburg after the first barracks were built in 1838.[6] It is a symbol of America's backbone and a place where any man would be proud to receive training in how to defend his country.

Admission to Plattsburg is an honor for which there is stiff competition. Every day for the last three years, Americans have been reading of the German atrocities inflicted upon Europe and the senseless, tragic loss of good lives. With both patriotism and disgust for the war running high, New Yorkers have been flooding the officer recruiting stations with applications for Plattsburg. When I applied for service, the recruiting officer stressed that, at 36 years of age, I could not be required to fight in this war, as the cutoff age was 31 years.[7,8] I explained that I believed in the cause, believed that I could quickly learn the art of war, and believed that I could provide leadership that would minimize the loss of good lives on the battlefield. This along with information on my education, health, and family background was taken, and I was moved along.

By April 26, 1917, there were already 10,000 applications for the 2,500 spots. The recruiting office at 19 West 44th Street stayed open until midnight that night to pro-

---

1 "First 10,000 Officers for First Army of 1917," *New York Times*, May 6, 1917.
2 *New York Times*, April 24, 1917.
3 *The Battery Book: A History of Battery A 306th F.A.*, edited by Francis L. Field and Guy H. Richards (New York: The De Vinne Press, 1921), p. 4.
4 "The Plattsburg Idea," by Penelope D. Clute, *New York Archives*, Vol. 5, No. 2, Fall 2005.
5 Yale biographies for Holland Duell, Class of 1902.
6 http://en.wikipedia.org/wiki/old_stone_Barracks.
7 Yale biographies for Holland Duell, Class of 1902.
8 *The Battery Book*, p. 4.

cess the 300 hopefuls who were still in line at 8:00 p.m.[1] Everywhere in the country there is a feeling of excitement about the war. There really has not been such a universal call to lay one's life on the line for king and country, and now for the welfare of the entire free world, since the days of the great crusades, and many now view the prospect of joining the fight as that of a great adventure. It was announced that no more applications would be accepted after May 4, 1917. As a result, that day saw a mob of applicants who wanted to become officers, which the police estimated between 5,000 and 10,000. Army staffers attempting to whittle down the crowd walked the line and ejected everyone who looked too young or had a physical makeup that appeared to be below Army standards. The final thinning of the crowd resulted from questions such as "What college did you attend? What business are you in? Married or single? Previous military service?"[2]

Finally the application process was closed, and shortly afterwards I received a card in the mail. I am to be one of the lucky 2,500 to attend Plattsburg Officer Training Camp. But let there be no confusion. Passing this first hurdle, and it is a big one, has only gotten my one foot in the door. The officers who graduate Plattsburg will train the troops, and the outcome of that training on the battlefields of France and Germany could determine the fate of the free world. America therefore wants only the best and brightest officers, and to facilitate that goal, it has predetermined that only one out of every four men will graduate from Plattsburg as an officer.[3]

It seems that more than 90% of the first "Plattsburgers" are to be college graduates, many coming from Princeton, Harvard, and Yale. Notable volunteers are the Mayor of New York City, the city chief of police, the former Secretary of State,[4] and the sons of former president Theodore Roosevelt.[5]

The train departing for Plattsburg was scheduled to leave from New York's Grand Central Station on May 11, 1917. As the first group of 1,250 men assembled there for a half-hour reception, one was left with little doubt that the military knew well how to screen for good officer material. Athletic ability was obvious when one noted the well-proportioned physiques, and the atmosphere of conversations was sharp and often quick witted. The station was packed with mothers, wives, sweethearts, fathers, and family and friends, all saying good-bye in their different ways. There were a few tears, but overall the atmosphere was upbeat and jovial. After all, no one was going off to war just yet. This was simply a three-month study in the academia of war. A patriotic touch was added when the 22nd Company of Boy Scouts paraded through the concourse with their band and guns. At 9:40 p.m., the first train departed to many waves and blown kisses and last glances back.[6]

The train was hot and stuffy and very crowded. It was an overnight ride. The whole train was one big smoking car, and near me was a very noisy poker game.[7] About

---

1   "8,000 to Apply Here for Officers Corps," *New York Times*, April 26, 1917.
2   "Swamped by Rush of Officers Corps," *New York Times*, May 5, 1917.
3   "Active Service Sure for Plattsburg Men," *New York Times*, June 20, 1917.
4   "The Plattsburg Idea."
5   "Roosevelt's' Sons on Duty," *New York Times*, June 20, 1917.
6   "Plattsburg Party Departs for Camp," *New York Times*, May 12, 1917.
7   *At Plattsburg* by Allen French (New York, Charles Scribner's Sons, 1917), p.6.

7:00 a.m.,[1] the train drew to a stop alongside a contingent of barracks ornamenting a wide and gentle sloping field, which was obviously a large drill field.[2] On the other side was Lake Champlain,[3] and a cold northeast wind blew across the lake, carrying with it drenching showers and hail, occasionally interrupted by patches of blue sky.[4]

Before our arrival, camp officers had organized the new arrivals to form into fourteen groups of about eighty men each. I was preassigned to Company 14.[5] All companies went to their corresponding barracks to check in, and then we marched as a platoon to the gymnasium and stood in line to receive uniforms and bedding.[6]

Plattsburg is located on the west bank of Lake Champlain in northern New York, close to the Canadian border. The view is picturesque, with pine trees growing down to the sandy banks of the lake.[7] About 200 carpenters were busy working to finish up the eleven new barracks that had been added to house the incoming students. Their design embodied simple functionality. Each barrack—250 feet long, two stories with bunk beds—housed about 167 men. Together with the existing 200-foot-long original stone barracks, they framed an immense 120-acre drill field.[8,9]

The next three months were to be a crash course in military life and specifically in leading men. Accordingly, our days were typically a minimum of ten hours. For the first month we did repetitive drills—"squad left," "squad right." The first week, Ralston turned in the wrong direction, tripped over his rifle, and fractured his cheekbone.[10] The daily news from the European battlefront described men in trenches, wild charges at the enemy under machine gun fire and across barbed wire defenses, and rapid fire artillery barrages. It was a fluid environment of action and reaction. With images of that landscape in our minds, it was hard to embrace the practicality of spending so much time in this drilling that seemed designed to create marching parade soldiers. But the reasoning, as I would find out later from personal experience, was sound. It was very sound.

The first order of building a soldier, that which comes well before training him to march or shoot a gun or thrust a bayonet, is getting him to check his self-serving interests and personal life at the front desk and embrace that, as a soldier, he is a selfless component of a bigger machine. Until that has been achieved, all other training is a waste of time. As University of Pennsylvania Professor Dr. Charles W. Burr articulated, "Unless the American boy is taught obedience, unless he learns to submit to authority, unless he learns that the highest manhood is to obey, unless he learns that work is a blessing, not a curse, this country is doomed."[11] The Plattsburg Training

---

1   "Plattsburg Camp Ready," *New York Times*, May 12, 1917.
2   "8,000 to Apply Here for Officers Corps."
3   *At Plattsburg* p.8
4   "2,500 Arrive in Rain at Plattsburg," *New York Times*, May 13, 1917.
5   "Plattsburg Roster," *New York Times*, May 9, 1917.
6   "2,500 Arrive in Rain at Plattsburg."
7   *The Autobiography of a Regiment: A History of the 304th Field Artillery in the World War*, by James M. Howard (New York, 1920), p. 4.
8   "Roofs for Plattsburg," *New York Times*, April 24, 1917.
9   "Plattsburg Can Take No More Applicants," *New York Times*, May 18, 1917.
10   "Reserve Officers Chosen," *New York Times*, May 16, 1917.
11   "The Plattsburg Idea."

Manual additionally stated: "Never forget that you lose your identity as an individual when you step into the ranks; you then become merely a unit of mass."[1]

The importance of instilling the "spirit" of a soldier was continually stressed at Plattsburg. On the evening of May 14, 1917, General J. Franklin Bell visited the camp and addressed the men, saying, "On the battle line its character that wins—not ability or knowledge so much as character. You know what I mean. You have only one life to live and one life to give, and it does not matter when a soldier leaves this life, but it does matter how he leaves it. A soldier must think only of his duty and must do it in a way that all who survive him will be proud of the way he gave up his life."[2]

Being able to instill this mindset in the new recruits I was eventually to train would prove to be a formidable challenge after which even the most complex, technical training would come easily. And so looking back to what, at the time, seemed excessive, repetitive, and mundane drilling of "squad left" and "squad right," now I see clearly that the exercises provided an almost tangible doorway of transition, a phase of metamorphosis in which a civilian first submits to becoming a soldier.

During this first month, everyone was trained to be an infantryman—or a "doughboy," as they were called. Most mornings, we had one to three hours of drilling followed by a half-hour of brisk calisthenics. The rest of the day might include rifle range; bayonet practice; hikes of several miles, initially light, but later with full packs and equipment; semaphore signaling, the technique of visually communicating with someone at a distance by waving two hand-held flags in coded motions; and skirmishes, charging at top speed and jumping to a position of lying flat on the stomach. It was cold and wet and dirty, as most of the month of May was punctuated with rain. This made landing on one's stomach in the mud unappealing, yet we knew it paralleled the reality of what awaited us in Europe.[3,4,5,6]

The rains had a particularly unpleasant effect on the trench work. An elaborate system of trenches had been constructed, identical to those on a sector of the French front. They were deep enough to stand in, and in France, infantrymen could peek over the top and direct rifle fire at the opposing enemy trench, hoping not to have their heads blown off. At the camp, to simulate actual living conditions, students were required to spend their full time in the trenches regardless of the weather, of the rain, of the standing water and mud and altogether wet, cold, dirty, miserable conditions.[7] On June 5, 1917, Charles Willard died in the post hospital from pneumonia caused by exposure.[8]

Our nights were filled with lectures as well as classes in French so that we future officers would become proficient with military terms used by the allied armies.[9]

---

1   *The Plattsburg Manual* by Olin O. Ellis and E.B. Garey (New York, The Century Co., 1917), p.17.
2   "Bell at Plattsburg," *New York Times*, May 14, 1917.
3   "Leaves Plattsburg to Rest in Trenches," *New York Times*, May 17, 1917.
4   "Hard Bayonet Drills for Plattsburg Men," *New York Times*, May 24, 1917.
5   "Plattsburg Men Hike," *New York Times*, June 2, 1917.
6   "Plattsburg Drills in Mud," *New York Times*, May 30, 1917.
7   "Plattsburg Adopts Strict Trench Life," *New York Times*, June 18, 1917.
8   "Plattsburg to Drop 700 Rookies," *New York Times*, June 5, 1917.
9   "Plattsburg Drills in Mud."

Throughout this time, instructors kept on file a card for each man, on which he was assessed and ranked in aptitude, conduct, capacity for command, military bearing, and zeal. On June 5, 1917, the first weeding out by this ranking method was announced as being imminent. On June 15, 1917, after ten very anxious days, 700 men were dismissed from Plattsburg Officer Training Camp.

With the first month of basic training now complete, the instructors used these same score cards to classify the men according to the branches of the service for which they were best suited. The men had no say in whether they were assigned to be engineers or infantrymen or artillerymen. It was determined that I was best suited for the field artillery—the big guns, the howitzers, the modern version of the cannon. Along with 199 other men, I was assigned to the Third Battery Field Artillery.[1]

There was immediate uncertainty about our future because it had just been announced that a school for artillery was being opened in Syracuse, New York.[2] At the time, Plattsburg had no guns, no horses, and no equipment for the artillery to train with and could not order any until the Adjutant General in Washington sent his decision about where the artillery would train.[3,4] Following a week of uncertainty, we were elated when, on June 23, 1917, word came down that the artillery was to remain and train at Plattsburg. This meant that we would continue to train side by side with the officers of the other branches, such as the infantry and engineers, with whom we would eventually partner on the battlefields of Europe. The instructors believed that maintaining these working relationships would prove invaluable when we finally went to war.[5]

The artillery training schedule called for an average of 60 hours a week.[6] On July 3, 1917, howitzers to train with arrived at camp,[7] and on July 14, soldiers from the New York National Guard First Field Artillery who would instruct us arrived. They encamped in a field south of the barracks. The rows of brown tents, the corralled horses, and the cooking shacks of the guardsmen presented a picturesque contrast to the long wooden barracks of the student officers.[8]

There were many sore arms among the students that day, as we had just received our second in a series of typhoid shots. But training commenced and went well despite temperatures that were, by the end of July, reaching 95 degrees in the shade.[9]

On August 15, 1917, three months after we came to Plattsburg, commissions were announced. In a characteristically short speech, Captain Rehkopf addressed the candidates: "Gentlemen you enter the service to become representatives of the American Army. It has been very difficult to choose among you. I trust I may be able later to say that I have chosen wisely."[10]

---

1   Give New Roster of Plattsburg Camp," *New York Times*, June 29, 1917.
2   "Drop 23 Plattsburg Men," *New York Times*, June 9, 1917.
3   "Plattsburg Men Going to Belvoir," *New York Times*, June 13, 1917.
4   "Candidates Await Orders," *New York Times*, June 14, 1917.
5   Artillerymen to Stay," *New York Times*, June 23, 1917.
6   "Candidates Await Orders," *New York Times*, June 14, 1917.
7   Artillery at Plattsburg," *New York Times*, July 4, 1917.
8   "Militiamen at Plattsburg," *New York Times*, July 15, 1917.
9   "98 in Shade at Plattsburg," *New York Times*, July 24, 1917.
10 *The Autobiography of a Regiment*, p. 6.

Where we all had been comrades of equal standing, each successful candidate was now to take on the rank commensurate with the ability he had proven to possess. Yet a fellowship had grown up in those three months that differences in rank could not efface. It was a group of friends who separated on August 15 for a brief vacation and with orders to report for service at the end of the month to the new training camp on Long Island, Camp Upton.[1] We left with the motto "Brave men shall not die because I faltered,"[2] and I left with the rank of captain.[3]

Camp Upton Troop Training Camp
(SEPTEMBER 1, 1917 – APRIL 22, 1918)

Army training camps were springing up across the country. In early 1917, the newspapers reported that for one of these future cantonment sites, the government had purchased 30,000 acres of land in the township of Yaphank, on the eastern side of Long Island, New York.[4] Although within the limits of the township, the site was completely isolated, being a full five miles away from the village itself.[5] The entire 30,000 acres was purchased for the sum of one dollar. Six months later, some 30,000 men pulling stumps on every acre of that bleak terrain agreed that the government had been cheated and that the man who had sold the land should be arrested as a profiteer.[6]

The Long Island Rail Road extended its tracks for two miles[7] to facilitate the building of what would be Camp Upton, named after the Civil War General Emory Upton, who wrote numerous books on U.S. military policies,[8,9] including *The Military Policy of the United States*.[10]

On June 24, 1917, the U.S. government awarded Thompson Starrett Company the construction contract for the new camp,[11] and in the spirit of the haste of the country,

1 *The Autobiography of a Regiment*, p. 6.
2 http://www.texasescapes.com/southTexasTowns/Leon-Springs-Texas.htm.
3 "Last of Commissions from Plattsburg," *New York Times*, August 13, 1917.
4 http://en.wikipedia.org/wiki/Yaphank,_New_York.
5 *Camp Upton*, by Roger Batchelder (Boston: Small, Maynard & Company, 1918), p. 4.
6 *The History of the 306th Field Artillery: Compiled by the Men Who Participated in the Events Described* (New York: Knickerbocker Press, 1920), p. 7.
7 http://www.trainsarefun.com.
8 http://www.bnl.gov/bn/web/history/camp_upton.
9 http://en.wikipedia.org.wiki/camp_upton.
10 *Camp Upton*, p.6.
11 http://www.trainsarefun.com.

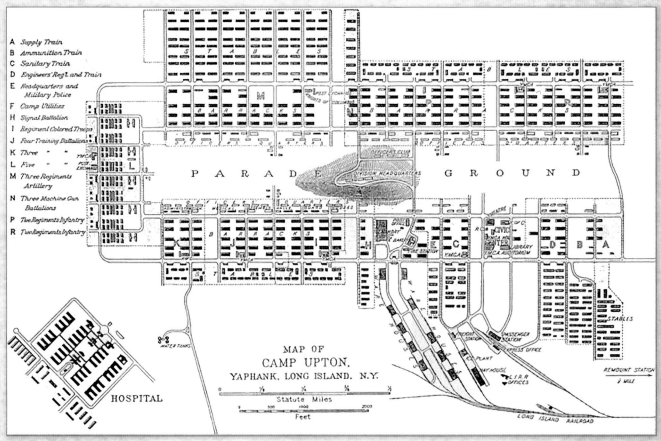

A   Supply Train
B   Ammunition Train
C   Sanitary Train
D   Engineers' Regt. and Train
E   Headquarters and
     Military Police
F   Camp Utilities
H   Signal Battalion
I   Regiment Colored Troops
J   Four Training Battalions
K   Three   "   "
L   Five   "   "
M   Three Regiments
     Artillery
N   Three Machine Gun
     Battalions
P   Two Regiments Infantry
R   Two Regiments Infantry

MAP OF
CAMP UPTON.
YAPHANK, LONG ISLAND, N.Y.

HOSPITAL

✳ *Diagram of Camp Upton*

construction commenced at a frenzied pace. The mammoth workforce, which had to be brought in from New York City, varied between 5,000 and 15,000 workers on any given day.[1] Carpenters were paid $0.63 per hour, and laborers were paid $0.38 per hour. The workers were of all nationalities. Many were immigrants who spoke little or no English,[2] and many were thugs and profiteers with no regard for laws or the well-being of anyone but themselves. To help police them, a large number of detectives and men with police experience had to be hired, resulting in 1021 court cases with imposed fines of $2,700, and jail sentences of 900 days.[3]

Working conditions that summer were almost unbearable. The extreme heat was exhausting. The almost daily rain turned the temporary roads into a series of mud-holes, and clouds of mosquitoes were a continual and maddening annoyance. After experiencing the difficult working conditions, many of the workers turned around and returned to New York City.[4]

Nonetheless, buildings went up in the space of hours, not weeks. An assembly line method had a gang of foundation men setting all of the wooden foundation posts

1   *Camp Upton*, p.5.
2   http://www.bnl.gov/bn/web/history/camp_upton.
3   http://www.longwood.k12.ny.us/history/upton/upton.
4   *Camp Upton*, p.5.

required for a barrack 30 inches into the ground, then the next gang would come in and lay the floor framing and floorboards. Next, the framing gang would frame the walls that lay flat on the floor, and at the sound of a whistle, forty or more men with the aid of block and tackle would hoist the walls into place.[1] Hammers flew, men scrambled aloft, and the roof was on. A few more hours saw the plumbers and electricians provide the buildings with electricity and hot and cold running water. Work ran steadily at this pace night and day, 24 hours a day. In less than two months' time, by August 1917, Camp Upton, while not complete, was a sprawling city of wooden buildings. Over 5,740 train car loads of lumber were used for the construction of the camp.[2]

✳ *"The Hill," Divisional Headquarters, Camp Upton (old postcard)*

The flat landscape as far as the eye could see was dotted with rows of long, rectangular, two-story wooden barracks laid out symmetrically on streets with names like 16th Street and Upton Boulevard[3] and Fifth Avenue (along which the 306th Field Artillery was to have its barracks).[4] The total conglomerate of barracks with names such as P-58 and J-43 was laid out in the form of a gigantic rectangle that was open at one of the small sides.[5]

In the middle of the rectangle was a small hill, which rose to an elevation higher than the rest of the camp. On this hill was located the Division Headquarters building, which became known simply as "The Hill."[6]

In all, there were 1,400 buildings designed to accommodate some 40,000 troops, and there were thirty miles of roads. By all measures, this was a city. Aside from barracks, there were offices; storehouses; kitchens and mess halls; stables; warehouses; a filtration plant; a church; a library; a YMCA; a complete utility system for sewer, electrical, and running water; a base hospital; a police force comprising one hundred and forty "bluecoats"; a fire department with forty firemen; a complete telephone system; a post office; one of the largest laundries in the world; several restaurants; a theater; a hotel; a telegraph office—everything needed to be self-sufficient.[7] The landscape, if one's perspective afforded a view beyond the edge of the city—consisted of thousands of acres, some barren, some wooded with pine trees and scrub oaks, but most flat to rolling, on which military exercises and training would be conducted.

By September, Camp Upton was about two thirds complete. It was described as a howling wilderness of stumps, lumber piles, civilian workmen, ditches, and half-finished buildings. The lumber was strewn in wild confusion all over the camp, and the

---

1 http://www.longwood.k12.ny.us/history/upton/upton.
2 *History of the 77th Division*, p. 11.
3 *The Battery Book*, p. 8.
4 *The History of the 306th Field Artillery*, p. 11.
5 *The Battery Book*, p. 8.
6 *History of the 77th Division*, p. 11.
7 *Camp Upton*, p.6.

❊ *Camp Upton 1919*

workers swarmed like hordes of ants.[1] But in our country's whirlwind of preparations to mold an army, this phase of construction was deemed to be "close enough" to begin moving troops in. So on September 1, while construction was still in full swing, I along with 2,999 other officers arrived at Camp Upton and moved in.[2,3]

Most of these officers, like myself, had just graduated from Plattsburg Officer Training Camp, and with our three months of training and no prior military experience, we were preparing to meet the troops whose lives we would hold in our hands as they went into battle.[4] Upon detraining at Camp Upton, we were escorted by military police to "The Hill," where we reported to the commanding officer, Major General J. Franklin Bell.[5] The 61-year-old veteran of the Spanish-American War had fought Indians on the Western Plains with Custer's 7th Cavalry and had also fought with distinction in the Philippines. He had served under President Taft and his good friend former President Theodore Roosevelt. As Major General Bell assigned each new officer to a regiment, which had yet to be formed, the officers heard for the first time the number of the battalion that they would command.[6] I was assigned to command the 2nd Battalion of the 306th Field Artillery.

When the United States had declared war on Germany, on April 6, 1917, Congress had passed the Selective Service Act, whereby every male citizen between the ages of 21 and 31, with certain exceptions, should be available for induction into military service. On June 15, 1917, all men of this age filled out registration cards, and each registrant was given a number. Numbers were selected by rotation in Washington, and those whose number was selected received an imposing "Order of Induction into Military Service of the United States," also known as a pink card. The cordial greeting from the President of the United States in that notice read, "Having submitted yourself to a local board composed of your neighbors for the purpose of determining

1 *The Autobiography of a Regiment*, pp. 6–7.
2 *The History of the 306th Field Artillery*, p. 7.
3 http://www.longwood.k12.ny.us/history/wwi/longwood.htm.
4 *The Autobiography of a Regiment*, pp. 6, 9.
5 *History of the 77th Division*, p. 11.
6 *History of the 77th Division*, 1919, p. 11.

the place and time in which you can best serve the United States in the present emergency, you are hereby notified that you have now been selected for immediate military service." At the given date and hour, the new recruits reported to their "district leaders" and undertook a journey that concluded with a train ride to Camp Upton.[1]

As the train full of recruits arrived at Camp Upton, we new officers, overflowing with enthusiasm and excitement, boarded the train with our shiny gold and silver bars[2] and an eager curiosity toward what we hoped would be strong and eager young bucks who would serve gallantly under our leadership. As the officers called out to the "district leaders" to surrender the records of the men in their groups,[3] there was probably both awe and consternation on both sides. The recruits (for the officers had been ordered to refer to them as "recruits" or "enlisted men," not as "drafted men")[4] now stood as soldiers, their homes, families, and friends behind them. Some of the men were drunk and boisterous, some were quiet. Some men seemed filled with nervous excitement while others were indignant at being forced into a service they did not wish to participate in.[5]

What the officers, many of whom were refined, well-educated graduates of Yale, Princeton, Harvard, and the like, saw was not the stereotypical image of the clean-cut, square-jawed all-American soldier we had hoped for. What we saw was a cross section of every imaginable race, sect, color, trade, occupation, and class of society, freshly delivered from the melting pot of New York.[6] Representing at least twenty-five national backgrounds and as many different languages,[7] there were Italians, Russians, Spanish, Lithuanians, Germans, Chinese, Turks, Austrians, Irish, Dutch, Swedes, Danes, and

---

1   *The Battery Book*, pp. 4,6.
2   *The History of the 306th Field Artillery*, p. 7.
3   *The Battery Book*, p. 6.
4   *New York Times*, September 15, 1917.
5   *The Battery Book*, p. 6.
6   *Camp Upton*, p. 7.
7   http://www.bnl.gov/bn/web/history/camp_upton.

* *Newly arrived recruits at Camp Upton (old press photo in personal collection)*

French, to name a few.[1,2,3] They hailed from the East Side and the West Side of New York, from Third Avenue and Central Park West, from the Bronx and Yonkers, from Brooklyn and Eastern Long Island.[4] It is doubtful whether there had ever been a stranger assemblage for the making of an army. A camp survey of occupations showed that the group included a chemist, a banker, machinists, plumbers, politicians, cooks, miners, lawyers, horse shoers, bookkeepers, draftsmen, electricians, druggists, actors, musicians, professional athletes, policemen, veterinarians, chauffeurs, laborers, the unemployed, boys just out of school, and—of course not listed by occupation in the official survey but ever present—gunmen and gangsters. In coming weeks, members of the toughest gangs such as the Hell's Kitchen Gang, the Gas House Gang, and the Gopleen Gang showed up in numbers. Admirably, they declared a truce with each other in order to better fight the Germans.[5]

A newspaper article had announced that all civilian clothes of arriving recruits would be thrown away upon issuance of their new uniforms at Camp Upton. Conse-

---

1 *History of the 305th Field Artillery*, by Charles Wadsworth Camp (Garden City, NY: The Country Life Press, 1919), p. 10.

2 *The Battery Book*, p. 8.

3 *New York Times*, May 4, 1919.

4 http://longislandgenealogy.com/campupton/upton.htm.

5 "The Camp Upton Story, 1917–1921," by Norval Dwyer, *Long Island Forum*, February 1970.

quently, most of the new arrivals were dressed in their shabbiest attire.[1,2] Some carried straw hats, umbrellas, tennis racquets, or musical instruments, and nearly all carried souvenirs given to them by friends and relatives at their send-off. To top it all off, many of the passengers had seen this train ride as their last breath of freedom and had taken advantage of the chance to belt a few shots of whisky during the transit.[3] So this was the officers' first look at the untrained men who, in six months' time, would have to be forged into a battle-ready unit. The men were escorted by the officers, and resembling the immigrants' line at Ellis Island, they marched along the dusty roads to their mustering stations.

The scene resembled the wildest days of a Gold Rush boomtown. Hammers rapped, saws ripped, and workmen rushed past, bound in all directions. The laborers seemed to add a Wild West element of danger to life at Camp Upton. Foremen and civilian guards, galloping back and forth on horseback, looked like Old West cowboys—lean, bronzed and gaunt, arrayed in broad-brimmed hats, and "packing guns."[4]

At the mustering stations, the recruits were checked in. Each man was issued two heavy army blankets, a long white bed sack, a mess kit, and a large agate cup and was assigned a barrack and cot number.[5,6] En route to the barracks, the men were directed to a large hay pile and were given instructions to use only a small ration of the hay to fill their bed sacks. But visions of soft, billowing mattresses fueled a spirited competition to see who could stuff away the most hay.[7]

The barracks were large, rectangular two-story buildings of unpainted white pine. The entire upper floor was used as a dormitory. With bunks about two and a half feet apart, each barrack could house 250 troops. Downstairs was a large mess hall furnished with tables and benches; a kitchen, pantry, and storeroom; a large recreation room[8] with a potbellied stove for heating;[9] and rooms for the sergeant, supply sergeant, and orderly. Beside each barrack was a separate building in which there were ten showers and numerous other toilet arrangements.[10]

Next, the men registered into the camp and, after completing many forms, fell into line for physical inspections. Everyone had heard the cliché that when you entered the military, you became just a number, and this was confirmed when each man's number was literally written on his arm before he underwent inspections that recorded his fingerprints and the location of every scar to help identify his dead body in case his tags were blown off as he departed this life.[11] Finally, after inoculations and vaccinations against typhoid and diphtheria (complete with the dreaded

---

1 *History of the 305th Field Artillery*, p. 9.
2 *The Story of Battery B 306th F.A.—77th Division*, by Roswell A. De La Mater (New York: Premier, 1919), p. 13.
3 *The History of the 306th Field Artillery*, p. 7.
4 *History of the 77th Division*, p. 11.
5 "The Camp Upton Story, 1917–1921.".
6 *The Autobiography of a Regiment*, p. 10.
7 *The Story of Battery B 306th F.A.—77th Division*, p. 13.
8 *The Autobiography of a Regiment*, p. 10.
9 *The Battery Book*, p. 9.
10 "The Camp Upton Story, 1917–1921.".
11 *The Battery Book*, p. 8.

*❋ Camp Upton dormitory,
1918. (Courtesy of Longwood
Public Library, Thomas R.
Bayles Local History Room)*

malaise that accompanied the shots),[1] induction into the army was complete.

Few soldiers will ever forget the first nights spent in the casual barracks and the sudden change from beds and rooms at home to bunks, blankets, and hollow, echoing, bare wood dormitories.[2] The bugler played evening taps at 10:00 p.m.[3] "Lights out" was followed by some brief horseplay and hilarity, but soon the place quieted down, and in the dark strangeness of the dormitory, with a breeze playing in and out through the knotholes and gaps in the open framed clapboard walls, each man was left to his own turbulent thoughts.[4] One by one, the chorus of snores grew louder until that was the only sound to be heard.[5]

Mornings began at 5:45 a.m. with the sergeant's whistle ringing shrilly through the barracks, followed by the blare of the bugle outside at 6:00.[6,7] After that dreaded reveille, troops assembled outside for morning roll call, which, with such a mix of nationalities might sound something like this:

OFFICER: "Krag-a-co-poul-o-wiez, G."
SOLDIER: "Do yuh mean me?" (heavy New York accent)
OFFICER: "Silence! Simply answer, 'here.'"
SOLDIER: (in disgust) "Then I ain't here. That's all. I ain't here."[8]

This chain of command was new to the men and to most of the officers. Before the recruits had arrived, we newly commissioned officers had role-played, each taking turns giving the others roll call and drill orders.[9] After roll call, the recruits marched back inside, had breakfast, washed their own mess kits, and then did "police duty," which meant housecleaning: making the beds, sweeping the floors, scrubbing the showers and lavatories, disposing of the garbage and peeling potatoes and onions.

At Saturday morning upstairs dormitory inspection, on each man's bunk— in perfect accordance with the diagram posted on the downstairs bulletin board—was required to be a properly folded blanket and mess gear laid out with such precision that the prongs of the fork and the points of the spoon and knife took the approved direction as further detailed in the *Book of Pass Regulations*. Each man's shoes had to be polished and placed with mathematical exactness under his bunk, and the floor of the dormitory had to be scrubbed every Friday night and kept clean for the morning. When an officer walked into the room, if "Attention" was not called or if the man

1   *History of the 77th Division*, p. 14.
2   *The Autobiography of a Regiment*, p. 12.
3   *The Battery Book*, p. 18.
4   *The Autobiography of a Regiment*, p. 12.
5   *The History of the 306th Field Artillery*, p. 8.
6   *History of the 305th Field Artillery*, p. 10.
7   *The Battery Book*, p. 18.
8   *History of the 305th Field Artillery*, p. 10.
9   *The Autobiography of a Regiment*, p. 8.

called it called out in a weak voice, he was made to repeat "Attention" until he could call it loudly enough to satisfy the officer. Any soldier who did not snap to his feet at this call would gain much practice in the art of doing jumping jacks. If an officer was addressed as "Cap" or "Sarge," the offending soldier was immediately charged with a violation of all the articles in and out of the *Manual of Court-Martial*.[1] It was a harsh contrast from civilian life, and there were frequently instances of resistance and even insubordination.[2]

The emotions behind that resistance were very familiar to Private Irving Berlin. Berlin had been born Israel Baline in Russia in 1888, and although he had moved to the United States with his family in 1893, he did not became a citizen until February 1918. His song "Alexander's Ragtime Band" had swept the world six years before and made his name a household word. Although Berlin had no formal music training and required a transcriber to write down his tunes, he composed both the music and lyrics for hundreds of songs, which earned him $100,000 a year in royalties. Almost 30 years old and a celebrity, he hoped that the military would pass him over. Shortly after gaining citizenship, however, he had the "painful shock" of being drafted into the United States Army and being ordered to Camp Upton.

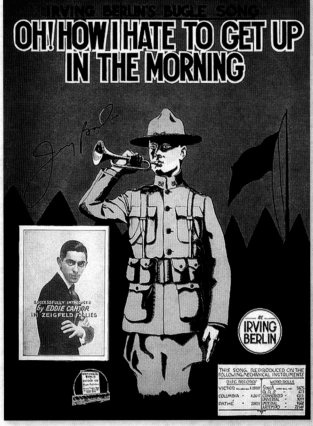

✳ *Cover of the sheet music of "Oh! How I Hate to Get Up in the Morning" (By Irving Berlin (Johns Hopkins University) [Public domain], via Wikimedia Commons)*

Irving Berlin didn't like a lot of things about army life, and foremost among them was reveille. "I hated it," he said later. "I hated it so much that I used to lie awake nights thinking about how much I hated it." He channeled that energy into composing a song that put a humorous spin on the early-morning reveille and perhaps helped him and his fellow soldiers to hear that bugle in a different light. "Oh! How I Hate to Get Up in the Morning" became an instant hit and eventually sold over one and a half million copies.

The first order of business for the officers at Camp Upton became the challenge of instilling in the recruits a positive attitude, a sense of teamwork, and respect for their commanding officers, the camp, and the military way of life. Absent these basics, all the weaponry and combat knowledge in the world would not make a unit competent. Most of the new recruits knew little or nothing of military discipline and the duties of a soldier. Being used to absolute freedom of mind and deed, they were decidedly unaccustomed to dictatorial treatment at the hands of men who democracy had taught them were no better than themselves. Many of the recruits were immigrants who could not speak English and, having only very recently obtained citizenship, now

---

1 *The Battery Book*, p. 28.
2 *The Autobiography of a Regiment*, p. 20.

resented being asked to fight for a country they did not feel they should have to die for. The rather unreceptive attitude of the enlisted men was evidenced in the term "ninety-day wonders,"[1] their nickname for the officers who, before our 90 days of training, had had absolutely no military experience what so ever.

Drills, routines, and discipline would become the daily bread, and only when they achieved their objective would the unit move on to specialized training. That first week, even the roll calls were frustrating. The scrub oaks, which had yet to be cleared, grew practically right up to the barracks. And what space there was for roll call was subject to stiff competition from piles of construction lumber, trenches and holes, and hundreds of rather aggressive, unpleasant civilian laborers as well as the troops from the other barracks.[2,3] The uniforms had not arrived. The troops were frustrated by the lack of organization, and the officers were frustrated by the complete lack of teamwork in everything from pulling stumps to learning regimental songs to scrubbing floors.[4]

For the first few weeks, the enlisted men were put to work side by side with the laborers to help complete the camp,[5,6] utilizing all their skills for everything from masonry to carpentry to the ever-hated stump pulling. Fourteen hundred acres of stumps, each stump measuring up to 6 feet in diameter, both from the original hard-wood forest and from the freshly cleared trees and undergrowth, had to be removed.[7,8] After those first few weeks, stump pulling became reserved for recruits whose actions had earned them disciplinary punishment. These men were jokingly referred to as "the chain gang."[9] It was said later, during the war in France, that pulling an 8,000-pound howitzer out of knee-deep mud paled by comparison to the chore of pulling those stumps at Camp Upton.

About a week after their arrival, the new recruits received their uniforms. We were a country going to war on the fly, so the soldiers got whatever they got. There were no custom tailors. These were uniforms made by the million.[10] Many men came out wearing baggy uniforms or uniforms that were too small, and many, because there was nothing even remotely close to their size, walked away with perhaps an extra set of shoelaces and tags and were put on the waiting list for the rest.[11] Yet from a distance, when all were assembled in olive drab uniforms for the first time, the group lost some of their queer, mismatched look and assumed a more unified military appearance.[12,13]

The second group of recruits arrived about a week later. Things seemed to go much more smoothly with this group because they arrived in a camp that had an

1 *The Battery Book*, p. 15.
2 http://longislandgenealogy.com/campupton/upton.htm.
3 *The Autobiography of a Regiment*, p. 14.
4 *The Autobiography of a Regiment*, p. 21.
5 http://www.bnl.gov/bn/web/history/camp_upton.
6 *The Battery Book*, p. 10.
7 http://www.longwood.k12.us/history/upton/upton.
8 *The Battery Book*, p. 10.
9 *The Battery Book*, p. 10.
10 *The History of the 306th Field Artillery*, p. 8.
11 *The Battery Book*, p. 13.
12 *The Autobiography of a Regiment*, p. 20.
13 *The History of the 306th Field Artillery*, p. 8.

established life, with men already there to set the pace for them.[1] The veteran soldiers (veterans of a whole two weeks) looked with disdain on the new recruits and taunted them with greetings of "Hey rookies" and "Oh Boy, wait till you get the needle" (a reference to the temporary illness and sore arms induced by typhoid shots).[2] In some small way that went unnoticed by all, this signaled a sort of bonding within the original unit. The "veterans" made proud displays of being seasoned soldiers. They spoke of K.P., chow, reveille, close order, and fatigue with fluency and nonchalance. Their salutes were punctilious, and they added a bit of swagger to their walk. This curious military pride, which the officers had worked in vain to extract from the fledgling soldiers, now emerged spontaneously. At first, the "rookies" were duly impressed, but it was not long before they too dissolved into the melting pot, and for the first time, the men started to show pride in their units.[3]

For an hour after breakfast every morning, the men would do exercises followed by close order drill, the noise of bulldozers and hammers cutting across the voices of the sergeants. Performing "squads left" and "squads right" and "right face" and "by the left flank" and trying to hold formation in whatever space could be found, while dodging stacks of lumber and grumbling laborers, was a challenge in the early weeks of life at Camp Upton. During every break, the whispers of soldiers could be heard as the recruits questioned each other: "Do you start off with left? No, right, then pivot."[4,5,6,7]

The art of saluting was the subject of much schooling. Lectures were actually given on the subject. Captain Dick gave a speech in which he described the terrible Canadian losses in Europe and emphasized that "they lost—they lost heavily—they lost because they didn't have discipline. We must have discipline." There were many occasions at Camp Upton when a battery was taken to some side road or field to practice the subtle, angular art of saluting. From the starting position of "at ease," with feet spread apart, came the command "Attention—hand," at which point the hand was raised to the saluting position, then "Salute," and the hand was snapped down. This was followed by "At ease." The drill was repeated over and over again.[8]

Afternoons were set aside for brisk five-mile hikes in the invigorating air of the country. The resulting sweat and aching muscles contributed perhaps more than any other activity to the physical conditioning of the men. One day of every week was set aside for an all-day hike with instruction on castrametation, the art of making camp. This consisted of pitching tents, mounting guard, preparing food on the field range, and policing the camp area.[9]

The Department of War had decided that Camp Upton was to be the base for the 77th Division. An entire division typically consists of about 27,000 men and 1,000

1   http://longislandgenealogy.com/campupton/upton.htm.
2   *The Story of Battery B 306th F.A.—77th Division*, p. 13.
3   *History of the 77th Division*, p. 15.
4   *The Battery Book*, p. 24.
5   *The Autobiography of a Regiment*, p. 15.
6   *C" Battery Book: 306th F.A., 77th Div., 1917–1919*, by John Foster (Brooklyn, NY: Braunworth & Co., 1920), p. 10.
7   *The Story of Battery B 306th F.A.—77th Division*, p. 15.
8   *The Battery Book*, pp. 11–18.
9   *The Battery Book*, p. 24.

77th Division *division = 27,000 men*

153rd Infantry Brigade

Brigade = 6000 men

305th Infantry Regiment
306th Infantry Regiment
304th Machine Gun Battalion

154th Infantry Brigade

Brigade = 6000 men

307th Infantry Regiment
308th Infantry Regiment
305th Machine Gun Battalion

152nd Field Artillery Brigade

Brigade = 4500 men

304th Field Artillery Regiment
(1500 men, 24 guns (75's))

305th Field Artillery Regiment
(1500 men, 24 guns (75's))

306th Field Artillery Regiment
(1500 men, 24 guns (155's))

- *152nd Depot Brigade*
- *306th Machine Gun Battalion*
- *302nd Engineers*
- *302nd Field Signal Battalion*
- *302nd Supply Train*
- *302nd Trench Motor Battery*
- *Ambulance companies: 305th, 306th, 307th, 308th*
- *Field Hospitals: 305th, 306th, 307th, 308th*

306th Field Artillery Regiment

Regiment = 1500 men, 24 guns (155s)

1st Battalion = 500 men

A battery = 250 men, 4 guns
B battery = 250 men, 4 guns

Major Holland Duell Commands 2nd Battalion

2nd Battalion = 500 men

C battery = 250 men, 4 guns
D battery = 250 men, 4 guns

3rd Battalion = 500 men

E battery = 250 men, 4 guns
F battery = 250 men, 4 guns

officers. A division is composed of brigades. Brigades are composed of regiments. Regiments are composed of battalions, and battalions are composed of companies, which are the smallest groups, usually containing about 250 men each.

An artillery battalion has about half as many men as an infantry battalion. I would command the 2nd Battalion of the 306th Field Artillery, comprising 500 men.

The 77th Division was organized as shown in the diagram on the facing page:[1,2,3]

At different camps around the country, plans were to form, train, and send to Europe 100 divisions by the end of 1919. A division goes to war as an interdependent family. The different branches of the division rely on each other for survival. The infantry are the men with rifles and grenades doing hand-to-hand combat at the farthest point of advance. One of the engineers' many challenges might be to replace a bridge that a retreating enemy has blown up so that the men of the infantry may continue the pursuit. During the rebuilding, the engineers depend on the infantry to protect them from enemy snipers who do not want the bridge replaced. Perhaps as the infantry resumes the advance, casualties are inflicted by enemy machine gun nests. At that point, the howitzers of our artillery brigade would be called upon to pound those enemy positions ahead of the infantry. The depot brigade must at all cost keep the gunners constantly supplied with ammunition, for without ammunition, the lives of the division would be at risk. And of course the division must internally meet its needs for meals, medical care, and a multitude of other logistics. Because a division is trained to support itself, it usually travels in a relatively tight geographical proximity.

It would become vital to the overall performance and survival of the division that every single soldier could be counted on to perform his duties and carry out his orders with determination and without question such that the division could operate as a single coordinated unit. Allowing for anything less would be to invite disaster. It would now be the job of the commander of the 77th Division to bring his new group of 27,000 of New York's most mismatched, diverse, unlikely individuals together into a group of companions who would interact not only with camaraderie and an overall knowledge of the division's operational mechanics but also with a mastery of the positions for which they were to train.

1 *Memories of the World War: 1917–1918*, by Robert Alexander (New York: The Macmillan Company, 1931), p. 100.
2 *The Battery Book*, p. 5.
3 *The Victorious 77th Division (New York's Own) in the Argonne Fight*, by Arthur McKeogh (New York: John H. Eggers Co., 1919), p. 9.

So with the melding of the division as the immediate priority and the instilling of technical proficiency as the next order of business, training began. At Camp Upton, one major general was in charge of 1,000 subordinate officers who would in turn mold 27,000 men into soldiers. One has only to contemplate that the challenges confronting the 77th Division were being faced by dozens of other divisions in camps around the country to understand the enormous and immediate burden in terms of manpower, materials, and money being placed on our country. Our aspiration for an immediate million-man army was an enterprise of appalling complexity and magnitude. And in the spirit of "when it rains when pours," nine days after General Pershing requested his million-man army, he revised the figures and requested an army of three million men.[1]

The declaration of war, which made necessary the equipping and maintenance of this tremendous army, made a sudden and pressing demand on the industries of the country. At first, the ability of industry to wrestle with and meet those demands was slow to develop.[2] We now had a partially complete camp where we could begin training. Recruits were starting to pour in but materials were woefully absent.[3] Gas warfare was a new, deadly, and barbaric technology of this war. Yet for training this division of 30,000 men, the camp was able to secure only twelve gas masks. We had no rifles until early spring of 1918.[4]

The 77th Division Artillery would be trained to fight with 75-millimeter and 155-millimeter howitzers. These large guns had inside barrel diameters of 3 inches and 6 inches, respectively and were each pulled by a team of eight horses. The crews would have to learn about the different types of charges to be fired, how to calculate firing coordinates, and how to transport the guns across different types of terrain, not to mention how to handle horses and a multitude of other very specific and very essential details. However, there was nothing available that closely resembled the howitzers for which we were supposed to be receiving such specialized training. What we had was one photograph of a 6-inch howitzer (the inside barrel diameter was 6 inches) and several manuals on the nomenclature of the piece.[5]

Eventually, the camp obtained four old 3-inch guns. They were castoffs from some National Guard unit but looked as though they had been used in the Civil War.[6] These guns were shared among the different artillery batteries. Each battery got all four guns one day a week. On the other days, standing gun drill was conducted by means of laying four wooden planks on the ground to represent the muzzle, wheels, and trail of a real gun.[7]

✳ *Old 3-inch gun used for training at Camp Upton, 1918. (Courtesy of Longwood Public Library, Thomas R. Bayles Local History Room)*

1   http://europeanhistory.about.com/od/worldwar1/p/ww1101.htm.
2   *The Battery Book*, p. 12.
3   *The Autobiography of a Regiment*, p. 13.
4   *The Battery Book*, pp. 22–23.
5   *The Story of Battery B 306th F.A.—77th Division*, p. 15.
6   *The Autobiography of a Regiment*, p. 15.
7   *The Battery Book*, 1921, p. 21.

Perhaps the most humorous problem was the lack of any horses that could be used as mounts or to pull the howitzers as well as the many ammunition and supply carts. The high command's solution was to construct training horses made of long, hollow wooden cylinders mounted on four sticks. With these horses, we executed commands such as "Stand to horse," "Prepare to mount," and "Mount." To mount the wooden horse (which had no stirrups), somewhat of a mounting jump was required, which resulted in an uncomfortable, forceful landing on a hard wooden imaginary saddle.[1] When the unit was given the order to go into action, the drivers would carry the wooden horses from their stalls to the firing range, the cannoneers would lay out the planks to form a makeshift howitzer, and the executive officer would come out with a handful of manuals. The camp was also completely lacking in the specialized instruments required for calculating and adjusting the direction of fire from the big guns. There was much discussion of what B.C. telescopes, range-finders, and goniometers might look like. Then mock-ups were fashioned out of scrap lumber or tin cans.[2]

On the battlefield, the linemen roll out sometimes miles of telephone wire across all sorts of terrain to connect the different spread-out units. At this point in our training, the linemen ran wires through the barracks, around posts, up and down staircases, through windows, and through holes drilled in walls, which, on occasion, allowed for some jovial and perhaps unauthorized, after-hours conversations between barracks and from floor to floor.[3]

It probably sounds like a fun children's game of playing soldiers, but it was a frustrating time for men who were trying to get a crash course in skills that would keep them alive on battlefields where there would be real guns and real bullets. But as a country we were "winging it." We had made the decision to go to war. We weren't quite sure how it was going to play out, but we had conviction, and most of the men were starting to stand behind that spirit.

Thus went the training from early September until October 22, 1917, by which time the men had hardened up, learned how to do close order drills, and could salute properly. They were light-years from being soldiers, but it was forward progress, and the spirit of "team" was starting to shine through. On October 22, 1917, we began a sixteen-week period of intensive training that would cover basic weaponry and combat techniques and specialized training specific to the different companies.[4] European officers, who had seen action at the front, taught the techniques of protecting ourselves from machine gun fire, crawling through barbed wire entanglements, and throwing grenades as well as the technique of trench warfare.[5]

Sprawling outdoor spaces were set up to mimic the landscape of the actual battlefields.[6] The men were divided up into "ally" and "enemy" groups, and by hand they would dig opposing trenches deep enough to stand in. The trench was each side's "front line," and each group would do everything possible to defend that territory

---

1 *The Battery Book*, p. 24.
2 *The Story of Battery B 306th F.A.—77th Division*, pp. 15–16.
3 *The Battery Book*, p. 21.
4 *The Battery Book*, p. 20.
5 http://longislandgenealogy.com/campupton/upton.htm.
6 *History of the 77th Division*, p. 17.

from the other side, and occasionally "go over the top" and attack their opponents' front line trench.[1] Professional boxers taught the men hand-to hand-combat.[2]

There was much practice in riflery, including practice in slow and rapid fire.[3] The rifle range was completed in January, and despite cold and mud and frozen ground, it was crowded every day.[4] With bayonets clipped onto the ends of the rifles, there were drills in which the men performed "On Guard," "Short thrust," "Withdraw," "Long thrust," and "Butt strike" until their arms were about to fall off, then make wild dashes in platoon front across open lots, yelling—in compliance with instruction— like Cherokee Indians.[5,6]

There was a series of lectures by British officers who had survived some of the bitterest fighting of the war. They described in vivid detail the ghastly effects of the mustard and phosgene gas being used by the enemy. Understandably, we took the drills with gas masks very seriously.[7] The gas mask was a sort of heavy olive-colored canvas hood that covered the entire head and neck, with built-in big, round goggles and a fat hose running from the mouthpiece to a filter. The air inside was oppressively hot and stuffy, the goggles would fog, and the wearer took on the appearance of an alien or a gigantic fly.[8]

The drills consisted of testing the mask for imperfections, rapid adjustment, dismount drills, and running courses while wearing the mask as well as first aid in case of being gassed. With only twelve gas masks for the whole of the camp, men were faced with the disagreeable situation of having to use a mouthpiece that had just come out of the previous man's mouth. An effort to sanitize the mouthpieces was made by wiping them down with a nauseating solution of creosote.

Finally, when the commanding officers felt that the men were ready, we were treated to the gas house, a wooden shack near the machine gun range. The Scottish sergeant in charge of training at the gas house addressed the soldier students as follows: "We got to ha'a wee bit o' luck this afternoon. We carried out thu-ree corpses this marnin', and they only allow me fower for a full day."

The commanding officer instructed us to laugh, lest we hurt the sergeant's feelings. So we laughed at his joke. It was more like a cry for help.

The gas sergeant then said, "I'm going to loose a killing mixture of chlorine, so it would be well to inspect your masks carefully." Then, after opening the valve, he said, "Come close so you can smell the stuff. Then you'll know I'm not putting anything over on you."

Our lungs refused to breathe the sickly air, and we were inspired to follow our training to the letter as we donned our gas masks. We were imprisoned in the gas house for ten minutes. The gas caused the air in the room to have a bluish appearance,

---

1   http://longislandgenealogy.com/campupton/upton.htm.
2   http://www.bnl.gov/bn/web/history/camp_upton.
3   *The Battery Book*, p. 23.
4   *History of the 77th Division*, p. 17.
5   *The Battery Book*, p. 23.
6   *"C" Battery Book*, p. 11.
7   *History of the 305th Field Artillery*, p. 27.
8   *World War I (DK Eyewitness Books)*, by Simon Adams (New York: DK Publishing, 2001), p. 44.

but the air in our lungs was pure, and we gained confidence in our training and equipment. Of course, on exiting the gas house, we cracked gruesome jokes for the benefit of the men who were about to enter.

The gas masks were miserable to wear. They were hot and cumbersome, and they obscured our vision. But the absolute necessity of donning them when called for was duly impressed upon us, and without a doubt, our thorough training saved many a life on the battlefield.[1,2]

The depth of education the men were receiving on a crash course schedule was staggering. A list of all of the basic drills and training programs would fill volumes. Added to that, officers were taking French lessons in the evenings,[3] and immigrants who spoke and understood so little English that they had trouble learning and performing their duties were required to take English classes.[4,5]

There was much additional training during this same period that was specific to our artillery brigade, though the training was greatly lacking in substance. We never had possession of anything closely resembling the actual howitzers that we would be using. Instead we trained with a limited number of quite ancient guns and basically played make-believe with a lot of explanation of how the real thing should be operated.

After more than three months with only our homemade wooden horses to train on, eighty-seven real horses arrived on December 10, 1917. In a way, they resembled the first recruits who had stepped off the train. They were shaggy and unkempt. Some seemed overburdened with life. Others were full of a zestful enthusiasm to have a go at the green equestrians, many of whom had never mounted a real horse in their lives.

Two days later, the 305th Field Artillery conducted the first live target practice. The four old guns were hitched up to four teams of eight horses each. Perhaps the bitter cold of the unusually severe winter agitated the horses, for they were not inclined to behave. Some pulled, some ambled, some objected vocally while prancing from side to side, which almost caused one gun to overturn. But the group made it to their destination, the horses were unhitched from the guns, and a total of nineteen rounds were fired. The following day, the 305th Field Artillery again went to the range and fired ten more rounds.[6] After three months of training, the 305th Field Artillery had fired a total of just twenty-nine rounds and would have to wait another three months, until deployment in Europe, to fire additional training rounds. By contrast, on the actual battlefield, it was not uncommon to fire hundreds of rounds a day. But the 305th fared better than the 304th Field Artillery regiment and our own 306th Field Artillery regiment, which never fired a single round at Camp Upton but had only the training benefit of watching the 305th Field Artillery shoot off their twenty-nine practice rounds.

On Washington's Birthday, Friday, February 22, 1918, though still far from being a well-greased military machine, the 77th Division paraded in New York City.

---

1 *The Battery Book*, p. 23.
2 *History of the 305th Field Artillery*, p. 33.
3 *The History of the 306th Field Artillery*, p. 9.
4 *The History of the 306th Field Artillery*, p. 67.
5 *The Battery Book*, p. 25.
6 *History of the 305th Field Artillery*, p. 21.

✻ *77th Divisional insignia*

From that day forward, it bore the title of "New York's Own," the "Liberty Division," accompanied by the new divisional insignia that the men wore so proudly on their uniforms: a gold image of the Statue of Liberty on a blue background.[1,2]

To complement this, the regiment now had its own marching music. In 1917, Lieutenant George Friedlander of the 306th Field Artillery asked John Philip Sousa, the world's most famous march composer, to create a march for the 306th Field Artillery. The result was "306th Field Artillery March," which became wildly popular and was later renamed "Field Artillery March" for all military artillery units to enjoy. The recording of the march sold over 750,000 copies.[3,4]

VERSE:

> *Over hill, over dale*
> *We have hit the dusty trail,*
> *And the Caissons go rolling along.*
> *In and out, hear them shout,*
> *Counter march and right about,*
> *And those Caissons go rolling along.*

REFRAIN:

> *For it's hi! hi! hee!*
> *In the field artillery,*
> *Shout out your numbers loud and strong, 3-0-6![5]*
> *And where e'er you go,*
> *You will always know*
> *That the Caissons go rolling along.*

VERSE:

> *In the storm, in the night,*
> *Action left or action right*
> *See those Caissons go rolling along*
> *Limber front, limber rear,*
> *Prepare to mount your cannoneer*
> *And those Caissons go rolling along.*

REFRAIN:

> *For it's hi! hi! hee!*
> *In the field artillery,*
> *Shout out your numbers loud and strong, 3-0-6![6]*

---

1 *History of the 77th Division*, p. 17.
2 http://longislandgenealogy.com/campupton/upton.htm.
3 *The History of the 306th Field Artillery*, p. 69.
4 http://www.skyways.org/orgs/mcb/Library/M0126.htm.
5 *The Story of Battery B 306th F.A.—77th Division*, p. 54.
6 *The Story of Battery B 306th F.A.—77th Division*, p. 54.

And where e'er you go,
You will always know
That the Caissons go rolling along.

Verse:

Was it high, was it low,
Tell me where did that one go?
As those Caissons go rolling along
Was it left, was it right,
Now we won't get home tonight
And those Caissons go rolling along.

Refrain:

For it's hi! hi! hee!
In the field artillery,
Shout out your numbers loud and strong, 3-0-6![1]
And where e'er you go,
You will always know
That the Caissons go rolling along.

The men were finally dropping the "self" that had defined who they were in the outside world. In this military, they were all the same. The millionaire in camp was no better off than the immigrant who could speak no English.[2] A hard shell had been broken and cast aside, and the men had come to truly enjoy each other's company. In one of the barracks, they had purchased a pool table, rented a piano, purchased chess and checker sets, and organized a small library of books and magazines.

Unsupervised time brought the welcome opportunity to hang out with pals. There was considerable talent within the ranks of the division,[3] and the men organized and put on many shows and concerts for their own entertainment. Sports became a favorite pastime, and much energy was put into competitions between teams from different batteries. The regiment promoted twenty recreational activities such as boxing, wrestling, baseball, soccer, track, football, glee club, orchestra, pool, volleyball, chess, and checkers.[4]

✳ *YMCA at Camp Upton, 1918. (Courtesy of Longwood Public Library, Thomas R. Bayles Local History Room)*

---

1   *The Story of Battery B 306th F.A.—77th Division*, p. 54.
2   http://www.longwood.k12.ny.us/history/upton/camp.htm.
3   *The Autobiography of a Regiment*, p. 22.
4   *The History of the 306th Field Artillery*, pp. 9, 68.

✳ *Camp Upton Liberty Theater auditorium. (Courtesy of Longwood Public Library, Thomas R. Bayles Local History Room)*

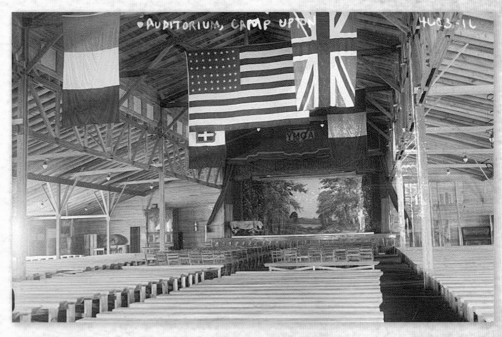

✳ *Hostess House at Camp Upton, 1918. (Courtesy of Longwood Public Library, Thomas R. Bayles Local History Room)*

On December 20, 1917, Camp Upton was declared officially complete.[1] New buildings had been opened for our enjoyment. The YMCA offered writing tables and motion-picture shows. The YWCA set up three "Hostess Houses," which provided comfortable, lounge-type environments in which the men could socialize with sweethearts, friends, and family and hold dances. There were rugs on the floors, comfortable easy-chairs, reading material, and a canteen where much delightful and dainty food afforded relief from the unpalatable army fare.[2,3] The Liberty Theater was an auditorium with seating for 3,000.[4,5]

1   http://www.bnl.gov/about/history/campupton.php
2   *The Battery Book*, p. 25.
3   http://www.longwood.k12.ny.us/history/upton/camp.htm
4   *The History of the 306th Field Artillery*, p. 9.
5   *History of the 77th Division*, p. 14.

Every Sunday, the camp was transformed from a drill ground to a picnic park. Thousands of friends, relatives, mothers, wives, and sweethearts would come to visit the soldiers. There was always a sightseeing tour, which introduced the natural scenic points of interest as well as the different areas of the camp, including Headquarters Hill. The more adventurous would climb the water tower atop the hill for a magnificent bird's-eye view of the camp.[1,2] There were dances, and local talent filled the air with lively ragtime. Abundant food included lots of homemade pies. For the men, a Sunday at camp was far from being a punishment.[3,4]

Almost every visitor who came to Camp Upton remarked that the fresh-baked bread was the best they had ever tasted. At the camp bakery, 440 pounds of the finest white flour, 3 pounds of yeast, 4 pounds each of sugar and salt, 26 pounds of lard, and 28 pounds of water were blended in one giant electric mixer. After rising, the dough was hand formed into two-pound, three-ounce loaves that were baked in coal-heated ovens. This single-batch recipe was repeated over and over in the 24-hour bakery, which was manned in three 8-hour shifts and produced 30,000 pounds of bread a day.[5] When viewed in the context of overall camp operations, this one monumental achievement gave visitors a perspective on the enormity of the overall war effort.

After months of hard work and training and forward progress, we were hit with a series of setbacks. An order was issued that we would be changed from a regiment using horse-drawn howitzers to having the howitzers pulled by tractors. Most of the officers had elected to serve in the artillery because they wanted to be with horses. In fact some had previously served in the U.S. Calvary on the Mexican border. With this order, riding boots and spurs would become obsolete, and bitterly sarcastic quips were made about the officers trading in their riding crops for monkey wrenches. All the preparation and training to this point, which had been centered on horses, would go out the window as wasted time.

A number of officers and men were to be sent away to motor school in Peoria, Illinois, to learn tractor maintenance and repair. Meanwhile, an automobile engine was set up in an empty room for the fledgling motorists to study, and a number of dummy instruments were constructed to give a touch of reality to some of the special work. But in all the training, the imagination played a large part. Everything had to be simulated. It was like little boys playing soldiers.[6]

In November, to the disgust and disappointment of the entire camp, orders came down for a sweeping transfer of 500 men from Camp Upton to the 82nd Division at Camp Gordon in Atlanta, Georgia. The 304th, 305th, and 306th Field Artillery battalions were required to transfer out about 100 men each. After the months of drilling and training and team building, to fracture the units and remove part of those teams was not only a logistical blow, it was also a morale blow to both the officers and the men. The men being transferred out were issued blue duffle bags to pack their things

---

1 *The History of the 306th Field Artillery*, p. 10.
2 *History of the 77th Division*, p. 16.
3 *The History of the 306th Field Artillery*, p. 10.
4 *History of the 77th Division*, p. 16.
5 *Trench & Camp Newspaper,* Camp Upton, L.I., Vol 2, No. 47, August 26, 1919.
6 *The Autobiography of a Regiment*, p. 19.

in. From that point out, any sightings at the camp of "blue bags," as they became known, were enough to inspire everyone with legitimate attacks of anxiety.[1,2] In the spirit of facing adversity with levity, transfers became treated as a standing joke. If, for example, during a YMCA show, an announcer called, "The following men will report at once to their orderly rooms," there would always be a shout of laughter and cries of "Blue bag!," "Goodbye Billy!," or "See you in France."

In December, we received replacement troops to bring us back up to full ranks. This was our first quota of men from outside New York City. They came from "up-state," mostly from the relatively rural area of Olean and Buffalo. When they first ar-rived, these "hicks" furnished considerable amusement to the city boys. Undoubtedly, they were a different breed, yet they added a certain element of wholesomeness that soon won them a place in the hearts of the regiment. Many of the new recruits were accustomed to outdoor life, and they infused a healthy attitude toward cold winds and snowstorms.[3]

On January 7, 1918, I was promoted to major.[4] As a battalion, we again began to feel like a solid, well-trained, close-knit unit.

All the logistical plans and itineraries of the military were cloaked in secrecy, and we were given no advance notice as to our own timetables. However, in early April, all indications were that we would deploy to Europe any day. Then one day we awoke to find one of the infantry regiments absent from the camp. The following day, a machine gun battalion disappeared, and then another infantry regiment. Our excitement now rose to a concert pitch as we expected our travel orders any minute. Then came the final blow.

The War Department, without a word of warning, made a last-minute change of plan and sent down orders for the artillery brigade to, at once, transfer 500 men to the infantry. Shortly afterward, the call was upped to 698 men. The order had devas-tating ramifications. We had trained as a unit for six months, each man had become proficient at a specific job, and the unit depended on him doing that job proficiently. How could we possibly hope to be competent as a unit now, with so many of our men removed? Every single man was vital to our ability to function in a competent capac-ity. At that point, we would not have been able to spare even twenty men! And after the painstaking efforts we had made to nurture the spirit and camaraderie that now existed in the unit, it was infuriating that some unseen branch of the military could sucker punch us and, with no discussion, rip away part of our team—our pals!

Then, from those dark depths, came rumors that the entire artillery brigade would be converted into infantry—that our monumental achievement of growing into an artillery unit in six short months had been for nothing. It was demoralizing. It was frustrating. It was insulting. It was maddening that such plainly illogical, ill-planned ideas could be handed down from a faceless bureaucracy with which there could be no debate. No one wanted our team broken up, and no one wanted to be

1   *The Autobiography of a Regiment*, p. 17.
2   *The Battery Book*, p. 27.
3   *The Autobiography of a Regiment*, p. 22.
4   Yale biographies for Holland Duell, Class of 1902.

taken away from the "big guns." There had grown in the men a stubborn pride in the name "Field Artillery," and all wanted the opportunity to use their skills on the battlefield to help save the free world. But the order was complied with. We had no choice. We transferred the 698 men to the infantry and waved goodbye as they went off with their blue duffel bags. But this time there were no "blue bag" jokes. We didn't see any of the men again until we arrived at the front lines in France.[1,2,3,4] Some we never saw again, as they had paid the supreme sacrifice and now lay buried in France.[5]

The newspapers were filled with details of the vast German offensive of the spring of 1918, and we could understand the pressing need for infantry troops to help hold the front lines.[6] But to fill those infantry "muscle" positions with highly trained artillerymen and sacrifice the might and power of artillery support defied any reasonable logic. One could only go back to the enormity of the U.S. war effort and conclude that there were just too many details and too many tactical decisions to be made and handled properly, which meant that mistakes would be made—sometimes grossly negligent and glaring mistakes. And we were witnessing one of them.

On Monday, April 15, 1918, the rumors that the artillery would be converted to infantry seemed to be supported. We were told to unpack a great deal of equipment. Then, as if the Army was trying to break us psychologically, on Wednesday we were told that nothing more was to be unpacked and that everything we had unpacked had to be repacked. On Thursday, we were resuscitated in yet another huge about-face.[7] We were informed that trainloads of men from Camp Devens in Massachusetts and Camp Dodge in Iowa would be coming to Camp Upton at once. The 77th was to remain an artillery division. Our quota of the incoming recruits would fill our ranks back up to full strength, and we would ship out in four days.[8] We would receive howitzers and ample training time in Europe.

On Friday, April 19, 1918, the replacement troops arrived, and our officers met them at the train. They were welcomed in perhaps a gentler manner than was customary in the military, for our officers were sensitive to the fact that these men had also been training hard for the past six months and that this last-minute change of plans left them feeling as if they too were having the rug pulled out from under them.

It was four o'clock by the time the replacement troops reached our barracks. The officers had escorted them through the cool fog, which had hung on throughout the day. The barrack was filled with the odor of warming coffee as we set about getting acquainted with each other. We searched for any reason to hope that we would not have to start training from square one.

Only a very few of the new men had training in artillery. Most we would have to retrain, as they had been trained to serve as infantrymen. How unjust that instead

---

1   *The Autobiography of a Regiment*, p. 32.
2   *The History of the 306th Field Artillery*, p. 11.
3   *The Battery Book*, p. 32.
4   *History of the 305th Field Artillery*, p. 36.
5   *"C" Battery Book*, p. 13.
6   *History of the 305th Field Artillery*, p. 36.
7   *History of the 305th Field Artillery*, p. 37.
8   *The Battery Book*, p. 32.

of simply waiting a week and sending these infantry troops to the front line as replacements for the depleted infantry, we had been forced to sacrifice so many of our highly trained artillerymen. The front line infantry was now faced with retraining our artillerymen to be infantrymen, while we were faced with retraining infantrymen to be artillerymen. It made no sense. Too many decisions, too few commanders, not enough communication—whatever it was, it was bad for morale, and that showed on the sleepy, grim faces of the replacement troops.

Some of the new men stared at the unpainted, studded walls of the downstairs mess hall. Some toyed with the corn bread and coffee that had been served to them on the bare pine tables.

A sergeant cried out with good humor, "We're not going to bite you. Talk up! Haven't you got a song?"

A few of the men grinned. There was no song. Some sporadic conversation sprang up but just as quickly died away. In a corner, a little fellow, bronzed from the western sun, sat before his untasted bread and coffee. The corners of his mouth began to twitch. For a moment, we thought he was going to laugh, but instead he began, silently and with difficulty, to cry.[1]

Such was the spirit of our artillery brigade when life was breathed back into it and the thought of converting to an infantry unit was dropped. There was no loud rejoicing, no shouting and throwing of hats in the air. By that point, everyone had been so beaten down by having their lives turned upside-down on an almost daily basis that a good night's sleep became the most immediate focus. However, as the days passed, the reality that we were to remain an artillery unit and that we would immediately deploy to Europe sank in. And with that and from each day forward, the morale, the skill, and the strength of the unit grew.

Sunday, April 21, 1918, was our last opportunity to say our farewells to friends and family. No passes were granted, so visitors had to come to camp. They began to arrive shortly after 9:00 a.m. in torrents of rain that never let up for a moment, blown by a cold, penetrating wind. Troops had to be present at 11:00 a.m. as Supply Company trucks backed up to the barracks and loaded the blue bags. After that, the men were free to visit until 8:00 p.m., when the camp was cleared of visitors.[2,3]

The atmosphere during those goodbyes was expectedly somber. All of the Hostess Houses were full. Women dressed soberly. At each opportunity, their men would sit with them. For many, there seemed nothing left to say except "Goodbye, I love you."[4] For others, especially among the families of the foreign born, grief was unrestrained, and loved ones wept openly together.[5]

For lice control, the straw-filled dormitory mattresses had all been removed and burned by the men in preparation for the next wave of recruits to train in the camp.[6,7]

---

1 *History of the 305th Field Artillery*, pp. 36–38.
2 *The Battery Book*, p. 33.
3 *The Autobiography of a Regiment*, p. 37.
4 *History of the 305th Field Artillery*, p. 38.
5 *The Autobiography of a Regiment*, p. 36.
6 *History of the 305th Field Artillery*, p. 39.
7 http://www.worldwar1.com/dbc/schneider_ws.htm.

So on Sunday night, we all slept on the wooden floor with nothing more than blankets and overcoats. Wake-up was sounded at 1:00 a.m., and there followed a hurried breakfast, final cleaning of the barrack, and stowing of all items in our packs. Before we left, many signs were painted on the outside of the barracks doors:

"Summer Home For Rent. Owners spending the warm season in France."

"Goodbye Upton! Hello Berlin!"

"Wipe your feet. We're off to kiss the Kaiser, and can't do it for you,"

"To let—Inquire Uncle Sam."

"Goodbye Upton—Will return in the Spring."[1,2,3]

At 3:00 a.m. on Monday, April 22, 1918, the rain had stopped, and our 306th Field Artillery and the 304th Field Artillery marched in darkness through mud and a heavy morning fog to the trains. The 305th Field Artillery left camp a few days later, destined for a different transport ship.[4] We boarded the railway cars, each marked with the names of the units to occupy them, and sat three men and their packs and rifles to each double seat. The train drew out at 5:55 a.m. and whizzed past the familiar stations of Hicksville, Mineola, and Jamaica.[5,6] At last, this was it. It was real. We were on our way, and our destination was the front.

---

1 *The Battery Book*, p. 33.
2 *History of the 305th Field Artillery*, p. 40.
3 *The Story of Battery B 306th F.A.—77th Division*, p. 17.
4 *History of the 77th Division*, p. 25.
5 *The Battery Book*, p. 35.
6 *The Autobiography of a Regiment*, p. 38.

Part 2
Events Leading to War

The European conflict that began in 1914 has ushered in a new era in warfare. Artillery has progressed from crude cannons to precision machines for the delivery of explosive projectiles, which are now being put to the test for the first time in history. A race had been going on for years between different countries to develop huge inventories of these weapons, which could blow up the landscape many miles away. From small mortars with light shells to large howitzers with 90-pound shells to the monster- size guns that are so large they are fitted with train wheels for transport on railroad tracks and use shells weighing hundreds of pounds that have to be loaded with winch systems, the sheer inventory of weapons and stockpiles of munitions that exist is staggering.

✳ *Thousands of artillery shells in munitions factory*

Far from being limited to advancements in artillery, implements of killing now include previously unseen machine guns, poison gases, navies with steel warships, bomb-dropping airplanes and zeppelins, and submarines armed with torpedoes. It is by far the most massive buildup of weaponry and killing power the world has ever seen. Countries are armed as they have never been armed before—but not just with weapons, also with soldiers. Before this time, countries fought wars with tens of thousands or, at most, hundreds of thousands of troops. The whole of the Roman army comprised an estimated 350,000 troops.[1] By contrast, there were 59 million troops in the armies of 1914.[2]

Germany as we know it did not exist before 1871; it was a confederation of twenty-six different states. In 1870, Prussia and the German confederacy united to attack and defeat France in the Battle of Sedan (a major French city), and in 1871, Prussia and all of the German confederate states unified into the German Empire.[3]

Until that time, Germany was largely an agricultural nation.[4] But as spoils of the war, Germany gained not only the hatred of the French, but also an area in northwest France known as the Alsace-Lorraine region, which Germany wanted in part because it was strategically positioned militarily but, more important, because of its vast resources of iron ore, which would support future ship and weapons production for Germany.[5] Alsace-Lorraine was the size of the states of Connecticut and Rhode Island combined; it consisted of 5,600 square miles that were home to 1,700 villages, towns, and cities and 1,600,000 human beings, the consent of not one of whom was either asked or given.

France had always treated the citizens of Alsace-Lorraine extremely well, and in return, they had a deep love and loyalty for France.[6] But on September 30, 1872, Germany forced its government and its will on the people and demanded that they pledge allegiance to Germany or depart the area. In response, 45,000 people sorrowfully left homes that had been occupied by generations of their ancestors. Simultaneously, the teaching of French in elementary schools was outlawed in Alsace-Lorraine, and the young men of the area were ordered by conscription into the German military.[7]

To the embitterment of the citizens of Alsace-Lorraine and France, Germany ruled the area by oppression for 45 years and benefited greatly from the natural resources. In fact, in 1913, out of 28 million tons of iron ore mined by Germany, 21 million came from the mines in Lorraine.[8] By 1914, iron, coal, steel engineering, and shipbuilding industries had turned Germany into the third largest industrial country in the world.[9]

---

1 http://en.wikipedia.org/wiki/battle_of_chalons.
2 http://europeanhistory.about.com/od/worldwari/p/wwi101.htm.
3 http://encyclopedia.farlex.com/German+unification.
4 *World War I (DK Eyewitness Books)*, by Simon Adams (New York: DK Publishing, 2001), p. 7.
5 http://encyclopedia.farlex.com/alsace_lorraine.
6 *Source Records of the Great War*, Vol. 1 (I
7 *Source Records of the Great War*, Vol. 1, p. 166.
8 *Source Records of the Great War*, Vol. 1, 1931, p. 163.
9 *World War I (DK Eyewitness Books)*, p. 7.

Germany's power was surging, and Kaiser Frederick Wilhelm ruled with lofty aspirations for a mighty navy and army and for territorial expansion.[1] Germany entered a race for colonies, raising flags over parts of Africa and on islands in the Pacific.[2] Germany had spent years developing bigger, stronger weapons and now had massive stockpiles of weapons and ammunition. Having entered into a naval arms race with Britain and, at a cost that strained her economy, Germany now had a navy to rival the largest in the world: that of Britain. In the midst of this fierce European arms race, many Germans felt that war with neighboring France and Russia was inevitable and therefore they should go to war sooner rather than later, while they still had an advantage over their major enemy, Russia.[3]

Germany's ruler, Kaiser Wilhelm II, is very self-conscious about a birth defect that left him with an emaciated left arm. In public, he always tries to conceal the defect with certain outfits or by holding his left hand with his right or with a number of other tricks. Wilhelm has a quick intelligence that is overshadowed by a cantankerous temper leading to emotional outbursts. He is also noted for his immeasurably exaggerated self-confidence, impatience, and megalomania. In an interview for a British newspaper, Wilhelm was quoted as saying, "You English are mad, mad, mad, mad as March hares." The German Chancellor, Otto von Bismarck, has said that Wilhelm "brashly wanted to play the part of the supreme warlord." When war did finally break out, Wilhelm titled himself "Supreme War Lord" and *Allerhochste* (All-Highest). He has been observed to be concerned less with gaining specific objectives than with asserting his will. Many Europeans had feared that war was inevitable in part because of Wilhelm's temperament, in part because of the race Germany had entered into to become a world power, and in part because of France's 40 years of resentment and desire to regain the territories she lost to Germany in 1870.[4]

Consequently, for years, maybe decades, Germany and France had both drafted elaborate "what if" war plans. Germany had already mapped out the specific route she would take if she invaded France, including timelines and exact battlefield movements. The Schlieffen Plan mandated the taking of Paris within forty days, since the city was the major railway hub for all of France. A country's transportation is vital for troop and munitions movement, and by crushing transportation, an enemy can defeat a country. France had analyzed every different possible German invasion scenario and had drafted defensive and counteroffensive war plans for each contingency. With tension high on all sides, the countries of Europe were understandably nervous and formed alliances with one another, agreeing to back each other up should one country be attacked by another country. Germany, Italy, and Austria-Hungary formed one such alliance, known as the Triple Alliance. Britain, France and Russia formed another alliance, known as the Triple Entente, which had secondary members including Serbia.[5] Europe was a powder keg waiting to be ignited. The spark came on June 28, 1914, with perhaps the most famous assassination in history.

---

1 http://en.wikipedia.org/wiki/wilhelm_II,_German_Emperor.
2 http://militaryhistory.about.com/od/worldwari/a/wwicauses.htm.
3 http://europeanhistory.about.com/od/worldwar1/p/ww1101.htm.
4 http://en.wikipedia.org/wiki/wilhelm_II,_German_Emperor.
5 *World War I (DK Eyewitness Books)*, p. 7.

Tensions had existed between Austria-Hungary and neighboring Serbia for years. Serbia was a country of farmers, 86% of the populace being peasants whose lives revolved around tending their farms. There was basically only one class: the working class. There were no landlords to collect rents and no royalty to tax the poor. Consequently, Serbia experienced no internal revolt, rebellion, or discontent; rather, there existed a sense of unity.[1]

Serbia's main product for export, her main source of national wealth, was the pig. Yet without a seaport, Serbia was dependent upon the goodwill of her neighbors to provide access across their countries to the sea. Bulgaria, to the east, was also a country of pig farmers and, understandably, barred Serbia from transporting product across her lands. So for years Serbia gained access to seaports by crossing through neighboring Bosnia to the southwest. Friendly Bosnia and Serbia had in effect operated as one country, with Serbia feeling that it had a controlling influence over Bosnia.

That ended in 1909, when Austria annexed Bosnia, claiming it as her territory. The Bosnian Serbs felt enslaved by Austria.[2] Austria prevented uprising by drafting all young Bosnian men into its armies, and all Bosnian leaders were sent to prison or into exile.[3] With the annexation, Austria prohibited the transport of Serbian pigs across Austrian territories, effectively dooming Serbia to economic destruction and imprisoning her within her own borders.[4]

In pent-up retaliation, the powder keg finally blew wide open on June 28, 1914, when the young Serbian terrorist Gavrilo Princip assassinated Archduke Franz Ferdinand, the heir to the throne of Austria-Hungary. The motive, aside from retribution, was to prevent Franz Ferdinand's planned reforms from being implemented when he assumed office. He hoped to allow the Slavs who were now part of the empire, such as the Bosnians, to have a voice in government; this would give them less reason to make common cause with Serbia.

Franz Ferdinand's wife Sophie, born a Czech aristocrat but not to one of the dynastic families of Europe, was treated by the Austrian courts as a commoner, though granted the title Duchess of Hohenberg. Emperor Franz Joseph had consented to the marriage only on the condition that the descendants of Franz Ferdinand and Sophie would never ascend the throne. In short, Franz Ferdinand had married for love alone.

On this June day, the couple had planned to travel to Bosnia to observe military maneuvers and then to Sarajevo to open a new museum. Unbeknownst to the couple, clandestine Serbian groups had other plans for them. Dragutin Dimitrijevic, the chief of Serbian military intelligence, had, together with Danilo Ilic, leader of a Serbian terrorist cell, coordinated an assassination plot to be carried out by six young Bosnian Serb assassins.

On the morning of June 28, 1914, Franz Ferdinand and his party proceeded by train from Ilidza Spa to Sarajevo. Departing the train, the party then boarded a motorcade of six cars. Franz Ferdinand and his wife Sophie were in the third car. They sat

---

1 *Source Records of the Great War*, Vol. 1, p. 189.
2 *Source Records of the Great War*, Vol. 1, p. 188.
3 *Source Records of the Great War*, Vol. 1, p. 185.
4 *Source Records of the Great War*, Vol. 1, p. 176.

together in the back seat of the Graf & Stift Double Phaeton convertible sports car, which had its top folded down.

With advance public knowledge of the motorcade's route to the military barracks, Ilic had placed the six assassins in strategic positions. The first two, Muhamed Mchmedbasic and Vaso Cubrilovic, lay in wait in front of the garden of the Mostar Café. Vaso Cubrilovic was armed with a pistol, and each of the two men carried a bomb. However, when the motorcade passed their position, both men failed to act.

A little farther down the road, on the opposite side of the street by the Miljacka River, waited Nedeljko Cabrinovic, armed with one bomb. As Franz Ferdinand's car approached at 10:10 a.m., Cabrinovic threw his bomb, but it bounced off the folded back convertible cover and detonated under the following car, disabling that car and wounding twenty people. Cabrinovic immediately swallowed a cyanide pill and jumped into the Miljacka River, but his failures continued: The cyanide only induced vomiting, and the river at that spot was less than a foot deep. The police quickly apprehended Cabrinovic, and he was severely beaten by the crowd before being taken into custody. The motorcade sped off, leaving the three remaining assassins—Cujetko Popovic, Gavrilo Princip, and Trifun Grabez—unable to act because of the high speed at which the cars were moving.

Although the archduke and his party were shaken, the motorcade proceeded as planned to a scheduled speech at the Town Hall. After reading the speech from the blood-stained text, which had been in the damaged car, Franz Ferdinand and Sophie decided to cancel the rest of their plans in favor of visiting the bombing victims in the hospital.

In the meantime, the cause now seemingly lost, Gavrilo Princip had gone to a nearby food shop, Schiller's Delicatessen. At the same time, Franz Ferdinand's driver, en route to the hospital, took a wrong turn. Realizing his mistake, he stopped to back up. Upon reversing, the engine stalled—by sheer coincidence directly across the street from the delicatessen. As Princip exited the shop and saw the car, he did not hesitate to take advantage of the second chance that fate had bestowed upon him. Pistol in hand, Princip approached the car, pistol-whipped a bystander who was in his way, and, from 5 feet away, fired two shots. One shot hit Sophie in the abdomen. The other hit Franz Ferdinand in the jugular, but his only concern was for his beloved wife as he called to her, "Sophie! Sophie! Don't die! Live for our children!" As the car sped toward the governor's residence for medical aid, Count Harrach, who was also in the car, asked Ferdinand his condition, to which Ferdinand replied several times, "It's nothing. It's nothing." Sophie was dead by the time they reached the governor's residence. Ferdinand died ten minutes later.

All six assassins, as well as members of the Serbian military intelligence and the terrorist cell, were captured. Later, after being tried, most of the leaders were hanged. The six young assassins were given prison sentences of 10 to 20 years, 20 years being

✻ *Assassination of Franz Ferdinand and Sophie. Copertina della Domenica del Corriere Anno XVI n. 27 del 5-12.7.1914 illustrata da Achille Beltrame, [Public domain] via Wikimedia Commons*

✱ *Austro-Hungarian troops*
executing Serbians

the maximum allowed for men under twenty years old. Gavrilo Princip died in prison of tuberculosis in April 1918.[1]

The news of the assassination shocked the world. Anti-Serb rioting broke out in Austria-Hungary. Thirsting for revenge, Austria–Hungary began to plan an attack on Serbia and asked Germany to back her militarily if she should get into trouble and need help.

For Wilhelm, the request was a dream come true. Despite the massive military buildup he had orchestrated to forward his aspirations of European domination, history had taught him that to win the full support of his own people, he must not appear to be an aggressor, yet to win battles, he must be fully prepared to launch unexpected attacks at a moment's notice. Austria-Hungary was now volunteering to be the target of world scorn for starting a war, and Germany could simply play the role of a good Samaritan coming to the aid of an ally.

On July 5, 1914, Kaiser Wilhelm gave secret assurance to envoys from Austria-Hungary that if their country should attack Serbia, he would support Austria-Hungary to the utmost and lend it the full strength of his armies. He was fully aware that this would bring about the war he had wanted. On the very same day, German officials were alerted that this pledge to Austria made war an almost certainty and instructed that every preparation must be made to ensure instant readiness.

Within the inner German circles, however, a two-week delay was insisted upon. This would give German financial leaders a chance to sell foreign securities, which would be impossible to liquidate once a war started. Another reason for the delay had to do with the untimely (for Germany) fact that the President of France was currently in Russia, and his personal presence there could allow the two allied leaders to

---

1   http://en.wikipedia.org/wiki/assassination_of_Archduke_Franz_Ferdinand_of_Austria.

orchestrate a swifter military retaliation against Germany once war broke out. It was decided that any declarations of war must wait until President Poincaré returned to France. In the meantime Kaiser Wilhelm departed on a vacation on his private yacht, so to all the world, he appeared not to have a single warlike thought.

When all was ready, on July 23, 1914, Austria hurled a war ultimatum at Serbia— one that was so purposely demanding and unreasonable that there was no chance that Serbia would comply in full.[1] Five days later, on July 28, 1914, Austria-Hungary declared war on Serbia, and a giant chain of dominos began to fall:

June 28, 1914:   Gavrilo Princip assassinated Franz Ferdinand, heir to the throne of Austria-Hungary.

July 28, 1914:   Austria-Hungary declared war on Serbia.

July 29, 1914:   Russia, Serbia's ally, mobilized troops on the Serbian border in support of Serbia.

August 1, 1914:   Germany, in support of Austria-Hungary, declared war on Russia.

August 3, 1914:   France, in support of Russia, declared war on Germany and Austria-Hungary.

August 3, 1914:   Germany retaliated and declared war on France.

August 3, 1914:   Italy surprised Germany by declaring neutrality and refusing to deploy any troops. Unbeknownst to Germany, Italy (which Germany considered an ally via the 1882 Triple Alliance agreement) had entered a secret agreement with France in 1902, promising to be neutral in any war in which France was involved.[2]

August 4, 1914:   Germany declared war on Belgium,[3] and in accordance with an existing German battle plan called the Schlieffen Plan, Germany invaded neutral Belgium with the intention of arriving in Paris within 40 days for a quick knockout punch of France.[4] The same day, Britain, which had an agreement to defend Belgium's neutrality, declared war on Germany.[5]

August 6, 1914:   Serbia declared war on Germany.[6]

August 6, 1914:   Austria-Hungary declared war on Russia.

August 12, 1914:   France and Britain declared war on Austria-Hungary.

---

1   *Source Records of the Great War*, Vol. 1, 1931, p. xxxv.

2   http://www.enotes.com/topic/Italy_in_World_War_1.

3   *Personal Perspectives: World War I*, edited by Timothy C. Dowling (Santa Barbara, CA: ABC-CLIO, 2006), p. 323.

4   http://europeanhistory.about.com/od/worldwar1/p/ww1101.htm.

5   *World War I (DK Eyewitness Books)*, p. 8.

6   *Personal Perspectives: World War I*, p. 323.

In short order, the European Conflict had begun.

Germany was faced with major enemies on two sides: France on the west and Russia on the east. Bloody German offensives began, and quick progress was made on the Western Front as Germany plowed straight through Belgium and deep into France. Perfectly in line with the Schlieffen Plan, Paris looked as though it would fall to the Germans in short order.

On the Eastern Front, the undersized German Eighth Army simply wanted to defend its border from Russia until France could be taken, at which time German troops in France could be transported to the Russian Front, where they would join with the German Eighth Army for a powerful assault on Russia. However, Russia, having no intention of waiting for Germany to gain the upper hand, acted to defend her border while her army still outmatched the opposing German troops. The German Eighth Army, commanded by the previous war heroes Hindenburg and Ludendorff, was outnumbered by two Russian armies about 16 to 9. The Russians were to the east, with the Russian First Army to the northeast of the Germans and the Russian Second Army to the southeast.

The Russians planned to advance into Germany and surround the German Eight Army. However, the Russians had a habit of using radio communication to transmit the next day's battle orders. The Germans were able to eavesdrop on these transmissions, which, amazingly enough, were unencrypted. Having advance knowledge of the Russians' intentions, the Germans were able to set a trap, and on August 26, 1914, they surrounded the Russian Second Army and destroyed it. In this engagement, known as the Battle of Tannenberg, 78,000 Russians were killed or wounded, 90,000 Russian prisoners were taken, and the Second Army's entire artillery was captured. Sixty trains were required to transport the 500 captured guns. Follow-up battles destroyed most of the First Army as well.[1] It was a staggering defeat for Russia and a huge early and unexpected gain for Germany on the Eastern Front.

On the Western Front, a month after beginning their offensive drive, Germany was right on track to take Paris[2] within forty days. By September 4, 1914, the Germans had pushed through Belgium and were within 23 miles of their target. In anticipation of the fall of Paris, its citizens were being evacuated, and the French government had already left Paris to re-establish itself in Bordeaux. The defending French and British forces were near exhaustion after having retreated continuously for eleven days under pressure from the rapid German advance.

By September 6, 1914, German forces looked poised to break through the beleaguered French lines, but on September 7, in a "do-or-die effort" that will go down in history, 6,000 French reserve troops were rushed to the front in a convoy of 600 taxicabs. In fierce fighting over the following few days, the Germans fell back 40 miles. There, in a stalemate, both sides dug in and built fortified trenches, which still remain as the front line. The bloody six-day Battle of the Marne, which drove the Germans back across the Marne River, cost the French 250,000 casualties.[3] By the end of the year, these front line trenches had grown to over 400 miles in length, stretched from the north coast of France to Switzerland, and had been the scene of 3.5 million casualties.[4]

✳ *Crater from a zeppelin bomb in Paris*

Aside from scoring strong gains on the battlefield, Germany's new weaponry has been striking fear and terror into her enemies on their home soil. On January 19, 1915, Germany conducted its first zeppelin raid on the British mainland, killing two people and injuring sixteen. At the outbreak of the war, Germany had seven zeppelins. By 1917, that number had risen to close to one hundred.

A zeppelin raid on London on May 31, 1915, killed seven people and injured thirty-five. On March 21, 1915, two zeppelins raided Paris, killing twenty-three people and injuring thirty. The airships are slow moving, and as the war has progressed, they have become ever larger in size, allowing them to fly so high that they

1 http://en.wikipedia.org/wiki/battle_of_tannenberg_(1914).
2 http://www.worldwar1.com/dbc/schneider_ws.htm.
3 http://www.firstworldwar.com/battles/marne1.htm.
4 http://europeanhistory.about.com/od/worldwar1/p/ww1101.htm.

can be neither seen nor heard. The bombs, ranging from small up to many hundreds of pounds, have terrorized Europeans, crashing down into tranquil noncombat zones with no warning whatsoever, spreading death and chaos. The zeppelin attacks, while not practical from death toll standpoint, have had a profound psychological impact on the Allies and have obligated the British to tie up twelve squadrons of planes for home defense.[1]

On January 31, 1915, Germany conducted its first use of poison gas on the battlefield. Mustard gas, phosgene gas, chlorine gas, and a host of others all deliver the worst suffering imaginable. One will blind you. One will cause the skin to peel off in painful blisters. One will cause the lungs to shrink and collapse, leaving the victim to suffocate in his own blood. It is a terrifying threat to even the bravest of souls.

As the war progressed, other countries were drawn into the hostilities. On November 5, 1914, Turkey joined forces with Germany and Austria-Hungary, and on September 6, 1915, Bulgaria also joined the Central Powers.

On April 26, 1915, Italy signed the Treaty of London. Both Germany and the Allied forces wanted Italy to join the fight on their side, which sparked something of a bidding war, each side offering Italy territories. The Allies won out, and in the treaty, Italy received a loan of $50,000,000 lire immediately and the territories of Trent, Southern Tyrol, Istria, Gorizia, and Dalmatia after the war.[2] Italian troops entered the fight on May 23, 1915.

On August 27, 1916, Romania joined the Allies and declared war on the Central Powers. Greece remained neutral for two years, reluctant to fight against Germany because Queen Sophia, wife of King Constantine of Greece, is the sister of Kaiser Wilhelm, Emperor of Germany. The political reverberations of this situation almost ignited a civil war in Greece. It was not until the British and French forces threatened to bombard Athens if King Constantine did not step down that there was finally a transition in Greek leadership. On July 2, 1917, Greece joined the Allies and declared war on the Central Powers.[3]

The first American casualty of the war was 31-year-old Leon Thrasher from Massachusetts. He was killed on March 28, 1915, when a German submarine torpedoed the cargo-passenger ship *Falaba*, and 104 passengers and crew drowned.[4] In an effort to block the import of war materials that could be used against her from reaching Britain, Germany had previously imposed a submarine blockade around Britain.

Only a month before its attack on the *Falaba*, Germany changed its submarine policy to unrestricted submarine warfare. In other words instead of attacking only navy ships or cargo ships, even then only after evacuating the crew and passengers to safety, German submarines would freely target any ship, anywhere, any time with no warning and no regard for the lives of the men, women, and children aboard. Most Americans were appalled by this indiscriminate disregard for civilian lives.

------

1 http://www.firstworldwar.com/airwar/bombers_zeppelins.htm.
2 http://istrianet.org/istria/history/1800-present/wwi/1915_treaty-london.htm.
3 http://en.wikipedia.org/wiki/greece_during_World_War_1.
4 http://www.history.com/this-day-in-history/first-american-citizen-killed-during-wwi.

A little over a month after the sinking of *Falaba*, on May 7, 1915, the Cunard passenger liner *Lusitania* was sunk by a German submarine with the loss of 1,198 lives, among them 124 American passengers.[1] On August 15, 1915, the British passenger liner *Arabic* was torpedoed, resulting in the loss of forty lives including two Americans. After President Wilson threatened to cut off diplomatic relations, Germany agreed, in the Arabic Pledge, to stop attacking unarmed passenger ships without warning and to provide for the safety of the crew and passengers of vessels under attack.

✳ *Lusitania (Old postcard)*

Germany's submarine fleet was still very small at the time. Until it could be brought to full fighting strength, the Germans did not want to provoke the United States into entering the war.[2] But on March 24, 1916, a German submarine torpedoed the French ferry *Sussex*, with eighty casualties, including twenty-five Americans.[3] Still wishing to keep the United States out of the war, Germany made the Sussex Pledge to the United States on May 4, 1916, promising to stop sinking merchant ships without warning.

Wilson perhaps dreaded the prospect of the United States being dragged into the European conflict even more than Germany feared our joining in on the side of the Allied forces. For two years in his first term, Wilson had done everything he could to keep the United States out of the war, even after the 1915 German sinking of the *Lusitania* and the sinking of the *Arabic* and the *Sussex*. Not only did Wilson resist participating in the war; he also resisted any precautionary military buildup, fearing that Germany might view such a move as a sign of aggression. Former President Theodore Roosevelt criticized Wilson for refusing to at least build up the army[4] and accused him of cowardice.[5]

On November 7, 1916, Woodrow Wilson won a second term in office by the closest electoral vote in U.S. history. His campaign slogan had been "He kept us out of the war."[6] One reason for Wilson's reluctance to deploy troops to Europe was the need for troops at home to guard our own border with Mexico.

Mexico had seceded from Spain in 1821. With independence, Mexico needed settlers and welcomed any Americans who would take an oath of allegiance to the Mexican government to come settle in the Mexican territory that would eventually become Texas. Many Americans populated the area, but being used to American democracy, the new "Texicans" soon became unhappy under the rule of Mexico's President Santa Anna. Through a series of bloody battles, including the Battle of the Alamo, in which legendary Davy Crockett was killed, Texas declared its independence in 1836. Border fights continued for almost a decade. Then on July 4, 1845, Texas joined the United States.

───────

1 http://europeanhistory.about.com/od/worldwar1/p/ww1101.htm.

2 http://www.u_s_history.com/pages/h1095.html.

3 http://www.firstworldwar.com/atoz/sussex.htm.

4 http://en.wikipedia.org/wiki/woodrow_wilson.

5 http://millercenter.org/academic/americanpresident/wilson/essays/biography/3.

6 http://www.legion.org/magazine/3368/great-reversal-wilsons-decision-war.

The following year, Mexico and the United States went to war over where the border between Texas and Mexico was supposed to be drawn. The United States desired a complete military victory over Mexico and deployed what was at the time the largest amphibious military force in history, landing 12,000 troops in Veracruz, Mexico. They soon took complete control of Mexico City while the U.S. Army captured the Mexican cities of Monterey and Los Angeles in what is now California. By 1848, the United States had achieved its desired complete victory, and both sides signed the Treaty of Guadeloupe Hidalgo, in which for a sum of $15,000,000 the United States acquired the states of California, Nevada, Arizona, and Utah from Mexico.[1]

As the war in Europe intensified in 1915, so did hostilities along the Mexican border, led by bandit Pancho Villa. When the United States refused to support him in a run for the Mexican Presidency, an angry Villa swore revenge and began murdering Americans. Initially, the bloody raids took place along the border and in Mexico, but on March 9, 1916 (shortly before the German sinking of the Sussex), Pancho Villa and 500 of his *pistoleros* attacked the 13th U.S. Cavalry near Columbus, New Mexico, and then shot up the town of Columbus for three hours, killing fourteen soldiers and ten civilians. President Woodrow Wilson deployed 75,000 National Guardsmen to protect the Mexican border and sent General Pershing with 10,690 men and 9,307 horses into Mexico to pursue Pancho Villa. A new Mexican-American war could very well have broken out at this point had it not been for the escalating situation in Europe. Not wanting to split the American military between two continents, Wilson was probably waiting as long as he could before committing to one conflict or the other.[2]

By that time, the Central Powers consisted of Germany, Austria-Hungary, Turkey, and Bulgaria; the Allied forces were those of Britain, France, Russia, Italy, Romania, Serbia, and Greece. Despite the strong Allied opposition, Germany and the Central Powers were stronger and were inflicting demoralizing damages on the Allies. On November 23, 1915, Serbia fell to the Central Powers. On December 9, 1916, the Central Powers defeated Romania, gaining vital supplies, including oil and grain. During the Great Retreat in the summer of 1915, German armies forced Russian troops to retreat 100 miles and captured the Russian portion of Poland (the country had been partitioned among Russia, Prussia, and Austria-Hungary in the late eighteenth century). In the Battle of Verdun, which lasted from February 21, 1916, to December 18, 1916, German forces attack the French garrison town of Verdun. During the long back-and-forth battle over this territory, there were 550,000 French casualties.[3]

One of the bloodiest battles of the war, the Battle of the Somme (named for the Somme River) commenced on July 1, 1916. The line of the German Western Front ran from the north coast of France in a southerly direction for about 400 miles. The line was distinguished by well-fortified German trenches about 30 feet wide. The French and British shelled the trenches of the Somme Valley mercilessly for seven days. The logic was that after such a barrage, totaling 1.7 million artillery shells, French and British forces would be able to practically walk over and take possession from any

---

1 http://www.historyguy.com/Mexican-American_War.htm1.
2 http://www.hsgng.org/pages/pancho.htm.
3 http://europeanhistory.about.com/od/worldwar1/p/ww1101.htm.

shell-shocked survivors. However, unbeknownst to the French and British, during the two years the Germans had been in possession of the trenches, they had constructed cement-fortified bunkers, many as deep as 20 feet. Consequently, the German soldiers simply hunkered down when the barrage commenced and were mostly unaffected by the shelling.

When the barrage stopped, 100,000 French and British troops with 70-pound packs advanced slowly across open grass fields to the German trenches. Intact barbed wire, which the shelling was supposed to have destroyed, impeded their progress. When the German machine guns emerged from the underground bunkers, it was a massacre. On the first day of the battle, British troops suffered 60,000 casualties, mostly in the first hour. A battle that was supposed to culminate in hours lasted four months. By November, British troops had advanced only about 6 miles at a cost of 420,000 British troops and 200,000 French troops.[1]

Europe was desperate for the United States to lend assistance, yet Wilson continued to sit on the sidelines. By 1917, the German submarine fleet had grown to be a formidable force, which Germany felt was ready to be fully unleashed. The final straw that broke the back of U.S. reluctance to go to war came on February 24, 1917, when the British government released to President Wilson the so-called Zimmermann Telegram, which the British had intercepted and decoded. With her submarine fleet at full force, Germany planned to resume unrestricted submarine warfare on February 1, 1917, and feared that this would draw the United States into the war. In anticipation of that, on January 16, 1917, Arthur Zimmermann, Foreign Secretary of the German Empire, sent a coded message to the German ambassador in Mexico. The ambassador was instructed that should the United States appear likely to enter the war, he was to approach the Mexican government. If Mexico would agree to fight against the United States, Germany would arm Mexico and allow her to reclaim the states of Texas, New Mexico, and Arizona, which Mexico had lost in the Mexican-American War of 1848.[2]

On April 2, 1917, Wilson made his war address to Congress. Citing mainly

Decoded Zimmerman Telegram (National Archives and Records Administration 302022)

TELEGRAM RECEIVED.

FROM 2nd from London # 5747.

"We intend to begin on the first of February unrestricted submarine warfare. We shall endeavor in spite of this to keep the United States of America neutral. In the event of this not succeeding, we make Mexico a proposal of alliance on the following basis: make war together, make peace together, generous financial support and an understanding on our part that Mexico is to reconquer the lost territory in Texas, New Mexico, and Arizona. The settlement in detail is left to you. You will inform the President of the above most secretly as soon as the outbreak of war with the United States of America is certain and add the suggestion that he should, on his own initiative, invite Japan to immediate adherence and at the same time mediate between Japan and ourselves. Please call the President's attention to the fact that the ruthless employment of our submarines now offers the prospect of compelling England in a few months to make peace." Signed, ZIMMERMANN.

---

1 http://www.historylearningsite.co.uk/somme.htm.
2 http://en.wikipedia.org/wiki/zimmerman_telegram.

✳ *President Wilson requesting Congress to declare war (Library of Congress, LC-USZC4-10297)*

the loss of civilian lives due to German unrestricted submarine warfare, which Germany referred to in the Zimmermann Telegram as the "ruthless employment of our submarines" and Wilson referred to as a "warfare against mankind," Wilson asked Congress for a declaration of war on Germany. He stated that he wanted it to be the "the war to end war,"[1] a phrase coined by British author and social commentator H. G. Wells and a concept scoffed at by many, including British Prime Minister David Lloyd George, who said, "This war, like the next war, is a war to end war."[2]

On April 6, 1917, the United States declared war on Germany.[3] On July 2, 1917, General Pershing, who had pursued Pancho Villa in Mexico and who would lead the American forces in Europe, requested a million-man army. Nine days later, he upped

---

1 http://en.wikipedia.org/wiki/woodrow_wilson.
2 http://en.wikipedia.org/wiki/The_war_to_end_war.
3 http://europeanhistory.about.com/od/worldwar1/p/ww1101.htm.

the request to 3 million. The first draft since the Civil War was implemented. "Liberty" war bonds were issued to help finance the fight, and the long process of preparing for war began.[1]

The situation in Europe has steadily deteriorated as we have scrambled and labored to build our fighting force. The Second Battle of the Aisne (named after the river by which it took place) began on April 17, 1917. In this battle, 1.2 million French troops in northeastern France put all their might into attacking the German front line in hopes of pushing the Germans out of France and back across the border into Belgium. Very little ground was gained, and the offensive was abandoned on May 9, 1917, the French having suffered a crippling 187,000 casualties. Worse yet was the loss of morale. After suffering 40,000 losses on the first day alone[2] and having already endured three long years of casualties upon casualties, many of the French troops could take no more, and mutinies became common. A total of 35,000 French soldiers were involved in mutinies. This could not be allowed; 2,873 prison sentences were handed out, and fifty-seven men were executed.[3]

By the end of 1917, German submarines had sunk over 6,000 ships[4] with a loss of over 20,000 lives.[5] The German aspiration to have their submarine blockades starve Britain out of the war has proven dangerously successful and threatening. Wheat supplies for the entire country have been so drastically reduced as to potentially be depleted in only a few weeks' time.

On December 15, 1917, Russia and Germany signed an armistice at Brest-Litovsk, which took Russia out of the war. Germany had won the Eastern Front and could turn its entire attention to the Western Front.[6]

That is the state of the war in Europe as we prepare to cross the Atlantic to join in the fight. Serbia has fallen, Romania has fallen, Russia has just fallen, millions of Allied lives have been lost, and the Allies who have been doing battle for four years are so weak, physically and in morale, that the French and British no longer have the strength to mount offensives and are in the fight of their lives simply trying to maintain their defensive positions. They are pleading with America for help and have expressed that they will not be able to hold out much longer without fresh troops. And so we go, ready or not.[7]

---

1 http://en.wikipedia.org/wiki/woodrow_wilson.
2 http://www.firstworldwar.com/battles/aisne2.htm.
3 http://www.historylearningsite.co.uk/mutiny_french_army.htm.
4 http://uboat.net/wwi/ships_hit/losses_year.html.
5 http://www.uboat.net/wwi/ships_hit/greatest_loss_of_life.html.
6 http://europeanhistory.about.com/od/worldwar1/p/ww1101.htm.
7 *Memories of the World War*, by Robert Alexander (New York: Macmillan, 1931), p. 34.

Part 3
Enroute to the War Zone

Leviathan

(APRIL 22, 1918 – MAY 2, 1918)

We detrained at Long Island City at 8:40 a.m. and crowded aboard the ferry boat *George Washington*. After departing the slip, we passed down the East River and then up the Hudson.[1] It was a beautiful April morning with a slight haze obscuring Manhattan. The sun soon broke all the way through, and as we passed under the Brooklyn Bridge, a group of teamsters, seeing the ferry congested with soldiers on every square inch of her decks, waved their hats, cheering heartily.[2] After a four-hour trip, we pulled up to the piers of the Army's transport docks at Hoboken, New Jersey, where lay docked the small freighter *Mercury* and the monster Leviathan.[3,4]

 Mercury looked as if she would be lucky to make it as far as Albany, New York, so the prospect of a trip aboard her all the way to Europe made us all nervous. Needless to say, a sigh of relief went up when we found that we would be traveling on the *Leviathan*.[5] She so dwarfed anything else in the water that we could view *Leviathan* only by looking practically straight up at the mammoth structure with her three huge smokestacks. Her black hull had been painted with a razzle-dazzle array of giant white geometric shapes and slanted lines with the intent of cloaking the image of her massive profile from the view of enemy submarines.

---

1 *The Battery Book: A History of Battery "A" 306th F.A.*, edited by Francis L. Field and Guy H. Richards (New York: The De Vinne Press, 1921), p. 35.

2 *The Autobiography of a Regiment: A History of the 304th Field Artillery in the World War*, by James M. Howard (New York, 1920), p. 38.

3 *The Battery Book*, p. 35.

4 *The History of the 306th Field Artillery: Compiled by the Men Who Participated in the Events Described* (New York: Knickerbocker Press, 1920), p. 1.

5 *The History of the 306th Field Artillery*, p. 11.

✳ *Leviathan with camouflage paint (Naval History & Heritage Command, # NH 71*

Built as the *Vaterland* in Germany in 1913, she was at the time the largest passenger ship in the world. Her itinerary had her in New York when the war first broke out in Europe. She was subsequently moved to Hoboken, New Jersey, where she was laid up for three years. When we declared war on Germany in 1917, the United States officially seized the ship, and President Wilson named her *Leviathan*.[1]

We had a long wait before disembarking the ferry and another wait under the great sheds on the dock.[2] We stood in line on the pier for several hours while each man's name was checked individually by the embarkation officials.[3] Having awakened at 1:00 a.m., having had nothing to eat since 2:00 a.m., and having stood for hours with our heavy packs wearing on our backs, we were all tired and hungry. In that state, we viewed the women from the Red Cross as angels when they greeted us and served us coffee and two small buns apiece, accompanied by friendly smiles and warm farewells. We will remember that fondly for a long time.[4,5]

At last, at about 3:30 p.m.,[6] the line moved up the gangplank, and we received our dunk ticket with a bunk assignment.

What a maze of stairways and corridors![7] The conversion to a military transport had removed any trace of luxury from the ship. All the stateroom doors had been removed.[8] Bunks had been built in every conceivable corner of the vessel and were so close together that two men passing each other in the narrow aisles had to walk sideways. The bunks were made of canvas stretched on frames of iron pipes, four tiers

1 http://en.wikipedia.org/wiki/SS_Leviathan.

2 *The Battery Book*, p. 36.

3 *The Story of Battery B, 306th F.A.—77th Division*, by Roswell A. De La Mater (New York: Premier, 1919), p. 17.

4 *The Battery Book*, p. 36.

5 *The Story of Battery B*, p. 17.

6 *The History of the 306th Field Artillery*, p. 12.

7 *"C" Battery Book: 306th F.A., 77th Div., 1917–1919*, by John Foster (Brooklyn, NY: Braunworth & Co., 1920), p. 17.

8 *The History of the 306th Field Artillery*, p. 12.

✳ *Leviathan dunk ticket (Naval History & Heritage Command # NH 104240-KN)*

✳ *Leviathan troop bunks (four high) (Naval History & Heritage Command # NH 73249)*

high. The lowest bunk was about six inches off the floor, and the highest was about two feet below the ceiling.[1] They seemed the last word in discomfort.[2] They would accommodate, packed in like sardines, 14,500 men for this voyage.[3]

Finally, with great relief, we removed our packs from sagging shoulders, deposited them on the bunks, and went to explore the ship. Everything was excessively crowded, the ship was dirty, the floors were unswept, and the heavy, stale air was unpleasant to breathe.[4,5] There was no mistaking the conversion from luxury passenger liner to military transport ship. Four huge 6-inch guns (inside barrel diameter) were mounted on specially built gun decks forward, and four more were positioned aft.[6]

The below decks were packed with bunks. There were plenty of showers but only with salt water.[7] In the mess hall, all the formal dining tables had been replaced by long, narrow tables running the full length of the hall, at which men ate standing up.[8] But not all signs of opulence could be removed. The mess hall, formerly the ballroom, was accessed by taking the grand stairway down from the balcony and was adorned

✳ *Leviathan, 6" Deck Gun (Naval History & Heritage Command # NH 41706)*

1   *The Battery Book*, p. 36.
2   *The Autobiography of a Regiment*, p. 40.
3   *"C" Battery Book*, p. 18.
4   *The Battery Book*, p. 36.
5   *The Autobiography of a Regiment*, p. 40.
6   *The Autobiography of a Regiment*, p. 43.
7   *"C" Battery Book*, p. 19.
8   *The Battery Book*, p. 37.

✳ *Leviathan troop mess hall (Naval History & Heritage Command #NH 104690)*

with mirrors[1] and hand-painted art on the walls and ceiling.[2] The grandeur of the decor was an odd contrast to the thousands of troops who would eat their meals in the room from their mess kits in a standing position, afterward washing the mess kits in large, rectangular communal tubs of water.

So great was the crowd on the ship that it was found to be impossible to serve more than two meals a day: breakfast at 8:00 a.m. and supper at 2:00 p.m. [3,4] Meals were always hurried affairs, with a guard continually calling out, "Come on, get that food in you and get out." The food was excellent but would have been more enjoyable if we could have eaten it in a less stressful environment.[5]

The first two nights on board were spent in Hoboken harbor.[6] Everyone was given a postcard called a "Safe Arrival Card" to address to our loved ones saying that we had landed safely in Europe. The postcards were stamped and left behind on shore, and we were told that if we should complete the crossing without falling victim to an enemy submarine, they would then be mailed out. We were allowed to make no mention of our whereabouts or the name of our ship.[7,8]

On Wednesday, April 24, 1918, we were awakened at 5:30 a.m. by the vibration of the giant ship engines. With the usual cloak of secrecy surrounding movements of our military, all troops were ordered to remain below decks as tugs towed *Leviathan* down the river, past the Statue of Liberty, and out to sea.[9,10] It was a glorious morning, clear as crystal, yet somewhat clouded by darkness, for the war was now becoming real, and for the first time, many of us began to seriously contemplate all we would have to endure before setting foot on U.S. soil again.

The 3,000-mile crossing to Europe was to take eight days. [11,12] The spirit of the men was generally "making the best of it" and jovial. For the vast majority, this was the longest journey of their lives, and they were enjoying the adventure of the "outing."[13] Most felt that it was better to travel the thousands of miles to Germany than to someday have German soldiers pounding at the gates of America.

---

1   *"C" Battery Book*, p. 17.
2   *The History of the 306th Field Artillery*, p. 12.
3   *The Autobiography of a Regiment*, p. 46.
4   *"C" Battery Book*, p. 18.
5   *The Battery Book*, p. 37.
6   *The Battery Book*, p. 37.
7   *The Autobiography of a Regiment*, p. 41.
8   *The Battery Book*, p. 38.
9   *The Battery Book*, p. 38.
10 *The Story of Battery B*, p. 19.
11 *The Autobiography of a Regiment*, p. 41.
12 *The Battery Book*, p. 38.
13 *The Autobiography of a Regiment*, p. 47.

The secrecy of our movements prevailed, and we were not told our destination.[1] Throughout the entirety of the transit, the ship maintained a zigzag course, making it impossible to gain a hint of the true course steered or the ultimate destination.[2] About 36 hours after leaving port, with much relief, we picked up a convoy of four destroyers.[3]

---

1 *The Autobiography of a Regiment*, p.41.
2 *The Autobiography of a Regiment*, p. 42.
3 *The Story of Battery B*, p. 20.

Avoiding detection by enemy submarines was of the greatest concern. Therefore, after nightfall, no one was allowed on deck under any circumstances.[1] After sunset, all water-tight doors and portholes were closed so that no light could escape. The only illumination below decks was a feeble, dim blue light emitted by small incandescent bulbs. When we had boarded the ship, all flashlights, matches, and cigarette lighters had been confiscated.[2,3]

The first five days were uneventful but far from being a luxury cruise. Military routine still reigned supreme, with morning reveille, calisthenics, abandon-ship drills to prepare us in the event of being torpedoed, inspections, and in general full days. In the evenings, the mess hall was converted to a theater, and the men who were lucky enough to find space in the packed room enjoyed silent movies.[4] On the sixth day out, as we approached the submarine danger zone, the terrifying prospect of being torpedoed weighed heavily upon the imaginations of all.

A firsthand account of the torpedoing of the Cunard passenger liner *Laconia* had been written by passenger Floyd Gibbons and published in newspapers around the country just weeks before the U.S. declaration of war. On February 17, 1917, the *Laconia* was en route from New York to Liverpool, England, with a crew of 216 and seventy-three passengers: men, women, and children. At 10:30 p.m., as Gibbons wrote,

THE SHIP GAVE A SUDDEN LURCH SIDEWAYS AND FORWARD. There was a muffled noise like the slamming of some large door at a good distance away. The slightness of the shock and the meekness of the report compared with my imagination were disappointing. Every man in the room was on his feet in an instant. "We're hit!" shouted Mr. Chetham. … Up and down the deck passengers and crew were donning lifebelts, throwing on overcoats, and taking positions in the boats. … There was a tilt to the deck. It was listing to starboard at just the right angle that would make it necessary to reach for support to enable one to stand upright. … "Lower away!" Someone gave the order and we started down with a jerk towards the seemingly hungry rising and falling swells. Then we stopped with a jerk. … The stern of the lifeboat was down, the bow up, leaving us at an angle of about forty-five degrees. We clung to the seats to save ourselves from falling out. … A hatchet was thrust into my hand and I forwarded it to the bow. There was a flash of sparks as it crashed down on the holding pulley. One strand of rope parted and down plunged the bow, too quick for the stern man. We came to a jerky stop with the stern in the air and the bow down …. as the entangling ropes that held us to the sinking *Laconia* were cut away …. Some shout … caused me to look up. … A man was jumping,… he passed beyond us and plunged into the water three feet from the edge of the boat. … "Get away from her [the ship]," [a crew member in our lifeboat] kept repeating. "When the water hits her hot boilers, she'll blow

1 *"C" Battery Book*, p. 20.
2 *The Autobiography of a Regiment*, p. 43.
3 *The Battery Book*, p. 36.
4 *The Autobiography of a Regiment*, p. 46.

up, and there's just tons and tons of shrapnel in the hold!"… It was bedlam and nightmare. … Thirty minutes after [the first torpedo] another dull thud … told its story of the second torpedo dispatched through the engine room. … We watched silently during the next minute, as the tiers of lights dimmed slowly from white to yellow, then to red, and nothing was left but the murky mourning of the night. … The ship sank rapidly at the stern until at last its nose stood straight in the air. Then it slid silently down and out of sight. … The black rim of clouds looked ominous. There was good promise of rain. February has a reputation for nasty weather in the North Atlantic. The wind was cold and seemed to be rising. Our boat bobbed about like a cork on the swells. … [After six hours in the open boats] we saw the first light, the first sign of help coming, the first searching glow of white brilliance. … We pulled lustily, forgetting the strain and pain of innards torn and racked from vain vomiting, oblivious of the blistered hands and yet half-frozen feet. … We floated off its stern of the British mine sweeper H.M.S. Laburnum for a while as it maneuvered for the best position in which it could take us on with the sea that was running higher and higher. … One minute the swell lifted us almost level with the rail of the low-built patrol boat and mine sweeper; the next receding wave would carry us down into a gulf over which the ship's side glowed like a slimy, dripping cliff. … Wet bedraggled survivors were lifted aboard. Women and children first was the rule. … The scenes of reunion were heart-gripping. … a frail little wife of a Canadian chaplain who had found one of her missing children delivered up from another boat. She smothered the child with ravenous mother kisses while tears of joy streamed down her face. Boat after boat came alongside. The waterlogged craft containing the captain came last. … I saw the hysterical French-Polish actress, her hair wet and bedraggled, lifted out of the boat and handed up the companionway. Then a little boy, his fresh pink face and golden hair shinning in the morning light, was passed upward, followed by some other survivors, numbering fourteen in all, who had been half drowned and almost dead from exposure in a partially wrecked boat that was just sinking. This was the boat in which Mrs. Hoy and her daughter lost their lives and in which Cedric P. Ivatt of New York, who was the manager for the actress, died. … One of the survivors of this boat was Able Seaman Walley. … "Our boat—No. 8—was smashed in lowering," he said." I was in the bow, Mrs. Hoy and her daughter were sitting toward the stern. The boat filled with water rapidly. It was no use trying to bail her out—there was a big hole in the side and it came in too fast. It just sunk to the water's edge and only stayed up on account of the tanks in it. It was completely awash. Every swell rode clear over us and we had to hold our breath until we came to the surface again. The cold water just takes the strength out of you. The women got weaker and weaker, then a wave came and washed both of them out of the boat. There were life-belts on their bodies and they floated away, but I believe they were dead before they were washed overboard."[1]

---

1   http://www.skaneateles.org/laconia1.html.

The story, in vivid detail, painted frightful images of being torpedoed that the troops on *Leviathan* knew represented the fate that could befall us at any moment as we proceeded into the submarine zone.

The reality of this ever-present risk elicited the strictest measures of preparedness and precaution. No refuse whatsoever could be thrown overboard during daylight hours, for it might leave a visible trail for submarines to follow.[1] The "no lights after dark" order was enforced without exception. The men were absolutely forbidden from going near the portholes (spies could signal submarines). A colonel gave the following solemn and blood-curdling warning: "No one must dare go near or touch a porthole. The guards have instructions to shoot. Every man's blood is upon his own head. Take heed, take heed."[2]

We were ordered to sleep fully dressed with our life jackets on.[3] There was no paranoia in these actions. The threat of being torpedoed was very real. For Germany to turn the ship that had been seized from her into a death trap for 14,500 soldiers of the offending country would be a monumental conquest, both logistically and psychologically. It would be as crushing to Allied morale as it would be sensationally uplifting for German morale.

There was no lack of eyes scouring the water for periscopes, and the gunners all stood at the ready at their positions, headsets keeping them in constant contact with the bridge.[4] Our convoy of destroyers became very active. One would shoot ahead, cut across our path, then fall back and presently scoot around behind us and take its old place again. On the seventh night out, the signal lights on the bridge of our ship were seen flashing messages to the destroyers. This was observed by some of the enlisted men on our ship who could read Morse code, and the secret was out: "O-u-r o-r-d-e-r s c-a-l-l f-o-r B-r-e-s-t." We would land in Brest, France![5]

---

1   *The Battery Book*, p. 41.
2   *The Battery Book*, pp. 41–42.
3   *The Battery Book*, p. 41.
4   *"C" Battery Book*, p. 21.
5   *The Autobiography of a Regiment*, p. 47.

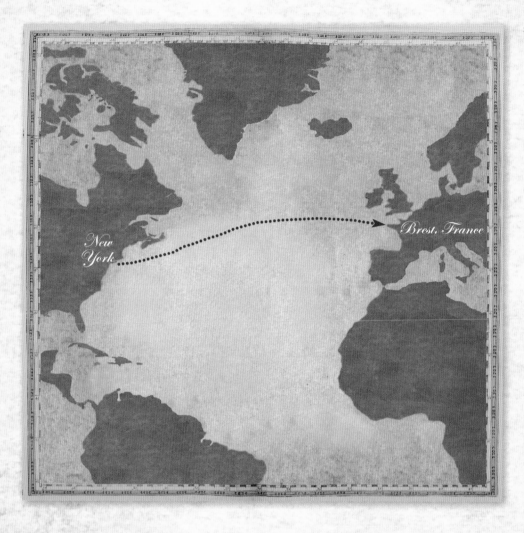

Brest, France

The next morning, May 2, 1918, we awoke to a fog so dense that, from the deck of our ship, we could not even see the destroyers. As the fog gradually began to lift and a radiant tint of golden yellow sunlight spread through the skies, we caught our first glimpse of France. Soon the fog was gone altogether.[1] Our mammoth ship was far too great in size for the small docks,[2] so at 7:15 a.m., we dropped anchor in the beautiful harbor of Brest.[3] The sky was cloudless, the hills wonderfully green, the water smooth as glass.[4] It was an odd contrast to see small wooden schooners sailing about in this tranquil setting in the presence of our ship and destroyers, which now shared the harbor with some French cruisers and French submarines.[5] As if set back in time, the city

---

1   *The Autobiography of a Regiment*, p. 48.
2   *The Story of Battery B*, p. 21.
3   *"C" Battery Book*, p. 121.
4   *The Autobiography of a Regiment*, p. 48.
5   *The Story of Battery B*, p. 20.

lay at the foot of the hill ahead of us, surrounded by rich green pasture lands and quaint cottages. There was a huge stone windmill, cylindrical in design with a funnel-shaped roof and very long blades. The base was bigger than an entire house, and it stood two or three times as high. Also plainly visible from the ship were the remains of some ancient stone fortifications.[1] The scenery now before us was that which one envisions when daydreaming of the French countryside.

There was an atmosphere of serenity in the air that almost overshadowed the presence of the military ships, yet a distinct nervousness was evidenced by a French blimp-like observation balloon, its long tether allowing it to hover high above the city.[2] Observation balloons have become a standard form of aerial reconnaissance in this war. A single observer high up in a balloon can spot an approaching enemy from far away.

In the early afternoon, like ants, we streamed through the corridors to gang-planks on both sides of the ship and were packed like sardines into British lighters (shuttle boats). As we were ferried to shore, the regimental band on board burst into "La Marseillaise," bringing cheers from sailors on French boats. Moments later, when we reached the docks, the band switched to "The Star Spangled Banner." One could not help but feel the thrill of the moment.[3,4] At 5:00 p.m.,[5] we became the first artillery regiments of the National Army to set foot in France.[6] In the excitement of the moment, no doubt many a soldier, taking a last glance back at *Leviathan*, said a silent prayer, thankful for the good fortune of having passed safely through the peril of the German submarine gauntlet.

---

1   *The Autobiography of a Regiment*, p. 48.

2   *The History of the 306th Field Artillery*, p. 13.

3   *The Autobiography of a Regiment*, p. 50.

4   *The Story of Battery B*, p. 21.

5   *The Battery Book*, p. 43.

6   *The Autobiography of a Regiment*, p. 49.

Ahead of us, at an undisclosed location, lay the two months of specialized training we had been longing for. This time, we would have live horses and real guns, the
actual guns that we would be using on the battlefield. However, the trains would not
be available to transport us for six days, so for now, we would have a rest stop at a camp
outside of town. We immediately formed ranks on the street by the docks and began a
three-mile hike to the rest camp.[1]

To say the least, the short hike was unusually difficult. The sun was intensely hot;
the hill from the docks to camp was exceedingly steep; the men were carrying heavy
packs, winter overcoats, rifles, hundreds of rounds of ammunition, and canteens full of
water; and the week at sea had left us all in less than peak condition.[2] But the scenery
provided diversion from our physical woes. As we began our hike past the town, little
boys and girls swarmed about our feet, running and jumping and begging for pennies
and "a cigarette for z papa." It was shocking at what an early age the rascals started
smoking.

✳ *French boy smoking*

Crowds of people gathered to watch us as we marched by, and from those onlook-
ers and others who waved from windows came the cheer "*Vive l'Amerique.*" One soon
became aware that many of the women were wearing black veils, some were visibly
moved to tears as we passed, and more and more we could spot, by the loss of an arm
or a leg, the men who had already played a part in the great conflict. Also noticeable
was the complete absence of healthy young men of fighting age. It was impossible not
to feel a sad empathy for these beautiful people in this beautiful land, and it filled our
hearts with the importance of the work that awaited us.[3,4]

Past the town, the grass was long and luscious, the trees had put forth their leaves,
the shrubs were in blossom, and flowers were blooming gaily by the wayside. When
we took a short rest, little girls came up to us and offered us tight little fistfuls of tiny
flowers they had gathered.[5] We continued and managed to survive the rest of the hike,
arriving at the Pontenezen Barracks about 8:00 p.m.

Pontenezen
(May 2, 1918 – May 7, 1918)

The quaint two-story stone barracks had been built in the middle of the sixteenth century as a monastery.[6] It was later used as a prison,[7] and at one time it housed Napoleon
and his troops.[8] At the southern end of the camp, we found whipping posts, a gallows,

---

1 *The Battery Book*, p. 43.
2 *The Autobiography of a Regiment*, p. 50.
3 *The Story of Battery B*, p. 21.
4 *The Autobiography of a Regiment*, p. 50.
5 *The Autobiography of a Regiment*, p. 52.
6 *The Battery Book*, p. 43.
7 *History of the 77th Division: August 25th, 1917–November 11th, 1918* (New York: The 77th Division Association, 1919), p. 26.
8 *The Battery Book*, p. 43.

a strongly built guardhouse, and a wall in which could still be found bullets from Napoleon's firing squads.[1] The camp was very run-down—a "rummy bunch of stone houses," as Private Lawrence Foster put it,[2] which probably had not been improved since the days of Napoleon.[3] The interiors were damp and gloomy[4] and had been stripped of beds, so we slept on the floor. An old bathhouse that accommodated only two squads of men at a time was located a good distance from the barracks, requiring us to undress in the barracks and walk the 300 yards sporting only shoes and over-coats. As soon as each man's allotted time had passed, the water was shut off and the shower was over, whether the man was still lathered up or not.

After six days of "rest," which translated into lots of drills and hikes with some time for sports such as ball games, we set off back to Brest at 7:00 a.m. on May 7, 1918, to board a train to the training camp.[5] The dirty little four-wheeled French freight cars were unlike any type of train car we had ever seen. They were so tiny that they looked like toys. Painted on the side of each car was "*Hommes 40, Chevaux 8*" (maximum forty men or eight horses per car). We somehow managed to pack forty men into each car with standing room only.

The countryside was beautiful, but the trip was grueling, and it seemed to worsen with each passing hour. We traveled south along the French coast for 43 hours with only a few brief rest stops.[6] On this trip, we were first introduced to "iron rations": hard bread (hardtack), corned beef, tomatoes, beans, and—if we were lucky—cheese and jam. It was survival food at best, and we never grew to like it.[7] At the occasional stops, guards were posted with orders that the men were not to buy wine, but many a clever French smuggler secured us some awful *vin rouge* at a price of one dollar per bottle.[8]

✳ *U.S. troops on a French freight car en route to the front (U.S. official photogravure in personal collection)*

The railroad cars had no springs, and trying to sleep standing up or leaning against a wall or box of supplies proved all but impossible. Convulsive attempts were made periodically by each man to extricate himself from the tangle of arms and legs by pushing in every direction at the same time, a contortion that invariably ended by damaging someone's face. Any snore that escaped from a delirious soldier would elicit a shove and a "Hey, Buddy, not in my ear!!"

About midnight on May 8, 1918, after passing through the towns of Landernau, Chatteaulin, Quimper, Rosporden, Quimperle, Lorient, Hembont, Vannes, St. Nicholas, Pontchateau, Nantes, Chason La Roche, Marans, La Rochelle, Rochefort, Saintes, Pons Janzac, and Bordeaux,

---

1 *The Story of Battery B*, p. 21.
2 *The History of the 306th Field Artillery*, p. 14.
3 *The Story of Battery B*, p. 2.
4 *History of the 77th Division*, p. 26.
5 *The Story of Battery B*, pp. 21–22.
6 *The Story of Battery B*, p. 23.
7 *"C" Battery Book*, p. 23.
8 *The Story of Battery B*, p. 22.

we detrained at the town of Bonneau, two hours south of Bordeaux, and hiked three miles in total darkness to our destination of Camp de Souge, arriving at 3:00 a.m. on May 9, 1918.[1]

Camp de Souge
(MAY 9, 1918 – JULY 15, 1918)

Some men did not even wait to find bunks but simply dropped to the concrete floor and fell asleep immediately.[2] Compared to the ancient fortification from which we had just departed, Camp de Souge, previously inhabited by French troops during their training, was more along the lines of Camp Upton back home. Although much smaller, it too had rows of long, rectangular wooden barracks and vast expanses of dry, dusty,

---

1   *The Story of Battery B*, p. 23.
2   *The Battery Book*, p. 45.

barren terrain. French entrepreneurs were allowed to operate outside the front gate to the camp, and the comedic scene reminded one of Coney Island. There stood a gaudy wagon that promised gaudy cinema entertainment when the gaudy engine ran. Beside it were pushcart vendors with oranges, nuts, cherries, and dates. Opposite stood a complete *mercerie* on wheels offering a thousand souvenirs of no value at exorbitant prices. And of course there was wine.[1,2]

Despite its simple style of construction, the camp was comfortably built, and the barracks were well ventilated. But to our dismay, we discovered that the soldiers were not the only inhabitants of the camp. In the middle of the night, when all the lights were out, an army of a different type could be heard. The memory of that first night remains vivid, when the noise from the scurrying feet and gnawing teeth would reveal what antics the rats were up to. One might be raiding the pantry while another was chewing a hole in the sole of a shoe. As soon as I fell asleep, something that felt the size of a small cat scampered across my blanket. One must experience this in person to appreciate the sensation. As it was a nightly occurrence, most of us armed ourselves with clubs for self-protection.

Our daytime companions were smaller but made up for it in numbers. The millions of flies that covered the walls to the point of disguising the wall color seemed to be lethargic or dormant. In reality, they were well trained, for they moved very little until a meal was served, and then the air was full of them buzzing in all directions and racing about on foot to such a degree that the tables appeared to be moving. All you could do was eat with one hand and continually swat with the other.[3]

This would be our home for the next two months.

At last, we were to immerse ourselves in the specialized training of howitzer operations, our final schooling before taking the sum of our new knowledge and training to the battlefield for the final exam of do or die. The howitzers to be used by the 304th Field Artillery and the 305th Field Artillery were called 75s because the inside barrel diameter measured 75 millimeters, or about 3 inches. Their full complement of guns was waiting for them when we arrived at Camp de Souge, so they started training immediately. Our 306th Field Artillery would have to wait because our 155s (6-inch guns) had not yet arrived.[4]

Soon after our arrival at Camp de Souge, we were floored by one last bewildering, infuriating decision from the War Department. The 306th was originally designed to be a regiment of horse-drawn howitzers, and we all, officers and men, felt the blow when, at Camp Upton, we were informed that we would be a regiment of tractor-drawn guns instead. We threw out our months of equestrian training, trained to operate with tractors, and trained mechanics to repair the tractors. After all that, we were now being informed that we were to be an equestrian unit after all![5] Initially, our delight at the news was somewhat dampened by our frustration at the ever-changing,

1   *The History of the 306th Field Artillery*, p. 15.
2   *History of the 77th Division*, p. 27.
3   *The Story of Battery B*, p. 25.
4   *The Battery Book*, p. 48.
5   *The Autobiography of a Regiment*, p. 58.

counterproductive mandates from the War Department, but that was short lived. Soon we all looked forward to the arrival of the horses.

The anticipation turned to consternation when, at the end of May, twelve hundred horses arrived at the camp.[1,2,3] These horses were not your amiable milk wagon nags, but great, raw, burly, snorting untamed monsters for pulling the heavy guns and scraggly, mean, vicious mounts for the officers and special detail men.[4] Many of the horses had to be broken, and then instruction was given in feeding, grooming, and general care of horses, after which methods of harnessing were taught, followed by instruction in riding first single mounts, then teams, and finally teams paired together.[5]

At first, we rode bareback to acquire a sense of balance. As French horses didn't understand English, the word used to make them start was "*allez*," meaning "go," but for the first few times, we didn't know the French word for "stop," and there were many "Paul Reveres" around the field.

Our instructors stressed the value of the horses to our unit and stated that on the battlefield, one horse was worth four men. The lengths to which we were encouraged to go to care for the horses can probably be perceived by studying what we called instructions for "grooming by numbers."[6]

1	*two minutes*	Front legs, from knees down
2	*two minutes*	Hind legs, from hocks down
3	*four minutes*	Nigh side, neck, shoulder, arm, elbow, back, side, flank, and croup
4	*three minutes*	Nigh side, chest and between forelegs, belly and between hind legs
5	*four minutes*	Off side; same as No. 3 above
6	*three minutes*	Off side; same as No. 4 above
7	*one minute*	Head, ears, and throat
8	*three minutes*	Forelocks, mane, and tail
9	*two minutes*	Eyes, nostrils, and dock
10	*two minutes*	Clean feet
11	*four minutes*	Unfinished work

---

1 *The History of the 306th Field Artillery*, p. 17.
2 *The Battery Book*, p. 47.
3 *History of the 77th Division*, p. 28.
4 *The History of the 306th Field Artillery*, p. 17.
5 *The Battery Book*, p. 48.
6 *The Story of Battery B*, p. 29.

❋ *Gas masks*

❋ *Playing soccer with gas masks*

Given the nature of the horses and the swiftness and strength of the hoofs that would occasionally strike out, the job was not without risk.

Special gas masks had been made for the horses. The flannel hood covered the horse's nostrils and almost reached to his eyes. In the event of a gas attack, our completely serious standing orders were that gas masks were to be put on the horses first and that the soldier was a secondary consideration.[1]

To say that the horses added an extra burden and element of work to our lives would be a gross understatement, but as Lieutenant Ketcham put it in a lecture to us, "When this war is over and the Hun has been licked and you go back to civil life, there will be one thing you will miss more than anything else, one thing above all others that you will hate to leave behind, and that is your horse!"[2]

On June 6, 1918, gas masks arrived by the case. Each man was individually fitted, as it was imperative to have a perfect fit with a tight seal around the face. Of all the helpless, suffocating, strangling sensations known to man, there are few that compare with the first attempts to wear a gas mask.[3] At first, very few of us could breathe through the mouthpiece even for a few minutes without gagging. With practice and daily drilling, we became more accustomed to the masks, although after wearing them for an hour, almost everyone would be blue in the face. Many surprise alarms were given, even in the middle of the night, with a six-second deadline for having the mask in place. Each soldier carried his gas mask in a special case, which was on his person AT ALL TIMES! We hated those masks, yet the terrifying prospect of gas made us value them above almost all of our other personal equipment,[4] and by the time we finished training at Camp de Souge, we were playing baseball games and running relay races with those hideous things strapped to our faces.[5]

Our graduation test in gas training was "The Tank," a huge concrete structure with one small, gas-tight doorway. We were each required to don our gas mask and

1 *The Story of Battery B*, p. 29.
2 *The History of the 306th Field Artillery*, p. 17.
3 *The Autobiography of a Regiment*, p. 64.
4 *The Story of Battery B*, p. 27.
5 *The Autobiography of a Regiment*, p. 64.

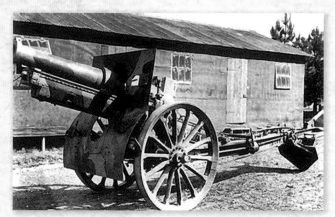

✳ *(above) French-made 155-millimeter Schneider howitzer;*
(right), American artillerymen and a new 155-millimeter Schneider
howitzer

spend ten minutes in the tank, which was filled with a nasty concentration of tear gas.[1] Tear gas has an immediate effect on the eyes, making them water in pain,[2] and the ten minutes seemed an intensely long period of time. Our complaints were mitigated by the consoling knowledge that this was a very weak concentration of gas. In fact, we all knew full well that this was child's play compared to what was being used on the battlefields. We had developed a deadly serious respect for gas by this point in the game.

June 8, 1918, was a memorable date, for on that day our French-made 155-millimeter Schneider howitzers arrived, and everyone gathered around to admire the massive weapons that were to be our comrades on the battlefield.[3,4,5]

The term "155 millimeter," which is equivalent to slightly over 6 inches, refers to the inside diameter of the barrel, which measures in excess of seven and a half feet in length. The cannon-like barrel is mounted by axle to two wood-spoked, metal-reinforced wheels that are over four feet tall.[6] It is an awe-inspiring weapon, and a short pep talk by one of the officers enlightened everyone at the gathering about the capabilities of the guns.

The maximum range of this howitzer was about seven miles with a 96-pound projectile. The gun was not designed to fire at line-of-sight targets as a rifle is; rather, it had a high angle of trajectory that would allow it, while concealed in a valley or depression, to lob shells up and over a hill at an unseen target on the other side.[7] Precision of fire was an absolute necessity, as our front line infantry would often be in close proximity to enemy targets. So the bulk of our training by French instructors would address the multitude of calculations, observations, and factoring in of variables re-

---

1 *The History of the 306th Field Artillery,* p. 17.
2 *The Story of Battery B,* p. 30.
3 *The Story of Battery B,* p. 27.
4 *The Battery Book,* p. 48.
5 *History of the 77th Division,* p. 28.
6 *The History of the 306th Field Artillery,* p. 75.
7 *The Story of Battery B,* p. 28.

quired to land a shell on its target. There would also be training on many other aspects, including the logistical challenges of transporting an 8,000-pound gun across every type of uncooperative terrain imaginable.

Transportation of the gun requires a team of eight horses, and firing of the gun requires a team of eight men.[1] The beauty of the gun was the simplicity of its construction. The entire gun could be broken down into parts without the use of a single tool.[2] In operation, the breech (the hinged door at the rear of the gun) was opened, a greased projectile was inserted, immediately behind that was placed the powder charges, the breech was closed, the lanyard (a small rope attached to the firing pin) was pulled, and the gun fired. The powder charges are canvas bags filled with explosives. The size and corresponding strength of the charges had a range of 00, 0, 1, 2, 3, 4, 5, with 5 being the weakest charge and 00 being the strongest. The projectiles also contained explosives and a fuse at the tip that would cause the projectile to explode on impact. There were many different types of projectiles to choose from. Depending on the effect desired, a projectile could be used with a fuse that would detonate immediately or one with a delayed fuse for concrete busting. In the case of demolition, a steel shell would be used. If shrapnel was desired for the purpose of inflicting injuries, a cast iron shell would be used. A projectile could be selected that would produce large pieces of shrapnel, or a different one that would produce smaller shrapnel. There were projectiles that would release poisonous gas upon exploding, and to that end, there was a choice of many different types of poisonous gases. Here alone was an almost infinite number of variables that had to be calculated in order to hit the desired target with the desired effect.

But, additionally, the size of the charge to select had to account for the weight of the shell, mass of the shell, angle of desired trajectory, and distance to the target. If there was any wind, an adjustment had to be input allowing for the deflection that was expected as a consequence of the given wind speed over the calculated range. Shells actually travel at different speeds through different levels of atmospheric pressure, so that had to be factored in, as well as the effect of air temperature on the shell traveling through the air and even the effect of the air temperature on the strength of the powder charge.[3] The training would be intense, but the lives of Allied soldiers would depend upon our ability to carry out the precision targeting that would be demanded of us. To be off target and hit our own infantrymen with whom we had trained back at Camp Upton would be every man's worst nightmare. Each one of us took this training with the utmost seriousness and dedication. We were determined to become no less than master sharpshooters of these giant guns of war.

Yet the training ahead would go well beyond that required of the eight-man gun crews. They were simply one part of the bigger weapon: our regiment. There were many other players behind the scenes without whom the delivery of a shell to its target would be impossible. Most times, the gun crew cannot see where their shot detonates relative to their target, and without the aid of an observer, they would not know whether to adjust the following shots to the right or left or whether they needed

1 *The History of the 306th Field Artillery*, p. 74.
2 *The Autobiography of a Regiment*, p. 59.
3 *The History of the 306th Field Artillery*, p. 74.

to make them longer or shorter. Normally, a gun crew sends forward one or two observers who simply try to find the highest ground from which to observe where the shells land and then report back to the gunners. It might be a hilltop, a tree, or any other good vantage point.

Somewhere in close proximity but to the rear of the guns are the P.C.s (posts of command). From there, the majors each oversee the operations of the eight guns in their battalion. Somewhere to the rear of the P.C.s, a regimental headquarters is set up where a colonel and his aides supervise the actions of the subordinate three majors and their battalions of gun batteries.

Still farther to the rear is the echelon. The echelon (a French term meaning literally "step")[1] is an encampment that is far enough to the rear of the big guns to be mostly out of range of enemy artillery fire. Bulk ammunition, food supplies, and wagons are warehoused here. Once the guns have been hauled into place, the horses are withdrawn back to the echelon for safekeeping during firing operations. The supply men who transport wagonloads and truckloads of food and ammunition to the forward gun positions are understandably prime targets for German planes.

All of these different posts have to be connected by temporary telephone lines laid in the field. The lineman's existence is a constant struggle to lay communication lines fast enough between all these posts of the regiment. When the regiment advances, the lineman, armed with spools of wire, wire cutters, and electrical tape, lays new phone lines, and as wires are broken by incoming artillery or cut by the enemy, he risks his life on repair missions.[2] During this two-month training period, everyone would train in every last detail to make us battle ready as a unit.

Many hours of every day were spent firing off hundreds of live rounds under the hot June sun and fine-tuning our skills at calculating firing data.[3] Accuracy of fire was paramount. Close behind that in importance was speed. A normal rate of fire is two shots per minute. A maximum rate of four to five rounds per minute is possible but cannot be maintained for more than a few minutes because it causes extreme heating of the gun.[4] We had competitions for speed and accuracy of fire, and no other regiment of artillery had ever done so well at Camp de Souge as our 306th Field Artillery.[5]

All was going well until June 20, 1918, when one of the guns of the 305th, training on the same field, exploded from faulty ammunition. Privates Jeremiah S. Lynch and Harry J. Posner were killed instantly. As the ambulance took the bodies away, an officer called out with battlefield callousness, "Brace up! You'll see plenty of other men killed before you get through with this war. Get on the job now. Firing will resume."[6]

There were overnight hikes with full packs and the teams of horses pulling the guns.[7] During this time, word came from the front that on May 27, 1918, the Germans had begun a great new offensive and were close to the gates of Paris. They wanted to

---

1   *The Autobiography of a Regiment*, p. 76.
2   *The Autobiography of a Regiment*, pp. 77–78.
3   *History of the 305th Field Artillery*, by Charles Wadsworth Camp (Garden City, NY: The Country Life Press, 1919), pp. 50–51.
4   *The History of the 306th Field Artillery*, p. 74.
5   *The History of the 306th Field Artillery*, p. 17.
6   *History of the 305th Field Artillery*, p. 54.
7   *The Battery Book*, p. 49.

put a swift end to the war before the Americans could join in. There were rumors that
the French government had moved from Paris to Bordeaux a second time.[1] Understandably, the residents of Bordeaux went into a temporary panic when, one hot June
day, our artillery practice set off a fierce brush fire, which sent up columns of thick
smoke that was visible across much of the countryside. Hundreds of us fought and
conquered that fire with no more than picks, shovels, and rakes.[2]

On the Fourth of July, the entire brigade marched two miles to Bordeaux and
paraded in the streets there, the big guns being hauled by teams of eight horses. It was
an impressive spectacle, and the sidewalks and every window were packed with spectators all waving flags, cheering the soldiers,[3] and throwing flowers. After the parade,
the majority of the men received passes permitting us to visit Bordeaux.[4] How we ate
in Bordeaux! How we starred! And since this is an accounting of actual history and
the truth, oh, how we drank![5] It was a fitting end to our training at Camp de Souge.

A few days later, on July 15, 1918,[6] we marched an hour to the railway station in
Bonneau and boarded train cars en route for the front to join in the war.[7] There was a

1   *History of the 305th Field Artillery*, p. 51.
2   *The History of the 306th Field Artillery*, p. 18.
3   *The Autobiography of a Regiment*, p. 7.
4   *The Story of Battery B*, p. 30.
5   *The History of the 306th Field Artillery*, p. 17.
6   *The Story of Battery B*, p. 31.
7   *The Battery Book*, p. 55.

need for increased aid from the Allies and especially for speed if we did not want to be too late to save the cause from defeat.[1]

We had not boarded a train as a fully equipped unit before. Loading the howitzers and wagons onto the flatcars was relatively easy compared to the challenge of loading the horses into the boxcars.[2] The horses often rose on their haunches and cried out their disapproval. Some men would pull on the halter while others pushed the horse from behind. The stallions were the main problem. If you put them in together, they would fight, and if you put them in with a lesser horse, they would kick at it and bite it.[3] One group of stallions had kicked a hole through the side of their car before the train left the station.[4] The advice "Get 'em in so tight they can't fight" worked fairly well. With time, we got to know which horses could travel amiably together, and this simplified matters.[5] Some of the mules had to be blindfolded, led in circles, and backed suddenly into the train.[6] However willing or unwilling, whether led, cajoled, or pushed aboard by brute force, they went with us. Three bales of hay and two men to act as guards were placed in each car.

Just about dusk, the little old French train gave two sharp, shrill whistles, and we were on our way to the war.[7] We were not to fight as an American army just yet. The French General Ferdinand Foch was in command of the entire allied military—all armies of all nationalities— for it had been decided that to have well-ordered coordination of so many troops, there must be but one person with ultimate power of command. General John Joseph Pershing was in command of the American troops and wanted adamantly to command them as an American army, but Foch ordered that until we could prove ourselves on the battlefield, the different divisions of our army would act under the direction of units of the French army. So while the French would dictate the missions for the different divisions of our army, General Pershing would give the divisional commanders—in the case of our 77th Division, Major-General George B. Duncan—orders on how to carry out those missions.

As we rolled along, we must have resembled some sort of gypsy circus. There were horse heads hanging out of windows, men dangling legs out of boxcars, big guns and wagons on flatcars, and on one flatcar the rolling kitchen with the cooks hard at work, smoke billowing out of the chimney as the train rumbled along the tracks.[8] This train was much nicer than our last. With only twenty men per car instead of forty, there was room to stretch out and sleep on the floor,[9] upon which we laid the bed sacks we had used at Camp de Souge.[10] Our meals consisted of the usual corned beef from cans, hard bread, and the occasional treat of jam or cheese.[11]

---

1   *The Autobiography of a Regiment*, p. 68.
2   *The Battery Book*, p. 55.
3   *History of the 305th Field Artillery*, p. 58.
4   *The Autobiography of a Regiment*, p. 72.
5   *History of the 305th Field Artillery*, p. 58.
6   *The Autobiography of a Regiment*, p. 72.
7   *The Story of Battery B*, p. 31.
8   *History of the 305th Field Artillery*, p. 58.
9   *"C" Battery Book*, p. 27.
10   *The Battery Book*, p. 57.
11   *The History of the 306th Field Artillery*, p. 20.

It cannot be said that the trip was entirely uneventful. During a brief stop at the town of Perigueux, through an error of the railroad authorities, the car containing all of our instruments used for calculations and fire control of the big guns was detached from the train. This was not discovered until we reached the next town, at which time a mad scramble was made to recover the car as quickly as possible.

Just outside of Chaumont, Private Folvig, who was on guard duty in one of the horse cars, was kicked out of the car by one of the horses and received a severe gash on the head. No one saw it happen, and the train rattled on, leaving him on the tracks. He made his way to an infantry camp and was transported to a hospital.

Early the following morning, a mare that had managed to get loose from her halter chain fell out of the moving car.[1,2] Many men saw the horse land catlike on her feet and, in a confused state, follow the train down the tracks at a full canter, whinnying. The train rolled to a stop after three miles,[3] and the horse was hog-tied and hoisted aboard.

Despite those mishaps, we traversed eastward in warm, delightful weather through the middle of France toward the German border. Many of us took turns riding outside on the open flatcars, breathing deeply the fresh summer air. We shall never forget those green and well-kept fields and the little villages of gray stone buildings with red-tiled roofs clustered about their church towers.[4] We passed old mills with their wheels turning beside beautiful ponds, a superb chateau with towers rising out of a wood, field after field of golden wheat ready for harvest, and flowers everywhere: goldenrod in full bloom, scarlet poppies and thistles, and purple asters.[5] Then,

1   *The Battery Book*, p. 56.
2   *The History of the 306th Field Artillery*, p. 20.
3   *The Battery Book*, p. 57.
4   *The History of the 306th Field Artillery*, p. 20.
5   *The Autobiography of a Regiment*, p. 74.

at the last station before our destination, we saw our first carload of German prisoners going the other way.[1] From that point on, the signs of war became increasingly obvious: houses burned or with ragged holes in the roofs and walls, broken bridges, and little brown crosses scattered along the roadsides, marking the spots where defenders of this country had died in battle.[2]

On July 18, 1918, after passing through Bordeaux, Labourne, Perigueux, Limoges, Chateauroux Bourges, Nevers, Casne, Clamecy, Auxerre, Brienon, Tonnerre, Chatillon-sur-Seine-Chaumont, Neufchateau, Minecourt, Epinal, and St. Die,[3] we arrived at the town of Baccarat. We had traveled for three days and two nights and had covered a distance of 310 miles.[4] We were immediately struck by the presence of German and Austrian prisoners working in the railroad station.[5]

✳ *Route from Camp de Souge to Baccarat.*

1 *The Autobiography of a Regiment*, p.74.
2 *The History of the 306th Field Artillery*, p. 20.
3 *The Story of Battery B*, p. 31.
4 *The Battery Book*, p. 57.
5 *The Story of Battery B*, p. 31.

Part 4
Chéry-Chartreuve

(July 18, 1918 – September 4, 1918)

Baccarat

(July 18, 1918 – August 1, 1918)

Our train arrived at Baccarat in the middle of the night. In the darkness, we unloaded the guns, wagons, supplies, and horses. After hitching the horses to the guns and wagons, we were ready to move out. To avoid being spotted by German aerial reconnaissance, almost all of our marches would be made at night with strict orders forbidding lamps, flashlights, lighting of matches, smoking, or any other illumination that could tip off the enemy to the position of our unit.[1]

We would spend the next two weeks in the vicinity of Baccarat. In 1914, when Germany invaded, Baccarat was the scene of intense fighting, and everywhere we saw the crumbled remains of buildings that had been blown to bits, with no attempt to rebuild.

Bibliotheque Nationale de France ark:/12148/btv1b6908662h

✳ Baccarat

---

1 *The Battery Book: A History of Battery "A" 306th F.A.*, by Francis L. Field and Guy H. Richards (New York: The De Vinne Press, 1921), p. 58.

The town, at the foot of the Vosges Mountains, was now on the outskirts of the active front. Although it was subject to occasional harassment from enemy planes, the threat of enemy infantry or artillery attacks was low. But the fact that death could be delivered at any time inspired us all to strive for perfection in the areas in which we had been trained. It was a perfect environment for the gradual immersion of our newly trained unit into war conditions that would soon threaten our mortality on a daily basis.

The utmost secrecy was always employed when units were moved around the battlefield because Germany had many eyes, constantly searching to detect our activities. Since this area was near the border of Alsace-Lorraine, the territory that France had lost to Germany in 1871, about half the populace spoke French and half spoke German. Sometimes one wondered whether one was in France or Germany. Spies easily blended in and abounded everywhere.[1] Many German spies even spoke perfect English and had attended the finest colleges in America. Tales came to us from the front of the common practice of spies crawling to our lines in the dead of night and tapping their telephones into our communication wires to eavesdrop. Therefore, all conversations used code names to refer to locations, units, and officers' names.[2]

We ran into some of the 77th Division infantrymen with whom we had trained at Camp Upton, who had arrived about two weeks before us. Aside from telling us harrowing tales of the front lines, such as the ghastly casualties caused by poisonous gas and flame throwers,[3] they illustrated to us what a problem the German spies in the area were. When those infantrymen had arrived to replace the 42nd Division infantry, in what they thought was a concealed and stealthy fashion, the Germans had greeted them by hanging a sign from an observation balloon that read, "Good-by, 42nd—Hello, 77th."[4] In contrast to our army, which was newly trained with no experience, the German army was one of the most skillful and experienced armies in the world. If they wanted to intimidate us, sending the message that they knew our every move in advance probably had the desired effect.

We were told of a skirmish in which a man in American uniform, speaking perfect English, ran down the ranks of an American unit telling the troops that the commanding officer had stated that they were overpowered and had given the order to surrender. Consequently, 140 of the 190 American soldiers surrendered, while the rest either retreated or were killed. In fact, the troops had not been overpowered, and no commanding officer had given such an order. A report of the incident was handed up to General Bullard, who stated, in written Order No. 561, that a person who spreads such an alarm is either an enemy in our uniform or one of our own troops who is a traitor. "WHOEVER HE IS, HE SHOULD BE KILLED ON THE SPOT."[5]

---

1   *The Story of Battery B, 306th F.A.—77th Division*, by Roswell A. De La Mater (New York: Premier, 1919), p. 33.
2   *The Autobiography of a Regiment: A History of the 304th Field Artillery in the World War*, by James M. Howard (New York, 1920), p. 83.
3   *The Autobiography of a Regiment*, p. 76.
4   *The Battery Book, p. 57.*
5   *History of the 305th Field Artillery*, by Charles Wadsworth Camp (Garden City, NY: The Country Life Press, 1919), p. 121.

So with a few butterflies in our stomachs and under cover of night, we headed off to the east on our first night march of the war.[1] The order specified a 160-foot interval between carriages so that if the German bombing planes appeared, they would do a minimum of damage.[2] Over unfamiliar country roads and past strange darkened villages, eerie from the absence of any lights, we hiked until just before dawn, when we pulled off the road into the protective cover of the woods. Horses were tied up, tents were pitched, and we slept well into the daylight hours.

On waking, we were greeted by a land of rolling hills, dark thick woods of birch and hemlock, and, in the midst of it, golden fields of ripe wheat as orderly and well tilled as any we had seen, all under a sky of the purest shade of blue.[3,4] French farmers—men, women, and children callused by four years of war—worked defiantly in their fields.[5,6] We spent the next few days preparing gun pits, positioning the guns and covering them with camouflage netting, running communication lines, setting up command posts and mess kitchens, and in general establishing our position.[7] When we had completed these tasks, one of our reconnaissance planes took aerial photos and reported that we had done our job so well that there was no indication of our presence and the film showed no difference from the photos taken before our arrival.[8]

Throughout our stay in Baccarat, all gunners had the opportunity to fire a few of their first real wartime shots. I believe that every gun crew wrote their names or a greeting message in chalk on the first shell they sent over to the Germans. The farmers did not run away when the thunderous booms of our guns commenced. Instead, we had to warn them and shoo them off the fields in much the same way that a parent keeps children from playing in the street.[9]

Like a troupe of dancers making a nervous and imperfect first stage performance, we did some fumbling. As Battery A fired off their first shots and, with a terrific roar, the gun leaped back in recoil, the camouflage netting caught fire. Operations had to be halted while the fire was put out. When the second gun fired, the concussion carried to the mess kitchen 25 yards away and knocked over a can of soup and a boiler of stewed tomatoes, putting out the fire underneath them.[10] Some of D Battery's shots fell short, with the unintended effect of plowing holes in a local potato field. A wrath-filled farmer ran up to the gunners and gave them a stern reprimand in French, stressing the value of his *pommes de terre*.

Most shots ended up being inconsequential, as they were fired at empty trenches and positions that had been abandoned by the enemy. However, a report came in one day, extracted from some German prisoners, of a huge stockpile of enemy

---

1 *The History of the 306th Field Artillery: Compiled by the Men Who Participated in the Events Described* (New York: Knickerbocker Press, 1920), p. 21.
2 *History of the 305th Field Artillery*, p. 61.
3 *The History of the 306th Field Artillery*, p. 21.
4 *History of the 305th Field Artillery*, p. 65.
5 *The History of the 306th Field Artillery*, p. 21.
6 *The Autobiography of a Regiment*, p. 86.
7 *The Battery Book*, p. 60.
8 *The Story of Battery B*, p. 34.
9 *The History of the 306th Field Artillery*, p. 22.
10 *The Battery Book*, p. 60.

artillery munitions hidden in a church. The 3rd Battalion of our 306th Field Artillery Regiment was given the target.[1] The shot was plotted by the sound-ranging method. The first data was given in the following form:

> Base deflection — Right 171 (correction left 12)
> Shell — OA
> Fuse — SR
> Charge — 0
> Site — plus 6
> Elevation — 480
> Method of Fire — At my command.[2]

The church was annihilated. It was our first real contribution to the war. Each one of those enemy artillery shells that added to the colossal explosion and fireball had been manufactured for the sole purpose of killing Allied troops. Even though our achievement was slight in the context of the overall war, to a small degree we had just reduced the enemies' ability to hurt us, and after a year of training for such duty, it was exhilarating to see the real-life results. To us, it verified the credibility, worth, and strength of our regiment. We had done damage to the enemy. Unfortunately, the enemy swiftly acknowledged it. That night, the Germans retaliated by sending their planes over and bombing our entire sector all night long. No lives were lost, but many nerves were.

A man's first thoughts upon going into action are whether he will have the guts and be able to show the real fighting spirit that is expected of him. This self-questioning was at the forefront of our thoughts. In retrospect, the pandemonium that was inspired by the bombing that night could be viewed as somewhat comical. Men flung their helmets on, dived into foxholes, and needlessly choked and sweated in their confining gas masks as unfounded gas alarms were recklessly sounded. The horses, which we had been adamantly instructed should be given gas masks before the men, were left on their own and were completely ignored as all hunkered down, solely focused on our own survival. Interestingly, many of our munitions dumps, which we had thought to be well concealed, were targeted so precisely by the bombing that it became obvious that the enemy had known their locations all along. In this somewhat inactive sector, there were not a lot of initiating attacks, but should one be conducted against the other side, a retaliatory attack could generally be expected.[3]

When we heard the daytime drone of the German reconnaissance planes for the first time, foolish curiosity drew everyone to the edge of the woods to catch a glimpse of the small silver speck high in the sky. Like mother hens, the officers quickly shooed everyone back under the cover of the woods with a reprimand to show more discipline and professionalism.[4] The Germans ruled the skies, and we almost never saw an

---

1   *The History of the 306th Field Artillery,* p. 23.
2   *The Battery Book,* p. 60.
3   *The History of the 306th Field Artillery,* p. 23.
4   *The History of the 306th Field Artillery,* p. 21.

Allied plane. The German planes were very busy during the day, not just doing visual reconnaissance but also taking regular and systematic photographs of the terrain. It was amazing how much information could be gleaned by comparing these photos to previous photographs of the same place. If, in pulling off from a main road to find cover in the woods, a unit marched across a dry grass field or wheat field, an aerial photo would clearly show the beaten path across the field where no path had existed in the previous day's photo. As seen from the air, the trail would clearly lead to the unit, though it would be completely unobvious to anyone on the ground.

Throughout our stay, there were more night bombings (a harassing German tactic to deprive their enemy of much-needed sleep) and numerous false gas alarms.[1] As we became more seasoned, our reactions shifted from counterproductive panic to calmer, more logical defensive actions. The value of our participation in the Baccarat sector was not to be measured by any real damage we inflicted upon the enemy; rather, the value was in the final melding of our regiment under actual battlefield conditions. We were our only salvation from the death our enemy intended for us. Every man's life depended upon every other man's ability to do his job. It is amazing how quickly one learns by immersion. The practical skills that we perfected during two weeks under battlefield conditions eclipsed months of "classroom" training at Camp Upton or Camp de Souge. And under these conditions, we came together. No one wanted the enemy to win. No one wanted to die and no one wanted to see one of his comrades get killed, so we worked together with strength and determination and skill and confidence AS A UNIT.

2 Weeks en Route to the Front
(AUGUST 1, 1918 – AUGUST 15, 1918)

Early on the evening of August 1, 1918, we began our march to a new sector. For two nights in a row, we hiked all night from sunset to sunrise. We had all heard of forced night marches, and now we had the opportunity to experience them. It is a world unto itself and, for those who have never been there, probably not a place most would ever have cause or occasion to try to imagine. Even for the most prime physical specimens among us, it was an ultimate test of endurance.

The nighttime darkness adds a weight and burden to one's soul and, in sharp contrast to daylight conditions, has a crushing effect upon both the spirit and the body. In the absence of light, each and every footstep could terminate in an unknown landing or unexpected slip,[2] accentuated by the weight of a 50-pound pack,[3] possibly in ankle-deep mud. The mental frustration and the wear and tear on the muscles from unexpectedly jerky slips or falls is exponentially fatiguing in contrast to a day march. The men who hiked behind the horses, in the splattering of mud thrown up by their

---

1 *The History of the 306th Field Artillery*, p. 23.
2 *The History of the 306th Field Artillery*, p. 94.
3 *The Autobiography of a Regiment*, p. 95.

✳ *Hauling the guns*

✳ *Marching on foot*

✳ *Howitzer stuck in mud*

hoofs and in the path of the steam that snorted from their nostrils against the icy gray mists of the valleys, could almost see the night's chill slowly draining the energy from all. The animals suffered. The men suffered. The men on the animals suffered.

It was commonplace to see riders slumped forward, their heads resting on their horses' necks, managing a state of sleep or perhaps simply unconsciousness in spite of the agitated, lurching motion of their mounts. Men afoot, worn down, would stagger from side to side and oftimes hold onto the back of a wagon, dazed and exhausted, as their feet mechanically shuffled along trying to keep up with their bodies. From the packs that burdened them so, they jettisoned every ounce of nonessential weight. We left behind us a trail of extra sweaters mothers had sent along and books that the men had hoped would offer them a diversion from war in moments of rest. Although it was against regulations, at times of desperate fatigue, a man would sometimes commission his pack as a stowaway on one of the supply wagons.

The situation could easily evoke images of a gypsy caravan: wagons piled high with all sorts of supplies, lanterns, pitchforks, saddles; pots and pans strapped to the sides, clanking to the rhythmic lurches of the wagons; the clanking of the harnesses; the skludge-skludge of the heavy, muddy hoofs of the horses; the background rumble of a multitude of carts and wagons and, to the rear of the column, the cannoneers. The only thing that was missing was a palm reader!

Invariably, each night's travails would include at least one howitzer that had become stuck in the mud or, worse yet, had slid off the side of an embankment. To a soldier whose exhaustion and fatigue threaten his ability to simply keep up with the march, the prospect of physically muscling an 8,000-pound howitzer out of the mud in the pitch black of night is not a pleasant one. In a steady rain, the order would go out: "Cannoneers at the wheels. Gather your horses, use your heels — Ready — Heave!" As the men strained to push on the slippery wheel spokes, the horses danced and plunged in place, and often the gun refused to budge even one inch. If needed, a second team of horses and more men would be added until eventually the gun was freed. This excruciating scene played out over and over again, testing the limits of both the men and the horses.

Given that most troop movement was restricted to nighttime and that there was much activity in this area, as American divisions and French divisions rushed to different battlefields, congestion on the roads was unavoidable. It was an infuriating aggravation for an officer to have his column split up in the dead of night because another unit at a crossroad, in hasty impatience, cut in rather than waiting for the entire column to pass. This led to many heated exchanges between officers of different units. Usually, it was the loudest and most authoritative voice that would win the right of way.

✳ *Howitzer stuck in mud*

> "What outfit is this?"
> "What y' doing here?"
> "Wha' d' ya' mean cutting in?"
> "Hold up that column!"[1]

After two grueling all-night westerly hikes, both of which ended at sunrise, we arrived at the village of Loromontzey at the foot of the Vosges Mountains. Mere description can do but scant justice to the striking beauty of the Vosges. Summit after summit, valley after valley unroll before one, each seemingly more beautiful than those that have gone before. Each peak is crowned with forest to its summit, and in each valley, villages nestle in the shadow of the protecting hills. Pages could be written in an effort to do justice to their splendor.[2]

We had a four-day layover here in constant rain and ankle-deep mud while we awaited the trains. On August 8, 1918, after a short two-hour hike north to the town of Bayon,[3] we spent four hours loading guns and equipment, and then we boarded trains bound for yet another unknown destination.

The trip was comfortable, with only twenty-five men per car.[4] After traveling west toward Paris for thirty-six hours, we detrained at the town of St. Simeon[5] on August 10, 1918. Coincidentally, on this day, the First American Army came into official existence on the battlefield. The newly promoted French Marshal Ferdinand Foch, in command of all Allied troops, had finally gained enough confidence in our military to relinquish full control to General Pershing.[6]

✳ *General Pershing*

For three days, we hiked to the east, traveling during the night and resting during the day.[7] It was by far our hardest march yet.[8] We were now close on the heels of the Germans. We were passing through towns where fierce battles had recently taken place. Halfway to our destination, we camped on the banks of the historic River Marne, the bright moonlight glistening on its waters.[9] We awoke in tall, wet grass that grew in abundance about the place, looking over the beautiful wide, deep, slow-

1 *The History of the 306th Field Artillery*, pp. 94–97.
2 *Memories of the World War*, by Robert Alexander (New York: Macmillan, 1931), p. 48.
3 *The Battery Book*, p. 63.
4 *The Story of Battery B*, p. 37.
5 *The History of the 306th Field Artillery*, p. 26.
6 *Memories of the World War*, p. 153.
7 *The History of the 306th Field Artillery*, p. 26.
8 *The Story of Battery B*, p. 37.
9 *The Battery Book*, p. 66.

✳ *Blown up bridge at Chateau Thierry (Press photo in personal collection)*

flowing river with tree-studded shores. A few hundred yards up the river lay a bridge, wrecked beyond use, with parts of its span hanging down into the water.[1]

Camping near us were the 304th and 305th Field Artillery Regiments. It was a warm, sunny Sunday, and in what can probably be looked back on as one of our happiest moments of the war, 3,500 of us proceeded to strip off our clothes and, like young boys in the Hudson, swim and play and splash in the cool water. A great many of us then lay under trees or in the sun, even falling asleep at times until the order was finally given to "roll your packs."[2]

With regrets about leaving, we began our march and crossed the Marne River on temporary pontoon bridges the engineers of the 302nd had constructed.[3] Some of the horses were nervous and spooked, and the 304th had one of their mules fall in the water, the rescue of which took quite some time.[4] Nearby, buried nose down in a meadow under beautiful, clear, sunny skies was an American plane that had crashed the day before, carrying its pilot to his death.[5,6]

Beyond the river, the town of Chateau Thierry was a scene of destruction that represented an epic landmark in this war. On March 21, 1918, the Germans had launched a powerful offensive drive toward Paris with the goal of capturing Paris, crushing France, and ending the war before the Americans were able to fully mobilize on the side of the Allies. The strength that the Americans would infuse into the fight

---

1   *The Battery Book*, p. 65.
2   *The Autobiography of a Regiment*, p. 97.
3   *The History of the 306th Field Artillery*, p. 27.
4   *The Autobiography of a Regiment*, p. 98.
5   *The Battery Book*, p. 65.
6   *The Story of Battery B*, p. 37.

was well recognized by Germany, whose drive was conducted with a "do or die" effort. Like a steamroller, the German army pressed forward day after day, and the threat to France grew so great that, for a second time, the government was evacuated from Paris to Bordeaux.[1] By May 27, 1918, the Germans had taken the town of Chateau-Thierry, only 59 miles from Paris.

Although the American soldiers were not fully prepared for such a battle, the emergency warranted rushing in any available troops to aid the exhausted French and British. So great was the urgency that the infantry, under the command of General Pershing, hurried ahead and joined in the battle before the support of their artillery could arrive. On May 30, 1918, when the Allies managed to halt the German advance, the tip of that wedge-shaped German offensive rested on Chateau-Thierry. It was the dire need for Allied troops to help repulse this German offensive that had prompted military leaders to initiate the painful emergency transfer of 698 of our artillerymen to the infantry back at Camp Upton. By mid-July, the rest of our American troops were in full readiness, and on July 18, 1918, they joined the Allied forces in a counteroffensive that reversed the direction of the German drive, chasing them out of Chateau-Thierry to reorganize farther back in their lines.[2,3]

No German artillery was captured, but in the haste of their retreat, the Germans were forced to leave behind huge dumps of artillery shells, obviously slated for a further advance toward Paris. A typical stack could be 150 feet long by four boxes wide and four boxes high. Occasionally, a brave German aviator would dart in and destroy the ammunition so that it couldn't be used against his side.[4]

We were now rushing in to add our muscle to the effort of the exhausted French and American units and to rock the Germans back further while they were still off balance.

Many buildings in Chateau-Thierry were in complete ruin with hardly a wall intact. Any homes still standing were riddled with bullet holes, testimony to the firestorm that had taken place. Evidence of the bitter hand-to-hand combat could be found in articles strewn about on both sides of the road: broken rifles, helmets, packs, gas masks, ammunition, overcoats, countless little wooden crosses, and a scattering of the unburied bodies of friends, foes, and horses,[5,6] accompanied by the pervasive odor of death. Off in the distance, for the first time, we could hear the roar of giant guns, growing ever louder as we marched on.

✲ *Town in rubble*

---

1 *History of the 305th Field Artillery*, p. 51.

2 *Memories of the World War*, pp. 60–64.

3 *The Autobiography of a Regiment*, p. 106.

4 *Memories of the World War*, p. 70.

5 *The History of the 306th Field Artillery*, p. 27.

6 *"C" Battery Book: 306th F.A., 77th Div., 1917–1919*, by John Foster (Brooklyn, NY: Braunworth & Co., 1920), p. 31.

On the road, we passed a column of infantry who were leaving the front for a short rest period at the rear. One man stopped right beside my horse, leaned over, and vomited. Then, in a matter-of-fact, disgusted way, he exclaimed, "God-damned gas!" There were many encouragements for us from the column: "Give 'em Hell!" and "They'll need all the guns they can get up there!"[1]

On the morning of August 14, 1918, the Forêt de Nesle (Nesle Forest) came into view. The sloping fields that we traversed on the way were dotted with graves, most marked by rough crosses on which hung German helmets. The horses were unequal to the slope of the hill, and with the command "Cannoneers to the wheels," we crowded in, each finding room to push on a wheel spoke until at last we summited the hill,[2] and the entire regiment made camp in the forest.[3]

Everywhere were signs of the bitterly fought battles that had pushed the Germans back just recently. Every square yard of ground had its "funk hole" that some infantryman had clawed into the ground to escape the threat of flying shrapnel. Accenting that landscape were great, gaping craters caused by enemy artillery.[4] Every now and then, we saw one whose bottom was yellow with spewed mustard gas that had failed to volatilize.[5] The ground was littered with the helmets, gas masks, rifles, and uniforms of the retreating Germans as well as with heavy packs that had been cast away by our American boys to hasten their speed in the fury of pursuit. In the midst of this crazy scene were an officer's mattress, a pair of boots, a down-turned box supporting some empty wine bottles and some dirty glasses, and a broken, mud-caked rolling kitchen covered with filth, its pots still partially filled with the remains of a half-cooked meal. Overwhelming all of this was the smell of death.[6] Many of the soldiers tended to congregate toward the edge of the forest in an effort to escape the stench of the bodies of decaying horses that littered the area[7] and those of German soldiers that lay in so many shallow graves throughout the woods.[8] It all left the impression of a catastrophic destruction of life, an almost spontaneous mass extinction. It was a surreal scene for which no mind could be properly prepared.

It was obvious to the Germans that American troops would be flooding into this area, so it was the target for their aggressive bombardments. That night, the air was filled with the constant drone of German bombers and earsplitting explosions accompanied by great flashes of light. Luckily, they were concentrated closer to the village of Nesle[9] in the valley below,[10] to the southeast of our position, and the only casualty we suffered was a lack of sleep and some frayed nerves.[11] Six gas alarms in rapid succession contributed to our lack of sleep. Each terrifying sprint to protect ourselves from agonizing death entailed leaping out of bed, donning gas masks, putting gas masks

---

1   *The Autobiography of a Regiment,* p. 100.
2   *History of the 305th Field Artillery,* p. 98.
3   *The History of the 306th Field Artillery,* p. 27.
4   *The Story of Battery B,* p. 43.
5   *History of the 305th Field Artillery,* p. 95.
6   *The Story of Battery B,* p. 43.
7   *The Autobiography of a Regiment,* p. 104.
8   *The Battery Book,* p. 68.
9   *The Battery Book,* p. 68.
10 *The Story of Battery B,* p. 39.
11 *The Battery Book,* p. 68.

on the horses,[1] and finally waiting for the commanding officer to give the order "Gas masks may be removed"[2] before we could try to go back to sleep.[3] Each turned out to be a false alarm.

✳ *Men and horses with gas masks*

Finally, after all our long months of training, that at times made it hard to remember civilian life before entering the army, this was "it." This was the real deal. All training was behind us and now, for the first time, we were about to participate in all out, fierce, "fight to the death" battles. We were officially in the war zone. Every step forward from here would require active fighting. Any forward progress would be at the expense of German lives, and to save their own lives, they would be trying aggressively to end ours. This being our first experience with battlefield conditions, when there was a lull in the excitement and a brief opportunity for sleep presented itself, our ears would nervously prick up at the rustle of leaves in an evening breeze, the neigh of a horse, the snap of a twig, or the whisper of a sentry on guard duty. In processing the sounds, an accompanying chill often went down the back of the neck.[4] Tempers were short before the night was over.[5] We were short on sleep and long on thoughts of battlefield stories that were constantly pouring in.

One of the men had conveyed an account of an ambulance driver by the name of Ernest Hemingway who, before the war, worked as a reporter for the *Kansas City Star*. On July 8, 1918, while handing out chocolate and cigarettes to Italian soldiers in the trenches, this young man was seriously injured by an incoming Austrian mortar shell. He was knocked unconscious with 200 pieces of shrapnel in his legs while one Italian next to him was killed and the other had both legs blown off. In describing the incident, Hemingway said, "There was one of those big noises you sometimes hear at the front. I died then. I felt my soul or something coming right out of my body, like you'd pull a silk handkerchief out of a pocket by one corner. It flew around and then came back and went in again and I wasn't dead anymore." He told his nurse in Milan that he plans to write a book about it.[6] We also heard a story about a German soldier, a dispatch runner named Adolf Hitler, who seemed to have a gift for dodging death. He had belonged to a regiment of 3,000 men of whom 2,500 were killed in battle near Ypres. He came out without a scratch and was awarded the Iron Cross 1st Class.[7]

In the morning, the regiment split up and took different positions. My 2nd Battalion consisted of C Battery and D Battery. Each battery was a group of four howitzers. Each howitzer required a firing crew of eight men and a support crew of another

---

1   *The Battery Book*, p. 67.
2   *The Autobiography of a Regiment*, p. 103.
3   *The Battery Book*, p. 67.
4   *The Story of Battery B*, p. 40.
5   *The Battery Book*, p. 67.
6   http://www.lostgeneration.com/wwI.htm.
7   http://www.historyplace.com/worldwar2/riseofhitler/warzone.htm.

eight to ten men for such jobs as transporting ammunition.[1] So together with all of our supporting linemen, cooks, medics, mechanics, and the like, my 2nd Battalion was about 500 men strong.[2,3]

Our 306th Regiment consisted additionally of the equal-sized 1st Battalion and 3rd Battalion. The 1st Battalion was located to our west, the 3rd Battalion to the northeast of us, and our own 2nd Battalion positioned itself in the nearby village of Chéry–Chartreuve, keeping the position in the forest as the echelon.[4] The echelon served as a concealed location to house the horses and the men who were too tired or too sick to fight.

The echelon also held the reserve stockpiles of food and ammunition, and from there the drivers would make nightly trips in wagons and trucks to deliver food, ammunition, and other supplies to the individual gun batteries. Although the roads couldn't be seen at night, the Germans knew that they would serve as nighttime supply routes for munitions and therefore conducted routine nighttime shelling of the roads.[5] While transporting shells to one of the gun batteries one night, four drivers and a sergeant from the 304th came under fire. They pulled over and, seeking shelter,

✳ *Route from Camp de Souge to Chéry-Chartreuve*

1 *"C" Battery Book,* pp. 2–4.
2 *"C" Battery Book,* pp. 2–6.
3 *The Battery Book,* pp. 189–196.
4 *The History of the 306th Field Artillery,* p. 27.
5 *The Autobiography of a Regiment,* p. 121.

huddled under a fallen plane. A German shell scored a direct hit on the wrecked plane. Four of the men were killed.[1] Drivers never knew when or where a shell might hit. They performed a dangerous but absolutely vital job.[2]

Chéry-Chartreuve
(AUGUST 15, 1918 – SEPTEMBER 4, 1918)

The quaint village of Chéry–Chartreuve was surrounded by gentle, rolling hills of wavy green grass and yellow flowers that stretched out mile after mile, occasionally accented by clusters of dense, tall, dark green forests. In the village, houses were scattered about, more in the style of a hamlet than an organized grid composed of rows of streets and houses. In the middle of the village stood a lovely stone church. The picturesque building with its steep roof, arched windows, and towering spire would best be described as "charming old-world France."[3,4]

Many buildings in the village had obviously been constructed long ago, some by skillful masons who had neatly cut stones into large rectangular blocks and added

✱ *Chéry-Chartreuve, France. (Photos courtesy of Marco de Boer)*

1 *The Autobiography of a Regiment*, p. 111.
2 *The Autobiography of a Regiment*, p. 121.
3 *"C" Battery Book*, p. 34.
4 *The Autobiography of a Regiment*, p. 107.

ornate detail to the arched doorways and circular attic windows. Other buildings and roadside walls looked to be constructed simply of smooth river rocks that a lesser mason had plopped down in wet concrete. Most of the wood framing and beams of the steeply pitched red tile roofs consisted of either raw logs or ones that had been hand shaped to have flat sides. Some of the buildings had a coat of white plaster over the stonework, stained, cracked, and peeling from years of neglect. The buildings with nicer stone work for the most part were left unplastered, and Mother Nature had accented the mottled gray rocks with pleasant shades of orange, sea green, yellow, and olive green lichen. Many of the streets of dirt and fine sandy gravel were carpeted with a thin covering of grass.

In peacetime, the thought of relaxing in this picturesque village with a glass of wine under deep blue skies would have had strong allure. But with the present ravages of war, the poor little village was in a state of ruin. Many houses were reduced to one or two standing walls. The streets were littered with demolished stonework and other debris left by the hostile artillery fire.

We moved into positions in Chéry-Chartreuve on the night of August 15, 1918. Our battalion command post was situated on the east side of the town in the cellar of an old building that had previously been leveled by a German shell, making it a low-odds target.[1] Battery D positioned itself in the immediate vicinity. The position selected for Battery C was to the west side of the town, a little more than half a mile to the southwest.[2] The gun pits were dug: 3 to 4 feet deep, 25 feet wide, and 30 feet long, with hundreds of sandbags piled up around the front and sides.[3] The horses hauled the guns into position and were then unhitched and taken to the echelon in the forest.

A tactic of the Germans was referred to as an elastic front line. A front line by its nature is always vulnerable and unstable. Any time the Germans would make a substantial advance of their front line, they would expend substantial resources in heavily fortifying what had previously been the front line. Should their new, active front line fail, they would then have an impregnable rear line of defense to fall back to. One month previously, the strong German offensive drive had been turned around by Allied counteroffensives at Chateau-Thierry, and the Germans had now fallen back to just such a stronghold.

The Germans, who liked to utilize natural barriers, were now behind the Vesle River, about three and a half miles to the north of us. The Vesle is a slow-flowing, snakelike stream only about 35 feet wide and 10 to 12 feet deep but with sheer banks, in places 5 feet high.[4,5] Immediately across the river is a large open and exposed grassy expanse and then the key village of Bazoches.

Bazoches, a railroad and supply center, was of major importance to the Germans.[6] It was the artery through which ammunition and supplies were fed to the

---

1 *"C" Battery Book*, p. 34.

2 *The History of the 306th Field Artillery*, p. 48.

3 *The Story of Battery B*, p. 34.

4 *The Victorious 77th Division (New York's Own) in the Argonne Fight*, by Arthur McKeogh (New York: John H. Eggers Co., 1919), p. 15.

5 *History of the 77th Division: August 25th, 1917–November 11th, 1918* (New York: The 77th Division Association, 1919), p. 40.

6 *The History of the 306th Field Artillery*, p. 30.

✳ *Battery of 155s setting up position*

area. Losing the village would reduce Germany's ability to fight, so the position was fiercely defended. The village itself had scores of machine gun nests in every conceivable location, as did the immediate nearby wooded areas.[1] Just beyond the village, the landscape became mountainous, and in those dominating heights,[2] the Germans had positioned massive concentrations of light, medium, and heavy artillery in the villages of Vauxcere, Perles, Paars, Blanzy, and Fismes. This allowed them to protect Bazoches from every conceivable angle of approach by the Allied forces.[3] Any invaders would first have to forge the Vesle River, which had been filled with barbed wire and across which all bridges had been destroyed.[4] Even if successful, such an accomplishment would only lead to the suicide mission of trying to storm across the flat, open expanse between the river and the village of Bazoches under the wrath of the German artillery fire. Repeated attempts in the past had all failed.[5]

---

1 *The Battery Book*, p. 84.
2 *The Autobiography of a Regiment*, p. 99.
3 *The History of the 306th Field Artillery*, pp. 27, 32, 48.
4 *"C" Battery Book*, p. 42.
5 *The Autobiography of a Regiment*, p. 107.

The Allied commanders decided that until the German artillery units in the mountain villages could be destroyed, leaving the way clear for us to take Bazoches, there would be no chance of further Allied advance. From Chéry-Chartreuve, those German artillery units would become our targets, and we undoubtedly would become theirs.

A flurry of operations went on at the same time that the gun emplacements were being established. Observation posts were being established as well as command posts, medical stations, and mess camps. Communication lines were being run to interconnect our regiment and to connect us to the other regiments and divisional headquarters.

Every effort is made to keep all phone lines operating, and the Germans make every effort to kill every observer and every lineman. These are not glorified positions. Although one rarely reads about linemen and observers in the *New York Times* war stories, their jobs are extremely dangerous and essential to our survival. When laying wires across areas where shelling could be anticipated, the lineman lays multiple wires of different colors, spread far apart so that if the blue wire is broken, the order can be given to switch to the red wire. To interconnect the segments of our regiment at this position, the lineman laid about 60 miles of wire.[1] The terminating end at our telephone post was in the small cellar of an old stone building. The incoming wires ran across the ceiling like an untidy spiderweb and were then bundled together and fed into three four-directional switchboards mounted against a wall.[2]

Two operators were on duty 24 hours a day. They tested the lines every two hours, and if a line went down, two linemen were sent out to fix the problem.[3] The linemen were a constant target. The countryside was full of German snipers, and because their observation was so good and they had so much artillery ammunition, they would not hesitate to use those expensive projectiles to target a single lineman.

Because lines are usually broken during enemy assaults, the repair skills of the linemen are usually called for at the most dangerous of times. Nonetheless, out he treks with his helmet and gas mask, wire, tape, pincers, and portable phone. He crawls through ditches in the dead of night, feeling along the wire for the problem. Occasionally, he taps his phone into the wire. If it still works, he knows the problem lies ahead; if it doesn't work, he has accidently passed the problem and has to backtrack. In the inky black of the night, he might as well have his eyes closed. The lineman works mainly by touch and feel, since any illumination from a lamp or flashlight would certainly trigger a hostile response from a German sniper or howitzer crew. Repairs are commonly called for during times of active shelling when poisonous gas fills the air and warrants the use of those miserable gas masks.[4] Casualties are common enough that it is policy for linemen to go out in pairs so that if one should be incapacitated, the other can return to camp for help.[5]

1   *History of the 305th Field Artillery*, p. 71.
2   *History of the 305th Field Artillery*, p. 64.
3   *History of the 305th Field Artillery*, p. 72.
4   *The History of the 306th Field Artillery*, p. 31.
5   *History of the 305th Field Artillery*, p. 72.

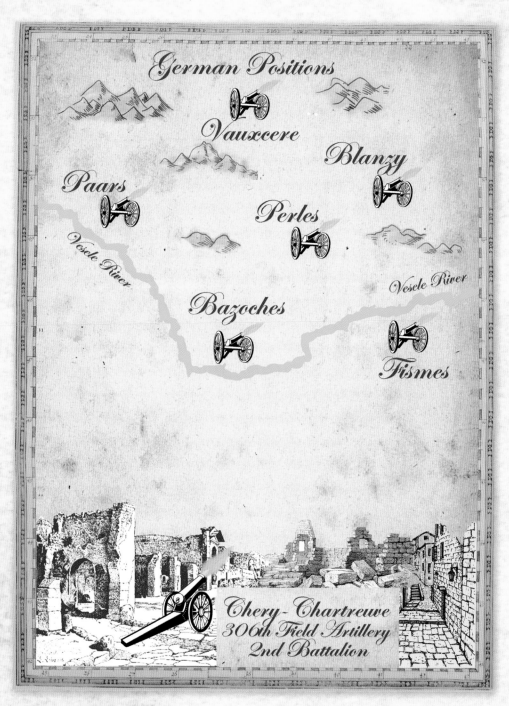

The morning light would provide German reconnaissance the opportunity to seek out our position. Aside from observation by their planes, which constantly circled above, off in the distance to the north, spread far apart from each other, was a row of six German observation balloons known as *Drachen* (German for "dragon").[1,2]

---

1 *The Battery Book*, p. 70.
2 *History of the 77th Division*, p. 45.

✳ *A German Drachen*

✳ *German gun pounding Allied positions*

The long, sausage-shaped balloons allowed the aerial observer not only to report potential targets to the German artillery units, but also to give feedback on the accuracy of their shots so that adjustments to the firing could be made.

As soon as our phones lines were established, connecting everyone together, the slugfest began. It was face to face, blow for blow, might against might, each side armed to the hilt and each determined to be the "last man standing." Observers were able to instantly give us the bearings of enemy muzzle blasts, and in record times of three and four minutes, we worked out the calculations and sent over the "adjustment shots." With further feedback from the observer as to how far off target we were and in what direction, we would make final adjustments and begin our barrage until the target was silenced. Our German targets were also trying to kill us before we could kill them. Speed and accuracy of fire determined the winner. Again we thanked our training at Camp de Souge, where we had held competitions between the gun crews to see who could fire the fastest and most accurately.[1]

The pace was relentless as the two sides hammered away at each other as fast as we could, both sides fighting for our very existence. At times, what should have been a landscape of stable terra firma seemed a sea of swirling perpetual motion with nothing still or stationary. Walls were falling, roofs were collapsing, exploding shells were sending dust and debris shooting high in the air to intermix with the drifting clouds of poisonous gas, and our 8,000-pound guns were rhythmically jumping back in the recoil of their thunderous firing. We recorded as many as 1,600 incoming high-explosive and gas shells a day.[2] There were no breaks. The pressure to keep the gunners supplied with shells never let up. The roads from the echelon to the positions were constantly shelled by the enemy, and on the last leg of the trip, the ammunition had to be carried by hand and by horses with special saddlebags carrying four shells on each side.

Day and night, the air whined, wailed, and whistled with the miscellany of shells the Germans sent over and with the drone of their planes.[3] Each type of projectile had its own distinctive incoming sound, and nicknames were chosen accordingly. The explosions from the much-hated high-velocity Austrian-made 105s, or "whizzbangs,"[4,5] shattered the air so close on the heels of the warning wail, *pfzzzz-z-z-BANG*, that

1   *The History of the 306th Field Artillery*, p. 17.
2   *The History of the 306th Field Artillery*, p. 27.
3   *The History of the 306th Field Artillery*, p. 27.
4   *The Autobiography of a Regiment*, p. 145.
5   *Memories of the World War*, p. 126.

the two were almost simultaneous.[1] A gas shell could be identified by the dull *Kur-r-r-r-Plun-n-k* sound it made upon hitting the ground[2] or by the wobbling whistle caused by the way it somersaulted through air as the liquid shifted inside it.[3] The shells of the *minenwerfers* ("mine launchers"), known as "iron mermaids" because of their fishlike tails, came in sounding like a mix between a locomotive whistle and a siren.[4] Everyone became familiar with many others such as "Jack Johnsons," "Whimpering Willies," "Tons of Coal," and "G.I. Cans." At times, Chéry-Chartreuve became an inferno of exploding shells, its streets alive with flying bricks and mortar and soaked with deadly gases, while the tumbling walls echoed and re-echoed weirdly with the shrieking of shells.[5]

✱ *Horses hauling artillery shells*

In addition to the 1st, 2nd, and 3rd Battalions of our 306th regiment, the 304th and 305th Field Artillery Regiments of our 77th Division, totaling about 72 howitzers, were spread out along the line directly opposite what were believed to be four German divisions. Additionally, on our right was the American 28th Division, and to our left were French units, all furiously battling the German divisions that were opposing their advance.[6]

It was a conflict of mammoth proportions. For miles along the Vesle River, literally tons of artillery shells were being lobbed back and forth. The earth shook to the tumultuous roars of the guns. It was the

✱ *Rapid fire artillery blasts*

war of the worlds in which it seemed that humanity was endeavoring to destroy itself. In Chéry-Chartreuve, we could not hear the thunder of the neighboring battles because the noise in our immediate area was so deafening. The battle cry was "Dig in." Little funk holes about two feet deep, just enough to get a man out of the horizontal flight path of flying shrapnel, saved many a life.[7] Anything that could be used to block the bits of deadly flying metal that could so easily tear through a man's body, causing searing pain and mutilating death, was utilized. Scraps of wood or corrugated tin adorned many of the funk holes. Sandbag walls were erected around the gun emplacements.[8] Sleeping hideouts in basements or behind stone walls that afforded protection

---

1 *The History of the 306th Field Artillery*, p. 28.
2 *The Story of Battery B*, p. 42.
3 *The Victorious 77th Division*, p. 14.
4 *History of the 77th Division*, p. 43.
5 *The History of the 306th Field Artillery*, pp. 27–29.
6 *The Battery Book*, p. 68.
7 *The History of the 306th Field Artillery*, p. 27.
8 *The Story of Battery B*, p. 41.

✳ *Every building destroyed by incoming artillery fire*

were carefully selected. It is common knowledge that a well-constructed shelter will provide safety—until it is the subject of a direct hit. No matter what we did to protect ourselves, every man lived with the unease that his life could be ended at any moment by a direct hit.[1]

While shrapnel had a limited range of travel, clouds of poisonous gas could fill the air and, with the breeze, travel great distances, gently wafting around obstacles and down into funk holes. The inhumanity of this tool of death cannot be overstated, and the fear it evoked in otherwise fearless soldiers—soldiers who refused to be intimidated by explosions, bullets, and flying shrapnel—could best be described as terror. Some gases, such as mustard gas, were designed simply to get men off the battlefield and into hospitals,[2] where the average treatment time was almost 42 days.[3] Others, such as phosgene, could kill with a single breath.[4] The first effects of gas were felt on the face and in the eyes, but within seconds, it entered the throat. Depending on the type of gas, some soldiers died very quickly. Others were blinded for life, suffered awful skin burns and blisters, or died a lingering death as their lungs collapsed and filled with liquid.[5]

The Germans were relentless in their use of gas at this position, and all suffered to some extent. Even when there were no active gas attacks under way, the little whiffs that one picked up from the residue lifted in the breeze had a cumulative effect. Typi-

---

1 *The History of the 306th Field Artillery*, p. 28.

2 *The Victorious 77th Division*, p. 14.

3 *Personal Perspectives: World War I*, edited by Timothy C. Dowling (Santa Barbara, CA: ABC-CLIO, 2006), p. 184.

4 *The Victorious 77th Division*, p. 14.

5 *World War I* (DK Eyewitness Books), by Simon Adams (New York: DK Publishing, 2001), p. 45.

✲ *Servicemen blinded by gas*

cal symptoms of this mild exposure were stomachache with nausea, violent diarrhea, and a general malaise that made it hard to fight.[1]

Every unit had some type of gas alarm. There was the shrill scream of the hand-cranked Klaxon horn or three shots from a rifle fired off in rapid succession,[2] but most commonly, the alarm consisted of several empty howitzer shell casings strung together, hanging from a tree with a hammer in the middle. At the earliest indication of gas, someone would bang the hammer against the shells as hard as he could. The clanging would set off a panic rush to don gas masks. If a neighboring unit heard the alarm, they would sound their alarm as well, and in this fashion, an alarm could often travel relay style for miles.[3,4,5]

During the day, the sun shone hot, and the men, who all sweated under the toil of their labors, could only race to adjust their gas masks and, after an hour of choking for air and sweating behind the fogged up isinglass faceplate, try to resist the violent urge to vomit even as their skin burned from the gas that had stuck to their perspiration.

In the midst of these attacks, the men had to continue to perform the back-breaking work of feeding 95-pound shells[6] into a howitzer that was too hot to touch. This was the exact time when their very survival required that they work the hardest and fire back at a marathon rate. There were no excuses. Even when the men were

---

1 *Memories of the World War*, p. 86.
2 *History of the 305th Field Artillery*, p. 79.
3 *The Battery Book*, p. 67.
4 *The Story of Battery B*, p. 33.
5 *The History of the 306th Field Artillery*, p. 27.
6 *The History of the 306th Field Artillery*, p. 75.

sick with fever, chills, and dysentery,[1,2] they could not slow the pace. If they let up, the Germans would send over twice the punishment. It was physically and emotionally torturous. It was an agonizing test of endurance that one could face only minute by minute, yet it went on hour after hour and then day after day.

At Camp Upton, many men had questioned why we would have to train for well over a year before going into battle. This was our answer. We each lived and breathed the training for our specific jobs, and every soldier in our unit knew his job so exceedingly well that at Chéry-Chartreuve, we were able to function as a mighty war machine even under what most people would consider unbearable and unlivable conditions. There was no longer any fumbling in our operations. No more learning. We had honed our craft, and now there was just acting and reacting.

The Germans were not the only ones inflicting misery upon us. The Spanish influenza, which, back in the spring, had made its first round globally with little serious impact, was now back for round two. This time, it hit with a vengeance, delivering the sudden onset of headache, backache, fatigue, sore throat, collapse, and even death.[3] Our survival at this position was our immediate priority. It was life or death. Accordingly, we lived in mud and dirt and filth, and lice became a problem. They were carriers of typhus, and some of the men suffered from the associated rash, fever, delirium, and depression. The filthy living conditions also proved life threatening to anyone with a moderate to serious injury. It was almost a given that a wound would immediately become infected. Gangrene spread within hours and caused many a poor soldier to needlessly lose an arm or leg that could have been saved in a germ-free hospital.[4] I doubt any one of us will ever in his lifetime have a worse memory than the hell of Chéry-Chartreuve.[5] The thrill of war we had all imagined and anticipated while at Camp Upton turned out not to be what one experiences in real war. At the front, in action, in the mud, uncomfortable or suffering, and perhaps both hungry and in the dark, there was no thrill in war.[6]

The fighting was bitter, and every unit of our regiment suffered casualties. In two weeks, the 306th suffered 158 casualties.[7] On August 20, 1918, Battery F had forty men badly gassed. Many were blinded.[8] Every day, hundreds of infantrymen were evacuated after being gassed.[9] Many of the men who were not gassed themselves suffered an agonizing sense of helplessness when they came to the aid of a gas victim. A more horrifying and pitiful sight one cannot imagine. Gas that enters the lungs causes chemical burns to the tissue, thus damaging the small air pockets and enlarging the lobes. The blood thickens, causing the heart to work overtime. The victim, whose skin and lips would be ashen in color, possibly with a bloody liquid foaming from his

---

1 *History of the 305th Field Artillery,* p. 111.
2 *The Autobiography of a Regiment,* p. 116.
3 *Personal Perspectives: World War I,* p. 185.
4 *Personal Perspectives: World War I,* p. 178.
5 *The History of the 306th Field Artillery,* p. 29.
6 *The History of the 306th Field Artillery,* p. 78.
7 *The History of the 306th Field Artillery,* p. 60.
8 *The History of the 306th Field Artillery,* p. 29.
9 *History of the 305th Field Artillery,* p. 112.

nose and mouth, would suffer from uncontrollable convulsive spasms, coughing and vomiting. His skin would blister from the chemical burns, and his eyes would water painfully and profusely as his vision failed.[1] At Chéry-Chartreuve, not only did I witness the effects of gas on others, but I was also afforded the opportunity to personally experience the suffering delivered by that retched creation.[2]

On August 22, 1918, a German barrage scored a direct hit on A Battery with multiple high-explosive and gas shells. In the mayhem, it seemed that the world was about to end. Two men were killed, three were wounded, and nineteen were gassed. Lieutenant Reid, who was in command of the unit and was one of the best and most respected and loved officers in the regiment, was killed. Of ten horses tied up in the woods, three were dead, hanging at their harnesses, and three were so mangled that they had to be shot. The men of that unit later recounted that they were so beaten down and demoralized that had someone told them, at that point, that the entire American army had been overpowered and had surrendered, they would have believed it, and if the Germans had surrounded them, they would have surrendered with indifference and willingly submitted to incarceration and even torture.[3]

The following day, August 23, 1918, while taking several horses to be watered, Lieutenant Reid's orderly, Private Mongeon, was killed by a shell burst, along with two of the horses. Everyone liked Mongeon for his modest ways and genial nature. He is buried close to where he fell.[4]

F Battery of the 304th Field Artillery Regiment suffered a direct hit to one of their gun emplacements. Three men were killed and others were seriously injured, but the odd thing was that their 8,000-pound howitzer was blown completely out of its pit and landed on its wheels at a 90-degree angle to its original position without a scratch.[5]

One of the old stone buildings in Chéry-Chartreuve was being used as a YMCA, where we could get chocolate, cigarettes, and the like. August 28, 1918, found a long line of men waiting outside, including some visitors from other units as well as men from the infantry. Call it good German shooting or bad Allied luck, but an enemy shell landed in the middle of the line, causing eighteen casualties,[6] myself among them.[7,8] Private Rosalia of the 305th was killed,[9] as was Private "Wally" Madden of B Battery, who was waiting to get some chocolate. Wally had been with us since our earliest days at Camp Upton. He was a great bookworm and could lose himself in literature even when the world sounded like it was going to explode all around him. All enjoyed his quaint, attractive personality. He is buried on the side of a sunny little hill. On his grave, we placed a wreath of flowers, which we had gathered from a deserted

---

1 *Personal Perspectives: World War I*, p. 183.
2 Yale biographies for Holland Duell, Class of 1902.
3 *The Battery Book*, p. 78.
4 *The Battery Book*, p. 82.
5 *The Autobiography of a Regiment*, p. 114.
6 *History of the 305th Field Artillery*, p. 120.
7 Yale biographies for Holland Duell, Class of 1902.
8 *The History of the 306th Field Artillery*, p. 59.
9 *History of the 305th Field Artillery*, p. 120.

garden, and we hung a crucifix on the wooden cross that marks his final resting place.[1] These guys were more than statistics. They were more than good soldiers. They were friends. It's hard to lose a friend. It's harder to lose a friend who has died in a ghastly fashion, and this was disagreeably becoming a daily occurrence.

A Dying Soldier
By Clarence Masters

A dying soldier crazed with pain
Sent up the piteous cry:
"Oh! Mother come; kiss me once more
Just once more before I die"

A Red Cross angel bent over his cot
As she was passing by
"Mother is here!" she said
And kissed his lip
And heaven forgave the lie.[2]

The Germans still ruled the air, but some small Allied planes were starting to show up. Every day, the question was asked: "Why don't we have more planes?"[3] The little silver German specks high in the sky circled above us daily amid the white puffs of anti-aircraft explosives sent up by our "archies." Some of the German planes were taking aerial surveillance photos to help reveal our camouflaged position, while others were visually directing German bombers and artillery to our positions.

On August 17, 1918, two days after our arrival, the distant popping of machine gun fire drew our eyes heavenward. From a small group of planes, two darted toward the earth at ever-increasing speed. The first plane crashed nose down into the trees. The second seemed for a moment to have a chance of gliding to a landing, but at the last minute, it went out of control and also crashed. Members of the 1st Battalion were near the crash site and were dismayed to find that both planes were ours. They buried the bodies of the two pilots by the side of a rippling brook, their graves marked only with two small wooden crosses.[4,5]

Our lack of planes gave us no recourse against the enemy's observation balloons. All we could do was look at them in the distance as the observers monitored our every move through high-power telescopes. Our own observation balloons were engaged in an ongoing game of cat and mouse with the German fighter planes, which were constantly trying to shoot them down. Cables secured the balloons to winches on the ground. When an incoming German plane was spotted, the winch man would crank as fast as he could to get the balloon down before the plane came into firing range.

---

1 *The Story of Battery B,* p. 43.
2 http://www.historylink.org/index.cfm?DisplayPage=output.cfm&file_id=8858. Reproduced by permission of HistoryLink.org.
3 *The History of the 306th Field Artillery,* p. 28.
4 *The Battery Book,* p. 70.
5 *The Story of Battery B,* p. 41.

Shortly after our arrival, on a day when we actually happened to have two planes flying lookout above our balloons, an enemy plane made a speeding approach. As our two planes engaged it in a dogfight, the German plane appeared to be hit and going into an erratic free fall to earth. It turned out to be a trick. The pilot suddenly maneuvered into a steep, controlled dive, plummeting like an arrow toward our balloon, which he sprayed with a blast from his machine gun. The observer parachuted out of the balloon just before it burst into flames and collapsed to the ground. As our planes sprinted after the offender, he made straight for another balloon, which he destroyed in like fashion. Then, with incredible skill and daring, he shot straight up and disappeared into the clouds and across the border.[1,2,3]

✴ *Observer parachuting to safety after balloon is shot down*

After two long weeks, which felt like years, of relentless hammering at the enemy, a perception gradually began to emerge that perhaps the German artillery and machine gun positions in the hills that protected Bazoches were weakening. At last, infantry assaults on the village were scheduled. Aside from being guarded by the howitzers that we were targeting in the hills beyond the village, Bazoches itself was heavily fortified with machine gun nests and German troops.

On August 27, 1918, the 306th Infantry launched powerful assaults on the village of Bazoches. The Germans launched a counteroffensive while, at the same time, their heavy artillery cut off our infantry's rear, preventing withdrawal and support from reinforcements. Only a very few survivors escaped to tell the tale,[4] and two entire platoons simply disappeared without a single word or clue as to their fate.[5] In sum, the assault was a disaster.

The following day, August 28, 1918, command of the 77th Division was transferred from Major General George B. Duncan, who had led us since our landing in France, to Major General Robert Alexander, who had been promoted from brigadier general when given this command.[6] He had served under General Pershing in Mexico as a major and then a lieutenant colonel. When the United States had decided to join this war effort, Colonel Alexander had been a staunch critic of the war theory being taught to our troops by officers brought over from France. The French believed that the best strategy was to dig in and conduct stationary trench warfare. Alexander believed that if there was one tactical principal that absolutely had to be embraced, it was that the only operations that can be decisive are those that are carried out in the open, not in trenches. He believed that much valuable time had been wasted on teaching stationary

1 *The Autobiography of a Regiment*, p. 117.
2 *The History of the 306th Field Artillery*, p. 28.
3 *The Battery Book*, p. 80.
4 *Memories of the World War*, p. 110.
5 *The Victorious 77th Division*, p. 17.
6 *History of the 77th Division*, p. 161.

battlefield tactics, and we knew that under his leadership, we would undoubtedly feel the constant pressure to advance, advance, advance.[1] General Alexander had a sterling reputation. His career, which he had begun as a foot soldier, had gained him the respect of every soldier who knew him. We all welcomed his leadership.

General Alexander believed that it had been a huge mistake to send our infantry in to take Bazoches while it was still fortified with multitudes of machine gun nests and protected by the surviving artillery coverage from the heights above.[2] In advance of any follow-up attempts to take the town, he ordered an all-out artillery assault against it.[3] He impressed all with a firm sense of drive, strength, and conviction. On August 28, 1918, in his General Order #20, he stated, "for every shell that he [the Germans] fires at us, the division commander will see that at least two go back to him."[4] From August 30 to September 4, 1918, our regiment delivered a bombardment that reduced the town of Bazoches to rubble at an expense of 3,000 shells. Observers reported, on impact of our shells, seeing figures that looked like tiny specks scrambling out of nearby buildings in a dash for other cover.[5,6]

On September 2, 1918, as the town was crumbling and a successful takeover by our infantry became imminent, observation posts reported seeing fires at many of the German positions and the villages of Paars, Perles, Vauxcere, and Blanzy to the north.[7] During that night and the following day, the fires increased in intensity, accompanied by mammoth explosions that sent huge fireballs and billowing columns of smoke high into the air. The Germans were preparing to fall back, and they were destroying all munitions and weapons that they could not transport in their hasty retreat. The munitions dumps went off like the Fourth of July. Dugouts, headquarters, and any other shelters that could accommodate the Allies were burned down or blown up. The skies were filled with smoke and the air with deafening explosions.

German planes were everywhere, harassing our positions to prevent us from firing on the retreating divisions. Allied planes had finally started to show up in some numbers, and we witnessed many dogfights. On occasion, the skies could come alive with ten or twelve planes, all darting in different directions in the most amazing dives, spirals, and somersaults as tracer bullets flew in every direction. Three enemy planes were brought down near our position that day, while the Germans scorecard listed two of our observation balloons destroyed. All the while, the rat-tat-tat of machine guns and the continual pop-pop-pop of anti-aircraft guns punctuated the symphony of war sounds that filled the day.

The following day, September 4, 1918, dawned peacefully absent of the enemy under clear, sunny skies.

✳ *Planes amid anti-aircraft fire*

1 *Memories of the World War*, p. 2.
2 *Memories of the World War*, p. 110.
3 *The History of the 306th Field Artillery*, p. 30.
4 *Memories of the World War*, p. 113.
5 *The Battery Book*, p. 84.
6 *History of the 77th Division*, p. 45.
7 *The History of the 306th Field Artillery*, p. 31.

French cavalry units passed by our position at a trot, following the retreating Germans. That night, orders were given to advance in pursuit of the enemy, and in a day's time, camouflage nets were taken down, guns were placed in marching order, wagons were packed, and we were on the move. The jubilation of the moment was hard to contain. For almost twenty days, we had endured and survived what, at times, each man had considered might be his final moments. In this first real battlefield test of our fighting skills, we had driven back a skilled and seasoned enemy, and while we could not foresee whether the conditions at our next position would be any more pleasant, we were at least now relieved to leave behind the hellish nightmares of Chéry-Chartreuve.[1,2,3] And so Americans and Allies alike advanced on numerous fronts.

✳ *American artillery unit advancing. A 155-millemeter Schneider howitzer is in the center of the photo.*

---

1 *The History of the 306th Field Artillery,* p. 31.
2 *The Story of Battery B,* p. 45.
3 *History of the 305th Field Artillery,* p. 122.

Part 5
Chéry-Chartreuve to Vauxcéré

(SEPTEMBER 4, – SEPTEMBER 24, 1918)

Across the Vesle River and Through Bazoches

(SEPTEMBER 4, 1918)

All of us felt the thrill of being in pursuit of a retreating enemy. As the artillery pieces rumbled and clanked over the ridge and down into the valley of the Vesle River, our 302nd engineers were hard at work constructing bridges. We would now cross the Vesle and travel to the very heights from which the Germans had pounded our position for so long! The infantry had already gone across on hastily constructed foot-bridges, but the heavy artillery would require something much more substantial. Our engineers enjoyed a period of peace and quiet while constructing the bridge, as the Germans were too busy falling back and establishing their new position to harass us.[1]

※ *Construction of temporary bridge across Vesle River*

---

1 *The History of the 306th Field Artillery: Compiled by the Men Who Participated in the Events Described* (New York: Knickerbocker Press, 1920), p. 31.

The trip down into the valley was treacherous, and the utmost skill was demanded of the drivers. It was raining, and the road was dangerously pitted with gaping shell holes. In the mud, the guns would at times break into a dangerous skid. At other times, the wheels would sink into the mud down to their hubs.[1,2]

When it was time to cross the river on the narrow plank bridge,[3,4] the horses were unhitched from the guns and led across by the drivers while the cannoneers manned the wheels and pushed the guns across.[5] The Germans, by this time, were settling in and, having just left this area, obviously had accurate registration of every potential target. Accordingly, they began sending over a steady bombardment of very accurate artillery fire. At first, we were puzzled that the almost perpetual shriek and whirr of incoming shells was accompanied by a noticeable scarcity of explosions. It wasn't long, however, before we realized that the mud, we had just been cursing, was softening the impact of the shells to such an extent that many of the detonators did not engage.[6] The shells that did detonate shot geysers of mud high into the air in concert with a million splintered metal projectiles.[7] It was a nervous crossing, and at one point, one of A Battery's guns broke through the bridge railing and was in danger of plunging into the river, but the men managed to get it safely across.[8]

A gun from B Battery that had yet to cross was stuck in the mud. As men and horses worked to free it, a shell exploded between the two lead horses, killing both and sending up a colossal shower of mud and shell fragments. The dazed unit, expecting to find the blown-off arms and legs of their comrades, was relieved to discover that they had somehow escaped any human casualties. Extra teams were rushed to the gun,[9] and as they crossed the bridge, we became the first American artillery unit to cross the Vesle River.

From this very spot, our infantry had charged across the open ground to take the village of Bazoches following our multi-day artillery barrage. Everywhere, the scenery gave insights to the battle. The river was filled with barbed wire designed to slow invaders. Across the river, Americans lay dead in skirmish formation, showing how the German machine guns had mowed them down in the middle of their charge. There were German bodies too, lying where they had died, a grim testament to the fierce hand-to-hand combat that had taken place.[10] It would have been suicide

---

1   *The Story of Battery B, 306th F.A.—77th Division*, by Roswell A. De La Mater (New York: Premier, 1919), p. 43.

2   *The Battery Book: A History of Battery "A" 306th F.A.*, by Francis L. Field and Guy H. Richards (New York: The De Vinne Press, 1921, p. 85.

3   *The Battery Book*, p. 85.

4   *The Story of Battery B*, p. 46.

5   *History of the 305th Field Artillery*, by Charles Wadsworth Camp (Garden City, NY: The Country Life Press, 1919), p. 124.

6   *History of the 305th Field Artillery*, p. 123.

7   *The Story of Battery B*, p. 46.

8   *The Battery Book*, p. 85.

9   *The Story of Battery B*, p. 46.

10 *"C" Battery Book: 306th F.A., 77th Div., 1917–1919*, by John Foster (Brooklyn, NY: Braunworth & Co., 1920), p. 42.

to try to recover any of the bodies during the fighting, so many of them had been lying there for days, blackened by the sun.[1,2] The smell of death made the air foul and difficult to breathe.

There was also the grim discovery of charred bodies. Although they were burnt beyond any means of identification, we believed that this solved the mystery of the disappearance of the two battalions from the 306th infantry during the failed assault on the town a little over a week earlier: They had fallen victim to German flamethrowers.[3] Burial details were formed, and in a short time, many bodies were placed in shallow little graves.[4]

The village of Bazoches lay immediately beyond the river, and as we marched through it, we saw firsthand the effectiveness of our fire. What must have seemed to the Germans an avalanche of shells had reduced the once pretty town to a heap of crumbled stones with only a few scattered broken walls managing to remain standing. The desolate place had been afire as the Germans fled, and little curls of smoke still rose from the ruins.[5] Huge heaps of abandoned ammunition lay along the tracks on the western edge of the town.[6] We later had the pleasure of returning many of those shells to the Germans.[7] On the hill behind the town had been innumerable machine gun nests. The entire surrounding landscape was pockmarked with shell holes from our fire. In one nest lay four dead Germans.[8]

Vauxcéré

(September 4 – 15, 1918)

After marching north for two and a half miles, we arrived at our next position on the outskirts of the small village of Vauxcéré.[9] All of the villages that the Germans had held just days before—Vauxcéré, Perles, Paars, Blanzy, and Fismes—were now being taken over by different units of our artillery and had just become the new targets for the Germans.[10]

The Germans, having abandoned these towns and their defensive position at the Vesle River, had retreated further north about five and a half miles[11] to heavily

---

1   *The History of the 306th Field Artillery*, p. 79.
2   *The Autobiography of a Regiment: A History of the 304th Field Artillery in the World War*, by James M. Howard (New York, 1920), p. 129.
3   *The Victorious 77th Division (New York's Own) in the Argonne Fight*, by Arthur McKeogh (New York: John H. Eggers Co., 1919), p. 17.
4   The *History of the 306th Field Artillery*, p. 31.
5   *The Story of Battery B*, p. 46.
6   *"C" Battery Book*, p. 42.
7   *The Story of Battery B*, p. 47.
8   *The Autobiography of a Regiment*, p. 129.
9   *The History of the 306th Field Artillery*, p. 48.
10   *The History of the 306th Field Artillery*, p. 32.
11   *History of the 77th Division: August 25th, 1917–November 11th, 1918* (New York: The 77th Division Association, 1919), p. 52.

fortified towns just across the Aisne River, utilizing that natural obstacle as a defensive barrier.[1] The river is about 150 feet wide and 10 feet deep and is bordered on both sides by meadows and fields.[2] Again the Germans were in an excellent position to observe anyone approaching the river and had the advantage of fighting a defensive battle from carefully prepared positions, while we were fighting offensive warfare in unfamiliar territory. We Americans were volunteers in a foreign land, and we would be formidably challenged to fight with the same determination and vigor as the Germans, who were being pushed back in the direction of their homes, families, wives, mothers, and children whose safety they both feared for and were responsible for.

We established our position on the south side of Vauxcéré.[3] Life there was not pleasant. Day after day, it rained, and when the rain occasionally let up, it was replaced by mist. Most of the men grumbled as we waded through a sea of mud and tried to stay warm through cold, wet nights.[4,5] The village, which is surrounded by miles of wheat fields with no trees or other natural cover, is situated on a hillside[6] that slopes steeply down to the Aisne River.[7] Just below the crest of the hilltop, on the side away from the Germans, were a number of caves, which we utilized for command posts and sleeping quarters, as they afforded excellent protection from enemy fire.[8]

The Germans were relentless and sent over their bombers in droves.[9] We would hear the Zzzz-Zzzz-Zzzz of an approaching engine. Suddenly, a brilliant flare of white light would burst overhead and gently float down toward the earth. Every man and horse stood in bold relief, the men with faces upturned, the horses with their ears alert and eyes staring wildly. Then, as the flare died out, the plane would swoop down and release a half dozen bombs. With a thunderous *bang-bang-bang-bang-bang-bang*, the bombs would explode in quick succession, scattering debris and bursts of deadly shrapnel. A hurried head count would immediately follow, and with luck, all would be accounted for. But luck was not always with us, and there were many casualties from these bombings.[10]

In front of us, our infantry was having a difficult and bloody time advancing toward the Aisne River because of the multitude of rear-guard German machine gun nests that had been left behind to halt our advance.

✳ *German machine gun nest*

---

1 *The History of the 306th Field Artillery*, p. 32.
2 *History of the 77th Division*, p. 54.
3 *The Autobiography of a Regiment*, p. 131.
4 *The Story of Battery B*, p. 47.
5 *History of the 305th Field Artillery*, p. 126.
6 *The Autobiography of a Regiment*, p. 131.
7 *"C" Battery Book*, p. 47.
8 *"The Autobiography of a Regiment*, p. 131.
9 *The History of the 306th Field Artillery*, p. 132.
10 *The Autobiography of a Regiment*, p. 134.

These were our targets, especially the village of La Petite Montagne, upon which we fired almost continuously, day and night, from September 5 to September 14.[1]

Slowly, our infantry made forward progress until it reached a point where the main German opposition across the river halted any further advance. The Germans had placed some of their best troops in front of us. Many were well-known Prussian

---

1 *The History of the 306th Field Artillery*, p. 50.

divisions. They had been in the game for a long time and knew something about fighting.[1] Our high command ordered a general attack along the whole front in order to advance the entire line up to the river. Early on the morning of September 14,[2] we commenced a rapid-fire rolling barrage that continued nonstop for 40 hours. The entire landscape rocked with the tumult of our howling howitzers all in concert. The air was in such turmoil that it was impossible to hear anything but the loudest shouts.[3] The guns became so hot that more than one gunner, leaning over his piece to adjust his sights, had his face scorched.[4]

Below us spread as pretty and dramatic a sight as modern warfare affords. There in the valley grew a magic garden of shell bursts in two parallel lines like the neat rows of some garden plot. As fast as the wind dissolved the cloud of a burst, a new burst grew in its place. Behind this protecting shield, the infantry crept forward, and as the garden sown by the shells extended toward them, the Germans withdrew and began yet another retreat from another major stronghold.[5]

The strain on the men was terrific. They worked day and night at an incredible pace, shoveling 95-pound shells into the breach while enduring the nervous strain of being under fire. Many men did not know how they could hold out any longer. "If I could just get some sleep!" was the remark heard at every battery.[6] Finally, on September 15, 1918, with the barrage over and the Germans in retreat, we were relieved from the position[7] by the Italian Garibaldi Division.[8] We fell back to the echelon, and while waiting for dark so that we could begin our march out of the area, we were delighted to receive bags of mail from home.[9]

Fismes

(SEPTEMBER 15, 1918)

Our journey to a new, undisclosed position would take us back across the Vesle River, but this time, instead of crossing at Bazoches, we would cross at the town of Fismes.[10] When night fell, our entire 306th Regiment[11] rumbled down the road for three miles under a brilliant moon.[12] As we took the horseshoe curve at the northern entrance to Fismes, the shell-torn town came into view, nestled in a little valley with one long,

---

1   *The Autobiography of a Regiment*, p. 136.
2   *The Autobiography of a Regiment*, p. 138.
3   *The History of the 306th Field Artillery*, p. 33.
4   *The Autobiography of a Regiment*, p. 138.
5   *The History of the 306th Field Artillery*, p. 33.
6   *The Autobiography of a Regiment*, p. 141.
7   *The Autobiography of a Regiment*, p. 143.
8   *The History of the 306th Field Artillery*, p. 33.
9   *"C" Battery Book*, p. 61.
10 *The Autobiography of a Regiment*, p. 145.
11 *"C" Battery Book*, p. 61.
12 *The History of the 306th Field Artillery*, p. 34.

narrow main street preceded by a narrower bridge spanning the Vesle River. Off to our left, we could hear guns booming away at our enemy, and the lights and rockets from the trenches caused flashes, similar to lightning, to streak across the sky.[1]

As we were preparing to exit the area, traveling south through the town, a steady stream of Italian infantry and French artillery were pouring in toward us from the opposite direction. Such a concentration of soldiers in one confined area with no means of rapid egress provides an ideal target for the enemy, and the situation made every one of us uneasy. Only two weeks earlier, members of the American 28th Division had been in a nearly identical situation in the neighboring village of Fismette. The Germans had boxed them in with an artillery barrage and then descended upon them with machine guns and flamethrowers. Only 30 of the 230 American soldiers escaped.[2]

I objected to taking this route through Fismes, but higher command stood by the order,[3] so we formed a column.[4] The moon had now set, and we were in pitch-black darkness.[5] Men and horses stood motionless to avoid detection as some planes flew overhead.[6] Then the order was given, and the column pushed forward across the little bridge into Fismes, all hoping for an uneventful transit.[7]

Having to squeeze through the streets past the French and Italians going in the opposite direction made progress painfully slow and frustrating. Over the narrow valley, the atmosphere hung heavy with nervous anxiety. As the opposing columns passed by each other closely enough that our wheels repeatedly scraped against theirs,[8] a tense silence prevailed, only occasionally broken by a command from one of the officers.[9] At that worst possible moment came the shrill whistle of incoming 77s. The German shell explosions illuminated the landscape, bursting first ahead of us, then behind us, and then all around us. They were high explosives with gas, and in no time, the valley had been transformed into a death trap filled with gas and flying shrapnel.

Visibility, already low because of the darkness of the night, was further diminished by the cumbersome gas masks we wore, and men groped to keep to the road and out of the stream of opposing traffic, which was moving at a terrific pace. The streets of Fismes reverberated with terrible explosions.[10] Walls of houses collapsed and tumbled into the streets.[11] The shrieking screams of incoming shells were accompanied by the splintering and crashing of branches as the shells plowed through trees before exploding on the ground in black clouds of deadly debris.

---

1 *"C" Battery Book*, p. 61.
2 "Schwerpunkt at Fismette, August 27, 1918," http://www.army.mil/article/44329.
3 *The History of the 306th Field Artillery*, p. 79.
4 *The History of the 306th Field Artillery*, p. 24.
5 *The Story of Battery B*, p. 49.
6 *The History of the 306th Field Artillery*, p. 34.
7 *"C" Battery Book*, p. 61.
8 *The History of the 306th Field Artillery*, p. 33.
9 *"C" Battery Book*, p. 61.
10 *The History of the 306th Field Artillery*, pp. 33–34.
11 *The Autobiography of a Regiment*, p. 145.

The bend in the road ahead of us at the far end of the town was taking direct hits, which had the effect of blocking our exit. The Germans can be very methodical, and I observed distinct intervals between shots. I told the men that I would time the intervals and rush them through between shell bursts. On my command, Sergeant Hark's team raced with his 8,000-pound gun and disappeared in the smoke of an incoming shell. I raced on horseback to the spot and determined that they had made it safely. Immediately on the heels of the next explosion, the call was made for Sergeant Sheehan's piece, which followed through the fumes of the powder. As fast as

❋ Location at Fismes

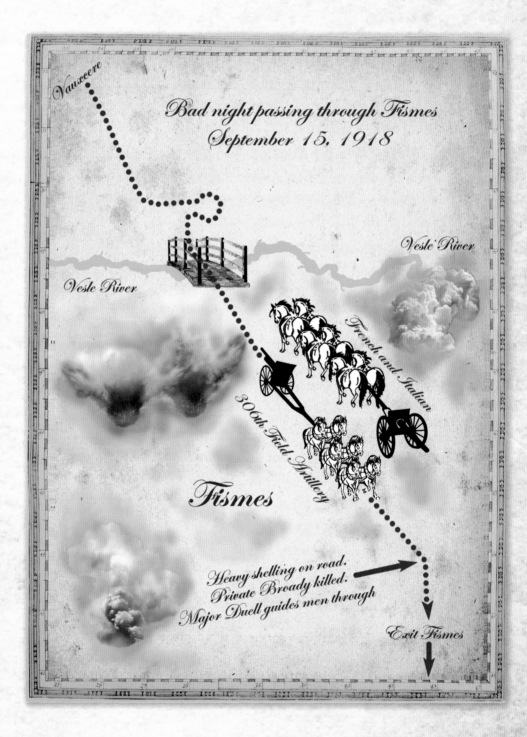

Bad night passing through Fismes
September 15, 1918

Vauxcere

Vesle River

Vesle River

French and Italian

306th Field Artillery

Fismes

Heavy shelling on road.
Private Broady killed.
Major Duell guides men through

Exit Fismes

was possible, I galloped up and down that road directing the guns and wagons and men until our unit had passed the bend.[1] My good horse was near exhaustion, and I myself struggled to continue against the uncomfortable and disabling effects of the continued gas exposure.[2]

Private Samuel Broady was mortally wounded on that corner. The last time we saw him, he was lying on the side of the road as a medic ran through the smoke to assist him. His loss was a tragedy, but everyone knew that it was nothing short of a miracle that we had escaped that valley with only one fatality that night.[3] Not until Fismes was several miles behind us did we slow our pace and realize just how quickly we had managed to scoot with those 8,000-pound guns.[4]

Nine-Day March
(September 15 – 24, 1918)

If our exit from Fismes was a sprint, ahead of us lay a marathon. For the next nine days straight, from September 15 to September 24, we marched south and then east. It is certain that not a single man who was on that march will ever forget it. It was a grueling test of the body, mind, and spirit. For nine to eleven hours per day, mostly at night, mostly in cold rain, always in mud,[5] we struggled up and over and down more hills than there are in the Rockies.[6] In nine days, we traveled 112 miles. It was the fastest trip for that distance ever made in any war by any artillery.[7]

There is a sense of nervousness when a long column maintains a brisk pace. In the darkness of night, with vision obscured by falling rain, drivers must be alert not to run into or slide into the wagon or gun ahead of them. On the muddy roads, such an event could easily lead to a ditched gun and the heartbreak of hours of backbreaking work trying to free it. Even without such delays caused by human error, the endless mud and rolling hills resulted in innumerable calls for "cannoneers to the wheels." At times, we felt that we were pushing the guns as well as the horses through the sea of mud. Such events, after marching for two to three hours at a time with only ten-minute breaks, were crushing.

Hiking in the rain at night is a battle between man and nature.[8] The already heavy 50-pound pack[9] and blanket sponge up the rainwater, which thus adds to the burden of the hiker. Every slogging footstep requires him to use his leg muscles to break the suction being applied to his foot and pull it from the mud, usually with the

---

1 *The History of the 306th Field Artillery*, p. 33.
2 Yale biographies for Holland Duell, Class of 1902.
3 *"C" Battery Book*, p. 63.
4 *The History of the 306th Field Artillery*, p. 33.
5 *The Story of Battery B*, p. 54.
6 *The History of the 306th Field Artillery*, p. 96.
7 *The Story of Battery B*, p. 54
8 *The Battery Book*, p. 98.
9 *The Autobiography of a Regiment*, p. 95.

✳ *Route of the Nine-Day March*

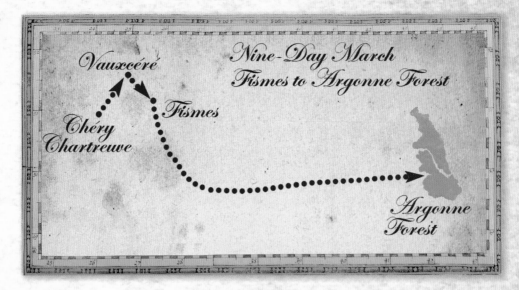

extra weight of a pound of clay clinging to his boot. Of course, his wet clothes weigh him down too. They also drain into his boots, causing water to squish from his socks with every step. The meals were not sufficient, and with hunger, the cold travels more easily into his bones. He shivers as he hikes, fighting off cramps and the overwhelming need to close his eyes for just one minute of sleep. His shoulders ache from the straps of his pack. At a halt, he sits in the mud and rests the bottom of the pack on the ground to relieve the strain on his back. Then the order "for'ard march" comes, and he drags himself upright again, praying for the first hints of daylight, which signal an end to the night's march. This ordeal continued step after step, night after night, until his mind began to numb and he marched in an almost hypnotic stupor.[1]

On September 24, 1918, we arrived on the outskirts of the Argonne Forest, bringing to an end a journey that had challenged every man on a personal level. What should perhaps be held as a very unpleasant memory was made a little sweeter as a consequence of our prideful triumph in the achievement and simply through the sheer relief of having had survived the experience. [2]

1   *The Battery Book*, p. 98.
2   *The Battery Book*, p. 98.

✳ *Route to the Argonne*

✻ The Hindenberg Line

Part 6
The Argonne Forest

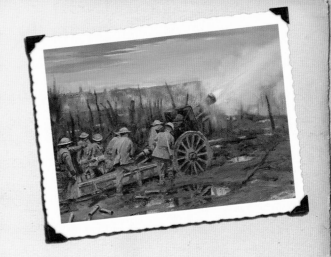

(SEPTEMBER 24 – OCTOBER 18, 1918

Opening Drive
(SEPTEMBER 24 – 26, 1918)

With the last few days of our march came rumors that the speed we were made to sustain was to ensure our arrival at a new front where our firepower would be needed in what would be the biggest "show" of the war. Talk of a huge collection of artillery units collectively aspiring to rock the Germans back on their heels floated about. There were stories of a huge offensive that would reach from "Switzerland to the sea." Indeed, we began to see miles and miles of marching troops, trains of motor transports, and an assortment of guns being pulled by horses and tractors, all moving in the same direction at a hurried pace.[1]

The plan was to confront the Germans who were now firmly entrenched in their most formidable line of defense, the Hindenburg line, which extended more than 300 miles.[2] General Pershing, in command of the American 1st Army and 138,000 French troops, 770,000 men in total, had committed to a front spanning a 71-mile section of the Hindenburg Line[3] and had assigned to Major General Alexander and our 77th Division the most heavily fortified portion of that section and the German defensive line: the Argonne Forest.

Construction of the Hindenburg line had been ordered by Field Marshal Paul von Hindenburg and General Erich Ludendorff when they took over command of the German war effort in August 1916.[4] It was designed and built to be so solidly

---

1 *The History of the 306th Field Artillery: Compiled by the Men Who Participated in the Events Described* (New York: Knickerbocker Press, 1920), p. 35.

2 http://en.wikipedia.org/wiki/hindenburg_line.

3 *The Story of Battery B, 306th F.A.—77th Division*, by Roswell A. De La Mater (New York: Premier, 1919), p. 55.

4 http://en.wikipedia.org/wiki/hindenburg_line.

entrenched and strongly fortified that, once it was completed, no Allied offensive would have a chance of penetrating it.

In the open, rolling farmlands on either side of the Argonne, the initial barrier the Allies would encounter consisted of large antitank ditches behind which were imposing barbed wire barriers. Next came a line of defense made up of forts and blockhouses heavily armed with machine guns. Behind these were an intricate system of zigzag trenches and, still farther back, two lines of artillery.[1] In places, the fortified line of defense was 15 miles deep and considered to be impenetrable.

In the Argonne, where the Germans took every advantage of the natural barriers of the forest, reinforcing them with constructed barriers, the defenses were even more deadly. The Argonne Forest is the largest expanse of woodland between the Mediterranean Sea and the Rhine River, stretching lengthwise a distance of 24 miles from the town of Sainte-Menehould on the south to Grandpré on the north.[2] The Hindenburg Line runs across the forest in an east-west direction beginning just above the southern edge of the forest, above La Harazée,[3] and continuing inward for a depth of about 4 miles to Binarville. Then begins the Kriemhilde-Stellung Line,[4] which is actually a series of heavily fortified barriers spanning an additional depth of 13 miles to the town of Champignuelles, just beyond the northern tip of the forest.[5,6]

Since completion of the Hindenburg Line in 1917, its perceived impregnability had been validated, as every attempted Allied assault on the line had failed.[7] Our immediate mission to break the Hindenburg Line, if achieved, would destroy the German offensive and put them into a purely defensive and withdrawing position. It would represent a monumental power shift that would deal a crushing blow to the spirit and morale of the German army.

Our ultimate objective was the German-held city of Sedan, 54 miles north of our upcoming position in the Argonne Forest and across the Hindenburg Line and the Kriemhilde-Stellung Line. The strategic importance of this position would be second to none on the Western Front. Sedan was a hub for a major railway system for the transportation of German soldiers and supplies and was vital to their war effort along the entire Western Front. Should the railway system be broken at that point, not only would the German war machine be broken, but their armies would have no transportation means for an escape and could be destroyed in France and Belgium.[8,9,10]

---

1   http://en.wikipedia.org/wiki/hindenburg_line.

2   *History of the 77th Division: August 25th, 1917–November 11th, 1918* (New York: The 77th Division As sociation, 1919), p. 59.

3   *History of the 77th Division*, p. 60.

4   *The History of the 306th Field Artillery*, p. 81.

5   *History of the 77th Division*, p. 95.

6   *The History of the 306th Field Artillery*, p. 82.

7   *The Battery Book: A History of Battery "A" 306th F.A.*, by Francis L. Field and Guy H. Richards (New York: The De Vinne Press, 1921), p. 101.

8   *History of the 77th Division*, p. 88.

9   *Memories of the World War*, by Robert Alexander (New York: Macmillan, 1931), p. 266.

10   *The Story of Battery B*, p. 55.

Our immediate objective en route to Sedan was to break through the Hindenburg Line and then the Kriemhilde-Stellung Line, which meant that we would have to advance through the entire length of the Argonne Forest and clear it of any German resistance, a drive of 14 miles from our point of entry at Sainte-Menehould, on a 5-mile-wide front.[1] The full responsibility for clearing the Argonne Forest had been assigned solely to our 77th Division. Should we succeed in this endeavor and prevail over what was accepted to be the most hostile and deadly portion of the German defensive lines, we would still be separated from our ultimate objective, the city of Sedan, by about a dozen German-held towns.

The assault on the Hindenburg Line would be a huge, coordinated Allied effort along the entire length of the line, but there was no question that, because of its strategic position, the most heavily fortified and fiercely defended section of that line lay within the forbidding confines of the Argonne Forest assigned to our 77th Division. It was also beyond question that the Germans would fight to the death to defend the Argonne because if it should fall, the Allied momentum toward Sedan, the most vulnerable part of the German underbelly, would become almost unstoppable, and the destruction of the German army would move ever nearer to being a reality. As the great French Marshal Ferdinand Foch stated, "The Allied Armies will strike at the door of Germany. To the American Army has been assigned the hinges of this mighty door [the Argonne Forest]; either you will push it open or you will tear it down."[2,3]

On the beautiful frosty night of September 24, 1918, our nine-day march ended with our arrival at the Argonne Forest. The 77th Division was to use the cover of the forest to advance our infantry and artillery northward to within striking range of the Germans. We entered the forest on its western side[4] after passing through the cobblestone streets[5] of Sainte-Menehould.[6] On our left, as we entered the forest, was nothing but dense blackness; on our right, we looked almost straight down into a steep ravine. At the bottom of the ravine, we could barely make out, at such a distance that they looked as if we were viewing them from an airplane, a small group of tents. Any misstep by the horses would certainly have meant death and loss of equipment.[7]

We hiked into the forest for hours and established the echelon. We then hiked another 6 miles and put our guns into position just north of the village of Florent.[8,9] The guns were covered with camouflage nets, the horses were picketed (bridled to a long rope strung between two trees), and the men got some much-needed sleep.

———

1 *History of the 77th Division*, pp. 7, 59.
2 *History of the 77th Division*, p. 7.
3 *The Battery Book*, pp. 101, 127.
4 *The History of the 306th Field Artillery*, p. 35.
5 *The Battery Book*, p. 97.
6 *The History of the 306th Field Artillery*, p. 35.
7 *The Story of Battery B*, p. 53.
8 *The History of the 306th Field Artillery*, p. 35.
9 *The Story of Battery B*, p. 53.

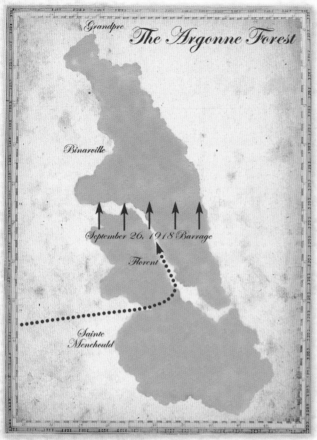

✳ *Position in the Argonne Forest*

The following day, the rest of the position was established. Ammunition was carried to the gun pits, telephone wires were run to all positions, and a host of other details were seen to. When we were in position, orders and details were given. A massive coalition of Allied artillery had assembled opposing the German front line, and in two nights' time, it would send the largest barrage of artillery ever delivered on an enemy in history.[1] Crowed into almost every available spot were approximately 3,500 pieces of artillery,[2,3] including the 200 guns under the command of our 77th Division.[4,5] On average, there was one gun for every 24 feet along the line.[6]

The attack was designed to come as a total surprise, as was the very existence of American troops in the area. Any indication of an American presence would undoubtedly cause the Germans to brace for attack, reinforce their positions, and send over preemptive strikes, so the utmost stealth and secrecy were observed. Any American reconnaissance forward was to be done in French uniforms. No English was to be spoken over the phone lines. The hope was for a massive opening barrage that would disable the German artillery before they would have the chance to take sight on our gun positions. The skies were now heavily populated with Allied planes, and time and time again, German squadrons would try to fly over to gather reconnaissance, only to be chased off by our planes.

We found our first real dugouts, which had been French defensive positions at the beginning of the war, before they had been overrun by the Germans. Some would hold 600 or 700 men and were well equipped with bunks, water, and electric lights. A single small hillside could swallow up an entire regiment and still yawn for more.

On the afternoon of September 25, we received our firing orders for the early hours of the following morning and feverishly completed the data calculations and arranged the shells and powder charges.[7] Although the towering trees in front of our guns were blocking our line of fire, they were left standing until the last moment, as they helped to conceal our gun positions from the enemy's view. The tree trunks had already been sawn most of the way through, and wedges had been hammered into

---

1 *The History of the 306th Field Artillery*, p. 36.
2 *The Story of Battery B*, p. 57.
3 *The Battery Book*, p. 103.
4 *The Battery Book*, p. 103.
5 *History of the 77th Division*, p. 61.
6 *The Story of Battery B*, p. 57.
7 *The History of the 306th Field Artillery*, p. 36.

the cuts. Soon after dark, the job was completed and the trees were felled.[1,2] For miles along the front, hundreds of giant beeches, which had effectively concealed the entire massive gathering of Allied guns in the Argonne, dropped to the ground. The entire forest echoed with the chorus of crackling, crunching trees followed by the heavy swish as they completed their fall. Each battery dropped about fifty trees,[3] and soon, as though a giant stage curtain had been removed, the path of fire was clear and the show was ready to begin.[4]

With moonrise, the bright blue sky gave way to silver streaks[5] of light from a full moon.[6] At 2:55 a.m. on September 26, 1918, our barrage began, and the entire sky lit up with the hellish red and orange illumination of a seemingly infinite number of muzzle blasts, accompanied by a continuous thunder of guns so great that it shook the ground and reverberated through every man's body, threatening to loosen joints and limbs.[7] So strongly did the concussions shake the earth that they threatened to collapse the walls of our dugouts and actually overturned many bunks and snuffed out candles that were inside.[8]

Bang goes a howitzer, and the hot barrel recoils smoothly up the cradle. The breech is opened on the way up and quickly washed with a wet cloth. The loading tray is placed on the runners. A shell—cleaned, greased, and fused—is immediately lifted onto the tray, which, with a hollow clank, is rammed into the bore. Up comes the powder bag, away goes the tray, slam goes the breech, in goes a primer, "Ready," calls the gunner, and the crew members stand clear and hold their ears. "Fire," calls the sergeant. *Bang* roars the howitzer, which leaps on its heavy wheels, vainly pushing its spade against the revetment. "Right two. Elevation 5-6-3," commands the sergeant, data book in hand, and the gunner manipulates his instruments and levels the bubbles. So it went, round after round, for three hours of the opening barrage. Then our infantry went "over the top," and we sent a barrage that preceded them at a rate of a 100-meter jump each five minutes. When the barrage reached a certain designated line, we shifted to zone fire, concentrating where enemy troops and material had collected farther to the rear.[9]

✳ *American artillery unit firing a 75-millimeter howitzer*

---

1 *The History of the 306th Field Artillery*, p. 50.
2 *The Autobiography of a Regiment: A History of the 304th Field Artillery in the World War*, by James M. Howard (New York, 1920), p. 160.
3 *History of the 77th Division*, p. 62.
4 *The Autobiography of a Regiment*, p. 164.
5 *The History of the 306th Field Artillery*, p. 36.
6 *The Story of Battery B*, p. 56.
7 *The History of the 306th Field Artillery*, p. 36.
8 *The Battery Book*, p. 102.
9 *The History of the 306th Field Artillery*, p. 50.

✴ *Canadian artillery unit firing a large howitzer*   ✴ *American artillery unit firing a 155-millimeter Schneider howitzer*

When we completed our fire, the eight guns of our 2nd Battalion alone had sent over approximately 2,000 high-explosive shells.[1,2,3] It was frightening to contemplate what life must have been like on the receiving end of the full complement of 3,500 Allied guns. By noon, it was reported that our infantry was advancing as the Germans retreated, and we were ordered to advance after sending over our part of a collective[4] 53,000 Allied shells.[5] We had succeeded in hammering the initial opening fracture in the Hindenburg Line.

Few names can conjure images as menacing and foreboding as that of the Argonne Forest, and rightly so. It is an old forest, dark, mountainous, and all but impassable. Ahead of us, the massive trees hid the sun from our view, and the light of day became dark. If mythical creatures such as ogres and trolls existed, this is where they would live. The entire forest blanketed an untamed landscape of hills and ravines and jagged cliffs and creeks and swamps. The base of the trees and the forest floor were obscured by snarled thickets of century-old underbrush. The impenetrability of that natural barrier would challenge the imagination of anyone who had not tried to forge a path through it. To forcefully attempt passage through the interwoven sharp sticks and thorny branches would be a futile endeavor, yielding little more than shredded clothing and bloodied skin. Averaging between 4 and 8 feet high, the undergrowth would be as hard to try to clamber over as it would be to crawl under.

Since the days of the Romans, armies have occupied and used the natural defenses of the Argonne in military operations as an obstacle against aggressors.[6] The Germans had done this in their turn. Except for this most southern portion of

1   *The Battery Book*, p. 103.
2   *The Story of Battery B*, p. 57.
3   *The History of the 306th Field Artillery*, p. 50.
4   *The History of the 306th Field Artillery*, p. 36.
5   *The History of the 306th Field Artillery*, p. 5.
6   *History of the 77th Division*, p. 144.

the Argonne, they had spent the last four years fortifying every inch of the forest. Every attempt by the Allies to penetrate it had failed. The Germans had positioned howitzers on the heights above so as to have artillery coverage over the entire forest. Narrow-gauge railway lines had been run throughout the forest to facilitate rapid transportation of artillery shells, munitions, and men, giving the Germans a huge advantage of being able to remain fully armed at all times.[1] Machine guns, one of their most effective killing weapons, had been positioned throughout the forest. Almost every road, path, trail, or avenue of passage through the forest was covered by numerous machine gun nests such that they would have intersecting paths of fire. Any Allies trying to approach and take out a machine gun nest would be in the crosshairs of several other machine gunners.

✳ *The Argonne Forest*

The strength of the established German defense system was superb. To further discourage any assaults, the Germans had deployed miles of rolled barbed wire as protective barriers. The barbed wire had gradually become hidden as the dense brush had grown in and around it, making it a deadly last-minute surprise for Allied infantrymen rushing a machine gun post—and making those flailing infantrymen sitting ducks for the machine gunners.

Throughout the forest were stockpiles of weapons and networks of dugouts housing soldiers to man those weapons. The Germans were prolific in their use of cement. They had built networks of reinforced trenches and saturated the forest with pillboxes; cement bunkers with rectangular slits on all sides through which the Germans could unleash their machine guns. Nothing about the German defensive position in the Argonne was temporary. The Germans had built it into a fortress that was designed to prevail for the long haul.[2] We would be entering this fight on their turf.

La Harazée
(SEPTEMBER 26–29, 1918)

As we started off and rumbled forward toward the next position, our 2nd Battalion became the first artillery of any caliber of any nationality to advance into this German-held section of the Argonne Forest. The French and American gun crews of the other organizations came out of their camouflaged positions to watch our heavy artillery lead the advance.[3] We began a short three-mile march over the ridge and down into the valley of the Biesme River toward our next position in the village of La Harazée.

---

1   *The Battery Book*, p. 101.
2   *The Battery Book*, p. 101.
3   *The History of the 306th Field Artillery*, p. 80.

❊ *American artillery advancing into the forest*

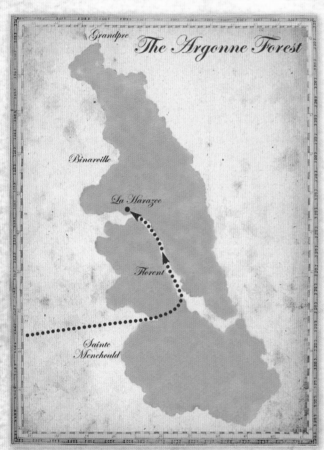

❊ *Position at La Harazée*

All along the roadside, we passed blown-up machine gun pits. Along the way, we stopped in the town of La Placardelle for mess and there saw German prisoners passing under guard to the rear.[1] After crossing the small Biesme River and arriving at La Harazée, we observed a dressing station that had been set up at the entrance to the town. It was pitiable to see how badly some of the poor fellows had been wounded.[2]

On September 27 and 28, 1918,[3] we remained in La Harazée and did minimal firing, as our infantry's advance was very fluid and their specific location often uncertain. Without specific, credible knowledge of their exact positions, firing upon nearby targets would be too risky. Life was exciting, though, as the Germans had good registration on our position and sent over a storm of very accurate fire. The first night, Lieutenant Klee and Private Valverde of C Battery narrowly escaped death as a shell burst directly behind them as they were seeking shelter in a shack causing their bodies to be silhouetted against the red flare of the burst. There was much mad scrambling that night in search of shelter from the flying shell fragments. The following day, I ordered the guns moved to a more sheltered spot farther up the hill where we found abandoned shelters built into the hillside with heavy reinforced steel roofs.[4]

❊ *La Harazée*

---

1   *"C" Battery Book: 306th F.A., 77th Div., 1917–1919*, by John Foster (Brooklyn, NY: Braunworth & Co., 1920), p. 66.

2   *The History of the 306th Field Artillery*, p. 36.

3   *The History of the 306th Field Artillery*, pp. 5, 36.

4   *"C" Battery Book*, pp. 66–68.

Pirate Gun

(SEPTEMBER 29 – 30, 1918)

By September 28, 1918, reports had come back that we had crossed the section of the Hindenburg Line assigned to us in the Argonne.[1,2] On September 29, we continued our advance, now toward the German-held town of Binarville and the forward edge of the Kriemhilde-Stellung Line, about three and a half miles to the north. The road leading in that direction through the forest had been rendered impassable by heavy shelling, so we traveled about a mile and a half to the west and then north along the western edge of the forest.[3]

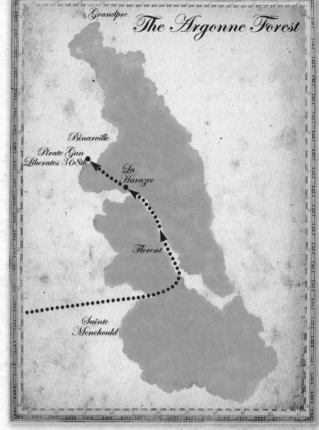

✳ *Position of Pirate Gun*

Our 77th Division was assigned to advance through the Argonne Forest. Far to our left, outside the forest, the advance was being conducted by the French Fourth Army. Filling the gap between our 77th and the French Fourth was the American 368th,[4] an all-black infantry regiment that had trained beside us back at Camp Upton as part of the all-black 92nd "Buffalo" Division, as they called themselves.[5] Having traveled north a little over a mile, we caught up to the 368th in their attempted advance.

They were in the company of one of their own machine gun battalions as well as the 2nd Battalion of our 302nd Engineers. Something had gone wrong in their advance, and they had allowed their flank (side) to become exposed[6] to a severe counterattack from the enemy.[7] For those who may not be versed in the mechanics of warfare, this can be the "kiss of death." In war, every effort is made to reduce the enemy's angle of attack to a frontal attack, which is the easiest to defend against. An enemy that can somehow get access to one or both flanks gains the upper hand, and mass casualties can be expected. This was the case on September 29, 1918. The 368th was pinned down and taking heavy casualties from swarms of German machine gunners who were fighting a desperate defensive battle and wanted nothing more than to see every one of our boys dead.

---

1 *The Victorious 77th Division (New York's Own) in the Argonne Fight*, by Arthur McKeogh (New York: John H. Eggers Co., 1919), p. 20.

2 *The History of the 306th Field Artillery*, p. 81.

3 *The History of the 306th Field Artillery*, pp. 51, 80.

4 http://.ranger95.com/divisions/92div_wwi_part1.html.

5 http://www.custermen.com/Itlaywwz/units/Division92.htm.

6 *The History of the 306th Field Artillery*, p. 81.

7 War Department, General Orders, No. 38, 1922.

Any failure of the 368th, at this point, to maintain the momentum of their advance could threaten the success of the entire Allied drive. If any unit was unable to establish continually advancing positions, neighboring advancing units would have their flanks exposed and could then themselves be cut off and surrounded by the Germans.

Our opening barrage three days earlier had rocked the Germans back. They were now scrambling to reestablish a strong, organized line of defense a little farther to the rear. They were wasting no time trying to get their artillery into position to fire on us again, and undoubtedly, their high command was rushing additional divisions to the area to reinforce the position. It was imperative that all Allied units maintain the momentum of the drive while the Germans were still off balance and deny them the opportunity to reorganize and launch counteroffensives against us. The 368th was ordered to keep up with the advance of the French Fourth Army to our left, and their failure to do so was now hampering the French advance, making it impossible for them to take their critical objective: the German-held town of Binarville. Something had to be done at once to ensure the success of the Allied drive.

Upon my immediate, urgent request, I received authorization to take one of our guns on an emergency support mission. While the rest of our battalion waited in reserve, I formed a small gun crew and dispatched Number 1 gun of D Battery[1] to a support position. The trip, which would have taken ten minutes on a sunny, peacetime day, took over two hours. It was raining, and the mud was knee deep. Major Green of the 302nd Engineers, to whose aid we were coming, later described the road as "one of the worst roads that ever crossed a torn and shredded No-Man's-Land." In our sense of urgency to come to the aid of our comrades, our frustration reached a peak when the gun slid into a water- and mud-filled shell hole, sinking to the axle. The men and horses that worked to free that Number 1 gun over the next hour did it by employing every ounce of brute muscle, will, and sheer determination that a soul and body might possess.

Despite impediments from the weather, the elements, and German machine guns, we finally summited the hill and threw our gun into action. There was no establishing of a position, no digging of a gun pit, no careful arrangement of ammunition. We had no phone lines and no command post. We were on our own, alone, our survival depending solely upon our own skills and speed. We were what is referred to as a "pirate gun."

Many of the machine guns that had been laying waste to the 368th now trained their sights on us. We did not deliberate about what targets to select. The machine guns that most severely threatened our mortality became our highest-priority targets. We struck first at those that were hitting us the hardest. Under a hail of fire and ricocheting bullets, we worked the firing data with the speed of a competitor in a trigonometry contest, slammed shells into the breech, and returned the punches with high explosives at a furious rate. The intensity was frightening. The volleys of bullets from different directions whirred and whizzed all about us, ending in muffled thuds as they splattered into the mud or high screeches as they glanced off our howitzer. Death under that rain

---

1 *The History of the 306th Field Artillery*, p. 81.

of bullets seemed inevitable, yet we knew that with every machine gun we disabled, the situation for the 368th would improve, as would the chances of our own survival.

Once again, we found ourselves in a slugfest; two sides letting loose with everything we had in a fight in which the winner would live and the loser would die. There was no strategy to this fight, no element of surprise, no trying to conceal a position behind a hill, no trying to hide our muzzle flash to avoid detection. Our gun stood alone on the top of a hill that had been ravaged by years of war.

At one time, there had been scattered trees about the area. On that day, there was not a tree in sight that had not been blown apart by years of artillery fire. All that stood was a scattering of trunks, shattered to half their original height, with ragged, splintered tops and no branches. In that barren landscape punctuated with water-filled shell holes and barbed wire entanglements, we stood in the open, a completely exposed target.

If ever there was a moment when all of the training from Camp Upton and Camp de Souge came together in triumph, when every man had mastered his job and completely devoted himself as an integral member of a team, a team that flowed with the skill and grace and efficiency of a precision fighting machine, this was it. As fast as the shells were fired, the observer was reporting back their proximity to the target, another man figured the corrections into the next set of firing data, another adjusted the gun sights, and again a shell was on its way. There was no taking cover from the machine gun fire. Every one of us knew that we could be killed at any moment. All we could do was stand toe to toe and utilize all our skills to take them out before they took us out. So we sent the shells over as fast as we could, one after another.

To hit a building or a large gathering of troops with a howitzer is routine. To hit a target as small as a machine gun nest is on par with a hitting needle in a haystack, but systematically we began to eliminate targets. The problem was the multitude of targets. Although the majority of the German machine guns were at first busy with the 368th Regiment, a completely unanticipated development overnight would change that. Under the cover of darkness, the 368th managed to slip out of their position, but rather than falling back to take a stand at our position, they fully retreated from the area, and dawn revealed that we were completely alone on the front line, now the sole target of the Germans. They were making an aggressive stand to block any further Allied advance toward the German-held town of Binarville two and a half miles to the north.[1] The intensity of their fire clearly signaled that they were backed against a wall and fighting for their lives.

The Germans may have felt the thrill of repelling the 368th into a retreat, but we were determined that we would maintain the pressure of our forward drive, so with our feet planted firmly, we continued the shoot-out with a now greater number of machine guns targeting us. The tempo increased when German artillery joined the chorus,[2] and an obvious call for air support resulted in a German plane swooping low over our position and dropping a bomb that landed in a colossal explosion exactly 30 feet from our position, yet we continued to live and, by some divine grace, without so much as one injury. Infantry troops from the French Fourth Army to our left soon moved into the area to fill the spot left vacant by the 368th. One by one, for a murderous two days and one night, we destroyed the machine gun nests and cleared a path along which the French would be able to advance and mount an assault against Binarville.[3]

At about this time, Major General Robert Alexander, who commanded our entire 77th Division, arrived at the outskirts of our position to take stock of the situation. His personal presence and need to assess developments underscored the critical importance of the situation. Accordingly, I dispatched a sergeant to the vantage point from which General Alexander was observing our fire, to confer on the status of events. The sergeant shortly returned with the general's praise of the entire gun battery for repulsing the enemy and resuscitating the floundering drive, as well as with his expressed intention to issue commendations for our gun crew.[4,5]

Shortly thereafter, behind our leading barrage, the French were able to advance and launch assaults against Binarville. The first two attempts failed, but on September 30, 1918, with the support of Number 1 gun of the 2nd Battalion, 306th Field Artillery, perched atop that barren hill, the French 11th Infantry succeeded in taking the town of Binarville and placing the opening crack in that portion of the Kriemhilde-Stellung Line through which, like water through a broken levee, Allied troops would soon pour.[6] Following the capture of Binarville, the grateful colonel of the French 11th Infantry verbally commended our Number 1 gun crew[7] and, later, made the recommendation that I be awarded the Croix de Guerre.[8]

---

1 *The History of the 306th Field Artillery*, p. 81.
2 War Department, General Orders, No. 38, 1922.
3 *The History of the 306th Field Artillery*, p. 81.
4 *The History of the 306th Field Artillery*, pp. 81, 83.
5 *Memories of the World War*, pp. 201–202.
6 *The History of the 306th Field Artillery*, pp. 81, 83.
7 *The History of the 306th Field Artillery*, p. 83.
8 Yale biographies for Holland Duell, Class of 1902.

✳ *"I was there." Number 1 gun, D Battery, the "pirate gun" in action. (Illustration from The History of the 306th Field Artillery, as recreated in oils by artist Greg Singley, © Chris Madsen.) Holland Duell was subsequently awarded numerous decorations for extraordinary heroism.*[1]

---

1   Among his many decorations, Holland Duell was awarded the Distinguished Service Cross with a citation directly from General Pershing "for distinguished and exceptional gallantry at Binarville." As stated in War Department General Orders, No. 38, 1922, "Although subjected to heavy machine-gun fire at short range and artillery fire he continued to direct the fire of his gun, and by his example of coolness and bravery encourage the gun detachment to remain at their gun, thereby assisting greatly in repulsing a severe counterattack of the enemy."

About 9:00 p.m. on the evening of September 30,[1] we resumed our advance, marching north toward Binarville. The night was so dark that it was almost impossible to see one's hand at arm's length.[2] It was cold and windy, and we were due for

---

1   *"C" Battery Book*, p. 69.
2   *The Story of Battery B*, p. 58.

a frost.[1] The road had been pulverized by relentless shelling from both sides. The guns, at times, sank to their wheel hubs in the mud. There were many calls for cannoneers to assist on the wheels of stuck guns and, shivering and chilled in the ankle-deep mud, to pull on the drag ropes. Several of the wagons carrying ammunition flipped over after sinking cock-eyed in the mud and had to be completely emptied before they could be righted.[2] Thus the men and the horses struggled forward.

When the order came to turn in for the night, we all tried to find shelter from the wind in the trenches at the side of the road, but we found them too full of barbed wire and water, so we rolled up on the roadside for the night. The unpleasantness of that night made it seem an eternity. After resting only a short time, one would become so numb that the only relief possible was dancing on one's toes to get the blood circulating. So deeply and painfully did the cold seep into the men's muscles and bones that the numbing ache, from which there was no escape, made one question how much the human mind and body could endure before failing and succumbing to death. No fires could be built so close to the front lines, and the night became a marathon of endurance as we waited for the warming sun to show its first light.

The landscape that was revealed, however, by that eagerly awaited dawn held nothing to lift our spirits. It was what is referred to as a "no-man's-land," the unclaimed span of territory between opposing artilleries where no man could survive; a barren wasteland of craters, shattered tree trunks, and barbed wire, uninviting and devoid of life, permeated by the smells of death. Such an environment infects its visitor's mood with an inescapable feeling of depression and despair. It carries the deep, bitter sadness of senseless loss and the foreboding that the end of the world is at hand. We all felt it as we packed up and marched on.[3]

✻ *No-Man's-Land*

Moreau Lager
(OCTOBER 1 – 10, 1918)

On October 1, 1918, we arrived at our next position, about a mile and a half south of the town of Binarville.[4] The spot was the German Moreau Lager (Camp Moreau), which only days ago had been abandoned by retreating soldiers of the German 9th Landwehr Division.[5] Located in the Moreau Valley,[6] the camp was designed to support infantrymen and weaponry on the front line a half-mile away through which we had

1   *"C" Battery Book*, p. 69.
2   *The Story of Battery B*, p. 58.
3   *"C" Battery Book*, p. 69.
4   *The History of the 306th Field Artillery*, p. 51.
5   http://www.washingtontimes.com/news/2008/may/26/white-markets-of-american-valor/?page=1.
6   http:///www.meuse-argonne.com/Randys%20Webpages/features_moreaulager.htm.

just crashed. The camp typically housed between 850 and 1,000 Germans who had just come from the front line, allowing them rest before rotating back to battle to replace those in need of a break.[1]

In this camp, we were introduced to one of the wonders of the war: the German dugouts. In the midst of the rolling wooded hills covered with thick under-growth, the only visible signs of a camp were a few small wooden shacks and some dugout entrances. A scattering of corrugated metal tubes tall enough to walk through marked the entrances to the dugouts, yet their nondescript presence gave no indication of the sprawl-ing expanse of the underground networks. An unaware observer could easily pass by the site, not realizing that he was anywhere near a massive military camp. In actu-ality, these few entrances led to an entire subterranean town of sleeping quarters, central mess establishments, a brigade headquarters, bathing and delousing facilities, and even a well to provide all the water needed. Rear exits existed in the event that artillery fire should col-lapse the front entrance. Generators provided electricity throughout, and many of the rooms were comfortably decorated with wallpaper, stained wood trim, solidly built furniture, beds with springs, built-in bookcases, and even open fireplaces to add to the charm.

Thus had the Germans been living before our ar-tillery barrage of September 26 and the ensuing infan-try advance drove them out.[2,3,4,5] The immediacy of the German retreat was evidenced not only by the unburied dead Germans outside the dugouts but also by the vol-ume of valuable items left behind inside. Tables in the command posts were still covered with classified maps and books and papers with field orders. It was as if the Germans had left everything to run for safety. There was much souvenir hunting. The men collected German helmets and rifles, most of which were eventually jet-tisoned to reduce weight under the strain of subsequent marches.[6]

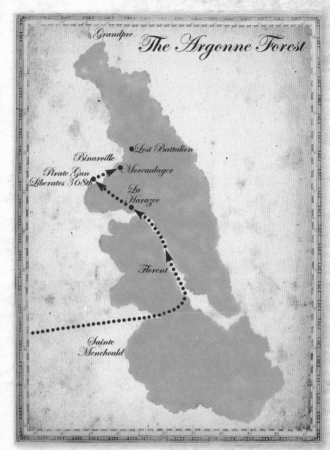

✸ *Position at Moreau Lager*

✸ *Moreau Lager (Photo courtesy of Rene Reuter, www.verdunbilder.de)*

1 http:///www.meuse-argonne.com/Randys%20Webpages/features_moreaulager.htm.
2 *The History of the 306th Field Artillery*, p. 37.
3 http://www.washingtontimes.com/news/2008/may/26/white-markets-of-american-valor/?page=1.
4 http:///www.meuse-argonne.com/Randys%20Webpages/features_moreaulager.htm.
5 *The Autobiography of a Regiment*, p. 18.
6 *The Battery Book*, p. 110.

We were to hold this position for several days and await orders. The infantry advance was rapid and fluid, and without confident knowledge of exact Allied positions, the upper command would not take the risk of assigning us nearby enemy targets, lest we shell our own soldiers instead. All of us were beyond exhaustion upon our arrival at Moreau Lager, and having just come from sleeping in wet, freezing, muddy conditions, we thought the comforts afforded here on a par with those of a luxurious resort.

As we waited, rumors, soon to be confirmed as facts, drifted in about what was to become one of the most publicized military dramas of this war. Our artillery barrage of September 26 and the aggressive ensuing infantry advance had been designed to be a lightning-fast, massively powerful punch that would cause the Germans to fall into a rolling retreat with no opportunity to regroup.[1] Maintaining the rapid charge and denying the Germans the opportunity to stop along the way and dig in were considered by General John J. Pershing, who commanded the U.S. forces, to be of critical importance. The significance of momentum was exemplified at the beginning of the war when the German charge toward Paris, which had at first looked certain to take the city in only 40 days, lost momentum and faltered. Once stalled, the drive was never able to regain forward trajectory. Instead, it deteriorated into a four-year standoff. Pershing warned General Alexander, who commanded the 77th Division, that he wanted no excuses and no slowdowns in the planned advance. Brisk forward progress was to be maintained "without regard of losses and without regard to the exposed conditions of the flanks."[2]

On October 2, 1918, as part of this advance and subject to this directive, Major Charles S. Whittlesey led 679 men, drawn from the 308th Infantry Regiment and the 306th Machine Gun Battalion, in an advance through the thickly wooded Argonne Forest.[3] The subsequent events would immortalize them as the "the Lost Battalion." Allied armies were lined up along a broad front with the same plan: a rapid coordinated advance to specific objectives, challenging the German defensive lines, and then holding those positions until all of the Allied forces had caught up with each other in the advanced positions, squeezing the Germans back in their defenses. The advance of Major Whittlesey and his men was very rapid. Protecting their right flank, the 77th's 153rd Brigade and the 28th Pennsylvanian Division met stiff resistance and were making no forward progress.[4]

To the left of Major Whittlesey's unit, the 368th Regiment not only had failed to keep up, but when we came to their aid on September 29, they turned tail and executed a completely unauthorized full retreat. Their conduct eventually led to five officers being court-martialed for cowardice, and four were sentenced to death.[5]

Whittlesey's 308th had made their advanced traveling up the Ravine de Argonne, a wide ravine with tall, steep embankments on both sides. Their assigned position was at the top of the ravine where it intersected the Ravine de Charlevaux,

---

1 *The History of the 306th Field Artillery*, p. 81.

2 http://www.americanheritage.com/content/lost-battalion?page=show.

3 *History of the 77th Division*, p. 206.

4 http://www.americanheritage.com/content/lost-battalion?page=show.

5 *Personal Perspectives: World War I*, edited by Timothy C. Dowling (Santa Barbara, CA: ABC-CLIO, 2006), p. 19.

another deep ravine, forming a "T." They fought their way to this position, losing about 90 men but capturing two German officers, 28 privates, and three machine guns. The plan was for the 368th on their left and the 153rd and 28th on their right to catch up and take possession of the heights above them, but neither of those units had managed to advance anywhere close to Major Whittlesey's unit. Realizing that this was not going to happen before dark and they would be on their own that night, Whittlesey and his men set up a defensive position in the shape of a large oval about 300 yards wide and 60 yards deep armed with machine guns and automatic rifles. This position later became known as "the pocket."

The Germans took advantage of the situation by calling in heavily armed troops who took up positions on the heights on all three sides above the Americans. Also during the night, the Germans silently blocked off the only escape route by laying rolls of barbed wire across the ravine downstream and fortifying the barrier with heavy machine gun coverage. By noon of the next day, Thursday, October 3, 1918, Major Whittlesey realized that they were completely surrounded by Germans.

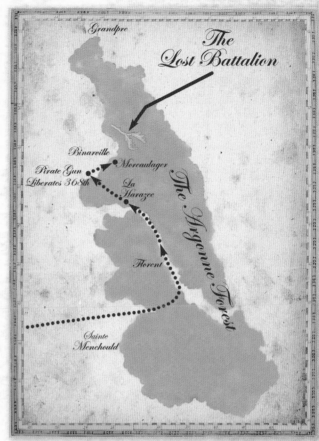

✳ *Position of the Lost Battalion*

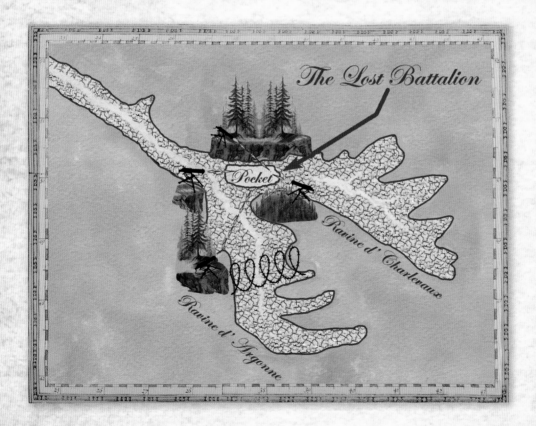

✳ *"The pocket," where the Lost Battalion was pinned down*

The trapped Americans released a carrier pigeon with an emergency call for help, which was received the same day by General Alexander. The rest of the day was carnage. From the dominating heights on three sides, the Germans were having a turkey shoot with rifles, machine guns, grenades, and trench mortars. All the Americans could do was try to claw out crude funk holes in the hard, rock-filled dirt and tend to wounds as fast as they were inflicted. At nightfall, Whittlesey released another carrier pigeon with the message that one third of his men had been killed or seriously wounded and all of his bandages and medical supplies had been used up. The 308th had brought only one day's food, which was now long since gone, and had not brought any blankets or overcoats. In the cold, damp weather, all were suffering from exposure and exhaustion as well as severe hunger.

In the dark, any noise or moan from the wounded would draw a burst of machine gun fire from the Germans. Captain George McMurtry cautioned one of the soldiers who had been shot through the stomach to try to be silent. "It pains like hell, Captain," the man said, "but I'll keep as quiet as I can." He died a half hour later without having uttered another sound.[1] By this time, the press around the world was sensationalizing the story, referring to the 308th, whose exact coordinates could not be ascertained, as "the Lost Battalion."

The next afternoon, Friday, October 4, 1918, the bloody assault by the Germans was interrupted when incoming artillery began hitting the German positions on the hills above. For some time, the fire was very effective, and it was the Germans' turn to bury their noses in the dirt. Then the fire slowly shifted, moving closer and closer until it finally landed directly on top of Whittlesey and his men.[2]

Battery E of the American 305th Field Artillery had been given orders to send over fire to harass the Germans and discourage more reinforcements from joining the attack on the 308th. Battery E had either been given the wrong coordinates or read them wrong because they were landing their 75-mm shells right on top of the 308th.[3,4] The cadence was fast; most who were there seemed to recall about twenty-five rounds per minute. The effect was both deafening and devastating. Dirt and rocks and shrubs and searing hot shrapnel flew through the air with each explosion. Many of Whittlesey's men were completely buried by dirt and sand upon shell impact and had to be dug out quickly before they suffocated in their unconscious state. Some men were killed instantly and disappeared from the face of this earth without so much as a helmet or piece of their uniform ever being found. Others died very unpleasant deaths after having flesh brutally ripped from their bones or limbs torn from their bodies.

The Germans, who must have thought Battery E's shelling a gift from the gods, sadistically joined in with volleys of grenades, trench mortars, and machine gun fire. Snipers cruelly cut down the men who tried to come to the aid of the wounded. It would be hard to envision anything that could surpass the horrific pain and suffering

---

1   The Lost Battalion, by Thomas Marvin Johnson, Fletcher Pratt, (Indianapolis, Bobbs-Merrill Co. 1938), p. 123

2   http://www.americanheritage.com/content/lost-battalion?page=show.

3   *Finding the Lost Battalion: Beyond the Rumors, Myths and Legends of America's Famous WWI Epic*, by Robert J. Laplander (Raleigh, NC: Lulu Press, 2006), p. 356.

4   *History of the 305th Field Artillery*, by Charles Wadsworth Camp (Garden City, NY: The Country Life Press, 1919), p. 135.

and the unconscionable brutality of that moment in the forest. It was obvious from the caliber of the shells and the direction of their origin that Whittlesey and his men were being shelled by American artillery. At 3:00 p.m., Major Whittlesey quickly wrote the following note:

> "We are along the road parallel 276.4.
> Our own artillery is dropping a barrage on us.
> For Heaven's sake, stop it.
> WHITTLESEY, MAJOR 308."

There were two carrier pigeons left. Whittlesey gave the note to Private Richards, but as he reached in the cage for a pigeon, a shell exploded nearby, startling them both, and one pigeon escaped. The devastated private could only say, "I'm sorry, sir" and immediately grab the last pigeon, a two-year-old black and gray bird named Cher Ami ("dear friend"). After attaching the note to the bird's leg, Richards threw him into the air, and with all eyes on him, Cher Ami flew two circles and landed in a nearby tree, too afraid to fly among the shell blasts. Richards threw sticks and yelled at the bird and was soon joined by several other men, whose united efforts failed to inspire the bird to flight. Finally, Richards climbed the tree, yelling at the bird the whole time. Not until he was able to shake the very branch on which Cher Ami was perched, did the bird fly off.

There followed a chorus of German rifles determined to shoot down what was obviously an emergency call for support. Just as it seemed that Cher Ami would make it to freedom, an artillery shell hit the ground, killing five American soldiers, and the percussion dropped the bird to the ground. But that stalwart little avian soldier quickly regained his composure and took to the skies, reaching his cage at the 308th regimental headquarters at 3:30 p.m. Corporal George Gault picked up the brave little bird, who was bleeding badly from the chest and missing an eye, and removed the message that was barely hanging onto the torn tendons of his shattered leg. The message was read, a few frantic phone calls were made, and by 4:00 p.m., the emergency intervention had stopped the shelling.[1]

With no more carrier pigeons and all attempts to send runners having ended with their capture or death, General Alexander had difficulty in establishing the precise coordinates of the 308th. Repeated Allied assaults in search and support of the 308th were turned back with heavy casualties caused by multitudes of skilled and well-concealed German machine gunners and snipers. Alexander knew that the 308th desperately needed food, medical supplies, and ammunition. Air drops of these were attempted, but the dense forest and deep ravine concealed the 308th well, and all the drops landed in German hands. Numerous small planes were sent out on flyover missions trying to establish the exact location of the 308th, and several were shot down. Day after day, the slaughter went on. Men died, and the wounded, soon infected with gangrene, became weaker and weaker. Bandages had to be removed from the dead to

1 *Finding the Lost Battalion*, pp. 348–358.

dress the wounds of the living. The nights were filled with the agonized moans of the wounded and dying.

Around noon on Sunday, October 6, 1918, the German General Wellmann, who had been orchestrating the assault on the Americans, received word that Allied forces were overpowering the Germans on the main front and that he was to pull back with all his troops in 36 hours. He had just received reinforcements of seasoned troops to finish off the Americans, but now his hand was being forced. He would have to deliver the death blow to the Americans within 36 hours. The Germans absolutely wanted all of the Americans dead before they fell back.[1] Meanwhile, American reconnaissance planes were finally able to spot the concentrations of heavily armed German troops massing on the heights above the ravine in preparation for their knockout blow. With precise enemy coordinates registered, an all-out artillery assault was ordered.

At 9:00 p.m. on October 6, 1918, we received from regimental headquarters Operations Order No. 23 as follows:

No.1 – With the purpose of relieving the battalion of the 308th infantry, which is at the present time cut off from the division, a special concentration will be fired by all guns of this regiment to cut the wire, destroy trenches and wipe out German troops occupying the trenches shown on the attached sketch and located to the S.E. of La Palette Pavilion. This fire will begin at 0 Hour, October 7th and continue until 4 Hour. During this period each battalion will fire 250 rounds, and the division of the trench and wire to be fired on by the battalion will be as per map attached hereto. From 4H to 6H the fire will be continued at the rate of 3 rounds per battery per minute (all B'N'S), and concentrated upon the southerly portion of the trench extending from approximately 4255 to 4456. At 6H this fire will cease.

No. 2 – The greatest possible care will be used in the preparation of the data for this fire, and coordinates will be taken from the 1-10000 Binarville map. Observers will be sent forward during the night so that from 4H on the fire may be controlled by direct observation.

No. 3 – To effect the destruction of the wire and personnel, and a partial leveling of the trench system, fuses will be used in the proportion of 75% I.A.L. and 25% S.R.

By order of Col. Winn,
E.E. Nelson, Capt., 306th F.A.,
Operations Officer[2]

---

1 *Finding the Lost Battalion*, p. 422.
2 *The Story of Battery B*, p. 61.

On the pitch-black[1] morning of Monday, October 7, at exactly 12:00 a.m., every gun in our regiment simultaneously fired their opening shots in a thunderous, booming chorus that continued until 6:00 a.m.[2,3] To say that we were ready for the mission would be an understatement. We had not been idle during our stay at Moreau Lager. We fired support missions as they were called in. But because of the rapid movement on the front, there was a scarcity of precise enemy coordinates, and we were easily able to keep up with the light demand for our support fire. Every minute we weren't firing, discussions and debates abounded about the most likely location of the 308th and potential positions of their assailants. We prepared firing operations for the multitude of possible scenarios. Data sheets were calculated in advance for scores of possible targets, and shells and charges were placed in neat, organized piles close to the guns.

In a military sense, we had grown up with the men of the 308th, as we had lived together and became soldiers together at Camp Upton. We had raised blisters side by side pulling stumps during construction of the camp. We had played sports together and enjoyed leaves to town on the same trains. We had overcome innumerable social boundaries to form many friendships, from drinking buddies and poker buddies to friends who performed in bands and camp plays together. On visitor Sundays, we got to know many of their families and sweethearts and, for some, children.

By the time the actual order came to us, physically and emotionally we were like a wound-up spring ready to explode upon the enemy. The release we felt from sending off that barrage was unlike any other we experienced during the war. Previous missions had been accompanied by feelings of nervousness and the fear of opening a hornet's nest, knowing that our opening shots were likely to invite a deadly counter-barrage upon ourselves. We felt no fear on this mission—none. It was more a feeling of "let us at them."

From the first pull of those lanyards, we sent the 155s over at a ferocious rate. We sent them over with emotion. We sent them over with a hate and a loathing for this brutal enemy who had imposed so much suffering upon this land and now threatened the lives of our fellow New Yorkers. For six long hours, we hammered the Germans' positions. The rate of fire rendered the guns dangerously hot. As the men rammed the 96-pound shells down the breeches of the guns at a rapid rate, their muscles hardened and cramped under the sweat of their labor.

With some limited airplane observation,[4] we first broke up large German infantry forces that were poised to attack from the south of the 308th. After a few hours, it appeared that those troops were regathering and joining other troops in what would be the main attack with grenades and the like from the north. As later described by the 77th Division Association: "In a miraculous way our shells leap-frogged the position of our own troops and fell on the crest to the north of them." The German troops that had amassed there caught the "barrage square in their faces, and their attack went to pieces."[5]

---

1 *The Story of Battery B*, p. 61.
2 *Finding the Lost Battalion*, p. 446.
3 *The History of the 306th Field Artillery*, p. 5.
4 *History of the 77th Division*, p. 205.
5 *History of the 77th Division*, p. 205.

An American infantry officer who was observing from his foxhole described it as a "beautiful barrage" that crashed into large numbers of the enemy massing for an infantry attack upon them.[1,2] For hours, the forest echoed with the heavy boom of our artillery and the moans of wounded Germans. Following our barrage, the Germans made some desperate attempts to keep the pressure on the 308th. For the first time, Germans descended into the ravine with flamethrowers. Of the men brutalized by these savage weapons, several died later from their painful burns,[3] but the men of the 308th fought back, and most of the operators of the flamethrowers were shot dead. A final long-shot attempt at victory came when the German Lieutenant Heinrich Prinz sent a captured American, Private Hollingshead, back to the pocket with a note stating the Germans considered it useless for the 308th to resist further and recommended that Whittlesey and the 308th surrender.[4] The recommendation was given no consideration by the 308th.

Shortly after 7:00 p.m. that evening, October 7, 1918, a unit from the 77th Division's 307th Infantry walked into the pocket without a shot being fired at them by the Germans. Unbeknownst to Whittlesey and the Lost Battalion, the Germans had silently pulled back and retreated shortly after sundown.[5] Their time had run out, and we had thwarted their last hope of a victory over the 308th. Now the Germans were under orders to fall back with the bitter frustration of not having been able to effect either the surrender or the annihilation of their opponent—an opponent that they

✳ *"Lost Battalion" survivors after being rescued (Whittlesey at bottom left)*

---

1 *History of the 77th Division*, p. 205.
2 *The Story of Battery B*, p. 62.
3 *Finding the Lost Battalion*, p. 429.
4 *Finding the Lost Battalion*, p. 473.
5 http://www.american heritage.com/articles/magazine/ah/1977/6/1977_6_86.shtml.

had fully boxed in on four sides and had outmanned and outgunned. The Americans, who had been determined to hold their ground "at all cost," had paid a huge price with blood, guts, and sheer New York stubbornness and determination, but they had held their ground in defiance of the German assault.

On the morning of Tuesday, October 8, 1918, the 252 survivors of the 679 who had entered the pocket walked out with their sick and wounded.[1,2]

The news of their liberation and the knowledge that our six-hour barrage had spared them[3] from what the Germans had planned to be a final death blow came as nothing less than an answer to our intense prayers and a source of jubilant relief to every one of us. It would be weeks before we would learn the horrific extent of the 308th's losses and gather the details of all the suffering they had endured, but for now, the knowledge that they had been freed energized us to electric levels and filled us with enthusiasm that a final death blow should be dealt, and it should be swift, but it should be dealt to the Germans, and we would be the ones to help deliver it.

On October 10, 1918, we bade farewell to the dugouts at Moreau Lager and headed north toward our next position. Our line of march took us through the woods to the left of the ravine where the Lost Battalion had been surrounded. Along the roadside lay entire groups of dead French soldiers, the obvious victims of machine gun bullets.[4] There had been no time to bury the dead in the wake of our rapid advance, and we saw lifeless bodies everywhere.[5]

✳ *Unburied casualties of war*

---

1 *History of the 77th Division*, p. 206.
2 *The Story of Battery B*, p. 62.
3 *The History of the 306th Field Artillery*, p. 55.
4 *"C" Battery Book*, p. 71.
5 *The Story of Battery B*, p. 62.

Grandpré and Saint-Juvin
(OCTOBER 10 – 18, 1918)

At long last, the German Kriemhilde-Stellung Line was at risk of falling. Ahead of us, on the Aire River, just beyond the northernmost fringes of the Argonne Forest, lay the two German-held towns of Grandpré and Saint-Juvin, the last two strongholds protecting that line. Grandpré was a small railway center that was much used in the movement of German troops and weaponry,[1] and both towns were well fortified and armed to the hilt. Previous Allied infantry attacks had repeatedly been turned back from the towns by machine guns, and many Americans had lost their lives trying to storm the positions.[2,3] The 77th Division was now planning an all-out assault on the two towns. Our artillery would give the infantry an infusion of muscle in the form of an opening barrage designed to decimate the German machine gun population and then be available for follow-up support as needed once their advance was under way. This would be some of the heaviest firing ever done by the battalion.[4]

After some time, we emerged from the western edge of the forest into open, rolling country and proceeded northward to our new position on the edge of the woods between the towns of Lançon to the south of us and Grandham to the north.[5]

At 6:30 a.m. on October 14, 1918, the attacks began, starting with our barrage on Saint-Juvin, which led to its bloody capture by that evening.[6] The following day, in a combined effort with the 3rd Battalion,[7] we hit Grandpré.[8] C Battery alone fired over 1,000 rounds in one 10-hour period.[9] Then the infantry went in. We had excellent observation, with posts situated about a mile in advance of our guns. As the infantry encountered machine gun resistance, reports were phoned back to us with exact coordinates, and we targeted the site until the resistance was silenced. It was a matter of one machine gun at a time and a matter of raw guts for the infantry.

After weeks in the forest, it was immensely gratifying to be out in the open and have the benefit of immediate and accurate feedback from the observation posts. From their vantage point, everything on the front line could be seen with perfect clarity.

By the evening of October 15, 1918,[10] we had achieved our objective of taking Grandpré. A main railroad line had been cut, huge stores of munitions had been captured, the Hindenburg Line was crushed, the Kriemhilde-Stellung Line was al-

---

1   *"C" Battery Book*, p. 77.
2   *The History of the 306th Field Artillery*, p. 81.
3   *"C" Battery Book*, p. 77.
4   *The History of the 306th Field Artillery*, p. 81.
5   *The History of the 306th Field Artillery*, p. 37.
6   *The History of the 306th Field Artillery*, p. 52.
7   *The History of the 306th Field Artillery*, p. 82.
8   *The History of the 306th Field Artillery*, p. 37.
9   *The History of the 306th Field Artillery*, p. 81.
10 *The History of the 306th Field Artillery*, p. 38.

most done for, and the mighty Argonne Forest was CLEARED OF THE ENEMY![1] The 77th Division had achieved what all others had failed to do,[2] a feat of which the French had said, "*Ce n'est pas possible*" ("It can't be done").[3] We had advanced to the front by smashing our way straight up the middle of the Argonne, the most heavily fortified, inhospitable stretch of territory on the Western Front.[4,5]

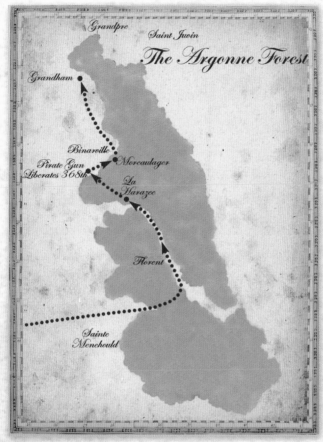

✳ *Position at Grandham*

1 *The History of the 306th Field Artillery*, p. 38.
2 *The Battery Book*, p. 110.
3 *History of the 77th Division*, p. 60.
4 *History of the 77th Division*, pp. 60, 144.
5 *Memories of the World War*, p. 156.

Part 7
The Final Drive and War's End

(OCTOBER 18 – NOVEMBER 11, 1918)

With the successful takeover of Grandpré came the immediate relief of the infantry units of our 77th Division, which were replaced by the 78th infantry.[1] It was a sobering sight as our infantry marched past our position, en route to a rest at the rear. After life-and-death struggles for nineteen straight days under exposure to night frost, mud, rain, and lack of food and sleep, they marched somberly, silently, and devoid of visible emotion. Their devastation was so plain a child could read it on their faces. There were no boastful stories of the front from these otherwise colorful, zealous New Yorkers, no marching songs, no eye contact. They looked neither left nor right but simply followed the man ahead in single file like a row of sheep.[2] Their silence spoke volumes about what they had endured.

We remained in this position for two days after their departure, providing scattered support fire as called for. It was not a pleasant two days, for the rains did not abate and the Germans did not wistfully relinquish the area to return to their fatherland. They mounted several strong counteroffensives,[3] in which we were targeted by their artillery fire. In a single barrage, the 1st Battalion lost their kitchen and had nine horses killed and several men wounded.[4] Luck alone spared us from losing any lives.

1   *The History of the 306th Field Artillery: Compiled by the Men Who Participated in the Events Described* (New York: Knickerbocker Press, 1920), p. 52.
2   *"C" Battery Book, 306th F.A., 77th Div., 1917–1919*, by John Foster (Brooklyn, NY: Braunworth & Co., 1920), p. 76.
3   *The Story of Battery B, 306th F.A.—77th Division*, by Roswell A. De La Mater (New York: Premier, 1919), p. 63.
4   *The Story of Battery B*, p. 64.

La Harazée   (OCTOBER 18 – 24, 1918)

Finally, on October 18, 1918, we were relieved by the 78th Division, 309th artillery and ordered into reserve in our prior position of La Harazée.[1,2] We were not as shell-shocked as the infantry, and with the joyous prospect of a rest away from the fighting lines, one could have viewed our fall back to La Harazée as a weird combination of mud wrestling and Roman chariot racing. We executed our moving orders with a vengeance. In civilian life, one takes clean clothes for granted, but for us, having worn and slept in the same wet, muddy, pest-infested uniforms for weeks, to the detriment of our irritated skin and noses, the mere thought of a clean, dry uniform and a shower energized every one of us to make the trek in record time.

As worn down as we were, our horses were more so. Large numbers of them were casualties of war, killed by artillery explosions or flying bullets. Many, under the strain of the task, had simply fallen dead of exhaustion in their harnesses. So depleted were they in numbers that we had to constantly shuffle them between guns when extra muscle was needed to summit inclines or tug through deep mud and shell holes. Yet we were determined to sleep in an actual rest camp that night, and by 9:30 p.m., we pulled into La Harazée.[3]

The only legitimate threat to our mortality here was that of aerial bombardment from planes, the probability of which was low. So for the first time in weeks, we slept through the night without the fear of being killed in our sleep. That one night of sound sleep probably equaled what we had had in the last ten nights on the fighting front. When we awoke, it was a new morning. We were recharged and, for the first time in weeks, relaxed.

The term "rest camp" may be something of a misnomer. "You have to do everything but fight camp" might have been a more fitting name. The days still started with reveille and morning roll call. We cleaned the guns, groomed the horses, and practiced drills. But it was heavenly. It was just the boys being boys and playing army, removed from the threat of being hurt. It took us back to the days of fun and frolic at Camp Upton, although we probably didn't realize there that we had been building pleasant lifelong memories. At

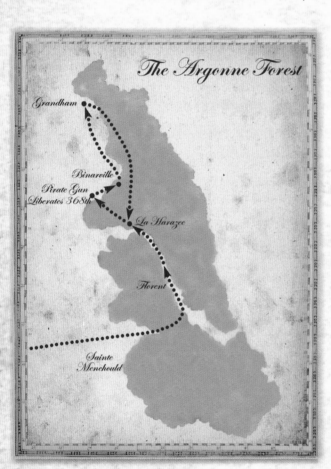

* *Route from Grandham to La Harazée*

1   *"C" Battery Book*, p. 77.

2   *The Battery Book: A History of Battery "A" 306th F.A.*, by Francis L. Field and Guy H. Richards (New York: The De Vinne Press, 1921), p. 121.

3   *The Battery Book*, p. 120.

La Harazée, we had three warm meals a day, consumed large quantities of nicotine, and had ample time to write letters home.[1]

In army style, the luxury of our long-awaited bath began with a stop at a delousing station in the shape of a bathtub.[2] Having lined up, discarded all of our clothes except for our shoes and identification tags, and passed through the delousing, we entered the shower tent. At the blast of a shrill whistle, ten naked, shivering men stepped under the trickling showers. "Five minutes to soap up," came the command, and at the expiration of that brief period, when we were all enveloped in a seething froth of soapsuds, a second order was yelled at us: "Three minutes to wash off." In the next tent, behind a table piled high with clothes, an orderly, after taking a flying glance at the naked soldier's proportions would throw him a clean uniform and, without giving the soldier time to check the size for proper fit, would bark out, "Move on" and "Hurry up, others behind you." But even if the fit wasn't quite right, what was more important was that we all had a hygienic, freshly washed feeling adorned with clean clothes, and that sensation was utterly delightful.[3]

✳ *Delousing station*

The officers were granted a three-days leave, and in the company of about a dozen other officers, I started off for Nice—via Paris, of course, for all destinations in France are routed through the hub of Paris.[4,5,6] A day's journey by truck and train put us in Paris, where I remained, parting company with the other officers, who traveled another day on the crowded Riviera Express to glorious Nice.[7] In Paris, I had a meeting with E.B. at the Ritz.

☙ I put down the diary and thought for a moment. Who was E.B.? I tend to be very detail oriented, and I appreciated the vivid detail of the diary—the scenes it painted in my mind, the emotions it allowed me to experience, and the answers it always provided to questions that arose during my reading. But "I had meeting with E.B. at the Ritz" seemed almost intentionally cryptic, and as I read ahead, the complete lack of any further reference to the statement left me with an irritating need and desire to know more. I made a note of it, as I had started keeping a follow-up list of things for further research, and continued reading. ☙

1 *The Battery Book*, p. 122.
2 *The Story of Battery B*, p. 65.
3 *The Battery Book*, p. 123.
4 *The Autobiography of a Regiment: A History of the 304th Field Artillery in the World War*, by James M. Howard (New York, 1920), p. 193.
5 *The History of the 306th Field Artillery*, p. 5.
6 *The History of the 306th Field Artillery*, p. 84.
7 *The History of the 306th Field Artillery*, p. 84.

"Rampant rumors swirled about during this time. It was hard to distinguish fact from fiction. It was amusing what confidence we placed in the enlightened individuals who carried word of new developments and what significance we attached to their pronouncements, especially if their reports aligned with our wishes. If one of them reported that the war would not end for two years, he was condemned as a "damned liar" who didn't know what he was talking about. But if a man knowingly claimed to have authentic information from another man who was told by a third man who had heard from somebody remotely connected with the general that the war would end within a week, then our elation reigned supreme, and our informer was held up as a model of integrity and the very personification of wisdom.[1]

We could not verify news that was coming in about the collapse of Bulgaria, Austria, and Turkey.[2,3] But the one thing that was a certainty now was that the German war machine was taking staggering blows from the Allies. There was no offense left in their fight, and their defense was looking more and more desperate every day. Battlefield developments were coming fast and furious, and no sooner had we commenced our leave than we received telegrams calling for our immediate return to the front.[4,5]

We rejoined the 306th Regiment in La Harazée, and early on the morning of October 24, 1918, we began a long, hurried march back to the front lines, this time toward the eastern side of the forest.[6] We took only what was absolutely necessary, for the horses were far too few and we needed to be prepared to advance quickly.[7] Ahead of us lay what remained of the formidable Kriemhilde-Stellung Line, the last vestige of the great German defensive system.[8] What we saw along the march told us, without a doubt, that we were to be part of a massive coordinated attack designed to knock the enemy to his knees and end this war once and for all. There were guns everywhere massing toward the front. The quantity of weaponry eclipsed even that of the massive coalition that had opened up the September 26 drive in the Argonne. There were great naval guns, the long 155-mm rifles, the enormous 9.2-inch howitzers that had to be hoisted onto and off their carriages by cranes, batteries of 120s and 90s, 155-mm howitzers like ours, an abundance of 75s manned by both French and American gunners,[9] and even a scattering of captured German guns.[10]

There was no mystery about this drive, as there had been in the Argonne offensive. There was no forest to cover us, and the troops, in double and even triple columns, were streaming along the great arteries of traffic in broad daylight. Division after division crowded in: marines, regular army, national army, and national guard. For the first time, vast squadrons of American planes soared overhead.[11] We camped

1   *The Battery Book*, p. 109.
2   *"C" Battery Book*, p. 78.
3   *The Story of Battery B*, p. 65.
4   *The History of the 306th Field Artillery*, p. 64.
5   *The Autobiography of a Regiment*, p. 195.
6   *"C" Battery Book*, p. 77.
7   *The History of the 306th Field Artillery*, p. 38.
8   *The Story of Battery B*, p. 65.
9   *The Autobiography of a Regiment*, p. 196.
10   *The History of the 306th Field Artillery*, p. 84.
11   *The Autobiography of a Regiment*, p. 196.

that night in pup tents in thick woods. There were incoming shells all night, but they were scattered and did no harm.[1]

Cornay and Champigneulle
(OCTOBER 25 – NOVEMBER 2, 1918)

With the morning came an early start, and by midday on October 25, 1918, we arrived at our position in the woods on the eastern edge of the Argonne Forest, west of the village of Cornay.[2,3]

It was a bright, sunny day,[4] and everywhere along the mile after mile of the Allied line, thousands of gun crews were preparing firing data for what was hoped would be a crushing blow to the Germans. There were many dogfights in the air, but our pilots managed time and again to penetrate the German lines and return with reconnaissance data, such as 800 German guns behind one hill or seven divisions behind another. All of this invaluable information was worked into the firing data so that when the attack began, every gun would be assigned specific and valuable targets.[5] That same reconnaissance also cautioned us that the Germans were amassing large numbers of troops with the evident determination to stop our advance at all costs.[6]

The battle plan for the 77th Division was issued. We would be responsible for a front twelve and a half miles wide.[7] At 3:30 a.m. on November 1, our artillery was to open up on the town of Champigneulle to the north. Our infantry was to "go over the top" at 5:30 a.m., and as soon as the town was taken, the artillery was to rush forward and take up new positions to support further aggressive and rapid advances.[8] The objective was to maintain a steamroller momentum that would push through every town to the north, driving the Germans back across the Meuse River and into the city of Sedan, where we would destroy the railroad, thus crushing the German war machine. This was to be

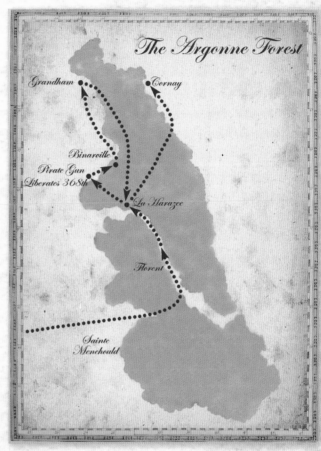

✳ *Route from La Harazée to Cornay*

---

1   *The History of the 306th Field Artillery*, p. 38.
2   *The History of the 306th Field Artillery*, pp. 5, 52.
3   *"C" Battery Book*, p. 77.
4   *"C" Battery Book*, p. 77.
5   *The History of the 306th Field Artillery*, p. 38.
6   *The Battery Book*, p. 127.
7   *The History of the 306th Field Artillery*, p. 82.
8   *The Autobiography of a Regiment*, p. 198.

the knockout punch, the death blow that we had vowed when liberating the 308th. It was the second half of what came to be referred to as the Meuse-Argonne Offensive.

The barrage opened right on time and eclipsed the opening Argonne barrage to become the largest, most destructive artillery barrage in the history of the planet.[1] The Germans had plenty of fight left in them, however, and were not going to roll up and blow away without resistance. They were under orders to hold at all costs,[2] and they fought so bitterly that our infantry was unable to take Champigneulle by dark as planned, and fighting continued through the night. The next morning, the infantry took the town,[3,4] and with its fall, so fell the last component of the mighty Kriemhilde-Stellung Line.

The Germans had turned tail to begin a full-fledged retreat to Sedan on the other side of the Meuse River, and we began a mad dash after them. This day marked our six-month anniversary since making landfall at Brest.[5]

We soon encountered streams of German prisoners being marched past us toward the rear—first hundreds, then thousands. The despair of defeat and exhaustion was written plainly on their faces. From them, we began to learn that they had been suspicious of some sort of possible offensive mission just before our opening barrage in the Argonne on September 26, but they never dreamed of the extent of the attack that was to be made upon them.[6] We also learned that throughout our entire drive, our artillery fire had been devastating to them.[7]

✳ *German prisoners by the thousands*

Seven towns, all major German strongholds, lay on the 23-mile road between us and Sedan, and we were determined to plow through them one by one. At times, it seemed that the entire American army was in competition for the same road space. There were columns of big guns, huge trucks piled high with ammunition, mess wagons, and medics, all trying to keep the hurried pace and, above all, not to get stuck and cause a miles-long roadblock. On occasion, when a truck would get bogged down in a muddy shell hole, chains, ropes, horses, and manpower would be applied in an endeavor to liberate it, but patience was short, and if the effort did not pay off in short order, a hundred men would combine their bodily force and simply roll the obstacle off the road into the ditch. The poor horses had given almost every last ounce of effort they had to give. They were literally falling in

1 *The History of the 306th Field Artillery*, p. 39.
2 *The History of the 306th Field Artillery*, p. 39.
3 *The Autobiography of a Regiment*, p. 201.
4 *The History of the 306th Field Artillery*, p. 5.
5 *The History of the 306th Field Artillery*, p. 84.
6 *History of the 77th Division: August 25th, 1917–November 11th, 1918* (New York: The 77th Division Association, 1919), p. 62.
7 *Memories of the World War*, by Robert Alexander (New York: Macmillan, 1931), p. 284.

✳ *Above and right, roadsides littered with abandoned howitzers, discarded equipment and dead horses (Courtesy Brett Butterworth Collection)*

✳ *Above, injured being evacuated to the rear while caravans of heavy equipment advance towards the front; left, muddy march past piles of abandoned equipment.*

their harnesses. When they did, the horses that had the energy to stand back up when unhitched were led off the road to the fields; those that could not stand were shot and dragged off the road.[1]

Thenorgues

(NOVEMBER 2 - 5, 1918)

By November 2, 1918, the 306th Field Artillery simply did not have enough horses left to pull all the guns and wagons, so the 1st Battalion was immobilized and remained behind in the town of Marcq. Of the battalion's original 180 horses, but 24 remained.[2] These were turned over to the 3rd Battalion.[3] By this time, our 2nd Battalion was

---

1 *The Autobiography of a Regiment*, pp. 202–203.
2 *The Story of Battery B*, p. 69.
3 *The History of the 306th Field Artillery*, p. 52.

Photograph Collection, New York Public Library, 114416

✳ *Town reduced to rubble*

left with only 100 horses,[1] so the following day, November 3, we combined all the horses from the two batteries, and Battery D assumed a reserve position in Verpel, while I proceeded forward with only Battery C under my command.[2] By now, the skies were filled with squadrons of Allied bombers.[3] On this day, we saw what we later learned were 182 American planes in formation. We watched as they dropped their bombs on and around the village of La Bezace[4] and then turned for home. The same day, we advanced to Thenorgues, having already passed through Marcq, Saint-Juvin, and Champigneulle.[5] These villages had been reduced to skeletons. Pounded by shells and gutted by fires, all that remained of the once beautiful old-world stone and wood towns were crumbling buildings or single, solitary walls surrounded by heaps and scatterings of mortar and broken rock.

Sommauthe

(NOVEMBER 5 – 9, 1918)

All along the roads were innumerable little wooden crosses with dog tags nailed to them, marking where our boys had been laid to rest. Far outnumbering them were hundreds of German graves marked by a stick shoved into the ground with a helmet hanging atop it.[6] On November 5, C Battery advanced farther north, passing through Buzancy before arriving at Sommauthe.[7]

In the fields on both sides of the road lay the unburied bodies of both Germans and Americans who had died in the previous days' fighting.[8] Many were blown to bits, presenting the indelible sights of scatterings of arms and legs. The fields were potholed with shell craters so evenly spaced, row after row, that they looked as if they had been laid out by a surveyor.[9] All along the way, we encountered huge piles of spent German artillery shells and ammunition that had never been used, so hurried and desperate had been the Germans' retreat.

Everywhere were items that the German troops had ditched to facilitate a speedier retreat. The road and fields were littered with helmets, rifles, packs, blankets,

1   *The History of the 306th Field Artillery*, p. 82.
2   *The History of the 306th Field Artillery*, p. 52.
3   *The Autobiography of a Regiment*, p. 196.
4   *Memories of the World War*, p. 280.
5   *"C" Battery Book*, p. 78.
6   *The Story of Battery B*, p. 70.
7   *The History of the 306th Field Artillery*, p. 52.
8   *The Autobiography of a Regiment*, p. 204.
9   *The Story of Battery B*, p. 70.

Photograph Collection, New York Public Library, 115873

✳ *306th Field Artillery passing through Buzancy*

✳ *Huge piles of spent German artillery shells*

shovels, overcoats, pistols, cartridge belts, reels of telephone wire, canned food, mess kits, and anything else that could be discarded to lighten the load.[1]

We camped among willows on very wet ground just below the town. It rained the entire time we were at this position, and we watched a steady stream of French refugees who had just been liberated after four years of virtual captivity behind German lines as they marched past us in the downpour toward the rear. It was a sad sight to see women the age of our grandmothers trudge by, bent over and straining to carry on their backs all that was left of their personal possessions; middle-aged people grown old and haggard from years of terror and hardship; sixteen-year-old girls who, by German soldiers, had unwillingly become mothers; and old men straining to push wheelbarrows holding their clothes and food and maybe an old clock or some pictures through the mud.

Yet despite their destitute state, many of these refugees dug into their possessions and, as a gesture of gratitude for our help, offered to share with us what meager amounts of food they possessed.[2,3] The generosity of these poor, beautiful people was both heartwarming and heartbreaking. It reinforced to all of us why we were in this fight, thousands of miles from our homes and loved ones.

✳ *War refugees*

---

1 *The Autobiography of a Regiment*, p. 204.

2 *The Autobiography of a Regiment*, p. 208.

3 *"C" Battery Book*, p. 81.

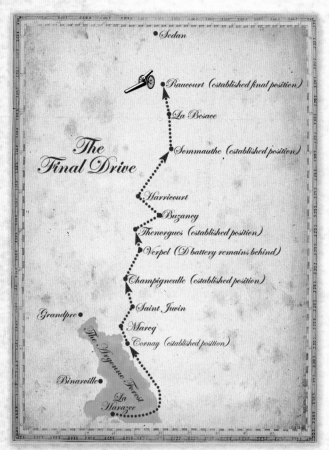

* *The Final Drivee*

Raucourt

(NOVEMBER 9 – 11, 1918)

On November 9, 1918, we advanced further north about eight miles to a position just south of the village of Raucourt. About five miles to the north of us[1] was the Meuse River. The Germans had retreated across the river and were now prepared to make a stand in the city that was our long-awaited target just on the other side of the river: Sedan. At last, it was in range of our fire, and from our elevated position, looking down across the valley and the river, we had a perfect view of the city. This is what we had crossed an ocean for, what we had traveled across France for. This was the reason we had clawed and scratched our bloody way through the entire length of the Argonne Forest and why we had mustered every last drop of our energy to make this final drive that had plowed through ten towns and 23 miles. Finally, we were in position to deal the death blow.

The Germans shelled the slopes all around us but to little effect. All our artillery units were under orders not to return fire so as not to reveal their exact positions[2] as preparations for the final thrust were made. By November 10, all our guns were in place, munitions had been readied, and reconnaissance teams had made it across the river and back with all the intelligence that was needed for the attack. We were just awaiting orders to fire. Then, on the morning of November 11, 1918, a beaming and breathless messenger brought Marshal Foch's message: "Hostilities will cease upon the whole front from the eleventh of November, eleven o'clock."[3] The Germans had had enough! On the eleventh hour of the eleventh day of the eleventh month, the war would be over.

For a moment, the news brought a stunned silence. We were all so full of adrenaline and so fully involved and consumed in readying our position to unleash the next assault that it took a moment for the monumental significance of those words to register clearly. Then, as if by spontaneous explosion, the entire battalion burst out in simultaneous cheers of joy.[4]

We had succeeded in our endeavor. It had been an epic journey. Having left our homes for Camp Upton, having crossed an ocean and then the country of France, we had fought our way to the Argonne Forest, which General Pershing had said "had been

1   *The Victorious 77th Division (New York's Own) in the Argonne Fight*, by Arthur McKeogh (New York: John H. Eggers Co., 1919), p. 29.

2   *The History of the 306th Field Artillery*, p. 82.

3   *The History of the 306th Field Artillery*, p. 87.

4   *The History of the 306th Field Artillery*, p. 39.

previously considered impregnable,"[1,2] and then our 77th Division had achieved what the French said would be impossible and what they had attempted unsuccessfully for over four years at a cost of 60,000 lives.[3,4,5] We had attacked head-on up the length of the forest, into a furious storm of machine guns, artillery, barbed wire and concrete, and the most hostile, impervious terrain imaginable. Through cold, wet weather and outnumbered, our one newly formed 77th Division, opposed by five veteran German divisions,[6] had fought inch by inch through 14 miles of forest,[7,8] capturing hundreds of German prisoners and machine guns[9] at a cost of 3,697 casualties[10] in what the papers are already referring to as "the Greatest Battle in American History." And our final drive had seen us pushing nine Germans divisions[11]

Photograph Collection, New York Public Library, 114399

✳ *Cheers at the announcement of the Armistice*

back another 23 miles,[12,13] through bitter fighting that had routed them out of ten towns in only ten days. In the process, we had liberated 10,000 French men, women, and children who had lived for four years under the Germans' daily rule.[14] We may have limped to the finish line, having had to leave many of our artillery units on the roadside, as our original complement of 1,200 burly horses[15] had been reduced to only 550[16] tenacious survivors. Many of the men had been able to survive only by supplementing their diets with cabbages and turnips foraged from fields[17,18] and drinking water from filthy shell holes,[19] but we had made it to the finish line nonetheless, and we were prepared to push on. We were ready to fight until the last man dropped. Now, on this last day of hostilities, nearer to the German front lines than any other American division,[20] we thankfully welcomed the fruit of our struggles. The largest war in the history of the planet, a war that had cost nine million lives, had just finished—right here, right now, at this very

1 *The Victorious 77th Division (New York's Own) in the Argonne Fight*, p. 1.
2 *Memories of the World War*, p. 170.
3 *The Victorious 77th Division (New York's Own) in the Argonne Fight*, p. 2.
4 *The Story of Battery B*, p. 55.
5 *Memories of the World War*, p. 156.
6 *History of the 77th Division*, p. 7.
7 *The Victorious 77th Division (New York's Own) in the Argonne Fight*, p. 1.
8 *History of the 77th Division*, p. 7.
9 *History of the 77th Division*, p. 82.
10 *The Victorious 77th Division (New York's Own) in the Argonne Fight*, p. 2.
11 *History of the 77th Division*, p. 7.
12 *The Victorious 77th Division (New York's Own) in the Argonne Fight*, p. 1.
13 *History of the 77th Division*, p. 7.
14 *The Victorious 77th Division (New York's Own) in the Argonne Fight*, p. 2.
15 *The History of the 306th Field Artillery*, p. 17.
16 *The History of the 306th Field Artillery*, p. 5.
17 *The History of the 306th Field Artillery*, p. 86.
18 *The Victorious 77th Division (New York's Own) in the Argonne Fight*, p. 28.
19 *The History of the 306th Field Artillery*, p. 39.
20 *History of the 77th Division*, p. 9.

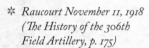
✳ *155-mm Schneider howitzer,
ready to fight*

moment, with the Germans raising their hands to us as they looked down the barrels of our loaded guns. The enormity of the moment was hard to absorb.

The surrounding landscape came alive faster than one would ever imagine news could travel. In the town of Raucourt below us, French citizens that we didn't even know were there emerged from buildings and poured out into the streets.[1] They had lived under German rule for four years. They had been lined up every morning by the unteroffizier and marched off to various occupations like serfs.[2] Watching the unfolding scene was like seeing a spring flower bloom open and full as life flowed back into the poor little battle-worn town. In no time at all, the streets were thronged with soldiers and citizens in what erupted into a spontaneous holiday atmosphere.[3,4] The French citizens laughed and cried hysterically as they embraced their liberators.[5] The French and American flags were hoisted, and a makeshift band played "The Star-

✳ *Raucourt November 11, 1918
(The History of the 306th
Field Artillery, p. 175)*

1 *The Autobiography of a Regiment*, p. 124.
2 *The Victorious 77th Division (New York's Own) in the Argonne Fight*, p. 29.
3 *The Autobiography of a Regiment*, p. 214.
4 *History of the 77th Division*, p. 95.
5 *The Victorious 77th Division (New York's Own) the Argonne Fight*, p. 29.

Spangled Banner" and "La Marseillaise."[1] To see those French men who, but a blink of the eye ago with all their worldly possessions upon their back, had impressed us as being the most pitiful, destitute, beaten-down souls in existence—to see them now infused with craziness and hilarity, running about madly, throwing their hats in the air and joyously shouting, "Fini la Guerre!"[2] and "Vivent les Americains!" and "Vive l'Amerique!" was a sight to behold. Fini la Guerre indeed! So it was true. The war was finally over.

Peace, a Different War, and Home

(NOVEMBER 11, 1918 – MAY 10, 1919)

During the peace negotiations, the French leader of the Allies, Marshal Foch, insisted that all conversations be conducted in French and not German, just as Otto von Bismarck had compelled the French to speak in German to discuss the terms of their surrender at the hands of Germany in 1870.[3] The final poetic justice came with the actual signing of the peace treaty, which took place in the Hall of Mirrors in the Palace of Versailles near Paris, where 48 years before, the German Empire had been proclaimed following the Prussian victory over France.[4]

The long process of packing up our army—returning weapons, congregating troops, and arranging transport ships—took much longer than any would have wished or imagined. The frustrating five-month wait in France was punctuated by a much celebrated ten-day leave in mid-December. For the most part, the enlisted men went to Aix-les-Bains[5] and the officers, including myself, went to Nice,[6] on the southern coast of France near the border with Italy.

✳ *Signing of the treaty in the Hall of Mirrors (National Archives and Records Administration 531150)*

Just minutes up the coast from Nice, in the principality of Monaco, is the city of Monte Carlo with its famous Grand Casino. And just minutes south, in a beautiful little bay where palm trees line the beach, is the yachting center of Cannes. This became our playground and little slice of heaven for ten days of leave.[7] I departed Nice two days ahead of the others to allow for a brief meeting with E.B. in Paris.

1 *The Autobiography of a Regiment*, p. 214.
2 *The History of the 306th Field Artillery*, p. 82.
3 http://www.mainlesson.com/display.php?author=usher&book=war&story=breaking.
4 *World War I (DK Eyewitness Books)*, by Simon Adams (New York: DK Publishing, 2001), p. 61.
5 *The History of the 306th Field Artillery*, p. 5.
6 *The History of the 306th Field Artillery*, p. 103.
7 *The History of the 306th Field Artillery*, p. 103.

For the second time in the diary, Holland Duell had made a glancing reference to "E.B." Later, I looked at personnel records, searching for any officer who might have those initials, but I had no success.

Before the transport ships arrived, before we could make the journey to our homes and our families, we were unexpectedly at war again, facing massive casualties on a grand scale. This time we faced an international enemy with no concern for borders or nationalities, an enemy against whom our weapons were useless. The Spanish flu had become a worldwide pandemic. It had gone around the world in the spring of 1918 with minimal effect. We felt the second powerful wave in August 1918 while at Chéry-Chartreuve. Now, in February 1919,[1] it was back for round three.

The Spanish flu was unlike any other flu in that it didn't target the young and the elderly. It wanted healthy young adults 20 to 40 years old. It wanted us, and we made all the better targets because of our close living quarters and perhaps because we were weakened from the stress of combat and from chemical attacks. For every ten people who were infected, one to two would die. It was estimated that a third of the world population was infected, meaning that about 50 million to 100 million people would die. The flu pandemic was being deemed "the greatest medical holocaust in history."[2]

Before the November 11, 1918, armistice, 58,000 Americans had died in battle in this war. This flu, it was estimated, would kill an additional 63,000 of my countrymen. Many men who had survived battle, while their families waited anxiously at home, were now being notified that it was some of those family members who had been destined to die as a consequence of this unforeseen enemy before they could be reunited. When Private William C. Schneider of the 305th Field Artillery, 77th Division, whom we all knew from Camp Upton, received a letter informing him that his young, vibrant girlfriend back home had died from the flu, he became just one of many examples of that painful irony.[3]

We were hit especially hard in early 1919, and many graves were dug in January and February. At times, the troops slept outside to minimize the spread, and when we slept inside, we all wore cloth masks over our mouths and noses.[4] Apparently, mine didn't do the job because I joined the ranks of the flu victims.[5] Give me a shrapnel wound any day. It was a bad flu—so bad that many cases were misdiagnosed as cholera or typhoid fever. The virus caused hemorrhaging, and it was common to see victims bleeding from the nose and ears and often with tiny hemorrhages on the surface of the skin. It was as a direct result of the bleeding and edema in the lungs, as well as secondary bacterial pneumonia, that so many people died.[6]

---

1 *Personal Perspectives: World War I*, edited by Timothy C. Dowling (Santa Barbara, CA: ABC-CLIO, 2006), p. 185.

2 http://en.wikipedia.org/wiki/The_Army_Goes_Rolling_Along.

3 http://www.worldwar1.com/dbc/schneider_ws.htm.

4 http://www.worldwar1.com/dbc/schneider_ws.htm.

5 *The History of the 306th Field Artillery*, p. 111.

6 http://en.wikipedia.org/wiki/The_Army_Goes_Rolling_Along.

The flu was not the ticket home that I would have bought of my own accord, but it did effect my evacuation back to a New York hospital.[1] The rest of the 77th Division finally boarded the Agamemnon, formerly the German Kaiser Wilhelm II, and sailed out of Brest, France, homeward bound, on April 21, 1919.[2] Thankfully, I did not become one of the 600,000 American fatalities of the flu, and having recovered before their landfall, I met my unit and the other men of the 77th on April 29, 1919, when, their ship pulled alongside the docks at Hoboken.[3] It was a warm reunion that culminated in a trip back to Camp Upton.

What a different world our old military home was this time around! What at the time had felt to us like a harsh, overbearing environment at Camp Upton now felt like a country club. It was good to see the old wooden buildings, good to dine in the old mess halls, good to take showers with hot water at leisure and not by the numbers.[4] It was a happy time, and the days passed quickly until, on May 6, the entire 77th Division assembled for the great parade of "New York's Own."

The day was clear and cool. Preceding the main parade by a half hour was a large banner with 2,356 gold stars, each representing one of the heroic dead of the 77th.[5] Then, promptly at 10:00 a.m., Major General Robert Alexander,[6] mounted on Captain,[7] a beautiful black horse, ordered the column forward and, followed by his staff, rode through Washington Arch and started up Fifth Avenue. The procession grew larger at each intersection as companies and battalions that were waiting on those side streets fell into formation at the rear of the parade until soon the street was filled from curb to curb with regiment after regiment. Every soldier carried his rifle with glittering bayonet fixed; everyone carried a light pack; everyone's arm displayed service stripes; everyone's helmet was fastened to the left shoulder; everyone's shoes were shined and clapped in unison on the hard black pavement[8] as 22,000 soldiers marched past millions of cheering, flag-waving New Yorkers.[9]

With the regimental band playing loud and lively, we proceeded five miles past flag-draped buildings, under the Arch of Jewels at Madison Square, and past crowded grandstands that extended the full length of Central Park to 110th Street. Here, General Alexander had pulled off to the side of the procession and proudly saluted each unit as it passed by.[10] So many times on the battlefields of France, we had optimistically and wishfully boasted,

✻ *Troops marching past New York Library (National Archives and Records Administration 533511)*

---

1 *The History of the 306th Field Artillery*, p. 111.
2 *The History of the 306th Field Artillery*, pp. 6, 111.
3 *The History of the 306th Field Artillery*, pp. 6, 111.
4 *The History of the 306th Field Artillery*, p. 112.
5 *The Story of Battery* B, p. 83.
6 *The Autobiography of a Regiment*, p. 244.
7 *The Story of Battery B*, p. 83.
8 *The Battery Book*, p. 162.
9 *The Story of Battery B*, p. 83.
10 *The Battery Book*, p. 164.

* *Troops passing through Washington Arch (Library of Congress LC-USZ62-64473)*

"When we go marching up Fifth Avenue …," and now that we were here, the moment lived up to every man's expectations.[1]

The 77th had been the first national army division to reach Europe, the first to be made responsible for a sector of the front, and the first to be ordered to an active part of the line.[2] No other division was on the front line during the start and the finish of the Meuse-Argonne offensive.[3] During the entire advance, we never gave back one foot of ground we had gained,[4] and no other division was closer to the German territory on the last day of the war.[5] On this day in May, New York certainly acknowledged our achievements and contributions in glorious fashion. It was an inspiring finish to a war that, for every soldier present, had been a life-changing experience.

On Saturday morning, May 10, 1919, we said goodbye to Camp Upton and military life forever. We marched to the quartermaster's office in a downpour of rain, turned in our blankets, received our transportation tickets, and marched to the Camp Upton terminal. As we passed through the gate, we were given our discharge sheets. Then we boarded the waiting train that was to carry us back to civilian life.[6,7]

Someday, years from now, when this has all become a fading, dreamlike memory—perhaps beside a fireplace on a rainy night, in the warmth of our homes—a faint voice from years long since past will whisper, "Take these coordinates," and the imagination will once again see the dim light from a single flickering candle, the wax running down upon a map scribbled with battle notations and targets and quaint old names almost forgotten. Perhaps we will once again hear the buzz of the voices figuring the firing data and then the tense stillness followed by the deep roar of the opening salvo. Oddly, mixed in with the hellish memories of war are heartfelt memories of personal bonds, achievements, and shared sacrifice. We had been woven together into a fabric that had provided a certain warmth and security and immense familiarity in a strange land full of difficult experiences. Now we were going our separate ways to rejoin our families. Although it was a family of a different type that we were leaving behind upon our departure from Camp Upton, the feeling that it was indeed a family was undeniable.

1   *The History of the 306th Field Artillery*, p. 112.
2   *History of the 77th Division*, p. 7.
3   *The Victorious 77th Division (New York's Own) in the Argonne Fight*, p. 2.
4   *The Story of Battery B*, p. 86.
5   *History of the 77th Division*, p. 9.
6   *The Battery Book*, p. 168.
7   *The Autobiography of a Regiment*, p. 247.

✳ *"Memories" (The History of the 306th Field Artillery, p. 71)*

Like a gigantic thunderstorm, the Great War had forcibly descended upon every one of us. We had played the role of slaves in the army, doing whatever we were told without question, for that is what makes a strong army. We had to come to terms with the reality that our lives could be cut short on the battlefield and that we might never return home. But of those who were lucky enough to survive and were about to return to civilian life, every single man, without question, now had a grateful appreciation and solid understanding of just how fleeting and precious life should be considered to be. We would never again take one minute on this earth for granted or lack the courage to pursue our dreams before time ran out.

The war had afforded us much time to question our priorities and to ponder which pursuits were the most individually enriching. We had all had promised ourselves rewards, should we survive this war. I had promised myself that if I returned home, I would enjoy more time on the water. That has always been my sanctuary, the place where I find peace as well as adrenaline-driven excitement. Whatever our individual dreams and plans, we all departed Camp Upton with the mindset that it was time to enjoy life once again and to live it to its fullest.

Hotel Majestic

Having finished reading Holland Duell's war journal, I gently set it down on the table, feeling a curious commonality with the men of the artillery units. Through reading of their experiences, I felt I had gained, in some small way, a sense of journeying beside them and of sharing all the life they had lived and all that they had been through as they traveled to France and back.

I went to *Rowdy*'s captain's stateroom and made the high step up onto the bed on the port side. It always offered a secure and comforting welcome. The head of the bed, from which I could reach out and touch the mast, was comfortably wide enough for two. Going forward, the foot of the bed narrowed somewhat on the left (port) side with the shape of the hull. The tongue and groove ceiling boards above the bed, painted a clean glossy white, were as smooth as a lacquered tabletop. On the starboard side of the stateroom was a maple countertop, supporting a stately library and liquor cabinet. The custom cabinet was mahogany framed with beveled, leaded glass doors and shiny brass latches of a patented Herreshoff design from 1916. Just aft of that was a mahogany hanging locker (closet). Soft light from two gimbaled brass wall lanterns brought out the rich, warm red color of the varnished mahogany bulkheads. When I lay in that bed, the feeling of the room was that of an inviting, warm, intimate hideaway, one in which I always slept very well. It was the perfect place to relax, absent the interruptions of the day, and entertain my thoughts and plans before drifting off to sleep.

✳ Rowdy, *Captain's stateroom*

As I lay there that night, the question that lingered in my thoughts was: Who was the mysterious E.B. to whom Holland had twice made glancing reference, with a complete absence of any other details? What were those meetings in Paris about?

By the next morning my curiosity prompted me to place a call to Hanny. When she answered, I told her that I had read everything and found it incredible and wonderful.

"I'm glad you read it," she replied. "It was a different time, and I think most people who didn't live through it probably can't fully appreciate all that happened."

"You must be very proud of your father," I said.

"Oh, I am. He was highly decorated by both the French and the Americans, and what you don't know from that journal is that after the war, when the record of his service was reviewed, he was promoted, eventually all the way up to colonel."

"I'm curious about something," I said. "In the journal, your father mentions someone with the initials E.B. Do you have any idea who that might have been?"

"In what context did he make the mention?"

"It was very, very brief. He simply noted having a meeting with E.B. in Paris on two different occasions while on leave."

"I probably know who that was." She paused. "But for me, it's a personal and rather painful subject." She paused again. "Can you can find that Fourth of July picture of *Rowdy* that you had framed?"

It was the one that I had enlarged, in which I had seen Holland Duell's face for the first time. I grabbed the picture and picked the phone back up.

"OK, I've got it."

"Do you see the little girl on the right?"

"Yes."

"As I told you, that is me when I was ten. The boy behind me is my brother Charles. Directly behind me is my mother, Mabel Duell. At the helm is my father, Holland Duell, and to the left of me, resting her chin on her hand, is Emilie Brown. I am quite sure she is the E.B. you are wondering about. I had never seen that picture before I saw it on your boat, and it is really quite incredible that of all the pictures in the world, you should have come up with that particular one to share with me. When I first saw it, I must admit, it hit me with a startling and rather involuntary jolt. A picture may be worth a thousand words, but it will require many, many more words than that to explain the story behind the moment that is captured in that picture.

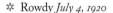 Rowdy *July 4, 1920*

There is so much that you cannot see or begin to imagine. It is a snapshot of a story that speaks volumes."

I sensed that this was important and that I should not ask questions but should let Hanny tell me in her own way.

"Emilie was my mother's first cousin.[1] Emilie and my mother had the same grandparents, James Ayers Brown and Ann Peet Brown.[2] James Ayers Brown was a leading textile merchant in London,[3] where he did business as a silk mercer, a dealer in silk fabric.[4] The couple had nine children,[5] among them Walter Peet Brown, who would become Emilie's father,[6] and Annie P. Brown, who would become my mother Mabel's mother.[7]

"The Brown family immigrated to St. Louis, Missouri, in 1867,[8,9] when Walter was twelve and Annie was ten. There, they ran a prosperous dry goods store, selling fabric such as cottons, woolens, linen, and silk. At the age of fourteen, Walter went to work in the store as an errand boy,[10] later becoming the bookkeeper.[11] In 1872, at the age of sixteen, he left the business and went to work as a traveling salesman for the Branch-Crooks saw company, a job he kept for over twenty years.[12]

"In 1880, Walter Peet Brown married Emily M. Miller,[13] not to be confused with their daughter-to-be, Emilie. Emily's father was a shoe and boot maker of German descent who had immigrated to the United States in 1854.[14] Walter and Emily's first daughter, Ann Louise Brown, was born on August 5, 1882.[15] Two years later, on May 17, 1884, the Emilie Miller Brown that you are curious about was born.[16] The girls were my mother's first cousins.

"On January 4, 1882, Walter Peet Brown's sister Annie P. Brown, who would become my grandmother, married my grandfather, Charles Eliezer Halliwell.[17] His family had also had immigrated to St. Louis from England, when he was three,[18] and he eventually became a very wealthy tobacco magnate.[19] On December 9, 1982, my mother Mabel Halliwell was born to Annie and Charles Eliezer Halliwell.[20]

* *James Ayers Brown (Photo courtesy Robert Melberg)*

* *Ann Peet Brown (Photo courtesy Robert Melberg)*

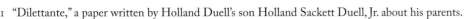

1 "Dilettante," a paper written by Holland Duell's son Holland Sackett Duell, Jr. about his parents.

2 1880 U.S. Census for St. Louis, Missouri, ancestry.com.

3 *New York Times*, March 13, 1902.

4 1861 England census, ancestry.com.

5 1880 U.S. Census for St. Louis, Missouri, ancestry.com.

6 Yale obituary for Holland Sackett Duell.

7 London, England, Births and Baptisms 1813–1906, record for Annie Peet Brown, ancestry.com.

8 1900 U.S. Census, City of St. Louis as stated by Walter Peet Brown, ancestry.com.

9 1900 U.S. Census, City of New York as stated by Annie P. Halliwell, ancestry.com.

10 1870 U.S. Census, City of St. Louis, ancestry.com.

11 1880 U.S. Census, City of St. Louis, ancestry.com.

12 http://home.comcast.net/~rkemps/Emily_Miller.html.

13 Samuel Henry Kemps Tree, ancestry.com.

14 http://home.comcast.net/~rkemps/Louisa_Ryan.hml.

15 Samuel Henry Kemps Tree, ancestry.com.

16 1916 passport, ancestry.com.

17 Missouri Marriage records, 1805–2002, ancestry.com.

18 1900 U.S. Census record for Annie B. Halliwell, ancestry.com.

19 *New York Times*, March 13, 1902.

20 1902 passport application, ancestry.com.

* *Charles Eliezer Halliwell (Photo courtesy of Holland Duell's grandson Robert Wood)*

* *Annie P. Brown (Photo courtesy of Holland Duell's grandson John Henry)*

"And that's who E.B. was: Emilie Miller Brown, my mother's first cousin. Her father was a traveling saw salesman, and her mother was the daughter of a shoe and boot maker. That's who she was as regards genealogy. The story of her life, however, and how she caused so many lives around her to be altered will take much, much longer to tell. But it is difficult for me to revisit those memories, Chris, and right now I need some rest, so I will leave anything further for another time."

After we said our friendly goodbyes, I pondered all that Hanny had told me, which perhaps posed more questions than it answered. As an adult, how did Emilie happen to be in Paris in the middle of a war so dangerous that the city had almost been taken by the Germans? And why did our discussion of Emilie seem to be so exhausting and unpleasant for Hanny?

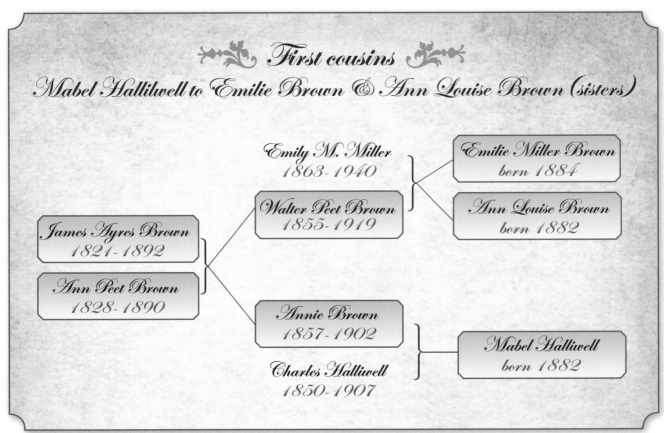

* *Family tree specifying how Emilie and Mabel are first cousins.*

Over the next few weeks, my work was focused almost entirely on *Rowdy*'s hull. I had previously replaced almost every plank on the boat, and the job of sanding the conglomerate of square-edged planks into a smooth, perfectly fair hull was monu-

mental. It required first ripping down both sides of the huge hull with a rough grit circular grinder, then switching to a vibrating sander, and finally using a hand-held long board sander, all in multiple steps with progressively finer grits of sandpaper. Each trip around the boat on different levels of scaffolding and assort-ments of ladders, while wearing goggles and a restrict-ing dust respirator, seemed an exhausting trip around the world.

As the sanding neared completion, I had heard nothing more from Hanny. I hoped that she had not considered my inquiry about E.B. to be improper or perhaps even rude, and my concern grew as time con-tinued to pass and I still had not heard from her. It had certainly not been my intention to be abruptly per-sonal, and while I certainly wanted to be respectful of her boundaries, I also wanted to get answers to what were now looking to be very personal questions about Emilie Brown. I decided that I needed to call Hanny, so the next morning, I sat down in the main salon of the boat, pencil and paper laid out on the table, as I always tried to take notes during our conversations, and dialed her number. Hanny answered and immediately put me at ease.

✳ *Top*, Rowdy's *hull before paint; and bottom, after being painted*

"Chris, I'm glad you called. Please excuse me for not getting back to you, but I did not want to call until I was ready. My father packed an amazing amount of life into his sixty-one years, and for much of his life, your boat was his center of gravity. Being on *Rowdy*, on the water, was his passion for years and years. He absolutely loved taking her out on Long Island Sound, where he was always able to find peace and the true inner happiness that would provide balance to his life. When life would challenge him, he always had *Rowdy* as a neutral corner. It was his sanctuary—a place of healing, a place where his stress faded away as soon as he stepped aboard. And on the water, he could regroup and recharge and come back ready to take on the world. In fact, the more stressful Father's life became, the greater was his need to sail aboard *Rowdy*. To me, Father's life and *Rowdy*'s history are synonymous, and I know you are curious about both. I know you have questions about Emilie, and you should be aware that Father also had two brothers and a sister. I have been struggling with how best to tell you all that you seem to want to know, and there is so very, very much. So many lives and stories were intertwined. If you have the time, I think it best that you sit down and make yourself comfortable, and I will tell you what I can."

Thus began my journey and immersion into the personal life of Holland Du-ell, the great sailor and war hero about whom I knew very little else. I savored subsequent conversations with Hanny, embracing every word as I hurriedly scribbled notes. I welcomed her many letters with the excitement a child feels on Christmas Day. I read them eagerly, reread them, and then reread them again countless times. In time, I came to know Holland and the circumstances of his life so well that I was actually able to feel in my heart the feelings he must have experienced at the time. It was as if that moment when Hanny suggested that I sit down represented the most marvelous opening of a stage curtain as it slowly began to rise and unveil the story of Holland Duell's life, a life so colorful and incredible that I could have never imagined all I was to learn. I was already sitting when Hanny began the first of what was to become many tales of Holland and his family:

"As you know my father was Holland Sackett Duell. My mother was Mabel Halliwell. Father came from the bluest of blue blood. On his mother's side, the Sacketts were among the first colonists in America, arriving with the Pilgrims at Plymouth in 1620.[1] His forefathers on both sides of the family had woven their lives into the fabric of this country as notable politicians, lawyers, and defenders of the nation, earning fame as far back as the American Revolutionary War.

"My father's mother, Harriet Sackett, was the great-granddaughter of Major John Buttrick, a hero of the American Revolution.[2,3] As you may remember from your history classes, on April 19, 1775, escalating tensions between Great Britain and the people of its thirteen colonies in North America erupted into armed conflict in the towns of Lexington and Concord in the colony of Massachusetts. About 700 British regulars had been given secret orders to capture and destroy military supplies that were reportedly being stored by the Massachusetts militia at Concord. As the British soldiers arrived at the North Bridge in Concord, they were opposed by 500 'embattled farmers' (to use Ralph Waldo Emerson's poetic term) under the command of Major Buttrick.[4] Major Buttrick then 'gave the famous orders to fire, and himself, fired the first shot'[5] from the patriot side, thereby starting the opening battle of American Revolution.[6] In his poem 'Concord Hymn,' Emerson referred to it as 'the shot heard round the world.' The British were driven back to Boston in defeat, and the battle went down in history as a famous and inspirational victory for the patriots, who the following year would declare themselves 'Americans.'

"Holland's great-great-grandfather on his father's side was Major Benjamin Ledyard,[7] who fought in the Revolutionary War at the battle of White Plains and at the battle of Monmouth,[8] where his horse was shot out from beneath him.[9]

---

1   *New York State's Prominent and Progressive Men*, vol. 6, by Mitchell Charles Harrison (New York: New York Tribune, 1900), p. 26.

2   *Boston Globe*, November 8, 1916.

3   *The Sacketts of America: Their Ancestors and Descendants 1630–1907*, by Charles H. Weygant (Newburgh, NY: 1907), p. 243.

4   Narrative from Elihu Root in his application for Sons of the American Revolution, ancestry.com.

5   Narrative from Elihu Root in his application for Sons of the American Revolution, ancestry.com.

6   *History of Westchester County, New York*, Vol. IV, by Will L. Clark (New York: Lewis Historical Publishing Company, 1925), p. 436.

7   *The National Cyclopaedia of American Biography*, Vol. XII (New York: James T. White & Company, 1904), p. 285.

8   Charles Holland Duell in his 1901 application for Sons of the American Revolution, ancestry.com.

9   http://www.worthpoint.com/worthopedia/1793-general-benjamin-ledyard-244051101.

"Holland's grandfather on his mother's side, was a lawyer by the name of William Augustus Sackett.[1] In the mid-1850s, he had been a member of Congress and had distinguished himself with his speeches against the expansion of slavery and his support of the bill to admit California into the Union. He joined the Republican Party immediately upon its formation and became a staunch advocate for the abolition of slavery. Following the commencement of the Civil War, his son of the same name, William A. Sackett, commanded the 9th New York Calvary at Gettysburg, the first Union troops to meet and check the Confederates.[2] The elder Sackett was later appointed to the position of Register in Bankruptcy under President Lincoln and, as Judge Sackett, administered bankruptcy proceedings.[3]

"Holland's paternal grandfather, Rodolphus Holland Duell, was one of the foremost lawyers in New York for over forty years.[4,5,6] From 1850 to 1855, he served as District Attorney of Cortland County, New York.[7,8,9] He denounced slavery and worked together with John C. Fremont to combat the Kansas-Nebraska Act, which promised to open up new territories to slavery. Their collaborative effort aided in the formation of the Republican Party,[10] and Rodolphus Duell served as a delegate to its first national convention, where Fremont was nominated as the Republican presidential candidate.[11] As a Republican Congressman from 1859 to 1863,[12,13] Duell gave powerful speeches denouncing slavery, was an outspoken supporter of the Civil War, and fought for proper equipping of troops in the field. After the war, he was an early advocate of the confiscation of Southern slaves and scoffed at those who hoped to restore the Union 'as it was.'[14] In 1868, he was a delegate to the Republican National Convention that nominated Ulysses S. Grant for president.[15] Duell was later appointed assessor of the Internal Revenue Service for the 23rd district of New York,[16] and in 1875, President Grant appointed him U.S. Commissioner of Patents.[17,18]

✳ *William Augustus Sackett, Holland's grandfather on his mother's side. (Our County and Its People: A Descriptive Biographical Record of Saratoga County, by The Saratogian, 1899, p. 499)*

✳ *Rodolphus Holland Duell, Holland's grandfather on his father's side*

1   *The Sacketts of America*, p. 242.

2   *History of Westchester County, New York*, Vol. IV, p. 436.

3   *Our County and Its People: A Descriptive Biographical Record of Saratoga County*, by The Saratogian (Boston: The Boston History Company, 1899, p. 499).

4   *Biographical Directory of the United States Congress, 1774–Present*, http://bioguide.congress.gov.

5   *Syracuse Evening Herald*, February 11, 1891.

6   *National Cyclopaedia of American Biography*, Vol. XII, p. 285.

7   *Biographical Directory of the United States Congress, 1774–2005* (Washington, DC: U.S. Government Printing Office, 2005), p. 985.

8   *Syracuse Evening Herald*, February 11, 1891.

9   *National Cyclopaedia of American Biography*, Vol. XII, p. 285.

10   Holland S. Duell is Named for the Assembly by Republicans," unidentified newspaper article archived at Westchester County Historical Society, French File, vol. 21, p. 131.

11   *National Cyclopaedia of American Biography*, Vol. XII, p. 285.

12   *Biographical Directory of the United States Congress, 1774–Present*.

13   *Syracuse Evening Herald*, February 11, 1891.

14   *Biographical Dictionary of the Union: Northern Leaders of the Civil War*, edited by John T. Hubbel and James W. Geary (Westport, CT: Greenwood Press, 1995), p. 154.

15   *National Cyclopaedia of American Biography*, Vol. XII, p. 285.

16   *Biographical Directory of the United States Congress, 1774–Present*.

17   *Biographical Directory of the United States Congress, 1774–Present*.

18   *Syracuse Evening Herald*, February 11, 1891.

Photograph Collection, New York Public Library, 1224517

CHARLES H. DUELL,
REPUBLICAN, ANTI-TAMMANY AND INDEPENDENT DEMOCRATIC CANDIDATE FOR THE ASSEMBLY IN THE THIRTEENTH DISTRICT.

✳ *Charles Holland Duell, Holland's father*

"Holland's father, Charles Holland Duell, a prominent New York patent attorney, was very active in politics. He served a term in the New York State Assembly representing the 13th District.[1,2] He was president of the McKinley League of the county of Onondaga, New York, during that campaign[3,4] and was later appointed U.S. Commissioner of Patents by President William McKinley.[5,6,7] He was known as one of the warmest and closest friends of President Theodore Roosevelt,[8] and he was the assistant treasurer of the Republican National Committee during Roosevelt's campaign for a second term.[9] In 1904, Roosevelt named him Associate Justice of the District of Columbia Court of Appeals.[10]

"It was as if the very genetic coding of Father's family had predisposed him to the practice of law and politics. So from a very early age, he knew that after graduating from Yale, he would attend law school and become a lawyer. Specifically, he would practice patent law, of which his father, Charles Holland Duell, was the foremost authority, having literally written the book on the subject: *Patents*, published in 1908.

"Unlike Father's family, whose lineage seemed to be rooted in the history of this country, both of my mother's parents were born outside of the United States and immigrated at a very young age: my grandmother Annie P. Brown, whose brother was Emilie's father, when she was ten and my grandfather, Charles Eliezer Halliwell, when he was three.[11] My grandparents, Charles Halliwell and Annie Brown married on January 4, 1882, in St. Louis, Missouri.[12] In December of that year, my mother, Mabel, was born to them, followed four years later by her brother Walter.[13]

"Not only were the Halliwells different from the Duells in being recent arrivals to this country, but unlike the Duells, who had built respectable wealth through generations of hard, scholarly work and wise investing, Charles E. Halliwell built a massive fortune within the short span of his own lifetime. The late 1800s were a very profitable time for tobacco companies. In 1890, a man named James B. Duke founded the American Tobacco Company and became hugely successful in marketing machine-rolled cigarettes. By 1899, the American Tobacco Company had eliminated the competition by buying most of the other tobacco companies in the United States. At that time, my grandfather Halliwell was in control of the Liggett & Meyers Tobacco Company in St. Louis. When American Tobacco acquired Liggett & Myers, Duke made Halliwell an officer of the company. He soon rose to the position of vice-

1 *National Cyclopaedia of American Biography*, Vol. XII, p. 285.

2 *Amsterdam Evening Recorder*, January 30, 1920.

3 *National Cyclopaedia of American Biography*, Vol. XII, p. 285.

4 *Syracuse Journal*, January 30, 1920.

5 *New York Herald*, January 25, 1898.

6 *Syracuse Herald*, January 30, 1920.

7 *National Cyclopaedia of American Biography*, Vol. XII, p. 285.

8 *Richmond Times Dispatch*, April 9, 1905.

9 *Amsterdam Evening Recorder*, January 30, 1920.

10 *New York Daily Tribune*, December 17, 1904.

11 1900 U.S. Census record for Annie B Halliwell, ancestry.com.

12 Missouri marriage records, ancestry.com.

13 1900 U.S. Census record for Annie B. Halliwell, ancestry.com.

president, second in power only to Duke.[1] To accommodate the busy merger business of the company, soon after becoming an officer of the American Tobacco Company, Charles E. Halliwell moved his family to Manhattan,[2] where he became one of the wealthiest men in New York.[3]

"Mother was about seventeen years old at the time, and the family, along with four servants,[4] took up residence at the eight-story Minnewaska, a luxury apartment complex bordering on Central Park, at 2 West 88th Street.[5,6] That was the first of four steps that had the consequence of eventually placing my parents-to-be in the same place at the same time. Otherwise, I wouldn't be here and we would not be having this conversation.

"At this time, Holland's father, my grandfather, Charles Holland Duell, Sr., was working in Washington as the U.S. Commissioner of Patents. He had been appointed on January 25, 1898, by President McKinley.[7,8,9] It was one of the rare cases when the president and not a senator had made the appointment.[10] Grandpa Charles had married Harriet Maria Sackett on November 11, 1879,[11,12] and together they had four children: my father, Holland, born on January 29, 1881;[13] Sackett, born in 1882;[14] Mary, born in 1885;[15] and Charles, Jr., born in 1889.[16]

"During his term, my grandfather reorganized the Patent Office, instituting many improvements and bringing the office up to date from a backlog of 15,000 applications.[17] By 1901, he had decided to return to private practice, and in March of that year, he announced that he would resign as Commissioner of Patents and would take with him from the Patent Office law clerk William A. Megrath and examiner Frederic P. Warfield to open a new law firm in New York City[18] under the name Duell, Megrath & Warfield.[19] My grandfather joked that he would 'leave enough behind to carry on Uncle Sam's work.'[20] In May 1901, he and his family moved into their new residence:

---

1 *Washington Post*, October 5, 1906.

2 Annie Brown Halliwell's obituary in the *New York Times*, March 13, 1902.

3 *The Morning*, February 13, 1903.

4 1900 U.S. Census for Manhattan, ancestry.com.

5 Annie Brown Halliwell's obituary in the *New York Times*, March 13, 1902.

6 1900 U.S. Census for Manhattan, ancestry.com.

7 *New York Herald*, January 25, 1898.

8 *Syracuse Herald*, January 30, 1920.

9 *National Cyclopaedia of American Biography*, Vol. XII, p. 285.

10 *New York Evening Post*, July 31, 1900.

11 *Syracuse Journal*, January 30, 1920.

12 *Syracuse Herald*, January 23, 1920.

13 Yale obituary for Holland Sackett Duell.

14 *History of the Class of 1905, Yale College*, Vol. 2, edited by Murray Sargent (New Haven, CT: Yale University, 1908).

15 1900 U.S. Census for Syracuse, New York, ancestry.com.

16 *Encyclopedia of American Biography*, edited by Winfield Scott Downs (New York: American Historical Company, 1955), p. 158.

17 *Syracuse Evening Herald*, 1901-0289.pdf, fultonhistory.com.

18 *New York Evening Post*, March 15, 1901.

19 The *Brooklyn Daily Eagle*, New York, April 8, 1901.

20 *New York Evening Post*, New York, March 15, 1901.

Hotel Majestic and Central Park West, New York.
Photograph Collection, New York Public Library, 836683

✳ *Hotel Majestic, 115 Central Park West*

✳ *Hotel Majestic Dining
Room (courtesy New York
Historical Society)*

✳ *Typical auto buggy*

the twelve-story Hotel Majestic at 115 Central Park West in Manhattan, less than a mile away from the Minnewaska, where the Halliwells lived.[1,2,3] That was the second step closer for my parents, Holland Duell and Mabel Halliwell.

"The Hotel Majestic was far from being what you probably envision when you think of a hotel. It was owned by Jacob Rothschild, one of the wealthiest merchants in New York. He had designed it to provide living accommodations that would surpass the expectations of even the most elite and most demanding members of New York society. Although the hotel offered some short-term accommodations, it consisted primarily of sprawling, luxurious suites that were designed to be permanent residences. The Grand Foyer, the Empire Dining Salon, and lounges throughout the Majestic were ornately decorated, complete with Roman columns, fine wood paneling, ceiling frescos, and towering arched windows. The cuisine ranked with that of the world's best restaurants, and every Sunday, there was a concert. Private balls were held there on Saturdays. The amenities featured private billiard rooms and bowling alleys, a 5,000-volume library, a stock brokerage, and a bank. According to a newspaper article, 'Every window offers a new panorama of delightful vistas. To the east stretch the broad, undulating acres of Central Park, rich in Autumnal foliage, animated by charming groups of pedestrians, equestrians and automobilists, and broken by lakes and ornamented by statues and towers.'[4]

"Holland was away at Yale at the time, living at Durfee Hall[5] since his admittance in to Yale in 1898.[6] He graduated in 1902 as one of the youngest members of his class. He was also one of the first to get a 'Benzene Buggy.'[7] It was a time when horse-drawn vehicles were starting to be replaced by early gasoline-powered automobiles. The competition for dominance in the auto field would be firmly decided in 1908, when the Model T burst onto the scene.

"Armed with his Yale B.A., Holland joined his family in Manhattan in 1902, moving in with them at the Majestic. This third step toward my mother had him

---

1 *New York Daily Tribune*, September 4, 1901.

2 *New York Herald*, April 27, 1902.

3 *Syracuse Herald*, September 1, 1906.

4 *New York Herald*, September 27, 1903.

5 1900 U.S. Census record for Holland S. Duell, ancestry.com.

6 *1902 Yale Autobiographies, Twenty-Five Years After, 1902–1927*, edited by James Wright (Newburgh, NY: Moore, 1927).

7 *Achievements of the Class of 1902, Yale College, from Birth to the Year 1912*, compiled by James Wright (New Haven, CT: Yale University Press, 1913), p. 256.

✳ *Holland Sackett Duell (Photo courtesy of Yale Class Book, 1902. Manuscripts & Archives, Yale University Papers, Yale Library)*

✳ *Durfee Hall, where Holland Duell lived while attending Yale*

living less than a mile from Mabel, but fate would have to work still harder. A few months previously, on March 11, 1902, Mabel's mother, Annie (Brown) Halliwell, had passed away at her home in the Minnewaska after a two-week bout of pneumonia.[1] It was heartbreaking for Mabel to lose her mother, and it was heartbreaking for her father, Charles Halliwell, to lose his wife. He knew that to continue to live at the Minnewaska would be too painful for either of them or his son Walter to endure. The fourth and final step was taken when Charles E. Halliwell decided to leave the Minnewaska and take up residence in the Hotel Majestic.[2] If fate's mission had been as simple as that, I might have been born a year earlier, but just as the Halliwells were moving in, the Duells were departing for an extended trip abroad. On July 24, 1902, the entire Duell family sailed for England aboard the *St. Paul* for a three-month vacation.[3,4] They returned from Europe in late September, and my parents-to-be shot off in different directions, never even having seen each other. Mabel went to the Miss Ely's School for Girls, a private boarding school overlooking the Hudson,[5] and Holland attended New York Law School at the southern tip of Manhattan.[6] But all good things come in time, and by the summer of 1903, the stars were in alignment for the tender collision of their hearts—or so seemed the case, until the last-minute introduction of a third player effected something of a love triangle."

---

1 *New York Times*, March 13, 1902.

2 Mabel Halliwell's July 8, 1902, passport application at ancestry.com lists the Hotel Majestic as her permanent residence.

3 *St. Paul* passenger list, ancestry.com.

4 *Achievements of the Class of 1902, Yale College, from Birth to the Year 1912*, p. 256.

5 "Dilettante."

6 *Achievements of the Class of 1902, Yale College, from Birth to the Year 1912*, p. 256.

Family Life

"My mother Mabel, as I told you, was a first cousin to Emilie Brown and Emilie's older sister, Ann Louise Brown.[1] Mabel and Ann Louise were very close in age, Ann Louise being older by only four months.[2,3] Growing up in St. Louis, the two had been close friends, and they had played with each other more than they had with Ann Louise's little sister, Emilie, who was two years younger. The friendship endured after Mabel moved away from St. Louis, and in the summer of 1903, Ann Louise, as any young woman of 21 would, gratefully and without hesitation accepted Mabel's invitation to visit her in the big city of New York and, at least for a while, leave St. Louis far behind. So as fate would have it, the first time Holland and Mabel found themselves in the same place at the same time, that being the dining room of the Majestic,[4] it was not simply a matter of boy meets girl. There were two girls, and Holland took equal notice of Mabel and Ann Louise.

"The dining room was something of a hub at the Majestic. Bumping into someone in other areas was hit or miss, but for many residents, the dining room was a part of the daily routine and a place where they were likely to see other people on a regular basis. It was formal and rather large, making casual introductions quite obviously forward and somewhat awkward. Rather than summoning the boldness required for such an initiative, on that morning when they first laid eyes on each other, Holland and the girls all chose the path of least resistance and simply enjoyed some casual back-and-forth glances with no introduction and no words spoken.

"From that moment forward, Holland became the main topic of conversation between Mabel and Ann Louise and a subject of equal infatuation. At 5' 11", broad-shouldered and narrow-waisted, he was as handsome as he was well proportioned. Had it not been for his intellectual ambitions, he most certainly could have pursued a career as a professional athlete. His strong jaw, prominent chin, and pensive eyes combined to give him the look of a man of power and intellect as well as a person of depth and sensitivity. The two girls immediately established that theirs would be a friendly competition for his affections, but with that, a most lively and spirited competition began in earnest.

---

1 "Dilettante," a paper written by Holland Duell's son Holland Sackett Duell, Jr. about his parents.
2 Ann's birth date was September 1, 1924, according to the passenger list for Samuel H Baer aboard *Leviathan*, ancestry.com.
3 Mabel's birth date was December 9, 1921, according to the *Aquitania* passenger list for Mabel Duell, ancestry.com.
4 "Dilettante."

* *Mabel Halliwell (Photo courtesy of Holland Duell's granddaughter Susan Duell and Mitch Higgins)*

HOLLAND S. DUELL.

* *Holland Sackett Duell (Westchester County in History, 1683–1912, by Henry T. Smith, Vol. 2, 1912, p. 265)*

* *Frederick Lewis Collins (12-14-1920 passport app. # 121121 at National Archives and Records Administration)*

"Mabel and Ann Louise studied Holland's schedule and made it a point to be in the dining room at the times when he took his meals. Perhaps he was unaware that he had become the object of their pursuit, but what man could object to being the quarry of two such attractive hunters? Shortly, familiarity led to flirtatious smiles, which in turn compelled an introduction. One might have thought that Ann Louise would have had the advantage, being the tall, blue-eyed German vixen, but what Mabel lacked in sexual presence, she made up for with personality. That was her edge. She knew it and she used it. She was small at 5' 2", and although her petite, unassuming figure did little to make an impression on a room, her distinctive auburn hair, which grew naturally in streaking shades of brown and copper, her huge deep brown eyes, and her extraverted personality and snappy sense of humor gave her magnetism in any crowd. It wasn't long before Mabel became the one to win Holland's heart,[1] and on September 19, 1903, Holland's parents gave a reception to announce the engagement of Holland Duell to Mabel Halliwell.[2]

"It was a fun time that was busy and full of life. There were many marriages and many babies. Ann Louise Brown wasted no time pining over Holland. On December 30, 1903,[3] she married chemist Samuel H Baer.[4] Mabel traveled back to St. Louis, where the wedding was held, and enjoyed sharing the position of maid of honor with Ann Louise's sister, Emilie Brown.[5]

"Frederick Lewis Collins and his fiancée, Elizabeth Everest Paine, who Mother and Father would not meet until 1910, at which time they would all become the very closest of friends,[6] were married on April 27, 1904.[7,8] There was some gossip, since in those days it wasn't common for the bride to be pregnant and entering her third trimester,[9] but few people resorted to being judgmental, and all wished the couple well. Holland had no way of knowing that the ensuing friendship would have a fuse attached to it, and despite the many years of enjoyable companionship, the association would have explosive repercussions.

1　"Dilettante."

2　*Sunday Herald* (Syracuse), September 20, 1903.

3　January 12, 1923, passport application for Samuel Harold Baer, ancestry.com.

4　Samuel Henry Kemps Tree, ancestry.com.

5　*St. Louis Republic*, December 31, 1903.

6　*Stilwell* v. *Duell*, Appellate Division of the New York Supreme Court, 1933, p. 199. Housed at New York State Library, Albany, NY, locator C31, vol. 164, citation 241 Ad 705

7　May 21, 1923, passport application for Elizabeth Collins, ancestry.com.

8　*25th Anniversary Report*, by Harvard College Class of 1904 (Norwood, MA: Plimpton Press, 1929).

9　*25th Anniversary Report*.

"Holland's bachelor party in September 1904 was reflective of the fine young men of Yale who dress impeccably, carry their heads high, always and without fail make dazzling conversation, and from time to time, perhaps in the confines of a private gathering , stand on chairs and let slip their mischievous side.

"Holland and Mabel were married at noon on September 29, 1904, at the Hotel Majestic.[1] It was an intimate wedding, the guests consisting mostly of family. Plans for a large wedding had been called off at the last minute and invitations recalled because of the serious illness of Mabel's paternal grandmother.[2,3]

"At Mabel's invitation, her cousins Ann Louise and Emilie Brown made the trip from St. Louis to attend the wedding. For most of the Duell family, including Holland, who had already met Ann Louise, it was their first acquaintance with Emilie.[4] She was charming—articulate, bubbly, vivacious, and full of positive energy. Her presence was enjoyed, but in the bustle of the main event, what for many in the family was a first introduction passed by almost unnoticed.

"After the wedding, Mother and Father traveled north about 100 miles to the Hotel Aspinwall in Lenox, Massachusetts, where they spent their honeymoon. The countryside along the way, for anyone unfamiliar with the area, was just that: country—mile after mile of gentle rolling hills, carpeted in grass that was kept green by nature, with no need for irrigation, and ran right down to the roadside. Everywhere were thickets of towering pines, maples, hemlocks, spruce, and birch as well as a multitude of lakes, both large and small. A novelty of the hotel was the serving of popcorn and cider, toasted marshmallows, and chestnuts in the afternoons.[5] When they returned to New York, the young couple moved into a house on Webster Avenue[6] in New Rochelle, in Westchester County.[7]

✳ *Holland Duell's bachelor dinner at the Yale Club, 1904. From right to left: William Sackett Duell, Holland Sackett Duell, unknown, Richard B. Tillinghast, William L. Chase, unknown, Frederic P. Warfield, Frederic R. Keator, and Walter M. Krementz. (Image MADID #10187018. Courtesy of Photographs of Yale alumni activities, 1889–1994 (inclusive). Manuscripts & Archives, Yale University.)*

✳ *Hotel Aspinwall, Lenox, Massachusetts (1912 postcard, Wikimedia Commons)*

---

1 *Syracuse Journal*, September 29, 1904.

2 *New York Daily Tribune*, October 2, 1904.

3 *Syracuse Herald*, September 18, 1904.

4 Holland Duell, as witness, stated that he had known Emilie since 1904 on her May 10, 1916, passport application, ancestry.com.

5 *New York Daily Tribune*, October 16, 1904.

6 "Dilettante."

7 *Westchester County in History: Manual and Civil List, Past and Present. County History: Towns,*

"It was a time for the Duell siblings to go out into the world and embark on their journeys as adults. Father's sister Mary would marry an army lieutenant, Otto Vaughn Kean.[1] In contrast to the tumultuous lives-to-come of her three brothers, Mary would lead such a normal married life in New Haven, Connecticut,[2] that there is really nothing more to say about her.

"Father's youngest brother, Charles, Jr., provided support for the theory that the youngest is often the most reckless and rebellious. After dropping out of Yale following his freshman year and attending New York School of Law,[3] Charles assumed a vocation as a high-profile political gladiator, only to switch tracks later in life, becoming a major player in the budding motion picture business.

"Father's other brother, William Sackett, who went by his middle name of Sackett, was younger than Father by one year. Six months after Holland's wedding, on April 19, 1905, Sackett married Louise Ensor Child in her hometown of Ashland, Virginia. Sackett, at the time, had been living in Lancaster, Pennsylvania.[4,5,6] He loved the country, and Pennsylvania was a land of spectacularly beautiful country.

"Sackett had tried to follow in his family's footsteps, having attended Yale for a time, the first step on the long road toward a law degree. But he was somehow different. The other Duell men seemed to thrive as legal warriors in the midst of the corporate, concrete city life of New York. They truly enjoyed a good battle and a struggle for dominance, the politics, the courtrooms, the ceremony of litigation. It was what excited them. Sackett was not particularly fond of confrontation and tended to view what to his family would seem an enjoyable challenge as an oppressive, stressful burden that he just wanted to go away. He knew he had been on the wrong path at Yale and felt lucky to have made it to the end of his freshman year, at which point he dropped out and went to work for Mother's father at the American Cigar Company, a subsidiary of the American Tobacco Company, in Lancaster.[7,8] The job necessitated a welcome move to Pennsylvania. Sackett's services were required from time to time at several of the company's plants throughout the tobacco-rich region, including the one in Richmond, Virginia where Sackett met his wife-to-be, Louise.[9] She was described in the newspapers as one of the most beautiful women in Virginia.[10] The wedding took place at the Duncan Memorial Chapel in nearby Ashland and was perhaps one of the most brilliant in the town's history.[11] In attendance were more distinguished visitors than could

✳ *Charles Holland Duell Jr.*
(Yale College class book 1911.
Manuscripts & Archives,
Yale University, p.355)

1   *Syracuse Herald*, March 23, 1908.

2   1930 U.S. Census record for Otho V. Kean, New Haven, Connecticut, ancestry.com.

3   *History of the Class of 1911, Yale College*, Vol. 1 edited by James Dwight Dana, Robert A. Gibney, and Harry S. Irons (New Haven, CT: Yale University, 1911).

4   *Times Dispatch* (Richmond, VA), April 20, 1905.

5   *History of the Class of 1905, Yale College*, Vol. 2, edited by Murray Sargent (New Haven, CT: Yale University, 1908).

6   *History of the Class of 1905, Yale College*, Vol. 6, edited by Boyd G. Curts(New Haven, CT: Yale University, 1930).

7   *History of the Class of 1905, Yale College*, Vol. 2.

8   National Register of Historic Places, Tobacco Buildings in Lancaster City, Section E, p. 16.

9   *History of the Class of 1905, Yale College*, Vol. 2.

10   *Times Dispatch* (Richmond, VA), April 9, 1905.

11   *Times Dispatch* (Richmond, VA), April 20, 1905.

be recalled in recent memory.[1] Father was the best man, and his brother Charles was one of the groomsmen.[2]

With marriages come babies, and on July 20, 1905 Holland and Mabel had their first, my brother, Charles Halliwell Duell.[3] Father's brother Sackett and his wife Louise followed up eight months later when William Sackett Duell Jr. was born.[4] Two months later, on June 30, 1906, my sister Helen Duell, was Born to Holland and Mabel.[5]

It was a happy time, and everyone's lives were very full and blessed with an abundance of love. Even Mabel's father, Charles E. Halliwell, who had been alone for three years since the death of his wife, was to once again fall in love, although not by the usual circumstances. In October 1905 he had undergone an operation for appendicitis.[6,7,8] In those days it was considered a severe operation with serious risks and long recuperation times. His doctor, in advance of the surgery, had recommended a nurse by the name of Ruth Alice Cole to assist him during what was expected to be a long, slow recovery.[9]

"Professionally trained and from Pennsylvania,[10] Ruth Alice was not only quite attractive but, at 29,[11] also very much Charles's junior, he being 55 at the time.[12] The convalescence took place at White Sulphur Springs, West Virginia, now the site of the world-class Greenbrier resort, at the base of the wondrous rolling, wooded Allegheny Mountains.[13] Established in 1778, White Sulphur Springs, became popular because of the generally accepted idea that drinking or bathing in spring water was a sure path to restored health and would cure anything from rheumatism to an upset stomach. By 1905, White Sulphur Springs had built a reputation as a resort of the utmost fashion and sophistication, attracting many of the nation's most influential and powerful families, including those of many Presidents.[14]

"My mother accompanied her father and Ruth Alice throughout the trip[15] and, through the time spent together, came to find that she truly enjoyed the company of her father's charming young nurse. After her father's recovery, which seemed quite complete at the time, Mother and Ruth Alice became very close friends and socialized frequently.[16,17,18]

---

1   *Times Dispatch* (Richmond, VA), April 9, 1905.

2   *Syracuse New York Post*, April 19, 1905.

3   *1902 Yale Autobiographies, Twenty-Five Years After, 1902–1927*, edited by James Wright (Newburgh, NY: Moore, 1927).

4   *History of the Class of 1905, Yale College*, Vol. 2.

5   *1902 Yale Autobiographies, Twenty-Five Years After, 1902–1927.*

6   *New York Times*, October 5, 1906.

7   *Utica Herald-Dispatch*, October 6, 1906.

8   *Syracuse Herald*, May 8, 1907.

9   *Utica Herald-Dispatch*, October 6, 1906.

10 *New York Evening Post*, October 4, 1906.

11 December 29, 1908 passport application for Ruth A. Halliwell, ancestry.com.

12 1900 U.S. Census for New York, New York, ancestry.com.

13 *Syracuse Herald*, May 8, 1907.

14 www.greenbrier.com.

15 *Syracuse Herald*, May 8, 1907.

16 *New York Times*, June 20, 1913.

17 *New York Herald*, February 12, 1909.

18 *Waverly Free Press and Tioga County Recorder*, June 27, 1913.

"It is not uncommon for a patient to become emotionally attached to his healer. Whether it was because of that or simply the allure of her beauty and the spark of her youthful energy, Charles found his heart once again being touched, and he made it a point to be at my parents' house in New Rochelle when Ruth Alice would visit.[1] The familiarity grew, as did a mutual comfort and fondness between Charles and Ruth Alice, so when Charles fell ill once more in early 1906, there was no question that Ruth Alice would again be his nurse during his convalescence, that time in Poland Springs, Maryland.[2] When he had healed that second time, Charles was a new man in more ways than one. The affection that he had felt in his heart for Ruth Alice had blossomed into a full-fledged mutual love affair, and when they returned to New York, they did so with plans of marriage.

"It is usually a daughter who asks her father's permission to marry, but in this case, when Charles asked his daughter Mabel, she gave her wholehearted approval both of Ruth Alice and of the wedding plans.[3] The wedding took place on October 4, 1906, at All Angels' Church in Manhattan.[4] It was intentionally small and unpublicized, and there were few guests other than the bride's parents, Holland and Mabel, and Mabel's brother Walter.[5] In fact, the whole affair was so private that many of Charles's neighbors at the Majestic were taken by surprise when his young nurse moved in with him as his wife. But she was found by all to be delightfully charming, and there was not a soul who was not happy for the couple.[6]

"Marriages and babies and newfound love aside, the Duell men were all very dynamic, and their pursuits during these years provided a constant source of energy and excitement in the areas of business and politics. Holland's father, Charles Holland Duell, Sr., had a passion for politics that was equal to his passion for law. He had helped to get William McKinley elected President by organizing the McKinley League of Onondaga County, of which he was president, and campaigning actively throughout the country.[7,8] When McKinley was assassinated in 1901 and Vice President Theodore Roosevelt assumed the Presidency, Charles Duell, Sr. became one of Roosevelt's strongest advocates and was known to be one of his warmest and closest friends.[9] In fact, the entire Duell family became intimately associated with Theodore Roosevelt, and Father and his brothers spent a tremendous amount of time and energy supporting Roosevelt's political endeavors. It wasn't just what he stood for politically that they took a liking to; it had more to do with the man, with his free-spiritedness, independent thinking, and utter lack of fear of failure. Roosevelt was one to do some-

---

1 *New York Times*, June 20, 1913.
2 *Utica Herald-Dispatch*, October 6, 1906.
3 *New York Herald*, May 7, 1907.
4 *New York Times*, June 20, 1913.
5 *Utica Herald-Dispatch*, October 6, 1906.
6 *Washington Post*, October 5, 1906.
7 *The National Cyclopaedia of American Biography*, vol. XII (New York: James T. White & Company, 1904), p. 285.
8 *Syracuse Journal*, January 30, 1920.
9 *Times Dispatch* (Richmond, VA), April 9, 1905.

thing because it made sense to him and it was the right thing to do, not because he was swayed by the prevailing crowd mentality or political pressure and bribery.

"Roosevelt had had an early start in politics, having been elected as a Republican to the New York legislature in 1881 at the age of 23. On February 14, 1884, both his wife and his mother died on the same day. That page of his diary was marked with a large "X" and the single entry "The light has gone out of my life." Following that loss, Roosevelt honored his position in the New York State Assembly until his term was complete, but he then immediately withdrew from public life. He went to his ranch in what is now North Dakota to heal himself by living a wilderness lifestyle. He hunted, ranched cattle, rode horses Western style, and learned to rope. He wrote articles on frontier life for Eastern magazines and wrote three books on hunting and ranching.

"In 1886, Roosevelt returned to public life and ran for mayor of New York, portraying himself as 'The Cowboy of the Dakotas.' He came in third. He later campaigned for Benjamin Harrison for President. After Harrison won the Presidency, he appointed Roosevelt to the U.S. Civil Service Commission, on which he served until 1895. The New York *Sun* described Roosevelt as 'irrepressible, belligerent and enthusiastic.'

"In 1895, Theodore Roosevelt became the Police Commissioner for the city of New York, which at the time had one of the most corrupt police forces in the country. He implemented massive reforms and made a habit of walking the officers' beats late at night and early in the morning to make sure they were on duty. In 1897, President McKinley appointed Roosevelt to the post of Assistant Secretary of the Navy. Roosevelt immediately moved to prepare the Navy for what he saw as the inevitable war with Spain, which would come as a consequence of tensions over the Spanish occupation in Cuba.

"Spain regarded Cuba as a province rather than a colony. Cubans had been revolting against Spanish rule since 1868. American newspapers printed stories of Spanish atrocities against the Cubans, who, it was said, were being treated like prisoners. In early 1898, a riot broke out in Havana, Cuba's chief port city. The United States had important economic trade interests in Cuba, specifically sugar. To protect those interests and American citizens in the wake of the riot, President McKinley dispatched the *USS Maine* to Havana.

"On February 15, 1898, the *USS Maine* sank in Havana Harbor following a large explosion, which was thought to be the result of Spanish espionage. Roosevelt campaigned strongly for the United States to take military action against Spanish military posts in Cuba to protect American interests there. Two months later, the United States declared a state of war with Spain. Roosevelt immediately resigned as Assistant Secretary of the Navy and formed the Rough Riders, a regiment of volunteer cowboys, Native Americans, college athletes, and ranchers, all of whom were capable on horseback and in shooting. Roosevelt's Rough Riders became famous for their uphill charges on entrenched Spanish positions at Kettle Hill and San Juan Hill outside Santiago, Cuba. At San Juan Hill, Roosevelt, on his horse Texas led the

✶ *Theodore Roosevelt, 1885*

✶ *Rough Rider Theodore Roosevelt, 1898 (Courtesy National Park Service, Theodore Roosevelt Birthplace)*

✶ *Theodore Roosevelt and his Rough Riders atop San Juan Hill, 1898*

charge, waving his hat in the air. He believed that the only hope for a victorious outcome was a swift and fearless charge on the Spanish fortified blockhouses atop the hill. The outcome was successful, and Roosevelt came back a colonel and a national hero but also a host to malaria, which would trouble him throughout his life. Theodore Roosevelt declared that it had been a 'splendid little war.'

"The peace treaty granted the United States almost all of Spain's colonies, including the Philippines, Guam, and Cuba. The United States subsequently allowed Cuba to gain her independence. Later in that same year of 1898, Theodore Roosevelt was elected Governor of New York, and in 1901, he became Vice President of the United States under William McKinley.

"On September 6, 1901, anarchist Leon Czolgosz stepped from a crowd at the World's Fair in Buffalo, New York, and, using a revolver hidden under his handkerchief, fired two shots at President McKinley, who died eight days later. Ironically, at that very Fair, Thomas Edison's newly invented device, the X-ray machine, which could have helped to save the President's life, was being exhibited. However, doctors were reluctant to use it on the President for fear of unknown side effects. On September 14, President McKinley died, making Theodore Roosevelt, at 42, the youngest President in U.S. history.

"Roosevelt was extremely constructive in his first term and ran for a second term in 1904. Charles Duell, Sr. aided Roosevelt in his reelection effort by taking the post of assistant treasurer of the Republican National Committee.[1] Roosevelt won by a landslide, and in December 1904, he appointed Charles Duell, Sr. Associate Justice of the District of Columbia Court of Appeals, the final court of appeals in all minor patent cases.[2]

"In January 1905, when Charles Duell, Sr. moved to Washington D.C. to fill the position, his law firm of Duell, Megrath & Warfield ceased to do business, and Father formed a new partnership with Frederic Warfield under the name of Warfield & Duell,[3,4] located on the nineteenth floor of the United States Express building at No. 2 Rector Street at the southern tip of Manhattan.[5,6] Warfield, a graduate of Hamilton College, had been a dedicated assistant to Charles, Sr. both during his term as U.S. Commissioner of Patents and afterward in private law practice. Warfield's attention to exacting detail and record keeping were appreciated as invaluable assets to the business, and his loyal friendship was enjoyed by the entire Duell family.

"The following years were full speed ahead. Father's law practice had gained a sterling reputation as well as an excellent balance sheet. By no means was he all work. He had many outside interests as well. Mother later mentioned to me that she had no idea how he found time for all those interests while maintaining his busy law practice. He loved learning and never let go of the constant pursuit of knowledge. An enjoy-

✳ *Frederic Parkman Warfield*
(Hamilton College Archives)

1 *Amsterdam Evening Recorder*, January 30, 1920.

2 *New York Daily Tribune*, December 17, 1904.

3 *1902 Yale Autobiographies, Twenty-Five Years After, 1902–1927*.

4 *Triennial Record, Class of 1902, Yale University*, edited by E. Carleton Granbery (New Haven, CT: Press of the Tuttle Morehouse, & Taylor Company, 1906).

5 *Westchester County in History*, pp. 266–267.

6 Holland's business card attached to Emilie Brown's May 10, 1916, passport application, ancestry.com.

able evening for Father might encompass hosting a meeting of the American History Club at home and reading papers on Thomas Jefferson and the Louisiana Purchase.[1]

"In late 1906, Father decided to expand out into politics. After a good campaign, on January 7, 1907, at 25 years of age, he won the election for assemblyman representing the 2nd District of Westchester County by one of the largest majorities ever given a candidate for assembly in that district.[2] He was following in his father's footsteps, as Charles Duell, Sr. had himself begun a political career representing the 13th District of New York in the State Assembly.[3,4] Father devoted himself completely to his responsibilities as assemblyman. He was a representative of the people, and he stuck to his campaign promise that he was under no pledges to any political organization and was absolutely free to carry out the will of the people.[5]

"The first bill that he introduced, in January 1907, would require newspapers to attach the names of journalists and editors to their articles in an effort to curb slanderous and erroneous stories, which were commonplace at the time.[6] A journalist from the *Syracuse Herald* who was fighting the proposed bill, wrote an article in which he said that Father's bill should be titled 'An Act to annoy honorable and responsible newspapers.' Amusingly, the journalist remained anonymous, as the article was not signed.[7] In April, the bill was passed into law.[8]

"Father worked tirelessly and had bill after bill passed, including the Bronx Parkway Bill, which reclaimed land along the Bronx River for Westchester County, to be improved and used as a public park. He engineered the bill so that three fourths of the expense was covered by New York City, Westchester having to carry only one quarter of the expense.[9]

"When it came time for reelection, Father was unanimously nominated as candidate for a second term. City Treasurer John H. Harmer made the nominating speech, which was frequently interrupted by great applause, and at the conclusion, the hall rang for several minutes with cheers and applause for Father.[10] In November 1908, he won reelection by a landslide majority of the vote, the largest ever given in the territory for assembly.[11,12]

"Father's second term was equally constructive. In 1909, he introduced a bill aimed at forest preservation. The bill made it a crime to cut down or intentionally kill any tree in the woodlands of New York that was less than 12 inches in diameter.[13]

---

1 *New Rochelle Pioneer*, March 31, 1906.

2 *Westchester County in History*, pp. 266–267.

3 *Cyclopaedia of American Biography*, Vol. XII, p. 285.

4 *Amsterdam Evening Recorder*, January 30, 1920.

5 *New Rochelle Pioneer*, October 17, 1908.

6 *The Syracuse Herald*, January 17, 1907.

7 *The Syracuse Herald*, January 19, 1907.

8 *Amsterdam Evening Recorder*, April 17, 1907.

9 *New Rochelle Pioneer*, October 26, 1907.

10 *New Rochelle Pioneer*, October 5, 1907.

11 *Westchester County in History*, pp. 266–267.

12 *New Rochelle Pioneer*, November 7, 1908

13 *Fulton County Republican* (Johnstown, NY), March 11, 1909.

He reorganized and increased the police force of the city of Mount Vernon.[1] He introduced a bill making conviction of a felony or being sentenced to hard labor for a term of two years or more absolute grounds for divorce,[2] and he introduced three bills related to automobiles, including one that made it a crime to drive at speeds that should be considered unsafe because of weather or road conditions even if the person was driving at or below the posted speed limit.[3,4]

"During this time, Mother and Father continued to live in New Rochelle while making plans for their future dream home. Their house in New Rochelle was a short drive away from the open water of Long Island Sound. Anyone who has never been to the Sound cannot appreciate the world-class sailing it affords.

"Long Island runs roughly from northeast to southwest, paralleling the mainland and connecting at its southwestern terminus to mainland New York. The Sound—the channel created between Long Island and the mainland—is an area on average about 100 miles long by 15 miles wide comprising innumerable small islands, wooded and beautiful, and secure coves that afford safe anchorage to recreational boaters. With names such as Turtle Cove, Pelican Bay, and Huckleberry Island, Long Island Sound is an exhilarating playground for boating of every type and is home to many of the premier yacht clubs in the world.

"In early 1907, Father had joined the New Rochelle Yacht Club[5] and bought a 33-foot AYC Raceabout named *Jolly Tar*,[6] 'tar' being a slang word for a deckhand. The Raceabout was a 1901 class of flush-deck, gaff-rigged sailboats, all built to the exact same dimensions and designed to race against each other in competitions.[7] *Jolly Tar* was kept on a mooring in Echo Bay next to the club and just minutes from Father's house.[8] He embraced the ceremony of sailing with a passion. From the very start, he loved everything about it, from racing to pleasurable, lazy day sails to the multi-day cruises of the various yacht clubs. He raced every chance he got and brought home trophy after trophy after trophy.[9]

"When Father and Mother started to plan their dream home in 1906, Father wanted to build nearby so that he would be near the yacht club and Long Island Sound. Mother wanted to build on the opposite side of Westchester County, in the city of Yonkers, about nine miles to the west, by the banks of the Hudson River. In the end, it was her wish that prevailed in determining the building site.[10]

"They bought a beautifully wooded 10-acre lot at 1161 North Broadway, which was part of a 60-acre development named Pinecrest Estates.[11] Their site was at the

---

1   *The Sun* (New York), May 26, 1909.
2   *Syracuse Herald*, March 3, 1909.
3   *Niagara Falls Gazette*, April 1, 1909.
4   *New York Times*, March 31, 1909.
5   *Westchester County in History*, p. 267.
6   *New Rochelle Pioneer*, June 22, 1907.
7   *The First 100 Years of the American Yacht Club: The Land, the People, the Boats, 1883–1983*, by Wallace W. Elton (Rye, NY: Centennial Book Editorial Board of the American Yacht Club, 1983).
8   *New Rochelle Pioneer*, June 22, 1907.
9   "Dilettante."
10 "Dilettante."
11 *Herald Statesman, Yonkers*, August 17, 1938.

highest part of the development and afforded stunning views of the Hudson from the hillside, some 300 feet above the river.[1] During the next four years, most of their spare time was occupied with permits, planning, and construction decisions.

"On Monday, May 6, 1907, the focus of all that happy planning was shattered when Mother received a call at their New Rochelle home informing her that her father had collapsed and was unconscious. He had been dining at a restaurant with his wife and a niece and was telling them a humorous story when his face suddenly became flushed, and he fell from his chair. When Mother got the call, he had already been transported to a private room above the restaurant, and physicians were in attendance. Mother and Father raced to the scene as quickly as they could and found the physicians working frantically to save the life of her father, who still lay unconscious. They worked on him for six hours until, in the company of my parents, Ruth Alice, and his niece, the grandfather that I never had the chance to meet died, never having regained consciousness. The cause was determined to be a cerebral hemorrhage, and the effect of his death was, for a prolonged period, crushing to poor Mother, who had been very close to her father.[2]

"Ruth Alice and Charles E. Halliwell had been married for only seven months. Previously, his will had specified the division of his estate 50/50 between his children Mabel, who was the apple of his eye, and her brother Walter, who, for some reason, Charles always viewed with disdain and a harsh, critical eye.[3] However, one month after Charles married Ruth Alice, he amended his will, still leaving 50 percent of his $5,000,000 estate to Mabel but splitting Walter's half, leaving him 25 percent of the estate and the remaining 25 percent to his new wife. After only seven months of marriage, Ruth Alice, who previously had been an unknown in New York, was suddenly worth 1.25 million dollars.[4] The newspapers got hold of the 'rags to riches' story and seemed to take great pleasure in presenting Ruth Alice as something of a celebrity, giving her the affectionate nickname "The Pretty Nurse."

✳ Ruth Alice, "The Pretty Nurse" (Washington Post, June 30, 1913)

"Mother and her brother Walter had never been close,[5] and she didn't seem to mind that half of his share of the family fortune had been left to Ruth Alice. Mother and Ruth Alice would remain close friends for many years and provided each other comfort while healing from the loss of Charles.

"Once Mother was able to return to planning our future house, she found the process to be healing and a source of much-needed positive energy. It was great fun working with architects and designing rooms and choosing styles. It put the focus back on the future, which seemed very bright. If they had lived well before, now they would live very well. To put the value of those 1907 dollars into perspective, the house that my parents had designed was a sprawling, colonial-style, 2 ½-story mansion, everything built of materials of the very finest quality, with many, many rooms, for a total cost of $50,000, an amount that would be equivalent to nearly $1,250,000 in today's

1 *New York Times*, April 3, 1910.
2 *Syracuse Herald*, May 8, 1907.
3 "Dilettante."
4 *New York Times*, May 12, 1907.
5 "Dilettante."

money.[1] The mansion was to be on the grandest of scales, yet with Mother's new fortune, she suddenly had the wealth to build fifty such houses.

"The house took almost four years from conception in 1906 to completion in 1910. Families kept growing the whole time. In June 1907, Sackett and Louise Duell had their second child, Robert Ensor Duell, in Syracuse, New York.[2,3] A year later, in June 1908, my parents, Mabel and Holland Duell, had their third child, my brother Holland Sackett Duell, Jr.[4,5]

"Charles H. Duell, Sr., had resigned from his position as Associate Justice of the District of Columbia Court of Appeals and had returned to New York to join Holland's firm of Warfield & Duell, which became Duell, Warfield & Duell and remained so for many years.[6,7,8] The firm possessed a mastery of the subject of patents and was without peer in that field.[9]

"But all of these are really secondhand stories, which were told to me by my parents. Although I was conceived in New Rochelle, my life began, I feel, at our new residence overlooking the Hudson River. That house, that beautiful sprawling mansion, which was surrounded by acres of the most marvelous woods in which to play, was the center of my life for many, many years. It represented, and still does in my heart, family and friends and social gatherings as well as success and power for my father and, in general, very happy, prosperous times. My prayers every night include thanks for my special childhood years there.

"In June 1909, Father announced that he would not be a candidate for a third term as assemblyman because he was moving out of the district,[10] and by early 1910, the finishing touches were being put on our future home, the estate that my parents named Ardenwold."

---

1 *New York Herald*, August 23, 1908.
2 *History of the Class of 1905, Yale College*, Vol. 2, 1908.
3 *History of the Class of 1905, Yale College*, Vol. 6, 1930.
4 *1902 Yale Autobiographies, Twenty-Five Years After, 1902–1927*.
5 June 7, 1924, passport application for Mabel Duell, ancestry.com.
6 *Washington Post*, September 2, 1906.
7 Yale obituary for Holland Duell.
8 *1902 Yale Autobiographies, Twenty-Five Years After, 1902–1927*.
9 Hamilton College biography for Frederic P. Warfield, c. 1916.
10 *New Rochelle Pioneer*, June 12, 1909.

Ardenwold

"With Mother pregnant and their new home nearly complete, my parents were busy planning the move so that my life would begin at Ardenwold. The last event of consequence in New Rochelle took place while Father was waiting for a streetcar and met Frederick Lewis Collins for the first time. A graduate of Harvard,[1] Frederick was an intellectual and worked in the publishing business as an editor and writer for the *American Home Companion* and *Collier's Weekly* magazines. He and Father hit it off immediately, and within a few weeks, Frederick and his wife Elizabeth and Holland and Mabel had become social friends.[2] It was in a way bittersweet given that Mabel was, for the fourth time, blossoming on the verge of motherhood, while only six months earlier, on June 5, 1909, Frederick and Elizabeth Collins had lost their only child, Barbara, who passed away one month before her fifth birthday.[3] Nonetheless, a bond was formed that not only evolved into a close friendship, but also later extended into mutual business ventures.

"In early 1910, while I was still in my mother's womb, the family moved into Ardenwold.[4,5] Shortly thereafter, my parents purchased the adjoining ten-acre lot, increasing the grounds of our estate to twenty acres.[6] It was a fairy-tale setting to be born into, and on April 7, 1910, I took my first breath.[7] I was very well cared for. Mother's love and devotion to family were unwavering.[8] Not only did she have a nurse to help with my needs, but there was also a cook, a butler, a houseman, a laundress, a couple of maids, and, outside, a chauffeur, a gardener, a chore man, and a couple of groundsmen.

Growing up at Ardenwold was enormously fun for a child simply on the merits of the enormity of its size.[9] It was 2 ½ stories high and 20,000 square feet[10] with thirty rooms.[11] After dinner, Mother and Father used to love to retire to the library and spend

---

1   *25th Anniversary Report*, by Harvard College Class of 1904 (Norwood, MA: Plimpton Press, 1929).

2   *Stilwell* v. *Duell*, Appellate Division of the New York Supreme Court, 1933, p. 302. Housed at New York State Library, Albany, NY, locator C31, vol. 164, citation 241 Ad 705

3   *25th Anniversary Report*.

4   1910 U.S. Census record for Holland S. Duell, ancestry.com.

5   *New York Times*, April 3, 1910.

6   *New Rochelle Pioneer*, April 23, 1910.

7   *1902 Yale Autobiographies, Twenty-Five Years After, 1902–1927*, edited by James Wright (Newburgh, NY: Moore, 1927).

8   "Dilettante," a paper written by Holland Duell's son Holland Sackett Duell, Jr. about his parents.

9   "Dilettante."

10   *New York Herald*, August 23, 1908.

11   http://www.hras.org/history.html.

hours filled with lively conversation and storytelling. There was also a billiard room, a sunroom, outside decks, a swimming pool, tennis courts, a three-car garage, and extensive well-tended rose gardens.[1] Of course, we had dogs, and Father had a horse that he loved to ride.

"I think Father had very much enjoyed our family's previous life in New Rochelle. It was on a simpler scale, he was closer to the water and to the recreation he loved, and he had time to relax and enjoy life. Mother, however, had visions of grandeur. Whatever drove her and motivated her, I was never really quite sure. Presumably, witnessing her father's rapid ascent to power, wealth, and recognition had set a

---

1 http://www.hras.org/history.html.

model for her of what a successful person of quality must aspire to. She was the typical woman who, as a little girl, had idolized her father and, as an adult, would use his success as a yardstick against which to measure her husband. She always had the very best intentions. Her love for her family was infinite, and she truly believed that her pursuits were necessary for the ultimate benefit and well-being of her family.[1] In the way that her father had worked hard throughout his life and built on his success until he finally hit the ultimate payday through the American Tobacco buyout, Mother felt that her life should be a road of empire building toward some type of equally spectacular ultimate payoff. The pursuit of that final goal at times seemed to be Mother's passion and her source of enjoyment and recreation.

"Father, by contrast, was a lover of life. He was extremely active in business, but he also had seemingly infinite interests outside of business that were tremendously enjoyable to him, none of which Mother shared. As you know, he had a passion for sailing, but he also loved tennis, golf, swimming, dancing, and horseback riding, to name a few. While life at Ardenwold, as I have said, seemed to me a fairy tale, for Father, this was a point at which his life, like a sponge, began to absorb more and more complications—things that required more and more of his time—until that balance sheet finally yielded very little time left for him and the things that he enjoyed in life. It was a problem, but 'I feel that for my emotional needs, I should have more time for my . . .' was not the type of conversation that Father was used to having or one that he would be particularly inspired to initiate. He was a man, and he was better suited to directing troops on the battlefield, defending a patent in the courtroom, or defining articles of incorporation to protect the assets of a business. So for years, he went along to the beat of Mother's drum, not simply working hard to maintain and enjoy their quality of life, but always aspiring and striving for higher status.

"Duell, Warfield & Duell became the preeminent patent law firm in the entire New York area and beyond.[2] Father was a brilliant and very active lawyer, earning about $85,000 a year,[3] which would be millions of dollars in today's money. He could afford to build a new Ardenwold every year and still have more money left over than most people's salaries. His legal representation of various companies gave him the opportunity to be on their boards of directors and to acquire stock in those companies, something that Mother encouraged, having seen the success that American Tobacco Company had enjoyed from taking an interest in as many other businesses as possible. Over the years, Father became:

> Director of American Sales Book Company, Ltd.[4]
> Director of the F.N. Burt Company, Ltd.[5]
> Director of William A. Rogers, Ltd.[6,7]

---

1 "Dilettante."
2 Hamilton College biography of Frederic P. Warfield, c. 1916.
3 *Stilwell* v. *Duell*, p. 427.
4 *1902 Yale Autobiographies, Twenty-Five Years After.*
5 *1902 Yale Autobiographies, Twenty-Five Years After.*
6 *1902 Yale Autobiographies, Twenty-Five Years After.*
7 *Achievements of the Class of 1902, Yale College, from Birth to the Year 1912,* compiled by James Wright (New Haven, CT: Yale University Press, 1913).

Director of Canadian William A. Rogers, Ltd.[1]
President of Klauder-Weldon Dyeing Machine Company[2]
Vice-President of *McClure's Magazine*[3,4]
Vice-President of the Noiseless Typewriter Company[5,6]
Director of Yonkers National Bank[7]
Director of Rampo Co., Oakland, N.J.[8]

"So at what seemed to Father the cost of precious leisure time, time that should be set aside for 'smelling the roses' and enjoying the short gift of life, the Duells' empire building continued on a steady course, year after year.

"The one area of his life that Father would not let Mother's ambitions encroach upon was sailing. That was what kept him grounded. That was his stress relief. That was what made it all worthwhile. Shortly after moving into Ardenwold, Father sold *Jolly Tar* and replaced her with another small sailboat.

"In the spring of 1905, the Herreshoff Manufacturing Company in Bristol, Rhode Island, built a new class of sailboats for the New York Yacht Club. They were named the New York 30s, or NY30s, because of the yacht club for which they were built and because they were 30 feet at the waterline. Eighteen of the little gaff-rigged sloops were built, all identical, to be raced against each other as a class exclusively by members of the NYYC. At $4,000 each, they came fully equipped with racing sails, awning, lead and lead line, two anchors, mattresses, pillows, bedclothes, stove, cooking utensils, and china in racks.

"Yacht design is one part advanced mathematical formulation, one part artistic expression, and an equal part of crossed fingers. It is not uncommon for a new design to hit the water and completely fail to meet expectations. When the New York 30s were launched, it was an instance of the concept on the design board coming together with the boatyard construction crews to produce nothing short of magic. The finished products were thoroughbreds. They were gems. They were little arrows that would slice through any kind of sea at exceptional speeds, often outpacing far larger boats. The prestigious owners, who included Vanderbilts, Roosevelts, and Morgans, to name just a few, held the highest appreciation for their craft, which were always popular and a main spectator attraction during cruises and regattas.[9]

---

1 *1902 Yale Autobiographies, Twenty-Five Years After.*

2 Yale obituary for Holland Duell.

3 Yale obituary for Holland Duell.

4 *Achievements of the Class of 1902, Yale College, from Birth to the Year 1912.*

5 *Achievements of the Class of 1902, Yale College, from Birth to the Year 1912.*

6 1922 directory for Noiseless Typewriter Company, Middleton, CT.

7 *Achievements of the Class of 1902, Yale College, from Birth to the Year 1912.*

8 *Westchester County in History: Manual and Civil List, Past and Present. County History: Towns, Hamlets, Villages and Cities*, Vol. 2, by Henry T. Smith (White Plains, NY: H.T. Smith, 1912), pp. 266–267

9 *History of the New York Yacht Club: From Its Founding Through 1973*, by John Parkinson, Jr. (New York: New York Yacht Club, 1975), p. 207.

✳ *New York 30* Rowdy, *1916 (photographed here as* Okee, *after being sold by Holland)*

✳ *New York 30* Rowdy

❋ *Trophies won by Holland Duell with his NY30 Rowdy (Photos courtesy of various members of the Duell family)*

❋ *1911 Yacht Racing Association of Long Island Sound Championship won by NY30 Rowdy (Photo courtesy of Holland Duell's grandson John Henry)*

"For five years, Father had admired the class and the spirited racing they provided when finally, in March 1910, he bought #12, which had originally been built for George M. Pynchon as *Neola II*. He renamed her *Rowdy*.[1] Obviously, that was not the *Rowdy* that you are now rebuilding. It was another six years before Father moved up in size to the larger *Rowdy*.

"Father had been voted in as a member of the American Yacht Club of Rye just before the purchase of *Rowdy*,[2] and once he took ownership, he raced her very actively, both in casual races and in more serious, long-distance races. On July 2, 1910, sailing for the American Yacht Club, he took part in the 280-mile Deep Sea Challenge Cup race held by the Brooklyn Yacht Club, finishing second, with a time of 64 hours and 50 minutes.[3,4] At the beginning of the race, he threw out a spinnaker sail so large that the handling of it would have been unnerving to most sailors. Not only did it allow him to run away from the rest of the fleet on the initial 50-mile downwind leg, but it later prompted talk of changing the rules to prevent the use of such large sails.[5]

"Father didn't join the New York Yacht Club immediately. You don't simply write a check and say, 'I would like to be a member of the club.' There is a formal application process, which includes a member having to sponsor for nomination the person interested in joining, followed by the club voting to decide whether or not to accept that person as a member. Finally, on March 23, before the start of the 1911 racing season, Father was voted in as member of the New York Yacht Club. He raced every chance he got.[6] His mastery of little *Rowdy* was almost immediate, and in 1911, he won race after race, including best overall for the season in the 1911 Championship of the Yacht Racing Association of Long Island Sound.[7] A shelf high up in the billiard room at Ardenwold displayed progressively more trophies, and through the New York Yacht Club, Father

1   *Yachting* magazine, January 1925, p. 30.
2   American Yacht Club yearbooks.
3   *New York Times*, July 6, 1910.
4   *The Sun* (New York), July 6, 1910.
5   *Evening Telegram* (New York), August 19, 1910.
6   New York Yacht Club yearbooks.
7   *Achievements of the Class of 1902, Yale College, from Birth to the Year 1912*, p. 256.

became friends with many people who were as revered for their sailing skills as they were for the financial and social status that they had achieved in life.

"Father was most charismatic and tended to make friends easily. He possessed in-depth, well-informed knowledge of an astoundingly broad spectrum of subjects and could always be counted on to add measurable substance to a conversation. Around the men, he was a man's man and was appreciated for his bright, sophisticated wit. In short order, he gained recognition both as a socially respected member of the club and as a highly skilled and talented sailor. It was the best of both worlds. The membership afforded Father the joy of sailing in the best yacht races and cruises in the area and also gave him the opportunity to interact with some of the most powerful businessmen in the nation.

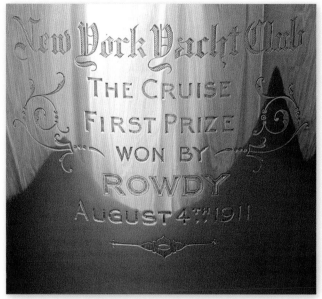

✳ *New York Yacht Club trophy won by NY30 Rowdy (Photo courtesy of Holland Duell's grandson John Henry)*

"Father's sailing was done primarily on weekends, as business matters allowed him little leisure time during the week. His legal schedule alone kept him very busy, not to mention the demands from the many businesses of which he had become a partner or director and stockholder. In 1911, he added another item to his workload, although perhaps more as a gesture of goodwill than as an actively sought-after business investment.

"Despite the half-hour distance between Ardenwold and their old neighborhood in New Rochelle, Mother and Father had kept in close contact with their friends Frederick and Elizabeth Collins. Frederick was working for the Butterick Company, a magazine publisher, as a writer and editor when he was approached by Cameron McKenzie, the son-in-law of S. S. McClure, founder of *McClure's Magazine*.[1,2] *McClure's* at that time was a very popular publication with distribution to a large percentage of households in the United States. The content was less in the form of articles and more in the form of stories. Each issue contained numerous short stories, which tended to be of a personal nature, allowing the reader to connect on an emotional level with the content. It was fun reading, but much of it was based on true life, and the aim was to keep the reader informed on the current state of events both at home and around the world. Founded in 1893, *McClure's* was well respected and was the first magazine to publish stories by H. G. Wells, author of *The Time Machine* and *The War of the Worlds*, and by Rudyard Kipling,[3] who wrote such works as *The Jungle Book*, *Rikki-Tikki-Tavi*, and *Gunga Din*.

"In 1911, the magazine business in the United States was going through a massive consolidation. Competitive pressures had made it all but impossible for a single magazine to support its own facility and printing press operation. Cameron McKenzie proposed to unite *McClure's Magazine*, the McClure's book publishing busi-

---

1 *Stilwell* v. *Duell*, pp. 304–306.
2 *The Sun* (New York), October 2, 1911.
3 *New York Times*, December 26, 1919.

ness, and the S. H. Moore Company, which published *The Ladies' World* magazine, under the umbrella of McClure's Publications, Inc., and he wanted Frederick Collins to head the operation as president.[1,2] Frederick accepted the position, McClure's Publications was incorporated, and McKenzie took the position of Vice-President. While an excellent and respected journalist, Frederick had no practical experience with corporate matters or balance sheets, and within two or three months, he came to the harsh realization that the company was going to fall well short of expected earnings and would not be able to make a $100,000 payment that was due on January 1, 1912. To get advice, a meeting was held at the Union League Club between Cameron McKenzie, Frederick Collins, his friend Holland Duell, and another attorney named Robert Walker.[3]

"While much of the friendship between Father and Frederick was based on intellect, common interests, and business matters, Mother and Elizabeth had bonded on a much deeper level. When they first met, Mabel had given Elizabeth emotional support as she tried to heal from the recent death of her almost five-year-old daughter, while at the same time, Elizabeth was gracious and selfless enough to take part in the joy of Mother's pregnancy with me. Now that Elizabeth was again pregnant and due to have her baby in four months,[4] Mother felt a need to protect and help her in any way she could, a sentiment that she very clearly articulated to Father. The bond of motherhood between the two women was heightened all the more by the fact that Mabel too was again pregnant and had almost the exact same due date.[5] When the four men met, Holland volunteered that if Frederick could raise $25,000, he would personally put up the remaining $75,000. This was done, and in return for Father's contribution, he became vice president of *McClure's Magazine*.[6]

"All major undertakings, upon successful fruition, deserve rewards. It was decided in advance that bringing the newly formed McClure's Publications out of the red—as a consequence of which Mabel, Holland, Frederick, and Elizabeth all became major stockholders in the venture[7]—and delivering two new babies into the world would certainly be worthy of a handsome reward. In the midst of adversity and struggle, it is uplifting to plan a celebration at road's end, and after many social evenings of fanciful ideas, the Duells and the Collinses unanimously agreed that a trip to Europe would be justified compensation. The babies were due in March 1912. By early that summer, at the latest, the Duell men would be obligated to the political campaign of Theodore Roosevelt, who had announced that he would run for a third term as President in 1912. If they were to fit their vacation into that small window of time, it would mean leaving newborns at home.

"For Mother, the solution was obvious. She would trust her baby with no one but family. Her cousin Emilie Brown in St. Louis had nursing skills, was not married,

---

1 *Stilwell* v. *Duell*, pp. 304–306.
2 *The Sun* (New York), October 2, 1911.
3 *Stilwell* v. *Duell*, pp. 304–306.
4 *25th Anniversary Report.*
5 *1902 Yale Autobiographies, Twenty-Five Years After.*
6 *Stilwell* v. *Duell*, pp. 304–306.
7 *McClure's Magazine*, January 1913 p. 241.

and, being the daughter of a traveling salesman, could certainly use the income.[1] Marjory Collins was born to Frederick and Elizabeth on March 15, 1912,[2] and three days later, on March 18, Mother gave birth to my little brother, Halliwell Ledyard Duell.[3] With five children, Mother thought about the benefit of having Emilie around the house and decided that, rather than simply asking for temporary assistance, she would offer Emilie a full-time, live-in position at Ardenwold, which Emilie gladly accepted.[4]

✳ *Emilie Miller Brown (May 9, 1916, passport application #23627 at National Archives and Records Administration)*

"Shortly after Halliwell was born, Emilie Brown came to live at Ardenwold.[5] I don't remember much personally of the time, as I was only two years old, but I know that my older brothers and sister were very fond of Emilie. She had such an energy about her. She was positive and vivacious, always with a half-teasing twinkle in her brilliant blue eyes and the most subtle hint of a smile at the corners of her mouth. She projected a playful persona yet always in a professional, sophisticated way and always in a kind way. She was engaging and fun, with a hearty, infectious laugh and a seemingly endless flow of lively, entertaining conversation. The entire family enjoyed being in her upbeat company.

"In the short time before leaving for Europe, Father became somewhat acquainted with Emilie. He had met her only briefly before, when she had attended his wedding. Being the nanny, she was expected to address her employers as Mr. and Mrs. Duell or Ma'am and Sir. The requirement to extend such formalities to her cousin and childhood playmate must have seemed a bit pretentious, but Emilie held no such feelings when using the address of 'Mr. Duell.' Having heard so many flattering descriptions of this 'beautiful, handsome man' from her sister Ann Louise, Emilie seemed to take pleasure in delivering the address with a subtle playfulness, placing an extra measure of emphasis on 'Mr.' and perhaps accompanying it with the slightest hint of a smile, as if to jovially suggest that she was not taking him as seriously as he was taking himself. Father found the playfulness refreshing and saw absolutely no offense in it. He enjoyed Emilie and had confidence that she could care for the children.

"Shortly after Emilie's arrival at Ardenwold, my parents and Frederick and Elizabeth Collins departed New York by ship, bound for Europe, where they spent two months in England and in touring the French countryside and Riviera by auto. Their return by ship in late April 1912[6] was clouded and perhaps made somewhat unnerving by the disaster of the *Titanic*, which only days before, on April 14, had sunk with such a huge loss of life. Aside from a few jitters, the trip home was pleasant. Emilie and the children had done fine, and Emilie remained in the household.

"The Duell men now rolled up their sleeves in preparation to campaign for Theodore Roosevelt. He had been a close family friend for so many years. It was good to once again embrace the possibility of his assuming the Presidency."

✳ *Theodore Roosevelt*

Library of Congress LC-USZ62-134760

1 http://home.comcast.net/~rkemps/Emily_Miller.html.

2 *25th Anniversary Report*.

3 *1902 Yale Autobiographies, Twenty-Five Years After*.

4 "Dilettante."

5 Ardenwold is stated as residence on Emilie Brown's January 10, 1913, passport, ancestry.com.

6 *Achievements of the Class of 1902, Yale College, from Birth to the Year 1912*.

Politics and Little Brother Charles

"In 1912, Theodore Roosevelt ran for President as the candidate of the new Progressive Party, and the Duell men swung into action. While Father immersed himself in the effort to elect Roosevelt,[1] his father, Charles Duell, Sr., assumed the position of chairman of the Roosevelt campaign committee of New York City.[2,3,4,5] Holland's brother Sackett was chosen as vice president for the Roosevelt campaign of Montgomery County, New York,[6] and Charles, Jr. went to Washington to be a member of Roosevelt's secretarial staff, traveling with him extensively[7] and managing his 1912 campaign tour.[8]

"Disaster struck on October 14, 1912, just three weeks before Election Day. Charles Duell, Jr. was with Roosevelt and the campaign team in Milwaukee, Wisconsin, where Roosevelt was scheduled to give a speech. Having just finished dinner at the Gilpatrick Hotel and getting ready to go to the Milwaukee Auditorium, Roosevelt passed through an admiring crowd outside the hotel. As he was stepping into his car, a man with a handgun, a saloonkeeper by the name of John Schrank, stepped forward and, aiming at Roosevelt's heart, fired point-blank.[9] It must have been Providence that had predestined the fifty-page copy of Roosevelt's speech as well as his steel eyeglass case to be situated in his coat pocket directly in the path of the bullet, which lost its lethal velocity as it ripped through both.

"Being an experienced hunter, Roosevelt knew that he was seriously wounded but also that, since he was not coughing up blood, he was not dying. With blood seeping from his shirt, he gave the entire campaign speech, which lasted ninety minutes. Afterward, X-rays showed that the bullet had traveled through 3 inches of tissue before lodging in Roosevelt's chest muscle. It would be too dangerous to try to remove the bullet, which remained deep in Roosevelt's chest for the rest of his life.

---

1 *Achievements of the Class of 1902, Yale College, from Birth to the Year 1912*, compiled by James Wright (New Haven, CT: Yale University Press, 1913).

2 *The Sun* (New York), June 2, 1912.

3 *Amsterdam Evening Recorder*, June 4, 1912.

4 *Amsterdam Evening Recorder*, January 30, 1920.

5 *Syracuse Herald*, January 30, 1920.

6 *Amsterdam Evening Recorder*, May 29, 1912.

7 *Encyclopedia of American Biography*, edited by Winfield Scott Downs (New York: American Historical Company, 1955).

8 *Evening Telegram* (New York), December 16, 1922.

9 *The Post* (Ellicottville, NY), October 16, 1912.

Roosevelt was in the hospital for a week. During this time, the other major candidates—the incumbent President, Republican William Howard Taft, and the Democratic candidate, Woodrow Wilson—suspended their campaigns, but they resumed as soon as Roosevelt was discharged. Roosevelt's convalescence prevented him from getting back on the campaign trail, and although he received more votes than Taft, Wilson won the election. At a time when world powers were saber rattling, the country needed a President who was a man of strength and action, and Roosevelt's defeat came as a frustrating blow to the Duells, who viewed the victorious Wilson as a man with little backbone.

"Charles, Jr. spent the next few years completely immersed in politics, and when Roosevelt departed for an expedition into the Brazilian rainforest in late 1913, he asked Charles to keep an eye out for a suitable candidate for Governor of New York in the upcoming 1914 election. Roosevelt trusted Charles. "I knew that Mr. Duell was absolutely sincere, absolutely straightforward, truthful, and responsible," he said later.[1] Charles was of course acquainted with then District Attorney Charles S. Whitman, having at one time worked as his assistant,[2] and felt that Whitman would make a good candidate for Governor. Charles began to campaign for him and announced in the newspapers that as soon as Theodore Roosevelt arrived home from his expedition, he would ask Roosevelt to endorse Whitman as the Progressive Party candidate for Governor of New York in the upcoming election.[3]

"Upon his return, Roosevelt immediately butted heads with Whitman, and his distrust for the man led to numerous heated arguments and newspaper articles filled with accusations and counteraccusations. In support of Roosevelt, leaders of the Progressive Party also opposed a Whitman candidacy on the grounds that they thought him "utterly tricky and insincere."[4] Poor Charles, still young, trusting, and idealistic, tried to act as a mediator and make peace between Roosevelt and Whitman. As a consequence, he himself was often placed in the hot seat by both the press and his own party. In the end, it was revealed that Whitman had never had any intention of supporting the causes of the Progressive Party and was simply using Charles Duell to try to gain an endorsement from Theodore Roosevelt. The betrayal infuriated Charles, who told the press that "the hypocrisy of the man in his now charged and newly announced candidacy for the Governorship should be exposed at once.... Either he lied then and he tells the truth now, or he told the truth then and he lies now. In either event the lie is there, whether it be in April or August—a Spring lie or a Summer lie. I, for my part, wouldn't believe him under oath."[5]

"It was a crushing blow to the Progressive Party's effort to put a governor into office. Their last-minute nomination of Harvey D. Hinman would prove futile against the Whitman campaign. It was also a crushing blow to what had been an ascending political career for Charles. He continued to be involved in politics but never on the same level."

✳ *Charles Holland Duell, Jr. (December 3, 1918, passport application #49906 at National Archives and Records Administration)*

✳ *Charles S. Whitman*

Library of Congress, ggbain 04989

---

1 *New York Times*, July 16, 1914.
2 *New York Times*, June 26, 1914.
3 *New York Herald*, May 5, 1914.
4 *New York Times*, July 16, 1914.
5 *New York Times*, July 30, 1914.

McClure's Goes to the Movies

"At the same time that Uncle Charles was facing his political challenges, Father also found himself being challenged, as a consequence of his business interest in McClure's Publications. Surprisingly, the war had a negative impact on the company's profitability. You would think that it would have been just the opposite. Everyone wanted to read stories about the war overseas, and *McClure's Magazine* ran many stories with wonderfully personal firsthand accounts. It was excellent writing and very popular reading. Unfortunately, German submarines plagued the ocean, and because of the resulting increase in shipping costs, as well as unfavorable economic conditions in Europe, the cost of paper had skyrocketed to the point of wiping out nearly all of McClure's profitability. Frederick Collins, Father's friend and business partner in McClure's, continually thought of other avenues the business could use to expand revenues. Despite the low profits, McClure's Publications was a valuable asset. *The Ladies' World* and *McClure's Magazine* had good circulation and loyal readership and were well respected in literary circles and by advertisers. The problem was that people were willing to pay only so much for a magazine, and demand simply would not justify a price high enough to cover the cost of paper and allow a profit.

"Motion pictures at the time were a relatively new phenomenon. The technology for projecting them onto screens in front of an audience had been developing rapidly since its inception in the 1890s, and there seemed to be almost daily advances in the art of film making as well. Movies were exploding onto the scene as a wildly popular form of entertainment and creating something of a gold rush. Companies stampeded into the industry in pursuit of overnight wealth and riches.

"Thomas Edison was the man of the day. Young people today hear his name and think, "inventor of the light bulb." But Edison was so much more. In the very earliest years of motion pictures, he invented the Kinetoscope, into which the patron placed a coin and then viewed, through the face plate window, movies averaging one minute in length. Not only was the machine Edison's invention, but the movies it showed were products of the Edison Company. Their debut in

* Kinetoscope parlor
(National Park Service,
Thomas Edison National
Historical Park)

New York City in 1894 at a penny arcade featured ten machines, and they were an instant fascination and success. Kinetoscope parlors soon popped up across the country. Their popularity spread to Europe, and all at once, the world was enamored of movies.

"Within a few years, movies were being projected onto screens. Once projection machines became affordable, Kinetoscope parlors went out of fashion, and nickelodeons swept the country. Still mom-and-pop operations, these nickelodeons were set up in small rented premises that held nothing more than a screen, a projector, and a handful of chairs, typically with a piano in the corner partially masking the clatter of the projector.[1] They charged patrons a nickel (thus the name, *odeion* being Greek for "roofed theater") to watch several short "flickers" usually totaling about a half hour.[2] Edison Studio's 1903 release *The Great Train Robbery* was an immediate success.

"All along the way, Edison had dominated the American market, eventually operating a full-scale production company and holding patents on many of the components that were essential to the filming and projecting of movies.

"Frederick Collins had researched the numbers and was fascinated by the potential profits that the motion picture business offered. He devised a plan that would benefit both McClure's and Edison.[3] He sold the Thomas A. Edison Company on a plan to create a story called "What Happened to Mary?" that would run as a series. Collins would first release the latest segment of the series in *The Ladies' World* magazine, and a short while afterward, the Edison Company would release the film version of the segment. It was the first series ever created, the concept for which Frederick was given full credit.[4] The cross-exposure and publicity benefited both companies, and the arrangement continued successfully with every appearance of a bright future. Frederick became increasingly fascinated by the motion picture business and took full advantage of his access to the Edison Studios to learn all that he could about the process of making movies.[5]

"Back in 1908, Edison had established the Edison Trust, consisting of a conglomerate of all the major American film companies, film distributors, and suppliers of raw film stock. Through this trust and aggressive legal enforcement of its patents, Edison controlled the motion picture market and the laws by which it had to abide. Perhaps for reasons involving cost control, the Edison Trust policed the industry, requiring domestic film makers to limit their movies to a length of about 13 to 17 minutes, just at a time when foreign films that ran as long as two hours were starting to be produced and American audiences were thirsting for longer films. On October 1, 1915, a federal court ruled that the actions of the Edison Trust went "far beyond what was necessary to protect the use of patents" and therefore constituted an illegal restraint of trade. With the ruling, the Edison Trust was ordered dissolved, and the arrangement between Edison and McClure's came to an end.

---

1   *The Movies, Mr. Griffith, and Me*, by Lillian Gish with Ann Pinochot (Englewood Cliffs, NJ: Prentice-Hall, 1969), p. 30.

2   *The Movies, Mr. Griffith, and Me*, p. 53.

3   *Stilwell* v. *Duell*, Appellate Division of the New York Supreme Court, 1933, p. 308. Housed at New York State Library, Albany, NY, locator C31, vol. 164, citation 241 Ad 705

4   *Photoplay* magazine, Vol. XI, No. 3, February 1917, p. 21.

5   *Stilwell* v. *Duell*, p. 308.

"Frederick Collins saw this as the perfect opportunity to stop outsourcing the film production to Edison and go directly into the business of making movies himself. He had developed quite a passion for it, and the numbers looked phenomenal. His assessment of the profit potential was borne out by research from the American Tobacco Company, to which my mother Mabel, as a major stockholder, had access.

"American Tobacco at the time had $100 million in surplus cash that it needed to invest. Benjamin B. Hampton, American Tobacco's vice-president (the position that Mabel's father had once held), had spent most of 1915 scrutinizing masses of data and had determined that the motion picture business offered investors fantastic growth potential.[1] Accordingly, in early 1916, American Tobacco invested $1 million dollars in Vitagraph Studios and took the company public, raising $25 million in capitalization.[2] Mother was enthusiastic about the numbers that Hampton had analyzed for the film industry and foresaw the movie business as a possible venture that could help Frederick and Elizabeth Collins to acquire wealth and fame. Her close friendship with Elizabeth had inspired her to take the couple under her wing, and considering wealth to be the biggest blessing she could wish upon them, she encouraged Father to help Frederick break into the business.

"Father couldn't deny the numbers, and when Frederick tried to convince him that they should go into the motion picture business as partners, it was an easy sale. With the breakup of the Edison Trust, full-length feature films were destined to become the new rage, and Frederick and Father saw a lucrative opportunity to enter the field, specializing in only movies of the highest quality. At the time, Frederick and Father had a joint lease on two floors at 19 West 45th Street. Father's office was on the upper floor, and a private stairway connected the two. He and Frederick saw each other every day, lunched together two or three times a week, and discussed the possibilities even when they saw each other socially every Saturday.[3]

"But that wasn't all that was on Father's mind. Herreshoff was about to introduce a new class of yachts, and Father was making plans to move up in size and order the yacht that you are now rebuilding."

---

1 *Dreams for Sale: The Rise and Fall of the Triangle Film Corporation*, by Kalton C. Lahue (South Brunswick, NJ: A.S. Barnes, 1971), p. 102.

2 *Dreams for Sale*, p. 109.

3 *Stilwell v. Duell*, pp. 310–314.

Rowdy's 2003 Launch

The history was fascinating to me, and if there had been two of me, I would have had one Chris Madsen doing full-time research while the other was busy readying *Rowdy* for her upcoming launch. I wanted to get her in the water as soon as possible, where I would then install the spars and complete the rigging and a number of smaller items.

It was a fun crowd in the boatyard, and there was always out-of-the-ordinary amusement. A married woman greeted me at my boat one day with "Excuse me." She wanted to know the location in the water of a boat owned by a woman named—let's call her Pamela. On the previous day, the married woman had come to visit her husband on his boat, only to find Pamela in an intimately shocking position on top of him. Speechless, she fled the scene in a dazed panic. Having had a day to compose herself, she now wanted to find Pamela to exchange a few words with her. I never heard a report of what words they exchanged, but I felt that I got more than my fair share of material for juicy boatyard gossip.

A big catamaran was ready to be launched, and no one who was present to see it begin its trip to the water will ever forget the scene. It was a seven-year, homemade labor of love, built from scratch and at last nearly ready to head for the South Pacific. It sat perched atop four 55-gallon drums, one at the front and one at the back of each of its double hulls. A harness had been attached, and as a huge crane slowly lifted the boat, it rose, somewhat cockeyed, off three of the drums, leaving the fourth drum bearing considerable weight. Before the crane operator could lift the boat above that last drum, the bottom of the drum slipped out across the asphalt, and as the boat shot the drum out like a watermelon seed, the catamaran lurched forward into a frantic, jerking swing that arced back and forth across a 30-foot span. In a panic to arrest the swing, the crane operator tried to ease the boat down so that he could use the ground as a brake, but his hand was too heavy, and the boat came down hard, bending the propeller shaft and doing moderate damage to the fiberglass. The screams from the owner's wife were unmistakable above the gasps of the crowd. Luckily, it was all fixable, and after a month of repairs, the boat was launched and did make it to the South Pacific.

Another 50-foot catamaran had been bought by a young man as a rebuild project. He paid yard fees for well over two years, but very little got done, and the boat's condition deteriorated. At one point, a beehive was established inside and caused enough problems around the yard that fumigators had to be called in. Eventually,

✳ *Top, Alan caulking the hull before the launch; bottom, Alan's caulking tools*

funds ran out for the project, and the boatyard had a bulldozer break the boat up and put it in a dumpster.

Relationships came and went. Employees came and went. In the spirit of a good soap opera, there were friendships and fights and rivalries and scandals. But despite the entertainment, it was not cheap lodging, and I was anxious to hit the water.

By March 2003, everything on *Rowdy* was done except the rigging and sails. Alan from Traditional Shipwright Services, who lent infinite talent and guidance to the project, checked the final boatyard item off the list by completing the caulking below the waterline. His assortment of antique wooden mallets and caulking irons looked as though they were right out of the Middle Ages.

Apparently, a good caulking mallet is like a fine violin in that it produces a certain tone and feel when the caulking is hammered in perfectly. Alan tried to impress on me how the sound from his vintage wooden caulking mallet gave him better feedback on his caulking than that of an equivalent modern wooden mallet—a subtle difference that I'm afraid I was never able to distinguish. He told me a story of showing up at one of his first jobs in proud possession of his own wooden mallet. His boss looked at it and then threw it in the ocean, telling Alan that the modern piece of junk would never give him the feedback of a good vintage mallet. Needless to say *Rowdy* got a perfect caulking job which would never leak a drop of water.

Finally, on March 14, 2003, I was ready to cap my hemorrhaging outflow of money to the boatyard. When I thanked them for throwing a launching party, they explained that it wasn't a party—it was a wake to mourn the loss of their best benefactor. The launch went smoothly, as did the first test of the propulsion system when, accompanied by a dozen friends, I motored *Rowdy* across the channel to her new end tie at a marina. After three and a half years in a boatyard, it was time for life on the water.

I had my sights set on the 26th annual McNish Classic, which was to take place in four months. It was a large race, reserved exclusively for classic sailboats, and had a good draw from areas quite far away. The next few months were a flurry of turnbuckles, mast, booms, rigging, sails, and the like—and, finally, sea trials.

On July 28, with the race five days away, I was driving back to the boat after a trip to Santa Barbara. Victoria Avenue is a straight six-mile-long road that runs from the freeway to the marina. On the right-hand side, toward the marina end of the road, was a small plant and flower shop called the Glasshouse Nursery. Had *Rowdy* not been in my life, I never in a million years would have been in the area and never would have

✳ *Chris Madsen christening* Rowdy *at the launching*

✳ *Rigging* Rowdy, *March 2003*

✳ Rowdy *during 2003 sea trials*

seen the slender woman walking into the shop who inspired me to make a U-turn at 50 miles per hour, park on the gravelly roadside, and say, "Hi, I'm Chris." Linda and I exchanged numbers, and I hurried back to the boat to ready her for the upcoming race.

The race took place on a perfect California coastal day. There was no fog, the seas were flat, and there was a fresh breeze. The race was made doubly enjoyable by the

✳ *Setting the spinnaker on the final leg*

✳ *Barreling down on the finish line, Chris Madsen at the helm*

large crew, made up of friends who had all cheered the project on, and triply fun by the fact that *Rowdy* placed first in her division, her first race in 50 years, and also won the Bristol Boat Award for the best-quality vintage yacht.

In the spirit of life keeping an interesting pace, Linda and I started dating right after the race, and in less than three months' time, on October 18, we were ecstatic to find out that we were going to have a child together. I had always wanted children, but for whatever reasons, it just never happened, and being 48 years old, I assumed that I had sadly missed the boat. Linda's wonderful, bubbly, beautiful five-year-old daughter Chloe said that the pregnancy happened because she had wished for a sister. Well, our first doctor's appointment on November 3 delivered double her wish when the ultrasound provided the first view of our *twin* daughters, Sophia and Claire.

The moment was both thrilling and terrifying. While my every emotion in connection with becoming a first-time father to twin daughters was joyous beyond imagination, my commitment to *Rowdy* had challenged me to my financial limit. As a bachelor, I had allowed myself the freedom to take financial risks, often with very beneficial results. But now that I was suddenly cast into the role of a responsible parent-to-be, I felt a burdening sense of urgency to sell *Rowdy* and return to a position of financial stability. Aside from a few minor finishing details and some routine maintenance, she was exquisitely ready to market, but I was now of the mindset that to find the perfect buyer, someone who would value her as much as I had come to, I would need to present her to the sailing world along with her complete history.

Sadly, on February 6, 2003, just one month before *Rowdy's* launching, Hanny's son Robert Wood called to inform me of his mother's passing. The news felt absolutely monumental. It was truly the end of an era. And as much as I was saddened by the loss, I was equally grateful that our two lives had the opportunity to touch, even for such a brief period of time.

The unfolding story of the Duells did not end upon Hanny's passing—far from it. During our friendship, she had introduced me to Holland's grandchildren and great-grandchildren, and through them and numerous other doors that opened up, information began to pour in as if from a waterfall.

Rowdy Arrives

olland Duell had sold his NY30 *Rowdy* in 1915[1], at the time when he and Frederick Collins were entertaining the prospect of going into the movie business together. Holland had loved the little boat but felt that he was ready for something larger. Herreshoff had added to his sterling reputation when he designed and produced the Thirties. These boats were universally admired in yachting circles, and by request, in 1913, Herreshoff had designed and built a new, larger class for the New York Yacht Club: the New York Fifties. Big brother to the New York Thirties and similar to them in many ways, the Fifties were 50 feet at the waterline and 72 feet on deck.[2] Like the Thirties, the Fifties turned out to be thoroughbreds, extremely fast and agile, and were well received by all their owners. The two classes were hugely popular, but there was a large gap between the two sizes, and soon there was talk of requesting a third class that would fill the gap. Holland was determined to be first in line when orders for the new boats became available.

By October 1915, Herreshoff had completed plans for the new class of sailboats, to be called the New York Forties. They would be 40 feet at the waterline and 59 feet on deck, with a beam of 14 feet, 3 inches and a relatively high freeboard. Unlike most racers of the day, whose pursuit of speed through minimum weight necessitated a somewhat stripped-down interior, the New York Yacht Club members had specifically requested Herreshoff to build the Forties with gracious interior accommodations, which Herreshoff was able to accomplish through the slightly wider beam and higher freeboard. Holland placed his order on October 14, 1915, for a price of $10,000 plus $280 for the wheel option instead of a tiller.[3] He again selected the name *Rowdy* for the boat. With the possible advent of war looming, there was some deliberation over whether to build the new class, but the general consensus was that Wilson showed every desire to avoid fighting alongside the Allies and would most likely retain that weak posture unless absolutely forced to take up arms.

Although the United States was not yet actively participating in it, the war was already having an impact on most people's lives. A large percentage of the country

1 *Yachting*, January 1925.
2 *History of the New York Yacht Club: From Its Founding Through 1973*, by John Parkinson, Jr. (New York: New York Yacht Club, 1975), p. 241.
3 Herreshoff order ledger book at Herreshoff Museum.

＊ *Red Cross Poster*

felt that the United States had a moral as well as a practical responsibility to join in the fight to protect the free world. Consequently, many civilians volunteered their services. Emilie Brown and Ruth Alice, the "Pretty Nurse," had become friends through Mabel and had traveled together to France back in 1913.[1,2] They had both fallen in love with that beautiful country and its people, and in 1915, feeling an obligation to help, Emilie left Ardenwold to serve as a Red Cross nurse in France.[3,4]

In her absence, it turned out that Holland missed her companionship more than he had expected. Holland worked hard and took things very seriously. He had to. He was involved in very important matters. Emilie, perhaps because of her nursing background, was more in tune with the fragility and fleeting nature of life and viewed every day as a gift that should be celebrated. She considered it essential to appreciate and enjoy every opportunity for happiness that comes one's way—even the smallest opportunities, such as sharing a smile in the middle of a busy day, actually taking the time to smell that rose, having a five-minute break for coffee and fun conversation, or simply doing something nice for someone.

Holland was the person to go to if you wanted assurance that your project would be completed in a satisfactory manner. He did not like things hanging over his head. He liked to "do it and get it done." He had a tendency to dive into projects with all his attention and energy and not surface for air until he had reached his objective. Mabel provided no balance. She encouraged the serious work ethic. In fact, it was often her ambitions that forced the need for his attention. Emilie, on the other hand, found a way of breaking through Holland's seriousness, which she respectfully but lightheartedly poked fun at. She found a way of pulling him out of his battle mode, if just for a moment, to focus on the beauty of the day he was living in and to put a smile on his face before sending him back on his mission. The mere act of those little interventions seemed to change the day's mood completely. It wasn't an effort for Emilie. That was just her nature. She was energetic and upbeat and playful, and she was always consistent in those qualities. She had brought a ray of sunshine and much needed lightheartedness into what, for Holland, was becoming a much more complicated and serious life at Ardenwold. Holland perhaps took that energy for granted while Emilie was living at Ardenwold, but he most certainly felt her absence when she left for France.

1　June 9, 1923, passport application for Emilie Brown, ancestry.com.
2　April 30, 1913, *Olympic* passenger list, ancestry.com.
3　"Dilettante," a paper written by Holland Duell's son Holland Sackett Duell, Jr. about his parents.
4　*New York Times*, November 2, 1925.

In late April 1916, the first of the New York Forties hit the water,[1,2] and by May 5, all twelve of the yachts had been launched.[3] The launching of the new class was celebrated with both excitement and anxiety. Everyone had crossed fingers that the Forties would perform up to expectations under sail. Sea trials were scheduled. Special races and captains' meetings were put on the calendar. The enthusiasm in the moment rivaled, for fully grown adults, what a child feels for Christmas. It was a time when Holland could have spent every moment with his new boat and his yacht club friends, had it not been for what felt to him like an utterly burdening work schedule. He was dealing with how to return McClure's Publications to profitability, the recently failed partnership with Edison, and the devising of a business plan with Frederick Collins to break into the movie business,[4] not to mention an already full workload from his law firm, the demands of being on the boards of several large businesses, and an active, multi-year case involving the family-owned Klauder-Weldon business, which Holland was battling through the courts to the New York Supreme Court.[5]

Mabel did little to help his situation. She was not particularly supportive of adding a new sailboat to their already busy lives. In fact, she was not supportive of anything outside the sphere of her vision of what their lives should be. This is in no way to fault the qualities of her heart or the moral fiber of her character. They were impeccable. She was perhaps the most devoted, best-intentioned, truly loving, caring mother a family could ask for. She was, without reservation, 100 percent selflessly and tirelessly committed to her family, and in her heart, she had only the best wishes for her children's happiness and well-being. The problem was that Mabel seemed to have a preconceived and completely inflexible vision of her perfect family and how to achieve their happiness. Anything that fell outside the framework of that vision, anything that did not contribute to the attainment of her goals and aspirations for family, she considered frivolous and altogether unnecessary. So despite all that Holland did in the way of work to support Mabel and the family, she felt that he shouldn't have a need for payback or reward outside of time spent with family. Family and the pursuit of ever higher success were all that she needed. Why should Holland need anything more? In that sense, Mabel added to Holland's feeling of being suppressed. He did not get support or encouragement from her to pursue his recreation; rather, she usually stood as one more obstacle between him and his passion for the sea.[6]

Emilie had returned from France shortly before *Rowdy* was launched. Planning to go back soon to resume her part in the war effort, she chose not to live at Ardenwold. Instead, she found a townhouse at 59 Gramercy Park, halfway between Central Park and the southern tip of Manhattan. She very much liked the location because it was almost next door to the Lexington Avenue residence of her friend Ruth Alice,

---

1 *New York Times*, April 27, 1916.

2 *Brooklyn Daily Eagle*, April 2, 1916.

3 *New York Times*, May 4, 1916.

4 *Stilwell* v. *Duell*, Appellate Division of the New York Supreme Court, 1933, pp. 308–314. Housed at New York State Library, Albany, NY, locator C31, vol. 164, citation 241 Ad 705

5 *Amsterdam Evening Recorder*, March 31, 1916.

6 "Dilettante."

the "Pretty Nurse," and Ruth Alice's third husband, Warren Van Slyke.[1] (Ruth Alice's second husband, whom she had married after the death of Mabel's father, had died in an automobile accident.) The location also had the benefit of the lovely, private, and fenced-in two-acre Gramercy Park, one of only two private parks in New York City. In 1916, when Emilie lived in the townhouse, in the center of the park stood a newly erected statue of the famous 19th century Shakespearean actor Edwin Booth, brother of the loathed John Wilkes Booth, who in 1865 had assassinated President Lincoln.

The entire Duell family was quite fond of Emilie, and she came to Ardenwold frequently to visit and to lend a hand when Mabel and Holland needed help with the children. Emilie had almost insisted to Holland that he give her a tour of his new *Rowdy*, and since he kept the boat at Rye, the two met first for lunch at the American Yacht Club there. It was a long lunch, as both of their lives had been very busy and eventful, and there was much to catch up on.

Emilie had spent several months working as a volunteer nurse in the French officer's hospital of St. Jean de Dieu in Paris and later working for a very small outpost, Hospital Militaire No. 43, in the town of Saint-Valéry-en-Caux on the northern coast of France. The hospital was run by volunteer surgeon Dr. Ralph Fitch, one assistant, and nine nurses. Accordingly, it was very busy,[2,3] and Emilie saw more than her share of the ghastly wounds inflicted by war.

The sheer volume and extent of injuries were hugely taxing on the medical personnel and facilities. Compound fractures and deep, ugly lacerations and amputations were the easy cases. They were straightforward and presented a welcome break. You simply set a bone and sewed up a gash. Unfortunately, the majority of injuries required creative solutions from physicians, who asked themselves, "How in the world do I begin to treat this?" What do you do with a man who can't breathe because all his airways are swollen closed from poison gas? How do you possibly remove shrapnel and the infinite amount of infection-causing dirt and debris that a mortar shell has pummeled through someone's abdomen?

The French, Emilie said, were beaten down to the point of breaking. They needed every bit of help they could get. No one over there could understand why the United States was standing by, watching the French defend the free world, at the cost of what every day was looking more and more to be their possibly annihilation, and doing nothing to lend assistance. Holland echoed the sentiment of the French that the United States should be involved. He had more than ample company in that regard. Roosevelt was slamming Wilson in the press for his pacifism and refusal to at least prepare the American military for the possibility of war.

Elihu Root, a cousin of Holland's (Elihu Root's mother and Holland's grandmother were sisters), had just finished a six-year term as a U.S. Senator.[4] Root also opposed President Wilson's policy of neutrality and actively promoted the Preparedness

Library of Congress, # LC-USZ62-100792

❋ *Elihu Root, 1902*

1   June 26, 1916, passport application for Warren Clark Van Slyke, ancestry.com.

2   *Eleventh Annual Report of the American National Red Cross for the Year 1915*, July 27, 1916, p. 23.

3   *New York Times*, September 2, 1925.

4   http://en.wikipedia.org/wiki/Elihu_Root.

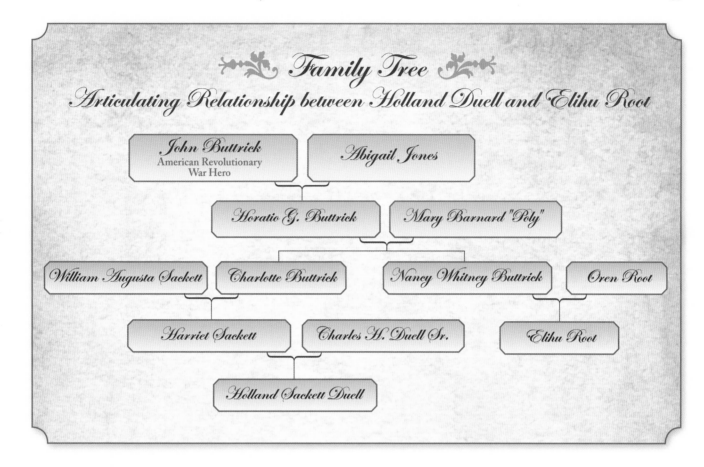

Family Tree
Articulating Relationship between Holland Duell and Elihu Root

John Buttrick
American Revolutionary War Hero

Abigail Jones

Horatio G. Buttrick

Mary Barnard "Poly"

William Augusta Sackett

Charlotte Buttrick

Nancy Whitney Buttrick

Oren Root

Harriet Sackett

Charles H. Duell Sr.

Elihu Root

Holland Sackett Duell

Movement to get the United States ready for actual participation in the war on the side of the British and French.[1]

Root was considered the prototype of the 20th century "wise man" who shuttled between high-level government positions in Washington, D.C., and private-sector legal practice in New York City. Besides his term as U.S. Senator, he also served at different times as Secretary of War and Secretary of State, was awarded the Nobel Peace Prize in 1912 as a result of his work to bring nations together through arbitration and cooperation, and in 1916 was proposed for the Republican presidential nomination but declined, stating that he was too old to bear the burden of the Presidency.[2]

Holland promised Emilie that if it did come to pass that the United States entered the war, he would be among the first to enlist and would make a point of finding her in France to share another lunch.

With that, the conversation turned to other things, including his new *Rowdy.* Holland filled Emilie in on all the business and legal ventures in which he was in-

---

1 http://en.wikipedia.org/wiki/Elihu_Root.

2 http://en.wikipedia.org/wiki/Elihu_Root.

volved and joked that now that he had the boat of his dreams, he didn't know how he was going to find time to sail her.

Emilie turned serious. "Holland, you love that boat, don't you?"

"I think we have potential together."

"Then play with it. Enjoy it."

"And as for the court case, shall I ask to be excused because I need time to relax and go sailing?"

"You simply find a different way to put it. I am sure you have arranged postponements for clients. Fight for yourself. Court can wait. Your movie business can wait. Frederick will do his best with the magazines. Let your law partners pick up some slack at the office."

"You certainly make it a simple undertaking to clear my calendar, Emilie."

"The determination is what makes those things easy. If you come to France for our lunch but end up getting killed by the war before your court case, will you be disappointed to miss it?"

"I would be delighted to miss the court case and would probably find in that some consolation for having to be a casualty of war."

"And if the same circumstances denied you the chance to ever sail *Rowdy*?"

"I would feel cheated, and that is a brilliant use of the 'Life is too short' strategy."

"Life *is* too short. Every day in France, I saw people who ran out of time, still having things they wanted and needed to do. My suggestion to you is to grab what you want while it is right in the palm of your hand." With that, she grabbed the palm of his hand and, with a huge, playful smile and half-questioning intonation, said, "Take me for a sail."

Holland chuckled. "As much as I would love to take you for a sail, *Rowdy* is a 22-ton yacht, and I regrettably did not think to bring a crew along."

"That's OK. I trust you," Emilie replied in playful defiance.

"Somehow I sense that you are choosing not to hear my answer."

"Well, I'm not particularly fond of 'no' if that happens to be your answer."

"Heaven forbid that should be my answer. Let me rephrase it to say that you will be expected to work."

Rowdy could be seen swinging on her mooring out in Echo Bay. Following a short row in a skiff, they were aboard.

The 1916 Racing Season

$\mathcal{S}$tanding on the deck of *Rowdy* was for all the world like being aboard a small ship. The distance from the bow to the stern coupled with the 14-foot beam gave the impression of an amazingly large area, perhaps seeming all the larger because there was no built-up cabin. With the exception of four hatches, *Rowdy* was all flush deck. Nevertheless, she was not flat and undimensional; rather, she was an artistic composite of aesthetically pleasing curves and cambers that ran harmoniously in opposing directions. The 60-foot sweeping curve that ran from a high point at the bow through the low amidships and back up to the high point astern was intersected by the large, arching camber of the deck, which was fully 6 inches higher at the centerline of the deck than at the port and starboard rails. The long 1 ½"-wide deck boards were sprung to conform to the curvature of the hull, so they worked in toward the deck's centerline like concentric layers of a halved onion. More beautifully sculptured art would be hard to find in a world-class gallery. And at 22 tons, *Rowdy* didn't bob like a small boat. She sat heavy and stable in the water and, when sailing, simply leaned on her rail and effortlessly pushed the ocean swells out of her way. Taking her out by himself without a crew might not have been the most prudent thing for Holland to do, but the warm afternoon breeze was steady and light, and Holland, who was an exceptionally skillful sailor, had no intention of hoisting enough sail to unleash *Rowdy*'s full speed. This would simply be a calm, relaxing cruise.

"I am going to throw off our mooring line, and while I am raising the mainsail, I want you to steer so the wind stays on our port side."

"Captain" Emilie laughed, "I'm not sure I know how to tell which direction the wind is coming from. Is that a problem?"

"If you are my entire crew, it very well could be. Let me show you before we cast off."

Holland came back to the cockpit where Emilie stood. A gentle breeze was luffing in from the port side of the boat.

"Look in this direction." He stood close behind her, his outstretched arm brushing against her side and pointing in front of her and off to port.

"Now relax and tell me, do you feel the wind on your face?"

"Ever so slightly, but yes, I do feel it."

He gently placed his hands on her cheeks and slowly turned her head to the left so that the wind lapped the right side of her face.

"Do you feel the wind on your ears?"

"I feel it on my right but not at all on my left."

Again he gently turned her head, this time in the opposite direction.

"Where do you feel the wind now?"

"Now on my left ear, but not at all on my right."

"Now I want you to turn your head from side to side until you feel the wind exactly evenly on both ears. Go beyond where you know you should be in both directions, feeling where you have gone too far, so that you can come back to that perfect point in the middle."

As Holland moved his hands from her cheeks to rest on her hips, Emilie slowly moved her head from side to side and, with her eyes closed, finally rested perfectly still with her nose pointing directly into the wind. The effect of an active lifestyle was easily evidenced in her graceful, slender figure, and Holland perhaps took notice of that even as Emilie may have noticed a perceptible lingering of the moment.

"There, you see," Holland said, "you're a natural."

"Thank you, sir. Actually, I think you get the credit for being an amazing teacher."

"If so, you might want to worry about a lesson in anchor duty." And then he barked jokingly, "Now prepare yourself, lass. We're going to sea."

Rowdy had no engine. The propeller drag and extra weight would hinder her speed when she was competing in races. Leaving port under sail alone is a nervous proposition for even the most experienced of sailors, but Holland's skillful maneuvering made the event feel as smooth and carefree as a summer stroll, and *Rowdy* managed a graceful exit from her mooring. Emilie held her at the proper angle to the wind while Holland hoisted the mainsail. The big wooden rings that circled the mast and secured the leading edge of the sail slid smoothly up the giant spar until *Rowdy* gently leaned on her side and began to slice through the water.

The day was perfect. Even on the water, they could feel the warmth of the sun on their skin. The seas were flat, and the breeze was just enough to keep the sail full and provide for a leisurely sail. Summer sea life abounded. Flocks of seabirds worked the boils of sardines and anchovies as they surfaced to escape the larger fish below. Occasionally, a large seal would join in the feast and add his bellowing bark to the hectic chorus of shrill seabird cries. Holland showed Emilie how to properly bring the boat back and forth across the wind, and she took great delight in standing at the helm shouting, "Ready about" and "Helm's a-lee" as she tacked the boat from port to starboard and back again.

Lashing the wheel in place with a short length of line, Holland asked, "Emilie, may I borrow you from the captain's seat for a moment?"

Playfully, she replied, "Might I ask, for what purpose, sir?"

"I would like to show you my favorite place on the boat."

"I really can't imagine there could be a better spot on the boat than this one, but yes, by all means, if there is, I would be honored to have you share it with me."

She followed as they crouched low to the deck and carefully walked to the bow of the boat.

"I want you to sit right there, facing forward." he said, pointing to the extreme tip of the bow. "Hold onto the forestay, and let your legs hang off both sides of the boat."

Emilie sat on the bow as one would sit astride a horse. The upward slope of the deck at that point elevated the bow well above water level such that her hanging feet were never in peril of getting wet.

"This is a special place to be alone," Holland said, "so while I steer the boat, you stay as long as you like and then let me know what you think."

It was a magical spot, the bow of that boat. It was a place where one went to be alone with oneself and the elements and the sea and the planet, and in the moment, there was almost a beckoning to contemplate one's place within that sphere and an allure to let slip away things of a trivial nature and to meditate on what was really important in this life. Perhaps it was a consequence of the simultaneous stimulation of all the senses: the smell of the salt air, the soft touch of the wind on one's face, the sound of the gentle bow wake lapping against the hull and the sight, as one leaned forward and looked down, of how gracefully and effortlessly the bow of the boat sliced through the water, galloping ever forward without mechanical power of any type, but simply dancing in harmony with the winds and the currents. It was mesmerizing, and what thoughts Emilie contemplated and struggled with as she sat there, her near-hypnotized gaze transfixed on the bow and bow wake, will remain for her alone to know, but when she came back to the cockpit, she made no attempt to conceal her awe.

"Holland, is this what sailing is about? I had no idea. I could never have begun to imagine how invigorating and almost spiritual it can feel. This has been the most incredible day. Oh, Holland, please promise me you will allow yourself proper time to enjoy all this. There will never be another first season. Your business can wait. Immerse yourself in dark, gloomy courtrooms when you are a stodgy old man. Right now, you're in the prime of your life. You've got your health. You've got money. You should be at every event sponsored for these boats. There must be so much energy and excitement among the new owners, and you should be sharing every minute of the fun with them."

"Unfortunately, I just happen to have a very full calendar at the moment—important things that require my time. I will be racing. I just won't make all the races. I think my father cursed me with his imparted wisdom of 'Holland, work before play.' No matter what the message, when you hear it enough at a young age, I think it becomes ingrained in you."

"Holland, you're all grown up. Some people never fully grow up. You certainly have. You're a big, strong businessman and a powerful attorney with lots of responsibilities. But somewhere inside you and every man, there is still a little boy who needs time to play. It's not only unhealthy but it's also irresponsible to ignore that side of yourself. I wish for you a long, healthy, happy life, but if that's going to happen, you need to nurture that child inside and take the time to play. Simply play—with things, with other people—but allow yourself ample time for play. If you look at elderly people, I think you will see most who have made it to 100 still have a rebellious, playful twinkle in their eye. You can see it on their faces as easily as you can see the aging effects on the faces of those who are 'all work and no play.' If I were your attorney, I would counsel you to enter every race and just have fun. Don't be so much your competitive self that you make sailing work and start to make it any less fun. Why, just look at today. It was just two of us playing around, and this is probably the most amazing fun I've ever had."

❋ *1916 photo of* Rowdy *(no bowsprit) (Photo courtesy Holland Duell's grandson Robert Wood)*

Holland had tried to show Emilie the joys of sailing, and she had reciprocated and held a mirror in front of him with a message of new insight, a message that he deliberated very seriously. Emilie was a breath of fresh air, a ray of sunshine for Holland, who was unaccustomed to having anyone advocate for his own personal enjoyments.

Sea trials had begun almost immediately upon the launching of the New York Forties, and on Tuesday, May 9, two days after Holland and Emilie's Sunday sail, Captain Nat Herreshoff and Holland Duell took *Rowdy* out on the Sound. Two dynamic men, they were probably equally fascinating to each other, with the consequence that the sail lasted over two hours.[1] The trial was good overall. *Rowdy* was fast, and her rigging all handled as indicated on paper. The only problem that both men noticed was that the boat's balance did not seem to be quite right. *Rowdy* seemed to have too much weather helm, meaning that she wanted to round up into the wind, requiring the captain to steer off the wind, thus causing an unwanted reduction in speed due to rudder drag. They discussed the possible solution of adding a short bowsprit, which would shift the sail plan 5 feet forward of the bow and, in the fashion of a weathervane, cause the nose of the boat to be pushed off the wind without the use of the rudder.[2] But much more sailing would need to be done before Herreshoff could decide whether to make such a modification to the entire class.

Memorial Day at the end of May was the opening day of the racing season for the New York Yacht Club, and races were held off the club station at Glen Cove in celebration of the event. It was the formal racing debut of the Forties, which was made all the more exciting by the presence of the New York Thirties and the New York Fifties. The three classes all sailed the same 18 ½-mile course in light winds under sunny skies.[3,4]

Shortly afterward, on June 3, Emilie and her friend and neighbor Ruth Alice Van Slyke sailed out of New York to resume their war work in Europe.[5,6] But in Emilie's absence, Holland took her advice to heart. He slashed his work schedule for the summer, and over the next three months, he sailed *Rowdy* every chance he found, participating in at least thirty-eight days of racing in events offered by the New York

---

1   *New York Times*, May 9, 1916.
2   *New York Times*, August 11, 1916; *New York Times*, September 21, 1916; *New York Times*, July 17, 1917.
3   *Rudder*, July 1916, p. 317.
4   *Rudder*, June 1916, p. 253.
5   1916 passport application for Emilie Brown, ancestry.com.
6   May 27, 1916, passport application for Ruth Alice Van Slyke, ancestry.com.

✳ *The New York Forties at
the starting line, 1916, with
Rowdy at far right*

Yacht Club, American Yacht Club, Larchmont Yacht Club, Manhasset Bay Yacht
Club, Seawanhaka-Corinthian Yacht Club, New Rochelle Yacht Club, Indian Harbor
Yacht Club, and Stamford Yacht Club. It was one of the most active racing seasons of
his life, and he never once regretted the decision to take Emilie's advice.

Of course, the premier event of the summer, as always, was the Annual Cruise
of the New York Yacht Club. Every year since 1844, when Commodore Stevens first
organized the club aboard his schooner *Gimcrack* and, three days later, a group of sev-
en yachts made a week-long cruise to Newport, Rhode Island, the New York Yacht
Club has hosted an annual cruise.[1] It is a ten-day affair that sometimes travels as far as
Newport and Vineyard Haven, Massachusetts, and occasionally around Cape Cod to
Marblehead or Gloucester, Massachusetts, or Bar Harbor, Maine. Each year, the varied
itinerary is released with joyous anticipation and excitement.[2] The days of the cruise are
filled with races from one port to the next, and the nights are filled with social events
at which some of the highest-standing members of society, far removed from the press
and the public, are able to lower their guard and partake in fully unrestrained merriment and good times.

The 1916 squadron of more than 100 yachts, which, in honor of the European
conflict, had assumed the name of the "Peace Squadron," assembled in Glen Cove
on Tuesday August 1, the night before the start of the cruise. The annual cruises are

---

1 *Rudder*, June 1916, p. 253.
2 *Rudder*, August 1916, p. 348.

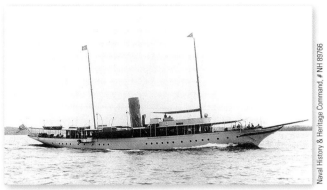

✳ *Viking, the 180-foot flagship owned by Commodore George F. Baker, Jr.*

✳ *J. P. Morgan's 223-foot yacht, Corsair*

run with military precision, and Holland made sure to be anchored in the crowded cove before the 6:00 p.m. arrival of Commodore George F. Baker, Jr. aboard the flagship, his 180-foot steamship *Viking*.

A cannon sounded as the commodore dropped his anchor, and in reply, every yacht dipped its ensign while *Viking* "dressed ship" by raising her ensign and all of her burgees and pennant flags to signal the official beginning of the cruise.

Glen Cove was a picturesque harbor with a scattering of summer homes and permanent residences to the west and east. The club's station #10, which was the first home of the New York Yacht Club, was situated on the inner portion of the cove. Defining the outer portion was a long breakwater that afforded protection to the boats within. Most of the racing fleet was tucked back into the inner cove, while a spectacular group of ten large luxury steamers anchored farther out. Close to the breakwater, Vice-Commodore J. P. Morgan's 223-foot black-hulled yacht *Corsair* anchored close to *Viking*. Both of these yachtsmen had their New York Fifties brought along for them to race during the day. Commodore Baker owned *Ventura*, and J. P. Morgan owned *Grayling*.[1]

At 9:00 p.m., Holland and some of his crew, including his friend and business partner Frederic P. Warfield,[2] attended a brief captains' meeting aboard the *Viking*, which was immediately followed by a reception that was merry but short, to accommodate the early racing start that was scheduled for the following morning.[3] With the evening's festivities over, *Viking* lowered her ensign, burgees, and pennant flags to the strains of "The Star-Spangled Banner." A flurry of launches ran from yacht to yacht, and then, one by one, cabin and deck lights were switched off until all that was left under the star-filled heavens were a hundred twinkling anchor lights that turned the harbor into a fairyland on the water.[4]

The 38-mile Wednesday race was from Glen Cove to Morris Cove in New Haven, Connecticut. From a starting line off Matinicock Point, the Thirties were sent away first, followed by the Forties and then the Fifties, followed by the other classes. The race became somewhat of a chess match, thanks to the light, variable winds, which would die out altogether and then come up from another direction. The fleet

1 *Rudder*, August 1916, p. 348.
2 *Rudder*, September 1916, p. 391.
3 *Rudder*, July 1916, p. 323.
4 *Rudder*, September 1916, p. 389.

soon split into groups that were taking different competing routes.[1,2,3] On a race course, a yacht sails a set route from buoy to buoy, but it is far different on a destination race, when one simply has to get from port to port. The captain has the flexibility to perhaps go off of the straight-line route to pick up a favorable current or expected wind shift. Strategy becomes a measurable factor, and sailors who choose wisely can claim a sizable margin of victory, but the flexibility is a two-edged sword for the losers.

Thursday held an enjoyable 39-mile run from Morris Cove to New London, Connecticut,[4] and Friday's 20-mile race to Fort Pond Bay near Montauk Point, New York, was celebrated with evening entertainment aboard the flagship *Viking* at 9:00 p.m., featuring a clever magician who entertained the guests for two hours.[5]

Saturday's race was certainly the most difficult leg: 62 miles from Fort Pond Bay to Mattapoisett, a small fishing port on Buzzard's Bay, seven miles east of New Bedford, Massachusetts. The wind was light, and despite a 7:30 a.m. start, the fleet did not arrive until ten to fourteen hours later, around 10:00 p.m.[6] Thankfully, Sundays on the New York Yacht Club cruises are set aside as days of rest and recreation, and the fleet had been given access to the Mattapoisett Golf Club and Tennis Club and to the Marion Golf Club.[7]

Sunday morning, the entire fleet dressed ship, as is customary on the Sunday of the cruise, and Holland and his crew[8] made the short seven-mile trip to the famous old whaling town of New Bedford to see the whalers and other odd craft that were always to be found there,[9] before returning to Mattapoisett for Sunday dinner.

Thick fog plagued Monday's 32-mile race from Buzzard's Bay to Newport, Rhode Island. Commodore Baker's New York Fifty, *Ventura*, ran ashore on Penikese Island and was stranded there for 24 hours until she was floated off with only a broken rudder and gouged keel.[10] *Rowdy* broke a spreader and sprung her mast but kept racing and finished third.[11,12]

The fleet remained in Newport for the next two days to enjoy the merriment of that town and to watch the races for the Astor Cups on Tuesday and the race for the King's Cup on Wednesday, after which, at sunset, the fleet disbanded,[13] bringing the 1916 racing season to a close. Holland hadn't been overly competitive during the season. He had decided to wait until the following season, when he hoped that the problem with the New York Forties' weather helm would be resolved, to race in real earnest. Instead, he did just what Emilie suggested and enjoyed every minute of it.

1 *Brooklyn Daily Eagle*, July 30, 1916.
2 *New York Times*, August 3, 1916.
3 *Rudder*, September 1916, p. 391.
4 *New York Times*, August 4, 1916.
5 *Rudder*, September 1916, p. 392.
6 *New York Times*, August 7, 1916.
7 *Rudder*, September 1916, p. 392.
8 *Rudder*, September 1916, p. 392.
9 *The Sun* (New York), July 30, 1916.
10 *Rudder*, September 1916, p. 392.
11 *Brooklyn Daily Eagle*, July 30, 1916.
12 *New York Times*, August 8, 1916.
13 *Rudder*, September 1916, p. 394.

Holland chose to race with a rotating group of good friends rather than putting together a serious crew—and, oh, what fun that turned out to be! The five sailors found *Rowdy* to be exceedingly spacious for their needs and luxuriously comfortable, with two heads, a full galley, and the large main salon, which hosted many late-night festivities. So although *Rowdy*'s first racing season produced only a middle-of-the-road record, it went down in Holland's memory as one of the most enjoyable.

On November 23, a dinner was given at the Larchmont Yacht Club with an assemblage of typically notable people, including Holland Duell, J. P. Morgan, and Harold S. Vanderbilt. At the meeting was made the formal announcement that 5-foot bowsprits would be added to the New York Forty class before the start of the 1917 racing season.[1] Little did anyone suspect that there would not be a 1917 racing season—or a 1918 or 1919 season. Because of the war, the brand-new New York Forties would have to wait almost four long years to get back into competition.

---

1 *New York Times*, September 21, 1916.

Superpictures, Inc.: Holland Goes Hollywood

olland had not been completely absent from work while sailing during the summer of 1916, for his life, it seemed, was always filled with high-profile events and with cases and business ventures that demanded his attention. He had simply made his sailing schedule his first priority and worked in the business matters when there was time. Just as the racing season was starting, Frederick Collins was becoming increasingly driven to break into the movie business, being both forced by the breakup of the Edison Trust and motivated by the positive financial analysis of the motion picture industry by American Tobacco vice-president Benjamin B. Hampton. The Duells had persuaded Hampton, who was very powerful in the movie industry, to help them and Collins in that pursuit and, with delightful success: Hampton managed to negotiate a powerhouse agreement for McClure's Publications to purchase Paramount Pictures Corporation.

On June 12, 1916, Holland's law office of Duell, Warfield & Duell secured an agreement between Collins and William W. Hodkinson, the president and founder of Paramount Pictures, for McClure's to buy Paramount for $12,000,000. It was beyond belief. With the acquisition, Collins would bypass the struggle, challenges, and headaches of building a business and reputation from the foundation up; instead, he would be instantly propelled to the helm of the premier motion picture company of the day. Unfortunately, the euphoria was short lived—very short lived—because the day after the deal was made, an election of officers was held at Paramount. Hodkinson was ejected from his position as president and Raymond Pawley from his position of treasurer, and the deal fell through.[1] To say that there were hard feelings would be an understatement. McClure's sued Paramount,[2] and, as legal wrangling went back and forth over the summer months, Holland, Collins, and the outsted Hodkinson, and Pawley had informal meetings to discuss how to proceed.

When the 1916 racing season ended, Holland decided to kick the business situation into high gear, and a decision was made for the four men to come together and form their own motion picture company, which would go into direct competition with Paramount.[3] Each of them would hold a 25 percent interest in the venture, which

---

1 *New York Herald*, June 21, 1916.
2 *Scarsdale Inquirer*, August 30, 1916.
3 *Scarsdale Inquirer*, August 30, 1916.

would be called Superpictures, Inc.[1] Hodkinson, with his vast experience from Paramount, would be the president; Collins would be vice-president; Holland Duell, who would arrange the financial backing, would be secretary; and Pawley would be treasurer.[2] On September 1, 1916, Duell, Warfield & Duell[3] filed the articles of incorporation,[4] and Superpictures, Inc. came into being.

A key component of their competitive business plan was to aggressively buy their way into the business. They would need to sell stock to raise money for the purchase and production of movies, but before making a stock offering, they wanted to be able to claim ownership of a major distribution outlet. This brought them to Harry Aitken.

As the motion picture industry evolved from small nickelodeons showing very short films to big screens and longer lengths, there was a race for dominance by those who made and distributed the movies. Everything was new. The film technology was new, as were the creative story lines and the methods for expressing those stories artistically and emotionally. The competitive struggle for survival and success was ruthless. This was the Wild West of a new industry for those with nerve enough to enter it. Businesses formed, merged, were bought out, sold out, changed names, went bankrupt, or achieved fame at a dizzying pace. Overnight, some individuals achieved fame and fortune while, in the same short period of time, others lost fortunes.

❋ *Harry Aitken (Photo Courtesy of Waukesha County Historical Society & Museum)*

Harry Aitken, who had previously been the operator of a nickelodeon,[5] entered the production arena in 1911 and had the good fortune to hire actress Mary Pickford.[6] His ambition to rise to the top of the pack was hampered by his shoestring budget, so the next four years comprised a tumultuous career that included many changes of businesses and business partners as well as wild gyrations in his finances and assets, swinging from millions in surplus to frightening deficits requiring infusions of investor money. By 1915, Aitken had devised a plan that would catapult him into the position of motion picture magnate by creating something of a monopoly in the industry. On July 19, 1915, Harry Aitken filed a certificate of incorporation in Richmond, Virginia, for the Triangle Film Corporation, which he would finance with $5,000,000 from Wall Street investors.

At the time, producers were very challenged by the question of how to physically get their movies before a national audience. Generally, each finished film was sold to a local salesman, who had exclusive rights to a certain territory. The films were usually sold for about 10 cents per linear foot, and the salesman rented them out as many times as he could until they became too scratched to show or literally fell apart. This system required producers to painstakingly maintain a network of salesmen, who would make greater profits by repeated rentals on the more popular movies, while the producers made money only on the initial sale.[7]

1   *Stilwell* v. *Duell*, Appellate Division of the New York Supreme Court, 1933, pp. 310–314. Housed at New York State Library, Albany, NY, locator C31, vol. 164, citation 241 Ad 705

2   *Dreams for Sale: The Rise and Fall of the Triangle Film Corporation*, by Kalton C. Lahue (South Brunswick, NJ: A.S. Barnes, 1971), p. 154.

3   *Stilwell* v. *Duell*, pp. 310–314.

4   *Scarsdale Inquirer*, November 1, 1916.

5   *Dreams for Sale*, p. 99.

6   *Dreams for Sale*, p. 19.

7   http://www.cobles.com/simpp_archive/statesrights.htm.

With Aitken's vision, Triangle would act as a business intermediary for every-thing between the film sets where movies were actually made and the theaters where the public ultimately watched them. Triangle would seek out producers and finance the production of their films, to which Triangle would have exclusive distribution rights. On the other end, Triangle would contract with theaters across the country, which would pay rental fees for the privilege of receiving and showing Triangle's films. In effect, the theater contracts were franchises, and theaters that did not hold a contract with Triangle could not gain access to any of its films.[1] This system would allow producers to focus solely on the creativity of movie making, relieved of the burden of marketing and business. At the other end of things, theaters would need to partner up with Triangle or get left in the dust without access to movies that the public would demand.

By April 1, 1916, Triangle had signed contracts with 1,600 theaters across the country and had an annual income of $6.5 million, but all was not roses. Expenses were high, and the money was pouring out faster than it was coming in.[2] Aitken's high risk business approach had gotten him into serious financial trouble, and by September, Triangle had a $600,000 lien against it.[3] The Superpictures quartet knew that for $600,000, they could pay off the lien, take a controlling interest in Triangle, and have an established, well-known, nationwide distribution outlet.

In November, Mabel Duell volunteered 1,600 shares of her American Tobacco Company stock for Holland and Collins to use as collateral for loans of $600,000.[4] The loans were soon secured, and Superpictures, Inc. paid off the $600,000 lien against Triangle,[5] thus gaining control of twenty-two Triangle exchanges, which were in effect full-service stores where they could market their films to theater own-ers nationwide, who would rent the films to play in their theaters.[6] Duell, Warfield & Duell immediately took Superpictures, Inc. public, raising $9,000,000.[7] It was a bittersweet month, marred by the death of Holland's mother at Ardenwold. She had been a loving mother for his entire life as well as a devoted wife to his father for thirty-seven years.[8]

The mission statement of Superpictures was to shop the world for films of such high quality that the company would probably be able to distribute only one such film per month. Superpictures would be completely independent, with no ties to any producers. They would be at liberty to acquire whatever films they considered to be the best of the best.[9] Throughout 1917, Superpictures was a successful enterprise and released seven films: *The Seventh Sin*, *Wrath*, *Passion*, *Sloth*, *Greed*, *Pride*, and *Envy*.[10]

---

1 *Dreams for Sale*, p. 49.
2 *Dreams for Sale*, p. 77.
3 *Stilwell* v. *Duell*, p. 313.
4 *Stilwell* v. *Duell*, p. 235.
5 *Stilwell* v. *Duell*, p. 315.
6 *Dreams for Sale*, p. 154.
7 *New York Times*, November 10, 1916.
8 *New York Herald*. November 8, 1916.
9 *New York Dramatic Mirror*, November 18, 1916.
10 http://www.imdb.com/company/co0053547.

It was an exciting time, and Holland and Mabel[1] and Frederick Collins and his wife Elizabeth were in San Francisco, finalizing plans for McClure's next movie and looking for a West Coast studio,[2,3] when the United States entered the war on April 6, 1917. On hearing the news, they immediately took a train back to New York, and Holland informed Frederick that he planned to join the military and aid in the country's fight in Europe.[4]

The escalation of the war had a serious effect on the movie business, as audiences worldwide stayed home rather than spending money on movies. Holland and Frederick became nervous that their substantial investment was in serious jeopardy, and the four owners decided that Superpictures, Inc. would liquidate its Triangle holdings if possible. At that same time, a suitor, an investor named Stephen H. Lynch, who was a large holder of Paramount securities, came to Frederick, inquiring about buying some of the stock the company held in Paramount. That opened up negotiations that lasted about a month, at the end of which Lynch bought not only the Paramount stock but nearly all of the assets held by Superpictures, Inc., including the Triangle interest, for $700,000.[5] Hodkinson resigned, and Frederick Collins became president of Superpictures, Inc.[6]

At the time the transaction was completed and funded, Holland was already away at Plattsburg Officer Training Camp, preparing for war. Collins, who wanted desperately to continue making a living in the movie business, sent a lawyer, Roy Frank, to Plattsburg requesting that Collins be allowed to use the $700,000 from Lynch as operating capital so that he could continue making movies through Superpictures. However, Holland had developed a lack of confidence in Collins's business ability, and because the $700,000 was needed to pay off loans backed by Mabel's stock, he certainly did not want to leave Collins in charge of the entire operation while he was away at war. Therefore, he refused Frank's request from Collins, and by June 1917, all Superpictures loans were paid off,[7] leaving the business with about $40,000 in cash.[8]

Still hanging onto hope, Collins played the friendship card and in July, along with his wife and Mabel, drove to Plattsburg, where they met up with Holland, and the four had lunch at the Hotel Champlain at Bluff Point.

Library of Congress ID: 73940

✳ *Hotel Champlain, Point Bluff (Old Postcard)*

---

1   "Dilettante," a paper written by Holland Duell's son Holland Sackett Duell, Jr. about his parents.
2   *Editor & Publisher*, March 24, 1917.
3   *Billboard*, March 24, 1917.
4   *Stilwell* v. *Duell*, p. 317.
5   *Stilwell* v. *Duell*, pp. 318–319.
6   *Dreams for Sale*, p. 170.
7   *Stilwell* v. *Duell*, p. 235.
8   *Stilwell* v. *Duell*, p. 319.

Collins expressed how much he wanted to continue in the motion picture business, which had become his principal business over publishing, and said that he would be ruined if he could not continue.[1] He made the case that it would be impossible to operate the business on the $40,000 in its current account and that he wanted to borrow $150,000 to continue operations.[2] It was an awkward moment, but Holland, always the type to be open and up-front, stated flatly in the presence of Mabel and Elizabeth that he had lost confidence in Frederick's business ability and was opposed to any further loans, especially since he was going to war and could not be there to deal with any business complications. Mabel immediately removed Holland from the lunch table and, pulling him aside, told him privately [3] that the Collinses were her very closest friends,[4] the friendship meant a great deal to her, and she wanted to extend the credit.[5] What more could Holland say? In support of her friendship with the Collinses, Mabel had used her money and power to trump Holland's best judgment and preferred business decision. It was an insulting affront to Holland, which, following the years of compromises on his part to fulfill Mabel's desires, threw a chill on their relationship. But bending once again to her will, he agreed to secure a loan once he graduated from Plattsburg. That day came in August 1917, and using Mabel's American Tobacco stock as collateral, Holland arranged for a $150,000 line of credit to be available to Collins personally and to Superpictures, Inc. through the Irving National Bank, with the stipulation that Collins not risk more than $50,000 on any one venture.[6]

Fueled up and fired up, Collins wasted no time. In the same month when he received the line of credit, he partnered with acclaimed Polish actress Madame Olga Petrova (who was in fact born Muriel Harding in England[7]), and together they formed the Petrova Picture Company with Collins as president. Collins told the press that Madame Petrova's salary was the highest ever paid to a motion picture actress and that the company was funded with "unlimited capital." The first picture that they produced was *Daughter of Destiny*, released on December 23, 1917.[8,9]

At just about that time, Holland was deployed for a time from Camp Upton to Fort Sill School of Fire to gain advanced instruction on howitzers. On his return in February 1918, Collins requested that the credit line be increased to $220,000, which Holland reluctantly arranged, again at Mabel's insistence.[10] That was one of Holland's last business dealings before shipping out to Europe. Soon he was to join a mass exodus of patriots, all putting their energies toward winning the war.

✳ *Madame Olga Petrova
(Photoplay)*

---

1 *Stilwell* v. *Duell*, p. 237.

2 *Stilwell* v. *Duell*, p. 320.

3 *Stilwell* v. *Duell*, p. 237.

4 *Stilwell* v. *Duell*, p. 199.

5 *Stilwell* v. *Duell*, p. 237.

6 *Stilwell* v. *Duell*, pp. 237–239.

7 http://en.wikipedia.org/wiki/Olga_Petrova.

8 *Dramatic Mirror*, August 18, 1917; *Dramatic Mirror*, October 27, 1917.

9 http://www.imdb.com/title/tt0007840/?ref_=fn_al_tt_2.

10 *Stilwell* v. *Duell*, p. 241.

Back in October 1916, Ruth Alice ("Pretty Nurse") Van Slyke[1] and Emilie Brown had returned home from their war work in Europe.[2] On August 11, 1917, Ruth Alice headed back to France aboard the *Espagne* to work as an auxiliary nurse for the American Girls Aid,[3] which had established a hospital on the Western Front.[4] One day after the United States declared war on Germany, Ruth Alice's third husband, Warren Clark Van Slyke, joined the Naval Reserves, although, at 43, he was beyond military age.[5] He rose to the rank of lieutenant commander in a few months and was transferred to Washington, where he became the Assistant Chief of Naval Intelligence under Rear Admiral Roger Welles, Director of the Office of Naval Intelligence.[6] Holland's youngest brother, Charles H. Duell, Jr., attended the 2nd Naval District Training school for four months, graduating as an ensign in December 1917.[7]

On April 24, 1918, Holland sailed from Hoboken, New Jersey, aboard the *Leviathan*.[8] One week later, Emilie departed New York aboard the *Espagne* to work for the Duryea War Relief in France.[9] Before departing, Holland lightheartedly reminded Emilie of the promise he had made to her before the start of the 1916 racing season: to find her in France if the United States went to war and to enjoy lunch together.

"You promise not to get hurt, Holland," she implored.

"I'll promise not to get killed, and you be careful too. Think about where a nice place for lunch might be."

1 *Kingston* (New York) *Daily Freeman*, October 7, 1916.

2 October 16, 1916, *Lafayette* passenger list, ancestry.com.

3 July 16, 1917, passport application for Ruth Alice Van Slyke, ancestry.com.

4 *Evening Telegram* (Elyria Ohio), September 11, 1917.

5 *Evening Telegram* (Elyria Ohio), September 11, 1917.

6 *New York Times*, April 8, 1925.

7 November 25, 1917, letter from Charles H. Duell, Jr. to Yale, provided by Association of Yale Alumni.

8 *The History of the 306th Field Artillery: Compiled by the Men Who Participated in the Events Described* (New York: Knickerbocker Press, 1920).

9 1918 passport application for Emilie Brown, ancestry.com.

Lunch at the Ritz Paris

For six long months, while Holland pushed the Germans back toward their homeland and Emilie busily tended to the needs of wounded and destitute civilians, it was a fun diversion to think about actually finding a way to turn their proposed luncheon into reality. The lunch date had been made more as a joke than anything else, but what a lighthearted treat and reward it would make! Granted, it would be small consolation for having to come to Europe under such circumstances; nonetheless, it would be fun to claim one pleasant event that certainly would not have transpired had it not been for the war. Holland and Emilie were able to manage occasional communications throughout the war. When the artillery unit had a lull that allowed for an outgoing bag of mail, Holland could send news to Emilie in care of the Duryea War Relief, which had a physical address in Dinard, France. Emilie could simply send Holland correspondence in care of his unit, whose whereabouts the military would determine for battlefield delivery.

The chance to meet finally presented itself on October 18, 1918, when the 77th Division was temporarily relieved of its position and ordered into reserve at La Harazée,[1,2] with news that the officers would be granted a three-day leave.[3,4,5] Luckily, a speedy mail service from that position allowed Emilie to receive Holland's news in time to get to Paris for his leave, and arrangements were made to meet for lunch.[6]

A day's journey by truck and train put Holland and his fellow officers in Paris, where he parted company with them, the others continuing on to Nice.[7] What more appropriate selection could Holland and Emilie have made for their luncheon than the luxurious Hotel Ritz Paris on the central square of the Place Vendome?[8]

---

1 *"C" Battery Book: 306th F.A., 77th Div., 1917–1919,* by John Foster (Brooklyn, NY: Braunworth & Co., 1920), p. 41.

2 *The Battery Book: A History of Battery "A" 306th F.A.,* by Francis L. Field and Guy H. Richards (New York: The De Vinne Press, 1921), p. 121.

3 *The Autobiography of a Regiment: A History of the 304th Field Artillery in the World War,* by James M. Howard (New York, 1920), p. 193.

4 *The History of the 306th Field Artillery: Compiled by the Men Who Participated in the Events Described* (New York: Knickerbocker Press, 1920), p. 5.

5 *The History of the 306th Field Artillery,* p. 84.

6 "Dilettante," a paper written by Holland Duell's son Holland Sackett Duell, Jr. about his parents.

7 *The History of the 306th Field Artillery,* p. 84.

8 August 30, 2011, letter from Dotty Henry, Holland Duell's granddaughter.

After four months at the front, how wonderful it was for Holland to walk into the lobby of the marvelous Ritz! The change of environment from war-torn battle-fields in an overnight blink of the eye bordered on surreal, and while it was almost hard to believe, it would most certainly be easy to acclimate to. It seemed that nothing could have dampened Holland's spirits, but when he checked in at the front desk, a message from Emilie awaited him, apologizing that her transportation had been delayed for twenty-four hours. She hoped, if it was at all possible, that he could wait for her until the following day. Such was war. Nothing was a given, and one simply had to work around such annoyances. Nonetheless, it came as a disappointment and raised the concern that the following day's transportation might fail as well, destroy-ing their plans to meet. The depth of his disappointment and sudden souring of his mood made it immediately obvious to Holland that he had been looking forward to meeting Emilie more than he had realized. He stopped for a minute and took time to ask himself why and to analyze consciously the thoughts or maybe feelings that he had perhaps been harboring deep inside, possibly for some time. Certainly he would stay, and he sent a message to that effect as he was checking into the hotel.

Despite the disappointment, it was hard to dampen the jubilation of being in Paris. Holland walked the streets and plazas. The reception he got, being in formal military uniform, was everywhere overwhelmingly friendly and thankful. French citi-zens vied for the opportunity to invite him into their homes with the allure of meals and drink and good company. The friendly gestures certainly had the desired effect of making an American soldier happy and proud to be there, fighting for the French people in their hour of need.

❋ *Place Vendome, Paris*

The next day, Holland took an outside table at the Ritz and, relaxing, simply savored Paris and the large outside piazza at the Place Vendome with its tower-ing central bronzed pillar, atop which stood a statue of Napoleon, a tribute to one of his greatest battles fought back in 1805. The sky was clear and blue, the air was pleasantly crisp and clean, and groups of pigeons busily pecked for bits of food stuck between the earth-toned paver bricks. Just before noon, several groups of pigeons were spooked to flight by the arrival of a taxi. Following a brief pause when the driver could be seen collecting fare, the cab door swung open, and out stepped Emilie Brown.

With a beaming smile, Holland quickly rose to his feet, drawing Emilie's attention as he raised his hands overhead, enthusiastically applauding her arrival. Laughingly, he called, "You made it! Bravo!"

Her reply lacked words but comprised a small, poised curtsy and an unrestrained smile, which radiated volumes of joy from every feature of her face. Their hug, cele-brating the realization of their long-awaited and much-anticipated arrival at the Ritz, was tight and joyous as Holland effortlessly spun Emilie around in several circles.

"Oh, Holland, I'm so glad you're alive!" Emilie blurted in joyous laughter, tears streaming down her face. "They told me you were wounded."

"I only promised not to get killed, and I'm fine. Don't worry about me. I'm a fast healer."

"We did it. We actually did it. I can't believe we're here!"

"I have a reservation. Would you do the honor of having lunch with me?"

"I've never had lunch with a major. I would be most delighted, sir."

The Ritz was without peer in world-class dining. Every facet, from the wine and cuisine to the décor and service, was five star, yet in the midst of it all, Holland and Emilie found themselves lost in the content of their own conversations. Emilie had become intimately involved in working with the Duryea War Relief, an organization that was representative of a small person's ability to achieve giant things.

✳ *"Hotel Ritz Paris," by Pierre Georges Jeanniot (Wikimedia Commons)*

In 1904, Nina Larrey Duryea had separated from Chester B. Duryea, her husband of six years. Soon thereafter, she took her two-year-old son to France with hopes for a happier life. The marriage had been strained by Chester's mental instability, and in May 1914, Nina read in a newspaper that Chester had killed his own father[1] and would spend the rest of his life in a hospital for the insane in New York.[2]

In August of that year, when the war began, Nina was residing in Dinard, France.[3] A few weeks later, she sent a letter to the *New York Times* expressing the pitiful state of the Belgian refugees who were flooding across the border into France and of the atrocities that had been inflicted on the women and children. "Not a man of strength or middle age among them," she wrote, "for they are dead or away fighting the barbarians who invested their little country against all honorable dealings.

"I saw sitting in a row on a bench in the shed seven little girls, none of them more than six. Not one of them now has a father, mother or home. None can tell me whence they came or to whom they belong. Three are plainly of gentle birth. They were with nurses when the horde of Prussians fell upon them, and the latter were kept—for the soldiers' pleasure.

"One young mother, who had seen her husband shot, tried to put aside the rifle of the assassin. She was holding her year-old baby on her breast. The butt of that rifle was beaten down; crushing in her baby's chest. It still lives, and I heard its gasping breath.

"I, an American woman, could weep for the inadequacy of my pen, for I beg your pity, your compassion, and your help."[4]

America heard Nina Duryea's cry for help, and the donations that poured in allowed for the formation of the Duryea War Relief organization at Dinard, France.

---

1 *New York Times*, May 5, 1914.
2 *Biographical Dictionary of Women in Science*, by Marilyn Ogilvie (London: Routledge, 2000), p. 389.
3 *Evening Independent*, March 16, 1916.
4 *New York Times*, September 14, 1914.

✳ *Emilie Miller Brown on chair in middle, Nina Duryea pouring tea behind her*

The mission, aside from nursing, was to collect money, food, clothing, and supplies that could be used to help war-torn villages on and behind the front lines. The organization grew and grew, eventually running offices in Paris and New York and distributing supplies by the ton for the benefit of thousands.[1,2] The organization was run with minimal management; consequently, Emilie's contribution had a large impact. She loved that. She loved that she personally was making a meaningful difference and that when she was not busy nursing, she was heavily relied upon and valued for her skills as an expert typist.[3] Her work and contributions were far from unrecognized, and it came as an honor when she was personally decorated by the French government.[4]

On August 18, two months before their luncheon, Holland's unit had taken a direct hit from an enemy shell at Chéry-Chartreuve that caused, in a single blast, two deaths and eighteen casualties.[5] Word had come to Emilie at the time that Holland was among the wounded.[6,7] She now told him how worried she had been when no one seemed to know the extent of his injuries, and she at last was satisfying an overdue need for information by discussing the day with Holland. He told her that he had no memory of the impact, as he had been knocked unconscious by the blast. As he

1   *Spokane Chronicle*, January 27, 1919.
2   *American Women and the War*, by Ida Clyde Clarke (New York: D. Appleton and Company, 1918), p. 483.
3   April 5, 1918, passport application for Emilie Brown and attached letters, ancestry.com.
4   *New York Times*, September 2, 1925.
5   *History of the 305th Field Artillery*, by Charles Wadsworth Camp (Garden City, NY: The Country Life Press, 1919), p. 120.
6   Yale biographies for Holland Duell, Class of 1902.
7   *The History of the 306th Field Artillery*, p. 59.

spoke, he deliberated about how much of the story he wanted to share with Emilie. He wasn't sure he fully understood all that had happened, and he had never shared it with anyone else.

At some point after the blast, while he lay on the ground, before he regained consciousness, Holland had entered a dream state, and everything was still and quiet and peaceful, far removed from the war. He was filled with a sense of serenity, as is sometimes recounted by people who had passed to the other side but then, at the last minute, were brought back to life. There were only two people in the dream. None of his friends were there, nor were his family or wife or children. It was only him and Emilie, and they simply danced. There was no music or talking or sound of any type, and everything was white—not a bright white, but soft tones of cream and ivory. His eyes were closed, yet he saw himself, as if watching a movie or looking down at a play from an elevated vantage point, dancing arm in arm with Emilie, very slowly and pressed together just tightly enough to feel a comfortable warmth between their bodies. Perhaps in his subconscious, he felt that Emilie, by consistently advocating for his best interests and personal enjoyments, was bringing peace into his life, and she personified that peace in the dream. Perhaps there was more. Perhaps mentioning the dream in their conversation would prove to be a mistake that he would not be able to take back. But, as was his nature, Holland usually took the course of laying his cards on the table for all to see, and so, at the risk of expanding the sphere of their conversation beyond what might feel comfortable and appropriate to Emilie, Holland began to describe to her the peaceful state he had experienced while unconscious. Before he was able to mention her part in the dream, however, their meal was interrupted by the delivery of a telegram. Battlefield developments dictated that the advance would resume momentarily, all leaves were being canceled, and every member of the 306th was ordered to return to La Harazée immediately.[1,2] Holland held his command with the utmost seriousness. Men's lives depended on him, and as terrible as the timing was, he had to end the luncheon abruptly and rush back to the front. He hugged Emilie as he left.

"Thank you for lunch, Holland," she said.

"We didn't even have the time to finish it, so naturally I must insist that you let me make it up to you."

"Better than lunch, Major, why don't you bring me back here for dinner?"

"At the earliest possible opportunity," he said gallantly.

"Be safe," she said and kissed him on the cheek.

---

1 *The History of the 306th Field Artillery*, p. 84.
2 *The Autobiography of a Regiment*, p. 195.

Christmas 1918 at the Ritz Paris

16

As soon as Holland returned to the front, the charging offensive began, which pummeled the Germans all the way back across the Rhine, terminating in the November 11 armistice. The following month was taken up with a hectic flurry of operations: packing up weapons, machinery, and gear and establishing troop camps where the men would await transfer back to New York. The first chance for Holland to take leave came in mid-December.[1]

Unfortunately, while the military was beginning to see light at the end of the tunnel, and operations were starting to be packed up, Emilie was busier than ever. The final offensive drive had opened up vast areas of France that, for years, had been under German suppression, releasing a flood tide of refugees who were in desperate need of aid. Emilie would not be able to get away as soon as Holland. At best, she could get a few days off for Christmas. While this was not ideal, their two times briefly overlapped, and through correspondence, they planned that Holland would take leave with his fellow officers in Nice in mid-December and, on the way back via Paris,[2] would meet with Emilie once again at the Hotel Ritz, this time for Christmas Eve dinner.[3]

When Holland arrived at the Ritz, the hotel was adorned for Christmas in its accustomed grandeur. A towering evergreen in the lobby was ornately decorated with handmade ornaments crafted by the finest French and Italian artisans. Garlands, mistletoe, and rich Christmas colors were warmly displayed throughout the hotel, and everyone's formal attire carried with it some statement of Christmas. While it most certainly would have been appropriate to show up in his best military dress, Holland chose not to. Instead, after stopping at a clothier down the street, he arrived in the Christmas spirit, dressed in a formal black and white tuxedo. Emilie had not checked in yet but had also left no word of any complications or travel problems, so Holland proceeded up to his room. Within minutes, the phone rang.

"Holland, it's Emilie. I'm downstairs in the lobby. I just arrived, and I'm dying to see you, but I'm also worn out from the trip. I've bought a beautiful dress. Do I have time to freshen up and get changed before dinner?"

---

1   *The History of the 306th Field Artillery: Compiled by the Men Who Participated in the Events Described* (New York: Knickerbocker Press, 1920), p. 103.

2   "*The History of the 306th Field Artillery*," p. 103.

3   "Dilettante," a paper written by Holland Duell's son Holland Sackett Duell, Jr. about his parents.

"I made a late reservation, just in case. Its 6:30 now, and our reservation is for 8:30."

"You're wonderful. Let's meet in the lobby at 8:00."

Holland set down the phone, feeling not a care in the world. The call had dissolved any fears of disappointment or letdown. There would be no recalled leaves this time. The war was finished, and they would be at complete leisure to celebrate together in the finest fashion.

Holland was waiting in the lobby when Emilie descended the stairs. Her describing the dress as "beautiful" was an understatement compared to the vision that she presented in it. It was a full-length black evening gown, sleeveless and accented by white silk gloves that fit tightly upon her forearms. Around her neck, she wore a white pearl necklace centered with a delicate cameo pendant. The entire patronage of the Ritz on that evening was dressed in their finest, with money as no object, yet Emilie stood out in the crowd. Her flashing blue eyes, radiant smile, and graciously poised figure were a compliment that no amount of money could buy. As she made eye contact with Holland, however, she had no thoughts of herself, her appearance, or how her outfit measured up against the other women's. Her sole focus, the entirety of her every thought and emotion, was centered on Holland and her happiness to see him.

"Congratulations, Major, you won the war," she greeted him. The familiarity of the kiss on the cheek, which had been established at their last farewell, was repeated as she gave him a welcoming hug.

"Let's say I played my part," he said.

"I heard you were recommended for many decorations."

"And you have already been decorated, so congratulations to you as well."

"Mine from the French, but yours, I hear, are from both the French and the Americans."

"While an honor, it is one I hope never to have the opportunity to repeat. Nonetheless, we must celebrate our victories."

Upon being seated at the table, Holland issued a command dispatching the waiter to bring two glasses of champagne.

Their conversation was quick and spirited. There was so much to talk about. The war had provided an abundance of once-in-a-lifetime true stories. There was talk of "when we go home" and rebuilding lives and New Year's resolutions.

As was to be expected, the cuisine was sumptuous, a procession of delectable yet teasingly small hors d'oeuvres, followed by chateaubriand for two with hollandaise sauce and a perfectly matched cabernet, with the crowning ceremony of crepes suzette flambéed at the table for dessert. Every morsel of it was savored—the food, the conversation, the ambiance of the setting—until somehow most of the evening had slipped away, leaving only a half an hour until midnight.

The initial excitement and energy had mellowed into a calm, peaceful, after-dinner contentedness. From the next room, muffled sounds of ballroom music could be heard.

"Holland, didn't you promise me a dance?"

"Well, if I didn't, I'm sure I certainly intended to."

As they walked to the ballroom, Emilie, in an action that felt most comfortable and natural, wrapped her arm around his. They made their way to the middle of the

✳ *Holland and Emilie: Christmas dinner at the Hotel Ritz Paris as portrayed in oils by artist Greg Singley, © Chris Madsen.*

dance floor just as the orchestra began to play. The smiles on their faces were barely perceptible except through their eyes, which radiated gentle warmth between them as they joined in a close embrace and danced ever so slowly to a beautifully emotional rendition of "Silent Night."

Holland closed his eyes, and suddenly everything was still and quiet and peaceful, far removed from the war. He felt a sense of serenity. The ballroom was gaily colored and well populated, but in the moment, to Holland, with his eyes closed, all of the tones and shades and colors in the room were a soft, velvety white, and he and Emilie alone occupied the large dance floor. He was living what he had dreamed while he lay wounded and unconscious in Chéry-Chartreuve. At that moment, nothing else in the world existed. Nothing else mattered. He had no wants or desires except to continue the moment in which he was living. And so they danced on in lingering bliss until, at the stroke of midnight, the hotel manager stepped through the door and greeted the room with "Merry Christmas to you, one and all!"

"Merry Christmas, Holland," Emilie said, and for the first time she kissed him on the lips. And for the first time in her life, she kissed a man with all her heart. A dam had burst in both of them, and nothing was held back. The kiss and tight embrace were long and passionate as Holland's fingers slid through Emilie's hair, cradled the back of her head, and pulled her close to him. But just as it had been Emilie who had initiated the kiss, it was she who ended it and, with startling suddenness, abruptly excused herself to retire to her room.

Somewhat dazed, Holland followed suit. In his room, as he slipped into his dressing gown, he wondered what conversations and direction the following day would bring. He wondered about Emilie's abrupt termination of the evening and the vast universe of questions and conflicts she must, at that very moment, be struggling with. Clearly, a boundary in his marriage had been violated. Clearly, they both recognized that their actions were inappropriate, and clearly, both of them felt something important enough toward each other to disregard all else. Holland would not have the opportunity to ponder the question "Does she want this to go further?" or "Do I want this to go further?" because at that moment, he heard a soft knocking on his door.

Securing the tie string around his dressing gown, he opened the door, and Emilie slipped inside. She stepped backwards, bumping the door closed behind her. No words were spoken, and for a lingering moment, they merely stood and looked at each other. Emilie had also changed into a robe, but not a woolen one like Holland's. Hers was made of delicate white silk and lace. It was beautifully sheer, very light, and conformed closely to her figure. It was in no way designed to accommodate modesty or to veil a woman's body. Its sole purpose was to accentuate her most alluring features, and Emilie was stunning. Holland's desire was spontaneous and immediate, yet he made no move to pursue it. Even in Emilie's daily attire, the blessings of the figure that had been bestowed on her were unmistakable and could not easily be concealed by clothing. Her broad shoulders and strong neck were accentuated by a beautifully prominent collarbone. The way in which her chest and unusually well-defined rib cage narrowed into perfectly proportioned waist and hips and long, athletic legs had, in the past, occasioned Holland to imagine how erotically she must present herself absent the confines of clothing. To see her at that moment, offering all of herself without reservation, was almost inescapably accompanied by feelings of disbelief.

The top of Holland's robe was open just enough to accommodate Emilie as she reached out and softly placed both outstretched palms on his chest, orchestrating them in slow, caressing motions across every feature of the beautifully formed pectoral muscles that she had secretly admired for years. The war had rendered him lean, defined, and strong by necessity. In contrast to their dance earlier, Holland's eyes were not closed now. He was holding back, but he was taking in everything. Emilie's arousal was evidenced in the firming of the features of her body, and viewing that effect upon her yielded an equal effect on Holland. It seemed an eternity since he had experienced physical intimacy, and in the moment—a moment that he didn't want to rush but envisioned savoring slowly, lovingly, and sensuously for hours—he could already feel the strains of holding back in the form of uncontrollable yet subtle muscle tremors that flashed across his body, bringing tingling goose bumps to the surface of the skin. It was utterly intoxicating. As he felt himself succumbing to the effects of altered blood flow, cascading hormones and pheromones, and all the other wonderful motivators of our species' propagation, the desire to touch Emilie became too great. She was not looking in his eyes now; rather, she was focused on his body, as he was on hers.

The sheer silk robe did little to conceal Emilie's breasts. As Holland ever so gently ran his hand across the material that lay so softly upon them, her eyes closed and her head tilted back with a slight shiver. In the next moment, he parted the front of the robe, which, when pushed back about her shoulders, slipped freely and effortlessly to the floor. He took her hands as their eyes locked together. As he raised her arms over her head and pressed himself against her, and her body against the door, their mouths met. This time, there was no abrupt end to what became a long and impassioned kiss.

As they paused to take a breath, Emilie freed her hands, slipped Holland's robe off his shoulders, and immediately relinquished control back to him. Again they kissed, and without the robe, he could feel every feature of her body against his. The gentle touching of their skin, like thousands of tiny fingers, each stimulating receptors in the brain, heightened the engorgement of those areas with which they toyed, elevating their impassioned desires to uncontrollable levels. It was clearly futile—indeed, utterly impossible—to endeavor further postponement. In surrendering to the inevitable, they moved to the sumptuous French provincial bed, where, not until hours later, in the early hours of Christmas morning, were all of their desires fully satisfied and all of their energies fully spent. The sleep that followed was deep and abundantly peaceful for both of them.

When the morning light arrived, it shone through bright, cloudless blue skies. The day beckoned Emilie and Holland, and they chose to take their breakfast at an outside table. Not a word was spoken of the future; they talked only of the moment, for the moment was perfect. It was everything they could ask for, and the future held only the obvious shadowy questions and uncertainties. But the future and their situation did need to be addressed, and after breakfast, Holland and Emilie walked the lovely streets of Paris. The shops were all closed on Christmas Day, leaving only the cafes to do business, but everywhere people walked about, looking in shop windows, merrily carrying on conversations, and greeting the couple with warm smiles and wishes of *Joyeux Noel*.

As usual, Holland spoke frankly. "Emilie, I want you to know that Mabel and I have not been close for some time. I love her, and I respect her. She is a good human being, but she is driven by an agenda that has nothing to do with the things that are important to me or bring happiness into my life, and it has pushed us apart. We live in the same house, but for the most part, we are traveling down two separate paths."

"Holland, I know you wouldn't be here if there weren't a reason."

"I just don't want you to think that I am in a perfect marriage and am here at the moment because I am simply greedy and want more and I think I can get away with it. I believe in fidelity. I enjoy the exclusive bond and partnership and loyalty between a man and a woman. I was brought up that way. My mother and father found perfect happiness in each other that carried throughout their entire lives. But in my marriage, the consequence of that philosophy has for some time been abstinence because our differences led, long ago, to the evaporation of our intimacy. Emilie, you are the most wonderful person who has ever come into my life. I feel with you what I saw between my parents. That is the type of love and intimacy that I have always desired in my life. You make me happy, and I don't want to lose that when we go back."

"I understand, Holland. You were young when you got married. Young men make rash decisions. You were a Yale man when you met Mabel, and I wager you had been schooled on how to analyze a business up, down, and sideways ad nauseam until you were certain that it was a wise long-term investment, suited to your personality. I will also bet that you bypassed any such intellectual analysis of Mabel as a potential partner and instead jumped in the way you would execute a cannonball—holding your breath, with your eyes closed, plunging in all or nothing, and hoping for a big splash. We've known each other for fourteen years, so the starting point of what we have is probably healthier, but as far as the rest of the world would be concerned, none of that would ever matter. If people discovered us to have a relationship, you could not possibly justify it to them by explaining that you had made a rash decision in your youth. And for all the world's eyes, no matter what, I would always be the other woman, the villain, the vamp trying to steal a married man away from his wife and children. No one would begin to sympathize or ponder honestly what they themselves would do in our situation. They would simply pass condemning judgments. I don't want to be judged. I don't want you to be judged like that. And in all honesty, I don't want to be the catalyst that breaks up a family."

"What do you need from this, then?" he asked. "What do you envision as the best course of action for your happiness when we get home?"

"In my absence, your family life would survive on its own, or it would fail on its own, and it's probably best to let that course play out. I would still like to be a familiar presence, and we can certainly continue to share the happiness and friendship that we have brought to each other in that capacity. But at the same time, I think I would curl up and die and blow away as dust if I were denied one ounce of the intimacy and closeness that we shared last night."

With that, the basic foundation of their clandestine relationship had been laid. Emilie returned to Dinard the following day, and Holland rejoined his unit. But in early January 1919, when Emilie learned that Holland was being invalided back to New York,[1,2] gravely ill from the Spanish flu, she resigned from her post with the Duryea War Relief and boarded the *La Lorraine*[3] to rejoin him in New York.

Through an enormous wealth of information, I had not only discovered who the mysterious E.B. mentioned in Holland Duell's war journal was, but I had finally gained clarity about the events that caused their two lives to become so deeply intertwined. In my mind, however, the dynamic of the relationship between Holland and Mabel and Emilie was one for which only the most optimistic and imaginative of dreamers could envision a survivable future. My feeling was that the developing events had brought these people's lives screaming right up to the edge of a cliff, but the momentum was still solidly locked in forward gear, and I was now, more than ever, eager to learn what happened next.

---

1   *The New York Red Book 1921*, edited by James Malcolm (New York: J. B. Lyons Company, 1921), p. 78.

2   June 8, 1921, passport application for Holland Sackett Duell, ancestry.com.

3   January 27, 1919, *La Lorraine* passenger list for Emilie Miller Brown, ancestry.com.

The Postwar Rebuilding

17

*M*ost wars, it seems, end in the fashion of an excessive drinking binge. There is a period afterward like a hangover when life just can't seem to get back on a healthy footing. The aftermath of the Great War proved no different. In 1919 alone, Theodore Roosevelt died of a heart attack, Holland's father had a stroke,[1] Sackett Duell's wife died,[2] Holland was hospitalized with the flu,[3] Emilie's father died,[4,5] Prohibition was instituted, the whole nation was so busy trying to get their lives back on track that there was an expected cancelation of the 1919 racing season, and the Duells were faced with a fiasco as a consequence of arranging and backing the line of credit for Frederick Collins.

The Petrova Pictures film *Daughter of Destiny* ended up being a financial failure.[6] Olga Petrova stared in four more movies through mid-1918, none of which improved the financial outlook for Collins, and the crumbling of the walls around him accelerated in late 1918 when Petrova decided to leave the motion picture business forever. There was a glimmer of light when Collins convinced the Duells' friend Theodore Roosevelt to let Collins make a film about his life. *Our Teddy* was completed just before Roosevelt died, and in early 1919, a desperate Collins traveled to Europe to try to bolster profits with additional marketing of the film abroad.[7]

While the movie about Roosevelt did not lose money, it also did not make the large amount that Collins had expected and needed in order to stay solvent.[8] When he returned to New York in June 1919, he had to face a dreaded meeting with Holland to go over the company's financial balance sheets. Through examining the numbers, Holland became convinced that Collins's operation had resulted in a loss of at least $150,000.[9]

---

1 *Syracuse Herald*, January 30, 1920.

2 Obituary, *Syracuse Herald*, July 20, 1919.

3 *The History of the 306th Field Artillery: Compiled by the Men Who Participated in the Events Described* (New York: Knickerbocker Press, 1920), p. 111.

4 Gravestone 1855-1919 in Bellefontaine cemetery, St. Louis, Missouri, ancestry.com.

5 Missouri certificate of death.

6 *Stilwell* v. *Duell* Appellate Division of the New York Supreme Court, 1933, p. 322. Housed at New York State Library, Albany, NY, locator C31, vol. 164, citation 241 Ad 705

7 *Stilwell* v. *Duell*, p. 323.

8 *Stilwell* v. *Duell*, p. 323.

9 *Stilwell* v. *Duell*, p. 237.

After Holland had addressed the situation with Mabel, they invited Frederick and Elizabeth to Ardenwold to discuss the matter. Holland pointed out to Collins that he had lost $150,000 as a result of breaking an agreement not to risk more than $50,000 on any one venture. In fact, as soon as Collins got the money, he had established the contract with Olga Petrova, which had resulted in almost the entire loss. Holland asked Collins for restitution because he had not stuck to their agreement. Collins refused. Holland told Mabel that he was going to compel Collins to make restitution. Mabel's response was "I don't want you to sue Fred. The Collins' friendship means a great deal more to me than the possible loss of $150,000."[1] Further investigation after that meeting revealed that Collins had in fact lost the entire $220,000.[2]

To discourage Holland from suing for the payback of the loan, Mabel volunteered to personally assume liability for the full amount of the loan. But Holland refused to let her shoulder the burden alone, and the two made decisions about what stocks to sell to raise the $220,000. Shortly thereafter, they paid off the loan that they had cosigned.

The payoff of the defaulted loan marked the end of Frederick Collins's participation in the motion picture business. The following year, he sold his entire interest in McClure's Publications[3] and retired from corporate life to become an author of books. Mabel and Elizabeth remained the best of friends,[4,5] while the friendship between Holland and Frederick soured quite abruptly. That discord presented an obvious awkwardness in regard to socializing, and the entire affair contributed to the toxic wedge that had splintered any loving or emotional bond between Holland and Mabel.

Holland's youngest brother Charles was one of the first to learn that Holland had become the unwilling owner of some expensive movie camera and filming equipment as a result of the defaulted deal with Collins. Charles's decision to relieve Holland of the equipment and try his hand at making a movie was probably more a matter of snatching a chance opportunity than it was of anything having to do with forethought. It was a snap decision, perhaps a rash decision, that would soon bring Charles spectacular fame, fortune, and romance. Yet if there were ever a decision in his life that he could simply wish undone, it would have been that one.

The postwar lives of the two brothers were extremely busy. Both ardent patriots,[6] they were not only occupied with getting their personal lives back on track, but also working tirelessly to assist in the nation's rebuilding. Charles became involved at high levels in the formation of the American Legion, assuming the position of the first Vice-Chairman of the American Legion in New York State.[7,8] He attended the St.

---

1 *Stilwell* v. *Duell*, p. 239.
2 *Stilwell* v. *Duell*, p. 220.
3 *The Sun* (New York), November 23, 1920; *New York Herald*, November 23, 1920.
4 Social sections of various newspapers.
5 Ardenwold is listed as Elizabeth Collins's residence on the June 23, 1926, passenger list for *France*, ancestry.com.
6 "Dilettante," a paper written by Holland Duell's son Holland Sackett Duell, Jr. about his parents.
7 *New York Herald*, May 3, 1919.
8 *New York Times*, September 6, 1921.

Louis Caucus as a delegate at large[1] and, on his return to New York, gave a talk at the New York Republican Union League, stating , "With the birth of the American Legion in St. Louis, there has been created in this country the greatest single instrument for the Nation's good, for the upholding of our American institutions, since the founding of the Republic."[2]

Holland was also involved in the American Legion and helped to establish a charter branch, which opened in Yonkers on June 3, 1919. He presided over the executive committee and was assisted by a new acquaintance, a man by the name of John Stilwell.[3] Stilwell, who was five years younger than Holland, was a lifelong resident of Yonkers and also a Yale graduate, from the class of 1907. Aside from the shared commonality of a Yale background, the two both enjoyed sailing, and their gallant service in the war would eventually take them both to the position of colonel.[4] In the absence of Collins's friendship, Holland and Stilwell came to socialize frequently, and John became a familiar presence at Ardenwold. He also came along on lighthearted sailing outings on *Rowdy*, and as Holland taught him to race, the two enthusiastically discussed participating in upcoming racing events.

It seemed that for the whole nation, as well as for most individuals, life had changed following the war, and there was a scramble to adapt to the new set of living conditions and challenges.

Sackett's wife Louise, whom he had married in 1905[5,6] and with whom he had had two sons,[7] had died on July 18, 1919.[8] She had been a beautiful, uncomplicated woman of simple needs. Her idea of an exciting social event was an afternoon bridge party, and she often was the recipient of club prizes.[9] She was a blessing to Sackett, and it stands as a testament to the family closeness that she was buried in the Duell family plot next to his mother.[10] Her name was engraved on that same headstone below his mother's, leaving room for only two more names: Sackett's and his father's.[11] Just as Sackett's temperament had not suited him to be a legal warrior or to live with the stress of city life, he found it crushingly difficult to live each day bearing the pain of his loss. Call it weakness or neediness, but for strength and for his well-being, Sackett desperately needed a woman in his life. He found that strength, or so he thought, in only a couple short months, and his life was forever changed when he met Annie Livingston Best,[12] known to all society as "Baby Best."

1 *New York Herald*, May 3, 1919.

2 *New York Herald*, May 12, 1919.

3 "20 years ago," *Herald Statesman* (Yonkers, NY), May 13, 1939.

4 *Herald Statesman* (Yonkers, NY), July 26, 1963.

5 *Times Dispatch* (Richmond, VA), April 20, 1905.

6 *History of the Class of 1905, Yale College*, Vol. 2, edited by Murray Sargent (New Haven, CT: Yale University, 1908).

7 *History of the Class of 1905, Yale College*, Vol. 6, edited by Boyd G. Curts (New Haven, CT: Yale University, 1930).

8 Obituary, *Syracuse Herald*, July 20, 1919.

9 *Amsterdam Evening Recorder*, March 25, 1914.

10 Obituary, *Syracuse Herald*, July 20, 1919.

11 photo, findagrave.com.

12 *Sandusky* (Ohio) *Register*, March 21, 1920.

Baby Best: A New Love for Brother Sackett

Annie Livingston Best was an only child, a princess cursed by the spoils of her upbringing. Her mother, Mary (Tooker) Best,[1] came from a most established and socially distinguished family.[2] When her parents passed, Mary Tooker became the beneficiary of a small fortune. It was nothing to rival the megafortunes of the Rockefellers, Vanderbilts, or Astors, but its worth was in the neighborhood of a million dollars.[3,4] Annie's father, Clermont Livingston Best, possessed no fortune, but he carried with him military fame.[5]

Clermont Best graduated West Point in 1847 as a second lieutenant in the artillery. He fought in the Mexican War, fought against the Seminole Indians in Florida, and battled bandits on the Rio Grande, all of which built his character for bigger things to come. In the Civil War, during 1861 and 1862, he not only commanded his own artillery battery but also was Chief of Artillery for the Fifth Corps. At the Battle of Cedar Mountain in Virginia, the artillery fire under his command was so accurate that the Confederates later reported that "it prevented Stonewall Jackson from making his victory complete." At Antietam, his artillery, stayed Stonewall Jackson's further advance. Finally, at Chancellorsville, Stonewall Jackson rode into the line of fire of the artillery of the Twelfth Corps under the command of then Major Clermont Livingston Best. When Major Best ordered an aggressive salvo, Stonewall Jackson broke and rode rapidly back toward his own Confederate forces. Mistaking him for a Union soldier, his own troops shot Jackson off his horse, mortally wounding him. At Gettysburg in 1863, Best was cited for gallantry and elevated to lieutenant colonel. By the end of the war, he was a full colonel.[6,7] In 1883, he was placed in charge of the Fourth Artillery and was stationed at Fort Adams in Newport, Rhode Island,[8] where he met Mary Tooker, who had a residence in Newport.

❋ Colonel Clermont Livingston Best (Photo from Arlington National Cemetery)

---

1 *New York Times*, May 24, 1923.
2 *Ogden* (Utah) *Examiner*, August 2, 1924.
3 *Kingston* (New York) *Daily Freeman*, October 1, 1884.
4 *Albany* (New York) *Evening Journal*, November 30, 1884.
5 *Sandusky* (Ohio) *Register*, March 21, 1920.
6 *History of the City of Hudson, with Biographical Sketches of Henry Hudson and Robert Fulton*, by Mrs. Anna R. Bradbury (Hudson, NY: Record Printing and Publishing Co., 1908), p. 163.
7 *The Family of Best in America of Holland Descent, with Copious Biographical Notes, 1700–1901*, by Charles Best Benson (New York: Knickerbocker Press, 1909), p. 52.
8 *History of the City of Hudson*, p. 163.

Newport was a playground for the rich and ultra-rich, a place where beautiful women strategized how to marry into wealth and power. But Mary was swept off her feet by the man that Colonel Claremont Livingston Best was. From the moment she met him, her heart swelled with a genuine love. She cared not that he didn't have a fortune,[1] and she cared nothing about the inevitable society gossip, she being 33 and he 50 and recently widowed. They were engaged within weeks of meeting, and they indeed did cause a stir when they almost immediately announced a wedding date.[2]

The wedding took place on September 29, 1884, at Mary Tooker's Newport cottage[3] "Inglenook"[4] on Bellevue Avenue and Perry Street. Although termed "cottages", the Newport summer residences of the wealthy were generally opulent estates, as evidenced by the Vanderbilts' "cottage", The Breakers, which had seventy rooms and was situated on a landscaped 13-acre oceanfront estate. The Tooker residence, while not palatial in size, was finished to perfection as if it aspired to be a work of art in itself. The house was adorned with expensive furniture, statuary, and fine oil paintings and of course was decorated for the occasion with ornate displays of flowers, tropical plants, and vines. The wedding was an intimate affair, limited to family and close friends. Mary was a beautiful sight in her white satin dress with point lace, a veil trimmed with orange blossoms, and jewelry of diamonds and pearls. Her bouquet was a sensational arrangement of white rosebuds, jasmine, and orange blossoms.[5] Colonel Best looked stately in full military dress.[6]

Despite the whirlwind love story, which caught much of local society off guard, Colonel and Mrs. Best were well regarded as a couple, well liked, and socially active in the Newport community. Mrs. Best had a passion for playing piano and often performed at social functions.[7,8] On July 21, 1887, their daughter Annie Livingston Best was born,[9] and on April 25, 1888, Colonel Best retired from the military to devote himself to his family.[10]

Annie was a beautiful baby from the day she was born, with sparkling blue eyes and shimmering blonde hair. As an only child, she was the center of her parents' attention; she was also thoroughly doted on by every relative and friend who was given an opportunity to coddle her. It was no surprise that this perfect infant garnered the pet name "Baby Best," which stayed with her throughout her life.[11] In fact, with the exception of one solitary experience, Annie's early childhood was one in which the universe seemed to revolve around her.

───────

1 *Sandusky* (Ohio) *Register*, March 21, 1920.

2 *Albany* (New York) *Evening Journal*, September 30, 1884.

3 *Kingston* (New York) *Daily Freeman*, October 1, 1884.

4 *Newport Historical Society*.

5 *New York Herald*, September 30, 1884.

6 *Kingston* (New York) *Daily Freeman*, October 1, 1884.

7 *New York Daily Tribune*, February 25, 1897.

8 *Sag Harbor* (New York) *Express*, November 26, 1896.

9 1921 *Baltic* passenger list, ancestry.com.

10 *New York Daily Tribune*, April 10, 1897.

11 *Ogden* (Utah) *Examiner*, August 2, 1924.

That one blemish—that one day on which Annie, who was just shy of two years old, experienced the opposite of adoration—fell on a Monday, July 1, 1889. Her mother had asked Delia McDermott, Annie's nurse, to take Annie out for a stroll. As the two were making their way along Parker Avenue, little Annie asked Delia to pick her a pretty flower that Annie had spotted on an overhanging bush in front of the cottage belonging to a Mrs. Clarke. Poor Delia had no idea that lying in wait on the other side of the bush was Mrs. Clarke's 22-year-old daughter, Fanny, who had been determinedly trying to catch the mystery culprit who had been pilfering flowers from their property. No sooner had Delia picked the flower than the slenderly built Fanny sprang out, grabbing the nurse by the hair and screaming at her for trespassing on the property. Unclear as to the motive for the assault and fearing for the safety of little Annie, Delia threw Fanny down on the graveled walk and pummeled her.

The screams and commotion had a dramatic effect, much like that of a screeching cat fight, and brought Fanny's mother racing from the house with a three-foot stick in her hand. As Delia broke from Fanny to turn her attention to the stick, Fanny sprinted back to the house and immediately returned, holding a revolver, which she fired once. The bullet inflicted no wounds, but smoke from the blast blackened Delia's apron. Before a second shot could be fired, Delia grabbed the hand with which Fanny was clutching the gun and yelled for help.

Colonel George R. Fearing, who happened to be passing by on a walk, rushed in, secured the pistol, and kept the peace until the police arrived. The chief of police cautioned Fanny about the use of firearms (rules were much looser in those days), and Annie's father, Colonel Best, later made a personal visit to the Clarkes but determined that the injuries they had suffered at the hands of Annie's nurse had been punishment enough.[1]

Thus were Annie's parents always there for her. She had the strength and security of an adoring war hero as a father and protector, and she had a cultured and refined mother who was determined that her daughter should grow up with all the same benefits that society had bestowed upon herself.[2]

The one thing from which Annie's parents could not protect her was heartache, and her first came when she was not quite ten. On April 7, 1897, Annie's father died at home after a week's illness from heart disease.[3] The funeral took place with full military honors and was attended by General Daniel Butterfield,[4] who had commanded Union troops in the Civil War and was the composer of the bugle call "Taps."

Seeing her daughter denied the blessing of a father as she grew strengthened Mrs. Best's resolve to fill Annie's world with happiness and the best things in life. She devoted herself to Annie fully and unconditionally. It was a mother-daughter bond that remained unwavering throughout Mary's lifetime. Annie was educated at the finest schools in France.[5] She was an accomplished linguist and, sharing her mother's

---

1 *New York Herald*, July 2, 1889.

2 *Sandusky* (Ohio) *Register*, March 21, 1920.

3 *The Family of Best in America of Holland Descent*, p. 51.

4 *New York Daily Tribune*, April 8, 1897.

5 *Daily News*, October 29, 1907.

love for piano, became an accomplished and celebrated pianist.[1] By 1904, Mrs. Best deemed Annie the picture of perfection. She was a beautiful young woman, refined and cultured, well-educated and charming, with impeccable social graces. She was ready for New York society, and it was ready for her.

In 1904, Mrs. Best hosted her daughter's debutante party in New York. Among the guests were Gladys Vanderbilt and Count and Countess Beroldingen.[2] The same year, Annie was invited to Mrs. William Astor's famous midseason ball at Beechwood, the opulent Astor estate in Newport.[3] The two-story, thirty-nine-room mansion on the low cliffs overlooking the Atlantic Ocean was the crown jewel of Newport and the site of the most exclusive social functions. Overnight, Annie had become a privileged member of "the Four Hundred," New York's premier social set. At the ball, Mrs. Astor's son, John Jacob Astor,[4] who would perish in the *Titanic* disaster in 1912, announced Annie Livingston Best for special attention.[5] With all her charm, Annie, whom the newspapers nicknamed "Baby Best," was described as "the most beautiful of all beautiful women"[6] and "society's most perfect blonde,"[7] and she was soon the darling of Mrs. Astor and many other society leaders who attended the ball. The newspapers couldn't get enough of "Baby Best," and she became a local, national, and international sensation. Members of the Four Hundred and ordinary newspaper readers alike delighted in speculating about which marriage proposal she might accept.[8]

✳ *Annie Livingston Best, 1907. (From THE SCRAP BOOK, First Section, Vol. IV, September 1907, p. 512)*

Everyone close to Annie assumed and hoped that she would marry into wealth, as she had been meticulously groomed to do. Yet following in her mother's footsteps, and to the chagrin of her mother, Mrs. Astor, and many of the Four Hundred, Annie followed her heart and fell in love with Alfred Holbrook, a perfectly charming young man of good family, good looks, and good social connections; in fact, he had everything but a fortune. For two years, they were inseparably in love, yet the outside pressure against the relationship was too great to allow Annie the courage to accept his marriage proposals. In the end, the couple was split apart through the interventions of Mrs. Best, Mrs. Astor, and other social sponsors, who formally and adamantly objected to the prospect of such a marriage. Seeing no possibility for a future with Alfred, Annie ended the relationship.[9]

1 *New York Herald*, November 4, 1906.
2 *New York Herald*, December 18, 1904.
3 *Sandusky* (Ohio) *Register*, March 21, 1920.
4 *Sandusky* (Ohio) *Register*, March 21, 1920.
5 *Sandusky* (Ohio) *Register*, March 21, 1920.
6 *Utica* (New York) *Globe*, June 5, 1908.
7 *Newport* (Rhode Island) *Mercury and Weekly News*, July 10, 1964.
8 *Sandusky* (Ohio) *Register*, March 21, 1920.
9 *Ogden* (Utah) *Examiner*, August 2, 1924.

Time heals all, and the wealth of suitors who pursued Annie eventually gained her attention. She was particularly drawn to Elizur Yale Smith, the son of millionaire paper manufacturer Wellington Smith and a descendant of the founder of Yale University. He seemed to fit both the requirements of what she wanted in a man and those of what society at large wanted for her as a husband. They were soon engaged.

Wanting to soften the blow to her first love, Annie delivered the news to Alfred Holbrook in person on October 18, 1906, before he heard it elsewhere. The gesture did not have the desired effect. Shortly after their meeting, Annie was staggered by the news that Alfred had returned to his hotel and ended his life with a single gunshot to the head.[1,2] Annie's subsequent marriage to Yale Smith did nothing to soothe her troubled heart and mind.

The day they were married, November 6, 1907, was one of the stormiest, most inhospitable days of the autumn. A mere ten days later, Mrs. Best received a telegram from Annie. As it turned out, Yale's father, although a millionaire, was of the old-fashioned mindset that a son needed to prove himself in the world before gaining access to the family fortune. Wellington was refusing to send money to Yale and Annie, and on their honeymoon, they had no means to pay for their hotel and travels. Mrs. Best wired the money. In the end, she even had to pay the bill for the diamond engagement ring.[3] A divorce decree was granted in June 1908,[4] and Annie moved back in with her mother in Newport.[5] A little less than two years later, Yale's millionaire father was crushed to death in a folding bed in a West 23rd Street rooming house. He was in the company of an unknown woman, who disappeared shortly after his death and was never fully identified.[6]

In 1910, Annie became engaged to Arthur Carroll, the son of General Howard Carroll, who had been inspector general for all New York troops during the Spanish-American War. The Carrolls were a socially prominent and very wealthy family with a stately mansion overlooking the Hudson River. However, although Arthur's parents entertained on a grand scale at home, his mother was an ultraconservative woman who looked down with contempt on the unrestrained, decadent, and perhaps immoral functions of the New-

ALREADY MAKING PLANS FOR THE WINTER SEASON WHILE ATTENDING THE AUTUMN WEDDINGS

MISS ANNIE L BEST
PHOTO BY CAMPBELL STUDIO

✴ *Annie Livingston Best, 1907 (New York Herald, September 22, 1907)*

1 *Evening Telegram* (New York), October 18, 1906.
2 *Sandusky* (Ohio) *Register*, March 21, 1920.
3 *Sandusky* (Ohio) *Register*, March 21, 1920.
4 *Utica* (New York) *Globe*, June 5, 1908.
5 *Sandusky* (Ohio) *Register*, March 21, 1920.
6 *New York Times*, June 8, 1911.

port and New York social circles. She pleaded and wept with her son not to marry into such a crowd, and General Carroll threatened to disinherit him if he followed through with the wedding plans. Love prevailed, and Arthur and Annie were married at her mother's house in Newport. Arthur's parents were noticeably absent.

* *Mrs. W. Sackett Duell (Photograph, Philadelphia Record Photograph Morgue (11626-V07), Historical Society of Pennsylvania)*

For several years, Annie tried as hard as she could to win over Arthur's family. She tried to blend into their stay-at-home lifestyle, and for some time, it seemed as if she were winning her way into their hearts. But there is a limited amount of time that one can pretend to be someone he or she is not, and eventually, Annie was socializing in her familiar circles. It was a gay crowd, utterly repugnant to the Carrolls. Annie finally broke completely with Arthur's family to be with her more spectacular friends, and it wasn't long afterward that she and Arthur brought their marriage to an end.[1] In 1915, Annie Livingston Best was awarded her second divorce decree.[2]

When the war came, although Sackett Duell registered for the draft,[3] he was not selected for service and did not go to Europe; instead, he did volunteer work at home. It was through this work that he happened to meet Baby Best, and the fact they planned to be married within three months of meeting[4] underscored Sackett's need for a wife and stability and peace of mind. His father, Charles Holland Duell, Sr., was in very poor health as a consequence of the stroke he had suffered in January. Accordingly, plans were made for a small wedding, which took place on January 21, 1920, at 4:00 in the afternoon in Annie's apartment at the Hotel Lorraine in Manhattan. The ceremony was private, with only relatives in attendance. Annie's beloved mother, Mary Tooker Best, had the honor of giving away the bride. Holland and Mabel were present, of course, and Sackett's brother Charles, Jr. was the best man.[5] The reception was larger, with about 250 guests.[6]

In 1916, Sackett had moved his family to Meadowbrook, Pennsylvania.[7,8] Meadowbrook is beautifully representative of Pennsylvania, with rolling wooded hills, and was perfectly fitted to Sackett's love of country living. The family lived in one of the

---

1 *Sandusky* (Ohio) *Register*, March 2, 1920.

2 *New York Times*, June 7, 1925.

3 Registration card for Sackett Duell from National Archives, Atlanta.

4 *Sandusky* (Ohio) *Register*, March 21, 1920.

5 *Amsterdam Evening Recorder*, January 22, 1920.

6 *New York Tribune*, January 22, 1920.

7 Registration card for Sackett Duell from National Archives, Atlanta.

8 *Amsterdam Evening Recorder*, March 31, 1916.

✳ *Annie Livingston Best, 1920 (Sandusky (Ohio) Register, March 21, 1920)*

✳ *Annie Livingston Best and Sackett Duell at the beach, 1924 (Ogden (Utah) Examiner, August 2, 1924)*

oldest colonial homes in the state. Their estate, Hillcroft, had been built on a grand scale, with huge rooms, exterior columns that presented statements of grandeur, and ornate gardens with white trellises from which hung flowering vines.[1] Although it was a vast departure from the environment in which she had been raised, Annie was determined that Hillcroft would provide the perfect setting for her happy new life.[2]

---

1 *Evening Telegram*, October 29, 1921.
2 1920 U.S. Census record for "W. Lackett Duill" [misspelling of W. Sackett Duell], ancestry.com.

There was obviously some part of Annie that wanted to settle down and lead a calm, quiet, sedate home life. Growing up in the social limelight had perhaps instilled in her a need for the energy and stimulation afforded by the Four Hundred's processions of balls, functions, and gala events, and that need might have contributed to her two failed marriages. She respected Sackett's life as being wholesome and admirable. He was a country gentleman who enjoyed the peace and tranquility of his Pennsylvania home, and her hope to fit into that lifestyle was as strong as Sackett's optimism that she would love the life that he wanted to show her and share with her. The presence of his boys and becoming a part of their lives would be added incentive for Annie to do things right this time. Also accompanying them in their new life would be Annie's mother, Mary Tooker Best, who was now close to seventy.[1,2] She had always been there for Annie, and it would now be Annie's turn to take care of her.

Holland may have questioned how well suited Annie and his brother Sackett were for each other, but there was no denying her healing effect on Sackett's depressed state, and everyone wished them well. It was a happy time, but unfortunately, there would be no happy ending.

✳ *Mrs. W. Sackett Duell, 1921 (Photograph, Philadelphia Record Photograph Morgue (11626-V07), Historical Society of Pennsylvania)*

---

1 *New York Social Register, Summer 1920* (New York: Social Register Association: 1920), p. 9.
2 *Albany* (New York) *Evening Journal*, September 30, 1885.

The 1920 Racing Season

On January 29, 1920, Charles Holland Duell, Sr. died at his son Holland's home, Ardenwold. Charles had lived there with Holland and Mabel for the past year since suffering a stroke that caused partial paralysis. He was a brilliant lawyer, and his quick-witted, engaging personality had earned him friends and admirers throughout his lifetime.[1,2] As a father, he had not only provided Holland with the love and support that is so nurturing to a child, but also set a sterling example of the respect and reputation a man can gain through proper education, hard work, and adherence to good moral principles. His monument, which towers above all others in Cortland Cemetery, N.Y. stands as a testament and reminder of the monumental achievements that Charles Holland Duell accomplished within the span of his own lifetime. His passing marked the end of an era, and the condolences were many, as were the feelings of profound loss among his children, to whom he left an estate of $300,000.[3]

Barring that one event, which overshadowed the year, everyone welcomed 1920 and happily bid farewell to "the lost year" of 1919. Holland and Emilie endeavored to manage a loving, supportive relationship, given what they had to work with. It was complicated both by their decision to conceal their love affair from the world and by the fact that they wanted to see each other constantly. Emilie perhaps struggled with it more than Holland did, or at least she struggled in a different way. He was certainly disadvantaged by the confines of his marriage, while Emilie had complete freedom to be available for him at any time. Before the war, Holland's life had always seemed to benefit from the positive influence of Emilie's presence, even under those very innocent circumstances. In making the best of the current situation, he wanted Emilie to continue to do things with the family as much as possible: help with the children, be a presence at Ardenwold, and, of course, socialize, as would normally be expected of a cousin.

That was an easy decision for Holland, being the only hand that he had to play. For Emilie, however, having to conceal her relationship while in the presence of Holland and Mabel and, at the same time, act out a charade of respecting that marriage felt entirely hypocritical and demeaning. Yet she knew that it was their only option if they wanted to maximize their time together, and she fully participated. The bored,

✳ *Charles Holland Duell Sr. monument, Cortland Cemebery, Cortland, N.Y. (Photo courtesy of Carol Darling)*

---

1 *Syracuse Herald*, January 30, 1920.
2 1920 U.S. Census record for Holland S. Duell.
3 *Syracuse Herald*, March 13, 1920.

* Rowdy, *July 4, 1920. Left to right: Holland Duell, his son Charles, Emilie Brown, Mabel Duell, Hanny.*

acquiescent look on her face during that Fourth of July sail in 1920 clearly reflected her sentiments. As Hanny had said, it was a picture that spoke volumes!

Any mortar that had previously held the foundation of Holland and Mabel's lives together and their ambitions on the same path was now rapidly crumbling, despite Mabel's seeming denial of that reality. She was unwavering in her pursuit of ever higher esteem and social stature, and she saw Holland's distinguished war record as an enormous asset in terms of electability for public office. She encouraged him to make a run for the state senate, but Holland was adamant that he was not going to miss the 1920 racing season. The two finally agreed that he would participate fully in the racing season and would then campaign for a seat in the New York Senate.

After four long years, serious sailing on Long Island Sound was about to resume. In perfect accompaniment to the local club races—and for the first time in 17 years—the Sound was to be the site of a competition for the America's Cup. English tea magnate Sir Thomas Lipton had been trying in vain to win the cup since 1899. The last race had been in 1903, when his *Shamrock III* lost to *Reliance*. His 1907 challenge to the New York Yacht Club ended in disagreement over how the two competing yachts should be rated for the race, and Lipton withdrew his challenge. His 1914 challenge was accepted, and in July of that year, his yacht *Shamrock IV* left Portsmouth, England, under tow, bound for New York. However, only a few weeks later, in early August, the war broke out in Europe, and the America's Cup was canceled.

May 22, 1920, was the date scheduled for the first of fourteen races between the American yachts *Resolute* and *Vanitie* to determine which would defend the cup.[1] Holland was sailing on *Rowdy* that day[2] and enjoyed watching the giant yachts as

---

1 *History of the New York Yacht Club: From Its Founding Through 1973*, by John Parkinson, Jr. (New York: New York Yacht Club, 1975), p. 265.

2 *New York Times*, May 23, 1920.

they knifed along, side by side. *Resolute* was some 300 yards ahead when she jibed at high speed around the second mark, and when the boom slammed to the opposite side of the boat, the large wooden mast shattered 10 feet above the deck, sending the entire rig and two men over the side. Luckily, no one was hurt, and the men were swiftly picked up in a dinghy. *Resolute* was towed into Bristol, where her former steel mast was restepped to the boat.[1] It was a thrilling start to a thrilling season.

Resolute prevailed in the trials and was chosen to represent the United States, but in her first race against *Shamrock IV*, on July 15, crew error caused the throat halyard to slip free. The resulting luff in the mainsail caused *Resolute* to lose speed and to lose the race.

✳ Resolute. *Broken mast. May 22, 1920.*

The second race, on July 17, was terminated when the yachts could not finish within the time limit because of a lack of wind. In redoing the second race on July 20, *Shamrock IV* and *Resolute* raced a 30-mile triangle in light variable winds. *Shamrock IV* was luckier in hitting the pockets of wind and won by a margin of 2 minutes and 26 seconds. She was one race away from winning the best in a series of five. Since acquiring the cup in 1857, the New York Yacht Club had never been in more danger of losing it.

The crew of *Resolute* fought with determination the following day in the third race and, in winds between 9 and 12 knots, held onto hope of not losing the cup after beating *Shamrock* by 7 minutes and 1 second.

The fourth race between *Shamrock IV* and *Resolute*, on July 23, was delayed at the start by fog and then proceeded under light winds punctuated at the end by a westerly rain squall. *Resolute* won by a comfortable margin of nearly 10 minutes, bringing the series to a cliffhanger. One last race would determine the winner.

At the scheduled start time of the final race on July 24, a gale was churning up very rough seas and 36-knot winds. The owners of both *Shamrock IV* and *Resolute*, finding the conditions too extreme, voted to postpone the race.[2]

On the same day, *Rowdy* was scheduled to sail in a 20-mile race, part of the Larchmont Yacht Club's Annual Race Week, on Long Island Sound. While yacht clubs sometimes postpone races for lack of wind, rarely do they call a race off because of too much wind, and that July 24 race was no exception. Ninety-eight yachts in total braved the boiling seas with winds that were never less than 30 knots. Holland won many races in such conditions because he simply ignored the threat of breakage and, with every inch of canvas stretched, sailed *Rowdy* as hard as she could be sailed. Pushing her to the limit of her design was exhilarating. Never once under those conditions, with one rail completely buried in the water, 22 tons of boat charging through the seas like a freight train, sending salty spray jetting through the air as if discharged from a fire hose, was anyone seen to yawn.

1 *History of the New York Yacht Club*, p. 265.
2 *History of the New York Yacht Club*, p. 268.

The New York Times

NEW YORK, SUNDAY, JULY 25, 1920.

98 YACHTS RACE IN 30-KNOT WIND

Several Accidents Mar Start of Larchmont Club's Regatta— 60 Cross Finish Line

ROWDY LOSES SPREADERS

Captain Knocked Overboard and Nearly Drowned

Duell's Rowdy carried away her spreaders and in taking in her topsail her Captain was knocked overboard. The skipper was finally rescued after he had almost gone down for the last time.

As was to be expected, there were many accidents that day. The NY40 *Monsoon* rammed *Shawara*, and on *Rowdy*, as she neared the end of the course, a loud crack from above signaled the failure of a spreader. A hurried effort was undertaken to reduce sail before the mast should be carried away. In taking in the topsail, Captain Duell was knocked overboard.

Luckily, Holland had planned to take this racing season seriously and, as a consequence, had on board a well-seasoned crew. Nonetheless, any sailor knows how difficult it is to bring a large sailboat around, return to a specific spot, and find something as small as a person's head bobbing in an angry sea. By the time they made it back to Holland, he was in serious trouble.

They say that a drowning person who slips under water as his strength fails can summon enough energy to make it to the surface for another breath before sinking a second time and then, in a dying effort, can make it back up for but one last breath before finally succumbing and going down for the third and final time. The crew aboard *Rowdy* scooped Holland from the sea as he was going down for the last time. Nonetheless, once aboard, Holland gave the order to continue the race, and *Rowdy* somehow avoided last place, finishing seventh, ahead of *Mistral.*[1,2]

Anticipation was high for the rescheduled final race in the America's Cup series. For the first time in the America's Cup, a series of five races had reached the fifth race. Ironically, on that day, a lack of wind prevented *Shamrock IV* and *Resolute* from finishing the course in time, and again the race was postponed.

Finally, on Tuesday, July 27, *Shamrock IV* and *Resolute* raced in light variable winds, and *Resolute* saved the America's Cup, winning by 19 minutes and 45 seconds.[3] It was a thrilling conclusion to what, for Holland, was a very active and successful racing season, during which he assumed the presidency of the New York Forty Association.[4]

After four years without racing, enthusiasm extended the 1920 season into late September. Even then, many of the owners could not get enough, and on Friday, October 1, a group of five New York Forties, including *Rowdy*, raced 42 miles

---

1   *New York Times,* July 25, 1920.
2   *Brooklyn Daily Eagle,* July 25, 1920.
3   *History of the New York Yacht Club,* p. 268.
4   *Rudder,* August 1920.

✳ *Resolute and Shamrock IV at the start of the 5th race. July 27, 1920.*

from Larchmont to New Haven. The group left their boats at anchor the next day to attend a Yale football game. On Sunday, they all raced back to Larchmont, and Commodore H. H. Raymond tendered a dinner as the last diehards officially ended a most enjoyable season.[1]

---

1 *Rudder*, November 1920, p. 48.

❋ *Left, 1920 New Rochelle Yacht Club Trophy, front view; above, 1920 New Rochelle Yacht Club Trophy, side view (Provided by Holland Duell's grandson Charles Duell)*

❋ *1920 trophies: six cups, six victories (Provided by Holland Duell's grandson Holland Duell)*

The New York Times.

NEW YORK, SUNDAY, JUNE 13, 1920.

ROWDY IS WINNER AMONG 40-FOOTERS

Captures Feature Event of Annual Regatta of Manhasset Bay Yacht Club.

MISTRAL FINISHES SECOND

Mallory's Yacht Is 2 Minutes 21 Seconds Behind Leader—Adios Shows Way to Alera.

Forty-six yachts sailed in the annual regatta of the Manhasset Bay Yacht Club on Long Island Sound yesterday. Unfortunately, the wind was not particularly strong, although it freshened as the afternoon advanced, giving the craft an opportunity of finishing within the required time limit. The start and the finish was off Execution Light, and the course sailed by the larger classes was from the starting line to a mark off Parsonage Point, thence to another off Week's Point and then home.

The feature division was the forty-footers of the New York Yacht Club. No less than five started. It was the largest representation in the division since 1916. The winner was Rowdy, the property of Holland S. Duell, which defeated P. R. Mallory's Mistrel by 2 minutes and 21 seconds over an eleven mile course. Among the thirty-footers of the same organization, Adonis, which has been purchased back by Fred L. Richards, was the first craft home, winning from Alera, which now belongs to F. W. Belknap.

The summaries:

NEW YORK YACHT CLUB 40-FOOTERS.
Start, 1:10. Course, 11 miles.

		Elapsed
Yacht and Owner.	Finish. H.M.S.	Time. H.M.S.
Rowdy, H. C. Duell	3:01:10	1:51:10
Mistral, P. R. Mallory	3:03:31	1:53:31
Schwara, Harold Wesson	3:06:28	1:56:28
Zilph, J. E. Hayes	3:08:08	1:58:08
Pamparo, H. H. Raymond	3:12:28	2:02:28

NEW YORK YACH CLUB 30-FOOTERS.
Start, 1:20. Course, 11 miles.

Adios, F. L. Richards	4:33:08	3:18:08
Alera, F. W. Belknap	4:41:00	3:21:00
Rowdy, C. Belsky	4:43:58	3:23:58
Mizpah, D. R. Richardson	4:50:31	3:30:31

NEW YORK, JUNE 27, 1920

ROWDY VICTORIOUS IN 40-FOOT CLASS

Duell Yacht First in Oyster Bay Regatta—Nahma and and Oriole Win.

Special to The New York Times.
OYSTER BAY, L. I., June 26.—The largest fleet that has sailed in a regatta of the Scawanhaka-Corinthian Yacht Club in years came to the starting line off here today for the annual Spring regatta of the organization. Although there were no big sloops or schooners that used to race off here before the war, the fleet had considerable class and included the 40-footers of the New York Yacht Club, the 30-footers of the same organization, Class P and the new Victory Class that originally was suggested by members of the Center Island Club.

The 40-foot class, which led the fleet, was won by Rowdy, the property of H. S. Duell. In Class P the speedy Nahma, entered by Hanan and Childs, was the winner. F. C. Pirie's Oriole was the winner among the 30-footers.

The summary:

NEW YORK Y. C. 40-FOOTERS.
Start, 1:50. Course, 14½ Miles.

		Elapsed
Yacht and Owner.	Finish. H.M.S.	Time. H.M.S.
Rowdy, H. S. Duell	4:22:20	2:32:20
Zilph, J. E. Hayes	4:22:42	2:32:42
Cockatoo, H. Chubb	4:25:25	2:35:25
Pamparo, H. H. Raymond	4:25:37	2:35:37
Shawara, H. Wesson	4:27:25	2:37:25

NEW YORK, JULY 11, 1920

ROWDY WINS ON SOUND.

Forty-Footer and Queen Mab Again Lead Eastern Y. C. Fleet.

Special to The New York Times.
NEW HAVEN, Conn., July 10.—The lightest of southwesters, with a favorable tide, wafted the Eastern Yacht Club fleet over 86 miles of the placid water of Long Island Sound today, and by picking up friendly slants and some of the stronger currents the 40-footer Rowdy, owned by H. S. Duell, and the schooner Queen Mab, owned by R. C. Robbins, captured the two prizes of the day. It was the Queen Mab's fourth victory on the cruise.

On the way from Bartlett's Reef to the Cornfield, Rowdy drew up to Mistral, and although the latter was well to windward the Duell boat drew by and took the lead. Just under her stern was Shawara, and as the air seemed stronger inshore both yachts gained on the rest of the fleet.

The wind began to fade as the yachts reached Branford Ledge, but there was air enough to bring all the yachts to the finish an hour before dark. Officers of the New Haven Yacht Club welcomed the fleet upon its arrival off the clubhouse.

The summary:

NEW YORK 40-FOOTERS.

	Elapsed	Corrected
	Time.	Time
Yacht and Owner.	H.M.S.	
Rowdy, H. S. Duell	5:00:38	......
Shawara, H. Wesson	5:02:50	......
Zilph, J. Hayes	5:03:26	......
Pamparo, H. H. Raymond	5:05:30	......
Sally Ann, S. Borden, Jr.	5:09:27	......

The New York Times.

NEW YORK, JULY 13, 1920

YACHTS COMPLETE 150-MILE CRUISE

Schooner Queen Mab Scores Six Victories—Rowdy Best Among Forty-Footers.

Special to The New York Times.

LARCHMONT, N. Y., July 12.—A fifteen knot southwester gave the racing portion of the Eastern Yacht Club fleet a good twenty-five mile run up the Sound to this port today as a fitting climax of the cruise of 150 miles along the southern New England and eastern New York shores. The winners for the day were the schooner Queen Mab and the New York Yacht Club forty-footer Rowdy. Queen Mab finished the cruise

The Sun and The New York Herald

SUNDAY, JUNE 13, 1920.

FORTY-SIX BOATS IN MANHASSET REGATTA

The 40-Footer Rowdy, N. Y. Y. C., First Home.

Forty-six yachts sailed in the annual regatta of the Manhasset Bay Yacht Club on Long Island Sound yesterday. Unfortunately the wind was not particularly strong, although it freshened as the afternoon advanced, giving the craft an opportunity of finishing within the required time limit. The start and the finish was off Execution Light and the course sailed by the larger classes was from the starting line to a mark off Parsonage Point, thence to another off Week's Point and then home.

The feature division was the forty-footers of the New York Yacht Club. Five came to the starting line, the largest representation in the division since 1916. As the wind came the yachts had a beat, a reach and a run. The winner was Rowdy, the property of Holland S. Duell, which defeated P. R. Mallory's Mistrel by 2 minutes and 31 seconds over an eleven mile course.

NEW YORK, AUGUST 29, 1920

ROWDY IS WINNER AMONG 'FORTIES'

Leads Pampero by Wide Margin ——New Rochelle Y. C. Regatta Has 72 Starters.

Special to The New York Times.

NEW ROCHELLE, N. Y., Aug. 28.—There were seventy-two starters in the New Rochelle Yacht Club's annual regatta, held off here today, on Long Island Sound. After two postponements of fifteen minutes each, because of lack of breeze, a light southwesterly wind sprang up. It held true throughout except close under the Long Island shore, where there were some treacherous soft spots.

New Rochelle Yacht Club fixtures are occasionally marked by extreme weather conditions, but today they were quite normal. The postponement was partly due to a desire to enable the Mistral of the "forties" to arrive. The Molloy cubical starting signals were used and, as on previous occasions, proved to be most satisfactory.

In most of the clashes the starts lacked dash and pep. The Corinthians seemed to be "recall shy," although there were two of the "forties" that did get away too soon. The Victory Class afforded the best getaway of the day. The number of starters was greater than at any other club this year, with the exception of Larchmont during race week. In the N. Y. Y. C. Forty Class H. S. Duell's Rowdy was the winner by a margin of nearly eight minutes, while Edmund Lang's Banzai of the "thirties" was first to finish.

N. Y. Y. C. FORTIES.
Start, 3:20. Course, 16¾ Miles.

Yacht and Owner.	Finish.	Elapsed Time.
Rowdy, H. S. Duell	6:30:12	3:10:12
Pampero, H. H. Raymond	6:44:08	3:24:08
Zilph, J. E. Hayes	6:46:55	3:25:55
Mistral, P. R. Mallory	6:48:58	3:28:58
Shawara, H. Wesson	6:53:20	3:33:20
Monsoon, F. D. M. Strahan	6:56:48	3:36:48
Cockatoo, H. Chubb	Did not finish	

The Senate Years

$\mathcal{H}$olland's ensuing run for the state senate overflowed with positive energy. The public loved war heroes, and earlier in the year he had been awarded the Silver Star Citation[1] and had been promoted to lieutenant colonel.[2] Holland was charismatic and had previously proved himself a man of action while serving as state assembly-man for New Rochelle. Of course, association with his brother Charles didn't hurt. Charles, who had built a career in politics, had many useful connections and was campaigning hard in the same race to elect Nathan L. Miller to the post of governor.[3] Election night brought victory: Miller won the governorship, and Holland was elected state senator for the 26th District.[4]

Probably no one felt the joy of that night more euphorically than Mabel. She had her children, her mansion, her war hero, and, with Holland's election to the state senate, the exciting prospect of even loftier political power and position to come. The fabric of her life was beginning to mesh with her ambitions and preconceived vision of her destiny.

As Holland rolled up his sleeves in preparation for busy service in the legislature, he sadly gave orders for *Rowdy* to be prepared for a year-long storage. There would be no time for racing in 1921.

Holland introduced bill after bill in the senate, many requiring amendments to the state constitution. He fought tirelessly for disabled veterans and introduced a bill requiring a constitutional amendment that would give disabled veterans preference in filling civil service jobs.[5] He also guided the passage of a bill creating the State Veterans Relief Fund, a fund for assisting disabled soldiers, for which he served on the finance committee.[6,7] In his spare time, he had published the book *The History of the 306th Field Artillery*; when it was completed, he formally presented the Syracuse Library with a copy.[8]

---

1 General Orders: GHQ, American Expeditionary Forces, Citation Orders No. 9, August 1, 1920.
2 Yale biography, "20 Years After."
3 *Evening Telegram* (New York), June 4, 1921.
4 *New York Times*, November 3, 1920.
5 *Daily News* (New York), April 15, 1921.
6 *Evening Telegram* (New York), April 16, 1921.
7 *Brooklyn Daily Eagle*, May 29, 1921.
8 *Syracuse Herald*, February 5, 1921.

In January 1922, Holland moved up in the senate to chairmanship of the Labor and Industries Committee.[1] He continued to work tirelessly and introduced the Duell Bill, which was aimed at reducing infant and mother mortality rates. At the time, every year nationally, 20,000 mothers and 200,000 babies died from causes that could have been prevented. In twenty-one New York counties, there was no agency whatever for instruction and supervision of maternity, not even a public health nurse. The Duell Bill would establish clinics, consultation centers, and public health nurses. The bill also provided help for the state in paying for the cost by mandating the federal government to provide matching funding.[2,3,4]

Another bill, the Industrial Relations Bill, was designed to prevent strikes and lockouts that were deemed harmful to the public. In case of labor disagreements, the state supreme court would act as the final arbiter. As Holland said, "I am confident that the public is sick and tired of being the victim of industrial disputes."[5]

Holland also introduced a bill aimed at preventing the deaths of pedestrians by automobiles. The operator of an automobile that injured a pedestrian would be guilty of assault, and a driver who caused the death of a person would be guilty of manslaughter, both punishable by time in prison.[6,7]

As a consequence of his accomplishments, Holland was rated the "ablest, most constructive and most independent" member of the legislature in the annual review[8,9] and was awarded the Distinguished Service Palm by the New York State Association.[10,11]

Holland continued to be honored with military decorations and was awarded both the New York State Conspicuous Service Cross[12,13] and the Distinguished Service Cross for "extraordinary heroism" at Binarville, France, on September 28–29, 1918.[14,15,16]

But enough was enough. Holland had owned *Rowdy* for six years and had been able to sail her for only two seasons. The 1921 season had been a spectacular one, but he had missed every minute of it while serving in the state senate. He told Mabel that he was not going to miss the 1922 season. In stunned disbelief, Mabel also dug in her heels. Holland was now just one step away from fulfilling her vision of his becoming a United States Senator. With his record, his electability was almost a given. He had

1 *Binghamton* (New York) *Press*, January 10, 1922.
2 *Geneva* (New York) *Daily Times*, March 4, 1922
3 *Gazette & Farmers' Journal* (Baldwinsville, New York), March 9, 1922.
4 *Otsego* (New York) *Farmer & Otsego Republican*, March 17, 1922.
5 *New York Times*, February 8, 1922.
6 *New York Times*, January 26, 1922.
7 *Brooklyn Daily Eagle*, January 26, 1922.
8 *New York Tribune*, July 24, 1922.
9 *New York Times*, September 2, 1925.
10 *New York Times*, November 26, 1942.
11 *1902 Yale Autobiographies, Twenty-Five Years After, 1902–1927*, edited by James Wright (Newburgh, NY: Moore, 1927).
12 Yale obituary for Holland Duell.
13 *New York Red Book* (New York: J.B. Lyon Company, 1921).
14 *Syracuse Evening Telegram*, October 25, 1922.
15 *1902 Yale Autobiographies, Twenty-Five Years After, 1902–1927*.
16 *New York Tribune*, October 20, 1922.

an impeccable family background, an honorable war record, and now an outstanding political record and credit for passing volumes of invaluable legislation. She argued in vain with Holland until, in final desperation, she offered him "half my fortune, IF you become elected United States Senator from New York."[1] To Mabel's dismay, Holland held to the adage "money can't buy everything," and in a speech before the Civic League at Tarrytown, he announced his retirement as state senator of the 26th District at the close of the year.[2]

With that, whatever mild warmth had still existed in the relationship between Holland and Mabel was replaced by a distinct chill. But for Holland, it came down to a matter of "being true to one's own self," and with Emilie's encouragement, he knew that he had to draw the line and protect his own happiness.

With the decision made and the action taken, the tension of the conflict soon lifted from Holland's shoulders, and his entire focus shifted to preparing for a busy racing season. For Holland, stepping aboard *Rowdy* was akin to stepping through a doorway—a magical doorway that stripped away all of life's troubles and worries. The effect was immediate; the burden of all the many worldly problems that tended to occupy his soul dissolved instantaneously. The joy of being aboard *Rowdy* on a sparkling sea so completely filled Holland's heart and mind that there was room for nothing else. It was emotionally therapeutic and healing to him as nothing else on this planet. Emilie joyfully watched as zestful enthusiasm was breathed back into his demeanor. The twinkling that returned to his eye as he got back on the ocean reflected how strong were his love for and need of the sport. The entire experience was utterly rejuvenating, and a part of Holland always credited Emilie for her consistent encouragement and support of his participation. Emilie's devotion to Holland was complete, and she gave of herself freely to him, never asking for anything in return. What a sharp contrast to his marriage it was, and the irony that Emilie was not the one wearing his wedding ring began to steadily inflate.

Rowdy sailed in dozens of races that summer, winning many, and Holland thoroughly enjoyed them all. The trophy was the bonus. The true prize was being able to simply blend with the elements of Long Island Sound in the spirited and brotherly company of like-minded sailors while at the helm of such a marvelous yacht as *Rowdy*. Holland's friend John Stilwell joined him for the August cruise of the New York Yacht Club,[3] and much of the conversation was centered on the happy news that John's wife, Mildred, had just become pregnant with their first child. Eight months later, however, his joy in the birth of little Jane on April 18, 1923, was sadly overshadowed by Mildred's subsequent death as a result of complications from the delivery. John found the combination of the permanent loss of his wife and the lifelong gain of a new daughter to be more than he could bear alone. Sympathetically, Holland opened the doors of his house, and for most of that summer, John, baby Jane, and the child's nurse lived at Ardenwold.[4]

---

1 "Dilettante," a paper written by Holland Duell's son Holland Sackett Duell, Jr. about his parents.
2 "10 years ago," *Herald Statesman* (Yonkers, NY), May 7, 1932.
3 *New York Times*, August 3, 1922.
4 "Dilettante."

It was in the same year that the nature of the relationship between Holland and Emilie came fully to the surface. After five years of happiness together, the desire and effort to conceal their relationship had eroded, probably to the point of wanting to be out in the open. In fact, by the time Mabel became aware of the situation, it had for some time been common knowledge among many people in Yonkers.[1] But that in no way lessened the impact of the event.

Holland was deeply and truly in love with Emilie. He felt safe with her. He felt with her a true bonding of souls and minds. They were perfectly matched in a way that is rare and special, and he felt blessed to be the recipient of her unwavering commitment, love, and support. With each passing day, the concealment of their love had become more of a burden, and in Holland's heart, the deception felt disrespectful toward Emilie and toward their relationship. With the disclosure of their love affair, Holland saw at last the chance to realize a life that he had always envisioned in his heart. It was a chance for a relationship filled with happiness, not through sacrifice or by means of undue compromise, but simply by the virtue of two lives meshing in a harmony of similar personalities. Now that everything was out in the open, he would return to Emilie the support and commitment that she had given him for the past five years.

While Holland met the event with relief and visions of happiness down the road, Mabel took it as well as one would take a direct bomb blast. She was shaken to the core but, oddly, not so much by the prospect of losing her husband's love as by the derailing of her agenda to achieve the status in life that she had envisioned and pursued for so long. Everything she had worked for, the entire sphere of her world, her image, and her place in society, was based upon a stable marriage and a husband of power and prominence. Mabel had become so focused on that next step of her aspirations—a husband who was a United States Senator—that it was almost impossible for her to back up and focus simply on salvaging what she already had. In the world that she had built for herself, there was no place to cast herself in the role of a divorced woman, and regardless of all else, she did not want that for her future.

The situation was obviously very complicated, and for nearly a year, Holland and Mabel discussed, argued, and negotiated over various possible outcomes. It was clearly one of those major life flare-ups that put all else on hold. Seeing no opportunity for sailing during 1923, Holland leased *Rowdy* out to S. G. Shepard, who raced her for the entire season.[2]

The obvious reality, to anyone viewing from a distance, is that such situations never have any type of amicable resolution. By the end of the year, the discussions, arguing, and negotiations terminated with Holland and Emilie sailing for France. It was a bold statement that their relationship was out in the open for all the world to see, and despite the consequences, despite any and all repercussions, the feeling was joyous and liberating. They had both been feeling the stress of the situation, and the voyage provided a much needed space in which they could regroup and plan the

---

1 "Dilettante."
2 *New York Times*, August 12, 1923.

course of their future as well as to openly celebrate their union at last. They wanted a life that was new and fresh, and by the time they boarded the *Leviathan* to sail home on December 15, 1923,[1] they had decided that they would build a brand-new house together. This time, Holland would be supported by a wife who shared his dream of living at the ocean's edge, and as soon as they returned, they would search for a lot along the shores of Long Island Sound. Holland would keep life simple: drop out of the political arena, concentrate his energies on his law practice, and reserve summers for sailing aboard *Rowdy*.

---

1 December 15, 1923, *Leviathan* passenger list for Holland Duell, ancestry.com.

The 1924 Racing Season

Upon Holland and Emilie's return from France, Holland felt like a man freed of restraints. When racing season approached, he put together a crew, including his friend Colonel John Stilwell,[1] and signed up for every race that was on the calendar. The 1924 racing season was a fabulous one, and *Rowdy* ended up sailing in over forty-three races—more than she ever had before. Her many victories culminated in winning the coveted 1924 Championship of the Yacht Racing Association of Long Island Sound.[2,3]

❋ *Eastern Yacht Club 1924 Annual Cruise Vice Commodore's Cup (Provided by Holland Duell's grandson, John Henry)*

❋ *Larchmont Yacht Club, 1924 (Provided by Holland Duell's daughter-in-law Nancy Duell)*

---

1 *New York Times*, August 11, 1924.
2 *New York Times*, October 31, 1924.
3 *New York Evening Post*, October 31, 1924.

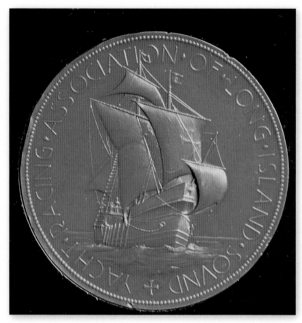

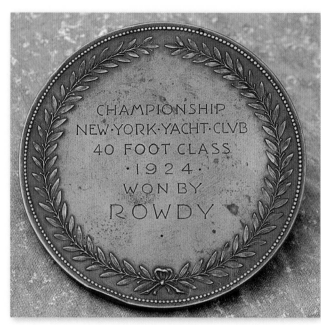

✻ *Yacht Racing Association of Long Island Sound, 1924 Champion (Provided by Holland Duell's grandson John Henry)*

✻ Rowdy *during the June 7, 1924, Larchmont race*

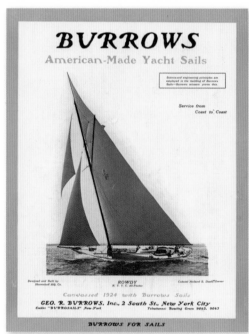

✻ Rowdy *featured in a full-page ad for Burrows Sails (Rudder, July 1924)*

The New York Times.

JUNE 22, 1924.

ROWDY HOME FIRST IN LARCHMONT RACE

Duell's Forty-Footer Leads Rivals Across Line in Annual Spring Regatta.

FLEET OF 78 TAKES PART

Largest of Season Meets Light Airs on the Sound—Grey Dawn and Minx Also Score.

LARCHMONT MANOR, N. Y., June 21.—Seventy-eight yachts, the largest fleet of the season, came to the starting line of the Larchmont Yacht Club off here today to sail in the annual Spring

George A. Corry's Little Dipper led home the Star boats. The International Six-Meter Class and the Victory yachts were the only divisions that had a real race. The light air suited them and, as a result, they finished hours ahead of the other craft. In the six-meter division the winner was Montauk, which belongs to W. A. W. Stewart. The first Victory home was Vindictive, which is owned by R. W. Fraser.

The summaries:

NEW YORK Y. C. FORTY-FOOTERS.
Start 3:55. Course 10¼ Miles.
                                    H.M.S.
Yacht and Owner.
Rowdy, H. S. Duell............7:11:24
Shawara, C. B. Seeley........7:11:43
Banshee, H. L. Maxwell.......7:12:26
Pamperom, C. L. Andrews......7:12:33
Mistral, W. B. Bell..........7:23:57

NEW YORK, SATURDAY, JULY 5, 1924.

ROWDY LEADS FLEET OF 95 BY 22 SEC.

N. Y. Y. C. 40-Footer Slightly Faster Than Banshee in Final Run at Larchmont.

DAUPHIN VICTOR BY 4 SEC.

6-Meter Yacht Attains Notable Triumph Over Lea—Allair

Star Winner by 19 Sec.

Forties Sail 18-Mile Course.

The New York Yacht Club forty-footers were sent away at 12:10 and sailed a course of eighteen miles, as did the Larchmont sloops and thirty-footers. The breeze was light from the eastward as the first class went away and held in this quarter throughout the racing. The first leg was a broad reach to the buoy north of Execution Light, then beat to Matinicock buoy on the Long Island shore, a reach across the Sound to Greenwich Point buoy, across the Sound again to a mark off Hempstead and home.

Rowdy and Banshee had a hard fight of it in the light airs, and only in the final run to the mark, under a cloud of canvas, did the Duell sloop, a bit faster than Banshee, gain the winning advantage.

There were ninety-five boats altogether in the race, making a new high record for the season, against ninety-four starters at the Seawanhaka-Corinthian regatta last Saturday. There were eleven New York Yacht Club thirty-footers starting in this class, in which Grayling, a Class Q sloop, sailed by J. P. Morgan, also went over the line. Edmund Lang's Banzai won her second race in as many days, going well in the light airs, defeating S. C. Pirie's Oriole by almost two minutes.

NEW YORK, September 21, 1924

ROWDY HOME FIRST BY ONLY ONE SECOND

Sets Spinnaker When Near Line and Beats Pampero Coming From Other Angle.

70 YACHTS IN THE REGATTA

Betty Takes Six-Meter Honors in Manhasset Event—Grey Dawn, Oriole and Vega Also Win.

Special to The New York Times.

PORT WASHINGTON, N. Y., Sept. 20.—A fleet of seventy yachts took part today in the Fall regatta of the Man-

Brooklyn Daily Eagle

THE BROOKLYN DAILY EAGLE.
NEW YORK, SUNDAY, JUNE 22, 1924.

ROWDY IS FIRST IN DRIFTING RACE OFF LARCHMONT

Lack of Wind Delays Start of Big Fleet on Sound. Little Dipper Wins.

(Special Cable to The Eagle.)
Larchmont Manor, N. Y., June 21—Seventy-eight yachts, the largest fleet of the summer, came to the starting line of the Larchmont Yacht Club off here today, to sail in the annual spring regatta of the organization. Al

Explosive 1925

In July 1924, Mabel had traveled to Lake Geneva in Switzerland, having given Holland the ultimatum that when she returned to New York, Emilie must be out of his life or he must have his possessions out of Ardenwold. When she arrived home, he had moved his things out.[1]

There seems to be something in the nature of tobacco heiresses with sprawling mansions that precludes them from remaining single for long, and by the end of 1924, John Stilwell was in the perfect position to take advantage of the vacancy left by his friend Holland. What more could Mabel ask for? She had known John for years, he was intelligent and successful, and, just like Holland, he was a colonel.[2] Their relationship developed and grew, further dissolving her ties to Holland, leaving only the final battle in the divorce courtroom to end the marriage and close that chapter of their lives. Holland and Mabel had spent twenty years together and had many shared assets, investments, and business ventures. It would indeed be a battle.

But that was not the only blow that life was about to throw at Holland. The year 1925 proved to be a stormy one for relationships. Both of his brothers met disaster in that year as a consequence of their love interests. So while in the midst of his own divorce struggles, Holland found himself additionally burdened in having to be there for his brothers' emotional and moral support. Furthermore, he was delegated by his youngest brother Charles to represent him in a colossal court case, one that would become the biggest battle of Charles's life.

Back in 1920, when Charles had decided, as a consequence of the Collins fiasco, to acquire Holland's unwanted motion picture equipment, his life's path had ricocheted off in an altogether new direction. The following years provided excitement for everyone around him as his adventures and successes led him to worldwide fame, fortune, and both marriage and divorce with a renowned Broadway star, followed by a steamy love affair with the leading actress of the day. But in 1925, with the sensational flair of a fireworks display's grand finale, all of that marvelous energy blew up in Charles's face.

---

1 "Dilettante," a paper written by Holland Duell's son Holland Sackett Duell, Jr. about his parents.
2 "Dilettante."

Inspiration Pictures: Charles goes Hollywood

Charles was born a social creature. He possessed not an ounce of shyness or timidity; rather, he exuded the self-confidence that Yale had instilled in him. He loved the collective energies of people and was magnetically drawn to group endeavors and team efforts. Before the war, Holland's involvement with Superpictures, Inc. had introduced Charles to the glamorous energy of Hollywood, and the allure was irresistible. It was a universe of which he longed to be a part. He had observed the pitfalls that his older brother had encountered, yet in 1920, with the war over, Charles felt that the environment for movies was much improved. With the acquisition from Holland of his modest amount of filming equipment, Charles began to socialize within the sphere of the motion picture populace.

It was when he became acquainted with the actor Richard Barthelmess that opportunity came to knock on Charles's door. When the two met, Barthelmess had just left the employment of acclaimed director D. W. Griffith. At a time when motion pictures were in an embryonic stage, Griffith's pioneering work was considered to be that of a visionary master. As actress Lillian Gish later said, "His genius lay in his understanding of the interrelationships of separate shots, each contributing to clarity and pace, adding substance, mood, and emotion to the bare story outline." He was driven to put what he called "the atmosphere" into the movie—to give the audience a feel of authenticity and involvement. He experimented with lighting and reflectors as well as zooming in and out and other technical methods for enhancing storytelling. Griffith also stressed the importance of getting suspense into a film. His axiom was "If the audience doesn't hang on every action or twist of the plot, you've lost them."[1]

Griffith had innumerable successes and created many stars. Among them was Lillian Gish, who had done many movies with him, including *Birth of a Nation*, which had secured her status as a movie star, though it gained her nowhere near the stature or paycheck of the leading actress of the day, Mary Pickford. Griffith had also elevated struggling actor Richard Barthelmess when he cast him alongside Lillian Gish in the 1919 film *Broken Blossoms* and then *Way Down East* in 1920. Still far from being among the top actors of the day, Barthelmess was determined to build on his success and become a star. He saw that such potential did not exist with Griffith, who was spread too thin between too many movies and was reluctant to pay Barthelmess the higher

---

1 *The Movies, Mr. Griffith, and Me*, by Lillian Gish and Ann Pinchot (Englewood Cliffs, NJ: Prentice Hall, 1969), pp. 61–70.

salary that he had come to command. So Barthelmess set out on his own.[1] It was an amicable split, and before he left, he purchased the screenplay *Tol'able David* from Griffith for $7,500, with aspirations to star in a film version of the story.[2]

Soon after Charles Duell and Richard Barthelmess became acquainted, Jim Williams, the head of First National, which distributed motion pictures, introduced Charles to director Henry King. Duell asked King whether he would be willing to produce the movie *Tol'able David*.[3] When King responded enthusiastically, the three—Charles Duell, Richard Barthelmess, and Henry King—formed the motion picture company Inspiration Pictures.[4,5,6] A contract was drawn up according to which King would produce seven movies between July 1921 and December 1922 and Charles H. Duell, Jr. would secure $250,000 seed money to fund the productions.[7] The bulk of the financial backing came from financier Averell Harriman, who deposited the $250,000 upon the inception of the company.[8] Inspiration Pictures was organized in Charles Duell's law office, Duell & Smith, with Charles H. Duell, Jr. as president and treasurer of the corporation and J. Boyce Smith, his law partner, as secretary.[9]

Inspiration Pictures became a New York corporation on May 3, 1921,[10] and, with that, Charles departed from the political life that had elevated him into the company of presidents and embarked on what would become an equally thrilling and powerful Hollywood journey.

---

1 *Hollywood on The Hudson: Film and Television from Griffith to Sarnoff*, by Richard Koszarski (New Brunswick, NJ: Rutgers University Press, 2008), p. 84.

2 http://www.silentsaregolden.com/featurefolder2/tolabledavidfeature2.html.

3 *Virginia Quarterly Review*, Autumn 1982, pp. 616–634.

4 *Hollywood on The Hudson*.

5 *Evening Telegram* (New York), May 9, 1921.

6 *Dramatic Mirror & Theater*, March–April 1921.

7 *Virginia Quarterly Review*, Autumn 1982, pp. 616–634.

8 *Medina* (New York) *Journal*, June 3, 1926.

9 *New York Times*, March 27, 1925.

10 Duell vs Gish, Los Angeles Superior Court, case 269864, 1929. Housed at Archives and Records Center, 222 N. Hill St., Los Angeles, CA.

The Cave Girl: A Love Interest for Brother Charles

The first movie that Inspiration produced, before *Tol'able David*, was *The Cave Girl*. Teddie Gerard, an American stage actress and dancer who, at the time, was most celebrated in the theaters of London and Paris, had been secured for the lead role. This would also be her debut in the motion picture business.

In *The Cave Girl*, a light comedy, Teddie played the role of Margot Sperry. Conditions had forced Margot to live in the forest under the dictates of her guardian, the eccentric, good-natured professor Orlando Sperry, who had chosen to live in a primitive mode. This wilderness lifestyle had made Margot forget completely about her pretty, feminine side, and her daily attire consisted of clothes such as a boy would wear.

One day, a Mrs. Georgia Case and her daughter Elsie (played by renowned Broadway star Lilian Tucker) arrived to winter at a camp in the mountains, accompanied by Mr. Divvy Bates, Elsie's wealthy and handsome fiancé. Mrs. Case, wanting her daughter to marry well, hoped that spending extended time together would strengthen the bond between Divvy Bates and Elsie, with whom he was not in love. As the winter snows covered the landscape, Margot, having difficulty finding food in the wild, began to steal provisions from the camp of Elsie, Mrs. Case, and Divvy. When Divvy and Margot met on one of her raids, sparks flew, leaving the audience with little question as to the chemistry between the two.

Later, a half-breed by the name of Baptiste (played by Boris Karloff, at the time a little-known actor who often had to supplement his acting career with

Reprint courtesy The Cumberland Times

297

construction jobs such as digging ditches and delivering plaster), who worked as a hired hand and guide for Divvy, Elsie, and Mrs. Case, was fired for stealing. Baptiste burned the camp in retaliation, and Divvy, Elsie, and Mrs. Case were forced to take shelter from the harsh winter with Margot and the professor.

The attraction between Divvy and Margot was obvious to Elsie. Feeling that she must do anything she could to retain her fiancé's affections, Elsie began to dress in boyish clothes like Margot's. When that had no effect, she covertly teamed up with Baptiste and, after kidnapping Margot, tried to eliminate the competition by sending her down the river in a canoe, bound at the hands and feet and headed toward certain death when the river reached a waterfall. However, cracking under the strain of her actions, Elsie confessed her plot to Divvy, who was able to save Margot just in time and secure a happy ending for the movie.[1,2,3,4]

The cast and crew spent much of the winter filming the movie in Yosemite National Park. The climactic rescue scene in which Margot was sent down the river, tied up in a canoe, was filmed in the heart of the park above Veronica Falls. The danger inherent in the shoot precluded any rehearsal or retake, so as insurance against missing the shot, it was filmed by six different cameras.[5]

The script had called for a mountain lion, and the crew had hoped that a park ranger could capture one for the filming. Forest Townsley, the rugged chief ranger of the park, told stories of capturing the animals with nothing more than a rope, for the use of guns in the park was discouraged. He explained that the large cats "when cornered fight with ferocity," and scars on his body bore out the statement. It was a time when the state of California and the federal government each offered a bounty for every mountain lion pelt, so the animals were aggressively hunted; consequently, no mountain lions could be found, and it was decided to use a cinnamon bear instead. Ranger Townsley located one, which, in Charles Duell's, words:

> immediately climbed the highest tree in reach. Chief Townsley, with only a rope to protect him, and undaunted by the signs that the indicated that the bear was in a fighting mood, went up after him. Then followed one of the most wonderful exhibitions of a fight in mid-air between huntman and animal. The bear would let go one of his forepaws and would try to hit Townsley, to knock him from the tree; Townsley having to duck and dodge the blows which were vicious enough to have crushed him. Four hours of this battle continued, until finally Townsley managed to get the loop over the bear's head.[6]

The realism that was brought to the screen in tandem with the grandeur of Yosemite and an imaginative, fast-moving storyline all combined to make the movie a success.

---

1 *American Institute Catalog of Motion Pictures Produced in the United States*, Vol. F2: *Feature Films 1921–1930* (Berkeley, CA: University of California Press, 1971), p. 115.

2 *Salt Lake Tribune*, July 3, 1922.

3 *Salt Lake Tribune*, July 2, 1922.

4 *Cumberland* (Maryland) *Evening Times*, April 25, 1923.

5 *Cumberland* (Maryland) *Evening News*, April 25, 1923.

6 *Oakland* (California) *Tribune*, September 25, 1921.

Lilian Tucker, who played the role of Elsie, was the daughter of a Norwegian mother and English father.[1] She was born in Chicago on September 21, 1894,[2] the day after her parents arrived there from Europe. Her mother was a talented concert singer, and Lilian inherited her beautiful voice, and was also taught to speak Norwegian by her mother. Lilian spent many years in American convent schools while her parents traveled back to Norway. The beautiful songs that she would sing within those walls gave indication to the sisters that she might someday be drawn from the convent by the temptations of Broadway. So constantly did they warn her about the evils of the stage that in 1904, at the age of seventeen, she rebelled and set off to experience that life firsthand.

Lilian joined George M. Cohan's musical comedy company in Chicago and began her career as an actress and soprano, rising quickly from the chorus to leading roles. She built a successful and established stage career, including a two-year tour in Australia.[3] She later earned wide acclaim for her performances in *Three Faces East*, which ran for a full season in Chicago in 1920.[4] She also appeared in seven silent films before *The Cave Girl*, although none were big box office hits.[5] Lilian was "said to be one of the most beautiful women in America"[6] and "has been described by artists and sculptors in this country and abroad as the typical Greek Goddess."[7] Charles H. Duell, Jr. and Lilian fell into a whirlwind romance and were engaged to be married within a few months' time.[8] Upon completion of *The Cave Girl*, Lilian dropped her first name and adopted her character's name of Elsie, which she used not only informally but also on formal documents such as passports.[9]

In March 1921, New York Governor Nathan Miller, whom Charles had helped to get elected, announced that he would support state legislation providing for strict censorship over all movies. As the governor put it, he saw "a picture in an advertisement that made me think I must have been living in the woods. It was a surprise to me that any newspaper or other publication would publish such a picture in connection with such an advertisement or that any institution would seek to make money out of such an appeal to the passions. I am in favor of anything that will put an end to that sort of thing, and you can't quote me too strongly." The bill provided for the creation of a three-person commission to prohibit the showing of films that were "obscene, indecent, immoral, inhumane or sacrilegious."[10]

Charles met with Governor Miller in early June 1921 at the Plaza Hotel in New York City and expressed to him that the film industry was concerned about the pro-

✳ *Charles Holland Duell, Jr. (February 28, 1920, passport application # 177031 at National Archives and Records Administration)*

✳ *Elsie Tucker (December 12, 1922, passport application #236670 at National Archives and Records Administration)*

1 *Sydney Morning Herald*, September 10, 1917, http://trove.nla.gov.av/ndp/del/article/15718001.

2 December 12, 1922, passport application for Lilian Tucker, ancestry.com.

3 *Sydney Morning Herald*, September 10, 1917, http://trove.nla.gov.au/ndp/del/article/15718001.

4 *New York Times*, September 6, 1921.

5 http://www.imdb.com/name/nm0875924.

6 *Utica* (New York) *Morning Telegram*, September 17, 1921.

7 *Evening Telegram* (New York), September 29, 1921.

8 *New York Times*, September 6, 1921.

9 Numerous pieces of correspondence and travel documents.

10 *New York Times*, March 4, 1921.

posed censorship of movies and wanted to get clarification as to what would and would not be allowed under the New York legislation. He also proposed a private screening of his newly completed movie, *The Cave Girl*, at the governor's mansion, which was agreed to.[1]

The premiere of *The Cave Girl*, Inspiration Pictures' first release, took place at the New York governor's mansion on Eagle Street in Albany on June 18, 1921. Assistant Secretary of the Navy Theodore Roosevelt, Jr. flew up from Washington for the premiere. Others of state and national prominence attending the event included Adjutant-General of New York J. Leslie Kincaid, State Engineer Frank M. Williams, Colonel James T. Lorce, the film's director Henry King, movie star Richard Barthelmess, Inspiration Pictures president Charles H. Duell, Jr., and of course Governor Miller and his wife. It was a black tie event complete with a seven-piece orchestra. Among the most enthusiastic in attendance were the governor's young daughters and some of their invited friends. Known collectively that night as "the Miller Girls," they were enamored with the glitz and glamour of the movie stars.[2,3]

Governor Miller afterward commented that the scenes in the Yosemite Valley, where the movie was shot, were spectacular, there was plenty of action, there were no dull moments, and it was wholesome and entertaining to both the adults and the children. "I think it is beautiful—it depicts the human emotions of conflict. To my mind, pictures of this sort should be encouraged."[4] With that, Charles was off and running with a new career in the motion picture business.

On September 5, 1921, Charles and Elsie announced their plans to be married.[5] The wedding took place on October 29 at Hillcroft, the home of Sackett and "Baby Best" in Meadowbrook, Pennsylvania. More than 300 guests attended, many having been brought in on a specially chartered train from New York and Boston. The plan to have the ceremony in the gardens had to be changed because of uncooperative weather. Instead, it took place in the huge reception room of the grand old house.[6]

Hillcroft was adorned with autumn flowers, foliage, and colors. In keeping with the fall theme, the bride and bridesmaids wore gowns of rich chrysanthemum hues.[7] Sackett was the best man, and Holland Duell was an usher. Following the ceremony, a dance for the guests was accompanied by music from a live orchestra.[8] When the evening concluded, Charles and Elsie departed for their honeymoon, which would include a stay at Hot Springs, Virginia, followed by a month of traveling.[9] On their honeymoon, they were received by President Warren Harding in Washington.[10] Upon returning to New York, Charles and Elsie made their home at the Ritz-Carlton Hotel.[11]

---

1 *Evening Telegram* (New York), June 4, 1921.
2 *Variety*, June 24, 1921.
3 *Amsterdam* (New York) *Evening Recorder*, June 28, 1921.
4 *Variety*, June 24, 1921.
5 *New York Times*, September 6, 1921.
6 *Evening Telegram* (New York), October 29, 1921.
7 *Amsterdam* (New York) *Evening Recorder*, October 31, 1921.
8 *Amsterdam* (New York) *Evening Recorder*, October 31, 1921.
9 *Evening Telegram* (New York), October 29, 1921.
10 *New York Times*, November 10, 1921.
11 *Evening Telegram* (New York), October 29, 1921.

✲ *Wedding of Charles Holland Duell to Lilian Tucker, October 29, 1921*

To the outside world, the three Duell brothers must have seemed to have it all: power, wealth, and spectacular women. One brother was married to a Broadway star, one to a society belle, and one to the heiress to a tobacco fortune. In reality, the romantic interests of all three men would prove to be powder kegs that, in short order, would explode, having thunderous repercussions on their lives.

Tol'able David: A Hollywood Success for Charles

Inspiration Pictures' second film, *Tol'able David*, was released at the end of 1921. It had been filmed in the small mountain town of Blue Grass, Virginia, an isolated backwoods community that proved the perfect location to portray the story's 1800s setting. Richard Barthelmess, who played the lead, stated that the citizens "rather gloried in having the world know that progress has not laid hands on that section of the country." Simply getting to Blue Grass was a feat, and of the car trip, Barthelmess said, "Never have any of us traveled such roads nor looked into such precipices as stared back at us gruesomely on that night. We were not altogether reassured when we saw our driver place in the car, within easy reach, a repeating rifle." The driver explained that on a recent journey, two wildcats had jumped from the trees.[1]

In pursuit of detailed authenticity, the cast and crew immersed themselves into the life of Blue Grass to absorb the mannerisms and ideas of the people. As Barthelmess put it, "we must live as they do, think as they do; and do as they do."[2]

In the film, young David Kinemon (played by Richard Barthelmess), the son of West Virginia tenant farmers living in a remote mountain community, longed to be treated like a man. This desire was lovingly rebuffed by his family; his mother told him that he was

* *Movie poster from* Tol'able David

---

1 *Virginia Quarterly Review*, Autumn 1982, pp. 616–634.
2 *Virginia Quarterly Review*, Autumn 1982, pp. 616–634.

* *Screen shot from* Tol'able David, *"looking up".*

* *Screen shot from* Tol'able David, *"with mom".*

still her baby, and his father refused him a cigar or drink on the occasion of family celebrations. He was constantly reminded that he was "tol'able" (tolerable) but not yet a man. David's older brother had a job transporting passengers to and from town and delivering the mail in a horse-drawn wagon. In those days, the delivery of mail was a huge responsibility, since the mail was the only link between the community and the outside world, and David longed for the day when he would be old enough to take on such a job.

David was sweet on pretty Esther Hatburn, who lived with her grandfather on a nearby farm. The peace of Blue Grass was shattered when distant cousins of the Hatburns, the outlaws Iscah Hatburn and his two sons Luke and "Little Buzzard," moved onto the Hatburn farm against the wishes of Esther and her grandfather. Esther cautioned David not to get involved, as he was no match for the ruffians. Even the sheriff didn't have the means to deal with such tough outlaws.

Tensions built when the outlaws killed David's pet dog and permanently crippled his older brother in an ensuing scuffle. Grabbing his rifle, David's father set out to administer vigilante justice, but before he could leave the house, he suffered a heart attack and died. David, now the head of the family, stormed out the door with the rifle to take care the Hatburns, but his mother grabbed him and pleaded with him not to go, saying that with his father dead and his older brother paralyzed, David must stay alive to take care of the family. And as Esther put it, "David, they'd mow you down like a clump of daisies." Listening to reason, David swallowed his pride and stayed at home.

Eventually, David got the job of driving the wagon, but one day, while it was rounding a corner, the mail bag fell off. By the time David realized what had happened, the outlaw Luke Hatburn had absconded with the bag and taken it back to the Hatburn farm. When David went there to demand the mail bag back, a fight broke out and David was shot in the arm. As Esther escaped the scene and ran to town for help, David managed to shoot Iscah Hatburn and "Little Buzzard." He then became embattled in a desperate and prolonged fight with Luke. As the townsfolk, whom

Esther had rallied together, prepared to hurry to David's aid, he arrived on the scene in the wagon, bloodied and injured but in possession of the mail bag. It was then clear that David had become a man.

The sets, mannerisms, and details had been made so painstakingly authentic that audiences felt as though they were experiencing the real events. The film was an instant success. America went wild for it. Europe went wild for it. Russian director and film theorist V. I. Pudovkin celebrated the movie, particularly for delivering what he called "color"—the sense of "that's the way it must have been." Director Henry King termed this "the atmosphere." Box office records were broken. Every major newspaper had nothing but the highest praise for the film, the *Chicago Journal* correctly predicting that *Tol'able David* would "go down in motion picture history as one of the greatest productions." It was Richard Barthelmess's first starring role in a movie, and after *Tol'able David* received the 1921 Gold Medal Photoplay Award as the year's best picture out of thirty-four candidates, Barthelmess was catapulted to the Hollywood stratosphere, second only to Rudolph Valentino. (In 2007, the Library of Congress selected *Tol'able David* for preservation in the National Film Registry for being "culturally, historically, or aesthetically significant."[1,2])

Richard Barthelmess took a copy of *Tol'able David* to share with D. W. Griffith and Lillian Gish, with whom he had previously worked. Griffith and Lillian were overwhelmingly impressed by the movie. With tears in his eyes, Griffith embraced Barthelmess and told him how proud he was. Aside from being happy with Barthelmess's performance, Lillian admired the skill and artistry of the director, Henry King, in making what she considered to be a beautifully artistic and expressive film.[3]

D. W. Griffith, while a visionary in the true sense of the word with regard to film making, unfortunately was lacking in common business sense. He was focusing so intently on the production of his movies that he spent little time contemplating the logistics of financing the projects. He borrowed money with abandon and accumulated staggering debt. Shortly after the release of *Orphans of the Storm*, he called Lillian into his office and said, "With all the expenses I have, I can't afford to pay you what you are worth. You should go out on your own. Your name is of as much value as mine with the public, and I think in your own interest you ought to capitalize on it while you can." It was a most cordial meeting. Of course, Griffith would have loved to have kept Lillian on at whatever low salary he could afford, but the two had become close friends, and Griffith truly cared about Lillian's best interests.[4]

It proved to be a challenging time for Lillian. With the war over and the reaction to Prohibition encouraging people to indulge their mischievous side, everyone was going a little wild. Fun was found in speakeasies, women smoked, and movies and plays were becoming less conservative as censorship was being relaxed. It was not a good environment for Lillian to market the virginal victim-heroine persona that had

1   http://en.wikipedia.org/wiki/Tol'able_David.
2   *Virginia Quarterly Review*, Autumn 1982, pp. 616–634.
3   *The Movies, Mr. Griffith, and Me*, by Lillian Gish with Ann Pinchot (Englewood Cliffs, NJ: Prentic Hall, 1969), pp. 251–252.
4   *The Movies, Mr. Griffith, and Me*, p. 247.

defined her career.[1] After she left Griffith, six months passed in which Lillian was unable to find a suitable employer. Her attorney, George S. Newgrass, who had tried to secure employment for her during that time, expressed doubt about her box office drawing power since leaving Griffith.[2]

In May 1922, Richard Barthelmess met with Lillian Gish to convince her to join Inspiration Pictures. He told her, "This is a little company, just starting—why don't you come with us?" Lillian replied that she would like to meet with the heads of the company if Barthelmess thought they would be interested.[3] Lillian had previously met and liked Charles Duell's wife Elsie, the former Lilian Tucker, which probably added some comfort to the prospective relationship.[4] A meeting was soon arranged that would open the most important chapter in Charles's life.

1 *Lillian Gish: A Life on Stage and Screen*, by Stuart Oderman (Jefferson, NC: McFarland & Co., 2000), p. 109.
2 *New York Times*, June 5, 1926.
3 *The Movies, Mr. Griffith, and Me*, pp. 251–252.
4 *Lillian Gish: Her Legend, Her Life*, by Charles Affron (New York: Scribner, 2001), p. 180.

Lillian Gish Enters the Picture

The meeting between Lillian Gish, her sister Dorothy, Charles Duell, his law partner and secretary of Inspiration Pictures Boyce Smith, and director Henry King took place in a relaxed luncheon atmosphere at the Ritz.[1] Lillian had a petite figure, which at times made her look frail and vulnerable. Her face, with large, sparkling eyes and a small, pouty mouth, exuded believable and endearing emotion in her roles of heroine or damsel in distress.

Within an hour, Charles had made Lillian an offer to star in two movies. Inside, he was bursting to put her budding star status behind the name of his small company, and he wooed her by saying that she could pick her own story for her first film. The salary portion of the offer, which was $1,250 a week, ratcheting up to $2,500 a week over three years, was far lower than a rival offer from Tiffany Pictures of $3,500 a week, but Inspiration was additionally offering Lillian 15% of her movies' gross profits and was also willing to hire her sister Dorothy.[2] While the weekly salary was important, Lillian knew that the only way in which she would become truly rich would be to take the lower salary, hope that the movies would be successful, and share in the profits. She was also intent on securing financial security for Dorothy.

❋ *Lillian Gish, June 29, 1921.*

To Lillian, money was everything. As she wrote to a friend, "If it makes money I may get some of it. If I could only get my hands on some, Nell, so I could put it away. This thing of having fame and no money is bad business."[3]

Lillian and Dorothy had grown up very poor. Their father had been an alcoholic who had never been able to support the family and had left them when they were

---

1 *Lillian Gish: Her Legend, Her Life*, by Charles Affron (New York: Scribner, 2001), p. 165.
2 *Life and Lillian Gish*, by Albert Bigelow Paine (New York: The Macmillan Company, 1932) p. 176.
3 *Lillian Gish: Her Legend, Her Life*, p. 166.

quite young. Those were very hard times. In 1902, their mother worked part time as a stage actress, and at the age of 9, Lillian, who was five years older than Dorothy, also took up stage acting to help support the family. The two girls spent many nights home alone after their mother had tucked them into bed and gone off to acting jobs. By 1905, their mother had saved enough money to open a candy and popcorn stand. At about this time, Dorothy fell off a pony and suffered a compound fracture of her arm, the candy and popcorn stand burned down at a total loss, and the family lost everything.[1]

Mother and daughters all went back to stage acting, and in one of Lillian's childhood roles, in the play *In Convict Stripes*, she played a little girl who was about to get blown up in a rock quarry by dynamite set off by the villain. The set was to be shattered by an actual blast on stage, and Lillian, who was to hide from the blast behind an artificial boulder, was then to be saved by the hero. During rehearsals, when it came time for the explosion, everyone said, "BOOM, BOOM" to simulate the blast. However, during the first live performance, the roar of the actual blast caught Lillian so off guard and so terrified her that she ran off stage screaming and crying.

In a different performance of the same play, a guard accidently dropped his shotgun, which discharged and peppered Lillian's leg. After being seen by a doctor backstage, Lillian came out and finished the performance. When the show was over, "the doctor used long needles to pry out the buckshot. It hurt badly, for he used no anesthesia."[2]

In 1909, Lillian suffered for many months from typhoid fever, and when she was 18, she received word that her estranged father was dying. She visited him in a hospital for the insane in Norman, Oklahoma, where he died on January 9, 1912, at the age of 36. The cause of death was "Gen. paralysis of insane."[3]

In June of the same year, while attending a nickelodeon in Baltimore, Lillian and Dorothy were quite surprised to see an old friend, Gladys Smith, on the screen. Eager to see her after the show, the sisters went to the Biograph Studio, where the film had been made, and asked for her, but no one recognized the name Gladys Smith. When Lillian described the girl in the film, they said, "Oh, you mean Mary Pickford." It was a time when being an actress in a nickelodeon movie was looked down upon with an utter lack of respect, so their friend Gladys had taken a stage name to protect her identity. Little did she suspect that the name Mary Pickford would soon become one of the biggest and most respected in Hollywood.

Pickford urged D. W. Griffith, for whom she worked, to put Lillian and Dorothy to work in the movies, and in a few days, they were on the payroll.[4] Their financial picture improved, but during the entirety of those early years, they still struggled for money and suffered from a lack of it. Lillian and Dorothy were affected differently by the experience. Once she acquired money, Lillian tended to save almost every dollar she earned. She shunned lavish purchases and an opulent lifestyle, and her compul-

---

1 *Lillian Gish: Her Legend, Her Life*, pp. 23, 33.

2 *The Movies, Mr. Griffith, and Me*, by Lillian Gish with Ann Pinchot (Englewood Cliffs, NJ: Prentice Hall, 1969), p. 10.

3 *The Movies, Mr. Griffith, and Me*, pp. 37, 39.

4 *The Movies, Mr. Griffith, and Me*, pp. 44–45.

sion for thriftiness was legendary. Dorothy used to tell friends that "Lillian lived to work," while she (Dorothy) "worked when she felt like it" and spent almost everything she made.[1]

During their meeting at the Ritz, Charles Duell sweetened his offer by promising to spend not less than $10,000 in advertising and promotion on each of Lillian's films, and should she be required to work outside New York, she would be provided a chaperone.[2] Lillian was pleased with the meeting. Charles had impressed her as being a suave and cultured gentleman,[3] but she wanted time to think it over. At the time, her personal holdings were very limited, and she accepted Charles's offer to loan her money to get by until she could make a decision.[4]

In 1922, Charles and Elsie had decided to summer in swanky Newport. Their villa, Rockry Hall, on Bellevue Avenue,[5] was on the southernmost tip of Rhode Island. Perhaps the most appealing part of the offer that Charles had made to Lillian Gish was the freedom to pick her own story,[6] and during the summer of 1922, she was a frequent house guest at Rockry Hall,[7] reading story after story in search of something exceptional.

✳ *Rockry Hall*

Newport Historical Society, #P9055

1 *Lillian Gish: A Life on Stage and Screen*, by Stuart Oderman (Jefferson, NC: McFarland & Co., 2000), p. 110.

2 *Lillian Gish: Her Legend, Her Life*, p. 166.

3 *Lillian Gish: Her Legend, Her Life*, p. 165.

4 *New York Times*, March 31, 1925.

5 *Ogden* (Utah) *Standard-Examiner*, October 8, 1922.

6 *Lillian Gish: Her Legend, Her Life*, p. 165.

7 *Evening Independent* (Massiollon, OH), February 11, 1924.

Newport represents—or likes to think it represents—the height of society, as if populated from a strainer through which pass only the wealthiest, most powerful, most cultured and socially proper of individuals. The community is the epitome of an inner circle, its members being most well established and coming from lineages of generation-spanning prominence. Everyone knows everyone and, for the most part, everyone's business.

Charles, being of blue-blood heritage and political notoriety, was graciously accepted into the community, but in the summer of 1922, when Elsie acted as Lillian Gish's social mentor, Newport seemed to raise a collective eyebrow. Lillian had been born into poverty, and Newport was not known for embracing the newly rich. Newport can be as catty as the gossip is cutting, but Lillian stood tall and dressed big. The local society columns described in detail her every outfit.

"Lillian went in often for jade green. Her wide hat and sash were of the shade, and her earrings, of that color, were set off against her yellow tresses. Another costume is described as a blue and gray sport suit, with a silk scarf in rainbow colors and a rolled brim hat of gray angora . . . . The spectators at the tennis tournaments missed any number of exciting rallies, considering Lillian the more exciting . . . . It almost seemed she wore a new gown every half hour. She had things appropriate to the beach, to the casino and to every other place."[1]

Lillian's every move was scrutinized, but in the end, her confidence and flair for fashion won her Newport's acceptance—or at least the admission that without her, Newport would probably have been rather dull that summer.[2]

During that summer, while staying with the Duells, Lillian read the 1909 novel *The White Sister* by F. Marion Crawford. She knew at once that it would make the perfect movie for her to star in.[3] Charles joyfully agreed and, on September 1, 1922, Lillian signed a contract with Inspiration Pictures.[4] Inspiration acquired the rights to the story for $16,000 just two weeks before William Randolph Hearst offered to buy the property for his mistress, actress Marion Davies.[5]

Charles wanted to begin production as soon as possible, and Inspiration Pictures purchased passage for twenty-four people for the November 18 sailing of the *S.S. Providence*, bound for Naples, Italy. As the departure date neared, all that was missing was an actor to play the male lead, and everyone embarked on a search. The cameraman reported seeing a promising young Englishman performing in the play *La Tendresse*. Lillian Gish and producer Henry King went to see the play and agreed that the handsome Englishman would be perfect for the part.[6] In a whirlwind, they had seen the play on a Thursday, on Friday they approved of a hurried screen test, and Lillian then personally called the play's producer and was able to obtain a release for the English actor in time for him to board the ship in New York with the company on

1   *Ogden* (Utah) *Standard-Examiner*, October 8, 1922

2   *Ogden* (Utah) *Standard-Examiner*, October 8, 1922.

3   *Lillian Gish; Her Legend, Her Life*, p. 166.

4   Duell vs Gish, Los Angeles Superior Court, case 269864, 1929. Housed at Archives & Records Center, 222 n. Hill St., Los Angeles, CA

5   *Lillian Gish; Her Legend, Her Life*, p. 167.

6   *The Movies, Mr. Griffith, and Me*, pp. 253–254.

Saturday. A relative unknown at the time, Ronald Colman was one movie away from becoming a national heartthrob.[1]

They became the first American film company to go to Italy. At the request of the captain of the *Providence*, an area of the small upper deck was enclosed in canvas, and there, over the course of the journey, daily rehearsals took place. Perhaps by coincidence or perhaps, as Lillian suggested, by the blessing of "some good angel," also aboard the *Providence* was Monsignor Bonzano, who was on his way to Vatican City to become a cardinal. When he learned that the planned film was to be a Catholic story, he promised the help of the Church. That gesture proved to be key to the success of the movie. In fact, when filming was under way, the Church advised on every religious scene, lending exacting authenticity to *The White Sister*.[2]

Charles and Elsie spent two months on the set, during which time Charles saw Lillian almost every day. Although Charles and Elsie had been married barely a year, problems were already developing. Elsie confided in her friend Lillian with intimate and personal details of her heartache. She never once suspected Lillian of being the other woman, yet that was developing into the sad truth. Elsie wholeheartedly wanted Charles's love and could neither bear nor understand his emotional withdrawal from the marriage. As Elsie poured her heart out, Lillian offered comforting and healing advice in a deception that went on for close to a year.[3]

Produced two years after the coup that had brought Benito Mussolini to power, *The White Sister* was filmed on location over six months in Rome, Naples, Sorrento, Tivoli, Mount Vesuvius, and northern Africa. Lillian's character, Angela, was devastated when her lover, army captain Giovanni (Ronald Colman), was reported killed by Arabs while on an expedition in Africa. In fact, Giovanni had only been taken prisoner, and he managed to escape two years later and return to Italy with plans of marriage, only to find that the heartbroken Angela has taken vows to be a nun—a White Sister. Soon afterward, Giovanni was killed while trying to save a mother and her children during an eruption of Mount Vesuvius. The movie ended with Angela praying to God to keep Giovanni safe until the two could be reunited in heaven.[4]

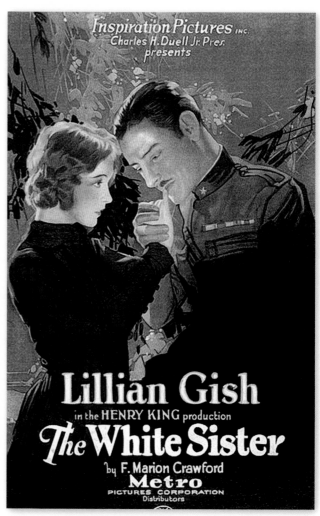

✳ *Movie Poster for The White Sister*

---

1 *Lillian Gish: Her Legend, Her Life*, p. 167.

2 *The Movies, Mr. Griffith, and Me*, p. 254.

3 Letters in the Lillian Gish Papers, New York Public Library for the Performing Arts

4 *Life and Lillian Gish*, p. 185.

✳ *Theater advertisement for The White Sister
(Reprint courtesy Tonawanda News)*

✳ *Movie Poster for The White Sister*

The filming of *The White Sister* took twice as long
as planned. The newly recruited Ronald Colman, except for having played a very small part in one movie
two years earlier, had never done film acting and came
across with the expected dashing looks but, unfortunately, a very reserved persona. To evoke the passion
and abandon necessary for the kidnapping scene, Hen-
ry King gave Colman whiskey throughout the all-night filming of that scene. The
stratagem worked. Lillian commented that at one point ,"Ronnie actually said damn,"
to everyone's surprise. The next day, he couldn't remember what had happened.[1]

---

1 *The Movies, Mr. Griffith, and Me*, p. 256.

No expense was spared on the sets, and as Lillian later said, "We built the most beautiful interiors I had ever seen. Our library walls were of solid carved wood, so beautiful that we wanted to put walls around them, and live in them. I think no other movie picture sets were ever as beautiful as those we built in Rome and Florence."[1]

Director Henry King was in a quandary as to how to portray the eruption of Mount Vesuvius by the Bay of Naples in what was scripted to be one of the most dramatic scenes of the movie. While filming scenes in Rome, he decided to transport his crew to the little village of Boscotrecase. Located at the foot of Vesuvius, the village is three layers deep, each succeeding village having been built on the ruins of one that had been buried in a previous lava flow.

After working for about three weeks, filming scenes in and around the crater, in King's words,

the old volcano began to rumble and shiver. . . ..I had to work fast, as lava in a molten state starts to flow with great rapidity. We had to figure our location so as to avoid those fiery rivers, and still be near enough to show the awe-inspiring torrent as it poured down the side of Vesuvius, consuming everything in its path, vineyards, houses and animal life; leaving nothing behind except the bubbling lava, like a scene from "Dante's Inferno." The fumes and gasses accompanying the eruption made us all sick; and a husky Italian cameraman, Fernando Recci, fainted from the effects. One of the cameras became so hot that the emulsion melted off the film and we lost about 1,500 feet of some very fine pictures.[2,3]

The stark realism, as huge black ash clouds billowed from Vesuvius and rivers of lava poured down her sides, was a magical complement to the scene and a glowing facet of the film.[4] In fact, the entirety of the movie beautifully captured the historic charm and feel of the centuries-old Italian surroundings. It was like no American picture that had ever been made. As Lillian wrote to a friend, "The very light from the heavens is so rich in coloring that it sheds a pink and yellow glow over the world so whatever you see seems to have the brilliancy of an oil painting done in high colors."[5]

Three months before filming was completed, Charles and Elsie returned to New York aboard the *Majestic*.[6] Charles remained there a mere three weeks before returning by himself to Rome[7] to rejoin the film crew and, in the absence of his wife, to begin a full-blown love affair with Lillian. Lillian later looked back at the period when *The White Sister* was being filmed and said that she had finally "found a man, well-bred, considerate and quietly effective, with whom I could identify myself in a personal as well as an artistic way." They shared "romantic interludes in the Villa Borghese gar-

1 *Life and Lillian Gish*, p. 180.

2 *Delmarva Star* (Wilmington, DE), March 2, 1924.

3 *Morning Herald* (Hagerstown, MD), July 21, 1924.

4 *Albany* (New York) *Evening Journal*, February 16, 1924.

5 *Lillian Gish: Her Legend, Her Life*, p. 169.

6 March 7, 1923, Majestic passenger list for Charles H. Duell, ancestry.com.

7 March 28, 1923, letter from Lilian (Tucker) Duell to Lillian Gish, in Lillian Gish Papers, New York Public Library for the Performing Arts.

dens, at the races outside Rome, the Opera, and brilliant cafes."[1] In later years, Lillian said that many of her fondest memories were of her time in Rome. Even the streets and walkways had a magical atmosphere as the sounds of scattered musicians, in competition for the attention of passersby, blended together. As Lillian later remembered, "at one place someone was playing a violin. Farther along someone was singing." Indelibly etched in her mind was an evening visit to the Coliseum under the soft glow of a golden moon.[2]

When Charles and Lillian departed for New York on June 6, 1923, they did so traveling together aboard the *Olympic*.[3] Meanwhile, poor Elsie still had no idea of the betrayal or the depth of involvement between her best friend and her husband.

WHITE STAR LINE
TRIPLE SCREW STEAMER
882½ FT.   "OLYMPIC"   46,359
LONG   TONS

Library of Congress LC-DIG-ppmsca-19060

---

1   *Lillian Gish: Her Legend, Her Life*, pp. 180–181.
2   *Life and Lillian Gish*, p. 182.
3   http://www.ellisisland.org.

From Elsie to Lillian to All Alone

27

*C*harles told Elsie that he wanted a divorce, yet she still held out hope, having no idea that there was another woman. In fact, Charles's infatuation with Lillian Gish had grown supreme, and in his quest for the freedom to pursue that relationship, he persuaded Elsie to sign a formal instrument of separation[1,2] in which he agreed to pay her $1,500 a month for life.[3] It was admittedly a large amount, but Charles believed that he was headed to the financial stratosphere and $1,500 would soon seem a mere trifle. With the separation agreement, he hoped that he and Lillian would be able to blossom out as a sensational public couple. Lillian, however, always the business-woman and always keenly aware of the public eye, was terrified of being viewed as "the other woman." Privately, their love was all consuming and without reserve, and she did accept and wear his engagement ring.[4,5] However, she insisted that any public hint of the true nature of the relationship between herself and Charles Duell must remain utterly nonexistent.

They went so far as to assume code names so that they could not be identified as the authors of romantic telegrams when they found themselves an ocean apart. Charles's love letters to Lillian from shipboard were addressed to "Blue," his code name for her.[6] Lillian's letters to Charles were addressed to "Carissimo" and signed, in code, "Love Blue, Yes, Blue."[7]

Lillian even endeavored—or perhaps especially endeavored—to conceal the relationship from Elsie. To keep from arousing Elsie's suspicions, Lillian continued their friendly and intimate correspondence. Shortly after Charles and Lillian's return to New York in June 1923, Elsie departed for Paris aboard the *George Washington*. Lillian ordered a basket of fruit and a message sent to her cabin. In reply, Elsie wrote back, "Now Lillian you must not worry about your mother. Take the time you spend worrying over (her) and consecrate to trusting God that she will be taken care of. . . . (For your ears only) Charles sent me some beautiful roses with the card 'A pleasant voyage.

---

1 *New York Times*, March 31, 1925.

2 *New York Times*, April 1, 1925.

3 *Duell v. Duell. U.S.* Court of Appeals 5/16/1949, F.2d 683, No. 9699, http://bulk.resource.org/courts. gov/c/F2/178/178.F2d.683.9699.html

4 *New York Times*, March 31, 1925.

5 *New York Times*, April 1, 1925.

6 *New York Telegram*, April 3, 1925.

7 *Lillian Gish: A Life on Stage and Screen*, by Stuart Oderman (Jefferson, NC: McFarland & Co., 2000), p. 126.

Don't worry, be cheerful. Charles.' I ask you, is that a message to send the lady you want to divorce?"[1] One has to wonder whether the gesture of roses and a kindly note caused Lillian, who had distrusted men her entire life, to suspect Charles of harboring residual feelings for Elsie.

After arriving in Paris, Elsie spent several months at the Hotel Ritz Paris, whence she sent Lillian the following correspondence:

> I have tried to rise above everything, look only on the good side, forget Charlie's madness, leaving him free to do his work. I have many, many lonely moments. Moments when things almost become unbearable—do become unbearable, but through it all I am calm, and trying to keep my health. I only know there is a great deal more good in Charles than anything else. I know too our marriage was right and our only trouble started when he double booked his company. So too, when he began making his contract with you and Dorothy. It really was too much for one man to stand, something had to be sacrificed, and at the moment he thinks more of his work than he apparently does of me. A real love can never really be killed and I simply know I will never love anyone but Charles. It will come out alright I am sure. I must prove a person of patience and poise.
>
> Lillian Dear my reason for going into detail about my feelings to you is because I have suffered very greatly in the last month. . . . You may not have the opportunity but if you do, I trust you to help the situation, by giving to Charles, not the opinion you had when we talked in New York, but a hopeful, constructive opinion. You and Dorothy, bless your hearts, have much happiness in your lives. I have only Charles. I have not a single, solitary soul in the world but Charles, and from loving him very dearly, he has suddenly dropped me, as it were, into the ocean and sent me out to swim. That I do not so much mind because that develops individuals and one should not cling. But divorce is drastic and should it ever come to that, I just do not know what to do. . . . I cannot talk to anyone because I do not want anyone to know, and I still trust you . . . . I am so terribly Lonely.[2]

Even as late as September 1923, poor betrayed Elsie, still completely unaware that her friend was "the other woman," continued to pour her heart out to Lillian:

> I do get lonely. Terribly lonely because I do not know a soul in Paris or France other than the waiter or the floor fare. . . . As marriage is very sacred to me and my ambition is to do that well, it is a jolt that marriage nowadays seems to be so unsacred to people—don't you think so? . . . Please keep my letters confidential as I asked you to do so in New York because I've written some pretty personal things. I trust you to do this. I do trust you Lillian and that trust has stood up against a good deal.[3]

---

1   1923 letter from Lilian (Tucker) Duell to Lillian Gish, in Lillian Gish Papers, New York Public Library for the Performing Arts.

2   1923 letter from Lilian (Tucker) Duell to Lillian Gish, in Lillian Gish Papers, New York Public Library for the Performing Arts.

3   1923 letter from Lilian (Tucker) Duell to Lillian Gish, in Lillian Gish Papers, New York Public Library for the Performing Arts.

A few months later, in January 1924, Elsie and Charles were granted a divorce.[1,2] However, the true reason for Charles's walking out on the marriage did not come to light until mid-1925, at which time Elsie sued Lillian Gish for $300,000 stating that Lillian had "willfully, wickedly and maliciously gained the affections of said Charles H. Duell" and that "at various times and places between July 1st, 1922 and January, 1924 defendant induced said Charles H. Duell to have sexual intercourse with her."[3]

The White Sister premiered as a gala event, with full orchestra, on September 5, 1923, at New York's 44th Street Theater.[4] Everyone at Inspiration Pictures knew going in that the film would be viewed as controversial and that it would be a battle to get it into theaters. It was the first modern religious story to be filmed, and just as expected, none of the major distributers would touch it.[5] Among those attending the premiere were New York Governor Al Smith, the Vanderbilts, the Whitneys, the Harrimans, and the Belmonts. President Calvin Coolidge sent a telegram to Charles H. Duell, saying, "I am glad to wish you every success in the production of your new picture."

The White Sister was an instant success and set house records.[6] Richard Washburn Child, the American ambassador to Italy, wrote to Charles, "I went to see *The White Sister*. What a wonderful piece of motion picture photography it is! Some of its scenes are as beautiful and as full of poetic feeling as anything I could ever imagine. . . . The art of Miss Gish rises at times into the realm of magic."[7] Metro-Goldwyn Pictures quickly dropped their reservations about *The White Sister* and picked up the movie for general release.[8]

Lillian Gish, who had previously been a C- or at best B-rated actress, and Ronald Colman, a virtual unknown, were catapulted to national stardom, and Lillian Gish became an idolized household name. On October 29, 1923, she appeared at a New York showing of *The White Sister* at the Lyric Theater, just off Broadway, "to bid au revoir to a monster audience, prior to her departure for Italy."[9] On November 6, she set sail for Italy to join the crew for the filming of her second movie with Inspiration Pictures.[10]

Charles was still basking in the glory of *The White Sister*. He had set a higher standard for movie makers around the world to try to match. He had truly broken new ground, and he was determined to raise the bar even higher with this next production, *Romola*. He had impassioned visions of creating a movie with sets that were more spectacular and sensational than anything the world had ever seen. Lillian, however, stressed to Charles that she wanted to make as much money as possible and was concerned about the high budget for *Romola*.[11] Before the filming of *The White Sister* had been completed, Inspiration Pictures had also produced five lower-budget films featuring Richard Barthelmess—*The Seventh Day, Sonny, The Bond Boy, Fury,* and *The*

---

1 *New York Evening Post*, January 26, 1924.

2 *New York Times*, January 31, 1925.

3 *Lillian Gish Papers, Box 25, Manuscript Division, Library of Congress, Washington D.C.*

4 *Lillian Gish: Her Legend, Her Life*, p. 173.

5 *The Movies, Mr. Griffith, and Me*, by Lillian Gish with Ann Pinchot (Englewood Cliffs, NJ: Prentice Hall, 1969), p. 252.

6 *Lillian Gish: Her Legend, Her Life*, p. 173.

7 *New York Times*, November 11, 1923.

8 *Lillian Gish: Her Legend, Her Life*, p. 173.

9 *New York Times*, October 30, 1923.

10 *Lillian Gish: Her Legend, Her Life*, p. 174.

11 *Lillian Gish: Her Legend, Her Life*, p. 174.

Bright Shawl—but none had been big money makers. The conflict between Lillian's quest for profits and Charles's quest for high quality adversely affected the couple on both business and personal levels.

To Charles's delight, a divorce was granted to Elsie (Tucker) Duell on January 24, 1924, in Paris on grounds of desertion in that Charles refused to live with her.[1,2] Rumors began to fly of an engagement between Charles and Lillian,[3] and Charles urged Lillian to go public with their intentions to marry. He had great plans for their future and proposed that they set up headquarters in Rome and embark on a round-the-world cruise the following year.[4] Although Lillian did introduce Charles Duell as her fiancé while at the Grand Hotel in Florence, Italy, she continued to resist making any public announcement and forbade Charles to reveal the secret.[5] Now her reason for not announcing an engagement was shifting from not wanting to be viewed as the other woman to fear of being married to a producer whose concern for the highest quality in his films could jeopardize profits—specifically, her paycheck.

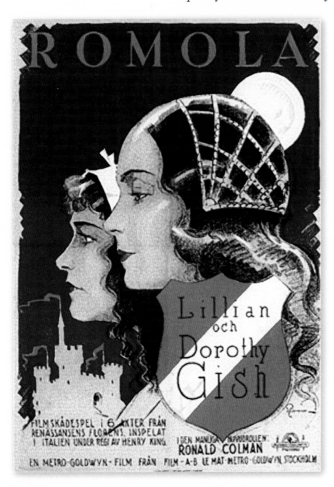

✳ *Left and above, movie posters for* Romola *starring Lillian Gish*

1 *New York Evening Post*, January 26, 1924.
2 *New York Times*, January 31, 1925.
3 *Evening Telegram* (New York), January 26, 1924.
4 *The Movies, Mr. Griffith, and Me*, p. 266.
5 *Evening Independent* (Massillon, OH), February 11, 1924.

The story of *Romola* took place in 15th century Florence, shortly after the 1492 departure of Columbus for the New World and while Florence was still mourning the death of its legendary leader, Lorenzo de' Medici. Lillian Gish played the leading character, Romola, and Ronald Colman played sculptor Carlo Buccellini, who was in love with Romola. Out of pure evil, the villain, a shipwrecked stranger, tormented the townspeople and blocked the union of the two lovers until his death at the end of the movie finally led to the couple's marriage and a happy ending.[1,2,3]

The realization that Florence, with its telephone poles and cars and the like, would prove too modern for the filming prompted the unplanned building of a huge seventeen-acre set. Local contractors and masons were hired to build the set in meticulous detail.[4] The skilled Italian masons had a love for their work, and the sets reflected it.[5] They could build anything, including a duplicate of the Piazza della Signoria and a cathedral with a 274-foot bell tower.[6] The textures of original stonework were replicated by taking plaster casts from the Davanti Palace. Bridges were built, and 15th century stone streets, lined with town shops that were true to the era, were constructed. No expense was spared.[7]

1 http://www.imdb.com/title/tt0015289/.
2 http://www.answers.com/topic/romola-film-1.
3 *Oakland* (California) *Tribune*, November 30, 1924.
4 *The Movies, Mr. Griffith, and Me*, p. 263.
5 *The Movies, Mr. Griffith, and Me*, p. 255.
6 *Lillian Gish: Her Legend, Her Life*, p. 175.
7 *Lillian Gish: A Life on Stage and Screen*, p. 120.

Charles also wanted *Romola* to be the first major feature picture to be filmed entirely on Kodak's new panchromatic film, which had a more sensitive visual spectrum but was almost prohibitively expensive and added frightfully to the budget.[1] Further compounding the production's financial woes were incessant rains, "about 19 days out of 20," as Lillian's sister Dorothy said. It was a very unusual winter, and the frustration was evident on a morning when the crew actually had to shovel a blanketing of snow off the set.[2] Coupled with a lack of equipment, the weather caused the final location filming to take three months longer than originally planned.[3] As the production costs skyrocketed beyond what had initially seemed to Lillian to be exorbitant, she agonized over her ever-diminishing paycheck and questioned her relationship with Charles all the more.

Charles, however, was more committed than ever to his desire to marry Lillian. As he crossed the Atlantic in early March, journeying back to New York aboard the *Berengaria*, he sent her love letters and telegrams urging her to agree to a public announcement of their engagement and encouraging her to wed him before her return to New York.

✳ *Below, part of May 16, 1924, letter from Charles H. Duell to Lillian Gish suggesting a wedding date (Lillian Gish Papers, Billy Rose Theatre Division, New York Public Library for the Performing Arts, Lenox and Tilden Foundations)*

Tomorrow we land (in New York)—the long voyage will be over—long because I have been these days without you. How short it would have been, had you been here. But you have been in my thoughts—so I was sustained. . . . Lillian! Almost two lovely years now! Through the stress and strain of life—together—you and I—building, building, toward an end that, as the years come and go, we will look back upon as our greatest heritage—our marriage—our children. . . . Such is surely the finest expression of love ever achieved by mortal mind. . . . Angel you must never worry now—you know I'll always lift you over every hill—whatever life brings—I'm your protector now. If I ever seem to fail it will only be to mount still higher.[4,5]

On March 16, returning to Europe aboard the *France*, Charles again emphatically professed his love, stressing that they should get married and suggesting the date of May 28, 1924, for the wedding.

---

1 *Lillian Gish: Her Legend, Her Life*, pp. 174–175.
2 *Life and Lillian Gish* by Albert Bigelow Paine (New York: The Macmillan Company, 1932) p. 195.
3 *Lillian Gish: Her Legend, Her Life*, pp. 174–175.
4 March 4, 1924, letter from Charles H. Duell, Jr. to Lillian Gish, in Lillian Gish Papers, New York Public Library for the Performing Arts.
5 March 6, 1924, *Berengaria* passenger list, ancestry.com.

Lillian I don't like these separations—do you? They're just awful. Never again if I can help it.... You are the only lovely person in the world for whom I would travel nine thousand miles quite by myself.... What does it mean? I'm afraid, Lillian, it means I love you very much—deeper perhaps than I had ever realized—it's the greatest thing in life. You taught me the oneness of it, which I had always believed.... Lillian I love—Love you, Love you. You make me happy.[1]

Lillian had become the center of Charles's focus, which, as it turned out, had repercussions for his business. Richard Barthelmess, who, through Inspiration Pictures, had risen in star status to a position second only to Rudolph Valentino's, became resentful that much of the attention and advertising that he felt he deserved from Charles was being lavished on Lillian. When Barthelmess was told that following *Romola*, he was to play second fiddle to Lillian in a production of *Romeo and Juliet*, it was the last straw.

On March 11, 1924, through his attorneys O'Brien, Malvinsky & Driscoll, Barthelmess announced that he would sever all ties with Inspiration Pictures. Thus not only did Inspiration Pictures lose one of its major moneymakers, but the fragility of the company's balance sheet was brought to light when Barthelmess complained that Inspiration Pictures owed him $35,000 in back wages.[2]

Lillian had been enamored with Charles for his eloquence and intellect, his social and political prominence, and his overall air of competence and ability to succeed at anything. Yet above all else, she required any potential suitor to be a man of solid financial standing. She had worked and suffered and struggled her entire life to attain her level of financial comfort, and the stinging memory of how easily and swiftly her father had lost everything for her family was permanently etched into her being. It was terrifying for Lillian to think that her stability in life could be jeopardized by romantic association with a man who was facing financial turmoil. With her defenses on high alert, the more she looked, the more financial instability she saw, and on April 2, 1924, she broke off the engagement.[3] She returned the engagement ring a few months later.[4] Broken-hearted, Charles wrote back to her, "Tomorrow the ring will be sold and my heart sent to its grave. What you have done to the honest love of a man who sincerely loved and meant to marry you, I hope God may spare you from ever knowing. Good-bye and good luck, Charles."[5]

Charles had no way of knowing that this good-bye note was far from being the end of his dealings with Lillian Gish. In fact, it was only the beginning of what would become the biggest battle in his life—and one more burden for his brother Holland in that difficult year of 1925.

---

1 March 16, 1924, letter from Charles H. Duell, Jr. to Lillian Gish, in Lillian Gish Papers, New York Public Library for the Performing Arts.
2 *The Bee* (Danville, VA), March 24, 1924.
3 *New York Times*, March 31, 1925.
4 *New York Times*, April 1, 1925.
5 Letter from Charles H. Duell, Jr. to Lillian Gish, in Lillian Gish Papers, New York Public Library for the Performing Arts.

Duell v. Gish

Following its release, *Romola* was praised for visually capturing historically rich and romantic settings that were, as the *New York Times* put it, "so beautiful that they in themselves are worth every instant one spends viewing this picture." However, the plot and pace of the movie were universally considered dull and slow moving.[1]

The final cost of production of *Romola* came to $700,000.[2] A year after release, the gross receipts were a disappointing $375,241. The losses from the movie wiped out much of the worth of Inspiration Pictures,[3] and the company soon began to liquidate assets. Charles convinced Lillian Gish—or, as she put it, tricked her—into transferring her contract to his newly formed movie business, Charles Duell, Inc.[4]

Lillian had previously encouraged Charles Duell to obtain the motion picture rights to *The Outsider* for her to star in, which he did at a cost of $55,000 but, as the extent of his financial failings and challenges came to light, Lillian lost all faith and trust in Charles and failed to show up for the scheduled December 6, 1924 start of filming.[5, 6]

The impact to Charles was no less jarring than that of having a financial dagger thrust into his back with brutal and malicious force. Beyond the $55,000 outlay for the movie rights, Charles had expended large sums of money for the use of the Metro-Goldwyn studios in Los Angeles, as well as for equipment, employees and other actors.[7] The planned pay back was to be a life saver. Back on October 9, 1924 Charles had entered into a written agreement with Metro-Goldwyn, in which they promised him a $400,000 advance as soon as the finished film could be delivered, which was expected to be in only six months' time.[8] It was the deal that Charles hoped would save his financial future. But without Lillian's star power, production of *The Outsider* would be impossible, and Charles would have to write off the entire investment as

---

1 *Lillian Gish: Her Legend, Her Life*, by Charles Affron (New York: Scribner, 2001), p. 177.
2 *New York Times*, March 26, 1925.
3 *Lillian Gish: Her Legend, Her Life*, p. 193.
4 *Lillian Gish: Her Legend, Her Life*, pp. 185–186.
5 *New York Times*, January 31, 1925.
6 Duell vs Gish, Los Angeles Superior Court, case 269864, 1929. Housed at Archives and Records Center, 222 N. Hill St., Los Angeles, CA
7 Duell vs Gish, Los Angeles Superior Court, case 269864, 1929
8 Duell vs Gish, Los Angeles Superior Court, case 269864, 1929

a catastrophic personal loss. As animosity grew between the two, Lillian threatened that she would soon work for another producer.[1] Whatever her feelings, Lillian was still under legal contract with Charles to appear in up to twenty-eight movies before January 1, 1930.[2] In a desperate effort to protect his interests, Charles hired his brother Holland Duell to file an injunction suit against Lillian Gish to prevent her from making motion pictures with any company other than his.[3] Lillian's public response, on February 13, 1925, was that she would never act in another movie if the only way she could do it was under contract with Charles H. Duell.[4]

Six days later, on February 19, things heated up when James Rennie, the husband of Lillian's sister Dorothy, grabbed Charles by the arm outside his office at 9 East 46th Street and said, "Duell, this situation is serious and must be stopped. You know what that means. I will go to the limit. Anything can happen. This is your only warning, and act quickly; I am giving you this chance to save yourself."[5] Charles pressed charges. Although the harassment had been witnessed by Charles's secretary, the charges of disorderly conduct were dismissed for lack of evidence because no crowd had gathered and no punches had been thrown. Rennie's counsel was instructed to advise Rennie not to annoy Duell.[6]

On Tuesday, March 24, 1925, the *Duell* v. *Gish* trial began. Throngs far greater than the capacity of Judge Julian W. Mack's courtroom in the Woolworth Building came to hear the case and see the witnesses. The disappointed majority were sent away.[7] Lillian Gish sat at one table with three attorneys, and Charles H. Duell, Jr. sat at an opposite table with his chief counsel, his brother Holland S. Duell.

Lillian, dressed in a dark blue serge suit with pleated sleeves and an embroidered collar, two strands of hair falling on her shoulders, looked more like a schoolgirl than a movie star. In her nervousness, throughout the proceedings, she took small nibbles from carrots, which "as every woman knows are accounted an excellent aid to the complexion." When asked why she kept a carrot concealed in her hand, she replied, with a slight laugh,

✻ *Charles Holland Duell Jr. in court during the 1925 Gish trial*

"Oh, I'm awfully nervous."

In his opening statement, Holland Duell described the case as one of "contract jumping."[8] He referred to the number of "star contracts" that had been violated in the motion picture industry and asserted that this "contract jumping still continues the

1 Duell vs Gish, Los Angeles Superior Court, case 269864, 1929.

2 *Lillian Gish: Her Legend, Her Life*, p. 182.

3 *New York Times*, January 31, 1925.

4 *Washington Post*, February 14, 1925.

5 *New York Times*, February 25, 1925.

6 *New York Times*, March 12, 1925.

7 *New York Times*, March 26, 1925.

8 *New York Times*, March 25, 1925.

principal menace to a sound development of this industry."[1] Although a well-known actress before joining Inspiration Pictures, Lillian Gish had never been sensational and had never earned any substantial wealth. Charles Duell's company had spent in the neighborhood of $1,500,000 on the production of *The White Sister*, which had propelled Gish to stardom. Charles had further elevated her reputation by starring her in the high-budget production of *Romola*. Over the course of the two years that she had worked for Inspiration Pictures, she had been transformed into the most highly acclaimed actress in the United States and had earned in excess of $250,000.[2] In effect, Inspiration Pictures had gained for Lillian Gish financial success and Hollywood stardom, and the court action against her was simply to enforce her loyalty to her contract.

Holland's opening statement marked the beginning and the end of his envisioned aggressive offensive against Lillian. From the moment her attorneys began to speak, the tables turned, and anyone sitting in on the rest of the trial might have believed that it was Charles Duell who was being tried for a crime. The underhanded war that Lillian's attorneys waged in their counterattack was nothing short of brilliant.

In the defense's opening statement, Max Steuer, the head counsel for Lillian Gish, came out firing from every angle imaginable. He charged Charles Duell with misrepresentation, stating that the contract Gish had signed was not in her best interest but she had signed because she trusted Duell and his law firm, Duell & Smith, with everything. Duell looked after her insurance and had drawn up wills for the entire Gish family, with himself as the executor. "He was God in her eyes," said Steuer, who then played the vulnerability card and said of Gish:

Although she is without a peer as an actress on the screen, she would sign anything that anyone . . . asked her to sign. . . . Probably you have never come in contact with a mentality so uniquely lacking in capacity to read or even analyze a document or understand figures. . . . I show this to show the domination exercised by Duell over this girl, and I am trying to show the amount of confidence which she reposed and the amount of power which he wielded.[3]

Lillian's defense team charged Duell with unethical conflict of interest for acting as Lillian's lawyer, trustee, and manager and influencing her business decisions while, at the same time, as president of a motion picture company, he was looking for every financial advantage for the company.[4]

Charles Duell's rebuttal would be that when he did discuss contracts with Lillian, he simply gave his personal opinion but did not advise as an attorney.[5] The crucial point in this explanation was that what Charles, as her fiancé, discussed with Lillian was his opinion of what he considered to be in their *mutual* best interest. Therefore, there was no self-motivated conflict of interest.

The response from the Gish team, in brazen disregard of the truth, was to flatly and adamantly deny that an engagement had ever existed. The subject evolved into a

---

1 *New York Times*, February 14, 1925.
2 *New York Times*, March 25, 1925.
3 *New York Times*, March 25, 1925.
4 *New York Times*, January 31, 1925.
5 *New York Times*, June 11, 1926.

major headliner during the remainder of the trial, and the Duell team, unprepared to have to prove what they had considered to be a given, struggled with the subject of "were they or were they not ever engaged?" as it was debated almost ad nauseam.[1]

Lillian covertly went to great lengths to quiet friends who had knowledge of the engagement. In a series of telegrams, she instructed them not to compose any affidavits and to "absolutely refuse to be brought into the matter." She advised, "Do not let them frighten you. They cannot force you in any way unless you are in New York State." She also cautioned, "Don't make any statements or sign any papers or write anything at all."[2] Yet throughout the proceedings, she postured in the courtroom, for all to see, as a vulnerable, injured victim.[3]

On Wednesday, the second day of the trial, testimony centered on a change in the contract between Gish and Inspiration Pictures after the completion of *Romola*, which happened to go over budget. The original contract called for Lillian Gish, in addition to her weekly salary, to receive 15% of gross receipts after Inspiration Pictures had recouped the production costs, which were estimated at $565,000. When the final cost of production came in at $700,000, Charles made a modification to the contract calling for Lillian to receive her 15% after Inspiration Pictures had recouped $700,000 rather than the originally estimated $565,000. The movie simply did not net as much profit as anticipated, so of course everyone should expect to walk away with less. In the spirit of the original contract, the modification was fair to both parties, but in bottom-line dollars and cents, it would mean a potential loss to Lillian's bank account of $60,000 if the movie was profitable. Lillian agreed and signed,[4] in what Lillian's defense team argued was a breach of trust orchestrated by Charles Duell.

On Friday, March 27, over 200 spectators gathered outside the courtroom doors for the afternoon session of the *Duell* v. *Gish* trial. When the doors were opened, "the crowd rushed forward. It carried one marshal like a chip on the crest of a wave. Women were flung against the rows of seats. They made no complaint but scrambled for places."[5] A water cooler was knocked over, causing veteran court attendant Abe Alder to receive four stitches.[6] When Judge Mack entered, he ordered all who were not in seats to leave the courtroom, saying, "This is a trial, not a show. Those who want to see the defendant perform must go to a theater."[7]

On Monday, March 30, much time was spent in presenting testimony to either support or refute the existence of an engagement between Charles H. Duell, Jr. and Lillian Gish. Charles testified that he and Lillian had become engaged in June 1923 after he had been separated from his wife by a formal instrument[8,9] and that he had

---

1 *New York Times*, January 31, 1925.

2 February 4, 5, and 7, 1925, Western Union telegrams, in Lillian Gish Papers, New York Public Library for the Performing Arts.

3 *Lillian Gish: Her Legend, Her Life*, p. 193.

4 *New York Times*, March 26, 1925.

5 *New York Times*, March 28, 1925.

6 *Daily Express* (London), March 28, 1925, in Lillian Gish Papers, New York Public Library for the Performing Arts.

7 *New York Times*, March 28, 1925.

8 *New York Times*, March 31, 1925.

9 *New York Times*, April 1, 1925.

bought Lillian an engagement ring. He continued that the engagement had become "official" in January 1924 when his divorce from his wife became final. The judge expressed confusion about the term "officially engaged" and pressed for clarification. Charles Duell explained that the two considered themselves to be "unofficially engaged" in 1923, pending his divorce (and noted that Lillian did wear his ring) and "officially engaged" in January 1924 once he received the divorce decree.[1]

On Tuesday, more time was spent extracting testimony relating to the alleged engagement. Under examination by his attorney, his brother Holland Duell, Charles testified that when he and Lillian became engaged, they shared with Lillian's mother the news that Charles was getting a divorce from his wife and that he and Lillian Gish were to be married shortly afterward. The engagement, however, did not endure, and was called off by mutual consent on April 2, 1924, and in June, Lillian returned the ring.

Under cross-examination by Gish's attorney, Max Steuer, there was no such relaxed environment in which Charles could tell his story. Steuer wanted only to extract specific words and answers that he could cut and paste into the form of damning testimony. When Charles, not wanting his responses to mislead anyone as to the true facts of the case, tried to include clarifying explanations with his answers, Steuer objected. Judge Mack, admonishing Charles, sarcastically asked, "Can you answer the question, Mr. Duell?"

Charles protested that he was trying to tell the truth—the *whole truth*.

"But I want you to answer the question," the judge continued harshly. "You may explain later." However, the promise of an opportunity to explain later was never honored.

The interludes continued, with Charles trying to respond to examination with the "whole truth," only to have Judge Mack elevate the level of his angry interruptions and warnings. At one point, Judge Mack stopped Charles and stated in a confrontational manner, "You have something on your mind that you want to tell me."

Charles insisted that there was nothing.

"There is," the glaring judge snapped back angrily.

Moments later, the judge interrupted Charles in the middle of testimony and practically shouted, "Be careful! I don't believe for a moment that you meant that. It's the first time that I've expressed an opinion in this case, but I'm doing it for your sake."

The tone of the judge from there on out was one of decided disdain for Charles Duell. Charles had definitely gone from being the hunter to the hunted.[2]

On Wednesday, the quarry in the hunt was slaughtered. In yet another grueling day of examining the engagement controversy, Max Steuer blindsided Charles with a trump card.

From the moment she had met Charles H. Duell, the last thing Lillian Gish wanted was for the world to view her as "the other woman" and a betraying "home wrecker." When, in 1924, a newspaper had printed an article announcing that Charles and Lillian were engaged, Lillian wanted an end to any such press and asked Charles

---

1 *New York Times*, March 31, 1925.
2 *New York Times*, April 1, 1925.

to deal with it. He drafted a letter in his hand, requiring only her signature (as was common practice during Charles's past career in political campaigns), stating that she was not engaged, and he went to a law firm to investigate the possibility of suing the newspaper for announcing their engagement[1] as well as for making slanderous accusations about Lillian with other men.[2]

Now Gish's attorney demanded of Charles, "As a matter of fact, did you not in February [1924] deny that you were engaged to Lillian Gish?"

Unsure of where Steuer was going with this line of questioning, Charles replied, "I do not recollect."

"Don't you recall that you wrote out in your own hand a letter given out for publication, signed by Lillian Gish and written by you?" Steuer persisted.

Charles was cornered, and he knew it. Obviously, Steuer had obtained a copy of the letter. The proper response would have been to explain that at the time, he was helping his fiancé to cover up the truth of their engagement at *her* request, to protect *her* reputation. Even if that had been allowed, though the judge would certainly have censored "whole truth" answers down to simple yes and no responses, the explanation would establish Charles Duell as being guilty of lying to the press about the subject that had moved to the very core of this case: the engagement. If he had lied to the press then, why should he be believed in court now? There was no way out, and Charles's disheartened response was "I do not recollect."

Steuer held up a note and read from it: "I am not engaged to marry Charles Duell or any other man. *(signed)* Lillian Gish."

"Didn't you write the body of that?" Steuer roared. "And didn't you hand it to her to sign, and then didn't you give it to the newspaper to publish, and didn't they publish it?"

Charles, shaken and beaten down, could muster no other answer than "I do not recollect," at which point Judge Mack growled that he "could not understand how the witness could have no recollection on such a matter."

If Steuer could debunk Charles Duell's claim of having been engaged to Lillian Gish and Charles could no longer claim that he had offered his opinion on business matters to Lillian in the capacity of her fiancé, which would have been appropriate, Steuer could then attack Charles for having a conflict of interest between giving his client advice and seeking the best deal for his production company. Steuer went at Charles with both barrels:

Am I to understand that at one moment you were sitting there as her lawyer acting in her interests, and the next moment you were sitting there—in the same chair—as President of Inspiration Pictures to gouge her out of her money? When was she able to know that you were her friend and when was she able to know that you were her enemy? Was she to believe up to 4:10 you were her friend and that at 4:15 she was to be on her guard against you? What was this—a sort of Jekyll and Hyde affair?[3]

---

1   *New York Times*, April 3, 1925.
2   *Lillian Gish Her Legend, Her Life*, p. 182.
3   *New York Times*, April 2, 1925.

Steuer had acted brilliantly. Given the corner into which Charles had been painted and the complete ineffectiveness of his testimony, Holland counseled Charles that it was futile to proceed any further with the trial. In private conference with the judge after court had recessed, they requested to withdraw the case.[1]

On Thursday, April 2, the courtroom was again filled to capacity, the previous day's request to withdraw the case not having been made public. Within a space of fifteen minutes, every person in the courtroom, with the exception of Judge Mack, was surprised and shocked by the explosive developments. First, the spectators were taken aback by the announcement that the trial was over. However, that proved trivial in comparison to the unexpected blow that Judge Mack delivered to Charles Duell.

Charles sat thunderstruck as Mack addressed the courtroom and first announced that the contract between Duell and Gish had been breached but not by Lillian; it had been breached by Charles Duell, and Lillian Gish was to be in no way further bound by the contract. The judge looked steadily at Charles as he continued, "In twenty-two years of judicial experience it has not been my fortune or misfortune to have had before me, with possibly one exception, any case of more flagrant, outrageous breach of trust and overreaching than has been shown on the plaintiff's own testimony in this case . . . nor more downright perjury committed on the part of the principal witness for the plaintiff, Charles H. Duell."

In wielding his might, the judge barred Charles Duell from ever bringing a case to federal court again, made a motion to have Charles permanently disbarred from practicing law, and began grand jury proceedings to have him stand trial for numerous counts of perjury. The judge also said, "I will hold the witness Duell to bail in the sum of $10,000."

Shortly after court was adjourned, U.S. Attorney Emory Buckner reined in Judge Mack's zealousness and removed any requirement for bail.

Charles left the courtroom with his brother in stunned silence, unable to utter a single word. Later in the day, he made a statement to the press, in which he said, "I am certainly the world's worst witness. I don't know why I couldn't understand the questions which were asked when I was testifying. I was utterly paralyzed and benumbed. . . . My intention was to be simple and direct, to freely admit the truth, and to clearly explain my position upon all points. The extent of my failure has come as a great shock." Charles was able to present to the press love letters from Lillian Gish that seemed to support his claim that they were engaged and a letter from Lillian's mother in which she said, "If Lillian makes as good a wife as she has been a daughter, your life together is going to be perfect."[2]

Charles emerged from the ordeal not only penniless, having lost the small fortune that his father had left him as well as the money he had made over three years in the film business, but also facing charges of perjury. In fact, the only way in which he was able to obtain legal representation in the perjury trial was through his connection with the American Legion, having been one of its original founding members.[3]

---

1 *New York Times*, April 3, 1925.
2 *New York Times*, April 3, 1925.
3 *New Hampshire Journal Courier*, May 21, 1925.

Unlike the first trial, the perjury trial was decided not by a single judge but rather by a panel of jurors. In this trial, attorney George W. Newgass, who had helped to negotiate the contract between Lillian Gish and Inspiration Pictures,[1] testified that in the original trial, he had been given very little time to prepare as a witness. As a result, he had given testimony with "considerable inaccuracy," and it was as a direct result of that testimony that Duell had been indicted for perjury.[2]

During the trial, Charles H. Duell's attorney, Nathan Burkan, mimicked the manner in which Gish's attorney, Max Steuer, had been allowed to shout questions aggressively at Duell. Burkan wanted this jury to understand how unnerving and distracting such a line of questioning was and how it had hindered Charles from presenting clear, well-organized testimony.[3]

When Charles took the stand in the perjury trial, he made the case that Judge Julian Mack had given him an unfair trial. In his three days on the stand in that trial, not only had Judge Mack allowed him to be peppered with "more than 2000 shouted questions, being interrupted an average of once a minute," but Judge Mack had himself contributed to the barrage with questions that were "more confusing than those of Mr. Steuer."[4] In closing, Charles Duell's attorney asserted that the first trial had been "bunk, bosh and buncombe,"[5] and out of a jury of twelve people, nine agreed, voting that Charles H. Duell was innocent of every one of Judge Mack's accusations of perjury.[6] The jury's stark difference of opinion from that of Judge Mack in the first trial caused the government to drop the case and all charges.[7]

Although somewhat vindicated, Charles was left a crushed man, out of work, penniless, and embittered,[8,9] and Holland was left battle-scarred and exhausted from the entire ordeal.

As if the seismic tremors in Holland's life from the Gish trial and his own divorce proceedings were not enough, exactly one month before the Gish trial commenced, Holland had received word that his other brother Sackett and "Baby Best" had been divorced.

For two years, Sackett had struggled to keep Annie happy in their marriage. He catered to her social needs by hosting functions at Hillcroft.[10] He took her on expensive vacations abroad[11] and, in general, made every effort to help her fit into his Pennsylvania life. Alas, finally she could take country life no more and pleaded with Sackett to move back to New York.[12]

---

1 *New York Times*, June 5, 1926.

2 *New York Times*, June 8, 1926.

3 *New York Times*, June 9, 1926.

4 *New York Times*, June 11, 1926.

5 *New York Times*, June 15, 1926.

6 *New York Times*, June 17, 1926.

7 *New York Times*, November 27, 1926.

8 *New York Times*, April 25, 1928.

9 *New York Times*, December 30, 1932.

10 *Amsterdam* (New York) *Evening Recorder*, October 31, 1921.

11 August 21, 1923, passport application for William Sackett Duell, ancestry.com.

12 *Ogden* (Utah) *Examiner*, August 2, 1924.

"Baby Best" still possessed the magic spell that had cast itself on so many hearts, causing them to value her above all else. How to run his business efficiently from New York was an unanswered question, but Sackett made Annie his top priority, and by 1923, they had sold Hillcroft and were in residence at 62 East 77th Street in New York.[1,2] The move to New York was bittersweet, for on May 23, 1923, Annie's beloved mother, Mary Tooker Best, died of heart disease at the Duells' home.[3]

Mary was the only person in Annie's life who had been there for her, always. A procession of men had professed their undying love and devotion for "Baby Best," only to turn around and disappear into obscurity. Throughout the instability of her life, Annie had had only one solid foundation that she could count on, and that was her mother. Mary had been the best mother a daughter could have asked for. Her unconditional love was a constant, and there was never a doubt that "Baby Best" was always her mother's first priority.

The void in Annie's heart was cavernous. She had Sackett, but the years had made her cynical, and deep inside, she really felt no sense of security with him. Desperate to heal her hurting heart, she immersed herself in social activities with the fervor of a lapsed alcoholic binging on spirits. Socializing was her drug. It was her stimulation and her euphoria. It was what she enjoyed.

But for Sackett, the pace of those social engagements, which he considered commitments and obligations rather than pleasures, was murderous. At first, he tried to keep up, but he soon felt himself betraying his own person for the sake of his wife's agenda. He pleaded with Annie to slow down, but that simply was not within her ability. The point was soon reached at which Sackett could no more keep up than Annie could consider slowing down.[4] It was not that one was good and one was bad. They had both tried, but their lives simply did not mesh together, and on February 15, 1925, Sackett and "Baby Best" were granted a divorce.[5,6] The reality was devastating for Sackett. He had neither the energy nor the desire to pursue further love interests. He had given everything of himself to make Annie happy and, in the process, allowed the finances of his business[7] as well as his own personal finances[8] to founder. The only thing that would numb his pain was alcohol, and he was in constant pain. A little more than a year after the divorce, Sackett died[9,10] from cirrhosis of the liver.[11,12]

Three brothers—three failed relationships. After his perjury trial, Holland's youngest brother Charles soon relocated out of New York, for all intents and purposes

1   *New York Times*, May 24, 1923.

2   1923 passport application for William Sackett Duell states that Hillcroft is sold, ancestry.com.

3   *New York Times*, May 24, 1923.

4   *Ogden* (Utah) *Examiner*, August 2, 1924.

5   *New York Times*, June 7, 1925.

6   *New York Times*, June 7, 1925.

7   *Amsterdam* (New York) *Evening Recorder*, June 12, 1926.

8   *Amsterdam* (New York) *Evening Recorder*, August 13, 1924.

9   findagrave.com.

10 Sons of the American Revolution, ancestry.com.

11 Obituary, *Syracuse Herald*, May 27, 1926.

12 Yale obituary for William Sackett Duell.

disappearing from Holland's life. His brother Sackett had died, and of course Holland himself had suffered an immense amount of stress in the process of his separation from Mabel. The recent avalanche of ill fortune and adversity had burdened a heavy cloud upon Holland's soul, and resulted in what was, undeniably, the most difficult period in his life.

Yet through it all Holland was grateful. He was grateful for the loving partnership that had been forged. He was grateful to have Emilie by his side as he struggled through adversity. It is a curious phenomenon the amount of strength and resilience a man can gain from the love and support of a partner of meek and diminutive power. For so long, Holland had wanted nothing more for his life than the reward of being with the woman who filled his soul, coupled with the freedom to sail *Rowdy* out on the Sound. For so long circumstances had continually yanked him back from that envisioned happiness in a frustrating denial of the life he knew that he was meant to have. But at last things seemed to be changing. Emilie was now a part of his life. She shared in his every emotion, and she had proven time and again that she would always be there for Holland and that she would always be his advocate. In fact it was for that very reason; it was through Emilie's support in the midst of all the craziness of 1925 that Holland Duell happened to participate in one of the most extraordinary races of his life.

Forties in a Squall

Only days after the conclusion of the Gish trial, Holland and Emilie purchased a three-quarter-acre lot on Beach Avenue in Larchmont. It sat right on the water's edge, with beautiful views of Long Island Sound, and was in walking distance of the Larchmont Yacht Club.

Holland put in an application at the Larchmont Yacht Club and was voted into membership on May 22, 1925.[1] Eight days later, he sailed *Rowdy* in her first race of the season.[2] It was to be another full racing season. By July 22, Holland and *Rowdy* had completed fifteen races.[3]

Wednesday, July 22, 1925, was the day of the third regatta of the Larchmont Yacht Club's Annual Race Week. The seas were massive and confused as a hard southwesterly blow carried in heavy rain squalls. From the moment the ninety-eight sloops and schooners crossed the starting line, every one of them had a rail buried in the water and endured sheets of flying spray.

To Holland, the explosive moment felt tauntingly equivalent to a metaphor for his life over the past three years; a life tattered by turbulence, at times being pummeled from so many different directions that he could find little recourse or resolution to the adverse situations. In stark contrast to his personal life, from the helm of Rowdy, Holland was in complete control and was able to fight back against this storm. And he did. As if striking out in defiance at the frustrations and injustices that life had piled upon him, he held nothing in reserve. By his command every sheet on the boat was winched down to a frightful tension. Anyone who has witnessed a guitar string that has been severely over tightened would recognize the danger, and probably appreciate the near musical tones rendered by plucking a finger across one of those sheets.

The constant stinging spray and horizontal flying water were punctuated by entire waves that would wash across Rowdy's huge flush deck as her bow plunged into the swells. The conditions, which were entirely unwelcome and most certainly unnerving to the majority of the captains, were readily embraced by Holland. The vicious, blustery environment provided him the perfect opportunity to finally unleash his emotions and frustrations in the way that felt most satisfying to him; from the helm of Rowdy - and he did so with an overwhelming and uncontainable determination to prevail in the race and to overpower the forces that were pushing against him.

Every inch of the race course seemed an uphill battle, the distance traveled probably doubled as a consequence of summiting and descending the huge swells and,

---

1 July 21, 2012, letter from Rosemarie Giuliani of the Larchmont Yacht Club.
2 *New York Times*, May 31, 1925.
3 Many newspaper references.

under those conditions, Rowdy had never looked finer. Her rail buried itself fully a foot beneath the water as she freight-trained through the swells, blasting the tops off whitecaps and sending plumes of water high into the air. But as so often happens in life, just when you think you are being tested to your limit, along comes something else to blindside you. The problem with adjusting a rig right up to the breaking point under a given stress is that if the stress is increased, something will break. And that's exactly what happened to many of *Rowdy*'s companions when the already blustery conditions were eclipsed by the arrival of a vicious 50-mile-per-hour squall that slammed the racing fleet from an unexpected direction.

Vice Commodore Phillip Johnson's 39-footer, *Grey Dawn*, could not react quickly enough to avoid an uncontrolled jibe, which caused her 60-foot mast to splinter about 5 feet above the deck. The entire rig and complement of sails went over the side, landing in the water, luckily without injury to the crew. The New York 30 *Nautilus* broke her boom and limped back to the harbor under her jib. *Manhassett II* also broke a boom, *Fifi* lost her spreaders, and *Mirage* broke her gaff. Through the chaos, *Rowdy* maintained as straight a line as an arrow in flight. Holland knew that if he held her to it, she was equal to the task, and he never wavered.

It was a day that the *New York Times* described as giving the contending yachtsmen enough thrills to last them until next year's Race Week.[1,2] Edwin Levick, the top marine photographer of the day, was at the right place at the right time on that day and captured an award-winning photograph of *Rowdy* pulling away from the pack

✳ *Edwin Levick's famous photo "Forties in a Squall," July 22, 1925,* Rowdy *at far right (Old poster in personal collection)*

1　*New York Times*, July 23, 1925.
2　*The Larchmont Yacht Club: A History, 1880–1990*, by C. Stanley Ogilvy (Larchmont, NY: Larchmont Yacht Club, 1993), p. 165.

just before winning the most grueling race of her career. The photograph, titled "Forties in a Squall," was made into a poster and sold nationwide.

As *Rowdy* charged across the finish line, it was as though all the oppressive resistance from the last three years of Holland's life was suddenly and miraculously blasted into oblivion. Whatever that moment was, whatever allowed for that monumental crescendo of human triumph over the elements, of personal triumph over adversity and emotion, it marked a turning point in Holland's life. The clouds that had darkened his life over the past years seemed to part suddenly, giving way to blue skies. Holland had loved his two brothers, but throughout their lives, their need for Holland's professional assistance had placed unrelenting burdens on his already busy life. Now those pressures had disappeared.

Another weight was lifted when, one month and three days after the race, Holland received the final decree of his divorce from Mabel.[1,2] Exactly seven days later, on Tuesday, September 1, 1925, Holland and Emilie were married in London, England, at St. George Hanover Square.[3,4,5] From that point for-

ward, Holland's life gradually assumed the track that he had always wished for, and with each passing day, Holland and Emilie's life together seemed to brighten.

Upon their return to New York, Holland and Emilie checked into the luxurious Ambassador Hotel.[6] They considered their stay there, while their new house was being constructed, an extended and well-deserved honeymoon.

It was a joyous and celebrated day when Holland and Emilie moved into Elm Court, the name they had chosen for their Larchmont estate. The new house was beautifully suited to their lifestyle. Every day greeted them with an over-the-water sunrise and ended in an equally spectacular front-row marine sunset. A chauffeur, a housemaid, a chambermaid, and a waitress staffed the sprawling Mediterranean mansion.[7] With six fireplaces and separate guest quarters, the residence enclosed an elegant cobblestone courtyard[8] that was romantically reminiscent of the Place Vendome outside the Hotel Ritz Paris, where they had first professed their love for one another. The front entry beckoned

✳ Elm Court" on Beach Avenue as it looks today. Cobble-stone driveway and courtyard are reminiscent of the Place Vendome in Paris.

1 *New York Times*, September 2, 1925.

2 *Syracuse Herald*, September 3, 1925.

3 England and Wales marriage index, 1916–2005, ancestry.com.

4 *New York Times*, September 2, 1925.

5 *Syracuse Herald*, September 3, 1925.

6 *New York Evening Post*, September 17, 1925.

7 1930 U.S. census record for Holland S. Duell, ancestry.com.

8 Unidentified February 4, 1994, newspaper clipping provided by the Larchmont Historical Society.

Mediterranean Mansion on secluded acre in Larchmont
Manor with spectacular views of Long Island Sound.
European grace with its cobble-stone courtyard and elegant
details. 6 Fireplaces, seperate guest quarters. Distinctive
dock/deep water mooring

✳ *Old real estate ad featuring the home that Holland and Emilie built on Beach Avenue*
(Courtesy The Larchmont Historical Society)

guests to share Holland's passion for the sea as they walked down a long hall that doubled as a gallery of sailing pictures.[1]

Emilie, of course, continued wholeheartedly to support Holland's enjoyment of sailing *Rowdy*. In the first eight years that he had owned the boat, he had been able to race her in only three seasons and never two years in a row. From the time he publicly began a life with Emilie in 1924, Holland raced *Rowdy* every season for eight years straight, fully satisfying his thirst for the sport and becoming one of the most respected and best-liked sailors on Long Island Sound.

For the rest of their lives, they enjoyed marvelous vacations together, including annual cruises to Europe[2] and trips to Panama,[3] Bermuda,[4] and the Bahamas[5] as well as stays at luxury country resorts in the United States. They frequented the world-class Greenbrier in White Sulphur Springs, West Virginia,[6] and the Bon Air Vanderbilt in Augusta, Georgia,[7] but perhaps their favorite was The Homestead in Hot Springs, Virginia.[8] It is a sprawling hotel and spa set amid rolling hills in the wooded Allegheny Mountains, featuring golf, tennis, horseback riding, trout fishing, canoeing, and many group activities, tournaments, and parties.

---

1 April 3, 2001, letter from Cherry Taylor.
2 Multiple passenger lists, ancestry.com.
3 March 17, 1938, *Britannic* passenger list for Holland Duell, ancestry.com.
4 *New York Times,* January 12, 1928.
5 *New York Evening Post,* December 16, 1928.
6 *New York Evening Post,* November 26, 1926.
7 *New York Evening Post,* January 8, 1927.
8 *New York Times,* April 4, 1932.

✳ *Holland and Emilie Duell*

Within every heart, at the core of every human soul, lies the yearning for a love as rare and as special as that which Holland and Emilie shared. Far apart coming into this life, they were brought together by fate, and, never looking back, they spent the rest of their days reveling in the blessing of their life together at Elm Court on the waters of Long Island Sound.

How accurate Hanny's words had been when, aboard *Rowdy*, she said to me, "You have no idea how much more there is to this story." Being involved in the restoration and racing of *Rowdy* was beyond amazing, but what I value above all else, and what I'm sure I will value for the rest of my life, is the window into *Rowdy*'s past that opened up and beckoned me inside. I could never have foreseen becoming so deeply immersed in learning a story that was almost lost to time. The entirety of the people's lives had already come and passed, yet I was able to find so many scattered pieces of the story that, as it came together and sprang to life once again, my familiarity with the characters grew until my connection to them became most wonderfully personal and intimate. I feel uniquely fortunate to have been gifted with the task of documenting the life of Holland Sackett Duell and especially privileged and grateful to be able to share this story and keep alive his memory and the memory of a most remarkable group of people.

My twin daughters were born happy and healthy in 2004, and with my "complete package" of *Rowdy*'s history in hand at last, I built a web site that told the story. It seemed no time before the perfect buyer was knocking on my door, and before long, *Rowdy* was transported to Monaco, where she once again became a world-class champion.

The End

✳ Rowdy *competing in Régates Royales–Panerai Trophy, Cannes, France, September 21, 2011 (James Robinson Taylor # JRT 7313)*

Epilog:
The Characters Continued

Holland and Emilie Duell

In 1927, Holland switched *Rowdy* from a gaff to a Marconi sail plan, requiring an entirely new rig with a towering mast. *Rowdy* was the only New York 40 to be thus modified, and she did not perform well in comparison to the others.[1,2] In 1928, she returned with her original gaff rig and had a very successful racing season, winning at least eight major races.

❋ Rowdy, *Marconi rigged, June 16, 1927*

❋ Rowdy, *Marconi rigged, June 16, 1927*

1 *New York Times*, June 19, 1927.
2 *New York Times*, June 24, 1927.

Holland seemed to excel in rough conditions. His sense of calm under pressure and his extreme confidence in *Rowdy* perhaps advantaged him with a little more nerve than many of the other captains. Such was the case on August 4, 1930, during a 31.5-mile New York Yacht Club race from Newport, Rhode Island, to Mattapoisett, Massachusetts. A vicious southwesterly wind and angry seas left a trail of damaged boats strewn across the course. Two of the New York 40s, *Mistral* and *Marilee*, were dismasted. The *Chinook* burst her ballooner sail as if it were a paper bag. *Pleione* lost both spreaders. Edward Cudahy, owner of the *Marilee*, cracked a rib as he was knocked overboard, and a crew member aboard *Weetamoe* was cast 15 feet into the air and landed in the sea after a whipping spinnaker line wrapped itself around him. Holland's unyielding determination added one more first-place trophy to *Rowdy*'s collection that day.[1,2]

The racing season of 1931 was Holland's last, and once again *Rowdy* won eight major races, including the 73-mile race of the New York Yacht Club's Annual Cruise from Vineyard Haven to Provincetown, Massachusetts. The Coast Guard had to rescue two boats that went aground in the thick fog, one being *Typhoon*, which laid over on her side as the tide went out. *Rowdy* won not only first place in class but also the annual Hayes Cup for New York 40s. She also won the Commodore's Cup for best overall.[3,4,5]

Back on May 21, 1927, just a month before Holland's first race of that season, Charles Lindbergh made history and won a $25,000 prize for completing the first solo transatlantic flight. The following year, Amelia Earhart, as part of a crew of three, made the same crossing. Aviation was becoming increasingly popular, and as a sportsman, Holland was bitten hard by the bug. In 1931, when not racing, he was attending Roosevelt Aviation School,[6,7] and in July 1931, he received his private pilot's license.[8] By the end of the year, he had written an enthusiastic article titled "Learning to Fly at Fifty," which was printed in *The Spur* and, in March 1932, in *Reader's Digest*.[9,10] Two months later, on May 20, 1932, the fifth anniversary of Lindbergh's solo transatlantic flight, Amelia Earhart became the first woman and only the second person in history to make the transatlantic flight solo.[11]

Holland bought an NC600Y open cockpit Waco airplane[12] and in June 1932 had the engine completely rebuilt at Jack Conklin's shop at Roosevelt Field.[13]

----

1 *New York Times*, August 5, 1930.

2 *New York Times*, August 6, 1930.

3 *New York Times*, August 16, 1931.

4 *New York Evening Post*, August 17, 1931.

5 *New York Times*, March 14, 1931.

6 *New York Evening Post*, July 29, 1933.

7 New York passenger lists, Holland Duell, August 21, 1932, ancestry.com.

8 *Who's Who in Westchester County* (Hastings-on-Hudson, NY: The Hastings News, 1931), p. 242.

9 *Readers Digest*, March 1932.

10 *Anniston* (Alabama) *Star*, September 15, 1932.

11 *New York Times*, June 21, 1932.

12 New York passenger lists, Holland Duell, August 21, 1932, ancestry.com.

13 *Brooklyn Daily Eagle*, June 17, 1932.

✳ *left, Holland Duell and his open cockpit Waco (Photo courtesy of Holland Duell's granddaughter Susan Duell and her son Mitch Higgins); right, Holland Duell's open cockpit Waco (Image courtesy of WACO Historical Society, Ray Blanden Collection)*

That same year, Holland joined the newly formed Westchester Aviation Club, which had just taken over the Armonk landing field on Long Island, formerly the Westchester Airport. Among the fifty-person membership were transatlantic flyer Amelia Earhart, speed record flyer Frank Hawks, William A. Rockefeller, former NY40 *Typhoon* owner Philip Morgan Plant, and former NY40 *Mistral* and NY50 *Istalena* owner George M. Pynchon.[1,2] With a spirit similar to that of the yacht clubs, it was a fun group of people, and the first air meet in August 1932 culminated in a dinner and dance. The dinner was served at tables on the concrete runway enclosed within a small semicircle of members' airplanes. The dance was held inside one of the hangars, which had been decorated with evergreens, oak leaves, and colored lights.[3]

In August 1933, seventy-five planes from the club departed Roosevelt Air Field on Long Island bound for Montreal to take part in the 5th Canadian Air Pageant. They flew in formation in groups of five and arrived in Montreal by 2:00 p.m. That evening, the group members were guests of the Governor General of Canada, Lord and Lady Bessborough, at a dance.[4]

Holland often flew long distances. Shortly after getting his plane, he flew 1,000 miles to Anniston, Alabama, to visit Colonel Frederic Smith, under whom he had served in the war.[5] In later years, Holland flew 2,000 miles, following railroads, to visit his son Holland Sackett Duell, Jr. and his four-year-old granddaughter Dottie at their ranch in New Mexico.[6]

---

1 *The Herald Statesman* (Yonkers, NY), August 13, 1932.

2 *New York Evening Post*, August 15, 1932.

3 *New York Times*, September 11, 1932.

4 *New York Evening Post*, August 18, 1933.

5 *Anniston* (Alabama) *Star*, September 15, 1932.

6 March 10, 2011, letter from Holland S. Duell, Jr.'s daughter, Dottie (Duell) Henry.

In 1933, Holland was granted a patent for a new type of amphibious landing gear,[1] and in 1934, he was issued a Royal Aero Club Aviators' Certificate (a United Kingdom aviator's flying license).[2]

After the Waco, Holland Duell owned a Stinson Reliant, and his last plane was a negative stagger biplane Beechcraft. He made numerous forced landings due to mechanical difficulties or marginal weather, all of which he got away with. He was never one to panic.[3]

Holland continued to sail *Rowdy* through most of his flying years but only for fun and never with a serious racing crew. He transferred her title to Emilie in 1936,[4] and the last public mention I found of her under Holland's name was on August 4, 1937, when *Rowdy* was in Newport to watch the America's Cup trials. The newspaper article additionally mentioned that *Rowdy* was decorated in celebration of Queen Elizabeth's birthday and the 147th birthday of the U.S. Coast Guard.[5]

In 1939, Holland Duell's son Charles Halliwell Duell founded the publishing company Duell, Sloan & Pearce, which later published, among other books, Dr. Benjamin Spock's groundbreaking and immensely popular The Common Sense Book of Baby and Child Care[6] as well as several books by famed architect Frank Lloyd Wright.

Holland S. Duell died at his home, Elm Court, on Beach Avenue, Larchmont, New York, on November 25, 1942, at the age of 61[7,8] from a cerebral thrombosis.[9] The funeral service was held at Elm Court on Friday, November 27, at 2:00 p.m., and he was buried on Monday, November 30, at Arlington National Cemetery outside Washington, D.C.[10,11]

After Holland's death, Emilie Duell lived in the Waldorf-Astoria Towers at Park Avenue and 50th Street in Manhattan.[12] She was friends with her neighbors General Douglas MacArthur and Elizabeth Taylor and dined with them on occasion. [13] Holland had been her world and the true love of her life, and although she lived another twenty-three years, she never considered remarrying. In her June 28, 1963, Last Will and Testament, Emilie left exacting instructions as to how her name was to be artistically added to the headstone that she and Holland would share for eternity. In the will, she warmly referred to a diamond bracelet "which was a wedding present from my beloved husband." In the following photo, taken thirty years after their wedding, Emilie is still seen affectionately wearing the bracelet."

---

1 U.S. patent number 1,929,630, 10-10-1933.

2 Great Britain, Royal Aero Club Aviator's certificates, 1910–1950, ancestry.com.

3 "Dilettante," a paper written by Holland Duell's son Holland Sackett Duell, Jr. about his parents.

4 Lloyd's Registry of Yachts.

5 *New York Times*, August 4, 1937.

6 *New York Times*, July 12, 1970.

7 *New York Times*, November 26, 1942.

8 *Syracuse Herald*, November 26, 1942.

9 Yale obituary.

10 *New York Times*, November 27, 1942.

11 Yale obituary.

12 Last Will and Testament of Emilie Duell, dated June 28, 1963.

13 March 10, 2011 letter from Holland's granddaughter Dottie Henry

* *Left, Emilie Duell, circa 1957 (Photo courtesy of Dottie Henry); above, grave marker for Holland and Emilie Duell, Arlington National Cemetery (Photo courtesy of Paul Hays)*

Despite having lost Holland, Emilie continued to live life fully, traveling abroad every year and spending her summers fondly at the Ritz Paris on the Place Vendome. Emilie was close to Holland Sackett Duell, Jr.'s daughter Dottie (Holland's granddaughter), with whom I was lucky enough to enjoy a wonderful correspondence, and Dottie was often Emilie's house guest. The two also enjoyed time together abroad and on cruises.[1]

Emilie died on April 16, 1965,[2] a month before her eighty-first birthday. She is buried with Holland at Arlington National Cemetery.

Mabel (Duell) and John Stilwell

After her divorce from Holland, Mabel Duell married her second husband, John Stilwell, on February 2, 1926.[3] Five months later, on August 1, 1926, while asleep in their bedroom at Ardenwold, the couple was robbed by the "second-story" jewel thief Arthur Barry.[4] His life story certainly warrants a separate book—which may very well prove to be my next project.

As World War II got under way in Europe, organizations were formed in the United States to help provide clothing for civilians in war-torn areas and hospital garments for the injured. Mabel Stilwell applied, and was granted permission, to start a local branch of one such organization, Bundles for Britain, in Yonkers, New York. She later opened a local branch of a similar organization, Bundles for

1 March 10, 2011, letter from Holland Sackett Duell, Jr.'s daughter Dottie.
2 New York Times, April 19, 1965.
3 *New York Times*, February 3, 1926.
4 *New York Times*, August 2, 1926.

* *Mabel Stilwell in 1942 (Photo from Herald Statesman, October 3, 1942)*

✻ *Lenoir Preserve in Yonkers,
former site of Ardenwold*

America, which grew from a one-woman beginning to having over 700 volunteer women working in Yonkers.[1] Mabel Stilwell died of a heart attack at her home, Ardenwold, on July 13, 1958.[2] Her husband, John Stilwell, died on July 26, 1963.[3,4]

After Stilwell's death, Ardenwold was purchased by the Julia Dyckman Andrus Memorial, Inc., under whose stewardship the house burned down. Fifteen years later, in May 1979, Westchester County acquired the 20-acre parcel of land as well as the 20-acre adjoining estate, Lenoir, which had been owned by Dr. and Mrs. Orrin Wightman. The two estates were combined to create the 40-acre Lenoir Nature Preserve, which is open to the public and renowned for its woodlands, spectacular views, and bird watching.[5]

Charles H. Duell, Jr.

As a result of the 1925 Duell vs Gish trial, Charles Duell Jr. lost everything; fame, fortune, his reputation, and any possibility of a political career. What Charles knew and used against Lillian going into that trial was the fact that Lillian breached her contract by refusing to show up for work - presumably because of their soured love affair, and because of Lillian's growing distrust of Charles and of his financial affairs. What Charles did not know at the time of the trial, and what he became firmly convinced of, after the fact, was that there had been much more to the story.

Based on new information, Charles filed a second law suit, in Los Angeles in 1927, claiming that Lillian had breached her contract with him because Metro-Goldwyn had secretly and maliciously seduced her away. Charles stated emphatically that, behind his back, Metro-Goldwyn, entered into secret talks with Lillian and offered her significantly more money than the salary he was affording her. [6] Throughout the entirety of Lillian's life, money and the desire for wealth had served her as the great almighty. The presumed outcome of Lillian's decision is no mystery. Charles' concurrent contracts with both Metro-Goldwyn, who would distribute his films and Lillian Gish who would act in them had left Charles particularly vulnerable to a hostile collaboration between the two. Those close to Charles knew that his financial survival was dependent on the production of The Outsider; the story which Lillian Gish had encouraged Charles to buy, and in which she would play the leading role. Given his heavy investment in the film, the simplest of strategies to ruin Charles financially

1 *Herald Statesman* (Yonkers, NY), October 3, 1942.
2 *Herald Statesman* (Yonkers, NY), July 14, 1958.
3 *Herald Statesman* (Yonkers, NY), July 26, 1963.
4 *Herald Statesman* (Yonkers, NY), August 1, 1964.
5 http://parks.westchestergov.com/lenoir-preserve.
6 Duell vs Gish, Los Angeles Superior Court, case 227232, 1927. Housed at Archives and Records Center, 222 N. Hill St., Los Angeles, CA

would require no more than Lillian's refusal to show up for work coupled with Metro-Goldwyn's refusal to distribute films for Charles.

The dagger was thrust and, in Charles' lawsuit, he held no reserve in detailing and condemning an outright conspiracy between Lillian and Metro-Goldwyn stating they "fraudulently, wrongfully, willfully and maliciously conspired together ...... for the purpose ..... of obtaining her services for themselves and of financially ruining the plaintiff" (Charles Duell). Charles stated to the court that, immediately prior to Lillian's breach of contract, Metro-Goldwyn did, in fact, threaten to discontinue distribution of his films and, on May 12, 1925, Lillian did, in fact, sign a contract to work for Metro-Goldwyn for approximately $8,000 a week.[1] Charles sued for $3,000,000 in actual damages and $2,000,000 punitive damages.[2] In his suit, Charles described details of the love affair between himself and Lillian Gish; details intended to be damaging to Lillian. Judge Tierney signed an order "striking out the allegations in paragraphs Fourth to Sixth . . . upon the grounds that these allegations were impertinent and scandalous." The judge further ordered that the contents were to be sealed under court supervision and the "plaintiff (Duell), his attorneys, clerks, employees and agents to be prohibited from directly or indirectly disclosing what matter was contained in the objectionable paragraphs."[3] In 1928, Charles lost the suit against the defendants.[4] Before the members of the jury were sequestered to deliberate the case, the judge had ordered them to render a verdict in favor of the defendants because all of the issues of the case had previously been addressed in federal court.[5]

In January 1929, Charles filed two suits against Lillian Gish: one for $32,578 and one for $3,217.[6] He announced publicly that he had written a tell-all book exposing the details of his scandalous affair with Lillian and that he planned to introduce the contents of the book as evidence in his new trial. Whatever the lurid details were, Lillian Gish's attorneys had spent years and great amounts of time and money negotiating with all the different media outlets to suppress the information. They also took steps to try to block the publication of any such book.[7]

Later the same year, Lillian Gish departed Europe bound for New York aboard the *Ile de France* only to find that Charles had bought a ticket the day after her. Upon seeing him on the promenade deck, Lillian fled to her cabin and radioed her attorney, Max Steuer, who in turn contacted the captain of the *Ile de France*. Two of the ship's crewmen were then assigned to follow Charles for the remainder of the voyage. Lillian remained in her cabin for the rest of the trip, having meals delivered to her.[8,9]

1 Duell vs Gish, Los Angeles Superior Court, case 227232, 1927
2 *New York Times*, June 24, 1927.
3 June 20, 1927, letter from Lillian Gish's attorneys, Chadbourne, Stanchfield & Levy, in Lillian Gish Papers, New York Public Library for the Performing Arts.
4 *Lillian Gish: Her Legend, Her Life*, by Charles Affron (New York: Scribner, 2001), p. 197.
5 *New York Times*, April 25, 1928.
6 *New York Times*, January 20, 1929.
7 1929 letters between Lillian Gish's attorneys and herself, in Lillian Gish Papers, New York Public Library for the Performing Arts.
8 *Washington Post*, August 21, 1929.
9 *New York Times*, August 21, 1929.

In late 1932, Charles lost his final appeal in his case against Lillian, which he had taken to the California state Supreme Court in San Francisco.[1,2]

With that, Charles finally let go, having at long last fallen in love again. On September 30, 1933, he married Edith E. Brisbane. He supervised the manufacture of a dispensing container that she had invented, and he became president of Brisbane Box Corporation. Charles Duell retired in 1945[3] and died of a heart attack in 1954, survived by his wife Edith and his sister Mary.[4,5]

In 2014, I nominated *The White Sister*, the 1923 film produced by Charles Duell that had made Lillian Gish a star, for inclusion in the National Film Registry at the Library of Congress.

✻ Mrs. W. Sackett Duell (Print, Philadelphia Record Photograph Morgue (11626-V07), Historical Society of Pennsylvania)

"Baby Best"

Only months after divorcing Sackett, Annie had married for the fourth time. That marriage, to businessman Charles Albert Smylie, ended in divorce in 1932.[6]

On October 1, 1932, "Baby Best" finally married the man of her dreams.[7] Vladimir A. Behr had grown up in Moscow, where his father had been a wealthy cotton broker. In World War I, Vladimir served as a heavy artillery officer and received several decorations for bravery. He was shell-shocked during the siege of Osovietz, one of the three fortifications guarding the approaches to Warsaw.[8] He subsequently fled to the United States during the 1917 Bolshevik revolution.[9] Eight years Annie's junior, Vladimir was a rock of a man, standing six feet, four inches and weighing 260 pounds.[10] The couple were perfect for one another. Soon after their marriage, they bought an estate in her old neighborhood and favorite spot in the world, Bellevue Avenue in Newport, Rhode Island. They remodeled the home, adding a third story, and named the estate Vladania—a combination of their two first names, Vladimir and Annie.[11,12] Situated

1   *Niagara Falls* (New York) *Gazette*, December 29, 1932.

2   *New York Times*, December 30, 1932.

3   *Encyclopedia of American Biography* (New York: American Historical Company, 1955), p. 158.

4   *Washington Post & Times Herald*, June 21, 1954.

5   *Encyclopedia of American Biography*, p. 158.

6   *San Antonio* (Texas) *Light*, August 21, 1932.

7   *Newport* (Rhode Island) *Mercury and Evening News*, April 4, 1952.

8   *Newport* (Rhode Island) *Mercury and Weekly News*, April 4, 1952.

9   *Newport* (Rhode Island) *Mercury and Weekly News*, July 10, 1964.

10 April 27, 1942 U.S. military registration card, ancestry.com.

11 *Newport* (Rhode Island) *Mercury and Weekly News*, April 4, 1952.

12 National Register of Historic Places Inventory for Bellevue Avenue.

✳ *Vladania (Newport
Historical Society, #P9070)*

on a little over an acre of the most prime Newport real estate,[1] Vladania hosted a ceaseless procession of social functions, which regularly included guests of notable title. Annie regularly filled the house with music that she played on a beautiful white Steinway grand piano.[2] She enjoyed performing with Countess Szechenyi, whose maiden name had been Gladys Vanderbilt. Annie also performed often at local functions and events.[3] Vladimir and Annie's love and energy and their common interests allowed them to mesh as perfectly as any two finely machined gears. They happily spent the rest of their lives together, their every anniversary being celebrated in the newspapers.

Ruth Alice Van Slyke

Dubbed by the press "The Pretty Nurse," Ruth Alice Cole became a millionaire as a consequence of marrying Mabel Duell's father, Charles Halliwell. Ruth Alice was in the newspapers once again in 1909, when she married wealthy William Porter, although the stories were far more sensational two years later when this, her second rich husband also died.

Porter had begun his career in 1881 as a cotton broker in Louisville, Kentucky. He later was involved with the American Tobacco Company, becoming general manager

1 *Newport* (Rhode Island) *Mercury and Weekly News*, September 19, 1952.
2 *Newport* (Rhode Island) *Mercury and Weekly News*, September 19, 1952.
3 *Newport* (Rhode Island) *Mercury and Weekly News*, July 10, 1964.

✳ *Foxcroft in the Ramapo Mountains of New Jersey*

✳ *View from Foxcroft of Lake Ramapo (Photo courtesy of Paul Neary)*

of sales[1] and one of Charles E. Halliwell's closest and most intimate friends.[2] Porter left the tobacco business in 1903 to join the stock exchange firm of Perkins, Erickson & Co.,[3] but he maintained his close friendship with Charles Halliwell, and that came to include the friendship of Ruth Alice when she married Charles. Their union following Charles's passing felt natural and effortless, and William and Ruth Alice lived in luxury at the twenty-story Plaza Hotel on Manhattan's 5th Avenue. They also owned a large tract of land in the Ramapo Mountains of New Jersey, where William had built his country home. It was a large stone and wood-beamed structure, called by many a castle, which William had named Foxcroft because it sat atop Fox Mountain.[4]

The house was surrounded in all directions by mile after mile after mile of lovely rolling wooded hills and afforded a bird's-eye view of the small lake just below. Ruth Alice, being a Pennsylvania country girl at heart, shared William's love of the peace and quiet and the natural serenity of Foxcroft, and they spent as much time there as their schedules would afford.

Ruth Alice had not accompanied William on his last trip to Foxcroft, in May 1911. William and three of his stock exchange friends were being driven by chauffeur from the country home back to Manhattan when their car approached a horse pulling a cart loaded with paving stones. The horse reared, causing the stones to roll out into the path of the car, which swerved and went off the road. The front tires jammed deep into the ground, which was soft and muddy, and the car flipped over. All of its passengers were ejected harmlessly except for William Porter, who was pinned under the car. He was rushed to the hospital in Paterson, New Jersey, in critical condition with two broken legs, a fractured pelvis, and a wound across his forehead.

---

1 *New York Times*, May 25, 1911.

2 *New York Times*, June 20, 1913.

3 *New York Times*, May 25, 1911.

4 *New York Times*, May 25, 1911.

✳ *Outside Foxcroft ruins, Ramapo Forest, New Jersey*
  (Photo courtesy Angela Mastrincola)

✳ *Inside Foxcroft ruins, Ramapo Forest, New Jersey*
  (Photo courtesy Angela Mastrincola)

At the time of the accident, Ruth Alice was returning from Europe aboard the *Lusitania*, which was scheduled to berth in New York the following day. Family members and friends decided to meet her at the ship with the news rather than sending a wire to her on the ship.[1] William Porter died as a result of his injuries seven days later.[2] Eight months earlier, he had doubled his life insurance with Etna, and for a total premium of $250, his policy paid out $58,607.[3] After William Porter's death, Ruth Alice took up residence at the Gotham Hotel in Manhattan.[4]

Her third husband, prominent New York attorney Warren Clark Van Slyke, whom she married in 1913, died on April 7, 1925, following surgery for gallstones.[5] Three years earlier, in 1922, he had busied himself by acting as counsel for relatives of the victims of the May 1915 sinking of the *Lusitania* and arguing claims against Germany for damages.[6,7] It was somewhat personal, he and his wife having traveled on the *Lusitania* only a year before the ship was torpedoed.[8] Ruth Alice remained friends with Mabel and her husband John Stilwell, inviting them to a dinner at the Madison Hotel in January 1928.[9] Ruth Alice survived her third husband by fifteen years and died on August 30, 1940, at Foxcroft.[10] The estate was sold in 1942, and the house, which was abandoned in the 1950s, burned down in 1959. Its overgrown two-story stone remains provide a marvelous spectacle for wilderness hikers in the Ramapo State Forest wilderness of New Jersey.

---

1 *New York Times*, May 25, 1911.
2 *Syracuse Herald*, June 1, 1911.
3 *Syracuse Herald*, June 20, 1911.
4 *New York Times*, June 20, 1913.
5 *New York Times*, April 8, 1925.
6 *New York Times*, April 25, 1922.
7 *New York Times*, April 8, 1925.
8 May 15, 1914, *Lusitania* passenger list for Ruth Alice Van Slyke, ancestry.com.
9 *New York Times*, January 12, 1928.
10 *New York Times*, September 1, 1940.

Major Charles Whittelsey

* *Major Charles Whittlesey (Photograph Collection, New York Public Library 437773).*

Following the war, Major Charles Whittlesey, who had commanded the "Lost Battalion," returned to his law practice in New York. What undoubtedly were haunting memories remained with him. In 1921, Whittlesey put his affairs in order, paid his landlady a month's rent in advance, and booked passage on the *S.S. Toloa* from New York to Havana, Cuba. On the evening of November 26, the first night of the voyage, Whittlesey dined with the captain and was last seen leaving the smoking room at 11:15 p.m. An unsuccessful search of the ship at 8:00 the next morning led to the conclusion that Major Charles Whittlesey had committed suicide by jumping overboard. Several letters to friends and family, along with instructions to the captain for the disposition of his luggage, were discovered in his cabin. His body was never found.[1]

Cher Ami

* *Cher Ami (courtesy Smithsonian Institution, Military History, image 2004-391199.01)*

Cher Ami (French for "Dear Friend"), the black carrier pigeon who helped to save the Lost Battalion in the Argonne Forest by getting a message out from them when all other means had failed, suffered life-threatening injuries as a result of his bravery. He was blinded in one eye, was shot through the chest, and lost one leg. Monumental efforts by army medics saved his life, and he was fitted with a small wooden leg. Once he had recovered, General John J. Pershing personally saw Cher Ami off when the pigeon sailed back to the United States, where he became the mascot of the Department of Service. Cher Ami was awarded the Croix de Guerre Medal with a palm for his heroic service in the war. After his death in 1919, his body was prepared by a taxidermist and entrusted to the Smithsonian Institution, where it is part of a display at the National Museum of American History entitled "The Price of Freedom."[2]

Christopher Madsen

My twin daughters were born six weeks early but 100 percent happy, healthy, beautiful babies. *Rowdy* was sold soon after their birth, and in order to spend as much time as possible with the girls, I embarked on a journey as a full-time futures trader, working out of my home office. I still take my current (much smaller) boat out to the Santa Barbara Channel Islands every chance I get.

---

1   http://en.wikipedia.org/wiki/Charles_White_Whittlesey.
2   http://amhistory.si.edu/militaryhistory/collection/object.asp?ID=10&back=1.

Rowdy's Continued History

During the rebuilding of *Rowdy*, I maintained a *Rowdy* website and placed ads in sailing magazines in order to get information about her history. Here is what I was able to piece together.

Rowdy Ownership

1916-1935	Holland Sackett Duell, Milton Point, NY
1936-1940	Emilie Duell, Larchmont, NY
1941	Frank Linden, City Island, NY
1942-1947	Kenneth W. Martin, New York, NY
1948-1950	Frank Zima, Bridgeport, CT (gas engine installed)
1950-1952	George (Red) Stacy, Detroit, MI
1953-1955	Dr. Chaignon Brown, Detroit, MI
1955	Donald Major, Detroit, MI
1955-1963	Aurelian F. Wigle, Detroit, MI (sailed her from Michigan to Florida, accompanied the Winns from Florida to Jamaica)
1963-1971	Frank Winn, Redondo Beach, CA (sailed her to from Florida to California)
1971-1973	John Barkhurst, Redondo Beach, CA
1973-1982	Marvin and Velma C. Stokoe, Oroville, CA
1982-1992	Gerry Purcell, Marina Del Rey, CA
1992-1998	Christy Baxter, La Canada, CA
1998	Blue Whale Sailing School, Santa Barbara, CA
1998-2006	Christopher Madsen, Santa Barbara, CA
2006-2013	Graham Walker, UK
2013-present	Howard Dyer, UK

1941-1950   After *Rowdy* left the Duell family in 1941, not much is known of her history until 1950.

1950-1952   In 1950, *Rowdy* was purchased by George (Red) Stacy in Detroit, Michigan. She carried a Marconi rig and no bowsprit, and her mast was weak from a repair or modification. Red was a well-known member of the Bayview Yacht Club in Detroit. He and his wife, Ann, lived aboard *Rowdy* at an end tie by the ways at Bayview. *Rowdy* stayed in the water all winter and was hauled out only for spring bottom painting. Red used to participate in the Mackinac Race, the longest annual freshwater sailing race in the world.

1953-1955   After Red Stacy, *Rowdy* was owned by Dr. Chaignon Brown. I was told by his son, Jim, that *Rowdy* was kept in the water year round: in the winter at Bayview Yacht Club and in the summer at the Detroit Yacht Club. Jim was the official skipper and spent every winter weekend aboard as well as the entire summer. He did a wealth of varnishing and said that the hull was in perfect shape but they did replace many of the deck boards. Because *Rowdy* drew too much for the Great Lakes, the Browns had 18 inches of lead cut off the bottom and put in the bilge. Lloyd's Register of American Yachts shows *Rowdy*'s draft changing in 1950 from 8'5" to 6'10". The Browns bought *Rowdy* with no mast and had one built by Pigeon Hollow Spar. They did not race her because they did not have a spinnaker, but Jim said that *Rowdy* was very fast. Dr. Brown died in 1954, and his wife sold *Rowdy* in 1955 to Donald Major.

1955   Donald Major of Detroit, Michigan, owned *Rowdy* in 1955.

1955-1968   The next owner was Aurelian Wigle, an ex-Navy diver and retired stockbroker. I have been told by several contacts that "Rill" (his nickname) was a very colorful character. Following a Bayview Yacht Club bowling party, Wigle won *Rowdy* in an all-night craps game over a $6,000 pot. He kept her at the Bayview Yacht Club in Detroit. He raced her in the Mackinac in 1959, 1960, and 1961. *Rowdy* had a plank for a makeshift bowsprit. I was contacted by Lynn Steadman in response to my ad in *Wooden Boat* magazine. He was aboard *Rowdy* as a guest on the night of Wednesday, December 12, 1956. They went out on Lake St. Clair to see the *Greater Detroit*, the world's largest side-wheeler, and a smaller boat that were being put out of commission by burning them on the lake. A news boat photographer captured *Rowdy* in the foreground, and the picture was published with the article in the *Detroit Free Press*. Lynn Steadman sent me the original photo.

✳ *"Rill" Wigle (Photo courtesy of Sharon Stewart)*

✳ Rowdy *in foreground, burning side-wheeler* Greater Detroit *in background, with article (Article reprint courtesy Detroit Free Press. Photo courtesy of Lynn Steadman.)*

DETROIT FREE PRESS

18 Friday, Dec. 14, 1956

The Night Was Made Like Day

"MAN IS BORN, lives and dies," said Capt. Frank Becker, "and it's the same with boats. They are launched, they sail and at last their day is done." Two boats died on Lake St. Clair Wednesday night. The Greater Detroit, world's largest sidewheeler and the biggest passenger boat ever to sail fresh water, and her smaller consort in the old D&C fleet, the Eastern States, were put to the torch by Capt. Becker. The purpose was to remove their wooden superstructure so that the metal of the hulls and engines could be cut up for scrap. It was difficult to burn the boats, both from a sentimental and a physical standpoint. Although they were soaked with gasoline, a flaming torch and several railroad flares burned out on the steel decks before a roman candle at last touched off the gasoline and the boats died in a twin blaze of glory, visible for many miles over the storm-tossed lake.

I also had a conversation with Steve Crook, a retired naval officer. He recalled that when he was a teenager, he and a group of friends pooled their money and chartered *Rowdy* from Wigle in the summer of 1959 and again in 1961. He still laughs about how anyone in their right mind could turn a 60-foot boat over to a group of wild teenage boys. Their main provision was a keg of beer. At bath time, they would put the dinghy on deck, fill her with water, grab a bar of soap and a mug of beer, and live the good life. A newsletter from Val C. Saph of the Bayview Yacht Club says that he was among the teenagers who chartered *Rowdy* for two-week trips and that *Rowdy* was known for her leopard skin interior and wild parties.

On November 15, 1961, Wigle departed Detroit with his 68-year-old mother and his brother and sister-in-law. They planned to take *Rowdy* to Fort Lauderdale, Florida, for the winter via the Barge Canal, the Hudson River, and the Inland Waterway. On the second day of the trip, Thursday, November 16, *Rowdy* lost power in a Lake Erie gale packing 55 mph winds and 25-foot waves. They sent out a Mayday call saying that they were in bad shape and had a couple feet of water over the floorboards. A 40-foot Coast Guard cutter that tried to reach them sank in the rough seas. Three Coast Guardsmen made their way a mile to shore on a raft and were taken to the Westfield Hospital suffering from exposure and shock. A second Coast Guard cutter, the 110-foot *Ojibwa*, reached *Rowdy* at 8:00 a.m. on Friday after *Rowdy* had been adrift in the storm for twelve hours. *Rowdy* was towed into Buffalo Harbor at 5:30 p.m. The elder Mrs. Wigle said that she had agreed to the voyage "for the experience." She quipped, "I sure got it." Undaunted, the four planned to continue along their way as soon as the storm damage could be repaired.

On Wednesday, November 22, with repairs completed, *Rowdy* departed Buffalo. However, Wigle missed the Barge Canal entrance and headed down the Niagara River straight for Niagara Falls. Gerald Wardell, who owned a River Road marina, spotted the mistake and raced out in a powerboat to turn *Rowdy* around. Wigle took *Rowdy* into the marina and tied up at Larry Wardell's boatyard to take on provisions, fuel, and water. The supplies lowered *Rowdy* so much in the water that she became stuck on the bottom and had to be pulled free by a truck and tow line. Back under

Tonawanda NEWS

Saturday, November 18, 1961

DRAMA ON ERIE: A tense life - and - death drama on stormy Lake Erie was brought to a happy climax late yesterday when the yacht Rowdy was towed into Buffalo Harbor by the U.S. Coast Guard. Four persons, who spent the night aboard the disabled boat are shown after their rescue in the photos above. Top left, is Mrs. Norma Marie Wigle and Mrs. Esther Wigle and in the next photo is Aurelan F. Wigle and Gordon Wigle, all of Detroit. The picture here shows the bow of the yacht which was damaged when the Canadian grain freighter Bricoldoc attempted to rescue the family on storm - tossed Lake Erie. (UPI)

✳ *Tonawanda News headline, November 18, 1961*
(Reprint courtesy of Tonawanda News)

TONAWANDA NEWS

*Serving the Tonawandas,
Kenmore, Town of Tonawanda*

Established 1880   River Rd. and Sommer St., North Tonawanda, N.Y.

Saturday, November 25, 1961

SLOOP IS HELD UP: The sloop Rowdy, owned by Aurelian F. Wigle of Detroit, is still in North Tonawanda today, 10 days after it left Detroit for Florida. The 60-foot vessel was battered by a Lake Erie storm, towed into Buffalo harbor by the Coast Guard, then went aground at a North Tonawanda marina, lost its propeller and drive shaft in the Barge Canal and ended in this ignominious, stern-up position. Capt. Wigle and his brother are making repairs to the Rowdy at the Richardson Boat Co. slip.

✳ *Tonawanda News
headline, November 25,
1961 (Reprint courtesy of
Tonawanda News)*

way, heading down the canal, *Rowdy* lost her propeller and drive shaft. Wigle and his brother lowered the outboard-powered dinghy and attempted to tow *Rowdy* back to the marina, but the dinghy fouled the tow line, threw the two brothers into the water, and sank. With assistance, *Rowdy* made it to the Richardson Boat Company, where she was hauled out of the water to have a new propeller and drive shaft installed (divers could not find the old ones).[1] On Sunday, November 26, at 9:00 a.m., *Rowdy* headed down the Barge Canal and continued her voyage toward Florida.[2]

The two-week ordeal was national news, and stories about it ran in newspapers in Michigan, Pennsylvania, Wisconsin, Virginia, Texas, Ohio, Arizona, New York, Oklahoma, and Indiana. In 1962, Bruce Bingham (who knew *Rowdy* from Detroit) saw *Rowdy* in Bradenton, Florida. She had no mast and was floating extremely high in the water. He was told that her ballast keel had been removed.

1963-1971   In 1963, *Rowdy* was purchased by Frank Winn of El Segundo, California. The Winn family's 50-foot schooner *Emerald* had sunk earlier that summer when she lost power while approaching King Harbor in Redondo Beach. Onboard were Frank, his 19-year-old daughter Sharon, his brother Bob, a black Labrador named Saltie, and his wife Carol, who was at the helm when the engine conked out. It took only minutes for the current to run the boat up against the breakwater, smashing a hole in the hull and sinking her in 35 feet of water.[3]

The family, including Sharon's 13-year-old brother Marc, also lost their home, for they had all been living aboard *Emerald* in King Harbor.[4] They collected the insurance money, and when they found *Rowdy* for sale in Florida, the whole family flew there to buy their new home and sail her back to California. Rill Wigle, the seller, helped the family to sail *Rowdy* on the first leg of the journey, but he parted company with them in

1 *Tonawanda* (New York) *News*, November 24, 1961.
2 *Tonawanda* (New York) *News*, November 27, 1961.
3 The book *Toward a Distant Island* by prolific author Leonard Wibberley (New York: Ives Washburn, Inc. 1966) details the sinking of *Emerald*, as well as Wibberley's undertaking, having purchased the salvage rights from Frank Winn, to raise her (via scuba tanks and 145 inner tubes) and completely restore the yacht.
4 *Daily Breeze* (Torrance, CA), June 8, 1963.

Jamaica before they made the 551-mile hop across to Panama because, as Sharon put it, "He didn't like to be out of sight of land."

Frank and Carol Winn have passed away, but I was lucky enough to establish correspondence with Sharon (Winn) Stewart, who made the trip on *Rowdy* when she was 19, and with Carol's half-brother, Gene Collard, who tape-recorded the Winn family's many stories of their trip. When Sharon moved residences in late 2012, the most miraculous thing happened: She found a forgotten box of over twenty letters that her mother had written detailing the trip as they advanced along their route. All of the letters had been written to Carol's sister, Jeanette Choate. Years after the trip, the box containing the entire collection of letters had fallen into Sharon's possession, where it remained, out of thought, until 2012. Sharon was kind enough to forward the entire box to me, and I was like a kid on Christmas, reading and rereading every letter. It still seems beyond belief that, not only did those letters survive 50 years, but they were all together in one collection—and they landed in my lap! They were postmarked from the Bahamas, Jamaica, Panama, Costa Rica, Nicaragua, and Mexico and, for the most part, were hand-written on old-fashioned, thin, crispy typewriter paper. For a guy like me, researching the history of the boat, it was a one in a million treasure trove.

Daily Breeze

THE ONLY DAILY NEWSPAPER IN THE SOUTH BAY AREA

Saturday, June 8, 1963

CREW SAFE

Schooner Sinks At Breakwater

STILL SHAKEN—Are Frank Winn (right), 41, and his wife, Carol, 37, after they were rescued from their doomed schooner, Emerald, which crashed yesterday on harbor rocks. Mrs. Winn, who had been at the helm, said the Emerald lost steerage afer she turned the craft into the wind preparatory to making a harbor entry.

✳ *Frank and Carol Winn were rescued when their schooner Emerald sank. (Reprint courtesy The Daily Breeze. Article provided by Sharon (Winn) Stewart.)*

✳ *Box of Carol Winn's letters describing the trip from Florida to California. Thank you to Sharon (Winn) Stewart, who, at age 19, was on that trip, for loaning them to me!*

﹡ Rowdy *tuning up in Fort Lauderdale, 1963 (Courtesy Sharon Stewart)*

﹡ *Frank and Carol's bon voyage party (Courtesy Sharon Stewart)*

﹡ Rowdy *leaving Florida, 1963 (Courtesy Sharon Stewart)*

✳ *Rowdy en route to California, 1963 (Courtesy Sharon Stewart)*

The Winns' voyage home, which began on September 15, 1963, and lasted for more than a year, had a bumpy start when the development of Hurricane Edith and then Hurricane Flora forced the Winns to hole up in the Bahamas for three weeks. One of the deadliest Atlantic hurricanes on record, with a death toll of over 7,000, Flora landed practically on top of the Winns as it slammed into Haiti before drifting up over Cuba and then moving away from them, heading far to the northeast and dissipating in the colder northern waters. The Winns continued south to Jamaica and then crossed 551 miles of open ocean, making it nearly to Panama before having to send out a Mayday call after losing power and taking on water. They were towed to port but lacked the funds to pay the tug and were forbidden to leave until the bill could be paid. A few months later, when the insurance money finally secured their release, they took *Rowdy* through the Panama Canal and sailed up the western coast of Central America, touching Costa Rica, Nicaragua, El Salvador, and finally Mexico, where they were disabled by more bad weather and towed into San Diego. Carol's letters painted such a wonderful picture of their journey that I decided to simply reproduce them word for word. "Pancho" in the letters is Frank's nickname. "Bob" is his twin brother Robert. All the letters were addressed to Carol's sister Jeanette Choate and family in Manhattan Beach, California.

Hi Choates,
I just wakened and watched a beautiful sunrise. The rest of the crew is still asleep.
We left Nassau nearly a week ago. Our first stop was Normans Cay. I thought

✳ *The first part of the September 25, 1963, letter.*

Hi Choates,

I just wakened and watched a beautiful
sunrise. The rest of the crew is still asleep.
We left Nassau nearly a week ago. Our first stop
was Norman Cay. I thought when we got in there
that it would surely be our last. The entrance to
the anchorage has a sand bar across with just 5
feet of water over it. We lined ourselves up with
the entrance, with wind abeam, healed over & went thru. The *Rowdy*
draws 6' 8" under power but less than 5' heeled. I kept wondering
what would happen if the wind stopped blowing half way across
that bar. Well it didn't & we sailed out the next morning the
same way. We spent the next night at Halls Pond Cay. We got there
too late to see the channel in so we anchored outside & rocked &
rolled all night, & next AM went to Staniel Cay. We were there
two days wandering around the little village, swimming, fishing &
visiting with other crews. While talking to the owner of another
boat we learned about the spot we are now in. It's called Compass
Cay. There are several small islands surrounding a beautiful
anchorage.

We are tied up to a small dock with the "Norma G." She is
another sloop, about 40'. We are the only boats or people we have
seen in 2 days. There is a path leading up the hill to a really
great club house. We cooked dinner up there last night & I even
cut loose & baked pies. From the house you can see for miles in
all directions, beautiful rolling hills of the surrounding cays,
sky & water. No telephone poles or TV antennas. We plan to stay
here till the weather report improves. There was a storm between
here & Haiti & we are waiting to find out where it's going. There
is a well-protected area about a mile from here & if this nasty
hunk of wind decides to turn into a hurricane we can go in there
& be reasonably safe.[1]

Ah! Another day. The weather report was good yesterday so
we untied dock lines & with a crew from the Norma G & 5 Bahaman
boys aboard as pilots, we threaded our way out of the channel.
Once outside, our pilots, all 7 of them climbed aboard their
outboard which we were towing & waved good bye. We sailed into

---

1 On September 30, 1963, Tropical Storm Flora developed into a hurricane, attaining winds of 145 mph.

Georgetown yesterday around 1:00 P.M. We spent the remainder
of the day cleaning up the *Rowdy* & boy did she need it. We were
beginning to look like a mud hole with crew to match. This AM the
top sides are nice & clean & white & the crew all smell good. I
can't say we look good, but we sure do smell good.

　　　We are all so black and covered with bites & heat rash etc.
that there is really not much we can do about looks. It's much
too hot to wear anything but a bathing suit & I've worn the rear
end out of the both of mine. They have been mended so much that
you can't tell the difference between mend and suit.

　　　By the way, if for some reason you should call us, don't
worry if you don't get an immediate reply. Our radio is playing
games. We receive beautifully, but there are times when we can't
send. We would receive your call but not be able to answer till
we get into port or in contact with another boat.

　　　I guess I'll close now. Skipper has a list of jobs to be
done today so we can make the jump from here to Jamaica & we want
to leave here tomorrow, so it's off to work I go.

　　　Bye Now

　　　Love

　　　Carol

Hi Jan

    Gads it was good to hear your voice.
There were a million things I wanted to say & I
couldn't think of any of them. I was glad to hear
that everyone at home is O.K.

    We have been working like mad trying to
repair the damage done during the storm.[1] We
loosened a few fastenings & scrapped the port
side while we were at the dock. It took an outboard plus 6 men on
the dock in addition to our own crew to get us off the dock when
the winds hit us. The bow is pretty badly chaffed from the anchor
lines. At least the anchor lines held so we won't complain. I've
never heard anything like the wind in the rigging & I hope I never
will again.

    Yesterday we took all the sail bags out of the forepeak &
dried the sails. It took all day. We also took all the clothes and
linens outside to air. It's necessary to do this about once a week
or they start smelling. This climate is a constant fight against
mold & rust.

    There was a pause here of several days. We got the necessary
repairs done & left Georgetown on Friday the 18th. We arrived in
Inagua & it's the 21st. We managed to get hit by a waterspout on
the way here. The only damage done was to the sails & our nerves.
I repaired the main sail on the way & I'll fix the jib today so we
can be ready to leave tomorrow.

    We need fuel & some food here. We will leave in the AM for
Jamaica. As you can see from your map we're only 40 miles from
Cuba. We will cut right between Haiti & Cuba. Hope our navigator
is on the ball.

    As I told you in my wire & here, our next main port is
Kingston, Jamaica. We should be there in a couple of days. It
depends on how much work there is to be done. We will stock there
for the jump to Colon at the Panama Canal. Our mailing address
there will be:

Yacht Rowdy
C/O Balboa Yacht Club
Balboa, Panama
Please hold

POSTMARK
25
Oct
1963

---

1 *Rowdy* had to hole up for three weeks in Georgetown to wait out Hurricane Edith and Hurricane Flora.

Our next mailing address will be Mazatlan. We will have many more stops before there but don't know addresses.

Mr. or Mrs. Frank Winn
C/O Sinora Cecilia Eimbcke
15 V Carranza Sur
Mazatlan, Sin, Mexico
Please hold

Tell everyone to write. I'm home sick.

I'm sorry to have had to ask for money. We have some in our savings but it would take nearly 2 weeks to get it. At least it took that long in Florida.

Oh yes — next time you write will you send Pat Keine (spelling) & Virginia Maynard's address. I'd like to drop them a card to thank them again for the clothes. I also don't have the Luke's or C.M.'s address.

As to Pancho's job? We just received on the 17th of October a wire from Standard[1] stating that his leave had been denied & that he was being considered AWOL. It was sure nice of them to let him know. They never said if they intended to take him back or not. He had been AWOL for a month before he got the wire.

We had a regular bird sanctuary on the way here from Georgetown. We had 3 birds, 2 were like sparrows only yellow. They were so tame they would walk right across our feet & kept us amused for 2 days. The other one was a tern who we named terd bird. He was with us a whole day and our deck will never be the same. Poor guy he was sick and couldn't fly. We lost him last night in a squall. He got washed over the side. I'm glad it wasn't me.

Lord you've never heard so much screaming. "Come on Carol stop writing & start cooking. We're starved. What do we do today, eat lunch instead of breakfast? Look Pancho, I'm losing weight, she's starving us." I give up. I'd better feed the slobs.

Bye now. I'll try to call & let you know when we get to Jamaica & I'll write.

Love
Carol
Be sure to give Ray and the kids a kiss for me.

---

1 Frank Winn worked for Standard Oil.

Hi Jan & all

     We got the money. Thank you. I'm sure it
should be enough to see us home unless something
very unusual happens.

     Jamaica is beautiful, lush & green & very
warm, but no bugs. Two men from the yacht club
have offered to take us for a drive tomorrow so
we can see some points of interest.

     We invited a large group to go for an afternoon sail today. They
have been so very nice to us & this was about the only way we could
repay their hospitality. There should be about 30 in the group.

     They are having a regatta next week starting Tuesday. They all
sail to Pigeon Isl. about 25 miles away, stay there Wed. then race
back Thurs., then small races Fri., Sat. and Sun. We were invited
to join them but we want to leave here Tues. if tropical storm
Helena will let us. Where Helena is right now we would go right
through it to get to Panama, so again we will wait and see.

     Jan you sound concerned about the hop from here to Panama.
DON'T BE. It is 551 miles of beautiful open water, no reefs, no
rocks, no hazards at all. I personally feel much safer in open water
than when we get in around shore. We can handle the water, its rocks
that frighten me. I almost developed an ulcer in the shallow water
of the Bahamas. We won't leave here until the weather report is
good. The trip should take around 6 days depending on the winds. We
carry enough water and food for 14 days without rationing. We carry
500 gallons of water in our main tank and have two 55 gallon kegs on
deck. Our navigation so far has been right on the nose. Our skipper
is the best & if I must say so the crew is pretty darned good too.
We have radio crystals for both Jamaica & Panama as well as 2182
(Coast Guard) so we won't be out of radio contact.

     It will be a couple of weeks at least before you hear from me
again. I'll try & call from Panama.

     Our hop from Inagua here was very interesting. We were checked
by US bombers, Germans off a carrier, small fighters from a land
base, destroyer escorts & helicopters. Many of each. We were also
checked by two large military vessels in the middle of the night.
One on each side of us within hailing distance but they didn't call
us and we still don't know whose side they were on. I'll say adios
for now. Give the kids & Raymond kisses for me. Thanks again for
the letters & the money. I don't know which I appreciate most. It
was so great hearing from you & Paula & Den. Thanks again

     Love Sis

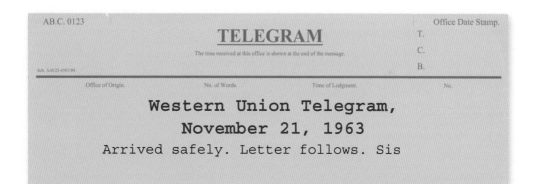

**Western Union Telegram,
November 21, 1963**
Arrived safely. Letter follows. Sis

Hi you lucky dry people

Boy oh boy this was just about the longest, wettest 551 miles in history. We left Kingston on Sat. the 9th & arrived here [Panama] on Mon. the 18th, then it took another day to clear customs & immigration. They finally let us bring the boat into a dock at their yacht club.

Our last few days in Kingston were a mess. Our skipper & crew members decided (with our complete agreement) to leave us. I wired the bank & got the last of our money to pay the skipper off. Unfortunately we had trusted him & had not drawn up an written agreement as to wages. When we went to pay him he claimed we owed him half again as much. We ended up having to give him all our remaining money including an airline ticket to Florida. Boy you live & learn!

We met 2 Australian boys at the yacht club who said they would like to join us. Since we really needed help & they said they would buy their own food, we signed them on. So far they have been just great. When we went to clear immigration on departure we found that Rill (skipper) had not properly entered us (as skipper this was his duty & again we trusted him. In fact customs & immigration won't let the owner clear the vessel & crew. It must be thru the master.) In fact we had been in Jamaica for 2 weeks illegally. There was so much discussion about fines & jail terms. Finally they decided it had not been our fault & since the skipper was already on his way to Florida, they would let us go.

We had beautiful sailing the first couple of days. Very heavy seas but a good, steady wind. Then the old sh*** hit the fan. At about 1:30 AM we were blasted out of our bunks by

Pancho's gentle bellers "all hands on deck." By the time we got
top side the main was in shreds & the jib had gone in 2 places.
He had been hit by a real squall &, being a dark night, he didn't
see it coming. It took all 7 of us to get the canvas off her.
We kicked over old Bessy & stayed under power till the wind died
to a normal breeze & then hoisted another jib. That day within
a period of 1hr & 20 min. we blew out 3 more jibs. All in light
air. The swells were so huge & the seas so confused that we would
heal way over, which would spill the air out of the sail, then we
would suddenly roll the other way. The sails would fill so fast
just from rolling that it sounded like a shot gun blast. This is
the day we also ran out of water in our main tank & had to drink
water from the kegs on deck which tasted foul. The whole crew
had diarrhea & were vomiting. Then we started taking on water
(salt). Our generator wouldn't run with us rolling so badly so
we couldn't use the 110V bilge pump. The starboard fuel tank
came loose & got water in the gas so our engine wouldn't run, so
we couldn't use the pump on it & we wore out the hand pump. We
started a bucket brigade & I got on the radio & started sending
a May Day for help. By this time we were within about 30 miles
of the Canal & when it would stop raining a little we could pick
up a 5 second flashing light that is just south of the Canal.
We got only one answer from our May Day & he was 125 miles from
us. The next evening we spotted a freighter (The Walter Rice).
We sent off rockets & flares & used a flashlight to signal SOS.
They spotted us & came along side at 7:30 PM. They asked if we
could send someone over to them in our dingy & guess who was
elected. This was my first & I hope my last experience with
a Jacobs ladder. Lindsey (one of the new crew) rowed me over.
The dingy would go way up on a swell, crash into the boat, then
drop way down again. Someone on deck told me to grab the ladder
when he gave the word. He yelled "grab" & I grabbed & much to my
surprise a minute later found myself on deck. By this time I was
shaking so badly I needed help to walk. The captain got all the
information as to the *Rowdy*'s condition & started calling for
further assistance. Then he sent us down to take hot showers &
gave us coffee. He finally got hold of a tug who said he could
get there by 3:00 AM. He suggested that we go back to the *Rowdy*
before another squall hit or we would not be able to. The cook

made up a lunch to take back. We went back down that horrible ladder & rowed over to the *Rowdy*. Walter Rice stood by us till 1:00 AM. They had picked up the tug on radar & said it should be there shortly. It finally arrived at 4:00 AM. It took them 14 ¼ hours to tow us in. They left us out on what they call the flats with just the water that the Walter Rice had given us & still no means of pumping. Like I said it took still another day to get permission to come in to a dock.

Oh yes, I broke a tooth and had an exposed nerve all this time. Immigration finally gave me permission to go to a hospital & have it pulled. We are now just sitting here waiting for a reply to a wire sent to the insurance company. The insurance surveyor was here yesterday & agreed to the damage we claimed; in fact he saw some things we hadn't seen.

Everything inside the boat is wet. We had water over the floorboards. I doubt if the carpet will ever dry. All the bunks & bedding are still wet.

We haven't gotten your mail yet. If there is any it should come from the other yacht club today or tomorrow. I'll write again & let you know when we are leaving and all. We are all feeling fine again. We're tired but as soon as we get the boat cleaned up we intend taking a whole day to just sleep. Everyone says hi! Marc wants to go home & go fishing with Paula. Pancho says he can almost taste the turkey. Sharon wants to reserve a hot bath for about a week. The Australians want to see the U.S.A. I just want to make it home by Xmas. I really miss you all.

Have you ever seen anyone who can get as fouled up as the Winns? Believe it or not we are all in good spirits & are looking forward to the rest of the trip. We have found out that Pancho as skipper is doing a better job than the old skipper & we are all much happier.

Love XXXXX

Carol

POSTMARK
25
Nov
1963

How about this, 2 letters in a week.
This is the darnedest place I've ever seen.
It's a maze of red tape & channels. One can't
do anything without permission. When I had my
tooth pulled I had to have permission from
Immigration & a letter from the secretary of
the yacht club stating that I was only in this
port temporarily aboard a foreign yacht. One can't buy even a
quart of engine oil (even if we had the money) without a courtesy
card, which we can't get because we are not employed in the Canal
Zone. Of course there are always ways of getting around this.
You find someone in the zone with a card & if he is not busy at
the time he will make the purchase for you, providing of course
that the purchase is not so huge as to arouse suspicion. I have
never seen so many government employees. They all have a job to
do & they go thru the motions of doing it. We were visited by 3
government launches at anchor. One checked our passports, one
our health card, and one checked for rats. When we did not have
anything to show that we had ever been de-ratted, the man gave
us 6 cans of roach killer and said not to tell anyone & left,
giving us a clean bill of health. Oh yes, the man that gave the
vaccinations also measured the *Rowdy* to determine the fee for
going thru the canal. Pancho & I also made 3 trips into customs
on further red tape. In order to be allowed to enter what they
(with straight faces yet) call the yacht club, we had to be a
member of a foreign yacht club. King Harbor Yacht Club doesn't
know it yet but they have 2 new members. Unfortunately we seem to
have lost our card but could send for a new one which might take
some time. It worked anyway. Our only other alternative was the
government dock, which for a small fee would allow us to tie up
there. ($10 per day in advance)

We have been drying sails and doing laundry, working on the
generator & engine etc. This drying bit is a laugh. In November
it rains an average of 20 days. So you can imagine how much
drying we're doing. I'll sure be glad to get out of here. I'll be
glad to get back to nice cold, sunny Calif.

Must go to the market before it closes.

Another day — On the way home from the market yesterday I

was approached by three separate groups of Panamanians, all with tears down their faces asking me if I had heard about our beloved president. I had not at the time heard anything. When I got back to the *Rowdy* I heard over the Radio (which is army operated as is TV) About Pres. Kennedy's death. We could hardly believe our ears. It's still hard to believe. All the shows, stores & places of entertainment are closed till after the funeral. There is no TV or radio either till then. I imagine it's the same in the states.

When we got into the Canal Zone Marc was running a slight temp. He was checked by the man with the shots who was to send a doctor to the boat. Last night Marc's temp went up to 104°. Today I reported it to the health department & even being Sunday it took about 10 minutes to have a doctor here. He gave Marc a very thorough exam & said he thought it was a case of the flu but in any case he can't leave the boat till his temp is normal for 24 hours. He feels pretty good today.

I called Balboa Yacht Club yesterday about our mail & the SOBs had returned it all to the senders. It was all I could do to keep from crying when I heard it. They said there was a whole stack too. I hope everyone will write again. We are really getting hungry for mail.

I stopped writing yesterday to watch another yacht come in. It's a beautiful Ketch out of Texas. When they tied up they were met by customs and doctors & men with inhalators & stretchers. There was a man aboard who had a heart attack. Boy & we think we have troubles.

Marc is much better today. His temp is normal. Darned kids just like to scare us to death.

Well I think I'll go take a shower then get back to work. Everyone but Marc is still asleep so I can get a shower before I cook breakfast for a change. Besides the sun is out & I hate to waste it.

Bye for now
Love
Carol

Undated

Dear Paula [Jeanette's daughter]

Yesterday I went over to Balboa Yacht Club & picked up the mail we thought had been lost. There was one from you. We really enjoy hearing from you. We do the same thing with your letters as you do with ours. Everyone just grabs & everyone reads all the mail over & over again.

Your letters are always our favorite.

Panama is a very interesting place. It's not as beautiful as Jamaica.

The other night a man took our whole crew up on a hill overlooking the Gaton Locks. We all laid on the grass for hours watching the boats being lifted up into lake Gaton. The man had a little dog just about like Specks. I had more fun playing with her.

Well honey I'd better get to work. There is much sanding & scrapping to do before we paint the bottom. Bye for now

Love & kisses

Aunt Carol

Hi again

I just received your wire. The address is correct. I hate like h*** having to have you send more money, but it looks like there is no other way.

We don't know as yet how much we will need. Our insurance is $250 deductable so this much plus gas & food we are sure of. The insurance Co. has told us to send the bills to them but the tug Co. says we can't leave until they are paid. I don't know yet how the yard or the sail maker will handle it.

Marc is fine today. Sharon is down now. I don't know if I told you but she got a reaction and secondary infection from her vaccination. When the doctor was here to see Marc he left a prescription for her. Pancho & the 2 Australians were going into town so I asked if they would get the prescription filled. The dumb clowns lost it. The doctor wasn't in yesterday, so bright & early this AM I took her to his office. He told me to take her back to the boat & he would get some penicillin & bring it down. He didn't have any in his office. He came down here and shot her with 1,800,000 units. She is pretty sick this afternoon and her arm is a mess but he guaranteed she will be OK in a couple days if she doesn't get a reaction to the penicillin.

We have had 2 dry days in a row & I have absolute mountains of dry laundry. Even the bunks and carpet are dry. Pancho and Glenn have the engine & generator torn apart. Lindsey is repairing and resetting the stanchions that got torn loose. Bob is tearing the winches apart and cleaning them. The sail maker is working on the main sail. Marc is getting in the way. Sharon is sleeping & I'm doing laundry, cleaning & running errands. By the way today I mailed 16 rolls of movie film & 7 rolls of 35mm to be processed & sent to your house. I hope the damp mess has not already gotten to it. It should take about a month to get to you. If it beats us there feel free to open it & have a look. I hope some of it will be worthwhile.

The prices here are horrible. Canned goods are beyond belief. A small can of tomato sauce is $.25. Chicken $.70 per pound. Eggs about $.60 per dozen (not bad). Milk $.30 qt. But meat is cheap $.35 per pound for good prime rib roast.

I want to get this in the mail so I'll close & call or write as soon as we know something definite.

Bye Again

Love Carol

January 18

Hi Jeanette & all

Yesterday I received your letter postmarked the 10th. Usually we get your mail in 2 days.

I imagine there has been some news in the papers about the situation here. If it's anything like the news here it's not too accurate. In the first place the riots all over Panama broke out within an hour or two of each other. These groups were too well organized to be spur of the moment. The Gatun Chamber of Commerce had a meeting 2 nights ago & showed movies of the flag episode in Balboa. They plainly show that the Panamanian flag was torn when a Panamanian student fell while he & a fellow student were carrying the flag. It was not torn by the Canal Zone student. Also the papers here have the big, bad Americans as the aggressors. We have pictures of our own taken with Bob's telephoto lens of the border between Colon & Cristobal. In Cristobal CZ our soldiers are down behind sand bags, they never expose themselves. They are in armor, ie: Breast plates & crotch plates. When they had to move from one point to another, they moved fast & ran a zig zag course. Now, unless our army is made up of 100% cowards, you'd think that maybe there was some danger from snipers or something. Right across the street from them in Colon, Panama, there were mobs on the street corner, women standing in doorways, small children playing on the sidewalks. The mobs were milling, shouting mobs, and yet there was no fear in the people around them. It seems to me that if our soldiers had been shooting their direction, they would have at least had their small children off the streets. Our soldiers were armed, they had one chip of amo each & orders not to shoot. They were allowed to use tear gas only & if the mobs still came they could shoot over their heads. I understand this did happen in Balboa but the tear gas kept them from crossing here.

Four ships from the U.S. Caribbean ready fleet just left yesterday. The captains & officers used the Yacht Club as a command post & after their meetings we were always invited to join them. We had them aboard the *Rowdy* & they in turn had us aboard their ships for lunch and dinners. They also helped us by keeping us supplied with food. For 6 days we were pretty well isolated here. Tom Clark brought down what food he could get, but it was difficult for him to get here, so the navy was very much appreciated.

Now for a point of humor. Your brother in law [Frank Winn] is now a jail bird. He spent 33 minutes in the Cristobal jail.

Commander Pitts of the "Unalde" asked us if it was possible for us to go for a sail. We said "no, we have orders from the port captain to stay here till our tug bill is paid." He asked us if we would like to go out if he could get permission. We said we would love it. He got on the phone, and in 5 minutes, he had the OK from Captain Cooney, acting port captain. We called Tom Clark (he has a license to operate a boat under 65'). Tom, Betty & their son Cris arrived about the time we had everything stored & ready to go. We also had with us, a marine Lt., a Swiss couple who are docked next to us, Pierre & Claudia Leonard (a friend) & Ike, a marine captain. We sailed around the harbor & ran across another navy ship. We invited their captain aboard & also a group of his men. This is an underwater demolition squad. We couldn't take all of them at once so they followed us in a launch and kept switching crew. About 4 PM a CZ police launch came along side & told us that we were not to return to the yacht club; that we were to go to the flats and anchor out. Commander Pitts had been told by Captain Cooney to stay inside the harbor & that he would be responsible for bringing the yacht back to the club. He immediately went below and got his hat and shirt which he had earlier taken off. The launch disappeared & about ½ hour or so later another police launch appeared with a warrant for Pancho's arrest. The commander asked if the owner could stay aboard till we got back to the club dock & they said yes they would follow us. They took Pancho off the boat just before we docked. The charges were for operating a boat inside the harbor without a licensed operator. As soon as we tied up Tom Clark & the commander went to the police department to be greeted by the desk Sgt. saying "Yes I know we goofed." Tom's reply was "in other words you have Mr. Winn here under false arrest." The Sgt. said "no I didn't say that." At any rate Capt. Cooney had not told his relief port captain, Capt. Allen, that he had given permission, & Capt. Allen neglected to ask if there was

a licensed operator aboard. They ended up calling in a judge &
holding court & dismissing Pancho. Capt. Cooney even offered to
post bail if they couldn't get the judge right away. Talk about
red faces. Pancho had been taken off the *Rowdy*, booked, finger
printed, photographed, tried, released & was back in the club in
33 minutes. I've heard that the port captain's office is a little
worried about a law suit. Pancho was just plain embarrassed. The
club was loaded with naval officers & it didn't make us very
happy to have him arrested in front of all these men.

 Must close now. Give all the kids kisses.

Bye now

Love + XXX

 The very *Rowdy* crew & its jail bird

Hi Choates

 Well today was a day for tears. Sharon &
I anyway.

 We received a very much needed & even
more appreciated check from the Choates. Then
we received a huge envelope from Herb Zalabak.
It had one of those paper Xmas trees in it.
Sharon & I promptly sat down on the floor & cried. We knew in our
hearts that we couldn't possibly get home this month but the tree
really brought it home.

 Then as if enough tears hadn't been shed, we had to wave
good bye to Glenn & Lindsay. They had to get going and just
couldn't wait any longer. They signed off the *Rowdy* & onto the
"Synfoni". The "Synfoni" came in here about a week or so ago &
the owner had had a heart attack. They needed extra hands to get
her back to Texas. This was made to order for the boys. We all
hated to see them leave. It not only leaves us shorthanded but we
enjoyed their company.

 The *Rowdy* is still on the ways. We will put her in the water
in the AM. We put a new boot cap on her — 2 coats & 2 coats of
bottom paint. We painted the freeboard up a couple of feet under

the counter. The rest of the freeboard we can get when she is in the water. She looks so pretty I hate to put her back in this oily water. There is another man coming to see if he can get the generator running. Our main sail is ready to be bent on & the engine is running.

As soon as we get the bill for the generator work, we can send all the bills along with our statement, the marine protest, and a list of damages to the insurance Co. Then we sit & wait to hear from them. I sure hope it doesn't take long.

Gads what we wouldn't give to be at Den's game tonight. Thanks for letting us know they are coming out anyway. We really are interested. This is the coldest group of people I've ever been around. There are a few that have really been great, but the rest let it be clearly understood that visiting yachts are not wanted. It's a far cry from Jamaica where at least 150 people came down and introduced themselves & welcomed us. These were all members of the Royal Jamaican Yacht Club.

I'd better not get started about this place or I'll still be raving tomorrow. I could go on and on about some of the things that have happened since we've been here. Sharon is sitting here waiting for the pen so I'll write again later. Thanks again.

Be good, write

Love

Carol

Postdated December 13, 1963

Hi Sis

There really isn't anything new to tell you. The bills & forms have been sent to the insurance company. We are getting all the odds and ends ready to leave even though we have no idea when it will be. We want to be ready any way.

Last Sunday 2 couples, Tom & Betty Clark and Lina & Monty Montgomery came down and said "come on *Rowdys* you need a day off." We were told to grab our bathing suits & climb in the cars.

They & their many children took us to see Fort San Lorenzo. This is the ruins of the fort that Henry Morgan took from the Spaniards in 1671. They were very interesting. I could have spent all day wandering around but our hosts had other ideas. We drove on the most beautiful road I've ever seen. It's cut right through the jungle. It is very rough, not paved, but nobody noticed the bumping. We ended up at Pina Beach which is at the end of the Chagues River, right across from Ft. San Lorenzo. They had everything for a wiener bake in their cars. We swam and ate all afternoon & evening. I was assistant cook. I sliced the buns. After this, as if it wasn't already enough, we went to the Clarks for pie & coffee, at which time I was led into the bathroom, handed a jar of bubble bath, & told to have fun. By the time I came downstairs, the Montgomerys had left & Betty had beds made up for us. Imagine a bath & a bed all in the same night. Tom accused me of sneaking back into the bath in the middle of the night but I really didn't. I guess this is about all for now. I'll write again – you too

Love Carol

Thanks for saving the letters

Dated December 19, 1963

Hi Sis

Ah! Peace & quiet! Pancho & Bob went with Monte to get a car running. Marc went in the dingy to visit some kids on another boat. Sharon is asleep. My boat wifely duties are all done. I have some varnish work to do but it will only take about an hour. I have one great problem. Shall I sleep or read?

Last night the Clarks & Montgomerys & Winns had a pot luck. Betty Clark had a huge standing rib roast & I brought apple pies. All the other food was Panamanian. The vegetable was Chiotes (a kind of squash). Instead of potatoes we had a yuka, scalloped just like you would do with a potato. Monty fixed sause, this is fresh pig's feet boiled with hot peppers & onions & then cucumber added. We ate these before dinner when they were just barely warm. Betty made a native drink, made with some kind of leaves or ginger root & cloves. Very good straight or with gin or what-have-you. We had a real nice time & as usual when we are at the Clark's, the whole gang ends up on the floor with many pillows, listening to records.

Your hostess dress sounds great. If it isn't summer by the time we get home, you'll have to wear it.

Is Den going with Pam again? Herb wrote last week & said that Uncle Frank would like to meet us & sail home. We have given our OK. I guess he will meet us somewhere in Mexico. How about you guys joining the good ship *Rowdy*, her crew & the other *Rowdy* fan clubbers in San Diego or points south & sail home? I don't think I can wait till we get to Portofino to see you. I don't know how many of the others will make it but it doesn't matter. There's plenty of room. We can divide into 3 watches, sleeping, working & drinking. This way we can have bunks for 27 people. Oh hell. Sharon just woke up. No more peace & quiet. I guess I might just as well get to my varnishing. Also I just had a call from the insurance surveyor. He wants me to check our policy to see if we can claim "lay time." Since we are being held here till the claim is settled he thinks they should pay dockage.

I just took time out to read the policy again & I cannot find a thing. They won't pay crew wages while being held up, but they don't say a thing about dockage.

I'll have to go call him back. Will write again

Love & Kisses & tears

Carol

Dated January 6, 1964

Hi again. I didn't even try to write over the holidays. I almost called Xmas Eve but I knew we would just spend the 3 minutes crying so I forgot it.

We were invited to a Dutch tug on Xmas Eve. We had a nice party & dinner. Xmas Day we went to the Clark's for dinner & drinks. We had a good time, these are wonderful people. For a whole week we were kept busy. One of the crowd would be here when we wakened in the AM with some place to take us or something new to see. We've had another beach party complete with the crew off the tug, the crew off a Swiss yacht, the Clarks, Montgomerys, Allens & Winns. We sounded like the United Nations. With Dutch, German, French, Spanish (Panamanian) & English.

New Year's Eve the Montgomerys had us over for dinner & a party. The dinner was really something. We all went out the day before and bought a pig. That is Monty bought a pig, had it slaughtered & we ate him at midnight, New Year's Eve. Monty's Panamanian wife "Tita" explained that there must be much food on the table when the New Year comes in if you are to prosper during the year.

We've been rock hunting down rivers, shell hunting on the beach, drives through the jungle. Someone asked us yesterday if we would like to make the 50 mile hike across the isthmus on the Las Cruces Trail. I nearly fainted.

In the first half of this letter I mentioned that Uncle Frank might meet us in Mexico. Well it looks like he might meet us here. If so, we've asked him to bring some of Sharon's clothes. They are in the luggage that we sent to you. She wants her blue dress, 2 cotton skirts with blouses, a black silk shirt & a white long sleeve blouse. He will be calling you I imagine. If he decides to come, that is.

Well I've gone as far as a stamp will allow so I'll close & write again later.

Love Sis

Hi Loves

    Again I must say thank you. The insurance company will pay for all of the repairs & replacements after we complete the work. We cannot get a number of items here so we will have to wait till we get home & then submit the rest of the bills. What a mess.

    We are like a bunch of cats on a tin roof.

    We checked food prices at the in-bond stores. Found them just about twice what the Canal Zone workers get theirs for. Several friends said "don't buy from them, we'll supply your stores." It's a riot. These poor people spend half the day finding what we need then sneak it to us late at night. This has been going on for over a week now & we are not finished yet. I hope we don't get caught.

    It's been so darned long since I've written that I don't know where to start. Abuelo [Frank Winn's Uncle Frank] arrived safely but very tired. The heat has bothered him some, but I think he will be OK.

    The bathing suits are both perfect. I'm glad you put my name on the red & blue one, I like it best.

    Our Xmas & New Years were sad and lonesome but the friends we have met here kept us so busy that they flew by.

    Marc shaved his peach fuzz off on New Year's Eve & thinks he's now a man. He has grown at least 2 inches. He's also lost some of his fat. Wish I could say the same.

    My dam*** back had been bothering me for about a month & it finally got bad enough that I went to the hospital for treatment, which they refused to give. They examined me and said it had the ear marks of a disk. They checked reflexes & length of right leg & muscle tone of same leg & said there was nothing that could be done without traction or surgery. I refused & said I'd take care of it at home. The Dr. said he thought if I stayed completely off my feet for a couple of weeks it would ease the pain. He also gave me codeine & something else to kill the pain. I came back to the boat & played Lady Astor for 2 weeks & lo & behold its better. I was afraid for a while I would have to fly home. This has created another problem though. It leaves the crew shorthanded with me not being able to pull or lift & the possibility of me ending up back in my bunk again. We have

finally decided to sign on a Panamanian [Dice] who has helped us
on the *Rowdy* since we have been here. He has been recommended by
the club & many separate members for his work & honesty. We've
seen him daily since we have been here & like him. He & Marc are
seldom apart & he treats Abuelo like his own father. He is 39
years old & is of Spanish-Indian descent. He wants to go & will
go for just his room & board. He has sailed quite a bit so he
should be all we need. He would like to stay in the states & work
but this is something to take care of when we get home. Abuelo
says he can find him a job at General Chemical. He speaks nearly
perfect English so a job shouldn't be too much of a problem.
If he doesn't get work, we will have to fly him home. But like
Pancho says 3000 miles is a long way to go with a boy & girl, 2
men & 2 invalids as crew.

     Anyway if we can get him entry papers we will bring him.

     The pictures are some that we got out of the photo shop
hours before it burned down. Please keep them in case our
negatives are bad.[1]

     We should be leaving next Thurs. AM. Our next mailing
address will be

     Yacht Club de Pescas
     Acapulco, Mexico
     Mark your letter "hold for the yacht Rowdy"
     The next address will be
     Senoria Eimbke
     15 V, Carranza Sur
     Mazatlan Sin, Mexico
     Mark your letters "hold for arrival"

     Bye now
     Love & XXX
     Carol

---

1   The camera shop was set afire during the rioting.

Undated[1]

Hi all you lovely land lubbers

Well we finally made it to the Pacific. It was a tough struggle but we made it. The *Rowdy* fan club, Panamanian chapter, was out in force. A group came down Wed. night with a load of ice & many cases of beer & harder stuff that filled the ice chest that sits on deck to the brim, said "see you in the AM" & took off. I made potato salad, baked ham, fruit salad, corned beef, michi bread (like pinch rolls), pickles etc. We got everything done except for gas pumped into the tanks, & collapsed at 2 AM. At 4:30 we were up again. Pancho filled the tanks, we got 3 of the 4 hand lines ready. (We required 4 lines 120 ft. long to hold us in the center of the canal, 2 starboard, 2 port). We could not find the 4th (it is now found). At 5 AM the pilot came aboard & started pacing back & forth. The port captain had told us we would leave at 6 AM. He paced & we stalled. At 5:30 Ronnie and Bob Nye came aboard with a huge birthday cake for Sharon. Not many gals transit the canal on their 20th, huh?[2] Arturo (one of the waiters from the Pan Canal Club) got there around 5:45. At 6 sharp the Clarks showed up. As they were running down the dock, the Pilot said "This is it. Leave now or not at all." So we threw off the lines slowly, letting the Clarks jump aboard. We were at the locks 20 minutes early. Tom & Pancho had a talk. They agreed Pancho should take the helm since he knew the handling of the *Rowdy* best & since Pancho had never gone thru the canal before, & Tom has had many crossings on small boats, he would be in charge of the line men (Sharon & Arturo on the starboard bow, Bob Winn on the port bow, Dice on the port stern, Bob Nye on the starboard stern, me hiding my eyes). The pilot was to give the orders to Tom & Pancho only. We motored into position in the center of the first lock (there are 3). The men on the wall yelled "Heads up" & 4 monkey fists [ends of ropes tied in knots that serve as weights, making the ropes easier to throw and catch] came hurling across our decks. Our lines were fastened to their throwing lines, then pulled up on the wall & made fast. As the water began to fill the lock, all four lines are pulled

---

1 February 21, 1964.
2 Sharon's twentieth birthday was on February 20.

in so that there is no slack in any line, this holds the ship
straight & keeps her from jerking & possibly breaking the lines.
Bud Allen who was working & couldn't transit with us, locked up
his control house & yelled his good byes' from the wall. When the
lock was full, the men on the dock took their end of the lines
forward, literally walking us to the next lock. Monty cheered
us thru this one & the 3rd, & ended up getting permission from
the port captain to join us at the end of the 3rd lock. When we
pulled over to pick him up, Dale Fontaine was with him. He had to
be to work at 8:30 but wanted to say good bye. The pilot wouldn't
let us sail across the lake so we motored. We got within 1 mile
of the first down lock & the engine stopped. The wind was on our
stern & we were still doing 3 knots when the line men got the
lines on her & stopped her in perfect position. Pancho discovered
that the spring on the points had broken and our spare set was
defective. We were towed into a small boat club called Pedro
Miguel & threw out the anchor. The pilot called marine traffic
& told them we were out of commission for the night at least. It
was now about 2 PM I think. A launch picked him up and he left.
Tom rowed over to a pipe line & walked the line into the club.
It was slimey & he fell in 7 times all told. We laughed till
it hurt. Most of us ended up ashore after that. The wonderful
people at the club started digging thru their spare parts & came
up with 2 sets of points. Pancho installed one set and old Bessy
started ticking away. We called marine traffic & got re-scheduled
for 9:20 on the last 2 down locks. Tom, as a licensed operator
took responsibility so no pilot was necessary. At 9:20 sharp we
entered the locks only to have the dock master charge down the
wall yelling "Get out! Get out!" It seems there was an error at
marine traffic & the traffic scheduled for 9:20 was too big. We
backed rapidly out of the lock & tied up on the wall just as the
big monster passed our bow. UGH! We tied up to a wall & waited
for the next lockage (about an hour). These 2 down locks were
uneventful. We tied up at a buoy at 12:30 AM. Oh yes, 5 members
of the Pedro Miguel Boat Club joined us from their club to the
Balboa Yacht Club. At about 1:30 most of these wonderful people
left us to go take a train all the way back to Cristobal. They
didn't get there till 6 AM & had to be at work at 7 AM. We were

so tired we could hardly make it to our bunks, in fact Marc didn't, he slept in the middle of the floor.

Pancho is at the moment at the Port Captain's office getting our final clearance. We will take on water & gas in the AM & be off.

We have met some really wonderful people here & if we had jobs or money it would have been great, but alas we had neither.

You'll hear from us in a couple of weeks. In the meantime, love to all. My back's fine
Love
Carol

Undated[1]

We left Balboa about 1:30 PM 2 weeks ago tomorrow. The wind was on our stern & the sea just a little heavy. We had a beautiful 3 ½ hour run, then things started to happen. The topping lift broke (a brand new one) and the boom parted from the gooseneck (this is the fitting that holds the boom to the mast). When the latter happened the boom came apart at the seams, literally. Our boom is a beautiful piece of woodwork. 27 feet long, made out of 8 fitted pieces, glued and rounded. It's hollow. Anyway after a he** of a struggle in the wind with no topping lift we got the sail down & a wailing crew started back for Panama. It took us 7 ½ hours to get back in using a jib & engine. We thought that this was the end of the road. A new boom would cost a fortune & this one looked beyond repair. We talked it over & decided to take it ashore where Sharon & I could scrape the paint off it so we could see what we really had. The end that fits into the gooseneck was beyond hope but the rest looked like with the right glue & stainless steel bands it could be saved. We inspected it inch by inch, decided on a plan of attack, called on several experts for advice (also received much non expert advice). I'm not going to go into detail about what we did but it's on the *Rowdy* again & looks stronger & better than ever. All this took us 9 days. The 9th night Major & Martha Dill invited the whole crew to their home for dinner. A quick one they assured us, & they would have us back aboard at 7:30 PM for a good night's sleep. Ha! This was Saturday night. Well it ended up with about 25 people & giant Sunday hangovers. So it was Mon. AM at 7:30 that we again left Balboa. We made 126 miles the first 24 hrs. & had only gone about 50 in the next 48 hrs. For the last 2 days we have passed the same point of land 3 times. We sail by in the afternoon then lose all the wind and drift back where we started. Tuesday AM we had the belt that drives the engine water pump and generator break & we can't use the engine. I should say couldn't. We now have made several rope belts, the first of which held for 1 ½ hrs. this AM. We spotted a turtle this AM while the engine was running so after it we went. Sharon maneuvered the *Rowdy* to within about 50 feet. Pancho went over the side, put a rope around it, after a fair attempt on the part of the turtle

---

1 March 7, 1964.

to relieve Pancho of his hand or a foot. It's now tied up on the deck. All I could hear while this was going on was "Turtle steak tonight." Now I can't find anyone to butcher him, and now they are trying to get the damn thing to eat. The kids have even given him a bath, he smelled fishy. His name is "Culo Dulce" which isn't very nice but we are running out of nice names for our pets.

I didn't tell you any more about our gift for Den, but I think it's left us so I'll give you the whole bit. Marc wanted to get an iguana for Den & I finally said OK, if he built the cage & took care of it. He didn't get one, he got three. Gads are they horrible. We have had them aboard for nearly a month. We named one Sheldon, one Cecil the seasick sea serpent & Bolivar Sanchez De Cordova. To begin with we don't know much about Iguanas because in the last month all three have laid eggs. Now can you imagine Sheldon laying an egg? To make matters worse they chewed through the wire on their cage & 2 have gotten out. We keep the cage in the dingy, but we also keep all our rope, buckets, ladder, brushes and several life jackets there. We know one is in the cage, one went over the side & when last seen was swimming for Punto Puerco, Panama. The third one could still be in the dingy, inside the boat or swimming. Frankly it makes me a little uncomfortable when I hit the sack to know that Sheldon might be there before me. In fact I've noticed nearly the entire crew straightening their beds very thoroughly when they get up & when they climb in.

It's the next AM about 10 I think. I came off watch at 8 AM, fixed breakfast (scrambled eggs & coffee), watched Abuelo & Marc each catch a bonito, & then retired to my favorite spot for writing, the forepeak. I lay across my bunk with my back against the bulkhead & prop my feet against the hatch. Normally this hatch is between & above the 2 bunks, but when we are sailing healed over like we are this AM, my feet are almost level with my hips & it puts me in a semi sitting position. Sounds comfy huh?

The Pacific so far has been very kind to us. Very calm & beautiful. In about an hour we will be passing the end of Isla Jicarita at which time we will change from our 265° heading to a 320° course. We will keep this heading for just about 120 miles into Costa Rica. I doubt we would stop at Gulfito except that we

need the belt I told you about. Last night we used the engine
for 6 hours & our home made belt held, but a rope belt is still a
rope belt & can't be depended upon.

Yesterday afternoon Abuelo gave Bob a haircut. Sharon gave
me one. Not every boat carries their own barber. The whole crew
keeps telling me to go put lipstick on so they can tell I'm a
girl. Now if they looked closely enough I'm sure they could tell.

Another day, another mile. I stopped writing yesterday when
the yell came from deck — fish. Pancho had hooked onto a blue
fin Tuna. It's more fun to maneuver under sail so someone can
land a good size game fish. Boy did we eat tuna. I've been half
sick to my stomach ever since. Nothing like being a pig. It did
accomplish one thing though, the old turtle got another days
reprieve. He has also been transported from Panamanian to Costa
Rican waters. The flag of Costa Rica went up at noon today. If we
keep going like we are now we should be in Gulfito by 8 PM.

Last night the whole crew was kept awake by the da** rope
belts. They kept popping off & we kept having to replace them.
While we were awake we were royally entertained by porpoise. If
they are cute or fun during the day, then you can only call them
beautiful at night. The water is loaded with phosphorescence &
you can watch their graceful maneuvers by the streak of light
they trail. These waters are absolutely alive with marine life.
Nearly any time of the day or night you can find at least one of
the crew hanging over the side watching the fish.

It's still bathing suit weather. I usually wear my nylon
Parka on my 4 to 8 watch in the AM. At the moment I'm sitting in
the shade of the main sail. The water is so calm that I'm sitting
in an aluminum patio chair that Marc caught while fishing in
Balboa. By the way that's all he ever caught there.

I thought we would never get out of Panama. We got in here
about 9 last night. It was a dark, dark night but we took it very
slow & easy, finally picked up the range lights & ended up in
the beautiful bay at Gulfito. Last night by the time the hook was
down it was so dark & we were so tired & hungry, I just opened up
canned stew, we ate & collapsed. I didn't waken till almost 7 AM
& when I stuck my head out of the hatch it was like being in a
green fairyland. The mountains are beautiful and they come right
down to the water.

Pancho & I rowed ashore & got clearance at customs, watched
one inning of a little league game, came back out to the *Rowdy*,

picked up the turtle & crew, and in 2 trips went ashore again where we got a lesson on butchering Tortuga. Yes, poor old Mr. turtle is in the pot. The kids gave him another bath so he would die clean. I nearly fainted when Sharon offered to help butcher. I do believe she is going native. A man just came along side with a beautiful bunch of bananas. A gift. His son had been by in the AM in the same dugout canoe & we had talked to him (mostly sign language) and asked him aboard to share our breakfast. Sharon & Marc & I are going to row our dingy up river a ways to see what we can see. More later.

It's the next AM. Yesterday when we went up river a man hailed us from his home which is built right on the edge of the water at high tide. He spoke English quite well. He introduced us to his 11 children, showed us his house which he had built himself, his well for water that he was very proud of because he had dug it & had a doctor check it & found it to be pure. He asked us if we had ever tasted wapa & we said no. He took us in his kayuka (dugout canoe) up river about ½ mile where he had banana trees, coconut & wapa. He climbed a tree & came down with ½ doz. or so of a fruit that is different than anything I have ever tasted. I wouldn't want it for a steady diet but they were quite good. By the time we got back to the *Rowdy* it was dark. In our absence someone had gone by, left us a pineapple, several fresh clams & some plantains. I can't get over the friendliness of these people.

The end has come for our friend the turtle. We felt like cannibals when we ate him, but I must say it was about the most delicious meat we have ever eaten.

I have to go fix breakfast now so the crew will get to work. Everything was closed yesterday so we will go ashore today & try to find our belt. We will also take the main ashore. I don't know where we will stop again. It may be a couple of weeks. We don't intend to pull into another port till we need fuel, water or repairs.

Everyone here is fine & healthy. How are the kids? We miss all of you & wish you could share the beauty of some of these places with us.

Bye now — Love & Kisses

Carol

I have to put this in 2 envelopes. I guess I got carried away.

Undated[1]

Hello you lovely people

We are on our way again. It's 9 AM and we are just about the point that is 16 miles outside of Gulfito. We pulled into the dock for water just after day break. We filled the water tanks while Marc ran into town to get some bread.

There were 50 to 75 people on the dock to say good bye. We thought we would never get Abuelo back aboard. He was like a honey bear with a jar of jam. It's good to feel wanted in a country again. Maybe Panama has made us appreciate this more. The customs officer or Aduano as he is called in Spanish, even offered to let us use the bath in his home. We did not accept his kind offer. We thought that this was just too much of an imposition. Instead we would put on bathing suits, grab a bar of soap & row ashore where there was a fresh water tap. In this climate one certainly doesn't need hot water.

When we left the dock we saluted the people with 3 long blasts from our conch shell horns & it was returned by a United Fruit Co. ship that was on the dock & the yells of "adios" "Via con Dios."

We went directly across the bay & waved & yelled good bye to Tom Claremont, his wife & 3 beautiful daughters. Now there is a man who has everything. He is completely happy & the most content person I've ever met. We had heard about him from Tom & Betty Clark & several other cruising people. They all said "be sure to meet Tom Claremont so you can learn how to live." He is an American who lost his right leg during the war. When he was discharged he bought a 110 ft. sub chaser from the war surplus with his mustering out pay. He ran the "Isle of Capri" for 10 years chartering, towing and running supplies. 8 years ago he was in Gulfito when his engines gave out & so did he. He ran the Isle of Capri onto the beach, built a house in front of it out of parts and material from her, met and married his wife, and settled down to raising children, coconuts, pineapples, chickens, pigs etc., etc., etc. The only thing he does not raise is his voice or his blood pressure. They live completely off his $140 per month pension.

---

1 March 30, 1964.

I stopped writing when Marc yelled "Tortuga off the starboard bow." We took a quick vote & decided we were ready for turtle steak again. Bob brought the *Rowdy* in close & Pancho went over the side & brought "Alfonce" alongside. I should say that Alfonce brought Pancho alongside. If you hold the shell just right then the turtle will tow you along.

Sharon butchered him while 2 of us held him. I filleted the steaks. Pancho & Sharon cooked them. We shared the meat with the 5 people from the motor sailor "Segura." We met the skipper & his wife in Balboa. They are delivering the Segura to her new owner in San Diego. They left Balboa nearly a week after us & are motoring all the way. We spotted them, & they us early yesterday AM & we merged courses. They offered to tow us till the wind picked up so we could conserve fuel. We tied on about 8 AM & even though the wind picked up around noon, they kept towing us all day & night. When we dropped the lines in the AM, we tossed them a bag of Tortuga steak, fresh pineapple & matches. They are having radio trouble & we are giving radio checks as we did all day yesterday until they can determine the trouble. They can receive but not send. More manana.

Happy anniversary to us — March 21 (1964)

It's much later than manana. We were just beginning to think that the ole Pacific had no spirit. We should have not doubted her ability. We ran into a Papa Gyro. This is a dry storm. Wind & heavy seas. We had heard and read that they can be nasty so we headed in for shelter. We were headed for El Union, El Salvador. We changed course & tried to make a run for a little bay called Bahia Elena, Costa Rica. We were 15 or 20 miles away from it when we decided to go in. It took us 34 hours running nearly full throttle to make it.

We got into the harbor & decided that the only thing we could do was sit it out.

Yesterday we had company: a Nicaraguan Coast Guard boat. We all thought, oh brother here we go. Up till this moment we were sure that we were still in Costa Rica. They circled us a couple times. There were 2 women & about 7 men aboard & they were fishing. We called them over to us and were greeted by a big "Hello, good morning" by the smiling gentleman in bathing trunks. He wanted to know if we needed anything. We said we would like a weather report & that we were nearly out of fuel. He suggested that we go over to Bahia Janillo where he could give us a drum of fuel also fresh water & meat if we needed them. He had one of the men from his boat come on the *Rowdy* to direct us. We asked him if this bay was still in Costa Rica & that we didn't want to enter Nicaragua because we had been told of unreasonable fees charged by the officials there. He assured us that we would still be in Costa Rica & even if we weren't there would be no fee. We complimented him on his beautiful English & asked where he learned it. His reply was West Point. He signed our log for us & we nearly fainted when we saw the name "General Anastasio Samoza" son & heir to Nicaragua dictator (ie till he was assassinated).[1] He jokingly told us that he was on a religious holiday with his secretary. What a beauty she is, only according to the General she can't spell.

We arrived in the bay in front of one of his homes & were invited ashore for showers, cocktails & lunch & dinner. He is a very likeable & charming gentleman. He is surrounded by guards, even his servants wear guns.

Marc & I were invited to go riding with his party this AM. We were ashore at 4:45 AM for breakfast then we went by jeep. 7 of us were followed by a Land Rover with 7 armed guards. We went about a mile to where the horses were saddled and waiting. We rode up the side of the mountains. Very rough & volcanic, where he checked some of his cattle & the water supply. We got back to the house at 11 AM with a very sore butt & badly cut up legs. I wore jeans & tennis shoes & the brush was thick.

Today we took all our sails ashore to dry them. While working with them, the General's pilot came over & asked if Sharon & I would like to go flying. We took off in Samoza's private plane, looked over some of the country, took pictures of the *Rowdy* & landed in the same cow pasture from which we took off. It was fun; my first time up.

After we got back to the boat Samoza's helicopter came by our stern & the pilot asked Sharon (sign language) if she would like to join him. Marc rowed her ashore where she was picked up. She loved it. She went back ashore last night after chow to help the pilot with his English (she said).

---

1 General Somoza was later President of Nicaragua and then de facto ruler of the country until 1979, when he fled to exile in Paraguay, where he was assassinated.

Must go now, I have to take the laundry ashore. There's a well clear at the back of the ranch where I can do the wash. Ugh!

Easter Sunday

Marc & I spent 6 hrs. washing clothes yesterday. My next boat will have a washer. We had cocktails with the General last night. You should have seen Sharon & him do the twist. He's a huge man & when he twists, he really twists. He gave us a paper giving us clearance into any port in Nicaragua without fees of any kind & said to conserve fuel (he gave us a drum of gas day before yesterday) he had his Coast Guard boat tow us to San Juan Del Sur. We got here at 9 AM. We left Bahia Janillo at 4:00 AM. The Coast Guard boat has a small repair to make & they will pick us up at 4 tomorrow morning & tow us to Curinto which is 120 miles from here & at the northern end of Nicaragua. I'm going to stick this in 2 envelopes & see if I can get the customs to mail them. If not I'll mail it Tuesday from Curinto.

Bye now

Carol

Still haven't found Sheldon

Undated

Hi you nice cool people

God it's hot here. We skipped El Union & came on to
Acajutla, El Salvador, from Curinto Nicaragua. I can't remember
exactly where I left off in my last letter. The Nicaraguan
Coast Guard boat was supposed to tow us from San Juan Del Sur
to Curinto. The men aboard her didn't want to do it and made it
very clear. They were supposed to get another tow rope after
they had broken ours three times. They said they couldn't get
one, then they managed to ram us 3 times on the port & once on
the starboard. We have nice long gouges down both sides & the
counter is torn off the stern. We finally got mad and told them
to go away. We sailed the 100 miles to Curinto & hoisted the O
flag. About a half hour after we got the anchor down, the reason
for small boats never stopping at Nicaragua came aboard—Customs,
health, sanitation, 3 other official looking men with white
shirts & brief cases. They asked for our ship's papers which we
gave them along with our letter from General Samoza. They were
not too happy to see the letter. This was one set of wings they
could not clip & it hurt them. They were very, very polite, even
refused a cup of my instant coffee. They told Pancho that he
would have to go ashore to see the port captain which he did. He,
even with our precious letter, signed some 28 different forms for
this gentleman. We checked around about fuel & water & finally
met a gringo named Mike who is dock master for a shrimp fleet. He
gave us permission to pull up next to their cleaning dock (here
the shrimp is taken directly off the boats, cleaned & taken by
conveyor to the freezing rooms). Mike made arrangements to get
us 159 gal. of gas & all the drinking water we needed. The rest
of the gang took care of getting the gas & water aboard while
Pancho, Sharon & I had dinner on a United Fruit Co. boat. While
looking for supplies in the afternoon we met one of the officers
& he invited us to dine with him, telling Sharon & I to bring our
largest bags. We had a nice dinner & then our bags were loaded;
5 lbs. bacon, 2 lbs. coffee, a cooked roast of beef, a carton of
cigs & some apples & oranges. Boy was the gang glad to see us.
Then to top it all off Mike gave us a 5 lb. bag of fresh shrimp.
During the day we had splurged & gotten 4 doz. Eggs & a couple
loaves of bread. We left the following morning after first having

a shrimp omelet. Delicious. We had beautiful sailing all morning & decided to have a cold curry rice & shrimp dish that I was taught to make by Claudia off of the "Holly." It's a French dish & very cheap & good & easy. I got sick right in the middle of it & had to make a mad dive for the rail. Boy was I sick. I thought Oh no sea sick again. Then the cramps started. It was almost a relief to know it was a bug. Anyway Sharon finished lunch & the gang said it was good. Marc started dinner. That evening Bob & Pancho split my watch. Marc had just heated the roast, opened canned peas & carrots & was fixing instant potatoes when a squall hit us. Poor kid, he had food all over the galley & dishes all over the dinette. You have never seen a mess till you've seen a galley when the cook is just to the point of putting food on the table and the boat lays unexpectedly on her side. If it had waited 10 minutes it would all have been on the table (which is gimbaled) & nary a drop would spill. Marc just said "Oh well that's life" & started cleaning up glass & food & dishes etc., etc., etc. Quite a change from the boy that left Calif. Huh? Not only that, he cooked another meal, served it & the water was really rough. He could hardly stand up in the galley, let alone cook. When the sh** hit the fan he had just stepped out of the galley to put the butter on the table. Well the butter ended up in the middle of the carpet but at least Marc was not in the galley & did not get burned. Ah for the life of a sailor. It makes you wonder where the marbles went.

This last short hop has finally discouraged Abuelo. He's heading home. Every time it gets rough & he gets nervous, his stomach gets upset & he gets diarrhea. Our diet doesn't agree too well either. He's used to Alice fixing all sorts of goodies for him & here it's impossible. We live on the fish we catch & turtle & rice or beans. Even if we had the money for the food he likes we couldn't cook them very often. Now & then we get lucky, like at Curinto & acquire extra food but this doesn't last too long. We run the generator just long enough to keep the batteries charged for running lights, so the refrigerator is cool but never cold. Fresh foods won't keep in this climate. When we get lucky like Curinto we eat like kings & then go back to our old standby. The rest of the gang never complains. I think they are too busy or tired to bother. I don't know how much I weigh, not as thin as I'd like but thinner anyway. Marc is not skinny but we can count

ribs. Pancho has gone way down. He must weigh around 180, he
looks great.

Day before yesterday Pancho & Cerillo [Dice] and I went
ashore to send a wire to Alice & to get airline information. We
were having a terrible time when we met 2 local men & their wives
& children. They asked if they could help us. We told them our
problem & they said if we would like to go to their home where
they would leave the women & children they would help us. They
took us to the wireless office & also made calls to the airlines
then brought us back to the dock. They asked if it would be
possible to see the *Rowdy*. We suggested they get their wives.
Marc would row them out. The women loved it, but the men got sea
sick. Marc rowed them back ashore. By the way they didn't speak
English. All this was done in Spanish sign language. Yesterday
about noon one of them hailed us from the dock & when Sharon
& Dice rowed over to see what they wanted, they lowered a huge
block of ice & about 25 cups of ice cream into the dingy & said
adios. We ate ice cream until we were sick, then had ice tea for
chow mmmmmm. They certainly found a permanent spot in our hearts
for their thoughtfulness. Now who else would think of ice & ice
cream for a gift, and it was just what we were hungry for.

We have to wait here to get Abuelo on a plane. Then we will
go straight thru to Acapulco. We can take longer jumps without
Abuelo. Poor old guy, he gets so tired that we've been stopping
about every 200 miles. Our next two hops will be about 600 miles
each.

Have you ever received our snaps? Have you seen any of the
other film? How are the kids? How is Dad? How is Ray? It should
take us a week to get to Acapulco so you still have time for a
letter there. Give everyone big kisses for me. I miss you all
　　　Love
　　　Carol.

Undated

Hi you clean unsalty people.

We finally made it to Central America. California here we come.

The sail from El Salvador, past Guatemala to Salina Cruz, Mexico was comparatively uneventful. The 356 miles took us 5 days. Not very good huh? We had the seas against us the whole way until the last night. The last night in the gulf of Tehuantepec the wind swung to the NE with such force that the surface current pushed us like mad, in the right direction for a change. We expected to get here around 6 AM & instead we arrived at 2 AM & had to run back up the coast until day light. Aside from the heavy seas & strong winds this is no harbor to enter in the dark. The entrance is very narrow & the swells break right across the entrance. This was a very uncomfortable 4 hours, in fact the whole night was bad. We took spray over the deck all night. We had to run just outside of the breaker line. When a Tehuantepecer is blowing, the advice of the Pacific Pilot Guide (our Bible) & also the people who we've talked to who have come thru here, including ship captains is that if you can't throw a rock ashore, you are too far out. In the afternoon we even had a shrimp boat come along side & tell us that we were too far off the beach & might get blown out to sea. We talked to one man in Panama who had been blown over 200 miles to sea by a Tehuantepecer.

The day before we got here was also a stinker. When I came on watch at 4 AM the engine was not running right & Pancho had to break the fuel lines & clean the filters. In Pancho's delicate words "I think all the **#!!*** gas in Central America has crap in it." Then before he could get to bed he had to get out the lube gun & grease the drive bearings & put oil in the transmission. These sound like simple jobs but on the *Rowdy* & especially at sea, they are next to impossible & these were not calm seas. Pancho, even with his weight loss, just barely fits into the area next to the engine in a prone position, wrapped around both the exhaust from the engine and the generator. These jobs took him a couple of hours & this after he had been at the helm for 4 hrs. Then the damned head stopped pumping & he had to dissect it. By the time this was completed it was noon & he went back on watch. In the meantime Bob was tracing down and repairing a short in the running lights & Dice was replacing a section of hose that goes to the exhaust from the bilge pump & was letting water into the boat like a stream from a fire hose every time we went on a starboard tack. During Pancho & Marc's afternoon watch, the seas got heavier & the genoa jib scooped water & put a 15 foot rip in it & Sharon & I went to work. This was all besides cooking, dishes & all the general up keep & cleaning jobs. Now I ask you—why the hell do people go to sea?

There are the brighter sides though. Like the morning that I went below to cook oat meal which we were going to eat without sugar (we ran out). I felt the boat change course & ran top side to see what was wrong. Marc had tied into a dolphin & Dice had brought the *Rowdy* into the wind to slow her down so Marc could land him. I turned off the stove - 2 minutes later Pancho caught one & we had fish breakfast, mmmmm. For lunch Marc caught a bonito which we had cold with curried rice for lunch.

Then there was the celebration when we took down the flag of Guatemala & hoisted our first North American flag, the green, white & red of Mexico. We toasted it with a drink of Lic Lack, a rum from El Salvador which some people from Acajutta gave us. Dice & I even did the Mexican hat dance around Bob's hat on deck. All this on one drink.

Salina Cruz is dry, arid & windy. The women wear very colorful floor length dresses & the men huge hats.

Pancho went ashore to get permission for us to go to the gas dock. While the men are taking on fuel Sharon, Marc & I will go into the Mercada for sugar, oil, fresh vegetables & meat, then we're off to Acapulco.

Bye & Love
Carol

The San Diego Union

SAN DIEGO, CALIFORNIA, SUNDAY, JANUARY 3, 1965

—San Diego Union Staff Photo

Sharon, Carol, Frank and Bob
Winn, with dog, Salty, sit around
wheel of the Rowdy after being towed
to San Diego from Mexican waters.

BATTERED BOAT ARRIVES

Florida To S.D.
—In 16 Months

By MIKE SHORT

Four Southern Californians
in a 43-year-old sailboat were
towed into San Diego Bay
yesterday at the climax of a
voyage that began in Florida
16 months ago.

The boat was the Rowdy, a
-foot-long veteran of New
York Yacht Club and Great
Lakes racing, more recently
the survivor of hard use as a
charter craft in Florida. Yesterday it was badly in need of
repairs.

The crew were Frank and
Carol Winn, their daughter,
Sharon, and Winn's brother,
Bob. Frank Winn, a former
weekend sailor, left El Segun-
do and a job with Standard
Oil Co. in 1963 to make his
first long cruise.

"It may seem strange," he

"It may seem strange," he
said yesterday, "but it's generally not rich people who
cruise. People with money
usually end up sitting at home
watching their holdings."

Winn stopped sitting at
home, flew to Florida and
found a boat with a racing
history that was proud even
though it ended 30 years
ago.

On Sept. 8, 1963, the Rowdy
headed into the Caribbean Sea
from Fort Lauderdale. Yesterday it was close to its final
destination, Redondo Beach.

The Rowdy sat at the guest
dock of the San Diego Yacht
Club yesterday, battered but
still watertight. The sails
were damaged, the motor
inoperable.

The bow was smashed.

missing. The living quarters
were soaked with salt water,
the result of encounters with
two Caribbean hurricanes and
recent northwesters off the
west coast of Mexico.

"This is a good boat," Winn
said, "but this Mexican coast
—I don't know. This was the
worst possible time to come
up."

In fact, his timing was un-
fortunate for most of the trip,
he said. The trip had hardly
begun when the Rowdy felt
the effect of hurricanes Edith
and Flora.

"Just the edges of the hurricane," Winn's blonde,
deeply tanned wife said, "but
that's enough."

After leaving the Caribbean

the Winns spent several
weeks in Panama. Demon-
strating timing that came to
be typical, they arrived at
the time of anti-American
rioting in early 1964.

At one point the Winns had
to stay in port six weeks to
have work done on the hull of
the Rowdy. When the craft
was seaworthy again they had
done most of the work themselves.

After entering the Pacific
Ocean they ran into storms.
The Rowdy survived one bout
with rough weather and put
into Cedros Island, about 325
miles south of here, for repairs.

When they left the island
the Winns were buffeted by 70-
mile-an-hour winds. The wind
blew the boat through a
"complete 360-degree turn,"
Winn said. They returned and
tried again a few days
later.

"For a few days out of
Cedros we had good
weather," Winn said, but then
bad weather and engine failure left them without power.

The Rowdy drifted 80 miles
in two days until the Winns
got in touch with another
boat, the 83-foot Western
Pride. The Western Pride
towed the Winns 220 miles to
San Diego.

The Winns planned to spend
several days in San Diego before heading north to Redondo
Beach. Winn will go back to
work, but his cruising is not
over.

The Winns' next course—
whether in the Rowdy or another boat—will be around the
world, he said.

The Winns made the 200-mile leg to Acapulco, then to Manzanillo, and then
to La Paz, where they hauled out in mid-October 1964 to take advantage of cheap
maintenance and repair rates before heading back up the coast. Rough weather and
a failed engine prompted another call for help and resulted in a 220-mile tow, all the
way to San Diego.

After their return to California, Sharon's half-brother, Gene Collard, spent the
better part of a week interviewing the entire family about the trip. He plans to turn
the taped interviews into a book, which I heartily look forward to reading.

I found a December 15, 1964, article in the *Press Telegram*, a Long Beach, California, newspaper. The article states that after passing through the Panama Canal,
Rowdy was damaged by a storm (for the second time) off the coast of Baja Califor-

nia and underwent extensive repairs in La Paz, Mexico. The focus of the article was that on the previous day, *Rowdy* had sent out a Mayday call from 370 miles south of San Diego. Aboard were Frank Winn, his wife Carol, Frank's twin brother Robert, Frank and Carol's daughter Sharon and son Marc, and their Labrador retriever Saltie (who had also been aboard when their previous boat *Emerald* sank). A Coast Guard plane dropped a pump to *Rowdy*, which was taking on water. She was towed partway to port by a Mexican fishing vessel, and a merchant ship later towed her the rest of the way into Asuncion Bay. The article mentioned that Carol Winn had spent 19 hours in a decompression chamber some time previously after her air supply ran out while she was scuba diving at Catalina Island (probably when the family lived on *Emerald*).

A phone call from John Barkhurst, who bought *Rowdy* from the Winns in February 1971 and sold her in 1973, as well as an e-mail from Marty May, who knew Frank Winn, confirmed the above and additionally included the information that the entire Winn family lived aboard *Rowdy* when they finally arrived at King Harbor in Redondo Beach.

1971-1973   After John Barkhurst purchased Rowdy from Frank Winn, he was floored on her first haul-out to see that she had no ballast keel. Her entire ballast came from internal pig iron. John kept Rowdy on a mooring at Redondo Beach and carried all materials for her repair needs out on a dinghy. He gutted the original interior, which was in bad shape, and spent months getting rid of roaches, which Rowdy had hosted since Panama. The deck had canvas over it but still leaked, so John added a layer of plywood and more canvas. He had the white brass winches chromed and replaced the worn wheel with a modern one. He still has the original wheel.

1973-1982   In 1973, John Barkhurst sold *Rowdy* to Marvin Stokoe, a hardwood flooring contractor from Orville, California. I was contacted by Marvin's son, Gere, who said that when his father bought *Rowdy*, she had no ballast keel but had pig iron in the bilge for ballast and that the previous owner had gutted the boat. Gere also reported that his father had replaced several planks and often took *Rowdy* to Twin Harbors, on Catalina Island. Marvin kept *Rowdy* on an end tie at Fleitz Brothers Marina in San Pedro, California, and eventually sold her for a used Oldsmobile Cutlass and $7,000 to $8,000 in cash.

1982-1992   In 1982, Gerry Purcell, a yacht broker in Marina Del Rey, California, found *Rowdy* at the end tie at Fleitz Brothers in San Pedro. He purchased her from then owners Marvin and Velma Stokoe and had her towed to the Windward Yacht Center in Marina Del Rey. Gerry owned *Rowdy* for ten years. Most of the structural work he did had been ripped out and redone when I acquired *Rowdy*, but he did have some very nice interior joinery work done, all of which was saved. And he took on the huge job of replacing the missing external ballast keel and keel bolts.

1992-1998   The last owner to attempt a rebuild was Christy Baxter from La Canada, California. Not knowing much about boat building, she was drawn into the deal by a business partner who volunteered the labor if she would put up the capital. The plan was to fix *Rowdy* up, sell her, and split the profits. I believe it was a 100 percent loss, and in the end, the boat was donated to a nonprofit corporation for a tax write-off.

1998   Blue Whale Sailing School was the nonprofit to which *Rowdy* was donated.

1998   In 1998, I purchased *Rowdy* from Blue Whale Sailing School for a modest amount. Her bilge pumps were running continuously, and she was one step away from being crushed up and thrown into a dumpster. For the next four years, I worked on *Rowdy* twelve to fourteen hours a day, seven days a week in the Channel Islands Boatyard, Channel Islands, California. Following the major renovation, *Rowdy* raced her first race in fifty years, the McNish Classic, winning first place in her division as well as winning the Bristol Boat Award for best classic yacht. I also sailed her recreationally in the Channel Islands.

2006-2013   I sold *Rowdy* to Graham Walker of the United Kingdom in March 2006, and on March 15, 2006, she sailed out of Channel Islands Harbor en route to a new life in Monaco. Her first stop was Long Beach, California, where her spars and rigging were removed. She was then put onto a custom-made metal cradle and hoisted onto a ship that transported her to the Mediterranean, where she has enjoyed an extremely successful racing career in the classic circuit. Her new owner raced her to twenty-seven consecutive victories in 2008 and won the most prestigious classic yacht race in the world two consecutive years, taking home the Rolex Trophy in Les Voiles De Saint-Tropez in 2008 and 2009, with a very close second in 2010. As of a March 20, 2012, e-mail to me from skipper Jonathan Greenwood, *Rowdy* had won in excess of 140 races in five seasons!

2013-present   In December 2013, Walker sold *Rowdy* to Howard Dyer, also of the United Kingdom, who plans to continue to race her.

If anyone has more information to help fill in the blanks, I would love to hear from you at rowdystory@yahoo.com. Hopefully, you will see your contribution in the second edition of this book.

Appendix

Rowdy's Racing Successes

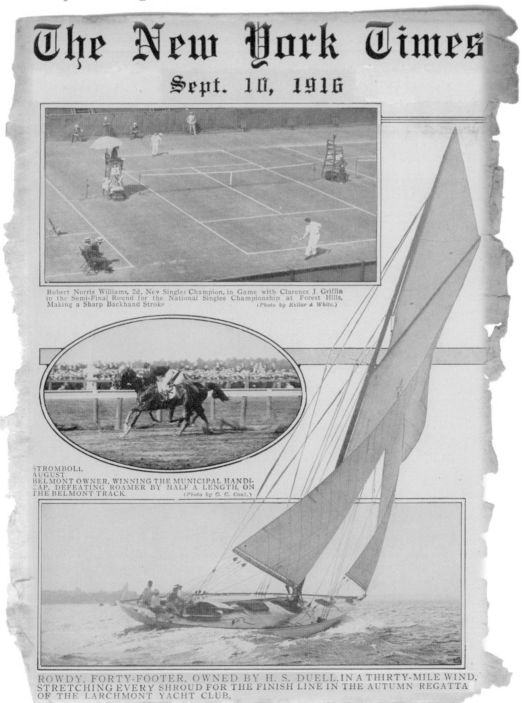

The New York Times

Sept. 10, 1916

Robert Norris Williams, 2d, New Singles Champion, in Game with Clarence J. Griffin in the Semi-Final Round for the National Singles Championship at Forest Hills, Making a Sharp Backhand Stroke (Photo by Kellar & White.)

STROMBOLI, AUGUST BELMONT OWNER, WINNING THE MUNICIPAL HANDI-CAP, DEFEATING ROAMER BY HALF A LENGTH, ON THE BELMONT TRACK. (Photo by G. G. Cook.)

ROWDY, FORTY-FOOTER, OWNED BY H. S. DUELL, IN A THIRTY-MILE WIND, STRETCHING EVERY SHROUD FOR THE FINISH LINE IN THE AUTUMN REGATTA OF THE LARCHMONT YACHT CLUB.

The New York Times.

NEW YORK, SUNDAY, JUNE 13, 1920.

ROWDY IS WINNER AMONG 40-FOOTERS

Captures Feature Event of Annual Regatta of Manhasset Bay Yacht Club.

MISTRAL FINISHES SECOND

Mallory's Yacht Is 2 Minutes 21 Seconds Behind Leader—Adios Shows Way to Alera.

Forty-six yachts sailed in the annual regatta of the Manhasset Bay Yacht Club on Long Island Sound yesterday. Unfortunately, the wind was not particularly strong, although it freshened as the afternoon advanced, giving the craft an opportunity of finishing within the required time limit. The start and the finish was off Execution Light, and the course sailed by the larger classes was from the starting line to a mark off Parsonage Point, thence to another off Week's Point and then home.

The feature division was the forty-footers of the New York Yacht Club. No less than five started. It was the largest representation in the division since 1916. The winner was Rowdy, the property of Holland S. Duell, which defeated P. R. Mallory's Mistral by 2 minutes and 21 seconds over an eleven mile course. Among the thirty-footers of the same organization, Adonis, which has been purchased back by Fred L. Richards, was the first craft home, winning from Alera, which now belongs to F. W. Belknap.

The summaries:

NEW YORK YACHT CLUB 40-FOOTERS.
Start, 1:10. Course, 11 miles.

Yacht and Owner.	Finish. H.M.S.	Elapsed Time. H.M.S.
Rowdy, H. C. Duell..........	3:01:10	1:51:10
Mistral, P. R. Mallory......	3:03:31	1:53:31
Schawara, Harold Wesson....	3:06:28	1:56:28
Zilph, J. E. Hayes..........	3:08:08	1:58:08
Pamparo, H. H. Raymond.....	3:12:28	2:02:28

NEW YORK YACH CLUB 30-FOOTERS.
Start, 1:20. Course, 11 miles.

	Finish.	Elapsed
Adios, F. L. Richards......	4:33:08	3:13:08
Alera, F. W. Belknap.......	4:41:06	3:21:06
Rowdy, C. Belsky..........	4:43:58	3:23:58
Mizpah, D. R. Richardson...	4:50:31	3:30:31

NEW YORK, JUNE 27, 1920

ROWDY VICTORIOUS IN 40-FOOT CLASS

Duell Yacht First in Oyster Bay Regatta—Nahma and and Oriole Win.

Special to The New York Times.

OYSTER BAY, L. I., June 26.—The largest fleet that has sailed in a regatta of the Seawanhaka-Corinthian Yacht Club in years came to the starting line off here today for the annual Spring regatta of the organization. Although there were no big sloops or schooners that used to race off here before the war, the fleet had considerable class and included the 40-footers of the New York Yacht Club, the 30-footers of the same organization, Class P and the new Victory Class that originally was suggested by members of the Center Island Club.

The 40-foot class, which led the fleet, was won by Rowdy, the property of H. S. Duell. In Class P the speedy Nahma, entered by Hanan and Childs, was the winner. F. C. Pirie's Oriole was the winner among the 30-footers.

The summary:

NEW YORK Y. C. 40-FOOTERS.
Start, 1:50. Course, 14½ Miles.

Yacht and Owner.	Finish. H.M.S.	Elapsed Time. H.M.S.
Rowdy, H. S. Duell..........	4:22:20	2:32:20
Zilph, J. E. Hayes..........	4:22:42	2:32:42
Cockatoo, H. Chubb..........	4:25:25	2:35:25
Pamparo, H. H. Raymond.....	4:25:37	2:35:37
Shawara, H. Wesson.........	4:27:25	2:37:25

NEW YORK, JULY 11, 1920

ROWDY WINS ON SOUND.

Forty-Footer and Queen Mab Again Lead Eastern Y. C. Fleet.

Special to The New York Times.

NEW HAVEN, Conn., July 10.—The lightest of southwesters, with a favorable tide, wafted the Eastern Yacht Club fleet over 36 miles of the placid water of Long Island Sound today, and by picking up friendly slants and some of the stronger currents the 40-footer Rowdy, owned by H. S. Duell, and the schooner Queen Mab, owned by R. C. Robbins, captured the two prizes of the day. It was the Queen Mab's fourth victory on the cruise.

On the way from Bartlett's Reef to the Cornfield, Rowdy drew up to Mistral, and although the latter was well to windward the Duell boat drew by and took the lead. Just under her stern was Shawara, and as the air seemed stronger inshore both yachts gained on the rest of the fleet.

The wind began to fade as the yachts reached Branford Ledge, but there was air enough to bring all the yachts to the finish an hour before dark. Officers of the New Haven Yacht Club welcomed the fleet upon its arrival off the clubhouse.

The summary:

NEW YORK 40-FOOTERS.

Yacht and Owner.	Elapsed Time. H.M.S.	Corrected Time
Rowdy, H. S. Duell......	5:00:38	......
Shawara, H. Wesson......	5:02:59	......
Zilph, J. Hayes..........	5:03:26	......
Pamparo, H. H. Raymond.	5:05:39	......
Sally Ann, S. Borden, Jr.	5:09:27	......

NEW YORK, July 4, 1922

CAROLINA OUTSAILS ISTALENA ON SOUND

George Nichols's Fifty-Footer Finishes Ahead of Rival by Nearly Eight Minutes.

ROWDY WINS AMONG 40'S

Unusually Close Races Mark Annual Regatta of American Y. C., Held in Steady Breeze.

Special to The New York Times.

RYE, N. Y., July 3.—The annual regatta of the American Yacht Club of Milton Point, Rye, was sailed today with eighty-one yachts going over the starting line off Scotch Caps. In contrast to the weather in which the Indian Harbor regatta was sailed on Saturday, the sun shone throughout the duration of the event no rain fell and the wind, which came from the south-southwest, held steady and true, with a velocity of about seven and a half knots.

Rowdy an Easy Victor.

A quartet of the 40-footers sailed today, also over the long course, and Holland Duell in Rowdy scored an easy victory, leading his nearest competitor, James E. Hayes's Zilph, over the line by a margin of several minutes.

NEW YORK, FRIDAY, AUGUST 11, 1922.

ROWDY IS WINNER IN 40-FOOT CLASS

Duell's Sloop Takes Close Race From Squaw and Sally Ann at Marblehead.

Special to The New York Times.

MARBLEHEAD, Mass., Aug. 10.—Apparently it is always good yachting weather off this port. At least it has been every day since the yachts making the annual cruise of the New York Yacht Club dropped anchor here. Yesterday's race for the King's Cup, which was won by Commodore H. S. Vanderbilt's schooner Vagrant, was sailed in a northeaster, and today, when three of the New York Yacht Club's forty-foot sloops sailed for a cup offered by the Eastern Yacht Club, the race was made in a northwester which had plenty of power. The

---

NEW YORK, JULY 13, 1920

YACHTS COMPLETE 150-MILE CRUISE

Schooner Queen Mab Scores Six Victories—Rowdy Best Among Forty-Footers.

Special to The New York Times.

LARCHMONT, N. Y., July 12.—A fifteen knot southwester gave the racing portion of the Eastern Yacht Club fleet a good twenty-five mile run up the Sound to this port today as a fitting climax of the cruise of 150 miles along the southern New England and eastern New York shores. The winners for the day were the schooner Queen Mab and the New York Yacht Club forty-footer Rowdy. Queen Mab finished the cruise

---

JUNE 22, 1924.

ROWDY HOME FIRST IN LARCHMONT RACE

Duell's Forty-Footer Leads Rivals Across Line in Annual Spring Regatta.

FLEET OF 78 TAKES PART

Largest of Season Meets Light Airs on the Sound—Grey Dawn and Minx Also Score.

LARCHMONT MANOR, N. Y., June 21.—Seventy-eight yachts, the largest fleet of the season, came to the starting line of the Larchmont Yacht Club off here today to sail in the annual Spring

George A. Corry's Little Dipper led home the Star boats. The International Six-Meter Class and the Victory yachts were the only divisions that had a real race. The light air suited them and, as a result, they finished hours ahead of the other craft. In the six-meter division the winner was Montauk, which belongs to W. A. W. Stewart. The first Victory home was Vindictive, which is owned by R. W. Fraser.

The summaries:

NEW YORK Y. C. FORTY-FOOTERS.

Starts 3:55. Course. 10¼ Miles.

Yacht and Owner.	H.M.S.
Rowdy, H. S. Duell	7:11:41
Shawara, C. B. Seeley	7:11:43
Banshee, H. L. Maxwell	7:12:26
Pampero, C. L. Andrews	7:19:36
Mistral, W. E. Bell	7:23:57

NEW YORK, AUGUST 29, 1920

ROWDY IS WINNER AMONG 'FORTIES'

Leads Pampero by Wide Margin —New Rochelle Y. C. Regatta Has 72 Starters.

Special to The New York Times.

NEW ROCHELLE, N. Y., Aug. 28.—There were seventy-two starters in the New Rochelle Yacht Club's annual regatta, held off here today, on Long Island Sound. After two postponements of fifteen minutes each, because of lack of breeze, a light southwesterly wind sprang up. It held true throughout except close under the Long Island shore, where there were some treacherous soft spots.

New Rochelle Yacht Club fixtures are occasionally marked by extreme weather conditions, but today they were quite normal. The postponement was partly due to a desire to enable the Mistral of the "forties" to arrive. The Molloy cubical starting signals were used and, as on previous occasions, proved to be most satisfactory.

In most of the clashes the starts lacked dash and pep. The Corinthians seemed to be "recall shy," although there were two of the "forties" that did get away too soon. The Victory Class afforded the best getaway of the day. The number of starters was greater than at any other club this year, with the exception of Larchmont during race week. In the N. Y. Y. C. Forty Class H. S. Duell's Rowdy was the winner by a margin of nearly eight minutes, while Edmund Lang's Banzai of the "thirties" was first to finish.

N. Y. Y. C. FORTIES.

Start, 3:20. Course, 16¼ Miles.

Yacht and Owner.	Finish.	Elapsed Time.
Rowdy, H. S. Duell	6:30:12	3:10:12
Pampero, H. H. Raymond	6:44:08	3:24:08
Zilph, J. E. Hayes	6:45:55	3:25:55
Mistral, P. R. Mallory	6:48:58	3:28:58
Shawara, H. Wesson	6:53:20	3:33:20
Monsoon, F. D. M. Strahan	6:56:48	3:36:48
Cockatoo, H. Chubb	Did not finish	

The New York Times

NEW YORK, SATURDAY, JULY 5, 1924.

ROWDY LEADS FLEET OF 95 BY 22 SEC.

N. Y. Y. C. 40-Footer Slightly Faster Than Banshee in Final Run at Larchmont.

DAUPHIN VICTOR BY 4 SEC.

6-Meter Yacht Attains Notable Triumph Over Lea—Alla'r

Star Winner by 19 Sec.

Forties Sail 18-Mile Course.

The New York Yacht Club forty-footers were sent away at 12:10 and sailed a course of eighteen miles, as did the Larchmont sloops and thirty-footers. The breeze was light from the eastward as the first class went away and held in this quarter throughout the racing. The first leg was a broad reach to the buoy north of Execution Light, thence east to Matinicock buoy on the Long Island shore, a reach across the Sound to Greenwich Point buoy, across the Sound again to a mark off Hempstead and home.

Rowdy and Banshee had a hard fight of it in the light airs, and only in the final run to the mark, under a cloud of canvas, did the Dueli sloop, a bit faster than Banshee, gain the winning advantage.

There were ninety-five boats altogether in the race, making a new high record for the season, against ninety-four starters at the Seawanhaka-Corinthian regatta last Saturday. There were eleven New York Yacht Club thirty-footers starting in this class, in which Grayling, a Class Q sloop, sailed by J. P. Morgan, also went over the line. Edmund Lang's Banzai won her second race in as many days, going well in the light airs, defeating S. C. Pirie's Oriole by almost two minutes.

The Boston Globe

THE BOSTON GLOBE

FRIDAY, AUGUST 11, 1922

ROWDY LEADS SQUAW BY ONLY SIX SECONDS

MARBLEHEAD, Aug 10—Probably not in all the six years that the New York Yacht Club one-design 40-footers have been raced have three of these Herreshoff cutters sailed a closer race than that of today under the colors of the Eastern Yacht Club.

They had a light northeasterly breeze that carried them in good time from the starting line off the red and black buoy outside of Marblehead Rock to the Eastern Point whistling buoy and return, a total of 16½ miles.

The course was a beat to windward to the whistling buoy off Eastern Point and then a spinnaker run back to the red and black buoy.

When they were started H. S. Duell had the Rowdy timed to the second as her stem was poked across the line just as the starting signal sounded from Robert Jordan's steam yacht Velthra, which was used as a committee boat by the regatta committee.

Right under her stern was John S. Lawrence's Squaw, so close and so directly in the Rowdy's wake that there was a question whether or not the jib-topsail stay of the Squaw did not hit the end of the Rowdy's boom. These two crossed on port tack, while the Sally Ann, on starboard tack, passed under the Squaw's stern, timed across less than half a minute behind the Rowdy.

Although the Squaw broke from both the Rowdy and the Sally Ann standing inshore for the first part of the beat to the whistler, when the three rounded the buoy they were in the same order as at the start and about the same distance apart.

The Rowdy finished first, just six seconds ahead of the Squaw, which in turn led the Sally Ann by 39 seconds. Thus only three-quarters of a minute separated the three at the finish. The summary:

NEW YORK YACHT CLUB, 40-FOOTERS (15M)

Name and Owner	El Time
Rowdy, H S Duell	3:44:20
Squaw, John S Lawrence	3:44:26
Sally Ann, Spencer Borden Jr	3:45:05

The Brooklyn Daily Eagle

THE BROOKLYN DAILY EAGLE.

NEW YORK, SUNDAY, JUNE 22, 1924

ROWDY IS FIRST IN DRIFTING RACE OFF LARCHMONT

Lack of Wind Delays Start of Big Fleet on Sound. Little Dipper Wins.

(Special Cable to The Eagle.)

Larchmont Manor, N. Y., June 21—Seventy-eight yachts, the largest fleet of the summer, came to the starting line of the Larchmont Yacht Club off here today, to sail in the annual spring regatta of the organization. Al-

New York Tribune

NEW YORK TRIBUNE,

TUESDAY, AUGUST 8, 1922

N. Y. Y. C. in 40-Mile Race

Provincetown to Gloucester

Rowdy Victor Over Squaw

The battling 40-footers had their usual rough and tumble tussel over the entire distance of forty miles, and six of them finished within nine minutes of each other. Seven of this doughty class started and H. S. Duell's Rowdy was the winner, defeating John S. Lawrence's Squaw by forty seconds.

The starts to-day were productive of many thrilling brushes up and down the line, even though position did not mean so much, due to the fact that the race was to be a run to leeward.

Istalena got away to a much better start than Harpoon, leading the later across the starting line by just about the length of time that Harpoon led her at the finish.

The New York Times

SUNDAY, JUNE 28, 1925.

87 Yachts, Including Several New Craft,
Compete in the Season's Biggest Regatta

ROWDY, WHICH COMPETED

IN FORTY-FOOT CLASS.

The New York Times.

NEW YORK, THURSDAY, JULY 23, 1925.

RACING YACHTS HIT BY 50-MILE SQUALL

Grey Dawn Is Dismasted, Mirage Breaks Gaff, While Others Suffer Minor Damage.

BANSHEE IS DISQUALIFIED

Finishes First, but Rowdy Wins on Foul in Third Regatta of Larchmont Race Meet.

By SEABURY LAWRENCE.
Special to The New York Times.

LARCHMONT, N. Y., July 22.—Racing in a hard southwest blow, accompanied by frequent heavy rain squalls, ninety-eight yachts crossed the line in the third regatta of the Larchmont Yacht Club's annual race week today and the contending yachtsman had enough thrills to last them till next race week. The sloops and schooners that raced were on their beam ends most of the time when sailing on the wind, big seas broke over them and when the racing crews were not being drenched by flying spray they were being deluged by torrential showers. Altogether it was a day long to be remembered by those who raced and it was not without its casualties among the racing boats.

The most serious accident occurred on Vice Commodore Philip Johnson's Larchmont 30-footer Grey Dawn, which was dismasted while running down the wind on the second leg of the 15½-mile course, her 60-foot spar splintering off about five feet above the deck, mainsail and all attendant gear going over the side in a mass of wreckage. This happened when the sloop was struck by a squall which blew at almost fifty miles an hour, just after she had passed Scotch Caps Buoy off Rye.

A sudden shift of wind had caused Sam Wetherill, who was sailing the yacht, to jibe his boom over and soon after this manoeuvre the crash came. Fortunately the tall spar fell over the side and no one on board was injured. The yachtsmen had a hard time getting the wreckage on deck in the heavy sea running, but finally did so, and the Grey Dawn was towed into the harbor by a power yacht which had seen the accident and stood by.

Other Yachts Damaged.

The same squall hit Mirage, which was racing with Grey Dawn and which was almost alongside, breaking the big sloop's gaff. The mainsail fell slack, but Mirage managed to keep going and covered the course.

Several of the other yachts suffered minor damage and had to pull out of the exciting race. The New York Yacht Club's thirty-footer, Nautilus, owned by J. H. Ottley Jr., broke her boom and came back to the harbor under a jib; Harry L. Maxwell's Fifi of the new R class, carried away a spreader; Manhassett II., another R class sloop, broke her boom, and the six-meter yacht Natka was damaged soon after the start and compelled to withdraw.

There were also some protests and disqualifications. Harry L. Maxwell suffered some more hard luck when his forty-footer Banshee, sailed by Jack Johnson, finished first in her class and was disqualified by the committee for fouling Shawara, while they were jockeying for the start. It was hard for the skippers to hold the forties with the breeze roaring along at thirty-five knots and while trying to keep his big sloop from crossing the line before the gun Captain Johnson bore down on Shawara, Banshee's backstay catching the Dunbaugh sloop's boom.

Banshee sailed a fine race and was almost a minute and a half ahead of Holland Duell's Rowdy after a hard battle in the rough seas. The committee was compelled to disqualify the Maxwell sloop because of the unintentional foul, the race going to Rowdy, with Mistral placed second.

In the thirty-foot class Vice Commodore Edmund Lang's Banzai, the winner of the race over a 15½ mile course, was protested by Blue Moon for forcing the latter off the starboard tack. The committee will hold a hearing on the protest tomorrow morning. In the Star Class two of the yachts were disqualified for infractions of the racing rules.

Ardette Wins Again.

In the new R Class six boats started and Ardette, owned by Donald H. Cowl of the Manhasset Bay Yacht Club, which yesterday captured the Childs trophy, was once more an easy winner, coming home over two minutes ahead of Commodore Robert Law Jr's Doress, with Commodore P. R. Mallory's Quiver about the same distance astern of the Indian Harbor boat. Ardette, with E. P. Alker at the helm, seemed to go just as well in today's rugged wind and seas as she had in previous races in light weather. Quiver, always supposed to be a light weather performer, surprised the experts by going well in the heavy blow and beating the Gardner sloop, Secret. Fifi and Manhasset were disabled and did not finish.

There were some close finishes recorded, the end of the race in the S Class being an especially tight fit. Guthrie Willard's Frolic, and Pandora, owned by Vice Commodore Harry M. Curtis, came down to the line almost abeam, with Frolic getting the verdict by four seconds.

The skippers of the game little Star boats showed their grit by coming out to race in the heavy going, an even dozen of the sloops being started in each division. In the first many of the Stars raced with full sail, and the winner was Duncan Sterling Jr.'s Vega, which captured her second race of the week. Sterling is one of Larchmont's youngest skippers and he beat Little Dipper, sailed by George A. Corrick, known as the Father of the Star Class.

There was a hot finish in the second division. Parry Hanson's Astral beating Ernest Ratsey's Irex III by twelve seconds, with Quamy thirty-eight seconds astern. When the Seawanhaka Fish boats finished the heaviest squall of the day was whipping the crests from the waves, but Shrimp came through it to win by twenty-one seconds from Arthur Iselin's Fly.

Photo#NYT07-23-25

The summaries:

N. Y. Y. C.—40-FOOT CLASS.
Start, 2:00 Course 15¼ Miles.

Yacht and Owner.	Finish. H.M.S.
*Banshee, H. L. Maxwell	4:38:04
Rowdy, H. S. Duell	4:40:29
Mistral, W. B. Bell	4:40:44
Shawara, Dunbaugh & Hoffman	4:51:45

*Disqualified.

LARCHMONT—CLASS C.
Start, 2:05 Course, 15¼ Miles.

Mirage, J. F. Mahlstedt	3:15:31
Grey Dawn, Philip H. Johnson	Dism.

N. Y. Y. C.—30-FOOT CLASS.
Start, 2:15. Course, 10½ Miles.

Banzai, Edmund Lang	5:06:42
Oriole, S. C. Pirie	5:07:20
Narcissus, Frank Page	5:08:09
Phantom, Flint & Halsey	5:08:33
Blue Moon, D. G. Draper	5:09:51
Silhouette, R. L. Amberg	5:14:36
Lena, O. Reid	5:17:16
Alera, H. F. Whitney	5:23:38
Nautilus, J. H. Ottley, Jr.	Disabled.

* Edwin Levick's famous
photo "Forties in a Squall,"
July 22, 1925, Rowdy at far
right (Old poster in
personal collection)

Edwin Levick's famous photo "Forties in a Squall," taken on July 22, 1925, during Larchmont Race Week, captured the excitement of racing. This race took place in a hard southwest wind and big seas. Intermittent squalls with 50 mph winds and torrential downpours wreaked havoc on the boats: One was dismasted, one broke her gaff, two broke booms, and one broke a spreader. It was described in this news article as "a day long to be remembered, with enough thrills to last until next year's race." *Rowdy* (on the far right in the photo) won first place. Levick's photo is also in the books *Sailing Craft, Yachts Under Sail*, and *History of the Larchmont Yacht Club*, and a framed copy is hanging in the Herreshoff Museum and the Larchmont Yacht Club.

The New York Times.

NEW YORK, September 21, 1924

ROWDY HOME FIRST BY ONLY ONE SECOND

Sets Spinnaker When Near Line and Beats Pampero Coming From Other Angle.

70 YACHTS IN THE REGATTA

Betty Takes Six-Meter Honors In Manhasset Event—Grey Dawn, Oriole and Vega Also Win.

Special to The New York Times.

PORT WASHINGTON, N. Y., Sept. 20.—A fleet of seventy yachts took part today in the Fall regatta of the Man-

---

NEW YORK, JUNE 2, 1931

YACHT ROWDY WAS VICTOR.

Regatta Officials Discover Shawara Did Not Finish Course.

In checking the results of the class races in the Harlem Yacht Club's regatta on Long Island Sound on Saturday the regatta committee learned that F. T. Bedford's "forty" sloop Shawara, which crossed the finish line far ahead of the rest of the fleet, had not covered the course through a misunderstanding of it. The winner in the class was H. S. Duell's Rowdy.

NEW YORK, JULY 13, 1931

ISTALENA IS FIRST IN CLASS M RACE

Leads Avatar to the Finish in Indian Harbor Yacht Club Regatta.

ROWDY HEADS 40-FOOTERS

Defeats Shawara and Typhoon Over 19½-Mile Course—Nachvak Wins 10-Meter Event.

Special to The New York Times.

GREENWICH, Conn., July 12.— More than 130 boats sailed today in the Indian Harbor Yacht Club's early Summer regatta. The weather was ideal, a good wind blowing steadily out of the north, and the sea was not too rough.

Holland Duell sailed his N. Y. Y. C. forty-footer Rowdy to victory for the first time this year, defeating F. T. Bedford's newly acquired Shawara and H. G. Leslie's Typhoon by 1:25 and 4:14, respectively, over the 19½-mile course. R. E. Fulton's Grey Dawn, a Larchmont O sloop, competed with those which took the rectangular course. Grey Dawn sailed with the forties, as there were no others in her class out.

NEW YORK, AUGUST 12, 1931

ROWDY LEADS FLEET ON DUCK ISLAND RUN

Duell's Craft First to Finish on Initial Leg of Indian Harbor Yacht Club Cruise.

METCALF'S SACHEM NEXT

Trails First Boat by 16:17 on the Thrash From Greenwich—Total of 27 Compete in Event.

Special to The New York Times.

NEW LONDON, Conn., Aug. 11.— Fanned along by a fairly good breeze, the fleet of the Indian Harbor Yacht Club arrived at Duck Island tonight, finishing the first leg of the cruising race from Greenwich, Conn., to Newport, R. I.

Holland S. Duell's New York forty-foot craft Rowdy led among the twenty-seven cruising and racing yachts that started, requiring eight hours and twenty-one minutes for the run.

The committee, headed by A. E. Luders, decided to postpone the start thirty minutes to allow some of the New York forties to arrive. At 9:40 o'clock the first class, cruisers racing for the Metcalf Trophy, was sent on its way. Fifteen minutes later the last of the fleet, the New York forties, were away and the long three days of racing was on.

A strong northeast-by-north breeze gave the fleet a good lift and stayed with it over the entire course of fifty-two miles from Greenwich up the Connecticut shore to Duck Island. The day was a dismal day on the water and with the spray and rain, the skippers and crews were drenched.

Rowdy finished at 6:21:11 with her lee rail awash, followed by Rowe F. Metcalf in his racing schooner Sachem 16 minutes and 17 seconds later.

WEDNESDAY, JULY 8, 1925.

VAGRANT IS LEADER IN EASTERN Y. C. RUN

Is First Into Rockland Harbor After 130-Mile Cruise— Rowdy Is Second In.

Special to The New York Times.

ROCKLAND, Me., July 7.—Led by the handsome Vagrant, with her old-fashioned gaff rig, and with the New York forty-footer Rowdy not many miles behind and a winner in her class, the Eastern Yacht Club fleet reached Rockland today after a fast run of 130 miles across the Gulf of Maine from Marblehead.

As it was very thick off the Rockland breakwater when the yachts finished, many of them before dawn, the Regatta Committee allowed each boat to take her own time, and the winners in the classes, except the forties, will not be known until later. After a few hours' stop at Rockland for provisions the yachts kept on up the bay and reached historic Gilkey's Harbor this afternoon. Tomorrow they will race again in the Western Penobscot for the benefit of the Islesboro cottagers. In the long run last night and this morning the yachts had varying conditions. Those which kept well off shore had a fine south-

NEW YORK, July 7, 1928

ROWDY LEADS COCKATOO

Scores by 26 Seconds Over a Leeward and Windward Course Off Marion, Mass.

Special to The New York Times.

MARION, Mass., July 6.—A twenty-five-knot Northeaster gave the boats in the Beverly Yacht Club's second regatta today an oilskin race with spray flying high, the larger yachts staggering under whole sail and the little fellows down to double reefs.

The Rowdy ran so far ahead of the fleet in the seven-mile slide down the breeze that it looked like a walkover, but when sheets were flattened for the climb home the Cockatoo, which had trailed far astern, began to gain, and half a mile from the finish had cut the Rowdy's lead to less than a minute.

Rowdy tacked a trifle too soon for the line and was pinched hard to fetch it, but the distance was too short to give the Cockatoo a chance for victory. The Rowdy wins the series in her class.

The Brooklyn Daily Eagle

NEW YORK, SUNDAY, SEPTEMBER 23, 1928.

ROWDY IS LEADER OF FORTY FOOTERS AT LARCHMONT

One Hundred Racing Yachts Start in Final Regatta of Season.

Larchmont, N. Y., Sept. 22—In the final championship regatta of the Long Island Sound Yacht Racing Association, sailed off this port this afternoon under the auspices of the Larchmont Yacht Club, a fleet of 100 boats started. Among the winners were Vice Commodore Clifford D. Mallory's Tycoon, in the 12-meter class; H. S. Duell's Rowdy, in the New York Club 40-foot class, and Robert A. Mahlstedt's Mirage, in the Larchmont O class.

The New York Times.

NEW YORK, JULY 25, 1931

Photo by Levick.

START OF THE NEW YORK YACHT CLUB FORTY-FOOT CLASS IN LARCHMONT REGATTA YESTERDAY.
Rowdy, Shawara and Typhoon Crossing the Line.

The New York Times

The New York Times
Published: August 3, 1930
Copyright © The New York Times

Rowdy

Photo Edwin Levick.

With All Canvas Spread: The Start of the Famous Forty-Footers' Race at Larchmont, N. Y.   Holland S. Duell's Rowdy Is Leading.

New York Evening Post

MONDAY, JUNE 2, 1930

AGAIN SAILS DOT THE SEA ROADS TO DELIGHT THE EYES. This fine picture shows the start of the fighting forty-footers of the New York Yacht Club in the Golden Jubilee Regatta of the Larchmont Yacht Club in the Sound. A puffing, lumpy nor'wester made racing difficult, some of the smaller boats continuously shipping water. Here, left to right, are H. S. Duell's Rowdy, the winner; the Chinook, owned by H. F. Whitney, and W. B. Bell's Mistral.

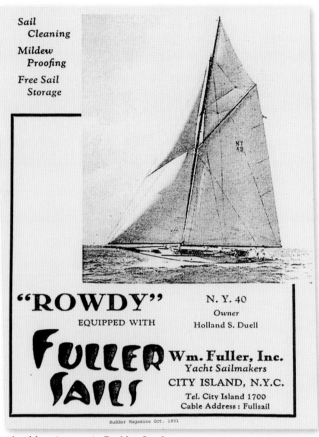

* *Advertisement in Rudder, October 1931*

* *Advertisement in Yachting, August 1927 (Reprint courtesy of Yachting magazine)*

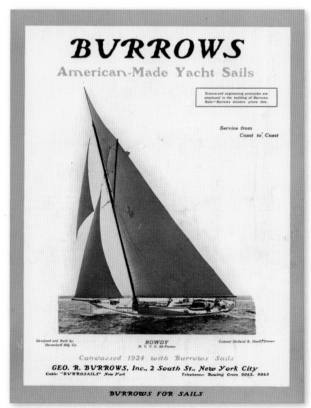

* *Advertisement in Rudder, July 1924*

* *Set of 1920 trophies (Photo shoot courtesy of Holland Duell's grandson, Holland Duell)*

* *1920 New Rochelle Yacht Club trophy (photo shoot courtesy of Holland Duell's grandson Charles Duell*

✳ *1928 Larchmont Yacht Club trophy (photo shoot courtesy of Holland Duell's grandson John Henry)*

✳ *Silver goblet and inscription on bottom of silver goblet trophy*

✳ *1922 Indian Harbor Yacht Club trophy, 1924 and 1928 Larchmont Yacht Club trophies (Photo shoot courtesy of Holland Duell's daughter-in-law Nancy Duell)*

* *1924 Eastern Yacht Club trophy (Photo shoot courtesy of Holland Duell's grandson John Henry)*

* *right, 1922 New York Yacht Club brass picture frame trophy (photo shoot courtesy of Holland Duell's granddaughter Susan Duell and her son Mitch Higgins); below, front and back of 1924 Championship medallion (photo shoot courtesy of Holland Duell's grandson John Henry)*

SANTA BARBARA NEWS-PRESS

FRIDAY, AUGUST 8, 2003

Madsen sails Rowdy to victory

YACHTING

● **McNish Cup:** Rowdy, a restored classic yacht that was orginally built for the New York Yacht Club in 1916, won the Class A sloop and cutters division at the 26th annual McNish Classic Yacht Race off Channel Islands Harbor.

Skippered by Chris Madsen of Santa Barbara, Rowdy also earned the Bristol Boat award for its magnificent restoration of the original design by famed marine designer and builder Nathanael G. Herreshoff in 1916.

✽ *This was* Rowdy's *first race in 50 years. (Article reprint courtesy Santa Barbara News–Press)*

Rowdy Documented First Place Finishes

May 29, 1920	Race for the New York Yacht Club 40-foot class[1]
June 12, 1920	11-mile race of the Manhasset Bay Yacht Club. First big race for the New York 40s since 1916[2]
June 26, 1920	14½-mile race of the Seawanhaka-Corinthian Yacht Club Annual Spring Regatta at Oyster Bay, Long Island[3]
July 10, 1920	36-mile race of the Eastern Yacht Club Cruise from New London to Morris Cove, New Haven, Connecticut, day four of six[4]
July 12, 1920	25-mile race of the Eastern Yacht Club Cruise. Final day of six-day, 150-mile cruise. For the entire cruise, Rowdy scored 2 firsts, 2 seconds, and 1 third.[5]
July 30, 1920	20-mile race of the Larchmont Yacht Club annual Race Week[6]
Aug 28, 1920	16¾-mile race of the New Rochelle Yacht Club 35th annual regatta on Long Island Sound[7]
July 3, 1922	16¾-mile race of the American Yacht Club of Rye Annual Regatta off Milton Point, Rye, New York[8]
July 16, 1922	Race of the Larchmont Yacht Club annual Race Week[9]
July 21, 1922	16¼-mile race of the Larchmont Yacht Club annual Race Week[10]
July 29, 1922	13¾-mile race of the Stamford Yacht Club annual regatta at Stamford, Connecticut[11]
July 31, 1922	39-mile race of the joint cruise of the Indian Harbor Yacht Club and the Larchmont Yacht Club from Morris Cove, New Haven to New London, Connecticut[12]
Aug 2, 1922	32-mile special NY40 race off Newport, Rhode Island[13]
Aug 7, 1922	40-mile race of the New York Yacht Club Annual Cruise from Provincetown to Gloucester, Massachusetts[14]

1　Photo of trophy.

2　*Brooklyn Daily Eagle,* June 13, 1920; *Sun & New York Herald,* June 13, 1920; *New York Times,* June 13, 1920; photo of trophy.

3　*New York Times,* June 27, 1920; photo of trophy.

4　*New York Times,* July 10, 1920; *New York Times,* July 11, 1920; *Rudder,* August 1920.

5　*Brooklyn Daily Eagle,* July 13, 1920; *New York Times,* July 13, 1920.

6　*Brooklyn Daily Eagle,* July 31, 1920; *New York Times,* July 31, 1920.

7　*Brooklyn Daily Eagle,* August 29, 1920; *New York Times,* August 29, 1920; photo of trophy.

8　*New York Times,* July 4, 1922.

9　*Brooklyn Daily Eagle,* July 18, 1922.

10　*New York Times,* July 22, 1922.

11　*New York Times,* July 30, 1922.

12　*New York Times,* August 1, 1922; *New York Tribune,* August 1, 1922; photo of trophy.

13　*New York Times,* August 3, 1922; *New York Tribune,* August 3, 1922; *New York Times,* August 7, 1922; *History of the New York Yacht Club: From Its Founding Through 1973,* Vol. 1, by John Parkinson, Jr. (New York: New York Yacht Club, 1975), p. 276.

14　*New York Tribune,* August 8, 1922; *New York Times,* August 8, 1922; photo of trophy picture frame.

Aug 9, 1922	15¾-mile race of the New York Yacht Club Annual Cruise off Marblehead, Massachusetts[1]
Aug 9, 1922	15½-mile race of the New York Athletic Club annual regatta off Execution Light on Long Island Sound[2]
June 9, 1923	13½-mile race of the Manhasset Bay Yacht Club Spring Regatta[3]
July 21, 1923	9½-mile race of the Larchmont Yacht Club Annual Race Week Race[4]
1924	Race for the New York Yacht Club 40 Foot Class[5]
1924	Race of the Eastern Yacht Club Annual Cruise, Vice-Commodore's Cup[6]
June 21, 1924	10½-mile race of the Larchmont Yacht Club Annual Spring Regatta[7]
July 4, 1924	18-mile race of the Larchmont Yacht Club 43rd Annual Spring Regatta[8]
Aug 3, 1924	40-mile race on the joint cruise of the Indian Harbor and Larchmont Yacht Clubs from Morris Cove to New London, Connecticut[9]
Aug 30, 1924	15½-mile race of the Knickerbocker Yacht Club Annual Regatta[10]
Sept 20, 1924	15½-mile race of the Manhasset Bay Yacht Club Fall Regatta[11]
Oct 30, 1924	Holland Duell was awarded the Season Championship Award in the New York Yacht Club 40 Class for the 1924 season[12]
July 7, 1925	30-mile Eastern Yacht Club race from Marblehead, Massachusetts, to Rockland, Maine[13]
July 11, 1925	Eastern Yacht Club race from Boothbay to Portland, Maine[14]

continued

1 *New York Times*, August 11, 1922; *Boston Globe*, August 11, 1922; *Brooklyn Daily Eagle*, August 11, 1922.
2 *Brooklyn Daily Eagle*, August 20, 1922; *New York Tribune*, August 20, 1922; *New York Times*, August 20, 1922.
3 *New York Times*, June 10, 1923.
4 *New York Times*, July 22, 1923.
5 Photo of trophy.
6 Photo of trophy.
7 *Brooklyn Daily Eagle*, June 22, 1924; *New York Times*, June 22, 1924.
8 *New York Times*, July 5, 1924.
9 *New York Times*, August 4, 1924.
10 *New York Times*, August 31, 1924.
11 *New York Times*, September 21, 1924.
12 *New York Times*, October 31, 1924; *New York Evening Post*, October 31, 1924; photo of trophy.
13 *New York Times*, July 8, 1925.
14 *New York Times*, July 12, 1925.

Rowdy Documented First Place Finishes

July 22, 1925	Larchmont Race Week, day 3. There were 50 mph winds and many damaged boats. Edwin Levick's famous photo "Forties in a Squall" was taken during this race.[1]
July 1, 1926	Race of the New York 40s at Marblehead, Massachusetts[2]
June 15, 1928	18½-mile race of the New York Yacht Club Spring Regatta[3]
June 25, 1928	Race of the New York Yacht Club special regatta off Newport, Rhode Island[4]
June 27, 1928	Special regatta off Newport, Rhode Island[5]
1928	Race of the Larchmont Yacht Club[6]
July 5, 1928	Race of the Beverly Yacht Club Annual Regatta[7]
July 6, 1928	Beverly Yacht Club Annual Regatta[8]
July 10, 1928	24-mile race of the Eastern Yacht Club from Buzzard's Bay to Vineyard Haven, Massachusetts[9]
July 25, 1928	3½-mile race of the Larchmont Yacht Club Annual Race Week[10]
Sept 22, 1928	Race of the Long Island Sound Racing Association, New York 40 class, sailed off Larchmont, New York[11]
July 4, 1929	Race of the Eastern Yacht Club Annual Regatta, 40 footers[12]
Sept 7, 1929	15½-mile race of the Manhasset Bay Yacht Club Fall Regatta[13]
May 31, 1930	13¼-mile race of the Larchmont Yacht Club Golden Jubilee Regatta on Long Island Sound to Great Captain Island off Greenwich, Connecticut[14]
July 12, 1930	*Rowdy* sailed in the 19½-mile race of the Indian Harbor Yacht Club Summer Regatta at Greenwich, Connecticut[15]

---

1 *New York Times*, July 23, 1925; *The Larchmont Yacht Club: A History, 1880–1990*, by C. Stanley Ogilvy (Larchmont, NY: Larchmont Yacht Club, 1993), p. 165.
2 *New York Times*, July 4, 1926; inscription on back of Lars Thorsen's oil painting of *Rowdy*.
3 *New York Evening Post*, June 16, 1928; *New York Times*, June 16, 1928.
4 *New York Times*, June 26, 1928.
5 *History of the New York Yacht Club*, vol. 1, p. 299.
6 Photo of trophy vase.
7 *New York Times*, July 6, 1928.
8 *New York Times*, July 7, 1928.
9 *New York Times*, July 11 ,1928; *New York Evening Post*, July 11, 1928.
10 *New York Times*, July 26, 1928; photo of trophy box.
11 *Brooklyn Daily Eagle*, September 23, 1928; *New York Times*, September 23, 1928.
12 *New York Times*, July 5, 1929.
13 *New York Times*, September 8, 1929.
14 *New York Times*, June 1, 1930; *New York Evening Post*, June 2, 1930.
15 *New York Times*, July 13, 1930.

July 21, 1930	Larchmont Yacht Club Race Week, day 2[1]
Aug 4, 1930	31½-mile race of the New York Yacht Club Cruise Race to Mattapoisett, Massachusetts, in gale conditions. Two New York 40s broke masts, one boat lost both spreaders, one burst a ballooner sail, and two men went overboard. Edward Cudahy cracked a rib when he was knocked overboard from *Marilee*.[2]
May 30, 1931	15½-mile race of the Harlem Yacht Club Regatta[3]
June 11, 1931	4.7-mile race of the New York Yacht Club race for the Glen Cove Cups[4]
July 12, 1931	Race of the Indian Harbor Yacht Club Annual Summer Regatta[5]
July 18, 1931	13¼-mile race of the Larchmont Yacht Club 33rd annual Race Week[6]
Aug 11, 1931	52-mile Indian Harbor Yacht Club Cruise from Greenwich up to Duck Island, Connecticut *Rowdy* won first place overall and first in class[7].
Aug 15, 1931	73-mile race of the New York Yacht Club Annual Cruise from Vineyard Haven on Martha's Vineyard over Nantucket Shoals and around Cape Cod to Provincetown, Massachusetts. *Rowdy* won first place in class and the annual Hayes Cup for New York 40s and won the Commodore's Cup for best overall.[8]
Aug 17, 1931	39-mile race of the New York Yacht Club Annual Cruise from Provincetown to Marblehead, Massachusetts[9]
Sept 5, 1931	13½-mile race of the Seawanhaka Corinthian Yacht Club 59th Annual Fall Regatta[10]

1   *New York Times*, July 22, 1930.
2   *New York Times*, August 5, 1930; *New York Times*, August 6, 1930.
3   *New York Times*, May 31, 1931; *New York Evening Post*, June 2, 1931; *New York Times*, June 2, 1931.
4   *New York Times*, June 12, 1931.
5   *New York Times*, July 13, 1931.
6   *Brooklyn Daily Eagle*, July 19, 1931; *New York Times*, July 19, 1931.
7   *New York Times*, August 12, 1931.
8   *New York Times*, August 16, 1931; *New York Evening Post*, August 17, 1931.
9   *New York Times*, August 18, 1931.
10   *New York Times*, September 6, 1931.

※ Lars Thorsen's oil painting of Rowdy *winning a race at Marblehead July 1, 1926. The inscription on the back reads, "*Rowdy *winning from* Shawara *and five other 40s July 1, 1926 at Marblehead. Presented by John Lawrence." (Provided by Holland Duell's grandson, John Henry)*

Artists

Lars Thorsen (1876–1952)

Lars Thorsen, sailor and artist, was a member of the Connecticut Academy of Fine Arts and of the Mystic Art Association. He was proficient in pencil, pastel, oil, watercolor, monotype, and drypoint etching, and he exhibited in the shows of the Mystic Art Association from the 1920s to his death in 1952. Typical of his work were small and large pictures of fishing boats and the docks of Noank, Connecticut, where he lived, and large paintings of historic ships of the romantic clipper ship age. Many of his works are registered in the National Archives, and many are in the collection of the Mystic Seaport Museum. Thorsen's work is being increasingly recognized for its beauty, freshness, and appealing qualities. His 1926 oil on canvas painting of *Rowdy* is nothing short of spectacular.

✳ *1916 watercolor of* Rowdy *by Frederic Cozzens (Provided by Tallant Smith, friend of the Duell Family)*

Frederic Cozzens (1846–1928)

Maritime artist Frederic Cozzens was born in New York. He began sketching marine scenes as early as 1868. Photography had not yet developed into a viable medium for mass media, and engravings made from artists' drawings were routinely used to illustrate stories in magazines. Cozzens's work appeared in this form in such publications as *Harper's Weekly*, *Leslie's*, *Century*, and *The Daily Graphic*. In 1880, the New York Yacht Club commissioned a set of six watercolors of yachting scenes that still hang in the club today.[1] By that time, Cozzens had become well established as a portrait artist who did watercolors of yachts on commission for many of New York's finest yachtsmen. His quick eye, trained hand, and technical knowledge produced works that conveyed the tension and excitement of the regattas. Collectors of his work speak in glowing terms of his ability to capture in watercolors the dampness of the ocean air or the blinding light of sun shining on wet canvas. L. Francis Herreshoff and his father, Nathanael Herreshoff, both considered Cozzens to be the most accurate portrait painter of individual American yachts. Cozzens is well known for his coverage of the America's Cup races. Some of his strongest works are in the books *American Yachts: Their Clubs and Races*, *Yachts and Yachting*, and *Frederic Cozzens: Marine Painter*.

✳ *1916 watercolor of* Rowdy *by Frederic Cozzens (Provided by Holland Duell's grandson, Robert Wood)*

1 http://www.philaprintshop.com/yachting.html.

✳ *Holland Duell's 1920 Christmas card depicting* Rowdy *(John Taylor Arms, American (1887–1953),* Merry Xmas, *1920, Pencil on paper, 6 × 4 1/8 in., Chrysler Museum of Art, Norfolk, VA, Bequest of Dorothy Noyes Arms, 55.28.127)*

✳ *Artist's proof for Holland Duell's 1920 Christmas card depicting* Rowdy *(John Taylor Arms, American (1887–1953),* Christmas Card for Mr. H.S. Duell, *1920, Etching, 5 1/8 × 4 1/8 in., Chrysler Museum of Art, Norfolk, VA, Gift of Mrs. John Taylor Arms, 54.51.75)*

John Taylor Arms (1887–1953)

John Taylor Arms studied architecture at the Massachusetts Institute of Technology and then embarked on a career as a successful graphic artist. He distinguished himself through his use of sewing needles and magnifying glasses to achieve exacting levels of detail. He served as president of the American Society of Graphic Artists and wrote *Handbook of Print Making & Print Makers*, published in 1934.

* Rowdy, *July 4, 1920*

© Mystic Seaport, Rosenfeld Collection, Mystic, CT, # 3872S

* Rowdy, *June 15, 1928*

© Mystic Seaport, Rosenfeld Collection, Mystic, CT, # 28544F

✳ *Above:* Rowdy *far left.*

✳ *1916 Larchmont race,*
    Rowdy *at far right.*

✳ Rowdy, *May 1931*

✳ Rowdy, *June 10, 1922*

✳ Rowdy *July 27, 1923*

❋ Rowdy, *July 1931.*

✻ *Above, Holland Duell at the helm of* Rowdy *(Photo courtesy of Holland Duell's daughter Harriet-Anne (Duell) Pierson)*

✻ Rowdy, *August 14, 1923*

✻ Rowdy, *1931*

✳ Rowdy, *1921*

Holland S. Duell's Military Career

The following military decorations were awarded to Holland S. Duell:

* *Major (later Colonel) Holland Sackett Duell (January 29, 1881– November 25, 1942). I bought this photograph on eBay from a man who had purchased a framed photo of a World War I general at an estate sale. Before selling the framed photo on eBay, he opened the back and found this photo of Holland Duell hidden behind the visible picture. What are the odds?*

> **New York Conspicuous Service Cross**[1]
> **Croix de Guerre**[2]
> **Distinguished Service Medal**[3]
> **Citation from General Pershing** "for distinguished and exceptional gallantry at Binarville"[4]
> **Distinguished Service Cross** from the hands of the Secretary of War in Washington, D.C., on October 19, 1922, with the following citation:[5]

> The President of the United States of America, authorized by Act of Congress, July 9, 1918, takes pleasure in presenting the Distinguished Service Cross to Major (Field Artillery) Holland S. Duell, United States Army, for extraordinary heroism in action while serving with 306th Field Artillery, 77th Division, A.E.F., near Binarville, France, September 28 - 29, 1918. While in command of the 2d Battalion, 306th Field Artillery, Major Duell voluntarily took one of the guns of his battalion forward to a position in advance of the immediate front line of the 368th Infantry. Although subjected to heavy machine-gun fire at short range and artillery fire he continued to direct the fire of his gun, and by his example of coolness and bravery encourage the gun detachment to remain at their gun, thereby assisting greatly in repulsing a severe counterattack of the enemy.
>
> *General Orders:* War Department, General Orders No. 38, 1922
> *Action Date:* September 28 - 29, 1918
> *Service:* Army
> *Rank:* Major
> *Regiment:* 306th Field Artillery
> *Division:* 77th Division, American Expeditionary Forces

> **Silver Star Citation** with the following citation:[6]

> By direction of the President, under the provisions of the act of Congress approved July 9, 1918 (Bul. No. 43, W.D., 1918), Major (Field Artillery) Holland S. Duell, United States Army, is cited by the Commanding General, American Expeditionary Forces, for gallantry in action and a silver star may be placed upon the ribbon of the Victory Medals awarded him. Major Duell distinguished himself by gallantry in action while serving with the 306th Field Artillery, 77th Division, American Expeditionary Forces, in action near Binarville, France, 29 September 1918, while directing the fire of a howitzer close up to the infantry line.

---

1   *The New York Red Book 1921*, edited by James Malcolm (New York: J. B. Lyons Company, 1921), pp. 79, 105.

2   *New Rochelle* (NY) *Pioneer*, November 30, 1918; *New York Times*, November 26, 1942; *Syracuse Herald-Journal*, November 26, 1942; en.wikipedia, "Recipients of Croix de Guerre (France)".

3   *New Rochelle* (NY) *Pioneer*, November 30, 1918; *New York Times*, November 26, 1942.

4   *Syracuse Herald*, February 5, 1921; *The New York Red Book*, p. 79; *The History of the 306th Field Artillery: Compiled by the Men Who Participated in the Events Described* (New York: Knickerbocker Press, 1920), p. 57.

5   http://military times.com; *New York Tribune*, October 20, 1922; *Syracuse Evening Telegram*, October 25, 1922; *Syracuse Herald-Journal*, November 26, 1942; *New York Times*, November 29, 1942.

6   http://military times.com.

General Orders: GHQ, American Expeditionary Forces, Citation Orders
   No. 9 (August 1, 1920)
Action Date: September 29, 1918
Service: Army
Rank: Major
Regiment: 306th Field Artillery
Division: 77th Division, American Expeditionary Forces

This letter, sent to Holland Duell's son when Holland died, was written by a soldier who had served under Holland. It conveys the respect and affection that existed between the men and their commander. It was provided to me by his daughter Harriet-Anne (Duell) Pierson.

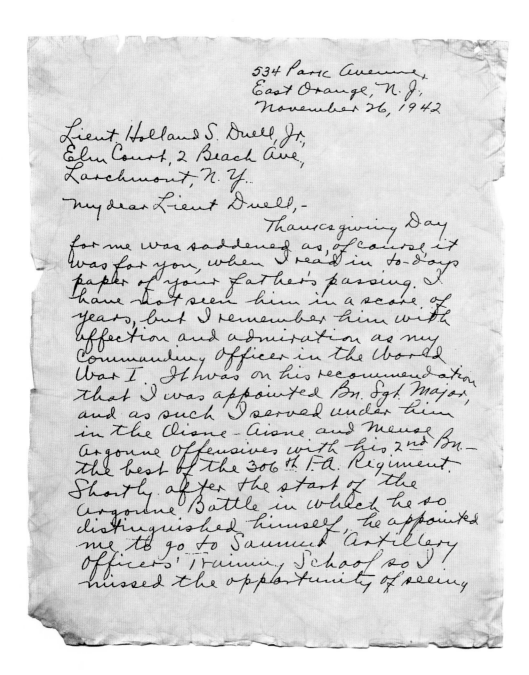

* *Letter written to Holland's son when Holland died, page 1.*

✳ *Letter written to Holland's son when Holland died.*

that 155 mm. howitzer which your father so splendidly took up to the front lines under cover of darkness and blasted at point blank fire a whole hill of machine gun nests.

He distinguished himself enough without any word of praise from me, but it is as a man who by his calm and cool courage under fire inspired his men and yet was a real friend to them, that I want to pay tribute to him.

One of my prized possessions is a copy of the Regimental History of the 306 F.A. with this notation "To 2nd Lt. F.L. Barry with the regard of Holland S. Duell, Maj. 2nd Bn. 306th F.A." I often read it and think that a soldier could ask no greater blessing than to serve under so fine a man and officer as Major [Later Colonel] Duell. I thought perhaps that you, now carrying on the torch which he carried during the last war, would be interested in knowing the reaction of one who served under your father in 1918. I was 22 years old; he about 37 — and that is how I remember him. The passing years may have made him 61 but I'll

✳ *Letter written to Holland's son when Holland died.*

bet his heart was young and as full of courage and daring as he was when he blew those German machine guns to bits.

Doubtless you have a copy of the 306 F.A. Regimental History. On Page 1 – Part I is a poem which your father improvised in the rhythm of "There's a long long trail goes winding." My copy is initialed "H.S.D." The words are an inspiration and it ends like this: "But we'll do our bit for honor
And all that life holds most dear
Until we've earned our peace, we'll meet
The Unseen with a cheer."

I hope shortly to again get into the Armed Services in some capacity – as active as they'll let a man of 47 serve, and if I do your father's memory will go with me as it has stayed with me all these years.

So when you stand at attention for the taps blown for Col. Duell and bid him a last farewell, salute him once again for me, won't you please – as he and I knew each other – from his Bn. Sgt. Maj. Barry, 2nd Bn.
Yours sincerely,
Fleroy Barry

Colonel Holland Sackett Duell (Photo courtesy of Holland Duell's grandson John Henry)

Following full review of his actions in France during the war, Holland Duell was promoted to lieutenant colonel in 1920 and to colonel in 1924. In 1920, Holland Duell compiled the book *The Regimental History of the 306th Field Artillery*. A quote in the book by Major Duell reads: "We who were members of the Second Battalion may reasonably feel that we belonged to the best battalion of the best regiment of 155 howitzers in the American Army. And we know that it was because of the everlastin teamwork of every bloomin soul. Holland S. Duell, Major, 306th F.A."

Holland S. Duell's Political Career

Assemblyman, 2nd District   On January 17, 1907, at 25 years of age, Holland S. Duell was elected assemblyman representing the 2nd District of Westchester County. He won by one of the largest majorities ever given a candidate for assembly in that district.[1]

Reelected Assemblyman, 2nd District   On November 7, 1908, Assemblyman Holland S. Duell won reelection by a landslide majority of the vote, the largest ever given in the territory for assembly.[2]

New York Senator, 26th District   On November 3, 1920, Holland S. Duell was elected New York Senator to the 26th District.[3]

Distinguished Service Palm   On July 24, 1922, New York Senator Holland S. Duell of the 26th District was rated as the "ablest, most constructive and most independent" member of the Legislature in the annual review[4] and was awarded the Distinguished Service Palm by the New York State Association.[5]

Holland S. Duell's Club Memberships

New York Yacht Club,[6] which he joined on March 23, 1911[7]
Larchmont Yacht Club,[8] which he joined on February 24, 1910[9]
Eastern Yacht Club[10]
Palisade Boat Club of Yonkers[11]
New Rochelle Yacht Club[12]
Saegkyl Country Club of Yonkers[13]
Westchester Aviation Club[14]
Union League Club[15]
Yale Club[16]
University Club[17]

---

1   *Westchester County in History*, by Henry T. Smith (White Plains, NY: Henry T. Smith, 1912), pp. 266–267.

2   *Westchester County in History*, pp. 266–267; *New Rochelle* (NY) *Pioneer*, November 7, 1908.

3   *New York Times*, November 3, 1920.

4   *New York Tribune*, July 24, 1922; *New York Times*, September 2, 1925.

5   *New York Times*, November 26, 1942; *1902 Yale Autobiographies, Twenty-Five Years After, 1902–1927*, edited by James Wright (Newburgh, NY: Moore, 1927); Yale obituary for Holland S. Duell.

6   *1902 Yale Autobiographies, Twenty-Five Years After.*

7   Club yearbooks.

8   *1902 Yale Autobiographies, Twenty-Five Years After.*

9   E-mail from club historian Timothy James.

10   *1902 Yale Autobiographies, Twenty-Five Years After.*

11   *Achievements of the Class of 1902, Yale College, from Birth to the Year 1912*, compiled by James Wright (New Haven, CT: Yale University Press, 1913), p. 256.

12   *Westchester County in History*, pp. 266–267.

13   *Achievements of the Class of 1902, Yale College, from Birth to the Year 1912*, p. 256.

14   *New York Evening Post*, August 15, 1932; *Herald Statesman*, August 13, 1932.

15   *1902 Yale Autobiographies, Twenty-Five Years After.*

16   *1902 Yale Autobiographies, Twenty-Five Years After.*

17   *1902 Yale Autobiographies, Twenty-Five Years After.*

Players Club[1]
Bonnie Briar Country Club[2]
Rockwood Hall Club[3]
Army & Navy Club[4]
Director Yale Alumni Association of Westchester County[5]
Presbyterian Church, Yonkers, New York[6]
New York Republican Club[7]
The City Club of Yonkers[8]

Holland S. Duell's Legal Association Memberships:

Holland graduated from New York School of Law with an LL.B.
in 1904. He was admitted to the bar the same year and went into
practice with his father, Charles, under the firm name of Duell,
Warfield and Duell. He belonged to the following bar associations:

New York Bar Association[9]
American Bar Association[10]
New York Patent Bar Association[11]
American Patent Bar Association[12]
Washington Patent Bar Association[13]
Westchester County Bar Association[14]
Bronx Bar Association[15]

What People Said About Holland Sackett Duell:

"Major Duell: Gentleman and soldier, cool, suave and debonair, respected and admired by every man in the second Battalion Detail."[16]

"Majors Duell and Smith, like good-natured Poppas of large families, never came
back from Baccarat without a load of chocolate and cigarettes for the boys."[17]

---

1 *1902 Yale Autobiographies, Twenty-Five Years After.*
2 *1902 Yale Autobiographies, Twenty-Five Years After.*
3 *1902 Yale Autobiographies, Twenty-Five Years After.*
4 *1902 Yale Autobiographies, Twenty-Five Years After.*
5 *1902 Yale Autobiographies, Twenty-Five Years After.*
6 Yale obituary for Holland S. Duell.
7 *Westchester County in History*, pp. 266–267.
8 *Westchester County in History*, pp. 266–267.
9 *1902 Yale Autobiographies, Twenty-Five Years After.*
10 *1902 Yale Autobiographies, Twenty-Five Years After.*
11 *1902 Yale Autobiographies, Twenty-Five Years After.*
12 *1902 Yale Autobiographies, Twenty-Five Years After.*
13 *1902 Yale Autobiographies, Twenty-Five Years After.*
14 *1902 Yale Autobiographies, Twenty-Five Years After.*
15 Yale obituary for Holland S. Duell.
16 *Hickoxy's Army: Being A Sort of History of Headquarters Company, 306th Field Artillery, 77th Division, A.
E. F.* (New York: J. J. Little & Ives Company, 1920), p. 94.
17 *Hickoxy's Army*, p. 31.

"He distinguished himself enough without any word of praise from me, but it is as a man who by his calm and cool courage under fire inspired his men and yet was a real friend to them that I want to pay tribute to him . . . . A soldier could ask no greater blessing than to serve under so fine a man and officer as Major, later Colonel, Duell."[1]

"Although subjected to heavy machine-gun fire at short range and artillery fire he continued to direct the fire of his gun, and by his example of coolness and bravery encourage the gun detachment to remain at their gun, thereby assisting greatly in repulsing a severe counterattack of the enemy."[2]

"All wondered how Major Duell missed being hit that night as he was continually around the shelled area seeing that we passed safely and with the least delay. He timed the shells and ordered the movements with such accuracy that due to his judgment we came through Fismes that night with the loss of only one of our comrades."[3]

As the troops of the 306th Field Artillery arrived home at New York aboard the Agamemnon, "Major Holland S. Duell, who had been in command of the second Battalion until illness caused his evacuation to a hospital, came aboard and was welcomed most warmly by the men who had loved him and fought beside him."[4]

In 1935, Holland Duell took 11-year-old Cherry Taylor on her first airplane ride in his open cockpit Waco, which he kept at an airport in Armonk, New York. They flew up the Hudson River to West Point and back—in her words, "just to be kind to a little girl of 11 who loved him. . . . Our family called him Uncle Holland and we loved him very much. He was a real charmer who loved getting the most out of life. . . . Uncle Holland loved to dance and ski. He always looked smooth in every activity. He had a good sense of humor and made everything lots of fun. He was a generous man who enjoyed doing things for other people."[5]

Holland learned to fly at the age of 50. "He had talent in pretty much the same way that he was a talented sailor . . . numerous forced landings all of which he got away with. He was never one to panic."[6]

"He is a progressive, dignified and energetic young man of professional standing and independence, who has the respect and liking of all the members of the legislature."[7]

---

1 Letter from F. Leroy Barry, who served under Holland Duell in World War I; a copy of the letter was sent to me by Harriet-Anne Duell.

2 Distinguished Service Cross General Orders: War Department, General Orders No. 38, 1922.

3 *"C" Battery Book, 306th F.A., 77th Div., 1917–1919,* by John Foster (Brooklyn, NY: Braunworth & Co., 1920), p. 35.

4 *The History of the 306th Field Artillery,* p. 111.

5 March 12, 2004, letter from Cherry Taylor.

6 Written by his son Holland Sackett Duell, Jr. and sent to me by Holland Sackett Duell, Jr.'s daughter Dotty Henry.

7 "The Palm to Senator Duell," *State Bulletin,* July 1922.

"His genial nature and intellectual cleverness gained him friends numerous; social and fraternal societies welcomed him to membership."[1]

"He is known to be a man of unbending integrity, high sense of honor, and of great moral worth. . . . his political opponents respect him as highly as do his most intimate party friends."[2]

Yale University: The Holland Sackett Duell (B.A. 1902) Memorial Scholarship Fund offers resources to talented and promising undergraduates who could not otherwise afford a Yale education.[3]

Holland learned to snow ski at the age of 60. Besides sailing and flying, he loved horseback riding, swimming, and playing tennis and golf. Holland owned *Rowdy* until 1940 (title was transferred into his wife's name in 1936), the longest possession by any of the original New York 40 owners. *Rowdy* is the only one of the original twelve New York 40s never to have had her name changed.

Cherry Taylor, who had known *Rowdy* and Holland Duell when she was a young girl, called me in response to my request for information in *Wooden Boat* magazine. She said that hearing the name *Rowdy* again was like revisiting a dear old friend. The call initiated a long and wonderful correspondence. Her father, Kirby Grafton, served with Holland Duell in the 306th Field Artillery. After the war, Holland rode horseback every Sunday with Cherry's mother while her father played tennis. Both her mother and father frequently raced and cruised aboard *Rowdy*.

✳ *Cherry Taylor at 11 years old, when Holland took her on her first plane ride. (Photo courtesy of Cherry Taylor.)*

✳ *Holland Sackett Duell at a fox hunt in Europe (Photo courtesy of Holland S. Duell's granddaughter Susan Duell and her son Mitch Higgins.)*

1 *Westchester County in History*, pp. 266–267.
2 *Westchester County in History*, pp. 266–267.
3 February 13, 2001, letter from Yale.

✲ *Letter from Cherry Taylor about Holland Duell to Chris Madsen*

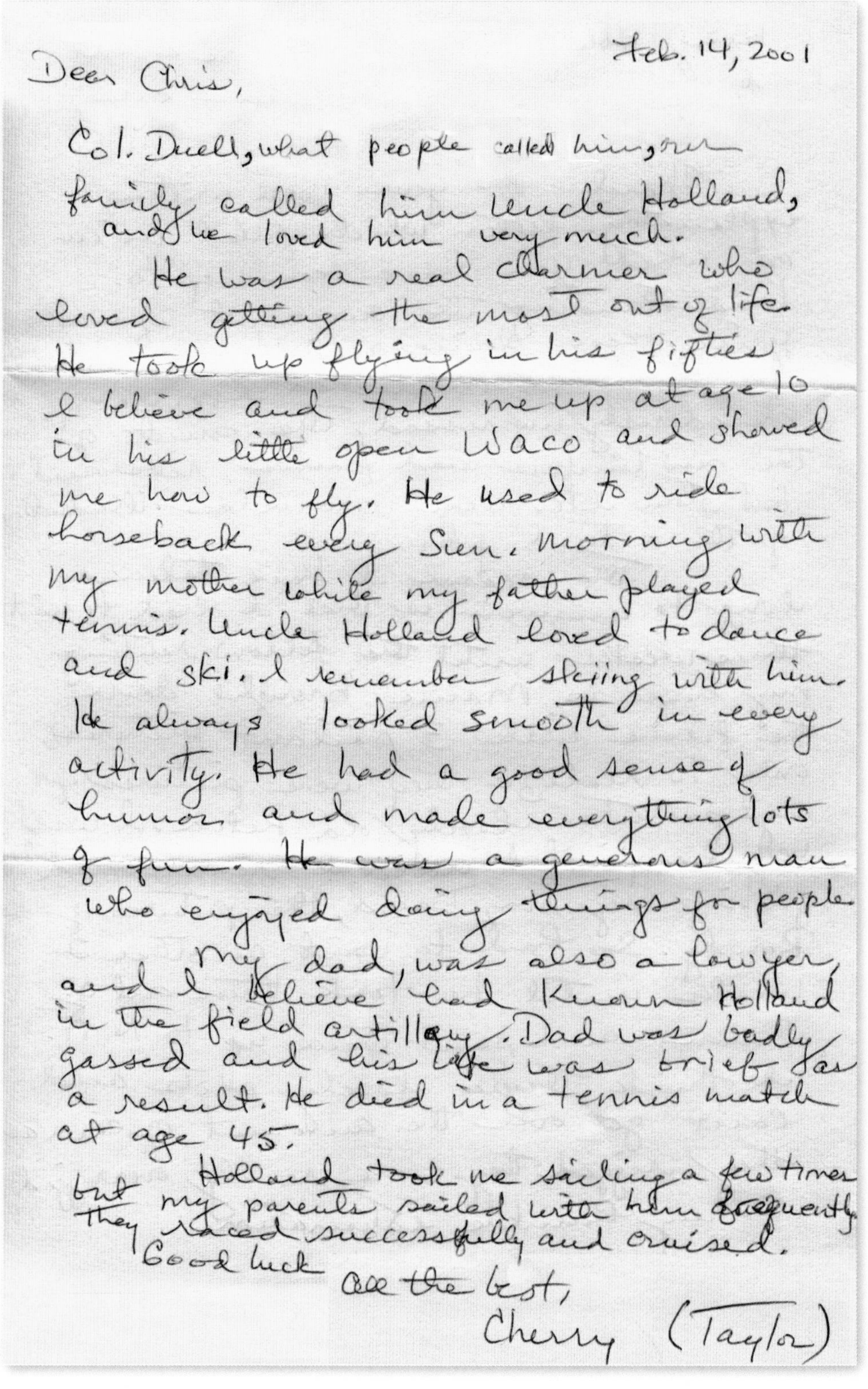

Feb. 14, 2001

Dear Chris,

Col. Duell, what people called him, our family called him Uncle Holland, and we loved him very much.

He was a real charmer who loved getting the most out of life. He took up flying in his fifties I believe and took me up at age 10 in his little open Waco and showed me how to fly. He used to ride horseback every Sun. morning with my mother while my father played tennis. Uncle Holland loved to dance and ski. I remember skiing with him. He always looked smooth in every activity. He had a good sense of humor and made everything lots of fun. He was a generous man who enjoyed doing things for people.

My dad, was also a lawyer, and I believe had known Holland in the field artillery. Dad was badly gassed and his life was brief as a result. He died in a tennis match at age 45.

Holland took me sailing a few times but my parents sailed with him frequently. They raced successfully and cruised.

Good luck

All the best,

Cherry (Taylor)

✳ Rowdy *being rebuilt, no deck*

✳ Rowdy, *view from mast look down at deck*

In 1999, *Rowdy* was put on dry land in Channel Islands Boatyard, Channel Islands, California. During the ensuing four years, she underwent an extensive 25,000-hour rebuild. The boat was reframed, over 90 percent of the planking was replaced and secured with bronze fasteners, internal steel hull strapping was replaced with bronze strapping, and the entire deck (including deck beams) was replaced. She was given a new bowsprit and a new rudder, and all new hardware, plumbing, electrical, propulsion, and electronics systems were installed. Only the finest-quality hand-selected woods were used. Painstaking efforts were made to restore *Rowdy* to her original condition and layout. I flew to the East Coast to research her sister ships *Rugosa II*, owned by Halsey Herreshoff, and *Marilee*, owned by a New York Yacht Club group. Copies of the original ships' plans were obtained from the Massachusetts Institute of Technology and cross-referenced with a large library of vintage photographs of *Rowdy*. New bronze deck and interior hardware pieces were cast using exact copies of the original Herreshoff patterns. When she was completed, Maritime Surveyors referred to *Rowdy* as an "American Maritime Treasure."

✳ Rowdy's *interior, captain's stateroom liquor cabinet*

✳ Rowdy's *interior forepeak;*

❋ Rowdy's *interior, main salon, port side*

❋ Rowdy's *interior, main salon, starboard side*

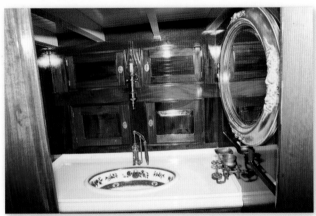

❋ Rowdy's *interior head sink*

❋ Rowdy's *interior galley*

※ *Facing page bottom, and above,* Rowdy *sea trials*

※ *Racing in the 2003 McNish Classic, owner Chris Madsen at the helm. In* Rowdy's *first race in fifty years, she scored a first place victory in her division. She also won the Bristol Boat Award for best restored yacht.*

※ *Hoisting the spinnaker during the McNish Classic*

❊ *In researching the history of* Rowdy *and Holland Duell during the years of rebuilding, I made friends with many of the Duell descendants.*
To help celebrate the completion of the project, Holland's grandsons and great-grandsons came from around the country for a reunion sail on
Rowdy *out to the Santa Barbara Channel Islands. Chris Madsen at helm. (Louise Ann Noeth)*

❊ *Duell reunion sail under*
a stiffening breeze (Louise
Ann Noeth)

✳ Rowdy, *competing in the Vela Clasica Menorca, Panerai Trophy, August 27, 2010, Mahon, Spain (James Robinson Taylor # JRT 7324)*

✳ Rowdy, *competing in the Vela Clasica Menorca, Panerai Trophy, August 27, 2010, Mahon, Spain (James Robinson Taylor # JRT 7405)*

✳ *Rowdy, competing for Le Voile d'Antibes, Panerai Trophy, Antibes, France, June 6, 2009 (© Ph. Carlhant)*

✳ *Owner Graham Walker (middle, holding trophy) and team accepting the Rolex Trophy at the 2009*
Les Voiles de Saint-Tropez (Photo courtesy Rolex/Kurt Arrigo)

In early 2006, I sold *Rowdy,* and she was transported by ship to Monaco. Her new owner, Graham Walker (middle, holding trophy), fine-tuned her to perfection and skillfully won race after race with her in the Mediterranean.

Classic Boat states "*Rowdy* was the fastest yacht in the Mediterranean, winning the overall season trophy (Vintage Class in the Panerai Series, Trophée Panerai) THREE TIMES"

Sandeman Yacht Company states "This yacht has indeed dominated her class at the classic regattas making her probably the most successful classic race winner on the Mediterranean Circuit EVER."

Among many other victories there, *Rowdy* won the coveted Rolex Trophy in Les Voiles De Saint Tropez in both 2008 and 2009. She tied for first place in 2010 but, after losing a pick from a hat to settle the draw, *Rowdy* accepted second place!! As of March 20, 2012, Rowdy had won in excess of 140 races in Europe.

About the Author

$\mathcal{M}$y parents were anthropologists and, as a child, I had the blessing of traveling the world with them and visiting many exotic, far-off destinations. My father, by the circumstances of his father's business, had grown up in the Philippines and for fun played in jungles and warm, tropical ocean waters. Consequently, I became infected at an early age with my father's love of the sea.

We moved to Santa Barbara, CA in 1967 when I was 11 years old. The Santa Barbara Channel Islands lie twenty miles offshore. To gain passage, I bought my first boat at the age of 18. For the past 40 years those islands have been my playground, and that nautical link is what put me in the same orbit as *Rowdy* when she became available for purchase in 1998. What followed changed my life, as can be gleaned from reading the book *Rowdy*. My twin daughters were born six years later, in mid-2004, and I sold *Rowdy* in early 2006 to give me the freedom to spend as much time as I could with them. I have a much smaller boat now but still need to get out on the water as much as possible, and I take the girls along every chance I get. Of course, they have adapted extremely well to life as little boaters, kayakers, swimmers, and fishermen—and, oh yes, they also love tropical vacations. After eight years of ownership, I assumed that the *Rowdy* project would end when I sold her, but it seems there was another seven years of work I needed to complete to satisfy the obligation I felt to share and keep alive this story. I hope you enjoy it as much as I have.

–Christopher Madsen

* *Chris, Claire, and Sophie at Lake Cachuma*

Index

Page numbers in *italics* are for images.